Introduction to International Development

Approaches, Actors, and Issues

Paul A. Haslam • Jessica Schafer
Pierre Beaudet

OXFORD
UNIVERSITY PRESS

OXFORD
UNIVERSITY PRESS

70 Wynford Drive, Don Mills, Ontario M3C 1J9
www.oupcanada.com

Oxford University Press is a department of the University of Oxford.
It furthers the University's objective of excellence in research, scholarship,
and education by publishing worldwide in

Oxford   New York
Auckland   Cape Town   Dar es Salaam   Hong Kong   Karachi
Kuala Lumpur   Madrid   Melbourne   Mexico City   Nairobi
New Delhi   Shanghai   Taipei   Toronto

With offices in
Argentina   Austria   Brazil   Chile   Czech Republic   France   Greece
Guatemala   Hungary   Italy   Japan   Poland   Portugal   Singapore
South Korea   Switzerland   Thailand   Turkey   Ukraine   Vietnam

Oxford is a trade mark of Oxford University Press
in the UK and in certain other countries

Published in Canada by Oxford University Press

Library and Archives Canada Cataloguing in Publication

Introduction to international development : approaches, actors, and
issues / edited by Paul A. Haslam, Jessica Schaefer, Pierre Beaudet.

Includes bibliographical references and index.
ISBN 978-0-19-542804-9

1. Economic development—Textbooks.   2. Political development—
Textbooks.   I Haslam, Paul Alexander.   II. Schafer, Jessica
III. Beaudet, Pierre, 1950–

HD82.I58 2008   338.91   C2008-904314-6

Cover image: Alternatives/Dominic Morissette

This book is printed on permanent (acid-free) paper ∞.
Printed and bound in the United States of America.

2 3 4 — 12 11 10 09

CONTENTS

LIST OF BOXES, FIGURES, AND TABLES

BOXES

FIGURES

TABLES

PREFACE

International development programs at the undergraduate level have burgeoned throughout the world in recent years. Formerly found on the margins of mainstream academic units and largely confined to graduate studies, these programs pioneered both *multi-disciplinarity* and *praxis* (the combination of academic analysis and real-world engagement with development issues) in the university and college setting. The appeal and common sense behind this approach, as well as the way development studies has connected with students' values, has brought development into the mainstream academy as an identifiable discipline.

Introduction to International Development sets out to respond to the particular needs of undergraduate international development programs—namely, their inherent multi-disciplinarity and their normative concern with praxis. Previous texts have typically been anchored within specific disciplinary traditions and have generally overlooked contributions from other disciplines to crucial debates in international development. Given that most international development programs of study are multi-disciplinary in nature, there is a clear need for a text that is explicitly multi-disciplinary in its approach to the key issues. Multi-disciplinarity has been at the heart of this project from the beginning; it has guided our selection of authors, who were drawn from disciplines as varied as political science, economics, sociology, anthropology, history, women's studies, and geography. Many of these authors have also been involved in working for and advising development agencies, are grounded by their solid experience of local realities, and represent the ideals of praxis to which our students aspire.

THE CHALLENGE OF MULTI-DISCIPLINARITY

Introduction to international development courses are often highly popular electives in the first and second years of Bachelor of Arts programs. This means that textbooks in international development need to serve a population with diverse disciplinary experiences and without a common theoretical or conceptual background. Typically, students do not come just from the diverse fields of the social sciences but also from the faculties of 'hard' or applied science and from other multi-disciplinary programs with no common core theoretical apparatus. The challenge of teaching development studies to an undergraduate multi-disciplinary audience is not simply one of providing multiple views on particular issues or exposing students to the diversity of issues in development studies; it is also more fundamentally about grounding students with a common theoretical and conceptual intellectual toolkit applicable to the multi-disciplinary nature of development problems. To our knowledge, there is no other textbook currently available with the explicit objective of grounding a multi-disciplinary audience in a way that permits the sophisticated understanding of development issues.

In this respect, the core mission of this book is to build a conceptual toolkit for first- and second-year undergraduate students with no prior knowledge of development and with diverse disciplinary backgrounds. It is for this reason that the book is structured into three sections: Approaches; Actors; and Issues. *Approaches* introduces the student to key concepts, historical contexts of development thinking and action, and theoretical approaches. A noteworthy feature of this section is the accessible account of post-modern and post-colonial approaches, which is rarely taught at this level but constitutes the fundamental epistemology for much recent work in development. *Actors* explains the various key external and internal forces that attempt to shape developmental outcomes. *Issues* applies the toolkit learned in the first two sections to a variety of issue areas. The book is designed to teach the student by establishing a series of layers that progressively deepen the student's knowledge of international development theory and practice.

At the end of a semester, the student has not just accumulated knowledge about 13 development issues but, much more fundamentally, has learned *how* to approach and study development issues.

We are honoured to be able to include an epilogue written by the prominent radical economist Samir Amin. This chapter offers students the opportunity to apply what they have learned in the theoretical, actor-oriented, and thematic chapters to an original text by one of the pioneers of the discipline reflecting on the future of development in the era of globalization and on the example of China. Students will find many of the themes of this book echoed in Amin's article and should use the skills and knowledge they have developed while studying the book to reflect, analyze, and critique his commentary.

FLEXIBILITY FOR TEACHING

In addition to the need to ground a multi-disciplinary audience with a common theoretical toolkit, an introductory textbook also needs to be pedagogically flexible. Some programs minimize exposure to theory in favour of problem-solving and case studies, while others introduce students to development theory early on. To cover these diverse situations found across undergraduate development programs, the three distinct sections of this book (Approaches, Actors, and Issues) offer the instructor considerable flexibility. He or she may follow the tripartite structure of the book, which progressively builds towards a more sophisticated integration of concepts, actors, and issues, or may pick and choose, perhaps preferring to twin actors and issues alone, or approaches and issues, or even to focus just on issues. Each chapter has been written to stand alone without requiring the assignment of previous chapters, although the collection is organized in such a way as to permit the instructor to draw connections between theory, actors, and issue areas when the student moves sequentially from the first chapters to the last. At the same time, the range of chapters makes it possible for an instructor to pick and choose the elements of the text that correspond with his or her 12- to 14-week course design.

The chapters follow a common structure to facilitate the book's use in undergraduate teaching. Teaching tools are provided in each chapter, including learning objectives, questions for discussion, and sources for further reading, including Internet sources. Textboxes draw on examples from a wide range of regional and historical experiences to illustrate the main text.

In this respect, we hope that *Introduction to International Development: Approaches, Actors, and Issues* will play an important role in providing students from multi-disciplinary backgrounds with the conceptual toolkit necessary to understand a wide range of development issue areas and help to launch them into this challenging and rewarding discipline that combines values, reflection, and action.

Paul A. Haslam, Jessica Schafer, Pierre Beaudet
School of International Development and Global Studies
University of Ottawa
July 2008

ACKNOWLEDGEMENTS

This book would never have seen the light of day without the generous contribution of time and effort by our colleagues at the University of Ottawa and enthusiastic collaborators elsewhere in the world. We would like to thank Cécile Coderre, vice-dean academic and secretary (Social Sciences) at the University of Ottawa, who enthusiastically supported this project from the very beginning and who found the financing necessary to employ a large and dedicated team of students in various stages of the preparation, translation, and copy-editing of this volume. A team of dedicated graduate and undergraduate students were important contributors to this project as translators and research assistants: Augusta Acquah, Alyssa Blank, Caroline Bouchard, Caleb Ficner, Pierre-Olivier Latrémouille, Émilie Senécal, and Mélissa Therrien. We also appreciate the considered and useful comments made by the anonymous external evaluators of this book. In addition, we would like to thank our editors at Oxford University Press: Kate Skene, who saw the potential of this book when it was only an idea in our heads, Dorothy Turnbull, whose excellent copyediting improved the manuscript, and Jennifer Charlton, who ably managed it to its conclusion.

ACRONYMS

ACP Group	African, Caribbean and Pacific Group of States	**DAC**	Development Assistance Committee (OECD)
ADF	African Development Fund	**DAWN**	Development Alternatives with Women for a New Era
AIDCO	EuropeAid Co-operation Office		
ALBA	Bolivarian Alternative for the Americas	**DFID**	Department for International Development (UK)
ALCA	Área de Libre Comercio de las Américas	**DG Dev**	Directorate General for Development (European Commission)
ANC	African National Congress		
ASEAN	Association of Southeast Asian Nations	**DPKO**	Department of Peacekeeping Operations (UN)
AU	African Union	**EA**	Effectiveness approach
AUC	United Self-Defence Force of Colombia	**EC**	European Commission
		ECA	Economic Commission for Africa (UN)
BHN	Basic human needs		
BIT	Bilateral investment treaty	**ECHO**	European Community Humanitarian Aid Department
BRICS	Brazil, Russia, India, China, South Africa	**ECLA/ECLAC**	Economic Commission for Latin America and the Caribbean (UN)
BSS	Basic social services		
BWI	Bretton Woods Institutions	**ECOSOC**	Economic and Social Council (UN)
CA	Capabilities approach	**EDF**	European Development Fund
CAMPFIRE	Communal Areas Management Program for Indigenous Resources	**EFA**	Education for all
		EKC	Environmental Kuznets Curve
CBNRM	Community-based natural resource management	**ENGO**	Environmental NGO
		EPZ	Export processing zone
CCAD	Central American Commission on Development and Environment	**ESCAP**	Economic and Social Commission for Asia and the Pacific (UN)
CCIC	Canadian Council for International Co-operation	**ESCWA**	Economic and Social Commission for Western Asia (UN)
CEB	COE Development Bank	**EU**	European Union
CEO	Chief executive officer	**EURODAD**	European Network on Debt and Development
CEPR	Center for Economic and Policy Research		
		FAO	Food and Agriculture Organization (UN)
CFE	Community forest enterprises		
CIA	Central Intelligence Agency (US)	**FDI**	Foreign direct investment
CIDA	Canadian International Development Agency	**FPI**	Foreign portfolio investment
		FRELIMO	Mozambican Liberation Front
COE	Council of Europe	**FSR**	Farming systems research
CSA	Community Supported Agriculture	**FTAA**	Free Trade Area of the Americas
		FTI	Fast Track Initiative
CSO	Civil society organization	**G-8**	Group of Eight
CSR	Corporate social responsibility	**G-20/G-21**	Group of 20/21

G-77	Group of 77	IMF	International Monetary Fund
GAD	Gender and development	INGO	International non-governmental organization
GATS	General Agreement on Trade in Services	INSTRAW	International Research and Training Institute for the Advancement of Women (UN)
GATT	General Agreement on Tariffs and Trade		
GDP	Gross Domestic Product	IOM	International Organization for Migration
GEF	Global Environmental Facility		
GNI	Gross National Income	IRD	Integrated rural development
GNP	Gross National Product	ISI	Import substituting industrialization
HDI	Human Development Index		
HIPC	Heavily Indebted Poor Countries	ISP	Internet service provider
HIV/AIDS	Human immunodeficiency virus/acquired immune deficiency syndrome	IT	Information technology
		ITT	International Telephone and Telegraph
HNP	Health, Nutrition, and Population (World Bank)	IUCN	International Union for the Conservation of Nature and Natural Resources
HPI	Human Poverty Index		
HSR	Health sector reform	IWGIA	International Work Group for Indigenous Affairs
HTA	Home town association		
HYV	High-yielding varieties	KMT	Kuo Min Tang, Chinese Nationalist Party
IBRD	International Bank for Reconstruction and Development		
		LDCS	Least developed countries
I/C	Income/consumption	LICO	Low income cut-off
ICA	International Coffee Agreement	M&AS	Mergers and acquisitions
ICDP	Integrated conservation and development programs	MAB	Man and the Biosphere
		MAI	Multilateral Agreement on Investment
ICT	Information and communication technologies		
		MBC	Mesoamerican Biological Corridor
IDA	International Development Agency	MCC	Millennium Challenge Corporation (US)
IDL	International division of labour	MDG	Millennium Development Goals (UN)
IDRC	International Development Research Centre		
		MDRI	Multilateral Debt Relief Initiative
IFAD	International Fund for Agricultural Development	MGE	Mainstreaming gender equality
		MIMP	Mafia Island Marine Park, Tanzania
IFBAN	International Baby Food Action Network		
		MINAC	Minister of Indian and Northern Affairs Canada
IFG	International Forum on Globalization		
		MNC	Multinational corporation
IFI	International financial institution	MNE	Multinational enterprise
IIA	International investment agreement	MST	Landless Workers Movement (Brazil)
IISD	International Institute for Sustainable Development		
		NAFTA	North American Free Trade Agreement
ILO	International Labour Organization (UN)		
		NAM	Non-Aligned Movement

NATO	North Atlantic Treaty Organization	SADC	Southern African Development Community
NGO	Non-governmental organization	SAP	Structural adjustment program
NIC	Newly Industrialized Countries	SCO	Shanghai Cooperation Organization
NIDL	New international division of labour	SDRS	Special Drawing Rights
NIEO	New International Economic Order	SE	Social exclusion
		SIDA	Swedish International Development Cooperation Agency
NWICO	New World Information and Communication Order	SIDS	Small island developing states
OA	Official assistance	SMS	Short messaging systems
OAS	Organization of American States	STABEX	Export earnings stabilization system
OCHA	Office for the Coordination of Humanitarian Affairs (UN)	SU/TCDC	Special Unit for Technical Cooperation among Developing Countries
ODA	Official development assistance		
OECD	Organisation for Economic Co-operation and Development	SWAS	Sector-wide approaches
OIC	Organization of the Islamic Conference	SYSMIN	System for stabilization of export earnings for mining products
OIF	Organisation internationale de la Francophonie	TCC	Teacher Creativity Centre (Palestine)
OIHP	Office international d'hygiène publique	TEK	Traditional ecological knowledge
		TNC	Transnational corporation
OLI	Ownership, location-specific, and internalization	TRIMS	Trade-Related Investment Measures
OPEC	Organization of Petroleum Exporting Countries	TRIPS	Trade-Related Aspects of Intellectual Property Rights
OSCE	Organization for Security and Co-operation in Europe	TRIPS-plus	Stronger version of TRIPS
		U5MR	Under-five mortality rate
PA	Participatory assessment	UCIRI	Union of Indigenous Communities of the Isthmus Region
PES	Payments for environmental services		
PNGO	Palestinian Network of Non-governmental Organizations	UN	United Nations
		UNASUR	Unión de Naciones Suramericanas
PPP	Purchasing power parity	UNCDF	UN Capital Development Fund
PRA	Participatory rural appraisal	UNCED	UN Conference on Environment and Development
PRSPS	Poverty Reduction Strategy Papers		
R&D	Research and development	UNCTAD	UN Conference on Trade and Development
RBM	Results-based management		
RENAMO	Mozambican National Resistance Movement	UNCTC	UN Centre on Transnational Corporations
RRA	Rapid rural appraisal	UNDAF	UN Development Assistance Framework
RTA	Regional trading arrangement		
RUF	Revolutionary United Front (Sierra Leone)	UNDESA	UN Department of Economic and Social Affairs
RWG	Redistribution with growth	UNDP	UN Development Programme

UNECE	UN Economic Commission for Europe	**USAID**	United States Agency for International Development
UNEP	UN Environment Programme	**USSR**	Union of Soviet Socialist Republics
UNESCO	UN Educational, Scientific and Cultural Organization	**WAD**	Women and development
UNFPA	UN Population Fund	**WCD**	World Commission on Dams
UN-HABITAT	UN Human Settlements Programme	**WCED**	World Commission on Environment and Development (UN)
UNHCR	UN High Commissioner for Refugees	**WFP**	World Food Programme (UN)
UNICEF	UN Children's Fund	**WGIP**	Working Group on Indigenous Populations (UN)
UNIDO	UN Industrial Development Organization	**WHA**	World Health Assembly (WHO)
UNIFEM	UN Development Fund for Women	**WHO**	World Health Organization (UN)
UNRISD	UN Research Institute for Social Development	**WAD**	Women and development
		WID	Women in development
UNRWA	UN Relief and Works Agency for Palestine Refugees in the Near East	**WIDER**	World Institute for Development Economics Research
UNV	UN Volunteers	**WSF**	World Social Forum
UPE	Universal primary education	**WSIS**	World Summit on the Information Society
		WTO	World Trade Organization
		WWF	World Wide Fund for Nature

CONTRIBUTORS

Erwin A. Alampay is assistant professor in the National College of Public Administration and Governance at the University of the Philippines.

Eric Allina-Pisano is associate professor in the Department of History at the University of Ottawa.

Samir Amin is an economist and president of the World Forum for Alternatives and the Third-World Forum.

Pierre Beaudet is a replacement professor in the School of International Development and Global Studies at the University of Ottawa.

Stephen Brown is associate professor of political science at the University of Ottawa.

Torunn Wimpelmann Chaudhary is project co-ordinator at the Chr. Michelsen Institute, Norway.

Radhika Desai is professor of political studies in the Department of Political Studies, University of Manitoba, Winnipeg.

Gavin Fridell is assistant professor of politics at Trent University, Peterborough, Ontario.

Natacha Gagné is assistant professor in the Department of Sociology and Anthropology at the University of Ottawa.

Joseph Hanlon is a senior lecturer in development and conflict resolution at the International Development Centre, Open University, Milton Keynes, England, and a visiting senior research fellow at the Crisis States Programme, London School of Economics.

Paul A. Haslam is assistant professor in the School of International Development and Global Studies at the University of Ottawa.

Anil Hira is associate professor of political science and Latin American studies at Simon Fraser University, British Columbia.

Cédric Jourde is assistant professor at the School of Political Studies, University of Ottawa.

Khalid Koser is fellow in humanitarian affairs and deputy director of the Brookings-Bern Project on Internal Displacement at the Brookings Institution.

Daniel Lavan is a doctoral candidate in the Faculty of Education at the University of Ottawa.

Richard Maclure is a professor and former acting dean at the University of Ottawa's Faculty of Education.

Nissim Mannathukkaren is assistant professor in the Department of International Development Studies at Dalhousie University, Halifax.

Andrea Martinez is associate professor at the Institute of Women's Studies at the University of Ottawa.

David R. Morrison is professor emeritus of politics and international development studies at Trent University, Peterborough, Ontario.

Joshua Ramisch is assistant professor in the School of International Development and Global Studies at the University of Ottawa.

Refaat Sabbah is director general of the Teacher Creativity Centre, Palestine.

Eunice N. Sahle is assistant professor in the Department of African and Afro-American Studies and Curriculum in International Studies at the University of North Carolina at Chapel Hill.

Jessica Schafer is assistant professor in the School of International Development and Global Studies at the University of Ottawa.

Ted Schrecker is associate professor of epidemiology and community medicine and principal scientist at the Institute of Population Health at the University of Ottawa.

Deborah Sick is assistant professor of anthropology in the Department of Sociology and Anthropology and the School of International Development and Global Studies at the University of Ottawa.

David Sogge is an independent analyst based in Amsterdam and a fellow of the Transnational Institute.

Astri Suhrke is senior researcher at the Chr. Michelsen Institute, Norway.

Marcus Taylor is assistant professor in Global Development Studies at Queen's University, Kingston, Ontario.

Henry Veltmeyer is professor of international development studies at St Mary's University, Halifax, Nova Scotia, and in the PhD Program at the Autonomous University of Zacatecas.

PART ONE

THEORIES OF AND APPROACHES TO INTERNATIONAL DEVELOPMENT

CHAPTER 1

MEANING, MEASUREMENT, AND MORALITY IN INTERNATIONAL DEVELOPMENT

JESSICA SCHAFER, PAUL A. HASLAM, AND PIERRE BEAUDET

LEARNING OBJECTIVES

- To understand the origins of different labels used to describe the developing world.
- To understand the relationship between national wealth, distribution of income, and poverty.
- To understand why development is considered a multi-dimensional phenomenon and to identify the major scholars associated with this approach.
- To distinguish the Human Development Index (HDI) from Gross Domestic Product (GDP) as a measure of development.
- To identify the ethical dilemmas associated with foreign aid and development practice.

WHAT IS THE DEVELOPING WORLD?

If you were a traveller crossing the countries and continents of the world, one of the features that would immediately strike you is the rich diversity of human experience and social organization. You would observe strikingly different landscapes, from sweeping deserts to lush forests, from scattered farmlands to densely populated cities. You would hear up to 6,912 different languages being spoken by the people you met (Gordon 2005). You would see people driving water buffalo, cultivating rice paddies in peninsular Malaysia; throngs in business suits shouting trade deals in the Hong Kong stock exchange; weavers producing intricate designs on hand-woven rugs in Isfahan, Iran; three generations of people driving tractors and feeding chickens in a communally run Israeli kibbutz; educated young people sitting at computers in call centres in Bangalore, India, answering customer service queries from London; and a myriad of other livelihood paths channelling human productive energies.

When the travelling made you hungry, you would be treated to *sadza* (cornmeal porridge) and *feijão nhemba* (beans) in Mozambique, *bibimbap* (rice with vegetable, egg, and other toppings) in South Korea, *empanadas* (fried turnovers with filling) in Chile, *haggis* (savoury pudding cooked in an animal's stomach) in Scotland, *holubtsi* (cabbage rolls) in Ukraine, and *pemmican* (dried meat) in northern Canada. In all of these places, you might also find soft drinks, fast-food restaurants, packaged breakfast cereals, and pizza. You would experience home life in many different forms: a nuclear family of four in a suburban house in the United States; a multi-generational family in a red-brick terrace on a housing estate in northern England; an extended family in a cluster of wattle-and-daub houses, led by a patriarch and his three wives in rural Tanzania; a family of recent migrants from the coast in a one-room wooden hut in a dusty clearing in the Brazilian Amazon; a single parent with four children in a high-rise apartment in Sydney, Australia; a group of nomadic Kyrgyz pastoralists in yurts on the Eurasian steppes. You would encounter a wide variety of political organizations: kingdoms, duchies, and principalities; federal, Islamic, and people's republics; tyrannical, oligarchic, and democratic regimes; commonwealths, unions, and emirates.

At the same time that you are impressed by this diversity, with your traveller's eyes you could not fail to notice that certain areas, towns, cities, countries, and regions exhibit signs of material wealth: sumptuously decorated buildings; abundant consumer goods; energy-intensive activities; a highly developed infrastructure of roads, telecommunications, hospitals, and schools. By contrast, others show evidence of poverty: human dwellings that do not protect inhabitants from the elements; absence of infrastructure for the movement of people, goods, and information; people with insufficient food and health care for survival. Similarly, you would begin to realize that some human beings appear to enjoy a wide range of opportunities and choices with respect to the way they live their lives while others appear to follow patterns of survival over which they exercise little control.

International development studies aims to explain both the diversity evident in the world in relation to human well-being and the patterns that emerge when comparing people, social groups, nations, economic and political systems, and regions of the world. Some explanations are based on historical evidence, finding the causes of today's poverty in the actions (and injustices) of past societies. For example, it can be argued that colonial conquest and occupation by European military and political powers caused poverty in colonized societies and left them with economic structures that made development progress difficult if not impossible (see chapter 2). Other explanations for worldwide patterns of wealth and poverty focus on the results of impersonal economic 'laws' and their functioning through individual rational action in impersonal market transactions. Still other theories of development hold that the economic logic of capitalism requires that some countries remain poor while others profit (see chapter 3).

Figure 1.1   Diversity of family organization: A chief and his three wives, Mozambique

Source: Jessica Schafer

But before we get to the theories put forward to explain global development, poverty, wealth, and human well-being, we will introduce you to some key concepts that will help you to understand the discussions in the rest of the book. We begin in the next section of this chapter with a discussion of the words and labels that scholars, practitioners, and the popular media use in talking about development. The third section will introduce you to different concepts of poverty and measurements of human development. The fourth and fifth sections of this introductory chapter address global ethics and ethical issues for development researchers and practitioners.

LABELLING IN INTERNATIONAL DEVELOPMENT

The words that have been used to describe people, places, and processes within international development reflect the evolution of thinking about poverty, wealth, and the relationship among nations. Critical theorists have pointed out that labelling plays at least two important roles: labels work to make existing practices appear legitimate, and they also shape future policy-making (Sachs 1993; Wood 1985). Understanding the history of

labels that have been used within the field of international development therefore helps to track the progression of key concepts and approaches.

The birth of the modern concept of 'development' is generally traced back to a speech by Harry Truman, president of the United States of America, in 1949. During this speech, Truman spoke of 'underdeveloped areas', a term still in common usage today.

If we unpack the term 'underdeveloped areas', the concept implies that there is a universal measurement of development and that nations can be assessed against this standard. Those that meet the standards are considered 'developed', while those that do not are considered 'underdeveloped'. In his speech, Truman suggested several criteria for measuring development: on the side of underdevelopment, he mentioned inadequate food, disease, primitive economic life, and poverty; on the side of development, he placed scientific advancement and industrial progress. The use of the word 'imperialism' also gives an idea of the areas to which Truman was referring when he made this speech: namely, the large number of countries in Africa and Asia still at that time under political rule by European powers and the countries of Asia and Latin America that had

BOX 1.1   TRUMAN'S POINT 4 SPEECH

We must embark on a bold new program for making the benefits of our scientific advances and industrial progress available for the improvement and growth of underdeveloped areas. More than half of the people of the world are living in conditions approaching misery. Their food is inadequate, they are victims of disease. Their economic life is primitive and stagnant. Their poverty is a handicap and a threat both to them and more prosperous areas. For the first time in history, humanity possesses the knowledge and the skill to relieve the suffering of these people . . . our imponderable resources in the technical knowledge are constantly growing and are inexhaustible. . . . The old imperialism—exploitation for foreign profit—has no place in our plans.

Inaugural address, President Harry S. Truman, 20 January 1949
(*Inaugural Addresses of the Presidents of the United States.* 1989)

emerged from European colonial rule over the course of the previous 150 years.

Prior to Truman's use of the term 'underdeveloped areas', it had been mentioned occasionally in international circles, but the terms 'backward areas' or 'economically backward areas' were more commonly used. The term 'backward' has faded out of use because it has come to be seen as derogatory and verging on supremacist. Nonetheless, it is worth asking ourselves whether 'backward' and 'underdeveloped' are entirely different ways of comparing countries, since both terms appear to imply a single, overarching scale on which to compare nations' success or progress in relation to each other. Both terms also imply the need for outside intervention by those who deem themselves to have achieved progress or development success on behalf of those who have not yet done so or who do not possess the necessary conditions to do so (see Cowen and Shenton 1996).

In 1952, the French demographer Alfred Sauvy used the term *tiers monde* (Third World) to refer to countries outside the two major power blocs of the West and the Soviet Union (Fry and Martin 1991). He used this term to draw a parallel with the *tiers état* (Third Estate) in pre-revolutionary France, which referred to the bottom layer of the social pyramid, beneath the clergy and the nobility. The Third Estate had a very diverse membership, from peasants virtually enslaved under feudal lords to bourgeois merchants with great wealth, who had little in common apart from exclusion from the nobility and clergy. Similarly, the Third World to which Sauvy referred in the 1950s included countries with diverse economic, social, and political histories, which were following widely varied trajectories of development. Gradually, though, the term Third World took on connotations primarily related to poverty at the national level.

The deepening hostilities of the Cold War during the 1950s meant increasing political tensions and rivalries between the ideologically opposed First and Second Worlds (respectively, the nations of the North Atlantic Treaty Organization and those of the Warsaw Pact or Soviet bloc). The Non-Aligned Movement (NAM) brought some political unity to the group of countries outside the two superpower blocs following a conference in 1955 in Bandung, Indonesia, and the first official Non-Aligned Movement summit in 1961 in Belgrade, Yugoslavia. In this context, the term Third World, like the NAM, suggested a political bloc that provided an alternative to the ideological power groupings (see chapters 3 and 10). Although the First and Second World designations became irrelevant with the fall of the Berlin Wall in 1989, the term Third World remains. Apart from a wavering degree of political unity provided through the Non-Aligned Movement—which does not include all of the countries often labelled Third World and whose membership and political role have fluctuated over the years since its creation—it is difficult to identify any enduring similarities among the countries that have been referred to under the category of Third World over the past 50-plus years. Although the term Third World is still sometimes used in international development circles, numerous questions have been raised about its value.

- Is it a sufficiently clear and useful term, given that there are no precise criteria to identify whether a given country falls within the category or not?
- Does the label have negative connotations? A glance at recent public discussions on the Internet about which countries should be considered Third World suggests that many people feel it is a pejorative term and therefore prefer their own country not to be included within the category.
- Is it ever possible for a country to move out of the Third World category, or is it a historically determined and static denotation? We might note that some eastern European countries with low scores on the Human Development Index (HDI, discussed in detail below) are not commonly referred to as Third World, whereas countries of South America may be automatically included even though some of them achieve high human

Figure 1.2 Old European elegance and modern design in Buenos Aires, Argentina

Source: Paul Haslam

development scores (for example, Argentina and Chile).

- Finally, many are unhappy with the way the term Third World seems to imply a world hierarchy and a unique path to development success, just as the term 'underdeveloped areas' did.

In the 1970s, a new label emerged as a result of economic transformation among a number of countries formerly considered part of the 'developing world': the Newly Industrialized Countries (NICs). These countries included Hong Kong, South Korea, Singapore, and Taiwan. More recently, Thailand, India, Mexico, Brazil, China, South Africa, Turkey, and Malaysia have been added to the NIC category. They are sometimes also referred to as 'emerging markets', a term that suggests they are perceived by the leaders of global capitalist enterprises as potential markets to target for profit but also that once they have shown willingness to embrace the rules of market economics, they may be admitted into the coveted circle of acceptable participants in global economic exchange. Fry and Martin list four economic criteria by which NIC status is determined: (1) manufactured goods contributing 30 per cent of GDP; (2) manufactured goods as 50 per cent of total exports; (3) a shift in employment from agriculture to industry; (4) per capita income of at least US $2,000 (1991, 151). This understanding of development will be explored further in chapters 3 and 7.

The term 'developing' country was proposed as a more optimistic term than either 'underdeveloped' or Third World. Its opposite is 'developed' countries, those deemed to have reached a certain level of economic success. A country's Gross Domestic Product (GDP) was the standard measure used in the past to classify countries as developed or developing, but this classification produced anomalies. A country's GDP is a measure of the value of goods and services produced in its economy and can be high as a result of natural resource wealth, even when other sectors of its economy and social well-being may not show signs of development such as industrialization, increased life expectancy, or higher levels of education. For example, Equatorial Guinea, an African country that saw its GDP shoot up in the mid-1990s with the discovery of oil reserves, would have been included in the 'developed' category simply on the basis of per capita GDP. Yet other key indicators of human well-being in the country remain very low, such as life expectancy and literacy. These problems with economic measurement are developed further in the following section of the chapter.

The World Bank has established its own system of classification, partitioning countries into low, middle, and high-income groups, as a basis for determining the loan programs for which a

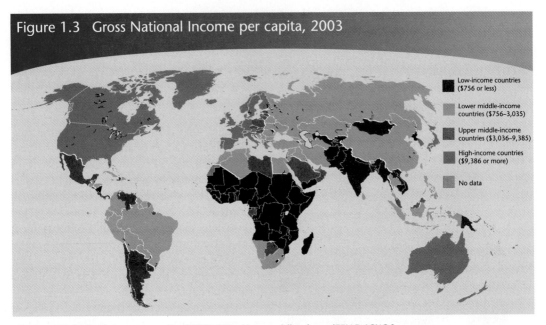

Figure 1.3   Gross National Income per capita, 2003

Low-income countries ($756 or less)

Lower middle-income countries ($756–3,035)

Upper middle-income countries ($3,036–9,385)

High-income countries ($9,386 or more)

No data

Source: World Bank. 'GNI per capita, 2003'. http://go.worldbank.org/7EIAD6CKO0.

country is eligible to apply. It uses a measure of Gross National Income (GNI), calculated according to its own formula but basically similar to GDP or GNP (Gross National Product). The World Bank has further subdivided the categories to include lower-middle-income and upper-middle-income groups. There is also a second category of high-income countries: those belonging to the Organisation for Economic Co-operation and Development (OECD). In World Bank reports, the term 'developing economies' is used to refer to low- and middle-income economies, but it officially recognizes that this terminology should not be taken to imply that these economies are in fact making 'progress' towards development or that those that do not fall into the two groups have already achieved 'development'. (See the World Bank website for more detail.)

The term **Fourth World** has more recently come into usage, although it is not yet common or central in the international development lexicon. It has been used in two quite distinct ways. One is to denote the poorest of the poor countries, often the 'failed states' of recent parlance,

which have experienced serious setbacks in human well-being and political governance, typically in connection with armed conflict. The other use of Fourth World has been to refer to Aboriginal peoples, whose status and citizenship rights vary considerably globally but who have frequently suffered dispossession and abrogation of political, economic, social, and cultural rights within countries where the dominant group acted as a colonizer (see chapter 23).

Discontent with 'Third World' and 'developing' or 'underdeveloped', for many of the reasons mentioned, has prompted people to adopt alternative words to refer to the subjects of international development, such as 'two-thirds world' and 'majority world'. These terms highlight the fact that the overwhelming majority of the world's population are the targets, subjects, or objects of development. The idea of strength-in-numbers underlies the hopefulness of these terms.

The label 'South' seems to provide a neutral way of referring to countries because it emphasizes geographical location over other characteristics. Yet using 'South' to refer to countries that

BOX 1.2   COUNTRY CLASSIFICATION

The International Monetary Fund (IMF), for its part, has classified countries according to their type of economy. In 1994, it listed three main categories: industrial countries (23); developing countries (132); and economies in transition (23). 'Economies in transition' referred to those countries formerly following an economic model in which the state planned and led development without participation from a private sector, in contrast to 'market-based economies' in which market forces were supposed to determine economic change.

By contrast, the World Bank focuses on income-based divisions between countries, as noted in the text above.

Under the General Agreement on Tariffs and Trade (GATT) system and now under the World Trade Organization (WTO), the principle of 'self selection' is followed, whereby members themselves choose their development status. However, in their publications, the WTO follows the UN country classification and for budget purposes also makes use of the income criterion adopted by the World Bank. This was also the case in the Uruguay Round Agreement (signed in 1994) where 'least developed' countries were defined as those with per capita incomes of less than US $1,000.

In terms of the per capita income classification, the UN categories are the following: industrial countries (46), developing countries (127), and least developed countries (45). The UN industrial countries category covers the IMF's similar category but also includes the IMF economies in transition grouping.

Modified excerpt from a report for the Organization of American States entitled *Small and Relatively Less Developed Economies and Western Hemisphere Integration*, http://www.dttc.oas.org/trade/studies/secon/small2E.asp.

---

qualify as the targets for development does imply characteristics beyond simply location in the southern hemisphere, since Australia and New Zealand, for example, are donor rather than recipient countries in international development, while some countries in the northern hemisphere receive aid and exhibit socio-economic characteristics similar to countries of the south. Grouping countries (which in themselves are historically constructed conceptual entities rather than simple geographical facts) under a label such as the 'South' implies a degree of homogeneity that both is too simplistic and may justify blueprint managerial approaches. Suggesting that large swathes of the world 'are inhabited by generic populations,

with generic characteristics and generic landscapes' can therefore be problematic, not just symbolically but also practically (Crush 1995, 15).

Global South has gained favour in the development community more recently and appears better able to incorporate the centrality of historical and contemporary patterns of wealth and power into a loosely geographically defined concept. The phrase may take better account of the fact that poverty and social conditions formerly identified with the Third World are in fact to be found throughout the world and not simply in one geographical region.

The following section explores in more detail how poverty and development have been measured and defined. Here, we will conclude the discussion of labels and development terminology by emphasizing that examining language and discourses of development helps us to illuminate the deeper ideas and beliefs underlying development practice and policies. We need to be aware of how the way we talk about development shapes and is shaped by our culturally informed assumptions and historical position, as well as by existing relations of power and knowledge. Words or labels that are apparently nonpolitical and appear natural or instinctively rational to us should be examined for the ways they may mask practices of control, regulation, and reproduction of particular power configurations or policy processes. There is also a danger that by superimposing new labels on existing practices, we create the illusion of reform while leaving power relations underlying the labels unchanged (Adams 1995). Yet at the same time, we should recognize the possibility for creativity in discursive practice and search for ways in which language can also be a force for transformation (Wood 1985). We should not assume that concepts or practices of 'development' are fully determined by those who believe themselves to be their architects. Instead, we need to recognize the agency exercised by those who have responded to, reacted to, and resisted being the objects of development (Crush 1995, 8).

GROWTH, INEQUALITY, POVERTY, AND DEVELOPMENT

Although we have discussed the vast diversity in the standards of living between, among, and within developing countries—and even within the developed world—it remains difficult to concisely define what 'development' is and how exactly to measure it. Different approaches to defining 'development' reveal different aspects of the problem: the need to distinguish between levels of industrialization, the need to consider different segments of the population, the need to look specifically at poverty, and the need to consider development as an 'ideal' or aspiration for betterment.

Growth

Development has most frequently been equated with growth of the economy over a prolonged period of time. This approach was most common during the 1950s and 1960s under the influence of theories such as Walt Rostow's *Stages of Economic Growth* (see chapter 3) but remains prevalent today. When the World Bank compares the level of development of different countries, it typically ranks them by their average income per inhabitant—or **GDP per capita**—although the Bank prefers the term Gross National Income. GDP per capita figures are also adjusted by **purchasing power parity** (PPP), which takes into account the different buying power of a dollar in different economies. This gives an average income per person that allows us to compare the annual incomes of, for example, an average American who earns $39,676 to the average Nigerian who earns $1,154. This kind of comparison reveals that the United States is the world's second richest country (after Luxembourg) and Nigeria is one of the world's poorest—154th out of 177.

GDP per capita is an extremely useful way of comparing levels of development. It also gives us the most widely used measure of how countries are improving (or deteriorating) in their level of development. GDP growth rates (the per cent change in national income between any two years) are like the Academy Awards of the developing world, clearly indicating which economies have been performing (in terms of adding wealth) and which have not. The top-performing economies in the developing world may have growth rates exceeding 10 per cent per annum—such as China in the early 2000s—but others may post negative rates, as was the case for much of sub-Saharan Africa during the 1980s and early 1990s. However, growth rates in developing countries are very volatile and may be high one year and low the next. In contrast, developed countries generally have slower GDP growth rates, usually between 2 and 3.5 per cent, but these rates are more stable over time. One of the world's most prominent development economists, Jeffrey

Sachs, has argued that the current gulf in wealth between the developed and developing countries is almost entirely caused by small differences in growth rates over the period since 1820. In 1820, he argues, the difference in GDP per capita between developed and developing countries was relatively small (only 4:1), but two centuries of differential growth rates have led to a 20-fold gap (Sachs 2005, 29–31).

Rapid growth in GDP is usually caused by rapid increases in productivity in agriculture, natural resource extraction, or industrialization. When GDP per capita reaches the level of a middle-income developing country, it usually means that a certain level of industrialization has been reached, including the production of manufactured goods such as textiles and consumer durables (refrigerators, cars) and of some intermediate goods such as steel and petrochemicals. It was generally assumed that growth of national wealth (as measured by GDP per capita) would 'trickle down' to the poorest segments of society in such a way that most people would benefit. In other words, development, viewed through the prism of increasing GDP per capita, was about copying the industrialization experience of the West.

But it should not be forgotten that GDP per capita is a measure of the *average* income in a country. There are many problems with GDP per capita, including the fact that it is an estimate that depends on the quality of information collected by government statistical agencies and that it fails to count the 'value' of non-market subsistence activities, which may be quite important in less developed rural areas (for a trenchant critique, see Seers 1979, 14–17). Although a good indicator of the degree of industrialization, the GDP tells us relatively little about the extent of poverty—specifically, what proportion of the population is extremely poor—or whether growth is in fact 'trickling down' to the poor. It is possible for countries to grow rapidly in GDP per capita but for only the richest segments of society to benefit. In this respect, development *cannot* be as simple as GDP growth, because growth does not necessarily reduce poverty.

Inequality

In order to know how many poor people there are in a given country and whether they are benefiting from the overall growth of the economy, we need to include another concept: the distribution of income. The **distribution of income** (also known as income inequality) is a measure of how the wealth of a country is distributed among its population: what share of that wealth is owned by the rich, and how much the poorest earn in comparison to the wealthiest. Indeed, income inequality is the direct link between GDP per capita and the number of people living in poverty.

There are two ways of measuring income inequality: a comparison of the income earned by different strata of the population and the Gini coefficient. Income inequality is often evaluated by dividing the population into five or ten equally populous strata, known respectively as 'quintiles' or 'deciles', and comparing the average incomes of these different strata to each other. A standard comparison is between the earnings of the wealthiest 20 per cent of the population and the poorest 40 per cent (first to fourth deciles). However, the Gini coefficient is the most commonly used measure of income inequality. It is a number between 0 and 1, with relatively equal societies such as the Scandinavian countries scoring around 0.25 while very unequal societies like Brazil score around 0.6.[1]

Income inequality is important in part because it forces us to confront the injustice in most developing societies: that a privileged minority lead luxurious lives while the vast majority of their own countrymen and women struggle in abject poverty. But income inequality is also an important constraint on development. It means that growth often comes from the richer segment of the economy and is less likely to translate into poverty reduction by 'trickling down' to the poor. Poverty is always eliminated more quickly when GDP growth is combined with improvements (greater equality) in the distribution of income.

Societies in developing countries tend to be much more unequal than societies in developed

Figure 1.4 A traditional Argentine *asado* (barbeque), a typical meal in Brazil and the Southern Cone of Latin America

Source: Paul Haslam

countries. Latin America, although an upper-middle-income area of the developing world, is also the region with the most unequal distribution of income. This means that the super-rich and the super-poor coexist in the same countries. Mexico, for example, has the third richest man on the list of the world's richest people, and citizens of the developing world as a whole occupy 19 of the top 100 places (*Forbes* 2007). Brazil, one of the most unequal countries in the world, has European-trained elites and a world-class aeronautics industry—but also *favelas* (Portuguese for 'slums') surrounding its major modern and cosmopolitan cities like São Paulo. By looking at the figures for the distribution of income in Brazil in 2002, we see that the top 20 per cent of the population earns 15 times more per capita than the average per capita income of the poorest 40 per cent. Brazilian GDP growth over the past 20 years has principally benefited the rich and barely reached the very poor, with the annual income of the poorest decile

growing by only 2 *reais* while the richest earned 385 more! Table 1.1 demonstrates the stickiness of distribution of income: very little changed in the 20-year period from 1981 to 2002.

The realization that income inequality makes the task of raising people out of poverty even more difficult has led to the current focus of international organizations and research on 'growth with equity', which seeks to combine the goal of GDP growth with the goal of distributing the benefits of that growth to the poor. Growth remains key because it 'grows the pie', but we must recognize that it is not enough in itself. Furthermore, there is some evidence that countries that grow faster do not always improve the situation of the poorest (such as Brazil), while countries with low growth rates and GDP per capita may succeed relatively well in reducing the vulnerability of the poorest segments in society (such as Cuba or the Indian state of Kerala). This means that high GDP growth is not strictly necessary for poverty reduction,

Table 1.1	The distribution of income in Brazil			
	1981		**2002**	
Deciles	**Income/capita**	**As % of average income**	**Income/capita**	**As % of average income**
1	27	8.9	29	7.6
2	54	17.7	65	17.0
3	78	25.6	96	25.1
4	105	34.4	131	34.2
5	137	44.9	171	44.7
6	177	58.0	224	58.5
7	233	76.4	291	76.1
8	322	105.6	399	104.3
9	499	163.6	617	161.3
10	1418	464.9	1803	471.2
Average income/capita*	305		382.6	

*Income measured in October 2002 *reais*.
Source: Coes 2005, 10.

although it may make it easier. It is also worth underlining that the poorest and those who are least likely to benefit from the 'trickle down' of growth are usually those who belong to disadvantaged ethnic, linguistic, and cultural groups. In Latin America, for example, this frequently means indigenous peoples and people of African descent.

Although inequality undermines the opportunities for the material advancement of the poor, it also has broader cultural effects on the rich. Dudley Seers writes, 'The social barriers and inhibitions of an unequal society distort the personalities of those with high incomes no less than those who are poor' (Seers 1972, 23). When inequality becomes part of a national culture, it undermines the broad and diffuse social trust, what Francis Fukuyama, among others, has called 'social capital' (Fukuyama 1995). Social capital refers to the extent to which individuals are willing to cooperate in the pursuit of shared goals and is usually thought to be essential to the development of a civic and democratic culture (see chapters 12 and 16). Public opinion polling in highly unequal societies such as Latin America demonstrates that peo-

ple trust strangers less than those in the developed world do. Gated communities and barred windows are commonplace. Furthermore, one may well ask if the traditional conservatism of elites in the developing world and their unwillingness to tolerate reformist groups or extend the rights of social citizenship to the poor comes from the fear of loosening their grip on the masses, who know very well who benefits from the status quo and who does not.

Although inequality is a common feature of most developing countries, it is very difficult to explain why this should be so in the first place. There are many possible reasons, some of which are discussed in more detail in subsequent chapters. At least three explanations seem plausible. First, the impact of colonial rule or neo-colonial economic relations may have forged or consolidated unequal social relations based on slavery, feudalism, and land ownership patterns that continue to influence the present (see chapters 2 and 3). Second, the characteristics of late industrialization—namely the use of inappropriate capital-intensive technology—reduce the employment potential of GDP growth (see chapters 7 and 24). Third, inadequate or non-existent social safety nets and regressive taxation systems prevent the redistribution of national income towards the poor and middle classes, as occurred in the developed economies after the Great Depression. The good news is that although income inequality makes development more difficult, it is not impossible to overcome. Targeted social programs have reduced the incidence of poverty while leaving inequality untouched.

What is poverty?

Income inequality leads us to the direct question of what proportion of poor people there are in a given country. (For a more detailed discussion of poverty and exclusion, see chapter 13.) Poverty, however, is a difficult concept to define. It is usually defined as an extremely low level of income. For example, the World Bank distinguishes between absolute and moderate poverty in much of its work. **Absolute poverty** refers to being below the minimum level of income required for physical survival. The World Bank defines this level as US $1 per day measured at 1993 international purchasing power parity—that is, adjusted for the buying power of one US dollar in the local market. **Moderate poverty** is typically considered to be an income of US $2 per day, a level at which basic needs are barely met but survival is not actually threatened (Chen and Ravallion 2007, 6).

In the 1960s, however, American sociologists such as Talcott Parsons and Kenneth Clark, addressing poverty and in particular the status of African Americans in US society, began to develop the concepts of **relative poverty** and social exclusion. Relative poverty refers to a kind of poverty that does not threaten daily survival but in which an individual may not have the income necessary to fully participate in his or her society (Thomas 2000, 13, citing Townsend). One may well imag-

Figure 1.5   Diversity of human dwellings

Source: Jessica Schafer

ine how an individual without computer access and knowledge would be seriously hampered in terms of his or her ability to access important information and even do basic tasks such as looking for employment. The poverty that we refer to in developed countries is almost exclusively, even for the very poorest, an issue of relative rather than absolute or even moderate poverty. A related concept is 'social exclusion' or social citizenship, which is discussed in greater detail in chapter 13.

Nonetheless, the concept of relative poverty reveals that poverty is not just about income levels; it also has social, political, psychological, and moral elements to it—and this is true in both the developing *and* the developed world. In other words, although GNP per capita is a good indicator of poverty as income deprivation, it does not tell the whole story. Consequently, alleviating poverty or *doing development* must also be much more complicated than simply economic growth or even reducing poverty. Three thinkers in particular have been fundamental in redefining how poverty, and therefore development, should be understood.

The idea that development was much more than economic growth or an increase in income per capita began to gain ground in the 1960s, promoted by development theorists and practitioners such as Dudley Seers and Denis Goulet. The arguments of these scholars have led to an understanding of poverty and development as *multidimensional*. In 1969, Seers rephrased the question of how to develop as 'What are the necessary conditions for a universally acceptable aim, the realization of the potential of human personality?' (Seers 1979, 10). He concluded that six conditions were necessary: adequate income to cover the needs of basic survival; employment (including any non-paid social role that contributes to self-respect and development of the personality); improvement in the distribution of income; an education, particularly literacy; political participation; and national autonomy (belonging to a politically and economically independent nation). Denis Goulet, writing at about the same time, asserted that development should

promote 'life-sustenance' (the basic requirements for survival—food, clothing, health, and shelter), self-esteem (or dignity and identity of the individual), and freedom (an expanded range of choice and freedom from 'servitudes') (Goulet 1971, 87–97; Seers 1979, 10–13; Todaro 1989).

It is evident that those closely involved in development were beginning to see growth as an inadequate measure of development and even entertained the possibility that rising incomes, although they improved the ability of individuals to meet basic physical needs, might not contribute to 'development' in its more sophisticated and multi-dimensional aspects. These ideas were further developed in the work of Nobel Prize–winning economist Amartya Sen. Sen argues that development should not be seen simply as rising income levels but rather as an increase in individuals' substantive freedoms. His approach is often called (after the name of his popular 1999 book) *Development as Freedom*, or the **capabilities approach** (CA). As Sen puts it, the real value of wealth and income is that 'they are admirable general-purpose means for having more freedom to lead the kind of lives we have reason to value' (Sen 1999, 14). In this respect, Sen sees poverty primarily as kinds of 'unfreedom' or deprivation of freedoms that limit the ability of individuals to improve their lives. Such unfreedoms may include a lack of access to health and welfare services, gender or ethnic **discrimination**, and limits on basic political, civic, and economic rights. According to Sen, lack of freedom can be the result of either processes (denial of rights normally considered 'procedural', like political, civic, and human rights) or the opportunities that people have (inability to feed themselves, receive an education, access health services, avoid premature morbidity) (Sen 1999, 14–17).

The key to Sen's argument, therefore, is the way in which the expansion of people's capabilities—that is, their ability to lay claim to or access various resources (such as civil and political rights and government services)—can improve their ability to make choices that they value. At the same time, an increased ability to make choices feeds back to build their 'capabilities'. One can imagine, for example, how the right to vote and participate in political decisions could lead to governmental decisions that increase local educational opportunities, which in turn could expand the choices of those who had participated in the political process by voting. Sen writes, 'Greater freedom enhances the ability of people to help themselves and also to influence the world, and these matters are central to the process of development' (Sen 1999, 18). Sen makes it clear, therefore, that level of income does not relate directly to 'development' and that poverty is better seen as the deprivation of basic capabilities or freedoms.

Sen points to a number of compelling examples to illustrate his argument, including the fact that African Americans (on average) have a lower probability of reaching old age than citizens of China, Sri Lanka, or Costa Rica despite having much higher incomes. Furthermore, male African Americans from Harlem are even worse off than the average, being less likely to reach the age of 40 than men in Bangladesh (Sen 1999, 21–3). In this example, Sen shows that African-American men suffer from restrictions on their 'capabilities' despite having incomes much higher than people in the other countries cited. It is important to underline that although freedom, for Sen, (including free markets) has intrinsic value and does not have to be justified in terms of outcomes, a significant part of the expansion of capabilities (ability to access freedoms) comes through access to government services. Therefore, Sen sees the ability to access education, health care, and unemployment insurance as key elements that expand people's capabilities. The inverse of this observation is that sometimes low income does not reflect the opportunities people have. This should be intrinsically clear to students in a university or college setting where their income (measured by summer earnings) would put them below the national poverty line. In no way does this income level reflect the real capabilities and freedoms commanded by students or the opportunities before them.

Sen's work has been instrumental (together with that of Seers and Goulet) in opening the door to more multi-dimensional measures of development that go beyond the ubiquitous GDP per capita. In defence of GDP per capita, it is easily measured, and levels of absolute and moderate poverty can be clearly established according to certain income cut-off points. Even one of its most ardent detractors, Dudley Seers, referred to GDP per capita as a 'very convenient indicator' (Seers 1979, 9). However, is it possible to measure a multi-dimensional concept like Sen's 'development as freedom'? Some authors have criticized such an approach as being impossible to quantify (Rist 1997, 10). Nonetheless, efforts have been made to construct measures that better capture the multi-dimensional aspects of development. The best known is the United Nations Development Programme's (UNDP) Human Development Index, or HDI, constructed with input from Amartya Sen.

The annual *Human Development Report*, which ranks the countries of the world by their HDI score, is the UNDP's flagship publication and was developed in 1990 as an alternative and more multi-dimensional measure of development than GDP per capita. Many people see it as an intellectual and philosophical challenge to the World Bank's annual publication, the *World Development Report*, which continues to use GNI per capita as a measure of development. The Human Development Index is a composite measure of three equally weighted factors: a long and healthy life, knowledge, and standard of living. A long and healthy life is measured by life expectancy at birth; knowledge is a composite of the adult literacy rate and the combined gross enrolment ratio for primary, secondary, and post-secondary schools; and standard of living is measured by GDP per capita. In this respect, the index recognizes that income levels are important but that other factors are also significant in human development. One may view the education and long-life measures as proxies that take account of the various government services that Seers, Goulet, and Sen see as crucial to expanding the range of individual choice. Indeed, the first *Human Development Report* (1990) was

Table 1.2   Countries ranked by HDI and GNP per capita

HDI ranking 2006	Country (according to World Bank categories)	HDI score	GNP/ capita (PPP US$)	GNP/ capita ranking
	High income (> $11,116)			
1	Norway	0.965	$38,454	4
5	Sweden	0.951	$29,541	16
6	Canada	0.950	$31,263	10
7	Japan	0.949	$29,251	18
8	United States	0.948	$39,676	2
18	United Kingdom	0.940	$30,821	13
20	New Zealand	0.936	$23,413	25
36	Argentina	0.863	$13,298	46
76	Saudi Arabia	0.777	$13,825	45
121	South Africa	0.653	$11,192	55
	Upper-middle income ($3,596–$11,115)			
38	Chile	0.859	$10,874	56
50	Cuba	0.826	$4,100*	110**
61	Malaysia	0.805	$10,276	57
69	Brazil	0.792	$8,195	64
81	China	0.768	$5,896	89
92	Turkey	0.757	$7,753	70
93	Sri Lanka	0.755	$4,390	103
108	Indonesia	0.711	$3,609	113
118	Guatemala	0.673	$4,313	104
146	Swaziland	0.500	$5,638	94
	Lower-middle income ($906–$3,595)			
122	Tajikistan	0.652	$1,202	152
126	India	0.611	$3,139	114
137	Bangladesh	0.530	$1,870	140
159	Nigeria	0.448	$1,154	154
171	Chad	0.368	$3,090	128
	Low income (< $905)			
143	Madagascar	0.509	$857	164
150	Yemen	0.492	$879	163
162	Tanzania	0.430	$674	170
176	Sierra Leone	0.335	$562	172
177	Niger	0.311	$779	165

Note: The countries are grouped according to the World Bank classification system.

*Cuba's GDP per capita at PPP (2006) as estimated by the CIA *World Factbook* (available at https://www.cia.gov/library/publications/the-world-factbook/geos/cu.html). Neither the World Bank nor the HDI offer estimates of Cuban national income.

**Estimated ranking.

Source: UNDP. *Human Development Report 2006.* http://hdr.undp.org/hdr2006/statistics.

explicit about this link, noting that 'Human development is a process of enlarging people's choices' (UNDP 1990, 10).

For the UNDP, countries with a HDI score of 0.8 or more are considered highly developed, while those with a score of 0.5 or less are considered to have low development. In the 2006 *Human Development Report*, classifications are given for 177 countries in the following categories: high human development (63), medium human development (83), and low human development (31), with HDI values ranging on a scale between 0 and 1. The HDI shows that many countries can do much better in 'human development' than average per capita income would predict. Even Norway, holding the number one spot on the HDI, does not do as well in converting GDP per capita to human development as neighbouring Sweden, which holds the number five spot but has a GDP per capita almost $9,000 less than Norway! Perhaps most importantly, the HDI has embedded the idea of poverty and development as a multi-dimensional phenomenon in the modern approach to development. New indicators such as the UNDP's Human Poverty Index (HPI) show that multi-dimensional approaches have entered the mainstream. Even the Millennium Development Goals (MDGs), the comprehensive framework that is supposed to focus the activities of all bilateral and multilateral aid agencies, can be viewed as operationalizing a multi-dimensional approach to development (see chapter 13 for an in-depth discussion of HPI and the MDGs).

GLOBAL ETHICS AND INTERNATIONAL DEVELOPMENT

You are reading this book because you have an interest in international development and, by extension, in the distribution of wealth and power, well-being and poverty in the world. It may seem obvious to you, therefore, that poverty and the negative consequences it entails for human health and well-being are on the whole a bad thing, both within your own country and in other countries throughout the world. You probably also believe that it follows logically from this belief about poverty that we should take action to avoid, mitigate, or reverse it wherever possible—and not just within our own country.

However, you may be surprised to discover that while few people would argue that poverty is not a bad thing in itself, the further belief that we should take action to address poverty is not universally shared. In addition, even among those who do accept that action should be taken to address global poverty, there are intense intellectual and political debates over how we can *justify* action on global poverty and *what* actions are justified. This section of the chapter will introduce you to some of these debates. We will look at several influential approaches to global poverty and examine their impact on international development as a field of thought and of policy action. Following this examination, we will explore dilemmas that you, as a student of international development, might face when assessing your options for action or when taking part in international development policy-making or practice.

Do our moral duties extend beyond our families, neighbours, and fellow citizens?

Over the course of the twentieth century, most Western societies developed systems of social support to ensure that no citizen would be left to die or suffer severe deprivation as a result of poverty. The welfare state was justified on both moral and pragmatic grounds. Morally, one argument for the social security system was a recognition that national economies based on the (relatively) free workings of the market left many individuals in a position of insecurity and deprivation through no fault of their own (that is, as a result of the system) (see Titmuss 1963; 1968). Society charged the state, therefore, with providing security for all citizens through programs such as national insurance, income assistance, universal health care, and education. Pragmatic justifications for the welfare state were that ensuring a minimum standard of living for all would prevent the proliferation of other social ills, such as crime, and that a healthy, educated population would result in a stronger economy. At the same time, geopolitical interests played a role in the formation of social assistance policies, since defenders of Western capitalism perceived a political threat from the socialist alternatives to market capitalism proposed by groups within these societies and pursued by other nations such as the Soviet Union.

In the mid-twentieth century, anti-colonial uprisings in Asia and Africa propelled that debate to a global level, prompting an ambiguous response from the Global North. This was the beginning of international development. Although tainted by self-interest and geopolitical considerations, development was also inspired by a perceived moral obligation to help the poor nations. In the beginning, there was tremendous excitement and enthusiasm about the idea of international development in both the North and the South. However, while the welfare state became ubiquitous among European and North American nations—although the interpretation of basic needs and rights of citizens has varied substantially among these nations (see Esping-Andersen 1990)—there has not (yet) emerged an equivalent global institution responsible for guaranteeing security and meeting the basic needs of all people through similar forms of wealth redistribution and universal public service provisions as exist at the national level. Yet many people feel that the principles of basic human rights and security should apply to all humans, regardless of where they happen to live in the world. Thus, we have moved from a time when most discussions about distributive justice were concerned primarily with distribution within states to a time when many are considering arguments surrounding distributive justice globally, or what has become known as **global ethics**.

Cosmopolitan arguments for global redistribution

Those who argue that principles of justice imply a moral obligation to address the needs of the poor not only within national boundaries but across and outside these borders largely fall within the philosophical category referred to as **cosmopolitanism**. According to cosmopolitanism, justice is owed to all people regardless of where they happen to live or where they happen to have been born and regardless of their race or gender, class or citizenship (O'Neill 2000, 45). National boundaries are therefore of little or no moral importance in considerations of justice. The majority of cosmopolitans also believe that some common values apply across humanity and some responsibilities exist towards all humanity (Dower 1998, cited in Gasper 2005, 9). Des Gasper's typology of global ethics (2007) points out, however, that belief in the low moral importance of national boundaries does not *always* entail a further belief that we have extensive responsibilities to promote pan-human values and responsibilities. Libertarians, for example, also accord low value to national boundaries but do not believe in strong duties towards others individually, nationally, or globally (see below for further discussion of libertarianism).

Nonetheless, it seems that the majority of cosmopolitan theorists believe that national boundaries are not of overriding ethical importance *and* that global justice entails a substantial set of responsibilities to people all over the world. Within this body of cosmopolitan thinking, Charles Jones (1999) identifies three main types of justification for global redistributive justice: **consequentialist** (as exemplified in the works of Peter Singer); **contractarian** (as in the works of Charles Beitz and Thomas Pogge); and **rights-based** (Jones's own position and that of Henry Shue).

Peter Singer's argument is that if we can take action that would prevent people from dying of starvation without compromising anything else of equal moral value, an impartial view of justice would clearly say that we are morally bound to take that action. Box 1.4 contains an example he offers readers to persuade them of the moral correctness of this position.

If Singer's position is correct, we can draw the conclusion that we should in fact be giving away

BOX 1.3   HOW TO JUDGE RIGHT AND WRONG: THREE PHILOSOPHICAL APPROACHES TO MORALITY

Consequentialist philosophy assesses whether an action is morally just on the basis of the goodness or value of the outcomes it produces.

Contractarian philosophy holds that moral norms are justified according to the idea of a contract or mutual agreement (as in the political philosophy of Thomas Hobbes, John Locke, and, most recently, John Rawls).

Rights-based philosophy justifies moral claims on the basis of fundamental entitlements to act or be treated in specific ways. Justifications for rights-based morality are complex, but they include the idea that we have rights because we have interests or because of our status.

all of the 'surplus' income we have as long as it does not cause us to give up something of *greater* moral value than the lives of people facing starvation anywhere in the world. One might characterize this as the 'Mother Teresa' approach (Doyle 2006) or radical sacrifice (Gasper 1986, 141), since it seems to require that we give up everything we have until we are in a similar position of poverty and have nothing left to give that would prevent another person from dying of starvation.

One objection to this position is that it is too idealistic. Surely it is not a good policy to argue in favour of a morality that seems so difficult to follow and is so unlikely to be taken up by the majority of people. Singer therefore argues that although we should accept the stringent moral duty as required by principles of justice, we could promote a more doable policy for people actually to follow. For example, everyone could be encouraged (perhaps required) to give a portion of his/her income towards preventing starvation, other serious suffering, and preventable causes of death.

Thomas Pogge (2005; 2002) argues for the moral duty to address world poverty using different justifications. He suggests that one of the key reasons we have a moral duty to alleviate global poverty is that we are in fact causally responsible

for the current situation. He supports this argument in several ways. First, he argues that the current situation of radical global inequality emerged as a result of the way today's wealthy countries ruled over poor countries during the colonial era: 'trading their people like cattle, destroying their political institutions and cultures, taking their lands and natural resources, and forcing products and customs upon them' (Pogge 2005, 2). Even if today's citizens of the world's rich countries are not responsible for what their ancestors did in the past, they equally have no claim to the fruits of their ancestors' actions—that is, the greater wealth they have inherited. Similar premises underlie the argument by Walter Rodney (1972), an influential Guyanese writer, that international development and assistance is simply a way to give back what already had been taken from the Global South.

Another argument Pogge provides takes a contractarian approach (see Box 1.3). He holds that an economic order should be considered unjust if it causes massive and severe human rights deficits that could be avoided under a different and in practice possible institutional arrangement. He argues that this is clearly the case with the current global economic order, which preserves the advantages of the wealthy and allows serious and avoidable deprivation among the poor, despite there being a 'feasible institutional alternative under which such severe and extensive poverty would not persist' (2005, 4). By preserving the current system, we (including citizens of wealthy nations, our governments, the corporations they run or support, and their participation in international institutions) are contributing to the causes of global poverty. Thus, according to Pogge, our obligation to address world poverty is based at least in part on our duty *not to harm* others.

What about the argument that national factors within poor countries are also responsible to some extent for problems of poverty, such as the greed of ruling elites, corruption, and poor planning? Pogge argues that these internal causes of poverty do not negate the fact that global institutions are *also* implicated in the persistence of seri-ous poverty and therefore bear some responsibility for it. He points to the asymmetrical rules of the World Trade Organization (WTO) that benefit wealthy countries and disadvantage poorer ones (Pogge 2005, 6). In addition, global institutions and/or Western governments frequently enable bad rulers to remain in power in poor countries by supplying money, weapons, or payments for resource exports. This support for bad rulers makes it difficult for citizens of those countries to address the national causes of poverty themselves by removing their corrupt leaders from power.

Rights-based approaches to global justice and the problem of poverty take the idea of human rights as implying duties for individuals, states, and other institutions to protect and aid those whose basic needs are not being met through contemporary global market economies.

BOX 1.4   THE DROWNING CHILD ANALOGY

Singer suggests that the following situation illustrates why justice requires us to act to prevent needless and extreme suffering regardless of national boundaries. Imagine you are walking to work and you see a small child fall into a pond. She is in danger of drowning. You could easily walk into the pond and save her without endangering your own safety, but you would get your clothing and shoes muddy. You would have to go home and change, causing you to be late for work, and your shoes might be ruined. Our moral intuition tells us that you should clearly put aside those minor inconveniences in order to save the child's life—and that if you ignored her and continued on your way, you would have done something seriously morally wrong. Furthermore, it should make no moral difference whether this little girl is your own child, your neighbour's child, or someone you don't know at all. But, Singer argues, are we not in the same position, morally speaking, when we choose to spend money on frivolous or luxurious items that are no more important than the muddy shoes in the example, rather than use that money to prevent someone from dying of starvation (for example, through donation to humanitarian agencies that have proven competence in delivering aid to the starving and needy)? And, he argues, this is clearly true even if that starvation is occurring in another part of the world, one we may never visit. Is that thousand-dollar bottle of champagne, that gold-encrusted tuna steak, that Tiffany diamond ring really more important, morally speaking, than a human life (or many of them)?

From Peter Singer. 2002. *One World.*

Charles Jones argues that the right to subsistence (principally food, shelter, and a level of health required for basic human functioning) is based on the recognition that these aspects of subsistence are universally shared human interests that are morally important. They are the most basic interests we have, because 'without food, shelter, and a reasonable level of health maintenance, human lives are simply not possible' (Jones 1999, 58). Furthermore, without the basic right to subsistence, a person cannot exercise any other rights, including those that have often been taken as fundamental in Western liberal democratic societies, such as freedom of expression or other political rights.

To say that a right exists is also to imply that there are corresponding duties: not to contravene the right, to protect the right from being contravened by others, and to aid the rights-bearer to attain the right. However, not all states are currently in a position to ensure the right to subsistence for all of their citizens, because some lack sufficient resources. This means that states with more than they need to ensure the fulfillment of the right to subsistence should redistribute wealth and resources to states unable to protect and provide subsistence rights to their citizens (Jones 1999, 70). Hence, a rights-based approach to justice can also provide moral justification for global redistribution of wealth in order to protect and aid all peoples in achieving the right to subsistence.

Arguments against global redistributive justice

The two main ethical positions opposed to cosmopolitan approaches to redistributive global justice are communitarianism and libertarianism. **Communitarianism** (exemplified in the works of Michael Walzer, Alasdair MacIntyre, Michael Sandel, and Charles Taylor) takes issue with the cosmopolitan assumption that national borders have no moral importance. Instead, communitarians believe that political and social community is morally relevant—in fact, some

feel that moral discussions (discussions about what is right and wrong) can only be understood among people sharing a common culture, language, history, and so on. In addition, some communitarians suggest that we are justified in giving (moral) preference to the needs of our fellow citizens, because membership in the nation creates special bonds, a kind of extended version of kinship. If we recognize that we can legitimately treat our family and close relationships with special care and attention and we believe that citizenship is a similar kind of kinship relation, then it is only right that we treat national borders as entailing specific rights and duties not extended to those outside the boundaries.

Another argument for the special moral importance of national boundaries is that citizens are taking part in a collective enterprise and therefore have a relationship of reciprocity among them that justifies special treatment of fellow citizens over foreigners (Callan 1997 and Feinberg 1998, cited in Singer 2002, 168–9; see also Miller 1998). In non-philosophical language, communitarian positions are sometimes referred to as *nationalist* (Gasper 1986, 138). In international relations theory, the *sceptical realist* or *international sceptic* positions also argue for the pre-eminent importance of nation-states and their actions in the international sphere. According to this view, 'countries (nation states/national States/. . .) overwhelmingly do and should pursue their own (long-term) interests, even when that involves breaking agreements' (Dower 1998, cited in Gasper 2007, 9). A state would only pursue global redistribution if it were in its own interests, without consideration of any impartial moral obligation.

Libertarian philosophy is best exemplified in the work of Robert Nozick, *Anarchy, State and Utopia* (1974), and it has been influential among a number of development theorists (for example, Deepak Lal and Peter Bauer) in the formulation of what is now known as **neo-liberalism** (see discussion in Gasper 1986; see also chapter 3 for discussion of neo-liberal development theory). Nozick argues for the primacy of the individual right to freedom and non-interference, and he places particular value on the right of individuals to acquire and retain private property. He famously characterized taxation as 'forced labour', and it is clear why this position would lead libertarians to oppose any form of obligatory redistribution of wealth, whether within one country or among countries.

Another aspect of Nozick's argument on justice is that we should not assess whether the current state of affairs is just on the basis of outcomes—i.e., wealth and poverty—but rather on the basis of just procedures (Gasper 1986, 143). If people obtain their wealth through free action in a market economy—rather than through brute force, for example—they have a right to that wealth and to dispose of it precisely as they wish. Thus, the simple existence of (even extreme) inequality of wealth and poverty does not indicate injustice; as long as the wealth was obtained legitimately, the situation should be deemed just. Individuals should be free to give donations to poorer people if they so choose, but there is no moral obligation to do so, and there should be no corresponding demand on the part of a state or other body.

We conclude this consideration of the various moral positions on justice and global poverty by examining briefly their implications for international development. If we look at statements by actors and institutions in national and international arenas, many suggest a widespread belief in universal human rights and transnational duties to protect and assist people regardless of where they live in the world. For example, the United Nations refers to common fundamental values and respect for all human rights as an important justification for adopting the Millennium Development Goals (UN General Assembly 2005); Jeffrey Sachs refers to poverty as an obstacle to people fulfilling their most basic human rights and achieving their individual potentials (2005); the G-8 posits that 'fighting poverty is both a moral imperative and a necessity for a stable world' (G-8 2000). These statements suggest a wide acceptance of a rights-

based and morally principled approach to global justice. 'Rights talk' is fashionable, and it would be virtually unthinkable for a political leader to deny the principle underlying universal human rights—that *all human life is of equal worth.*

Back in 1970, the United Nations set a goal for the world's wealthiest countries to dedicate 0.7 per cent of their GNP each year to development assistance by 1975, a goal that is still held up as a benchmark for countries to achieve. This goal can be seen to embody a belief in the obligation to redistribute wealth globally and hence suggests an acceptance of the idea of global redistributive justice. In contrast, much of the actual practice of Western aid allocation and broader approaches to global institutions seems to imply a far less consistent view of the moral obligation to address global poverty. A look at aid figures over the past few decades seems to provide evidence that 'despite the lip-service most people pay to human equality, their circle of concern barely extends beyond the boundaries of their country' (Singer 2002, 182). Development assistance is frequently allocated as if it were simply a matter for voluntary individual (or national) conscience and goodwill (if not purely a matter of self-interest) rather than a moral obligation. (Chapter 8 explores these issues in more detail.) The growth of the non-governmental sector relying on individual donations can also be interpreted as reflecting the principle that addressing global poverty is a matter of voluntary charitable action. We may think that it is a *good* thing to do but not that it is a *duty* to address the needs and rights of poor people internationally.

It is clear, then, that moral justifications are highly relevant to principles and practices of international development. It is equally clear that we, as individuals and as nations, appear to act in ways that are not always consistent with what we profess to believe is morally just. As you read this book, you should find yourself reflecting on what might be needed to bring our beliefs about justice and our actions in the global sphere more in line with each other.

ETHICAL BEHAVIOUR AND THE DEVELOPMENT PRACTITIONER

Development ethics also addresses the issue of how each of us should behave as development practitioners and researchers working in the developing world. As Des Gasper puts it, those who work on the front line 'need ethical frames by which they can better understand their situation, structure their choices, avoid debilitating degrees of doubt and guilt, and move forward' (1999, 6).

Although there are differences between the ethical responsibilities of researchers and those of practitioners, there are important commonalities between them that are required for work in developing countries. Researchers tend to be principally concerned with the issues of informed consent and respect for the privacy and confidentiality of those who participate in their studies, the implications of relationships of reciprocity with key local informants (what researchers owe them, if anything), and the benefits of the research for the community (including how to share the findings with them) (Marchall 1992, 1–3). An overriding injunction at all times is to 'do no harm'—to ensure that the vulnerable are not put at risk as a result of their participation in the research or project (Adams and Megaw 1997; Jacobsen and Landau 2003, 193). All of these ethical responsibilities are salient for practitioners as well, although informed consent usually translates as ensuring that participation is willing and voluntary in the development project at hand.

Above all, being ethical as a development worker or researcher suggests a kind of permanent self-critique and evaluation of one's actions and their effects, taking care to identify, privilege, and respect the rights of others over one's more narrow professional objectives (Adams and Megaw 1997). In other words, development ethics subordinates the goals (what we want to do) to the means of development (how we do it). In the rest of this chapter, we turn to ethical dilemmas related to positionality and lifestyle that development practitioners and researchers may expect to face in the field.

Power and positionality

We are always aware when we do not have the power in a relationship, but well-meaning people—like the typical development worker—are not always aware when they do! As Western middle-class citizens working for middle-class organizations in largely middle-class societies, many development practitioners are unprepared for the 'class shift' that occurs upon arrival in the Third World—suddenly they have cars with drivers, accommodation with servants and cooks, and people at their beck and call (Adams and Megaw 1997, 3). Beyond the novelty, these changes also indicate that because of education, country of ori-

BOX 1.5   ETHICS OF PARTICIPATORY RURAL ASSESSMENT

Robert Chambers's injunctions for participatory rural appraisal (PRA) may be viewed as good ethical guidelines for the development practitioner: 'ask them; be nice to people; don't rush; embrace error; facilitate; hand over the stick; have fun; relax; they can do it (i.e., have confidence that people are capable)' (Chambers 1997a, 1748).

gin, the agency represented, and perhaps race, practitioners are viewed differently by the locals with whom they interact and have more authority and power than they are used to having at home.

This situation is captured by the idea of **positionality**, which suggests that researchers or development practitioners must be aware of and reflect upon the social and power relationships in which they are embedded, particularly their position relative to the local people with whom they interact (Binns 2006, 19). However, the development practitioner's positionality is not always easy to assess, since all projects are 'riddled and crosscut by relationships of power', including funder/employer to researcher/practitioner, researcher to researched, as well as power disparities within the local community (based on class, literacy, ethnicity, gender, and so on) (Brydon 2006, 27). Choices made by researchers and practitioners—such as the social and political background of key assistants and translators, the non-governmental organizations (NGOs) they work with, and the political 'gatekeepers' who help them—all contribute to how local people interpret who they are and whose interests they represent.

In this respect, the development practitioner may become caught up in local struggles of which he or she is little aware. In conflict situations where tough battles are being fought for democracy, justice, and peace and where NGOs explicitly claim neutrality, they are nonetheless often seen by locals as belonging to one side or the other. The resources they introduce into poor communities and safe havens such as humanitarian corridors (for food and medicine) and refugee camps may become instruments used by combatants to further their own interests (Pouligny 2001). Even in 'normal' situations, development workers are part of the 'landscape' in which local people struggle to make ends meet. An anthropologist working in Guinea-Bissau wrote: 'We developed reciprocal relationships of "help", "trust", and "friendship" with some people in our neighbourhood. . . . In short we became intertwined with people's strategies for earning money' (Pink 1998, 9–10). How a project is carried out will affect the local balance of power in ways that are difficult to foresee. Taking positionality seriously, therefore, means that the development practitioner needs to reflect on the implications of his or her power position vis-à-vis local power structures and individuals' self-help strategies.

Lifestyle abroad

Lifestyle, dress, and behaviour abroad are important to local perceptions. In general, it is expected that development workers live modestly with the people they are supposed to assist. Professionalism and advanced technical capacity should go hand in hand with high moral and ethical standards based on transparency and democratic accountability. Most development experts see hiring and buying locally as an ethical obligation to spread the wealth. Likewise, participating in local cultural events, observing local standards of dress and modesty, and learning the local language are essential elements in building a healthy relationship with local partners (Apentiik and Parpart 2006, 39–40). Tony Binns offers some words of advice that apply equally to the researcher and the practitioner:

> . . . you are a guest in that community, and how you relate to individuals and groups will be likely to affect the responses you receive and can ultimately determine the success of your entire research project. Above all, you should respect local customs and make a determined effort to be unobtrusive, polite, and deferential. At the end of your fieldwork you should report back on your findings to the community, explaining how you intend to follow up the fieldwork after you have left (Binns 2006, 20).

Nonetheless, some development practitioners earn the derisory nickname of **development tourists** as they jet in and out of poor countries dispensing advice with little understanding of local conditions (Adams and Megaw 1997, citing Chambers 1997a). The generous per diems received by UN and national development 'experts' that compensate them for all the foreseeable risks and inconveniences of visiting a developing country are viewed by many as morally objectionable when contrasted with the poverty outside the consultant's five-star hotel (Gasper 1999, 20).

More listening and less talking

The personal modesty we discussed above also applies to the broader issue of how development actors engage with local people and communities. The ethical guidelines adopted by development NGOs increasingly point to the need to do more listening and less talking. The code of ethics of one prominent NGO asserts: 'development should enable people, especially the poor, the oppressed, and the marginalized, to organize and to improve their political, social, and economic situation' (CCIC 2004, 2.2 [c]). In other words, aid works when people work with other people as equals. Although such attitudes may appear self-evident, there are too many examples of development mission staff lecturing politicians from the Global South 'like schoolboys' in a (deliberate?) attempt to leave them powerless (Klitgaard 1991, cited in Gasper 1999, 24).

Today, anyone who wishes to be involved in international development cannot but experience a great sense of modesty as compared to the kind of intellectual arrogance that was prevalent in the past. Modesty can mean many things, including a sense that the 'Western' way is *not* the only way, that the achievements of richer countries are not necessarily replicable or even desirable in poor countries, that Western science and techniques are not always value-neutral, and that there are other narratives to explain reality and to change it in a pro-people way. Development agencies and practitioners should not assume that they can solve local problems from the outside when solutions exist at the local level, which is frequently the case. This growing self-critical attitude among contemporary researchers and practitioners in what we may term the *post-naive* era of development represents a welcome break from the simplistic interpretations of the past.

In lieu of conclusion, we may ask future development practitioners and researchers to reflect upon the words of Mahatma Ghandi: 'Recall the face of the poorest and the weakest man whom you may have seen, and ask yourself if the step you contemplate is going to be of any use to him. Will he gain anything by it? Will it restore him to a control over his own life and destiny? In other words, will it lead to *Swaraj* [self-rule] for the hungry and spiritually starving millions?' (Kerala 2003, 12).

QUESTIONS FOR DISCUSSION

1. Why is the term Third World sometimes viewed unfavourably? Which alternatives are most appealing?

2. Why is inequality the crucial link between GNP per capita and the number of people living in poverty in a given country?

3. Why is GDP an inadequate measure of development?

4. What is a 'multi-dimensional' approach to development?

5. Why should the rich 'help' those in poverty?

FURTHER READING

Allen, Tim, and Alan Thomas, eds. 2000. *Poverty and Development into the 21st Century*. Oxford: Oxford University Press and The Open University.

Desai, Vandana, and Robert B. Potter, eds. 2006. *Doing Development Research*. London: Sage.

Payne, A., ed. 2004. *The New Regional Politics of Development*. Basingstoke, UK: Palgrave Macmillan.

Sachs, Jeffrey D. 2005. *The End of Poverty: Economic Possibilities for Our Time*. New York: Penguin.

Todaro, Michael P., and Stephen C. Smith. 2006. *Economic Development in the Third World*. 9th edn. Boston: Addison Wesley.

Wood, G., ed. 1995. *Labelling in Development Policy: Essays in Honour of Bernard Schaffer*. London: Sage; The Hague: Institute of Social Studies.

INTERNET RESOURCES

World Bank country classification: http:www.worldbank.org/data/countryclass/classgroups.htm.

World Bank's *World Development Report*: http:www.worldbank.org/wdr.

United Nations Development Programme's *Human Development Report*: http://hdr.undp.org.

United Nations Conference on Trade and Development (UNCTAD): http://www.unctad.org.

International Development Ethics Association: http://www.development-ethics.org.

NOTES

1. The Gini coefficient is based on the Lorenz curve, which plots the proportion of national income accruing to each segment of the population. The Gini coefficient is a ratio of the area between the curve and a line representing total equality to the total area under the line of equality.

CHAPTER 2

IMPERIALISM AND THE COLONIAL EXPERIENCE

ERIC ALLINA-PISANO

LEARNING OBJECTIVES

- To identify at least two causes for imperial expansion.
- To specify at least three important consequences of colonial rule for indigenous societies.

'He was a sugar planter or something. Wasn't that it, Manuel?'
'Yes madam. He was sugar. He was sugar, wine, sugar brandy, coal, sardines, water, everything. . . . He took the water from the people and sold it back again.'
'You mean he developed the country.'

H.E. Bates. *Summer in Salandar*.

From 'First and Third World', to 'centre and periphery', to 'developed and developing', we have now arrived at 'Global North and South' to describe the world's uneven distribution of political and financial capital. Each of these paired terms has a history, and as much as the compass-oriented labels now in vogue strive to elide that history, they cannot, if only because some parts of the 'South' lie an inconvenient distance north of the equator. What each pair unsuccessfully attempts to euphemize is a separation of the world along a gradient, a separation whose modern history began with the creation of European empires in what is now known as the 'South'. There are, of course, exceptions to prove this rule, perhaps none more outstanding than the United States, a world superpower for much of the twentieth century, a state composed of former British, French, Dutch, Russian, and Spanish colonies.

We might trace the history of interaction between this Global North and South back to the fif-teenth-century explorations, led by the Portuguese and the Spanish, that gave rise to European expansion into the Americas and Asia. Yet the 'age of exploration', as it has sometimes been called, is something of a misnomer: by the time Portuguese sailor Vasco da Gama's sea voyage in 1497–9 turned Europe's contact with Asia into one of regular (if not rapid) exchange, people, goods, and ideas had been travelling along the great Central Asian highway known as the 'silk road' for centuries. Europeans besides Marco Polo had made the trip east, and Chinese and other inhabitants of Asia had gone west. This very long history of interaction was one reason that da Gama knew of his destination in advance: the world he entered was known to those who lived in it, if not to him (Newitt 2005, 2–3). Such earlier interactions notwithstanding, most exchange between Europe and Asia had taken place through intermediaries, with merchants and traders all along the southern and eastern portions of the Mediterranean Sea marketing Asian and African products to European consumers. Previously, it was the rare traveller who moved from one sphere into the other, but such movement now became more routine.

EUROPEAN EXPANSION AND CONQUEST

Southern Europe's interactions with largely Muslim traders were an important factor in

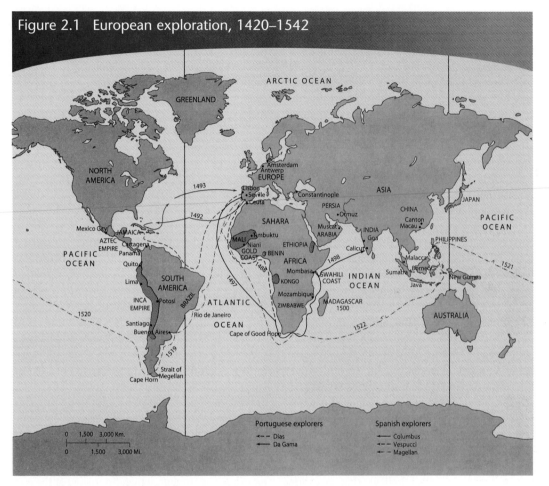

Figure 2.1   European exploration, 1420–1542

Source: Richard W. Bulliet et al. 2005. *The Earth and Its Peoples: A Global History*. 3rd edn, p.427. Boston: Houghton Mifflin.

Portuguese and Spanish decisions to embark upon the seafaring explorations that led to Europe's more direct contact with a wider world. The kingdoms of Portugal and Spain had only been established following the thirteenth-century military reconquest of the Iberian Peninsula, territory the Christian rulers had seized from its Muslim occupants. This foundational conflict was one impulse that led the Spanish and Portuguese to confront their North African neighbours. Accordingly, in 1415 Portuguese forces invaded Ceuta, a city whose wealth made it known to the Portuguese as the 'flower of all other cities of Africa' (Diffie and Winius 1977, 53). The assault was successful, and following their conquest and occupation of the city, the Portuguese learned more about the sources of its great wealth, such as its access to a gold trade that came from points south of the Sahara northwards into the Mediterranean world. The motives for expansion were thus at once political-religious, born of a competitive tension with Muslim neighbours, and economic, owing to ambitious Europeans' desire for more direct access to goods—not only gold but spices and textiles as well, much sought after in Europe's growing towns and cities, now beginning to recover from the ravages of the Black Death.

The desire for more direct trade with African and Asian societies, eliminating Muslim middlemen, was fulfilled in the vast seaborne expansion during the sixteenth century. Spain and Portugal established their previously unplanned presence in the Americas and created footholds in Africa and Asia. They were soon joined by the French, the English, and the Dutch, leading to several centuries of expansion, occupation, and competition among the European empire-builders for control over these far-flung sources of wealth, power, and glory. Over the next three centuries, the Spanish, French, Portuguese, and British founded—and mostly lost—vast colonial possessions in the Americas, while their holdings in Africa and Asia only grew.

If there is consensus on the motives for Europe's initial phase of expansion, the same cannot be said for the final burst of conquest and occupation towards the end of the nineteenth century. Following an interpretation offered by English scholar John Hobson and also strongly associated with Vladimir Lenin (the Russian revolutionary and theorist who helped end the rule of Russia's Romanov dynasty and launch the October Revolution in 1917, bringing forth the Soviet Union), many scholars believe that economic motives linked to the **Industrial Revolution** launched the classic 'high' **imperialism** of this period (Hobson 1902; Lenin 1920 [1916]). According to this view, the expansion of European empires was undertaken as part of a search for new markets: economic returns within Europe were dwindling, and industrial capitalism had to search abroad for new investment opportunities and consumers. Renewed expansion and the creation of new colonies were thus necessary, because most of Europe still practised protectionist trade policies. This economic explanation offers an appealing logic, and the emphasis on the role of capitalism dovetails neatly with the eventual exploitation, most especially of African labour, that followed during the era of high imperialism. The

Hobson–Lenin thesis nonetheless has its critics, among them economic historians who point to the limited investment made in the new overseas colonies, as well as other scholars who find the model places too much importance on impersonal economic structures in general and ignores any role Asians and Africans may have played in particular.

Another approach also focuses on Europe but combines political and economic factors to explain the rapid expansion of empire. According to this view, 'Great Power' rivalry, most especially between Britain, France, and Germany, drove Europe's statesmen in a rush to seize territories as yet unclaimed in Southeast Asia and Africa. European leaders saw the opportunity to expand as part of a zero-sum game, and in light of the tensions and rivalries that existed in crowded Europe, none were content to wait while any of their neighbours moved ahead, especially after the discovery of diamonds (1867) and gold (1886) in South Africa. Although a desire to secure access to strategically important industrial inputs, such as rubber, or to gain control over areas long believed to possess great riches, such as parts of tropical Africa, was not irrelevant, this understanding emphasizes the imperial powers' race to keep pace with their neighbours.

Associated with the Great Power explanation is the belief in the important role played by nationalist sentiment, which flourished at the end of the nineteenth century. Thus, the emergence of Germany and Italy as unified states was a key factor, especially for France, an older imperial power now concerned with its German neighbour's new expansionary activity. Nearly all of Europe's nations, however, were preoccupied with attaining the degree of prestige and sense of greatness they believed was their due. This explanation is often deployed to account for the outsized role played by Belgium and Portugal, two small and relatively minor European powers whose involvement in the 'scramble for Africa' had no clear connection to political or economic interests, yet both countries ended up with vast African colonies (for broad syntheses of these debates, see Sanderson 1974 and Kennedy 1977).

What none of these explanations include, however, is much room for the actions of what some historians call the 'men on the spot', a term most common in studies of British empire though just as useful elsewhere. These men—for they were all men—often took decisions to expand European activity and territorial claims, even when such moves (and the means by which they were achieved) went beyond or even ran counter to official metropolitan policy. Reacting to local crises or opportunities amid a wider atmosphere of tension and transformation, their improvisations may have had little immediate connection to industrial capitalism or domestic nationalism, but the effect was to expand the European field of action and build bigger empires.

Most scholars now accept the idea that each of these explanations can account for some important part of the history of empire-building. Although some may long for a theory that might explain all imperial expansion in the final third of the nineteenth century, the staggeringly far-flung extent of these endeavours, encompassing such very different parts of the world, with accordingly different political and economic conditions, defies any such attempt short of writing a 'total history' (Sanderson 1974; Kennedy 1977).

The debates over the causes of imperialism or **colonialism** are unfortunately matched by lack of consensus over just what either of the two terms may be said to mean. In common usage, imperialism refers to the era of European expansion that began in the sixteenth century, when first the Portuguese and the Spanish and then the English, French, and Dutch created empires of trade in the Americas and Asia and, to a lesser extent, Africa. African territory did not, for the most part, come under imperial control or witness **colonization** (outside of Algeria and South Africa) until the last quarter of the nineteenth century; some scholars target in particular the period from 1870 to 1914 as the era of 'high imperialism'. The word imperialism itself first came into use in the late nineteenth century, when it referred to the operation of Britain's empire: a political system by which colonies are ruled from a central seat of power in the pursuit of largely if not entirely economic goals (Williams 1983, 159). This meaning of imperialism neatly describes some of the earlier European empires (such as the Spanish, English, or French territories of the Caribbean and the Americas) as well as those that covered Africa and good parts of South and Southeast Asia from the last quarter of the nineteenth century through the mid-twentieth century.

Another meaning of imperialism, however, casts it not as a political system but as an economic one in which a state pursues 'external investment and penetration of markets and sources of raw materials' (Williams 1983, 159–60). This idea of imperialism is closely associated with the concept of neo-colonialism, by which the economies of formally independent countries remain subject to the control of others, often their former colonial rulers. Such a system may, of course, continue past the formal end of colonial rule, with the former imperial power continuing to exert strong control over a nominally independent ex-colony. In some uses, prior colonization is not considered necessary, such as might be the case when imperialism is applied to the involvement of the United States in the Middle East since the mid-twentieth century or of China's increasing influence in sub-Saharan Africa since the turn of the twenty-first century.

Colonization, in the sense of settling and occupying a specified territory, can refer to other contexts as well. Some scholars of early African history, for example, consider the expansion of African societies into unpopulated or sparsely populated areas as a process of colonization. Similarly, most evidence suggests that the earliest human societies in Madagascar were established by colonists who travelled to the island from Southeast Asia. However, neither of these instances of distant settlement took place as part of an imperial expansion or resulted in ongoing political or economic links between the society of origin and the society of settlement. The foundation of a colony may simply indicate the displacement and resettling of a population; colonialism implies the rule of some people over others (Cooper 2006, 28).

Figure 2.2   East African troops

Source: Northwestern University Library, Melville J. Herskovits Library of African Studies, The Winterton Collection of East African Photographs: 1860-1960.

The relationship between imperialism, colonial rule, and development has drawn great interest from scholars, politicians, and policy-makers alike, and many have sought to explain how European imperial expansion led to or prevented development in those areas of the world now considered to be developing countries. Few would question that colonial rule had an impact on economic development in colonized territories, but there is no consensus on just what kind of development European imperialism (and colonialism) brought about in Africa, the Americas, and Asia.

RIVAL EMPIRES OF TRADE

Ventures to the east brought Europeans into a crowded arena that joined together several regions, each one washed by the Indian Ocean. Local and regional trading networks had long linked South Asia to peninsular and island Southeast Asia and to the Arabian and Red Sea regions and the coast of east Africa to the west. After the Portuguese arrival in South Asia in 1498, Europe soon established a permanent presence with Lisbon's conquest of Goa, an urban trading centre on present-day India's western coast, in 1510. The English, Dutch, and French quickly joined the expansion into Indian Ocean waters, all hoping to dislodge the Portuguese from the position of dominance they had seized as European pioneers. The Dutch and English soon created **chartered companies**—the Dutch and English East India companies—in an effort to enlist private investment in the service of empire; the French did the same later in a belated effort to compete, while the Portuguese Crown retained more direct control over its eastern empire. The recruitment of private capital by the English and

Dutch proved a shrewd decision, for it broadened the financial base for expansionary activity and provided a sturdier platform that better withstood the cut and thrust of imperial rivalries.

Out of this seaborne scrum, the rivals began to carve out areas of influence: the Dutch soon assumed a dominant position in the spice trade out of the Southeast Asian islands (present-day Indonesia and Malaysia), leading the English East India Company to concentrate on the South Asian subcontinent. The French competed with the British on South Asia's east coast, while the Portuguese clung to their base on the west coast. The various European powers sought openings overseen by the Mughal emperors, the recently risen rulers of the South Asian subcontinent. The Mughals welcomed the outsiders' rivalry because the emperor could capitalize on the competition among them to demand better terms of trade, reversing the trend that had prevailed during the first decades of Portuguese monopoly when the newcomers had been able to impose trade terms less favourable to them.

The 'new' world that Europeans entered in the Americas differed greatly from the one they encountered in Asia. In Central and South America, European arrival and the labour practices imposed on conquered Amerindian societies produced a staggering population collapse, making any continuation of existing political systems a near impossibility. European sailors and explorers carried smallpox to the Americas; the indigenous peoples of the Americas had no prior exposure and virtually no resistance to the virus. The disease laid waste to the previously populous societies of Meso-America. Alongside this unintended biological assault, the Spanish, in their eagerness to acquire as much silver and gold bullion as possible from their rapidly growing empire, enslaved indigenous people by the thousands and worked them to death mining gold and silver. In some places, such as the island of Hispaniola (present-day Haiti and Dominican Republic), the death toll resulted in near extinction: the indigenous Taino people numbered at least one million (and perhaps as many as five million) in 1492 but by 1550 had disappeared. In present-day Mexico, the Aztec state collapsed as the population plummeted from perhaps 25 million in 1518 to just over a million in 1605 (Watts 1999, 84–90). No political institution could survive this degree of social destruction, and that fact ensured that any political system that might be created in New World empires would be cut from whole cloth.

Imperial expansion, especially in Spain's New World possessions, brought an unimagined wealth to the Iberian *conquistadores*. The captured Inca ruler Atahualpa, for example, offered his Spanish captors a ransom of 6,000 kilograms of gold and 12,000 of silver. (The Spanish eagerly took the ransom but instead of granting Atahualpa his freedom only gave him a choice between being burned at the stake and being baptized, then strangled as a believer in Christ. He chose baptism and strangulation.) The prospect of such immense wealth, together with the decimation of Amerindian societies, resulted in greater immigration to the Americas than to other imperial possessions. Spanish colonists sought their fortunes in gold and silver mining and wielded great power, staffing the viceroyalties of Peru and New Spain, as the Spanish territories were called. The large numbers and eventual strength of this colonial elite led to broad tensions with the Spanish Crown, which recognized the potential threat they posed to ongoing imperial control.

Meanwhile, along with gold diggers the Portuguese exported sugar cultivation, which they had pioneered on the Atlantic islands of Madeira and the Azores, to the New World. Sugar—and an important product thereof, rum—flourished in Brazil and especially on the Caribbean islands, becoming a major item in the so-called triangular trade with Europe and Africa. From the later 1600s, export of African slaves to the Americas grew enormously, largely to supply labour for sugar (and later cotton and tobacco) production. The elimination of the Amerindian population was a major factor in Europeans' decision to purchase millions of African slaves and export them to the Americas, although the ability of European merchants to purchase slaves in

Africa in exchange for relatively low-cost manufactured goods was also important. Towards the end of the seventeenth century, this forced African migration far outstripped European settlement, and colonial masters depended mightily on their black slaves, who built the foundations of the New World colonies and ensured their economic growth for centuries to come.

In contrast to Meso and South America and the Caribbean, South Asian polities remained robust in early and ongoing interactions with agents of European empire, both in defence of local sovereignty and in pursuit of economic interest. To a certain extent, agents of European empire were compelled to accept terms dictated by the Mughal emperor: as much as the Europeans held sway at sea—for the Mughals had no navy or merchant fleet—Indian rulers accepted no challenge to their dominance on land, strictly limiting the outsiders' rights even to self-defence. Unlike the situation in the Americas, Europeans arrived in Asia with no significant advantage in military technology, and local armies were more than their match.

The greater the number of European firms vying for access to Indian markets, the stronger the Indian negotiating position. The question of competition would come to be of great strategic importance in future years: as Mughal power began to fade around the turn of the eighteenth century, the British and French sought to expand their influence with the regionally based successor states that emerged. Through the first several decades of the eighteenth century, European trading companies found that by allying with and even fighting on behalf of the rulers of Indian states, they could secure valuable concessions, such as duty-free export rights, that could boost their profits significantly.

Through the middle of the eighteenth century, France and Britain vied for dominance in South Asia as in Europe and the Americas. Britain topped her rival in Asia, especially after the English East India Company gained control of Bengal province in 1765. Exploiting rivalries within Bengal's political and commercial elites, the company defeated the Mughal armies, and although Bengal remained part of the Mughal empire on paper, the company emerged as the real power in eastern India. The province was one of India's most economically productive, and the company now held the rights to Bengal's revenue as well as free reign to trade there. As much as it was a significant political evolution, this development also marked a key turning point in the economic history of imperial activity. Previously, the company had financed its purchase of Indian exports with gold bullion, but with rights to locally raised tax revenues, its operations were now locally financed. Thanks to its military adventures, the company now exercised an economic dominance as well and could rely on its ability to raise local revenue to fund its military actions, a practice known as 'military fiscalism'.

From this point forward, the company became a virtual juggernaut; although it ruled only a part of India directly, it wielded great influence over a much wider area through alliances with the princely rulers of individual states. With control over Bengal's vast revenues, the company expanded its military forces, creating a professional army that made it among the most powerful of any in the region. Having squeezed out its European rivals (French influence receded rapidly through the last third of the eighteenth century, and the Dutch East India Company was dissolved in 1795), the company held a commanding position in its relations with Indian elites—political, financial, and commercial—who saw in the company a powerful partner that could secure their own interests. For some, whose loyalties were locally rooted, the benefits that might come from alliance with the company were far more important than the consequences of such partnerships for people in other parts of the subcontinent or for the overall balance of power. Absent any broadly shared identity, ambitious individuals in South Asia had no reason to resist the company's influence if they might profit from its presence.

In tandem with the company's growing control over territory in South Asia came a more active role in economic life as well. No longer

BOX 2.1   AN 'ORIENTAL DESPOT': BRITISH COMPANY RULE IN SOUTH ASIA

Queen Elizabeth I's government created the English East India Company in 1600, granting it extensive powers and a measure of autonomy from the state. At the same time, the English state devolved the burden of raising capital and the inevitable risk of the distant undertaking to private investors. With a monopoly on British trade with Asia and the right to arm its trading fleet, the company possessed the economic and coercive force that would make it the most powerful actor in European imperial history.

For most of its first two centuries, the company jockeyed for position with rival Dutch and French companies. It also vied to create a more secure relationship with Indian rulers who controlled the company's access to the subcontinent's producers and to consumers. Outlasting its European competitors, whose position weakened in part because of a changing domestic political landscape, the company, powered by England's early industrialization, was alone in a position to challenge India's princely rulers in the last quarter of the eighteenth century.

Having spent nearly two centuries as a naval or at most a coastal power, the company expanded throughout South Asia in the late eighteenth and first half of the nineteenth century. Despite its new dominance, the company continued to recognize the Mughal emperor as a symbol of Indian authority and in individual states left princes on their thrones as figureheads. Doing so meant that the public, visible face of authority—embodied in the 'magnificence of princely courts [and] the gifting and patronage activities they sustained'—would remain Indian. Behind the throne, the company's resident officers controlled military forces, negotiated relations with other rulers, and oversaw revenue collection, often seizing vast fortunes for their personal enrichment (Metcalf and Metcalf 2006, 75). These 'men on the spot', as they became known, had tremendous latitude to make decisions independent of company policy, which sometimes lagged behind their improvisations.

This indirect rule preserved a veneer of indigenous authority over the reality of company power and it was in keeping with British beliefs that essential cultural differences between South Asian people and Europeans made European-style representative government impossible. The company (and later the British government, once the British Crown took charge of India following a rebellion in 1857) insisted on governance that represented a rule of law: a commitment to law, rather than the personal rule of a prince or emperor believed to characterize 'Oriental despotism', was part of the way that the company justified its writ. Yet in refusing any role for South Asian representation in government and in establishing a legal code that privileged colonizers' rights and interests and those of the wealthy local elite, it was the English East India Company (and eventually the British colonial state) that was the 'Oriental despot' until the end of colonial rule in 1947.

confined to importing and exporting goods, the company used its influence to begin reshaping the regional economy. Of signal importance was the extensive rail network constructed in the middle of the nineteenth century. Linking the vast hinterland to port cities (and the ports to one another), the railway greatly reduced transport times and costs, transforming the economy. In the process, however, it also laid down in iron rails the features of an underdeveloped economy:

an infrastructure suitable for the export of high-bulk, low-value products. It was a missed opportunity to develop closer ties among the subcontinent's different regions and to integrate potentially complementary economic sectors. Instead, the export-oriented network served the company's interests, and with financing from British investors, the system generated profits that left the country instead of producing revenue that might have been invested locally.

'HIGH' IMPERIALISM IN AFRICA

If South Asia's encounter with European imperialism was a case of conquest in slow motion, with the better part of three centuries elapsing between Vasco da Gama's arrival and the English East India Company's emergence as a territorial power, the creation of European colonies in Africa occurred at a breakneck pace by comparison. The last two decades of the nineteenth century saw Europeans burst forth from scattered coastal enclaves, some of which they had held for centuries, to seize the entire continent, except for Ethiopia. In this era of high imperialism, Africa occupied centre stage, with Belgium, England, France, Germany, Portugal, Italy, and Spain all establishing African colonies, albeit the last two limited to comparatively small territories.

However, Europe's imperial powers felt such ambivalence about the colonial endeavour in Africa that nearly all sought to find a way to draw non-state actors into the process, mostly by granting charters to private companies that undertook many of the initial (and sometimes more) steps. Perhaps the most famous of these companies was Cecil Rhodes's British South Africa Company, a vehicle for his continent-sized ambition, which the diamond baron used to seize present-day Zambia and Zimbabwe. But the British also used companies in Kenya (the Imperial British East Africa Company) and Nigeria (the Royal Niger Company), as the Germans did in Tanganyika (the German East Africa Company). Similarly, the French rented out a wide swathe of central Africa to concessionary companies, and the Belgian government was so uninterested in creating an African empire that King Leopold I on his own pursued a vast private fief in present-day Democratic Republic of the Congo, parts of which he leased out to private companies in return for a percentage of the profits. (Only in the face of international protest over the abuses committed there was the Belgian state persuaded to take over the territory from Leopold.) Most of these companies held their state-like powers for only a decade or so before being replaced by formal colonial administrations early in the twentieth century, but they carried out the strategically vital, expensive, and bloody tasks of conquest and construction of basic infrastructure. Rhodes's company lasted longer than most, ceding its powers only in 1923, although it was outlived by two companies Portugal had created in Mozambique in the 1890s, one of which endured until 1929 and the other until 1942.

The first generations of scholarship on the history of colonialism in Africa focused a good deal of attention on perceived differences between British, French, and Portuguese approaches to colonial rule. German rule, being comparatively short-lived (following World War I, Britain and France divided most of Germany's colonies, with Belgium taking Rwanda and Burundi; southwest Africa was something of an exception, being entrusted to South African rule under a League of Nations mandate), tended to be ignored in these analyses, as was Italian and Spanish, while Belgian rule was similarly overlooked. The focus on metropolitan differences, largely confined to the realm of formal policy, made much of an apparent difference between British **indirect rule** versus French direct rule. The Portuguese, on the other hand, were judged to have followed a third path, an especially hands-on and, according to some, more violent version of direct rule. Yet conquest across the board was prosecuted with violence, and all colonial rule was backstopped by violence or its threat; the variation in actual practice on the ground owed more to time and place than to the national origin of the colonizer. As one historian noted, indirect rule was associated with

BOX 2.2   THE 'SCRAMBLE' FOR AFRICA

The late nineteenth-century European conquest of Africa is often referred to as the 'scramble for Africa', a phrase that suggests both speed and disorder. On the eve of Africa's partition, European powers had only a handful of colonies on the continent despite having visited and traded with coastal African societies for more than 400 years. When German Chancellor Otto von Bismarck convened the Berlin Conference in late 1884 (with not a single African representative in attendance), the European powers agreed on ground rules for their land grab. Henceforth, a claim to African territory would be commonly recognized if the claimant had established 'effective occupation' of the area. The effect was to accelerate the process, with the scramblers rushing to put 'boots on the ground'. In the resulting flurry of activity, seven European states divided the continent into 40 colonies, leaving only Ethiopia unclaimed or unoccupied, while resistant African leaders clung to a fragile and dwindling independence.

The political and economic topography of late nineteenth-century Africa at the time of partition was markedly uneven. Large African empires with powerful centralized rulers, some controlling long-distance trade in ivory and slaves, existed in most regions of the continent, while smaller independent polities ruled by local authorities were also common. In some areas, notably coastal west and east Africa and their littorals, existing regional economic networks had grown ever stronger since the abolition of the slave trade earlier in the century, and through these networks, local producers (mostly producers of vegetable products sought by European industry but also elephant hunters who supplied ivory for growing middle-class consumers) were tied to international commercial networks. With their links to overseas finance, these areas became even more 'extroverted' in their orientation, while other parts of the continent were characterized by locally oriented self-sustaining economies.

In many instances, the European powers inserted themselves into areas fraught with tension, at times born of friction between expanding states and at others resulting from competition over trade. Amid such tensions, African leaders were eager to sign treaties with Europeans, hoping to gain an edge over their neighbours or enemies. In view of these existing divisions, the European powers employed less of a strategy of 'divide and rule', but they were deft in their manipulation of local rivalries. African rulers soon found that after a rival had been subdued or defeated, their erstwhile allies turned on them, now demanding their submission. Standing alone against encroaching European forces, sometimes reinforced by African troops drawn from among those already conquered, remaining African leaders faced a choice between signing treaties that presumed their submission or fighting to remain sovereign. Armed with the Maxim (machine) gun, fortified against malaria with quinine, and more manoeuvrable than ever before with easily assembled (and disassembled) steam-powered flat-bottomed riverboats, the scramblers' forces encountered few opponents who could withstand their attack.

Britain 'not so much because the British applied more indirect rule but because they talked more about it than others' (Kiwanuka 1970, 300).

The focus on the European origins of colonial policies misses the important ways in which policies imagined in London or Lisbon were transformed by the challenge of putting them into practice and by the opportunistic nature of many colonial administrators, who seized whatever openings were available in striving to meet their goals. Britain's policy of indirect rule for its African colonies was, in important respects, a product of failure more than anything else: an inability to break the power of local African rulers in northern Nigeria led the British administrator responsible for the region to declare instead his intention to keep them in place so that he might rule indirectly through them. If there was any genius to the policy, it was in public relations—in making virtue out of failure and proclaiming the result to be official policy (Cooper, Holt, and Scott 2000, 124–5).

Indirect rule in colonial Africa followed closely on the early model the British had established in South Asia. It was perhaps even more in this later case a decision based on practicality. By keeping local rulers in place (or creating them where indigenous authorities proved difficult to identify or co-opt), colonizers saved themselves the difficulty of establishing new forms of authority or the expense of employing large numbers of European administrators. European colonizers found quick profits in only a few parts of the continent, such as South Africa's gold and diamond strikes or the Congo Free State's short-lived rubber boom, and despite an enduring myth that African colonies would turn out to be another Eldorado, the colonizing powers were reluctant to

Figure 2.3   The sultan of Zanzibar

Source: Northwestern University Library, Melville J. Herskovits Library of African Studies, The Winterton Collection of East African Photographs: 1860-1960.

invest much or incur ongoing costs in Africa. In much the same fashion that the East India Company had done in South Asia, colonial administrators sought to identify and codify the 'customary' law that they believed governed African societies; their aim was to rule Africans indirectly through their own laws, enforced by their own leaders, who answered to colonial administrators. If they could incorporate local African rulers at the lower rungs of colonial administration, they could achieve at low cost a dominance that they believed would be viewed legitimately by the African population at large: a 'hegemony on a shoestring' (Berry 1992).

Colonial rule did not affect all colonized people in the same manner. Depending on their position in society, especially their exposure to specific economic or political practices, certain groups of individuals might lose (or gain) material or social capital. The clearest cases of such differential impact occurred with indirect rule, under which many local elites benefited: some helped to collect new tax levies and received a portion for their role, while others, with the tacit support of the colonial state, imposed new burdens on their subjects. But more broadly, the great political and economic changes associated with colonial rule created winners and losers, and some people gained influence over others in the process. The overall effect was to strengthen existing cleavages or to create new ones in indigenous societies, with resulting social tensions. Particularly towards the end of the colonial era (the 1930s and 1940s in Asia and the 1950s in Africa), political constituencies manoeuvred for position as independence approached, and these cleavages—along lines of religion, language, ethnicity, race, and class—became sources of heightened tension and outright conflict, at times very violently so.

COMMON THEMES IN THE COLONIAL EXPERIENCE

The colonial rule established under imperial systems of government lasted long enough—two centuries or more in South Asia and parts of the Americas, less lengthy in Africa, where some scholars emphasize the brevity of the colonial era by pegging it at 'only' eight decades—to transform indigenous societies in a fundamental manner. The breadth of change wrought in political and economic life was such that it is difficult to address overall in a cohesive fashion. (Central Asia is one area of colonial rule outside the context of colonization by western European powers and largely absent from comparative scholarship, with the exception of Beissinger and Young 2002. It came under Russian imperial rule in the eighteenth century, and the Soviet Union later asserted control. Empire and colonial rule thus may flourish in the absence of a capitalist economic system; many of the economic and political outcomes considered characteristic of post-colonial societies are evident in post-Soviet Central Asia.) Rather than attempting an encyclopedic coverage, this section focuses on three broad themes that reflect common elements of the colonial experience: European faith in essential cultural differences and the superiority of European peoples, often used to justify exploitative economic policies and violently abusive governance practices; metropolitan states' ambivalence regarding the overseas commitments of empire; and a movement, in the twilight years of colonial rule, towards the promotion of economic development in colonial territories.

Late nineteenth-century imperial boosters rallied others, including sometimes reluctant government ministers, to their cause with claims regarding the inferiority of peoples and cultures outside of Europe. Influenced by so-called social Darwinist ideas, which had little to do with those Darwin offered in *On the Origin of Species* in 1859, they applied the idea of evolution not to individual species but instead to human societies. They believed that European peoples represented a more evolved type of human being and human society, while other, darker-skinned people and societies were supposedly examples of still-surviving earlier forms. These beliefs powerfully shaped attitudes towards empire in two ways. First, with Asian or African cultures seen as inferior and even 'primitive', their sub-ordination and even destruction was easily jus-tified in the name of progress. Following on this, because indigenous African or Asian societies were regarded as backward, their transforma-tion, by force if necessary, was judged to be a moral duty of Europeans as the bearers of a higher civilization.

These secular beliefs were prosecuted with a zeal not unlike the longer-standing and persistent spiritual impulse to spread Christianity and 'save' souls from what was believed to be their unhappy heathen fate. The belief in indigenous inferiority was so tightly held that in its imperviousness to dispositive proof, it resembled faith. Thomas Macaulay, a senior British official who served in India from the 1830s, exemplified this stance, infamously expressed in his claim that 'the entire native literature of India and Arabia' was not worth 'a single shelf of a good European library'. The claim stands as a hallmark of European chau-vinism, all the more remarkable in light of Macaulay's lack of knowledge of any Indian lan-guage. He instead was a proponent of angliciza-tion for Britain's Indian subjects, supporting English-language education to create a 'class who may be interpreters between us and the millions we govern; a class of persons Indian in blood and colour but English in tastes, in opinions, in morals, and in intellect' (Metcalf and Metcalf 2006, 81; Bose and Jalal 2004, 67).

Imperial expansion did not always occur quickly or decisively, for metropolitan govern-ments were sometimes unsure of the benefits of expansion and leery of taking on new commit-ments, particularly overseas. Yet once imperial powers committed themselves to acts of colonial conquest—sometimes because they feared that they might be outmanoeuvred by a European rival—they prosecuted these wars with maximum force. In the imperial era of the late nineteenth century, particularly in Africa, this meant mar-shalling the resources of a modern industrial state against opponents nearly always outmatched in military terms. There were exceptions to this rule,

and one of the most successful cases of indigenous resistance was that of Samori Touré, the ruler of a large state in west Africa, who fought French forces tenaciously for the better part of two decades before succumbing to conquest in 1898. (Ethiopia's successful stand against the Italians, dealing their forces a devastating blow in 1896, is the single case of a European empire defeated in Africa.) Still, even once imperial powers estab-lished control over the territories they sought, they maintained an ambivalence towards invest-ment of the resources that would have brought the reality of colonial rule into line with the rhet-oric of the civilizing mission.

Those who examine colonial attitudes and policies towards indigenous peoples sometimes point to stated differences among French, Portuguese, and British approaches, such as the French intention to assimilate Africans and make them 'black Frenchmen' as opposed to the British commitment to creating 'civilized Africans'. Although formal differences existed among these approaches, all were based on a faith in the supe-riority of European culture and in the benefit it could bring to African societies. Additionally, for most of the period of colonial rule, these policies affected very few people: French 'assimilation' required attainment of, for example, literacy in French, an achievement beyond most people's means, given colonial neglect of African education. Instead, the underlying belief in cultural hierarchy and racial difference was used to justify a wide range of practices whereby indigenous people were forced—sometimes through great violence—to serve Europeans' objectives and needs.

Part of the progress that European powers claimed to be bringing to their colonial territo-ries was a transformation of economic life to the 'modern' level of European economies. What this meant in practice was an overwhelming orienta-tion of African economies towards production of raw materials for export. Mineral extraction—especially of copper, gold, tin, and diamonds—was enormously important in many parts of west, central, and southern Africa, but so were agricultural commodities. Africans produced sugar, cocoa, cotton, peanut oil, and other tropical products to supply European industry, setting the stage for longer-term economic dependencies and vulnerabilities.

The high imperial era looked somewhat different in Latin America. The Spanish colonies and Brazil had won their independence early in the nineteenth century, as local elites had chafed under and eventually challenged imperial rule successfully. Formal independence did not bring equal status between colonizer and ex-colony, however. For example, Britain and the United States—a new member of the imperial ranks—sought to control trade rather than territory. The British financed a vast expansion of South American rail lines, aiming to seal their access to the continent's large consumer markets for the sale of industrially produced machine goods and textiles and to speed export of agricultural products. Argentina, for example, was able to export great quantities of wool, wheat, and beef, generating important revenue for those who controlled these industries. Such a concentration of primary commodity production, however, along with the neglect of investment in domestic industry, produced structural imbalances and laid a foundation for future weakness.

It was only comparatively late in the history of colonialism—the early to mid-twentieth century for the most part—that colonizers began to institute policies that brought significant investment intended to benefit indigenous populations. The field of development, as a professionalized and self-conscious effort to transform economies outside of the industrialized West, dates from this time and still bears some remnants of its origin in the colonial era. In Africa, the end of the 1930s brought what historians used to call the 'second colonial occupation' but which is now seen as the emergence of the development era. The shift came amid realization on the part of colonial governments that their past practices had not yielded the expected results. Coercive labour practices—by which hundreds of thousands of Africans were

forced to engage in heavy manual labour without pay, a 'modern slavery' that often undermined their ability to support themselves or their families—and heavy-handed unequal treatment did not result in the 'civilized' Africans colonial boosters had promised but rather in an embittered and impoverished population.

World War II, a war in which Africans fought alongside Europeans for the right of European and Asian nations to **self-determination** and freedom from foreign rule, forced a re-examination of the colonial endeavour. Africans increasingly exhibited a new militancy, a refusal to remain confined to the narrow grooves cut by the traditional society imagined by colonial rulers, but rather made demands and articulated rights by drawing on metropolitan principles.

Part of the colonial response to such actions on the part of colonial subjects was a new approach, at least by Britain and France, to social and economic policy in the colonies. The British passed the Colonial Development and Welfare Act in 1940, and the French established the Investment Fund for Social and Economic Development in 1946. Both expanded the scale of colonial development activities in the postwar period, partly by increasing the flow of funds from the metropole, primarily through loans. Beyond the greater scale, however, they also changed the nature of colonial efforts to promote economic and social change. The plan for a 'modern future set against a primitive present' was part of an attempt to prolong empire amid growing anti-colonial mobilization; economic development would be the 'antidote to disorder' (Cooper 1997, 65, 67). Coming at the time it did, the shift did not have a great impact on Britain's or France's closing years of colonial rule in South or Southeast Asia, but it powerfully shaped Africa for the future.

Alongside the growth in scale came an associated increase in the personnel involved: local administrators (who may have improvised on their own initiative, perhaps on the basis of observations of and interactions with the Africans whose lives they administered) were now replaced with a

BOX 2.3   DEVELOPMENT PROJECT AS WHITE ELEPHANT: THE OFFICE DU NIGER

The French Office du Niger, a sprawling agricultural project planned for the French Soudan (present-day Mali), exemplified the ambition and oversight of colonial development planning. Conceived in the 1920s, the project signalled its outsized aims in the area targeted for development: 18,500 square kilometres, some of which fell within the Niger River's inland delta but much of which lay considerably outside of it. The plan called for the construction of several dams to irrigate vast tracts of land to be planted with cotton and rice. Planners did not speak of making the desert bloom, but their aim was to develop what they saw as underused land on the edge of the Sahara Desert. Yet because much of the area was arid and the population density accordingly low, many of the one million farmers imagined for the project would have to be resettled from elsewhere in French West Africa.

The plan had shortcomings sufficient to doom it from inception, chief among them poor 'expert' knowledge and a yawning gap between the projected objectives and the interests and desires of the Africans expected to participate. Of all the planning shortcomings, perhaps the most astonishing was that the irrigation network—the project's very backbone—provided inadequate or ill-timed water flows in some areas, making successful cultivation nearly impossible. Other problems abounded: some planned villages lacked wells, forcing settlers to collect water from irrigation ditches, while other wells were dry or contaminated (van Beusekom 2002, 89, 94).

A rejection of African farmers' considerable knowledge and experience was of a piece with the hierarchical nature of the endeavour. Volunteers for resettlement on the project were few; in 1938, one colonial official estimated that 90 per cent of those settled in the villages had been forcibly recruited (van Beusekom 2002). The forced labour recruitment prevalent in the French colonies was quite useful for this purpose, and to secure settlers for the project, the Office tapped into the lines of authority that extended down through district-level administrators to local African authorities. Amid the wider political setting of coercion under colonial rule, it is hardly surprising that most African residents had little interest in the project, where they could expect an especially high degree of surveillance and control.

As with other colonial projects, the plan imagined not only a transformation of African agriculture but also a re-engineering of African social and economic life, changing the way Africans farmed, the structure of their families, and the values that underlay the organization of work and community. In the end, the project fell far short of its goals, whether defined by the area cultivated, the number of settlers, the processes of cultivation, or the crops planted. To the extent that the African settlers on the scheme succeeded in creating a livelihood for themselves, it was owing to their insistence on choosing their own crops, cultivated according to unapproved methods and frequently outside the areas designated for planting. Many others fled the settlement scheme instead, and those who remained, forging their own path, found the freedom to do so after 1946, when France abolished forced labour in its colonies.

nascent bureaucracy charged with studying, planning, and executing projects conceived to meet priorities set by ministries based in Europe. Colonial intervention in agriculture, forestry, water supply, and livestock was not new, but there was now an emphasis on 'harnessing scientific and technical expertise' to such efforts (van Beusekom and Hodgson 2000, 31). It was a new approach to an older ideal—delivering modernity to 'natives', who were believed to be incapable of achieving such progress on their own. With the assistance of European experts, indigenous societies and cultures would thus evolve to the norm established by the West. Rather than continuing the mission, spiritual and otherwise, to 'civilize' indigenous societies in accordance with European norms, colonial rule in its final two decades shifted to the 'development' of those societies. In the effort to modernize African economies, the new form of colonial rule took aim not merely at farming techniques or livestock grazing practices but also at the social relations that organized those economic activities. As such, colonial development focused on indigenous social life, as much as on economic life, as being in need of modernization.

In the same way that an earlier generation of colonial policy-makers had aimed to foster cultural transformation and 'evolution' in indigenous societies, in keeping with a belief that the European model presented a natural path to progress, colonial planners now demonstrated faith that an economic makeover would set African societies on a similarly inevitable path. The increasingly advanced degree of political mobilization in postwar African colonies made colonial administrations wary of overly forceful implementation and occasionally responsive to African opposition to some projects. The turn towards development of indigenous societies came at a time when the inevitability of Indian independence was becoming clear, but in Africa, colonial rulers saw development plans in part as a way to return the

mercurial genie of nationalist sentiment back into its bottle (Cooper 1997). Still, the timing was crucial for the future, because the new development approach was bequeathed to a generation of African leaders who were mostly products of colonial education and had absorbed the associated idea of African 'backwardness'. Science and technology, held to have originated in the industrialized West, were the metric by which economic practices were to be evaluated. Although most post-colonial African leaders embraced African cultural practices, they were also enamoured of scientific knowledge as distinct from local knowledge and were thus sceptical of the practical experience of anyone who lacked a formal education.

The full turn towards development took place in a world divided by the Cold War, with the West—including all the colonial powers—arrayed against the Soviet bloc and its mission of 'exporting revolution'. Some leaders of nationalist independence movements in Africa and Asia sought and received aid, both military and financial, from the Soviet bloc. As anti-colonial mobilization intensified, the colonial powers reassessed their commitment to political control in their colonies. They questioned the financial benefits and feared the political costs, perceiving that continued denial of self-determination, and the greater oppression it would entail, might drive anti-colonial movements and newly independent states into the arms of the Soviet Union. Fiercely fought anti-colonial wars in Vietnam, Algeria, Cameroon, and Kenya—to name only a few—proved the limits to continued colonial rule. Economic links replaced colonial ministries as the means of influence, and delivering development to colonized peoples was seen as a way to present capitalism and the West in a good light. Looking forward into a post-colonial era, past colonial rulers and a new ally, the United States, sought to maintain the loyalty of former colonies as client states in the Cold War.

QUESTIONS FOR DISCUSSION

1. What continuities might be identified between economic conditions created under colonial rule and those that prevail today in former colonies?

2. How did colonial policies help to contribute, even if indirectly or unintentionally, to the end of colonial rule?

3. How might present-day conflicts in former colonies be seen as a legacy of specific colonial policies?

4. What ideas about indigenous peoples in Africa, Asia, or Latin America are still present in contemporary understandings of the 'Global South'?

FURTHER READING

Bose, Sugata, and Ayesha Jalal. 2004. *Modern South Asia: History, Culture, Political Economy*. 2nd edn. New York: Routledge.

Hochschild, Adam. 1998. *King Leopold's Ghost: A Story of Greed, Terror, and Heroism in Colonial Africa*. New York: Houghton Mifflin.

Kennedy, Paul M. 1977. 'The theory and practice of imperialism'. *The Historical Journal* 20 (3): 761–9.

Thornton, John. 1998. *Africa and Africans in the Making of the Atlantic World, 1400–1800*. 2nd edn. Cambridge: Cambridge University Press.

INTERNET RESOURCES

Harappa: The Indus Valley and the Raj in India and Pakistan: http://www.harappa.com.

Around the World in the 1890s: Photographs from the World's Transportation Commission, 1894–1896: http://memory.loc.gov/ammem/wtc/wtchome.html.

The Atlantic Slave Trade and Slave Life in the Americas: A Visual Record: http://hitchcock.itc.virginia.edu/Slavery/index.php.

Afriterra, The Cartographic Free Library: http://www.afriterra.org.

United States and Brazil: Expanding Frontiers, Comparing Cultures: http://international.loc.gov/intldl/brhtml.

Caribbean Views from the British Library: http://www.collectbritain.co.uk/collections/caribbean.

Parallel Histories: Spain, the United States, and the American Frontier: http://international.loc.gov/intldl/eshtml/eshome.html.

Oriental and India Office Collection from the British Library: http://www.collectbritain.co.uk/collections/svadesh.

Gallica Voyages en Afrique (French National Library): http://gallica.bnf.fr/VoyagesEnAfrique.

CHAPTER 3

THEORIES OF DEVELOPMENT

RADHIKA DESAI

LEARNING OBJECTIVES

- To trace the lineage of development as an aspiration back to the origins of capitalism and the role of the nation-state in it.
- To delineate key political tensions at the end of the Second World War, which birthed development as a project.
- To identify the main theoretical approaches to development in the post–Second World War era in their historical context.

As the twenty-first century opened, global humanity was divided into two unequal parts: less than one-sixth resided in the rich countries of western Europe and North America and in Japan, with high mean incomes and material welfare, and the rest lived in the predominantly poor countries of Asia, Africa, and Latin America, with low average incomes, low average levels of welfare, and large pools of poverty. Although income inequality had also grown within countries in recent decades, nationality remained a much stronger predictor of income and welfare than the class one belonged to.

It is generally agreed that the division of countries into rich and poor originated with the colonialism and imperialism that began more than five centuries ago—although one recent calculation placed its origin farther back in history (Maddison 2006, 46–50). The gap has widened more or less continuously. Although statistics provide only rough indicators, one writer estimated that average incomes in the rich countries were a stunning 23 times those in the rest of the world in 2000 (Freeman 2004, 47). The 'development' project emerged at the end of the Second World War to abolish this divide when it was a fraction of what it is today but was already considered politically unacceptable. Its present size is the clearest indicator of the failure of 'development'.

'Development' suffered its worst setbacks in recent decades. Neo-liberalism rolled back earlier meagre gains. Competing discourses and practices of 'globalization' and 'empire' sidelined it. Exercises in international showmanship such as the announcement, amid much fanfare, of the actually quite modest Millennium Development Goals forsook development's original ambitions. 'Post-development' currents rejected it outright as a worthy aspiration. Worse, the new reckoning of national incomes in 'purchasing power parity' (PPP) rather than in US dollars seemed to suggest that the problem was an optical, or rather statistical, illusion (see chapter 1 for an explanation of PPP). In PPP terms, the incomes of poor countries with low wages were systematically higher (since their citizens could afford to buy more of the goods and services produced by their equally low-income fellow citizens): it was development by statistical redefinition. Indeed, PPP added insult to the injury of low incomes by in effect congratulating a people for them! Needless to say, low income was precisely the problem that development was supposed to overcome.

However, the aspiration to development cannot be reversed, sidelined, diminished, rejected, or denied so easily. Although development acquired the distinctive form in which we know it today only after the Second World War, and the theories that then arose to comprehend the problems and prospects of development constitute the body of what is conventionally considered 'development theory', development has a long lineage. It is effectively the most enduring national and social urge of modern times. We begin our review of development theory by recalling that longer lineage and end it by asking whether and under what conditions development might once again be on the world's political agenda in a serious way.

In the next section, we trace the long lineage of the aspiration to social and national material progress that we now call development. Against this backdrop, we then examine the historical moment when development emerged as a project after the Second World War. A brief review of development's record in the following decades is essential before we go on to look at the succession of theories of development and their enduring contribution. In the conclusion, we assess their theoretical and analytical gains and ask whether and how development may once again become a realistic project in the future.

DEVELOPMENT AVANT LA LETTRE

The idea that all societies can progress or develop—change for the better—became widely accepted with the **Industrial Revolution** more than 200 years ago when people at the northwest corner of Europe were hurled into 'change' and 'improvement' at a faster clip than ever before, and similar changes seemed to be in store for other peoples. Before that, change had been slow, and the gains of one society or group seemed to come at the expense of another. The Industrial Revolution promised *absolute* and *rapid* increases in wealth. Theoretically at least, all individuals, groups, and societies could partake and hope to better their lives substantially within individuals' lifetimes.

However, the Industrial Revolution took place in a qualitatively new kind of society—**capitalism**. It organized production in units in which private owners of *capital* bought the means and materials of production and the

labour of those who had no other means of making a living on the *market*, and the product was also sold on the *market*, the main mechanism for matching labourers, producers, and consumers. Capital and markets had hitherto played only a small role in social production and distribution: they were either absent or constrained by social custom and more or less authoritarian political regulation. Under capitalism, they came to govern more and more of the social product, and custom and regulation came to serve rather than constrain them as new capitalist states became committed to creating and maintaining this type of productive order.

Production and human productive capacity, now unbridled by any social or political estimate of need, underwent a revolutionary expansion. As Karl Marx memorably put it, the new industrial bourgeoisie

> created more massive and more colossal productive forces than . . . all preceding generations together. Subjection of Nature's forces to man, machinery, application of chemistry to industry and agriculture, steam-navigation, railways, electric telegraphs, clearing of whole continents for cultivation, canalisation of rivers, whole populations conjured out of the ground—*what earlier century had even a presentiment that such productive forces slumbered in the lap of social labour?* (Marx and Engels 1967, 84–5, emphasis added).

Such prodigality and expansiveness nurtured the hope that all individuals and nations might benefit.

However, increased production required, and created, a constantly expanding world market, and all societies became part of it, whether through commerce ('the cheap prices of its commodities are the artillery with which it batters down all Chinese walls') or, more usually, through conquest. The nineteenth century witnessed the world's first industrial capitalist country—Britain—acquiring the largest colonial empire, one on which 'the sun never set', despite its commitment to 'free trade'. Both imperial control and the world market augmented the economic advantage of the colonizing nation and compounded the disadvantage of the colonized. Capitalism's geographical spread was uneven, creating agglomerations of wealth in some societies and pools of poverty and misery in others. This was only the first way in which industrial capitalist society's promise of generalized prosperity was broken. There were at least two other problems. First, capitalists paid workers only a fraction of the value of their product so, while production expanded, incomes from it were unjustly and unequally distributed. Second, market co-ordination of privately organized production units was liable to breakdown and crises that interrupted and occasionally reversed increases in production. Karl Marx's famous critique of capitalism focused on these internal problems. Never before in human experience had the fate of entire societies been governed by such a problematic, impersonal, and uncontrolled set of institutions.

Ideas of progress, what we now call 'development', emerged out of the tension between the tantalizing possibilities for general human welfare that **industrial capitalism** offered and their failure to materialize for a majority of the people in the world. Since then, these problems have been the focus of politics and geopolitics because, as Colin Leys so accurately put it, what was at stake was 'nothing less than whether human beings can act, collectively, to improve their lot, or whether they must . . . accept that it is ineluctably determined by . . . "world market forces" . . . over which they have, in general, little or no control (and least of all those who need it most)' (Leys 1996, 3).

Modern social thought is neither more nor less than a series of attempts to comprehend and master the deeply contradictory dynamic of capitalism for human societies. Except for short-sighted and vulgar celebrations and condemnations, all accounts of industrial capitalist society, whether 'economic' or 'philosophical', reflect capitalism's double-sidedness. Take Adam Smith's *Wealth of Nations* (1937 [1776])—a veritable manifesto of the Industrial Revolution. Smith clearly saw that industry had transformed economic competition from a zero-sum game to one in which general and

absolute increases in welfare were possible. He attributed this possibility to the market—the 'invisible hand' that deftly co-ordinated private efforts. All societies would eventually benefit, including those subjugated by Europeans:

> Hereafter, perhaps the natives of those countries may grow stronger, or those of Europe may grow weaker, and the inhabitants of all the different quarters of the world may arrive at that equality of courage and force which, by inspiring mutual fear, can alone overawe the injustice of independent nations into some sort of respect for the rights of one another. But nothing seems more likely to establish this equality of force than that mutual communication of knowledge and of all sorts of improvements which an extensive commerce from all countries to all countries naturally, or rather necessarily, carries along with it (Smith 1937 [1776], 590–1).

However, contrary to the dominant tendency in the interpretation of Smith's thought, he did not believe the market mechanism could successfully rule society: it violated the moral sentiments that constituted society's necessary human basis (Göçmen 2007). But industrial capitalist society replaced social bonds and norms with market relations—the dreaded 'cash nexus'—so rapidly that a mere four decades later, thinkers like the great German philosopher Hegel saw the state as indispensable for correcting and opposing market forces.

The idea that state regulation is necessarily socialist is mistaken. Because of the frequency of 'market failure', the tension between economic or market regulation and state or political regulation has pervaded social thought. Karl Polanyi captured this tension best in his idea of a 'double movement'. Market failure was endemic to capitalism, he argued, because it treated land, labour, and capital (i.e., social and productive organization) as commodities even though they were not produced for sale. He refuted the idea that markets can, *or ever have*, successfully regulated any economy. Historical evidence showed that 'no economy has existed that, even in principle, was controlled [purely] by markets' (Polanyi 1944, 44). No wonder, then, that the nineteenth-century spread of market society provoked a countervailing movement: 'While on the one hand markets spread all over the face of the globe and the amount of goods involved grew to unbelievable proportions, on the other hand a network of measures and policies was integrated into powerful institutions designed to check the action of the market relative to labour, land and money.' It was 'a deep-seated movement [that] sprang into being to resist the pernicious effects of a market-controlled economy. Society protected itself against the perils inherent in a self-regulating market system—this was the one comprehensive feature of the history of the age' (Polanyi 1944, 76).

While Polanyi focused mainly on the operation of the 'double movement' within societies, the emergence of nations and the problem of 'national development' can be seen as part of the operation of a similar sort of double movement at a geopolitical level. Although nations are usually seen as cultural artifacts, they are equally the product of a material dynamic—the globally integrated but geographically uneven development of capitalism. The origin of nation-states lay, as Tom Nairn clearly saw,

> in the machinery of world political economy. Not, however, in the process of that economy's development as such—not simply as an inevitable concomitant of industrialization and urbanization . . . [but in] the *uneven development* of history since the eighteenth century. This unevenness is a material fact; one could argue that it is the most grossly material fact about modern history. The conclusion, at once satisfying and near-paradoxical, is that the most notoriously subjective and 'idealistic' ideal of historical phenomena is in fact a by-product of the most brutally and hopelessly material side of the history of the last two centuries (Nairn 1981, 335–6).

Uneven capitalist development was expressed in imperialism and, for subjects or less powerful people, it was not a peaceable spread of development or prosperity but lack, deprivation, imposition, domination, and exploitation. Such people

> learned quickly enough that Progress in the abstract meant domination in the concrete, by powers which they could not help apprehending as foreign or alien. In practice as distinct from the theory, the acculturation process turned out to be more like a 'tidal wave' . . . of outside interference and control (Nairn 1981, 338).

Peoples could choose between being 'drowned' by such tidal waves and erecting barriers against them. The assertion of nationhood against such economic and political pressures has formed the underlying principle of the emergence of the nation-state system as Benno Teschke recently saw it:

> *Contra* Marx and Engels in *The Communist Manifesto*, the expansion of capitalism was not an *economic* process in which the transnationalising forces of the market or civil society surreptitiously penetrated pre-capitalist states, driven by the logic of cheap commodities that eventually perfected a universal world market. It was a *political* and, *a fortiori*, *geopolitical* process in which pre-capitalist state classes had to design counterstrategies of reproduction to defend their position in an international environment which put them at an economic *and* coercive disadvantage. More often than not, it was heavy artillery that battered down pre-capitalist walls, and the construction and reconstruction of these walls required new state strategies of modernisation (Teschke 2003, 265).

The nineteenth-century ideology of a seamless *economic* spread of capitalism worldwide was soon challenged by a new generation of thinkers who sought to promote the *national* development of their countries against Britain's industrial supremacy through political means. For thinkers such as Alexander Hamilton and Henry Carey in the United States and Friedrich List in Germany, free trade was the dogma and ruling ideology of

British supremacy. Free markets tended to concentrate and reinforce economic advantage as much as conquest. Both reinforced the division of labour among societies in which some produced goods of higher value—usually industrial—than others. The existing pattern of economic advantage could be challenged only by non-market, political means.

National development was thus about governments promoting industrial development and engineering a transformation of agriculture to support it. Its theorists rejected dominant free-market ideas and proposed state management of trade in order to protect and foster key industrial sectors and increase their capacity to produce higher-value goods. In particular, they questioned the idea of 'comparative advantage' in which the productive specialization of each nation—essentially, industrial powers producing industrial goods and colonies producing agricultural goods—created by the workings of the world market was to be accepted without question. Since this international division of labour was not the product of commerce alone but also of conquest, and since even commerce alone tended to reinforce existing inequalities, emerging nations would have to use political means to break out of the inherited specialization and produce higher-value goods, which were usually industrial goods. Finally, rejecting the breezy free-market idea that demand and supply would balance each other out—an idea that only served to disguise the critical role of colonies as suppliers and markets—the first generation of theorists of national development aimed to ensure the supply of industrial raw materials and the markets for their products, in part by creating and expanding formal empires.

This competition for empires intensified in the closing decades of the nineteenth century as other powers—principally Germany, the US, and Japan—arose to challenge Britain's industrial supremacy. These challengers emerged as they completed critical phases of their own national formation—the victory of the industrial North in the US Civil War; the Meiji restoration in Japan, creating a modern centralized state; and the unification of Germany. In the work of their leading thinkers, national development took a form that would be reflected in the development project of the second half of the twentieth century—with one critical difference. The 'developing' countries of the second half of the twentieth century had been colonies themselves and could not acquire colonies of their own to facilitate their industrial development. Not surprisingly, the question of 'development' and imperialism would remain intertwined. The way out of *potential* subjugation for these 'late industrializers'—Germany, the US, Japan—lay in a critique, intellectual and practical, of 'free trade'. The way out of *actual* subjugation for the developing countries of the latter part of the twentieth century lay in a critique, intellectual and practical, of imperialism—and that was much more difficult.

THE MOMENT OF DEVELOPMENT

The launching of development as a project of the US government, other rich-country governments, international institutions, and (not least) national governments of newly independent but poor nations after the Second World War marked a historic turnaround in relations between rich and poor countries. After centuries during which colonizers justified colonialism with racist rationales such as the **white man's burden** and 'civilizing missions', colonial and imperial exploitation, **oppression**, and plunder were at last recognized for what they were, and decolonization began to reverse them, while theorists and practitioners of development began to envisage the poor countries 'catching up' to the rich world's levels of income and material welfare.

This historical moment had been long in the making. The imperialist First World War inaugurated a '30-year crisis', 1914–45, spanning the two world wars and the Great Depression. It became the crucible of a new world order. Three massive changes produced and defined the 'moment of development' as this period of crisis came to an end. First, the US emerged the most powerful (capitalist) nation in the world by far. Already the largest single economy in 1913, it came to account for fully half of world production by 1945, thanks to the destruction that two world wars had caused in Europe and elsewhere. Previously, the US had stood at the margins of world development, which was dominated by Europe. While the Europeans had vast formal colonial empires, the US was forced to devise 'informal' methods of imperialism over the formally independent nation-states in the western hemisphere. This difference was definitely handy when, in the new circumstances after 1945, the US began to sponsor decolonization, reconstruction, and development to cut the formally imperial capitalist powers down to size and to expand the capitalist world-economy under its leadership.

The second change made development endeavours urgent. The Soviet Union, formed after a communist revolution against Russian absolutism in the midst of the First World War, had experienced remarkably successful industrialization based on state planning and direction while the capitalist world languished in depression in the 1930s. The Soviet Union's role made the difference between victory and defeat for the allies fighting fascism in the Second World War. Its power and prestige now balanced US power: along with similar communist regimes in eastern Europe and China, it truncated the size of the capitalist world and checked the exercise of US power in it, particularly in its poor parts, forcing it into 'altruistic' grooves to keep or wrest them from the attractions of communism.

Third, after the First World War, many national liberation movements, as well as the Bolsheviks in the USSR, had demanded decolonization. Only after the Second World War, however, did the US consistently support decolonization, thanks to its desire to lessen the power of its capitalist rivals and its need to compete against the Soviet bloc for the support of national liberation movements. Thus, the 'catch-up' of former colonies to the levels of prosperity of rich countries was placed on the world agenda. This was 'development'—in a critical sense the ransom that the capitalist world had to pay to keep poor countries from

communism. That the Cold War was fought 'hotly' only in poor countries—Korea, Cuba, Vietnam—provides the clearest evidence that they were real stakes in it.

While development meant many things—rising levels of education, political participation and democracy, urbanization, technology, health and welfare—higher incomes and greater material welfare were critical, and industrialization and state direction were seen as essential to achieving them. It is important to underline this, because populist, neo-liberal, and post-modern discourses that emerged in the late twentieth century and remain fairly influential today tended to be heavily biased against any state role and to portray industrialization as unnecessary, indeed positively harmful, for the poor nations (for a critique, see Kitching 1982). Originally, industrialization was considered the basis for higher productivity, higher incomes, and well-being. The poor countries were predominantly agricultural and the rich countries predominantly industrial. Industry provided the critical advantage in productivity. Thus, development involved industrializing predominantly agricultural economies, as had already happened in rich societies, and the state was its agent.

Intellectually, development was the product of the *confrontation* between capitalism and communism as much as of their *interaction*. By 1945, the success of state direction of the economy in the USSR and the failure of liberal capitalism in the West, which was starkly revealed in the two wars and the Great Depression, had taught

the politicians, officials and even many of the businessmen of the post-war West . . . that a return to **laissez-faire** and the unreconstructed free market were out of the question. Certain policy objectives—full employment, the containment of communism, the modernization of lagging or declining or ruined economies—had absolute priority and justified the strongest government presence. Even regimes dedicated to economic and political liberalism now could, and had to, run their economies in ways which would once have been rejected as 'socialist' (Hobsbawm 1994, 272–3).

A consensus had been forming during the inter-war period to favour planning, state ownership, a large state role in directing the economy in productive and egalitarian directions through welfare, and redistributive measures to remedy the undeniable ills of capitalism. After all, while liberal capitalism was in the throes of the Great Depression, the achievements of Soviet planning in industrializing a predominantly agricultural Russia formed an instructive contrast. The economist John Maynard Keynes, who diagnosed the Depression, recommended an important government role in preventing crises and/or rectifying them through macroeconomic means that intruded less on the private capitalist economy than Soviet-style planning. **Keynesian policies** formed the basis of important early ideas of 'development'. While the free market was abolished in the communist countries, its restriction and regulation in the advanced capitalist and developing economies laid the institutional basis of the 'golden age' of capitalism that was to follow. Ironically, the 'economy of private enterprise ("free enterprise" was the preferred name) needed to be saved from itself to survive' (Hobsbawm 1994, 273). Indeed, it had to be saved from itself with the ideological and policy toolkit of its enemy, socialism and communism.

Internationally, trade and finance came to be governed by the Bretton Woods institutions—the International Monetary Fund (IMF), the World Bank, and the General Agreement on Tariffs and Trade (GATT) being the most important—which were designed to enable the national economic management required for welfare states as well as development.

These arrangements were designed to permit national governments to manage their economies so as to maximise growth and employment. Capital was not allowed to cross frontiers without government approval, which permitted governments to determine

domestic interest rates, fix the exchange rate of the national currency, and tax and spend as they saw fit to secure national economic objectives. National economic planning was seen as a natural extension of this thinking, as were domestic and international arrangements to stabilize commodity prices. It is not a great oversimplification to say that 'development theory' was originally just theory about the best way for colonial, and then ex-colonial, states to accelerate national economic growth in this international environment. The goal of development was growth; the agent of development was the state and the means of development were these macroeconomic policy instruments (Leys 1996, 6–7).

Of the numerous terms and euphemisms for the poor countries of the world and what they shared despite their diversity of cultural and material endowments—developing, underdeveloped, post-colonial, less developed, backward, Southern, and so on—the term 'Third World' best captured the tensions of development's formative historical moment (see also chapter 1). First, these countries tried to strike a balance between the capitalist First World and the communist Second World in international politics. At the Bandung conference of 1955, the Third World was institutionalized in the Non-Aligned Movement (NAM), which sought independence from Cold War blocs in world politics and put issues of importance to development on the world agenda. Second, most nationalist leaderships and governments needed to strike a balance, domestically, between the political weakness of capitalist forces and the strength of socialist and communist force. In India, Egypt, and Indonesia, for example (Ahmad 1992, especially 297–304), the idea of a 'Third World' was connected with a 'third way' between capitalism and communism—a reformed capitalism pursuing development with planning and state direction. Although 'development' meant the development of capitalism, it was to be capitalism of a reformed sort: more productive and egalitarian than the liberal capitalism that had caused so much grief in the inter-war period. Indeed, so low had capitalism sunk in the minds of the public internationally that the capitalist world was now on the defensive and avoided using the term 'capitalism' when countering communist propaganda, using 'development' and 'free world' as substitutes.

DISPUTING DEVELOPMENT

The new institutions of global economic governance ensured a two-decade-long 'golden age' of growth unprecedented in tempo and duration. Third World economies were swept along, although problems such as low prices for their commodity exports were noted. And these problems were especially urgent because, despite Third World attempts to industrialize, too much of the growth in the 1950s and 1960s originated in high demand for primary products by the First World, perpetuating rather than breaking colonial economic relationships. (First and Third World dominant classes had vested interests in the continuation of these relationships and were able to keep them in place: clearly, decolonization and development marked breaks from the past but of an ambiguous sort.) In retrospect, this 'golden age', such as it was, was development's best. Neither world growth nor Third World growth has reached such long-term rates since then. These decades also represent a time when the most stimulating debates on the problems and prospects of development took place.

Table 3.1 outlines the major theories of development that have successively held sway since development became a project more than 60 years ago.

Development economics

Development economics was the first of the succession of theories of development that emerged after the Second World War. It was merely the contemporary form of the way that economics articulated its perennial questions.

For centuries economics was—at its very core—an art, a practice and a science devoted to 'economic development', albeit under a variety of labels: from an idealistic promotion of 'public happiness' to the nationalistic creation of wealth and greatness of nations and rulers, and the winning of wars (Jomo and Reinert 2005, vii).

Development economics was predominantly Keynesian and saw capitalist crises such as the Great Depression as products of cyclical deficits of demand. During such times, capitalists were reluctant to invest in productive plant, preferring to keep their capital 'liquid'. The state could counteract this cyclical tendency through fiscal and monetary 'macroeconomic' policies such as increasing the level of state spending and expanding credit at the beginning of a downswing in economic activity to buoy up demand and 'smooth out' possible troughs, restoring equilibrium at high levels of employment of labour and capital. A larger role for the state in terms of the provision of health, education, instituting unemployment insurance and public pensions, and the ownership of key industries was also envisaged.

Keynesians sought to accelerate growth in developing countries through an injection of capital and macroeconomic policies adapted to developing economies: assumptions such as decreasing returns to scale, labour scarcity, and 'perfect competition' were discarded, since the problem was how to get a process of growth going in contexts where certain factors were not fully employed and others, such as capital and technology, were very scarce. Discontinuities and disequilibria were necessary to achieve a quantum leap to a higher growth path in 'stagnant' economies in low-level equilibrium. As W.A. Lewis saw it, for example, largely agrarian labour-surplus economies had to be put on an industrial growth path such that labour absorption in industry made labour scarce enough for wages to rise (Ros 2005, 89–91). The scale of the initial shift onto a self-sustaining growth path invited comparison with an airplane taking off.

Launching a country into self-sustaining growth is a little like getting an airplane off

Table 3.1   Theories of development

Theory/ Theme	Emergence/ Dominance	Thinkers	Discipline/ Tradition	The Problem	The Solution
Development economics	1950s	Lewis, Rosenstein-Rodan	Keynesian economics	Low-level equilibrium	Injection of capital and management of disequilibria to put economy on a growth path to high-level equilibrium
Modernization theory	Late 1950s	Rostow, Shils, Pye, Almond, Huntington	Weberian/ Parsonian sociology	Traditional society	Modernization through diffusion of modern values and institutions
Dependency theory	1960s	Cardoso, Frank, Wallerstein, Amin	Prebisch, Economic Commission for Latin America, Marxism	Dependency within a world capitalist system	Delinking, fully or partially, or socialism
Marxism	1970s	Brenner, Warren	Marxist theory of modes of production	Articulation of modes of production	Not prescriptive but development of capitalist relations of production/socialism
Neo-liberalism	1970s	Bauer, Balassa, Kreuger, Lal	Neo-classical, marginalist economics, Austrian economics	State intervention	Free markets
Developmental states	1970s	Amsden, Haggard, Chang, Reinert	Listian national 'neo-mercantilist' political economy	Free markets	State management of the economy to increase productivity, equality, and technological upgrading

the ground. There is a critical ground-speed which must be passed before the craft can become airborne (Rosenstein-Rodan 1961, quoted in Ros 2005, 81).

While the Keynesian revolution made national economic management acceptable, its tools were macroeconomic. They paled in comparison with those of **Listian industrialization**, which had already been employed in the rise of the first set of nations to challenge the then-existing world division of labour, let alone the means employed in Soviet industrialization. Whether they would prove effective in overturning the even wider gap in incomes and productivity that now lay between the First World and the Third could be doubted, but it was not, because the new international economic arrangements were supposed to promote development and because the mood of the time was optimistic.

Modernization theory

Sure enough, by the late 1950s it was clear that, while most developing countries grew, none was launched on a path to self-sustaining industrial growth. Social and political factors largely outside the purview of development economics seemed responsible. Modernization theory now emerged, supplementing economics with sociology and political science to theorize the preconditions for, and obstacles to, a more encompassing vision, going beyond economics, of the 'modernization' of 'traditional' societies.

Walter Rostow's *The Stages of Economic Growth* was a transitional text between development economics and modernization theory in which economics remained central without being the exclusive focus. Relying on the growth experience of the developed countries and combining it with an appreciation of key social and political factors that facilitated growth, Rostow discerned five broad states through which 'traditional' societies passed to become modern 'high mass consumption' societies (the three states between 'traditional' and 'modern' were 'preconditions for take-off', 'take-off', and the 'drive to maturity'). Traditional agricultural societies were dominated by 'pre-Newtonian' attitudes towards nature, and thus suffered low levels of technology and growth. The preconditions for take-off began with a number of economic changes, including trade expansion and increases in investment, but the creation of a national state was critical. While these changes had occurred more or less autonomously in England and western Europe, in most countries they were the result of external pressures that undermined the structures of 'traditional societies'. Take-off was defined as the stage at which investment reached 10 per cent and both industry and agriculture became more and more productive, outstripping population growth. The drive to maturity featured further instalments of growth and modernization of the economy with the production of a more diverse range of goods, including those of greater technological sophistication, and greater integration into the world economy. High mass consumption society was the end state in which average incomes were high and consumption expanded beyond basic needs. Societies could then institute welfare states and also spend more on the military as they sought to project their power internationally.

Originally a set of lectures delivered at Cambridge University in 1958, Rostow's account bore all the foundational marks of modernization theory: consciousness of the stakes in the Cold War (he subtitled his work *A Non-Communist Manifesto*); an assumption that the First World was the model and end-state for the Third; optimism about the prospects for growth in the Third World; and an assumption that the First World would be instrumental in promoting it. He felt that the danger of communism was greatest when the preconditions for take-off were being met, because conflicts were most likely during that period.

While Rostow's theory was based on economic history, the principal modernization theorists who followed were sociologists and political scientists. Their work relied on Talcott Parsons's *The Structure of Social Action* (1937), an adaptation of Weber's complex and rather gloomy sociology of modernity in a radically more sanguine register. 'Modernity, Parsons believed, implicitly but fundamentally, formed a *coherent, unitary, uniform and worthwhile* whole, and had to be apprehended by a social science that shared these qualities' (Gilman 2003, 75). Parsons was not concerned with the Third World. However, the overall question that framed his study—'what made the West different?'—eminently suited the purposes of modernization theory in the Cold War circumstances of the 1950s. His 'pattern variables' distinguished modern from traditional societies by identifying the one with one set of characteristics and the other with their opposites. It only remained for modernization theory to produce an account of development as the 'diffusion' of modern characteristics—values and institutions, in addition to capital and technology—from the formerly imperial 'modern' to the ex-colonial 'traditional' countries until they matched the former as closely as possible. Table 3.2 details the pattern variables.

Figure 3.1   Construction of Cairo's subway system

Source: Robert Charbonneau, IDRC

Modernization theory focused on local and inherited obstacles to 'modernization', simply assuming away the history of imperialism. The ex-colonial countries were designated as merely 'traditional'—existing in a condition before capitalist development, which would now be brought to them through capital injection and/or 'diffusion' of modern values and institutions. Increasingly close contact—economic, social, political, and cultural—with former imperial countries was expected to be conducive for development. While a liberal wing of modernization theory assumed that modernization was inevitable and imminent and would lead to democratic orders, there was also a darker side to the theory.

Modernization theory was the work of ambitious scholars who identified closely with the world aims and activities of the US.

While, to their disappointment, modernization theorists never became influential in making US or World Bank development policy, they did generate well-funded programs of research, especially in 'area studies' departments, which the US government funded to create knowledge about the parts of the world that Washington found itself involved in. And the one policy area in which a couple of modernization theorists did become influential was US foreign policy. Walt Rostow served as head of the policy planning staff under John F. Kennedy and as national security advisor under Lyndon Johnson. He was widely known as the chief architect of the Vietnam War.

The Rostow Doctrine was the most far-reaching American political-military doctrine/strategy employed in South Vietnam. It combined Cold War toughness with Western-style

Table 3.2   Traditional society versus modern society

Traditional Society	Modern Society
Affectivity	**Affective neutrality**
Predominance of roles that give affective or emotional gratification	Predominance of roles whose performance is affectively neutral
Ascription	**Achievement**
Predominance of roles according to non-achievable status or attributes (sex, age, family position, etc.) indifferent to quality of performance	Predominance of roles in which achievement is the basis of status
Diffusion	**Specificity**
Predominance of roles in which a number of functions may be combined: e.g., family memberships and work on a farm	Predominance of roles specific to particular functions, as in a bureaucracy
Particularism	**Universalism**
Predominance of roles in which expectations are particular to the status of the performer	Predominance of roles in which performance is measured irrespective of the status of the performer
Collectivity orientation	**Self-orientation**
Predominance of roles oriented towards the collective, such as society or kinship group	Predominance of roles in which private self-interest is the prime motivation

economic modernization. Rostowians saw the world locked in a communist-capitalist struggle whose outcome would be decided in the developing areas. South Vietnam was the linchpin in this struggle. Under Walt W. Rostow's guidance, the Doctrine became the primary tenet of American policy toward the developing areas in the 1960s and the principal rationale for US intervention and conduct in Vietnam. . . . The international order depended on whether the developing areas could be 'modernized'—a process Rostow equated with Western-style economic development (Grinter 1975, quoted in Gilman 2003, 249).

One of the more prominent representatives of modernization theory, more ambitious than the others for political influence, Samuel Huntington never attained high office but did manage to exert a chilling influence on US policy in Vietnam. He had already given up on the possibilities of democracy in the Third World, preferring 'order' instead—he thought that 'the most important political distinction among countries concerns not their form of government, but their degree of government'. He advocated 'urbanization' in Vietnam by whatever means necessary, including bombing and defoliating, to undercut rural support for the enemy. In this period, one of his colleagues pointed out, 'Sam simply lost the ability to distinguish between urbanization and genocide' (Ahmad 1992, quoted in Gilman 2003, 233).

The mainstream of modernization theory may well have been a product of American liberalism, but it could always be overridden by anti-communism. Moreover, a certain acceptance of anti-democratic tendencies was built into its founding contrast between modern and traditional societies. When optimism about, and then patience with, traditional societies wore out, the natural conclusion was that contrasting outcomes could also be expected

(Gilman 2003, 45–63; see also O'Brien 1971; the key text is Huntington 1969).

Given that it was rarely the basis of development policy, modernization theory's validity remained protected from policy challenge. It remained the dominant paradigm governing the understanding of the Third World during the 1960s. By the end of that decade, however, the 'golden age' of capitalist growth had ended.

As it came to an end, the comfortable assumptions of modernization theory were soon challenged by dependency theory.

Dependency theory

Dependency theory turned a new corner in development theory. The *dependentistas* reinstated imperialism as a central factor in the understanding of development and the lack thereof. They took their task to be the theorization of *informal* imperialism, giving rise to terms like 'neo-colonialism'. Not surprisingly, perhaps, dependency theory originated in Latin America, the one region of the Third World where, although the vast majority of nation-states had been independent for more than a century, underdevelopment seemed just as endemic as it was in recently ex-colonial Asia and Africa.

Dependency theory overturned the central assumptions of modernization theory. Whereas modernization theory studied countries, dependency theory studied the whole capitalist 'world system'. Whereas modernization theory assumed that the problem of development was an original state of *non*-development, dependency theory argued that a single and integrated historical process had differential results for different countries, producing development in some and *under*-development in others. Whereas modernization theory assumed that development was a process through which 'traditional' societies would 'catch up' with 'modern ones', in its strongest forms dependency theory insisted that this was impossible under capitalism and that socialism was the only solution. Whereas modernization theory saw the elites of the 'traditional' societies as vectors for

the transmission of modernization, dependency theory saw them as collaborators in a process of underdevelopment.

Dependency theory was also a relatively diverse set of theories united in their conception of the world economy as divided not between 'traditional' and 'modern' societies but between an advanced industrial 'core' and a largely agricultural 'periphery'. It had two principal sources. First, there was the work of the UN's Economic Commission for Latin America (ECLA) under Raul Prebisch in the 1950s. Prebisch's work had challenged the assumption of conventional development economics in two key ways. First, he argued that there was a centre and a periphery in world capitalism and that with the application of conventional development economics, which encouraged trade between the two, inequalities between them would continue to grow. He pointed especially to the contrary experience of the two world wars and the intervening Great Depression when, at a time when trade between Latin America and the core countries was disrupted, Latin American countries diversified and industrialized. The gains of this period were being lost as, after the end of the Second World War, conventional economics justified the resumption of close trading relations with the core countries. Second, and theoretically, reflecting on the experience of the peripheral countries during the period of booming international trade, he took issue with conventional trade theory according to which trade between industrial and agricultural countries would, over time, favour the latter because they would benefit from advances in technology in industrial countries, which would reduce the prices of industrial goods faster than the prices of agricultural goods. In fact, he argued, instead of permitting the prices of industrial goods to fall in tandem with technological progress, advanced industrial countries kept the benefits of technical progress by keeping prices high.

The second major source of dependency theory was the work of Paul Baran. Baran adapted the classical theory of imperialism to understand the condition of the Third World in the second half of the twentieth century—an era when the poor parts of the world were formally independent nation-states, not colonies. The classical theory of imperialism was produced by early-twentieth-century Marxist intellectuals and leaders, including Lenin, whose outlook and politics were shaped by the intensification of imperialism and inter-imperialist rivalry of that time. As they sought to understand the relationship between imperialism and capitalism, they were forced to the conclusion that imperialism was endemic to, and necessary to, capitalism and that both would only be ended by socialism. In the second half of the twentieth century, Baran argued, underdevelopment was a product of capitalism, a hierarchical international system based on a transfer of surplus from underdeveloped to developed countries—a process in which multinational corporations played an increasingly important role, blocking industrial development and producing stagnation in the poor countries, a situation that could only be ended by socialist revolution.

Dependency theory covered a range of views: politically, many dependency theorists spoke as representatives of their own national bourgeoisie, 'chafing at its subordination to the interests of foreign companies and the influence of the US state in domestic politics' (Leys 1996, 12). Or they spoke as those who sided with the working class and other radical currents. Theoretically, Gabriel Palma (1981) classified dependency approaches in terms of the extent to which each theorist thought development possible. Some currents merely pointed to the difficulties of development, elaborating ECLA's concern with external obstacles to development. A second current, which included Palma himself, F.H. Cardoso, and Enzo Falletto, focused on 'concrete situations of dependency' and on how external obstacles were complemented by domestic class configurations to impede development. However, some capitalist development—'dependent development'—was still possible within these parameters. Peter

Evans (1979) made a major contribution to this approach when he analyzed how a 'triple alliance' of state capital, domestic capital, and foreign capital had determined the actual pattern of industrialization in Brazil. Finally, there were those—pre-eminently Andre Gunder Frank—who argued that no real development was possible without socialism and a delinking from the structures of world capitalism. To Palma's classification we must add the theories of Samir Amin, a major theorist of dependency whose origin and geographical focus lay in Africa. While he differed from dependency theorists when they claimed that underdevelopment was a capitalist condition, seeing it instead as the result of a combination of capitalist and pre-capitalist structures in peripheral societies, he agreed with some of them that delinking from the world economy (not autarky but as a selective form of linkage) could be combined with a broad-based and internally generated process of capitalist accumulation.

Any discussion of dependency theory is incomplete without mention of the related 'world system' theory. It drew on the work of the French *Annales* school of historians, in particular Fernand Braudel, whose rich historical work on the development of capitalism on a world scale drew on, but differed significantly from, Marxist analyses. For Immanuel Wallerstein, the most prominent representative of the world system theory, the capitalist world-economy was the product of a centuries-long expansion of European capitalism dating back to the fifteenth century. Despite the multitude of political and economic forms within it, it was from the start and remained a *capitalist* world-economy. No unit within it could be analyzed separately. It could have only one system-wide character, even though it generated

unequal development and therefore differential rewards, and unequal development in a multilayered format of layers within layers, each one polarised in terms of a bimodal distribution of rewards . . . there was the differential of the core of the European world-economy versus its peripheral areas, within the European core between states, within states, between regions and strata . . . (Wallerstein 1974a, 86).

This capitalist world-economy was divided into a core, a periphery, and a semi-periphery, and though at times the position of individual countries changed, the overall structure was unchanging.

Dependency turned out to be a mere mirror image of modernization theory: the one inevitabilist, the other impossibilist. It dismissed the idea of national autonomous development in the context of the powerful and varied structures and practices of imperialism and revived the concept of imperialism to theorize the reality of the now nominally independent nation-states of the Third World, still struggling, in many cases after two decades of independence, to foster 'development'.

Dependency theory's most important contributions came from its focus on the specific mechanisms of imperialist subjection and exploitation. After all, Marx's theory of exploitation was unrelated to these forms of surplus extraction, and they affected more working people than did those he so brilliantly uncovered. The wealth of writing on the operation of 'unequal trade' (Emmanuel 1969), multinational capital (Hymer 1972), and aid and official development organizations (e.g., George 1988; George and Sabelli 1994; Hayter and Watson 1985; and Payer 1991) is too vast to summarize here. This literature seemed to confirm the conclusions of classical Marxist theories of imperialism that imperialism and dependency were endemic to capitalism and that only socialist revolution could end them.

Marxism

Marxists understood capitalism as contradictory: an unjust, exploitative, and crisis-prone form of society that had nevertheless taken human social productive capacity to greater heights than ever before. Although they claimed to be Marxists, dependency and world system theorists focused on capitalism's former aspect alone. It was, however, the latter aspect that gave rise to the ideas of development and progress in the first place. A brief review of the Marxist critique of dependency makes the implications of this one-sidedness clear.

On the question of whether the inclusion into the world market of lands hitherto outside it could be expected to lead automatically to the development of capitalism, world system and dependency theories claimed that such inclusion was tantamount to the establishment of capitalism and, if the results were different, even opposite, from those in the core lands of capitalist accumulation, well, that was imperialism and dependency for you. Their Marxist critics argued that capitalism was a matter of the social relations of production (and not only exchange) and that not all forms of incorporation into the world market constituted the development of capitalism. They pointed, for example, to Latin American *latifundia* and eastern Europe's 'second serfdom', not to mention the still-numerous peasantries of the world, and argued that there were forms of world market incorporation that did not immediately or easily lead to the development of capitalist relations of production. While the 'articulation of modes of production' approach (chief works include Laclau 1977, Brenner 1978, and Banaji 1977) of these Marxists was theoretically rich, it also revealed clearly how counterintuitive the Marxist idea of capitalist exploitation as the extraction of surplus value was. As one writer, who perhaps most consistently attempted to apply Marx's law of value to the understanding of underdevelopment, pointed out:

> The radical critics of orthodox development theory were so keen to prove the ideological point that underdevelopment was the product of capitalist exploitation, that they let the crucial issue pass them by: capital created underdevelopment not because it exploited the underdeveloped world, but because it did not exploit it enough (Kay 1975, x).

In thus keeping open the possibility of an end to dependency—and therefore imperialism—through the implantation of capitalist relations of production, the Marxist critics of dependency were criticized for underestimating the problems of the Third World (Lipietz 1982). However, these Marxists were only dismissing the 'impossibilism' of dependency approaches and pointing to counter-indications in the evolution of the Third World over the postwar period. Chief among these counter-indications was the 'miraculous' rise of the East Asian economies by the 1970s and the more widespread phenomenon of industrialization of a great number of Third World countries in the 1970s and 1980s (Warren 1973; 1980).

Neo-liberalism

The 1970s marked a watershed in the story of development. While a small number of countries industrialized successfully, slow growth in the First World meant that aggregate Third World growth rates slowed perceptibly, in good part due to the unravelling of the Bretton Woods institutions, which had governed the world economy of the 'golden age'. This slowdown contributed to the further restructuring of these institutions and, by the 1980's, they took forms that were hostile to development. The slowdown was rooted in the postwar recovery of western Europe and Japan, which the Cold War had forced the US to sponsor. As these economies recovered, the US trade and balance of payments deficits widened, and the latter was compounded by the costs of the Vietnam War. When the US did not have enough gold to back the dollars with which it paid these costs, it simply broke the dollar's peg to gold at $35 an ounce, the keystone of Bretton Woods economic governance. All convertible currencies now floated against each other, creating great financial uncertainty. Although most Third World currencies were not convertible, a related development proved fateful for them.

The Organization of Petroleum Exporting Countries (OPEC) dramatically raised oil prices from approximately $2 per barrel to $39 by the end of the 1970s. While the devastating impact on all oil-importing countries made its own contribution to the slowdown in world and Third World growth, the oil price increases also facilitated a divergence in the fate of Third World countries as some relatively successful industrializers broke ranks to forge ahead while most others began sinking into a mire of economic stagnation or decline, political instability, and social disintegration that would worsen in coming decades. If the Third World was disparate enough to begin with, it would soon come to seem unmanageably so.

A rather unique conjuncture in world political economy accounted for the cases of Third World industrialization in the 1970s. International interest rates, never very high in the postwar period thanks to the 'repression of finance' in the Bretton Woods institutions, dipped even lower amid slow growth and low demand for capital. Indeed, as slow growth combined with inflation, real interest rates—the difference between the nominal interest rates and the rate of inflation—were even occasionally negative. With the vastly inflated revenues from oil sales deposited in US banks, these banks were eager, even desperate, to lend money (see also chapter 14). The 1970s witnessed a boom in private bank lending to sovereign Third World governments through open variable-rate loans. They financed the substantial spurt in industrialization in the Third World during the second half of the twentieth century and seemed to promise practically free capital and potentially high industrial growth for Third World countries with the state capacity and political will to foster it.

It was this prospect that the US's turn towards 'monetarism' ended and indeed, some would argue, was calculated to end. Monetarism prescribed raising interest rates to end inflation. Whether it ended inflation remained moot, but it certainly caused a sharp recession and delivered a harsh financial shock to Third World borrowers, who now faced higher principal and interest payments than anyone had originally anticipated. In 1982, the Third World 'debt crisis' broke as Mexico, Brazil, and Argentina defaulted on their debt. Although not originally designed to do so, the IMF and the World Bank stepped in to manage the crisis such that First World bankers' responsibility for profligate lending was never acknowledged and the whole burden of adjustment was imposed on borrowers, mainly Third World governments. Acting more like instruments of US and Western power than the multilateral institutions they were supposed to be, the IMF and the World Bank rescheduled debts to avert repudiation and imposed **structural adjustment** programs (SAPs), stricter, more market-friendly versions of the 'conditionalities' that the IMF was empowered to impose on countries in balance of payments difficulties (see also chapter 9). These programs severely restricted consumption and investment in favour of production of largely primary goods for export to repay debts.

SAPs marked a major change in the theory and practice of development. The neo-liberalism now ascendant in the IMF and the World Bank contested the original goals and methods of development—to which, as we have seen, state intervention to control and direct market outcomes had been central—in favour of dogmatically market-friendly policies. While in the rich countries neo-liberalism resulted in unprecedented rates of unemployment, poverty, inequality, and deindustrialization, ending the 'golden age' of the Keynesian welfare state, its effects on the Third World were far worse. While neo-liberalism and structural adjustment were anti-statist rhetorically and to a certain degree practically, in reality they entailed comprehensive state intervention to re-engineer whole economies in favour of private capital—foreign more than domestic, financial more than productive.

Although a number of debt-reschedulings followed and small parts of the debt were forgiven, little was done to alleviate the debt burden that had expanded so vastly with the interest rate increases. For the next two decades, countries under SAPs, a majority of Third World countries, were forced to expand exports of mostly primary commodities and low value-added industrial products to pay back the debt. Consequently, the market for these commodities was glutted, lowering prices. Even as this made debt repayment harder for Third World countries, First World consumers benefited as many tropical products, from higher-value teas and coffees to cotton, entered mass consumption in the First World in the 1980s for the first time. Contrary to all notions of development, neo-liberalism engineered a massive transfer of capital *from* the Third World to the First. The series of 'lost decades' of development, with negative growth rates in many Third World countries, are often blamed on poor government policies. However, with state spending restricted and interventionism ruled out, no attempt to break out of the production of low value-added products—in effect no development—could even be contemplated.

Neo-liberalism's anti-state and pro-market dogma proved the end of 'development' as originally conceived: with the nation-state as its chief agent and industrialization its key component. By the early 1980s, various commentators were pronouncing it at a 'crisis' or 'impasse'. In the 1990s, the dominance of neo-liberalism was reinforced by the discourse of 'globalization', which argued that nation-states were now irrelevant. Then, as the twenty-first century opened with 9/11 and the US's war on terrorism, a new set of discourses on 'empire' and 'imperialism' portrayed a number of Third World states as 'rogue states' and 'failed states' to be dealt with, if necessary by violence. Amid all this, development, industrialization, and 'catching up' to First World levels of prosperity remained a distant dream for most of the Third World.

Indeed, the story of development in its original sense seemed to have more or less ended in the 1970s when its promise was forsaken. It is yet to be redeemed.

By the early 1970s the vision of 'catching up' (culminating in Rostow's 1960 version, in a 'high mass-consumption' society, which implicitly included equity and democracy) had already given way to more modest ambitions: 'redistribution with growth'—i.e., some reduction in inequality but financed out of growth so that the better off in the developing countries might be less unwilling to agree to it—in a word, fewer illusions about democracy. And by the end of the 1970s, redistribution had given way to just trying to meet the 'basic needs' of the poor who, it seemed, would always be with us after all; the goal of equity had disappeared. Then came structural adjustment; to get growth, underdeveloped societies were to adjust themselves to the Procrustean bed allocated to them by the market, and for this purpose even basic needs must be sacrificed (Leys 1996, 26).

Neo-liberalism became a new orthodoxy not only among Western governments but also among those of the Third World where elites were impatient of the obligations to their own working and peasant classes implied by developmentalism. Its 'indentikit' policies involved cuts in state spending on welfare and subsidies, currency devaluation, deregulation of the economy and privatization, and restriction of the rights of labour. Neo-liberals argued against the most fundamental tenets of development, attacking the emphasis on industrialization by insisting that markets assured that each country would specialize in the economic activity—and it could be agriculture—in which it had a 'comparative advantage'. Any attempt by governments to work against the verdict of the market and to industrialize would lead to a decline in welfare. And they argued that governments, rather than being agents of development, were obstacles to it—profligate, corrupt, inefficient, and parasitic. Government intervention interfered with the market's way of 'getting prices right' and emitting the signals for optimum levels of economic activity.

Part of the reason that neo-liberal critiques worked was that governments in the Third World had never represented the interests of all the citizenry, only of its propertied. A great many development failures could indeed be placed at their door, and critics of neo-liberalism faced the difficult task of arguing that while that was true, in the right political circumstances governments were indeed capable of better. And the task of arguing that development was only possible under the right political circumstances and that in these circumstances democratic and accountable governments were an invaluable agent of development? Well, that just seemed too complicated in the face of the simplicities of neo-liberalism. Only in following decades, when a new generation became acquainted with the costs exacted by the oversimplifications of neo-liberalism and free-market thinking, would thinking about alternatives rekindle.

By the end of neo-liberalism's first decade, the high priests in its temples—the World Bank and the IMF—were already having to qualify their neo-liberal doctrine by admitting at least a limited role for the state. However, on the one hand, the political power of neo-liberalism prevented a real intellectual reckoning with its critics, while on the other, the increasingly unstable dynamics of the world order in which US dominance was in crisis, and consequently on the offensive, resulted in new discourses of globalization and empire, drowning out theories of development even in neo-liberal forms.

Today, development discourse seems to have petered out in a series of apparently similar discourses—whether of 'post-development' or NGOs, or esoteric reflections on the condition of various parts of the Third World—which differ from development discourse in one critical respect: they posit no project and address no agent.

Developmental states

While neo-liberalism attempted to claim development successes as products of free-market policies, new scholarship reaching back to the theorists of the late industrialization in the latter part of the nineteenth century (such as List and Carey, mentioned above) emphasized the role of government in these industrial success stories. The resulting literature on developmental states—states that consciously fostered more or less successful capitalist development, often benefiting sectors broader than the capitalist classes alone—converged with the Marxist critique of dependency in refocusing attention on the social relations of production, the political character of the states to which they give rise, the range of policy options available to such states, and the circumstances in which the more progressive options could be expected to be exercised. At the same time, it also confirmed dependency theory, arguing that South Korea and Taiwan were not the best examples to hold up to the rest of the Third World since their 'miraculous' development had been the result of exceptionally benign international conditions thanks to their position as frontline states against communism. In that sense, more modest instances of industrialization—in India or Brazil, for example—seem more worthy of study (good overviews can be found in Chang 2003 and Cumings 1999).

CONCLUSION: WHITHER DEVELOPMENT?

Does all this mean that development has no future? In answering this question, we should take note of two important phenomena. First, as we have already seen, the industrialization of some Third World countries has been a striking achievement in our time. Although many sober observers have noted that their industrial convergence has not been matched by income convergence, it is not clear whether this condition is endemic. Incomes are contingent on wage levels, and they in turn depend on the self-organization of labour.

> [T]he relocation of industrial activities from richer to poorer countries has more often than not led to the emergence of strong, new

labour movements in the lower-wage sites of investment, rather than an unambiguous 'race to the bottom'. Although corporations were initially attracted to Third World sites— Brazil, South Africa, South Korea—because they appeared to offer a cheap and docile labour force, the subsequent expansion of capital intensive, mass-production industries created new and militant working classes with significant disruptive power (Arrighi 2003, 36–7).

Second, despite all the gruesome shortcomings of what has been called 'development' since the end of the Second World War, the end of colonialism and the generalization of the nation-states system at least slowed the income divergence among countries. In his important survey of world income inequality, Branko Milanovic comes to the following conclusion about population-weighted national inequality in per capita incomes in the pre- and post-1950 periods.

> The first was characterised by (i) strong divergence between countries, (ii) relative decline of populous countries, (iii) increasing inequality among world citizens, and (iv) decreasing within-country inequality. In the second period, after 1950, (i) the divergence among countries continued though at a slower pace, (ii) populous and poor countries started to catch up with the rich world, (iii) inequality among world citizens moved slightly up, and (iv) the overlap [between the poor of rich countries and the rich of poor countries], and perhaps within-country inequalities, increased again. In other words, the features (i) and (iii) continued, but at a slower pace, while the features (ii) and (iv) reversed. In effect, it is the reversal of feature (ii)—namely, the end of India's and China's falling behind the rich world—that causes the increase in the overlap component, as some part of poor countries populations now 'mingle' with people from rich countries (Milanovic 2005, 144).

Figure 3.2   Coahuila state; rural electrification

Source: Denis Marchand, IDRC

This is the record of the whole period from 1950 to 2000, despite the radical reversal represented by the monetarist counter-revolution for the development of Third World countries. While much of the difference between the pre- and post-1950 periods may be attributed to the wild fluctuations in the economic fate of China since 1820, the record of India, the tortoise to China's hare, so to speak, is particularly revealing. Taking the twentieth century as a whole, the *most* significant break in India's growth record came following independence in 1947, when after stagnating for the first half of the century, the country experienced a clear step upward in growth.

There are two sets of growth rates for the period 1900-01 to 1946-47 based on two different estimates of national income. The Sivasubramonian estimates suggest that, in real terms, the growth in national income was 1 per cent per annum, whereas the growth in

per capita income was 0.2 per cent per annum. The Maddison estimates suggest that the growth in national income was 0.8 per cent per annum, whereas the growth in per capita income was almost negligible at 0.04 percent per annum. The growth rates for the period from 1950-51 to 2004-05 provide a sharp contrast. In real terms, the growth in GDP was 4.2 per cent per annum while the growth in per capita income was 2.1 per cent per annum (Nayyar 2006, 1452–3).

The reconfiguration of imperialism implied by decolonization was, then, central to the story of India's growth in the twentieth century. Surplus extracted from colonies such as India, indeed pre-eminently India, had contributed to the initial accumulation that had led to the Industrial Revolution in Britain and, a century later when Britain's industrial supremacy began to decline, had helped it to balance its payments against new rising manufacturing powers (see Arrighi 2005; Patnaik 2006, 2001). But for India, the whole panoply of the practices of colonialism had meant stagnation.

Without their own colonies to exploit, the industrial capitalist development of the former colonial countries of the South has been anything but spectacular. And where it has been, as in South Korea and Taiwan, it has been mainly because, as noted earlier, the exigencies of the Cold War forced the US to grant these two frontline states levels of aid, policy freedom, and access to US markets denied to all other ex-colonial countries. Nevertheless, industrialization in the South has been a widespread phenomenon. Moreover, at worst, national independence, and the national economic management that went with it, has prevented a worsening of inequality. In the early twenty-first century, there are signs that neo-liberalism's ascendancy is weakening. If it is reversed, the merits of the Marxist and 'developmental state' theoretical developments in understanding and rectifying underdevelopment can perhaps be tested.

QUESTIONS FOR DISCUSSION

1. Why did the post–Second World War project of development fail?

2. How and why is thinking about reviving development in the wake of neo-liberalism dependent on thinking about its lineage before the Second World War?

3. What is neo-liberalism? Why has it been so fatal to development?

4. What are the enduring contributions of dependency theory? What were its chief problems?

5. Do you think developmental states are the key to development's future? If we are moving towards a post-state future, who or what will be the agent of development?

FURTHER READING

Chang, Ha-Joon. 2003. *Kicking Away the Ladder*. London: Anthem.

Larrain, Jorge. 1989. *Theories of Development: Capitalism, Colonialism and Dependency*. London: Polity Press.

Leys, Colin. 1996. *The Rise and Fall of Development Theory*. Nairobi: EAEP; Bloomington: University of Indiana Press.

Polanyi, Karl. 2004. *The Great Transformation*. New York: Beacon Press.

Reinert, Erik. 2007. *How Rich Countries Got Rich and Why Poor Countries Stay Poor*. London: Constable.

INTERNET RESOURCES

International Development Economics Associates: http://www.networkideas.org.

The Bretton Woods Project: http://www.brettonwoodsproject.org/index.shtml.

Political Economy Research Institute: http://www.peri.umass.edu.

Economic Commission for Latin America and the Caribbean: http://www.eclac.org.

Focus on the Global South: http://www.focusweb.org.

The North-South Institute: http://www.nsi-ins.ca.

The Transnational Institute: http://www.tni.org.

CHAPTER 4

POST-DEVELOPMENT

EUNICE N. SAHLE

LEARNING OBJECTIVES

- To identify the historical context in which the post-development perspective emerged.
- To understand the core arguments put forward by post-development scholars.
- To understand the criticisms levelled against the work of post-development scholars.

As in other academic fields, the evolution of development studies has been characterized by shifting ideas about the economy, democracy, and the state. Thus, it has been marked by vigorous debates concerning our understanding of and the range of tools necessary for explaining social change in the Global South. From the late 1970s, the field has become highly contested, with the rise of new debates that challenge the way in which development has been conceptualized and practised since the immediate post–World War II period. These ideas have emerged from diverse sites in the academy, including economics, anthropology, political science, and critical feminist thought. This chapter's objective is to provide a discussion of the core claims by what has, since the 1980s, been commonly referred to as the post-development school in development studies. It is important to note from the outset that scholars associated with this school have different analytical entry points and stress a diverse range of concerns. Thus, this chapter puts together the core issues on which the understanding of these scholars converges as far as development theory and practice is concerned. To achieve this, the chapter is divided into three sections. The first section highlights the historical conjuncture that marked the emergence of the post-development school; the second discusses the core claims made by scholars situated in this tradition; and the third

offers responses from critical perspectives on the post-development turn in development studies.

THE POST-DEVELOPMENT TURN IN DEVELOPMENT STUDIES: HISTORICAL CONTEXT

Theories of development, or for that matter any theory of social change, do not emerge out of a political, cultural, intellectual, and economic vacuum. Examining the historical context that characterizes the rise of a given development perspective provides us with a broader lens through which to understand and interrogate the claims that it embodies. In the case of the post-development turn, it had its roots in the conditions surrounding the field in the 1980s and 1990s. Three developments are pivotal to understanding the historical conjuncture that marked its emergence: the crisis of post-1945 development theories; the perceived failure of development practices informed by dominant theories of development (specifically modernization and neo-liberalism); and the rise of post-modern thought in the academy.

The crisis in development theorizing and practice in the 1980s and 1990s

As other chapters have indicated, the 1950s saw the emergence of powerful ideas about the processes of social, political, and economic change in Asia, Africa, the Middle East, the Caribbean, and Latin America. These ideas, which came to be embodied in modernization theory, originated from various fields in the academy, although mainly in sociology, psychology, political science, and economics. In essence, while the colonial era was marked by the notion of 'civilizing' the savage 'other' in Asia, Africa, the Middle East, the Caribbean, and Latin America, the rise of a new world order after the Second World War, dominated by the geopolitics of the Cold War, as well as decolonization struggles in Africa and Asia, led to the reproduction of the same civilizing idea but under the non-offensive-sounding rubric of 'development'. As Arturo Escobar argues,

> This transformation took place to suit the demands of the post-war development order, which relied heavily on research and knowledge to provide a reliable picture of a country's social and economic problems. Development disciplines and sub-disciplines—including development economics, the agricultural sciences, the health, nutrition and education sciences, demography, and urban planning—proliferated (1995b, 213–14).

As discussed in chapter 3, the core elements of modernization theory's ideas and vision of economic and political change had, by the 1960s, been significantly challenged by dependency theorists, whose perspectives came to dominate development debates from this period until the 1970s. By the 1980s, modernization theory and the economic and political practices it informed, as well as the critical tradition in development studies generated by the rise of the dependency perspective, had begun to unravel. Beyond the conceptual blinders of modernization theory that were highlighted by dependency theorists, its envisioned Third World modernization project was considered a failure by a broad range of actors in the development community—a community defined by Colin Leys as 'a network of people professionally concerned with development', including the '"donor" and the recipient country's

development ministries, multilateral aid agencies, financial institutions and non-government organizations, and academic and non-academic [players]' (1996, 29).

The crisis of the Third World modernization theory and practice did not mean the end of what Gilbert Rist (2002) terms as the 'messianic' belief in the idea of development, which he argues is deeply rooted in Western ideas about progress and industrialization. The 1980s saw the ascendancy of a new development perspective, referred to as the neo-liberal approach because it was underpinned by core ideas of classical liberal economic thought. The neo-liberal development perspective reproduced the messianic belief in the possibility of development in the Global South—with a caveat: the old model of development that was informed by modernization theory and other ideas from the immediate post-1945 period had to be dismantled. For neo-liberal thinkers, the way forward for these countries was to institute measures that created favourable conditions for market-led development. For almost three decades, then, the neo-liberal development perspective has informed development policy and practice. Its core tenets are **privatization** of publicly owned enterprises; removal of tariffs and other bottlenecks that limit international free trade and foreign direct investment; focus on primary commodity export-led development strategy, with emphasis on the comparative advantage of each country; and deregulation (rolling back the state through such strategies as downsizing the civil service; removing subsidies in sectors such as agriculture; cutting government social expenditure in education, water, and health sectors; and devaluing local currencies).

Even as neo-liberal development theory and practice was gaining global ascendancy, orthodox (modernization, neo-liberal) and critical (dependency, Marxist) theories of development were increasingly challenged from various sites. In the academy, feminist scholars in development studies contended not only that these approaches were gender-blind but that the economic and political practices they envisioned had gendered effects—

i.e., they had different effects on women and men. Thus, such approaches offered very limited insights into political and economic processes because they failed to take cognizance of the gendered nature of these processes, particularly the ways in which they reconfigured power dynamics between women and men (Scott 1995; Cook and Roberts 2000; Cook, Roberts, and Waylen 2000; Sahle 2006). These theories—specifically modernization and neo-liberalism—were also seen to generate economic practices that contributed to the marginalization of women in the differentiated Global South, especially for women from lower social and economic classes and members of historically neglected communities, such as the low castes in India, indigenous peoples in Latin America and Asia, and peasant women in Africa.

From the standpoint of the critical tradition in development studies, development theorizing was considered to be at an impasse during the 1980s. For leading scholars in this tradition, the Marxist and neo-Marxist approaches to social change that dominated development theorizing during the late 1960s and for most of the 1970s had significant limitations. Scholars associated with the impasse debate felt that the limitations of these approaches stemmed from their economistic, essentialist tendencies and their epistemological roots. In the case of Marxist development theory, these scholars argued that social, political, and cultural realities and developments in what was termed the 'periphery' (Third World) were mainly analyzed as serving the needs of local and global power structures (Frank 1969). Furthermore, according to David Booth (1985), for instance, dependency theory and Marxist accounts of development represented capitalism in teleological and tautological terms: the ironclad laws of capital were unmovable, and the end results were known a priori. For these scholars, Marxist-inspired theories of development were similar to modernization theory in that they were marked by deep essentialism, resulting in the characterization of countries in Asia, Africa, the Middle East, the Caribbean, and Latin America as having the same political and economic features

and being destined to follow the same unilinear developmental path. The questions raised in the impasse debate generated a vigorous response from Marxists and within the impasse camp itself through most of the 1990s. The debate disrupted and problematized assumptions that had informed what was considered progressive and radical theorizing on the development question, including theorizing on the nature and role of the state in economic and political change.

The ascendancy of neo-liberal development theory and practice, like that of its earlier orthodox counterpart (modernization), was also facing major challenges from a diverse group of political movements by the mid-1980s. The rise of neo-liberalism and the economic practices it generated were considered a major failure by a range of social actors in the Global South. For example, Tunisia and Zambia, in 1984 and 1985 respectively, experienced riots as local people challenged higher prices for grain products and other commodities as a result of the implementation of neo-liberal economic policies, especially devaluation of local currencies. For many critical analysts and members of civil society groups, these neo-liberal-inspired economic practices had contributed to deepening economic stagnation, growing poverty, and a declining ability on the part of governments in the Global South to fulfill their traditional functions, such as the provision of public goods like education. Thus, from the 1980s onward, as the works of Edward Osei-Kwadwo Prempeh (2006), Benjamin Kohl and Linda Farthing (2006), and others have demonstrated, a number of political movements ranging from indigenous peoples' movements, women's movements, organized labour, students' associations, faith-based communities, and many more have been contesting the dominant development ideas and practices embodied in post-1945 modernization theory and the current neo-liberal development theory.

It was in that historical conjuncture in development studies that a new tradition emerged: the post-development school. While this conjuncture is crucial to our understanding the context in which the post-development school emerged, other scholarly developments are no less important. In particular, the rise of *post-modern* and *post-structuralist* debates in the academy greatly contributed to the emergence of the post-development perspective. Michel Foucault and Jacques Derrida, while not the only scholars mapping out post-modern and post-structuralist thought, are nonetheless considered key thinkers in the emergence of these developments in Western social theorizing and scholarly trends. In the context of development issues, post-modern and post-structuralist thought share the following common features, which are relevant to our discussion of the post-development turn in development studies:

- that language (words, concepts) is central not only to the understanding of social reality, or the 'world-out-there', but also to the making of the 'real world-out-there' (we will elaborate on this point later);
- that knowledge is socially constructed and thus not neutral and that knowledge is always situated in a local historical setting. Thus, attempts to universalize it lead to the colonization or subordination of other forms of knowledge. In this respect, scholars working within the post-modern and post-structuralist school challenge the notion of universal or totalizing knowledge that can be applied to all societies.

INTERROGATING POST-1945 DEVELOPMENT DISCOURSE: POST-DEVELOPMENT PERSPECTIVES

The questioning and disruption of the concept of development itself as it had been conceived and practised in the post-1945 period underwent a significant 'vivisection', to use James Ferguson's (1994) phrase, in the 1990s with the ascendancy of the post-development turn in development studies. While Frans Schuurman (1993) and others had conceived of the increasingly 'fragmentary' and limited nature of the dominant critical development theories of the 1960s and 1970s as

an impasse and were attempting to tease out possible openings in development theorizing, a new challenge emerged, mainly from anthropology, that called into question 'the myth of development', modernity, and other assumptions that had informed development discourse as it had been conceptualized and practised in the post–World War II period. Their texts, while focusing on diverse geographical sites of the development apparatus and marked by different analytical entry points, laid bare the structuring, colonizing, disciplining, and depoliticizing nature of post-1945 development discourses.

According to Ferguson, for example, development discourse cannot be ignored or trivialized just because whatever claims it makes are either 'untrue' or end up not achieving the objectives it upholds as its raison d'être: e.g., poverty alleviation, helping Third World societies become modern, and so forth. Ferguson contends that development discourse needs to be questioned, for like other forms of discourse in different historical conjunctures,

> it is a practice, it is structured, and it has real effects which are much more profound than simply 'mystification'. The thoughts and actions of 'development' bureaucrats are powerfully shaped by the world of acceptable statements and utterances within which they live; and what they do and do not do is a product not only of the interests of various nations, classes, or international agencies, but also, and at the same time, of a working out of this complex structure of knowledge (Ferguson 1994, 18).

Another core contention of scholars writing from the post-development perspective is that while the notion of development is not new, it took a different turn in the post-1945 period. Arguing along these lines, Escobar states:

> Behind the humanitarian concern and the positive outlook of the new strategy, new forms of power and control, more subtle and refined, were put in operation. Poor people's

ability to define and take care of their own lives was eroded in a deeper manner than perhaps ever before. The poor became the target of more sophisticated practices, of a variety of programs that seemed inescapable (1995a, 39).

While diverse in their approaches, scholars associated with the post-development turn in development studies converge on the following themes, which they consider as hallmarks of post-1945 development theory and practice: representation, knowledge-power, depoliticization, universalism, and homogenization. Further, the post-development school's critique of the concept of development is very different from that of other critical traditions in development studies, as will be highlighted later in the discussion on the notion of 'alternatives to development'.

Development discourse: Colonial representations, knowledge-power, and depoliticization

Following the post-structuralist idea that words or language and meaning contribute to political, cultural, and economic social reality, post-development thinkers argue that the texts, images, and concepts of development have facilitated the reproduction of the colonial imagery of societies in Latin America, the Caribbean, Asia, the Middle East, and Africa. According to these thinkers, the words we use generate meaning—of a place, a cultural practice, a person—and form a mode of representation. For post-development scholars, representation matters: it facilitates the production of the social reality that development institutions and theorists claim to be analyzing. What do these scholars mean by representation? Further, what is the role of language in the production of meanings embodied in systems of representation? Stuart Hall's (1997) discussion of the notion of representation and the role of language in the creation of meanings is worth quoting at length here to help us understand why post-development scholars are

concerned with these issues in the context of development studies (see Box 4.1).

For post-development scholars, representational systems were central to the political, cultural, and economic project in colonial times, and they contend that this trend has been reproduced in post-1945 development theory and practice. What do they mean by this? The central idea is that during the imperial era, colonial interests—as expressed by writers (e.g., Joseph Conrad, *Heart of Darkness*), travellers, missionaries, traders, government officials—created powerful narratives of non-European peoples that constructed them as savages, backward and subhuman. As some scholars have shown (wa Thiong'o and Sahle 2004, 64–5) in the case of Africa, for example, Georg W.F. Hegel, a leading nineteenth-century European philosopher, represented the continent as a place that 'exhibits the natural man in his completely wild and untamed state'. He counselled his fellow Europeans, whom he considered as the central focus of human history—'World-Historical individuals', as he termed them—to 'lay aside all thought of reverence and morality—all that we call feeling—if we would rightly comprehend [the African]'. For Hegel, all aspects of an African's life were governed by untamed desires and passions, 'volition in its rough and savage forms', features that consequently placed Africans outside 'the scene and sphere of universal history' (see Box 4.2 for an alternative post-colonial literary representation of Africans). Hegel's representational system enabled colonial authorities to construct African societies as being greatly in need of a civilizing political, economic, and cultural project designed and implemented by the Europeans—hence the coining of the expression the **white man's burden** during the era of European colonialism in Africa and elsewhere in the non-European world. Hegel's concepts and those of other European intellectuals provided colonial authorities with ideas to frame and legitimize their political, cultural, and economic agendas in Latin America, Asia, Africa, the Middle East, and the Caribbean.

BOX 4.1   STUART HALL ON REPRESENTATION

Language . . . operates as a *representational system*. . . . Language is one of the 'media' through which thoughts, ideas and feelings are represented in a culture. Representation through language is . . . central to the processes by which meaning is produced. . . . Sounds, words, notes, gestures, expressions, clothes—are part of our natural and material world; but their importance for language is not what they *are* but what they do, their function. They construct meaning and transmit it. They signify. They don't have any clear meaning in *themselves*. Rather, they are the vehicles or media which carry meaning because they operate as *symbols*, which stand for or represent [i.e., symbolize] the meanings we wish to communicate. . . . Signs stand for or represent our concepts, ideas and feelings in such a way as to enable others to 'read', decode or interpret their meaning in roughly the same way that we do. . . . The conventional view used to be that 'things' exist in the material and natural world; that their material or natural characteristics are what determines or constitutes them; and that they have perfectly clear meaning, outside of how they are represented. . . . Since the '**cultural turn**' in the human and social sciences, meaning is thought to be produced—constructed—rather than simply 'found'. . . . Representation [then] is conceived as entering into the very constitution of things; and thus culture is conceptualized as a primary or 'constitutive' process, as important as the economic or material 'base' in shaping social subjects and historical events—not merely a reflection of the world after the event (1997, 1, 5–7).

The colonial representational system had a significant and detrimental impact on Asia, Africa, Latin America, the Caribbean, and the Middle East, and yet colonization was represented as being of benefit to the people of these regions, given their savage and backward status. The gains that the European colonizing societies made in the process were erased in this representational system. But as Walter Rodney (1981) has demonstrated in the case of Africa, the extraction of resources and the establishment of unequal economic relations between the European colonizing powers and Africa had significant and long-lasting effects in both regions. While African countries contributed to Europe's economic development, colonial authorities established weak monocultural economic systems that saw African countries incorporated into the world economy on unequal terms, a historical development that continues to haunt the continent's economic processes up to the

contemporary era of neo-liberal globalization, as discussed in chapter 3. Further, the colonial representation of the European political project in Africa as laying the foundation for the emergence of civilized political systems and practices was very far from what was happening in actual practice. On the one hand, this language, enabled the legitimization of colonialism in Africa, while on the other hand it contributed to the emergence of despotic state forms, which have been succinctly analyzed by Mahood Mamdani (1996). In essence, the colonial representational system silenced any expression of the true political nature and economic, cultural, and political effects of the European colonial projects, a social practice that is in post-development studies referred to as **depoliticization**. The latter, examples of which will be offered shortly, refers to approaches that represent political and economic issues as technical problems. For post-development thinkers,

BOX 4.2   BEYOND THE HEGELIAN VIEW OF AFRICANS

Even prior to colonialism, through cultural practices such as epic poems, songs, mime, and armed resistance, Africans contested injustices and engaged in political and economic practices geared to creating and reproducing their communities. Thus, as in other societies, resisting and contesting power structures and ideologies were a feature of pre-colonial African societies. This tradition, which continued in the era of European imperialism, as examples of the legendary uprisings such as the 1905 Maji Maji rebellion in contemporary Tanzania and the 1915 Chilembwe uprising in Malawi indicate, disrupts the Hegelian view of Africans as docile simpletons without political agency. Following the end of formal colonialism, Africans have continued to 'speak truth to power' and demand accountability from members of the hegemonic ruling elites. Below is a literary representation of the political agency of members of a rural community in Kenya who decide to take a long trip to the city to challenge the neglect of their community by their local political representatives.

'They did not know it, but that night was to be the peak of their epic journey across the plains. It was true that Abdulla's feast, as they called it, had leased them new life and determination, and the following day, despite the sun which had struck earlier and more fiercely than in the other days, as if to test their capacity for endurance to the very end, despite indeed the evidence of the acacia bush, the ashy-furred leleshwa bush, the prickly pears, all of which seemed to have given in to the bitter sun, they walked with brisk steps as if they too knew this secret desire of the sun and were resolved to come out on top. . . . Abdulla's story had made them aware of a new relationship to the ground on which they trod . . . everything in the plains had been hallowed by the feet of those who had fought and died that Kenya might be free: wasn't there something, a spirit of those people in them too? Now even they of Ilmorog had a voice in the houses of power and privilege. Soon, tonight, tomorrow, some day, at the journey's end, they would meet him, face to face. . . . During the last election campaign, some recalled doubtfully, he had promised them many things including water and better roads. . . . Recalling, too, Abdulla's heroism in the past and also yesterday . . . they walked with eyes fixed on a possibility of a different life in Ilmorog, if not for them, at least for their children' (Ngugi wa Thiong'o 1977, 143).

political and economic processes are in the main political issues that are deeply embedded in national and international political-economic developments at a given historical moment.

A key factor that has facilitated the embedding of colonial and post-1945 representational systems of the Global South is the geopolitics of knowledge production and circulation. Thus, post-development scholars' concern with the question of representation is closely linked to the power of development knowledge production and circulation and the role it has played in the pro-

duction of Third World societies. Arguing along these lines and building from his contention that the notion of development and its attendant practices took a new form in the post-1945 period, Escobar states that 'the making of the Third World through development discourses and practices has to be seen in relation to the larger history of Western modernity, of which development seems to be one of the last and most insidious chapters.' He goes on to say that in the post-1945 era 'development can best be described as an apparatus that links forms of knowledge about the Third World with the deployment of forms of power and intervention; resulting in the mapping and production of Third World societies' (1995b, 213). Institutions such as the World Bank and the IMF have been crucial sites for the generation of development theory. Development knowledge produced in these sites is closely linked to hegemonic theories of development and the geopolitical conditions at the global level at a given historical moment. Consequently, for a comprehensive understanding of, for example, President Harry Truman's famous Point 4 (see Box 1.1), it is crucial to go beyond the emphasis on how the developed world was going to contribute to the eradication of poverty and underdevelopment in the various parts of the Global South and examine the political, intellectual, and economic conditions that marked the world at the historical juncture when the Point 4 schema was produced.

Going back to the notion of hegemonic theories of development, here are some thoughts on what, to a large extent, scholars mean by it. A hegemonic development theory sets the parameters of, for instance, how we think about the role of the state in social change, the market in the economy, democracy, and the role of development institutions in development processes in the countries in the differentiated Global South. A theory or idea is considered hegemonic when it is taken for granted and assumed to be articulating the truth about a social reality, such as the need for development, the domination and apolitical nature of Third World women, or the superiority of a given society when compared to others. **Hegemony** emerges when powerful actors in a given society or at the international level do not have to rely on force to get citizens to accept their visions of the good life, the common good, and, in the case of the Global South, the concept of development.

One of the ways in which this process—which scholars refer to as the offering of 'consent'— works is through the representation of the visions or other projects of ruling elites in neutral and apolitical terms. Thus, if you are a citizen of a country such as Bangladesh and you encounter the representation of your country as one of the least developed countries in the world, plagued by famine and so forth, the neutral language of development projects as communicated by the government and international development institutions might all sound very reasonable, since they are supposed to address the lack of development and the perpetual problem of poverty in your country. Consequently, even if a number of development projects in your country fail to address their technically stated objectives, the idea of development that is supposed to not only address poverty but also help your country 'catch up' with the developed world, which has reached the highest stage of development on the development ladder (as described by Rostow [1960]), may seem plausible. This process of consent formation occurs not only in local contexts such as Bangladesh but also within countries that extend development loans to the Third World. To a range of citizens in the developed world, having their countries 'help' poor countries in the developing world sounds very reasonable and morally right.

For post-development scholars, hegemonic theories of development have come to function as *discourse* akin to colonial European ideas on Middle and Near East societies, which were analyzed by Edward Said in his study *Orientalism*. Building on Michel Foucault's work, Said observed: 'Orientalism can be discussed and analyzed as the corporate institution for dealing with the Orient—dealing with it by making statements about it, authorizing views of it, describing it, by teaching it, settling it, ruling over it', and in the process producing 'the Orient politically, sociologically, militarily, ideologically, scientifically, and imaginatively . . .' (Said 1979, 3). From the perspective of post-development scholars, hegemonic theories of development such as modernization and, currently, neo-liberalism, which since the post-1945 era have informed government and international institutions such as the World Bank, function as discourse because they create 'a space in which only certain things could be said and even imagined' (Escobar 1995a, 39). For Escobar, 'discourse is the process through which social reality [political, cultural, economic] comes into being, . . . the articulation of knowledge and power, of the visible and the expressible' (1995a, 39). In the case of societies in the Global South, the entry point for the discourse of modernization development was

> the belief in the role of modernization as the only force capable of destroying archaic superstitions and relations, at whatever social, cultural, and political cost. Industrialization and urbanization were seen as the inevitable and necessary progressive routes to modernization. Only through material advancement could social, cultural, and political progress be achieved. This view determined the belief that capital investment was the most important ingredient in economic growth and development. . . . Moreover, it was absolutely necessary that governments and international organizations take an active role in promoting and orchestrating the necessary efforts to overcome general backwardness and economic development (1995a, 39–40).

It should be clear from our discussion so far that for post-development thinkers, knowledge production and its circulation are underpinned by power dynamics, and thus the generation of development theory—its circulation in various parts of the world and notwithstanding its technical and neutral language—is underpinned by power. Those who have power locally and internationally determine what relevant knowledge is, how it is used, and so forth at a given historical moment. Knowledge and power are two interlinked pillars that enable the crafting and dissemination of development representational systems and attendant development practices. Two examples from leading scholars in the post-development school will illustrate this point. Timothy Mitchell's work in Egypt since the 1980s has demonstrated the ways in which the representation of the country in development theory has enabled economic practices that have had significant political and social effects, even though they have been presented in technical and neutral

terms (see Mitchell 2002). According to Mitchell, development theory represents Egypt as an overpopulated country characterized by a geographical landscape—limited arable land and water sources—that significantly constrains the process of development. The representational system for Egypt includes the following features:

> The geographical and demographic characteristics of Egypt delineate its basic economic problem. Although the country contains about 386,000 square miles, . . . only a narrow strip in the Nile Valley and its Delta is usable. This area of 15,000 square miles—less than 4 per cent of the land—is but an elongated oasis in the midst of desert. . . . Crammed into the habitable area is 98 per cent of the population. . . . The population has been growing rapidly and is estimated to have doubled since 1947 (Mitchell 2002, 209).

This representational system underpins the view of development agencies involved in Egypt, such as the United States Agency for International Development (USAID) (Mitchell 2002, 209). Yet representing Egypt in this manner offers at best a limited understanding of the country's history and contemporary conditions. From a post-development perspective, the system represents Egypt as a place without history and not influenced by broader external forces, much as the colonial representational system did. For Mitchell, this representation is not only **ahistorical** but it opens a door for the development agencies to craft a development project that they believe will not only address Egypt's economic underdevelopment but move the country towards modernity. According to Mitchell, the 'poetic imagery' of Egypt as in the text quoted above creates 'the entire relationship between the textual analysis and its object'—in this case Egypt's development. Thus, the language facilitates the constitution of Egypt as a country that has population and natural resource problems even before development aid or economic development programs arrive in the country.

Egypt is not the only country in the differentiated Global South that has been represented in ahistorical terms. For instance, while Lesotho's colonial history and the rise of a migrant-labour-dependent economic system in South Africa resulted in its being incorporated into broader international and regional economic and political systems, it is represented as an enclosed society of peasant farmers surrounded by intimidating mountains and lacking development. According to James Ferguson, the 'development apparatus' operating in Lesotho generally represents the country in the following way (drawn from a World Bank report):

> Few developing countries faced such bleak economic prospects and were so ill-prepared as Lesotho when it gained independence in October 1966. . . . In spite of the fact that Lesotho is an enclave within highly industrialized South Africa and belongs with that country, Botswana, and Swaziland to the rand monetary area and the Southern African Customs Union, it was then virtually untouched by modern economic development. It was and still is, basically, a traditional subsistence peasant society. But rapid population growth resulting in extreme pressure on the land, deteriorating soil, and declining agricultural yields led to a situation in which the country was no longer able to produce enough food for its people (Ferguson 1994, 25).

The representational systems of countries in the Global South constitute a strong foundational framework for development agencies such as the Canadian International Development Agency (CIDA), USAID, the World Bank, and the International Monetary Fund to generate development projects aimed at what they consider undeveloped countries that need to get on the historical road and become developed like their counterparts in the industrialized Global North. Such representations provide these institutions with a rationale to intervene in the economic and political processes of these countries, yet their development projects are always represented in neutral and non-political terms. In the case of Lesotho, for instance, this approach facilitated the generation of a develop-

ment project focused on the mountain region during the 1970s. The mountain region—and Lesotho in general—is represented (as indicated above) as a geographical area lacking development and underpinned by what Ferguson calls an 'Aboriginal economy' dominated by peasant production. Building on this representational system, officials of the World Bank, the United Nations Food and Agriculture Organization (FAO), and CIDA, in conjunction with the Lesotho government, decided to institute a development project in the mountain region, costing about $15 million its first phase (Ferguson 1994, 75). The project's objective was to facilitate the development of the Thaba-Tseka area, which in the view of the parties proposing the project had lagged behind in development because of the lack of infrastructural modernization. The Thaba-Tseka journey to development was to be facilitated by the building of roads, a modern regional centre, and a farmer training centre, and the economy was to be modernized through livestock and cash crop production geared for the market. For the development institutions supporting the introduction of cash crop production, the driving assumption was that the non-modern farmers who had engaged in peasant production for so long would be keen on becoming modern commercial farmers once they had access to the market (FAO/World Bank 1975, Annex 1, 11, referenced in Ferguson 1994). All these efforts, as well as others such as the decentralization of political and economic authority, would empower local people in the rest of the country, who were poor and isolated from modern development processes.

As Ferguson relates, by 1979 the project's sponsors considered it a failure—especially CIDA, which pulled out. To be sure, the proposed road and regional centre were built, but the core aim of the project—to transform the Thaba-Tseka Aboriginal peasant economy from its traditional stage to a higher stage of economic growth—did not occur. It is important to note that a failure such as this is a common occurrence in the development industry. However, a close examination of the project reveals the ahistorical and depoliticizing nature of the hegemonic development theory that underpins it. For instance, the roles of the development institutions and the local state were represented in technical and neutral terms. Nonetheless, despite the neutral language, the project resulted in the expansion of the bureaucratic and coercive power of the state in a region of Lesotho that was a strong base for oppositional forces (Ferguson 1994).

As with Lesotho, the representation of Egypt as a traditional society led development agencies such as USAID to conclude that for Egypt to get on the world train to modernity, 'the impetus and the means must come from outside' (Mitchell 2002, 223). The need for 'outside' designers and implementers of Egypt's development project led in the 1980s to USAID having a central role in explaining and enabling the reconstitution of the country's grain production sector. Since the 1970s, Egypt had become increasingly dependent on imported grain. In USAID's view, this development was the result of high population growth that made it impossible for the country to feed itself, coupled with the lack of arable land for agrarian production, which contributed to a decline in food production. To respond to this agricultural development crisis, USAID, with support from the US government, provided 'at reduced interest rates more than three billion dollars worth of Egyptian grain purchases from the United States between 1975 and 1988, making Egypt the world's largest importer of subsidized grain', claiming that the grain was 'to help the poor' (Mitchell 2002, 216). Over the years, as the country's dependence on imported grain increased, the Egyptian government had to borrow money from other countries to cover the costs. This trend resulted in increasing external debt, which by 1989 amounted to $51.5 billion, placing Egypt among the most highly indebted countries in the world, a development that saw the US—based on its own geopolitical interests, mainly Egypt's support in the 1990-1 Gulf War—provide debt relief to the country (Mitchell 2002, 216).

The development representational system that led to this outcome, however, does not stand up to a historical and structurally grounded analysis. Egypt's rising dependency on exported grain had nothing to do with declining agricultural production or overpopulation. Analysis of the country's agricultural sector indicates that although it had sufficient production to keep up with population growth, with grain production increasing by 77 per cent and population growth standing at 75 per cent between 1966 and 1988, studies influenced by the hegemonic theory of development claimed that there was a decline in agrarian production during that period (Mitchell 2002, 215).

At the core of the grain importation trend was the nature of the country's social class dynamics, the nature of local state power, and broader international development issues such as the strategic role that Egypt had historically played and continued to play in the US geopolitical map (Mitchell 2002, 217). In social class terms, the historical processes of economic and political change that contributed to the formation of the contemporary Egyptian state also led to the emergence of various classes. Political, military, and economic elites emerging out of this process formed the privileged strata of Egyptian society and the social class configuration of the state. What did this have to do with the grain importation question? As Mitchell explains, changing consumption patterns among the Egyptian upper classes and the demands of tourists and other foreigners saw increased consumption of meat products. To service the consumption patterns of a powerful segment of Egyptian society, the local grain industry was reconfigured: 'Rather than importing animal feed directly, Egypt diverted domestic production from human to animal consumption. Human consumption of maize (corn) and other course grains (barley, sorghum) dropped from 53 per cent in 1966 to 6 per cent in 1988' (Mitchell 2002, 215). Thus, grains that had historically been available for human consumption were transformed to animal feed, a development that led to a crisis of food security for the majority of Egyptians while the 'needs' of the privileged minority were taken care of by the government in conjunction with USAID through the implementation of a new strategy in the grain industry. These sorts of strategies are what have led some post-development scholars to refer to development practices as 'planned poverty' (Illich 1997).

As the examples of development practices in Lesotho and Egypt indicate, at issue is development theory's construction of the state and international development institutions in depoliticized terms. In the case of the state, it is viewed as a neutral actor serving the needs of the citizens through the adoption of sound economic and political practices. Yet the state is a site of power, and state forms do not exist in local or international vacuums. In the main, and as Ferguson argues,

> [although] 'development' discourse tends to see the provision of 'services' as the purpose of government, it is clear that the question of power cannot be written off quite so easily. 'Government services' are never simply 'services'; instead of conceiving this phrase as a reference simply to a 'government' whose purpose is to serve, it may be at least as appropriate to think of 'services' which serve to govern (1994, 253).

While Ferguson's work and that of others demonstrate the ways in which so-called government services enable the achievement of the political objectives of ruling elites and in the process result in the expansion of state power, especially in authoritarian political contexts in the Global South, the same phenomenon occurs in the Global North. In liberal democratic political systems, ruling parties tend to represent their political and economic agendas as neutral, serving the interests of all citizens. For instance, a ruling party with neo-liberal ideological underpinnings may represent practices such as downsizing the public sector and privatization of publicly owned enterprises as being informed by neutral economic principles and geared to serving the needs of society at large. Yet these practices are not neutral, and further, they have social and political effects. For example, they lead to job losses and insecurity, and at the same time they serve the interests of a neo-liberal government's strong constituency: citizens who are fiscal conservatives

and may have a stake in large publicly owned firms that may be candidates for privatization.

The experiences of Lesotho and Egypt illustrate some of the central claims that post-development scholars make in their analysis of the power of the language of development theory. For these scholars, such language enables the design and implementation of development practices that are not only implicated in power dynamics from the outset but also have what Ferguson—building on Foucault's work—terms as 'instrument-effects', which means 'effects that are at one and the same time instruments of what "turns" out to be an exercise of power' (1994, 255). This exercise of power is not just limited to the local states in the Global South but includes international institutions, whose rhetoric remains focused on helping the poor and pushing recipient countries forward into a Western capitalist trajectory of development but who are very much implicated in their own country's geopolitical designs, as the case of USAID in Egypt indicates. As for CIDA, the 'failure' of a development project such as the one in Lesotho is also problematic on both the domestic and the international front. In terms of domestic economic and political dynamics, Canadian foreign aid, like that of other countries in the Global North, tends to be 'tied' aid, meaning that the receiving countries are required not only to pay the loans back but also to guarantee Canadian firms and other actors involved in the development industry, such as Canadian non-governmental development organizations, a stake in the implementation of the projects (see chapter 8). For Canadian businesses, this takes the form of contracts to supply machinery or other goods or services, depending on the project. At the international level, Canada has, since the early part of the last century, constructed itself as a leading actor in the creation and maintenance of multilateral institutions and in the post-1945 period as a generous and progressive provider of development assistance to countries in the Global South. Nevertheless, while institutions such as CIDA present their development intervention programs as neutral and for the 'service' of poor countries, Ferguson's idea that 'government services' are 'never simply "services"' can be applied to the role of Canadian development agencies and those of other countries, such as USAID.

Universalism and homogenization

The previously mentioned ahistorical approach that permeates development theory and practice has led to a strong tendency to universalize European and (since World War II) American processes of political and economic change as the reference point for countries in Latin America, the Caribbean, Asia, the Middle East, and Africa. For post-development scholars, this **universalizing logic** is not difficult to deduce, given the linear view of history that underpins hegemonic theories of development, which in turn inform development practices. From a post-development perspective, hegemonic development theories represent the European and American economic and political trajectory as the normal course of historic development, and it is this view—this 'logic'—that drives the promotion of the Westernization of the world (Sachs 1993, 4). In doing so, these theories ignore the historical specificity of the Western experience and the factors that contributed to the rise of their capitalist forms of modernity, such as colonialism of other regions of the world. But more important, the universalistic logic results in a denial of global diversity, since it recognizes only one way of thinking about the economy and political arrangements, one based on the Western experience. As Wolfgang Sachs contends, 'The worldwide simplification of architecture, clothing, and daily objects assaults the eyes; the accompanying eclipse of variegated languages, customs and gestures is already less visible; and the standardization of desires and dreams occurs deep down in the subconscious of societies. . . . The mental space in which people dream and act is largely occupied today by Western imagery' (1993, 4).

Closely linked to the universalistic logic is the tendency of hegemonic theories—e.g., modernization, women in development, and neo-liberal perspectives—to portray the diverse societies in Africa, Asia, the Caribbean, the Middle East, and Latin America as sharing the same history, cultural practices, and political and economic realities. This tendency, which post-development scholars refer to as **homogenization**, is reductionist and simplistic and does not facilitate our understanding of the complex and diverse histories and cultures of the various societies in these regions. Further, the tendency to homogenize has significant effects not only on development policy but also on the political and economic processes in these parts of the world. In the main, this trend has generated the creation of development blueprints that are informed by the logic of 'one size fits all': an economic development project crafted for Lesotho might also be applied to Malaysia. Such an approach, which, for instance, is embedded in neo-liberal development theory, informs structural adjustment polices and has significant political, cultural, and economic effects in the differentiated Global South, because what might work for Chile will not necessarily generate the same results in India, given the different historical and contemporary political, cultural, and economic trajectories of the two countries. For post-development scholars, historically grounded or 'place-based' analysis (to borrow a phrase from Arturo Escobar) has tended not to apply under hegemonic theories of development.

Post-development thought: Alternatives to development

When compared to other critical perspectives in development studies (such as dependency, Marxism, and even approaches promoting the notion of 'another development' as articulated by scholars such as Bjorn Hettne [1990]), the post-development school departs significantly from these traditions. While offering interesting insights into the limitations of hegemonic theories of development (such as modernization and neo-liberalism), these other critical traditions are still wedded to the concept of development. The

BOX 4.3   EXAMPLES OF ALTERNATIVES
TO DEVELOPMENT PRACTICES

A. Community Supported Agriculture

'Thousands of small grassroots groups are realizing that there is no need to "think big" in order to begin releasing themselves from the clutches of the monopolistic food economy. . . . Among the most promising solutions is the movement towards Community Supported Agriculture (CSA), inspired by both local thinking and action. It involves urban consumers supporting small local farmers who farm with wisdom and care for local soils, waters and intestines. And who, in doing so, simultaneously ensure that unknown farmers from far-away places like Costa Rica or Brazil are not exploited with inhuman wages and left sick with cancer or infertility. By taking care of our local food, farms and farmers, those of us who are members of CSAs are slowly learning to overcome the parochialism of "industrial eaters"—those who are "educated" to be oblivious to the harm done by supporting multinationals and others who "think big", destroying millions of small family farms across the globe' (Esteva and Prakash 1997, 280–1).

B. Community Economies

In recent years, the notion of 'community economies' (Gibson-Graham 2005) has been embraced by some post-development scholars (see Harcourt and Escobar 2005). These community economic practices take a range of forms—for example, the agricultural producer cooperatives in Kenya's Central Province, the coffee cooperatives among the Oromo community in the southern part of Ethiopia (see the film *Blackgold*). Here is another example—from Kerala in India, as described by Gibson-Graham.

'Currently Kerala is engaged in what they call the "Mararikulam experiment"—an adventure in generating local income and employment for the poorest of the poor . . . as part of this experiment, over fifteen hundred neighborhood savings groups made up of twenty to forty women are transforming themselves from credit associations to production cooperatives. The exclusive emphasis on women's involvement is a way of addressing issues of gender equity and women's empowerment in Kerala, developing women's productive power to enhance their social and political power. The first step has been to generate capital by organizing women to redefine some of their meagre earnings as a surplus to be saved and invested rather than as a part of the necessary consumption fund. . . . The Mararikulam experiment is both building on and going beyond the development approach of the Grameen Bank of Bangladesh, which has demonstrated the benefit that savings and small-scale loans can have on women's livelihoods. In Mararikulam the lending structure is organized and controlled by elected committees of the women's neighborhood groups, not an outside bank bureaucracy . . . the initial co-ops started by producing soap . . . by 2003 the second stage was underway, with co-ops producing semiprocessed foods. . . . The basic idea of the Mararikulam experience is that local 'wealth' can be collectively marshaled to bring people out of poverty' (2005, 151–3)

objective of scholars working within these traditions is to find better conceptual tools and development practices, not to transcend the discourse of development. For example, for dependency theorists, what is at stake is the understanding of the historical and structural conditions that have constrained development processes in the differentiated Global South. In the case of scholars such as Hettne, the concept of 'another development' is presented as a tool not only for the dismantling of the **Eurocentric** roots of hegemonic development theories but also for facilitating the instituting of economic and political practices that are underpinned by environmental concerns, local cultural practices, deeper forms of democratic participation in the development process, and self-reliance (1990). For post-development thinkers such as Escobar, traditional critiques in development studies remain entangled in the discourse they aim to interrupt. As he states,

> such analyses have generated proposals to modify the current regime of development: ways to improve upon this or that aspect . . . even its redeployment with a new rationality (for instance, socialist, anti-imperialist, or ecological). These modifications, however, do not constitute a radical positioning in relation to the discourse (1995b, 214–15).

In an effort to move beyond the hegemonic development framework, most post-development scholars promote the framework of 'alternatives to development' in economic, cultural, and political practices. For some advocates of this concept, the emergence of social movements discourse in various parts of the Global South represents an important development in the struggle to imagine a post-development epoch (Escobar 1995b, 216). These movements, while not monolithic, tend to engage in participatory forms of politics, value local ways of knowing and solutions, seek autonomy from the state and international development institutions, and promote pluralistic ways of thinking

in terms of economic and political practices. These features contrast sharply with hegemonic theories of development and practice, which have historically and currently pushed one way of thinking—or what post-development thinkers refer to as a 'regime of truth' (following Michel Foucault's writings)—concerning, for example, economic production and state forms. In the current era of neo-liberal development theory and practice, the idea that the invisible hand of the market should be the sole determinant of economic development is an example of a regime of truth.

According to scholars such as Escobar, through self-organizing knowledge-production practices (which tend to be underpinned by progressive research approaches, such as participatory action research) that focus 'on the encounter between modern and popular forms of knowledge' (1995, 224), social movements have the potential to contribute to the emergence of a new era in which the naturalized and depoliticized need to develop that has always been embodied in hegemonic development discourse is finally put to rest and replaced with new ways of thinking and practices in the economic, cultural, and political arenas. In addition to the practices of social movements, post-development scholars offer a range of economic practices that epitomize alternatives to development (see Box 4.3). Further, the World Social Forum process (see list of Internet resources) has since 2001 provided opportunities not only for challenging hegemonic theories of development but also for imagining a post-development era.

THE POST-DEVELOPMENT SCHOOL: BRIEF NOTES ON CRITIQUES

The powerful critiques levelled against the traditional development apparatus in the 1990s by scholars such as James Ferguson, Arturo Escobar, Jonathan Crush, Wolfgang Sachs, and many others made thinking and writing about development no longer 'business as usual', as a colleague in Malawi once stated, reflecting on Ferguson's work in Lesotho. Suddenly, the emperor of development had no clothes. Since its emergence, however, the post-development perspective has been criticized by a range of scholars in development studies. For some scholars, the perspective may offer scathing critiques of development discourse, but it does not provide concrete alternative models for development based on the Derridean deconstructionist roots that inspired its original claims (Watts 1993; 1995). Other critics contend that the post-development approach to the concepts and practices of development is ahistorical. Scholars of 'doctrines of development', writing from a historical perspective (e.g., Michael Cowen and Robert Shenton [1996]), argue that contentious debates about the concept of development, such as those prompted by the work of Ferguson, Escobar, and others, are nothing new. As an example, they note that similar debates were the hallmark of nineteenth-century writings by Saint-Simonians in France and others on the nature and definition of concepts such as progress and development.

The post-development perspective has also been charged with having a romanticized vision of non-Western societies. It allegedly fails to take account of complex histories (although its schol-ars claim that this is one of their concerns when they examine the totalizing hegemonic theories of development that are in the main underpinned by a universalistic logic). Seen through a historical lens, colonial political, cultural, and economic processes left indelible traces that have influenced identity formation (e.g., Christianity, class) and that continue to influence the diverse historical trajectories of countries in the Global South. Thus, for instance, a simple binary representation of a 'corrupt' Western and a 'pure and human' non-Western knowledge form does not capture the nuanced and multi-layered social reality of post-colonial societies. Arguing that post-development theory fails in that regard, Christine Sylvester states, 'Like most development thinking, it seems devoid of a sense of the devious ways that knowledge has been "worlded" by the forces of globalization such that local ideas become hybrid. It places faith in new social movements the way Marxists did in guerrilla movements of the 1970s.' Looking through a critical feminist lens, Sylvester accuses post-development scholars of neglecting the ways in which 'local struggles, such as those that are feminist and those that are patriarchal, can get in each other's way, work at cross-purposes, or amplify reactionary elements' (1999, 709).

QUESTIONS FOR DISCUSSION

1. What do scholars mean when they claim that development discourses are ahistorical and that they depoliticize political and economic processes in the Global South?

2. In what ways does a representational system influence development policy?

3. Why is it claimed that the question of knowledge production and circulation is central to students of development?

4. How could we rethink the concept of development in an effort to transform it from its colonial and neo-colonial roots?

FURTHER READING

Babbington, A. 2000. 'Re-encountering development: Livelihood transitions and place transformations in the Andes'. *Annals of the Association of American Geographers* 90 (3).

Crush, J. 1995. *Power of Development*. London: Routledge.

Escobar, A. 1995. *Encountering Development: The Making and Unmaking of the Third World*. Princeton, NJ: Princeton University Press.

Escobar, A. 1995. 'Imagining a post-development era'. In J. Crush, *Power of Development*, 211–27. London: Routledge.

Esteva, Gustavo, and Madu Suri Prakash, 'From global thinking to local thinking'. In Rahnema and Bawtree (below), 277–289.

Ferguson, J. 1994. *The Anti-Politics Machine: 'Development,' Depoliticization, and Bureaucratic Power in Lesotho*. Cambridge: Cambridge University Press.

Frank, A.G. 1969. *Capitalism and Underdevelopment in Latin America*. New York: Monthly Review Press.

Mitchell, T. 2002. *Rule of Experts: Egypt, Techno-Politics, Modernity*. Berkeley: University of California Press.

Rahnema, M., and V. Bawtree. 2006. *The Post-Development Reader*. London: Zed Books; Dhaka: University Press; Halifax: Fernwood; Cape Town: David Philip.

Rist, Gilbert. 2002. *The History of Development: From Western Origins to Global Faith*. London: Zed Books.

Sachs, Wolfgang. 1993. *The Development Dictionary*. London: Zed Books.

Sylvester, C. 1999. 'Development studies and postcolonial studies: Disparate tales of the "Third World"'. *Third World Quarterly* 20 (4).

INTERNET RESOURCES

World Social Forum: www.forumsocialmundial.org.br.

Arturo Escobar webpage: www.unc.edu/~aescobar/.

CHAPTER 5

GENDER AND DEVELOPMENT: ISSUES AND STRUGGLES OF THIRD WORLD WOMEN

ANDREA MARTINEZ

LEARNING OBJECTIVES

- To identify the different approaches to the field 'women, gender, and development'.
- To understand the historical and theoretical foundations of the field, including the principal concepts and debates.
- To grasp the links between the social construction of gender and other systems of power that block fair and equitable development.

This chapter offers an introductory analysis of the issues and struggles faced by Third World women in the context of development programs and policies over the past 50 years. While initially ignored by state development programs and international financial institutions sponsored by the rich countries, women have gone from being simple recipients of social assistance to 'objects to be integrated' into development and, finally, have become indispensable actors in the quest to eradicate poverty. From the 1950s to the present day, six main theoretical approaches have influenced successive—although sometimes overlapping—interventions: (1) the welfare approach; (2) women in development (WID); (3) women and development (WAD); (4) gender and development (GAD); (5) the effectiveness approach (EA); and (6) mainstreaming gender equality (MGE). While their outcomes have been variable, and generally unimpressive, our purpose is to take a critical look at each of these approaches in order to better understand why women have failed to benefit to the same extent as men from the 'trickle-down effects' of economic, political, and social development promised by the architects of international development policies. Beyond the good intentions, we will see that the history of targeting women for development seems to resemble an obstacle course. Before examining the theoretical foundations and central concepts that have marked this history, an overview of the living conditions experienced by millions of women and girls in the Third World will help us to assess the limits of development.

AN OBSTACLE COURSE

Despite numerous initiatives and statements by the international community intended to support and promote gender equality, statistics reveal that when it comes to poverty, women and men are far from equal. It is estimated that 1.2 billion people in the world are living in extreme poverty (subsisting on less than one dollar per day). Of this number, 70 per cent are women who are disadvantaged in terms of their access to property, housing, credit, inheritance, technology, education, health services, and quality jobs. In Africa, for example, where women are responsible for 75 per cent of agricultural work as well as for 60 to 80 per cent of the production and marketing of the resulting foodstuffs, they earn only 10 per cent of total revenue and own less than 1 per cent of the land (EU Commission 2007).

In terms of education, close to 85 million school-aged girls in the world are deprived of the basic right to education (representing 57 per cent of the total number of children who do not go to school), while women comprise two-thirds of the illiterate population (Bisilliat 2003). Despite a certain amount of progress globally since 1990, official statistics tend to demonstrate that literacy among women has been declining or stagnating in 54 countries of the South, including Pakistan, India, and 16 countries in sub-Saharan Africa (UNESCO 2003). As a result of low levels of education and the lack of a socio-political and legal structure favouring equality between the sexes, women are relegated to unstable employment for which they are generally poorly remunerated, most often in the urban informal economy and subsistence agriculture.

This situation increases their financial and material dependence on men while simultaneously exposing them to violence and sexual harassment. According to a study conducted in Kenya by the International Labour Rights Fund, more than 90 per cent of the women interviewed in the export trade sector (coffee, tea, and light manufacturing industries) claim to have been the victims of or witnesses to sexual abuse at their workplace (Karega 2002, quoted in Toroitich 2004). In addition, the World Bank (2003) has established a direct correlation between female

Figure 5.1   Household labour: Women carrying wood in the Amazon

Source: Caroline Heringer

literacy rates (the number of years spent at school) and birth rates (the number of children born). For example, in Mali, where the average number of children is seven per woman, only 16 per cent of women are literate.

With regard to health, 'of the over 800 million people suffering from malnutrition, the majority are girls under the age of five and women who are pregnant or nursing' for whom nutritional needs are of the utmost importance (Baeza-Rodriguez and Debos 2004, 103). Less well-nourished and cared for than boys, girls are more susceptible to developing health problems, such as learning disabilities, anemia, and obstetric complications. Tropical diseases, as well as sexually transmitted infections in general and HIV/AIDS in particular, compromise the health of women, which has serious consequences for national economies and families. According to the 2004 report on the global AIDS epidemic, Africa is the epicentre, with 25 million HIV-positive adults out of a total of 37 million HIV-positive adults worldwide (WHO 2004). Women and youth constitute the majority of new HIV cases as well as of deaths associated with AIDS. In sub-Saharan Africa, 57 per cent of HIV-positive individuals are women, and 75 per cent of the youth affected by HIV are girls. The World Health Organization estimates that young women between the ages of 15 and 24 are three to four times more likely to become infected than boys of the same age. The loss of this segment of the female population is all the more worrying because it further burdens the surviving women with the already weighty social responsibility of working and taking care of those afflicted with HIV/AIDS.

Meanwhile, the Declaration on the Elimination of Violence against Women, adopted by the United Nations General Assembly in 1993 and reinforced within the framework of other large-scale international meetings, is far from being actualized. According to Article 4 of the declaration, 'States should condemn violence against women and should not invoke any custom, tradition or reli-gious consideration to avoid their obligations with respect to its elimination.' Moreover, 'States should pursue by all appropriate means and without delay a policy of eliminating violence against women' (UN General Assembly 1994). In numerous countries of the South, however, women are still repressed by family honour codes and customary laws, rendering them second-class citizens. Under the pretext of cultural and religious beliefs, fathers, brothers, uncles, and male cousins seek to control women and their sexuality in both the public and the private sphere (the home). This patriarchal domination, which is exerted from childhood onward, justifies a range of repressive behaviours, from real or symbolic confinement, through violence, to the elimination of women and girls (see Box 5.1).

While the foregoing is by no means an exhaustive list, we should avoid falling into the trap of seeing women as perennial victims. Beyond the media clichés of the 'underdeveloped' woman, courageous in her misfortune and resigned to her fate unless rescued by the intervention of Northern benefactors, we must recognize that the category of 'Third World women' is not homogeneous. Contrary to the widely held belief that these women lag 'behind' those of the West, the diversity of female experience demonstrates that the cycle of misery, oppression, and exploitation does not affect everyone equally. Thus, a young working-class Mexican woman hired for a pittance in the agri-food industry of tortilla production does not have the same rights or privileges as a bourgeois Mexican woman who works in the government. Similarly, the latter situation cannot be compared to that of an illegal immigrant from Mexico (without proper documentation) who, responding to the winds of globalization, is recruited illegally and without any social protection into a textile factory in Canada or the United States. As we shall see further on, the extent and persistence of **discrimination** against women varies according to a complex

BOX 5.1 EXAMPLES OF UNJUSTIFIABLE REPRESSIVE PRACTICES

China, with its one-child-per-family policy that dates to 1978—but also India, Indonesia, Pakistan, Bangladesh, Taiwan, and South Korea—all have the unfortunate distinction of abnormally high rates of selected abortion of female fetuses, infanticide, and the abandonment of female children in orphanages. Because of a preference for boys, the Asian continent has a shocking demographic imbalance that has resulted in an estimated 90 million 'missing' women.

As well, globalization has stimulated an increase in the social plagues of sex tourism and international human trafficking. An increasing number of women and young girls have been bought or kidnapped and sold to brothels—in all corners of the world—by international networks of organized crime. According to UNICEF, approximately 1.2 million children, the majority of whom come from Asia (China, the Philippines, Thailand, Vietnam), the Caribbean (Cuba, Haiti, Dominican Republic), and Africa (Kenya, Madagascar, Morocco, Tunisia), are condemned to a life of forced prostitution each year. This estimate does not include war-torn countries, where rape and sexual slavery have become common.

In certain Muslim societies, misinterpretations of Koranic law have justified violence and crimes perpetrated inside and outside the family unit. For example, numerous recent *fatwas* (or judgments) have been passed by local religious councils in Afghanistan, Iran, Pakistan, Nigeria, and Saudi Arabia, condemning women who refuse to wear veils or complete *burqas* (clothing that covers the body from head to toe with a grill over the eyes that permits the woman to see but not be seen) or to be escorted by a man in public, along with those who commit 'adultery', to stoning, imprisonment, or capital punishment (Kian-Thiébaut 2006). In Uttar Pradesh (India), the same fate awaits the victims of rape, while the perpetrators are neither punished nor condemned (Khan 2006).

In Africa, although to a lesser extent than in the Middle East and Asia, genital mutilation constitutes another form of violence against women, with tragic physical (such as hemorrhaging, infection, or death) and psychological consequences. Often performed in unsanitary conditions, these mutilations consist of the partial (excision) or entire (infibulation) removal of the external genital organs of girls or women for cultural reasons without any medical justification. The WHO estimates that globally, 100 to 132 million women have undergone genital mutilation. Although some 15 countries have made this practice illegal, the laws are not always respected.

---

system of power relations (gender, social class, race or ethnicity, age, religion, and sexual orientation, among others) that challenges a number of the development theories reviewed in this book (see chapter 3).

The connection between **gender equality** and development may appear self-evident to us now, but it is in fact the result of a lengthy struggle by feminist movements and women's groups—initially from the North and eventually from the South—to valorize their rights in all areas of human activity. The following section traces the sometimes conflictual evolution of theoretical approaches that, pulled between feminist demands and donor requirements, have shaped the field of 'women, gender, and development'.

THE EMERGENCE OF THE FIELD 'WOMEN, GENDER, AND DEVELOPMENT'

A number of different theories with vaguely defined borders are grouped together in the scholarly literature under the ambiguous title of the field of 'women, gender, and development'. Irene Tinker (1980; Fraser and Tinker 2004) points out that in contrast to other areas of knowledge, this field was built through the contributions of three categories of women: academics, feminist activists, and development practitioners, whose concerns and roles occasionally overlapped (particularly in the case of the activists). In this chapter, we will examine six strands of thought in the chronological order in which they appeared, roughly speaking—although reality does not conform so neatly to this linear presentation. Indeed, development itself has not always advanced in a straight upward trend but instead has spurted forward and then fallen back.

Similarly, the term 'gender', credited to Ann Oakley in 1972, is the end result of a series of debates and reflections among anglo-American feminists regarding the asymmetrical power relations between men and women. In brief, the term distinguishes biological sex (physiological and biological characteristics such as genitals and the ability to breastfeed and bear children) from the associated socially constructed notion of sex (acquired sexual identities, such as femininity versus masculinity—i.e., gender). Although some feminists in France prefer the term 'social sex' to 'gender', the latter (gender) has progressively become dominant beyond linguistic borders, especially in the social sciences, as both a concept and a tool for analyzing inequalities between the sexes. Meanwhile, the rise of queer critiques condemning the 'heteronormative' feminist discourses (i.e., led by a dominant white heterosexual approach), coupled with scientific advances in sex change technology, is throwing into question the physical and hormonal markers of bodies and sexualities. These transformations support the emergence of new sexual identities (transgender, intersex, lesbian, gay, and bisexual), leading to a questioning of what was once thought to be the fixed nature of biological sex.

The introduction of gender into the international development arena coincided with the mobilization of feminists in the South. Determined to put an end to 'women's projects', they called for development policies and projects to take into account the sexual division of labour between men and women. International agencies such as the United Nations Development Programme (UNDP) and the World Bank, as well as non-governmental organizations (NGOs), quickly appropriated the concept of gender while emptying it of its original meaning. The first semantic elision was the increasingly frequent use of 'gender' interchangeably with 'women'. As pointed out by Rathgeber (2005, 589), 'When the development industry uses the word "gender", it usually means "women". Men are almost never analysed as part of the gender equation.' This was not a neutral process. In essence, little or no attention has been devoted to the social construction of gender relations within the existing patriarchal structures. On the contrary, it responded to considerations of a moral (avoid offending male sensitivities), pragmatic (attract funding), or political nature (avoid questioning the social structures that maintain the capitalist system). As the term 'gender' has become more common in everyday language, its meaning has stretched to include an increasingly vast range of sectors, such as politics, economics, environment, and health. This has led to a simultaneous normalization and bureaucratization of a concept that has become somewhat of a catch-all.

Social assistance

The 'welfare approach' that predominated from the 1950s to the 1970s was rooted in the context of the decolonization and political independence of numerous African and Asian countries. In the South, the formation of nation-states favoured the emergence of local **elites**, who were often more concerned with increasing their personal power than redistributing societal wealth. At the same time, the American military-industrial complex was spreading its influence across the globe along with its value system.

As discussed in chapter 3, international development at the time was strongly influenced by theories of modernization and the diffusion of technology. Economic growth, increased consumption, and strengthening of the nation-state were the guiding principles of United Nations activities in the postwar period. Achieving these objectives demanded intense efforts to contain the demographic explosion of the Third World, where population increase was believed to make economic advancement more difficult. The World Bank therefore adopted a Malthusian perspective, which sees family structures in developing countries as the 'greatest obstacle'—to quote the terms used by its president at the time (Robert McNamara, in 1969)—to the prescribed social and economic modernization. Specifically, the World Bank estimated that large families, characterized by early marriages, too many mouths to feed, illiteracy, and low incomes, were responsible for overpopulation, which was incompatible with 'development'.

Having underestimated the importance of local cultures and socio-political and economic modes of organization in Third World societies, other large international agencies (United Nations Population Fund [UNFPA], the Food and Agriculture Organization of the United Nations [FAO], United Nations Children's Fund [UNICEF], and the World Health Organization [WHO]) put in place population control initiatives, targeting female reproduction—i.e., maternity and child care. Social welfare programs based on initiatives such as the training of social workers, familial well-being, and community development attempted to implement family planning and to combat childhood malnutrition, though not without setbacks and slippages (see Box 5.2). Within this perspective, women were closely monitored. Their bodies became the focus of social control of fertility, while their thoughts, experiences, and sexual and reproductive health needs were ignored and marginalized.

According to the International Baby Food Action Network (IFBAN), the manipulation of

women found fertile ground in Nestlé's publicity campaigns. Active in many Third World countries, the multinational company took advantage of the wave of policies promoting maternal care for children to promote the substitution of powdered milk formula for breast milk. In addition to the added financial burden of buying this milk, which further strained the finances of families and impoverished single mothers, the mixing of contaminated water and overly diluted milk often proved fatal. According to research conducted in Brazil, the risk of death for babies under the age of one is 14 times higher among those who are fed artificial milk than it is for those who are breastfed. In spite of the establishment of the International Code of Marketing of Breast Milk Substitutes, which was approved by the World Health Organization in 1981, some organizations report that Nestlé continues to exert pressure to try and limit or circumvent its implementation (IFBAN; Baby Milk Action 2007).

Women in development (WID)

The approach *women in development* (WID) arose out of the liberal feminist movement and in the context of three key social phenomena that changed ideas about the 'feminine condition': the mobilization of feminist organizations in the North, the declaration of the United Nations Decade for Women (1975–85), and the publication of a seminal book regarding the role of women in development.

In North America and Europe, the movement for the emancipation of women began in the nineteenth century with the suffragettes (women who fought for the right to vote). The movement was then taken up by a new generation of feminists who refused to be objectified. The affirmation that the 'private is public' epitomized their rejection of the **patriarchal system** that placed women under the authority of fathers or husbands, thus reducing them to the subordinate position of 'minors'. These second-wave feminists demanded recognition not for their reproductive role but as full citizens and complete individuals. Their demands

BOX 5.2   THE CASE OF INDIA

India was the first country to adopt a public program to reduce its birth rate and used surgical steril-ization as a key weapon in its policy arsenal. This is a clear example of the perverse effects of the 'welfare' approach to programming. Beginning in 1951, the government offered monetary or in-kind compensation to those who underwent the aforementioned procedures. Meanwhile, the results of a 1961 census (a record high level of fertility, paradoxically attributable to medical progress in the fight against morbidity) prompted the central administration to take more radical measures in its strategies of control. With the help of the United Nations, the Ministry of Health increased its distribution of contraceptives and organized 'sterilization camps' for the rural population who lived too far away from family planning clinics. Media campaigns were launched to raise public aware-ness of the 'perils' of having a large family. However, it was the introduction of sterilization quotas between the years of 1975 and 1976 that epitomized the excesses of these population control poli-cies. In response to the pressures of meeting these targets, some overzealous civil servants demanded sterilization certificates as a prerequisite for obtaining governmental permits or employ-ment; others authorized police raids to forcibly sterilize women as well as poor men, primarily land-less peasants or shantytown dwellers.

Since that time, other countries have adopted this method of forced sterilizations. Between 1995 and 1998, Peru forcibly sterilized more than 300,000 poor indigenous women. Moreover, the means of population control have become more sophisticated thanks to the spread of more sub-tle new technologies, such as ultrasound scanning, which have enabled selective abortion of female foetuses (Guilmoto and Kulkarni 2004).

were political, economic, and legal: the right to study, work, divorce, control their own property, and freely express their sexuality (controlling their own fertility, exercising the right to abortion and to sexual pleasure). These claims did not go unno-ticed, given the challenges they posed to societal norms and taboos. The appearance of the logo 'women and equality' on millions of documents, clothing, and accessories (jewellery, key chains, badges) was symbolic of the bubbling up of the 'sexual revolution', as the period came to be known. The changes that feminists demanded were controversial and provoked vicious satires and anti-feminist insults. In spite of these attacks, feminists were remarkably effective in their lobby-ing of men, and later women, in power. As a result of their initiatives, the General Assembly of the United Nations organized the first global confer-ence on women, which took the first steps towards equality between the sexes. Held in Mexico in 1975, during International Women's Year, the con-ference sought to draw international attention to the need to develop strategies and action plans to support women's rights. To this end, the General Assembly adopted a World Action Plan, which would be implemented over the course of a decade, based on three objectives deemed priori-ties in orienting future aid targeting women:

• complete equality between men and women and the elimination of sex-based discrimi-nation;

• integration and full participation of women in development;

• a growing contribution by women to the quest for international peace.

Another fact of historic importance was that women themselves led the discussions. Of the 133 delegations representing member states, 113 were led by women. In addition, women organized a parallel NGO forum that brought together around 4,000 participants. The majority of the participants agreed on the fundamental challenges faced by women: education, health, nutrition, employment, housing, political participation, peace, and human rights, among others. Nonetheless, there were notable differences, reflecting the prevailing tensions of the time (the Cold War and demands by developing countries for a new international economic order—see chapters 3 and 10), which polarized debates. While women from the Soviet bloc prioritized the issue of peace, women from the West focused upon equality between the sexes, and women from the South stressed the importance of development processes. These differing emphases highlighted the cleavages that existed between the diverse strands of feminism of that period around which 'femocrats' (the term given to feminist bureaucrats) oriented their development work.

In spite of the existence of dissenting opinions and general divisiveness, the General Assembly managed to achieve a compromise. On the one hand, it established special measures to ensure that the action plan's recommendations would be implemented and to evaluate progress. On the other, it recommended that governments set up institutions and other national mechanisms (services, policies, research, and programs) to promote women and their participation in development. The General Assembly proclaimed the United Nations Decade for Women the same year.

The new interest in women's participation in development was fuelled by the publication of a key book, *Women's Role in Economic Development* by Ester Boserup, a Danish economist. Released in 1970, the book sent a shock wave through Northern development agencies and humanitarian organizations. Based on vast empirical research conducted in Latin America, Asia, and Africa, Boserup's work demonstrated that official statistics either ignored or underestimated the value of work performed by women. She argued that the increasingly specialized division of labour associated with development resulted in the deterioration in women's status. In the agricultural sector, for example, colonial policies of recruiting manual labour and then technical assistance approaches resulted in a radical change in gender roles. Whereas men had monopolized the use of new equipment and modern farming methods, enabling them to increase productivity, women were tasked with simple manual activities; for example, they cultivated food crops, which do not benefit from new technologies, leaving female productivity stagnant. A similar phenomenon of segregation was found in cities, where women were confined to the home or hired as the lowest-paid workers in factories or offices controlled by men. In other words, neglecting the female labour force only served to widen the chasm separating women's level of knowledge and training from that of men. This discrimination deprived women of an equal share with men of economic and social benefits.

Boserup was thus responsible for making women 'visible' as a distinct 'analytical category', preparing the way for the women in development approach. In 1973, following the concerted efforts of a feminist lobby, the US Congress voted in favour of the Percy amendment. This amendment modified the 1961 law regarding the allocation of American foreign aid, making it mandatory for the United States Agency for International Development (USAID) to include women in development initiatives. The new WID programs and services have only enjoyed limited resources, accounting for scarcely 2 per cent of US budget allocations towards foreign aid (Rathgeber 1994). Nonetheless, this example made waves, and soon other industrialized countries, also inspired by the action plan of the Mexico conference, opened WID units within their official development agencies. In 1976 in Canada, for example, CIDA set up a committee responsible for drafting WID guidelines. Even the international financial institutions could not escape this trend, as demonstrated by programs developed by the World Bank, among others.

Following in the footsteps of the dominant paradigm of modernization theory, WID addressed the **oppression** of women from the vantage point of transforming 'traditional' economic and social relationships in society. The principal means used were education and skills acquisition training for women and improving their access to credit and advanced agricultural techniques. The purpose of these interventions was to integrate women into the workforce and increase their productivity in order to improve their lives. However, the consequences of these so-called solutions for the emancipation of women have been called into question.

According to feminists from the South, WID is based on an inadequate understanding of the exploitation of women, reflecting the individualistic concerns of women from the North rather than the collective concerns of the poor women in the Third World. In this respect, by emphasizing the integration of women into the public sphere and not considering the inherent inequalities between men and women in the private sphere (such as daily tasks related to child care and domestic work), the approach neglected the real needs of the women it sought to help. Instead of contributing to the well-being of women, it imposed an additional burden of work on them. Furthermore, the WID approach failed to question the broader structures of development, particularly its insertion into the capitalist system, as well as differences in class, caste, and ethnicity among women. Moreover, as we shall see later on, revenue-generating and training projects for women were neither sufficient to alter the hierarchical structures of production engendered by the internationalization of capital, nor did they address the socio-cultural models that favour men over women.

Women and development (WAD)

Beginning in 1975, thanks to the debates at the United Nations conference in Mexico City, the concept of *women and development* (WAD) gained steam in development circles, where it was sometimes confused with WID. However, this theoretical perspective is categorically distinct from the way it was erroneously characterized by some development agencies and NGOs. Parallel to United Nations efforts on women's issues, WAD evolved out of the refinement of various interpretations of neo-Marxist thought, including dependency theory (see chapter 3), which provided it with its theoretical foundations. However, unlike dependency theory, which ignored the oppression of women, the WAD approach defined itself as a current of Marxist feminism. As such, it sought to explain the relationship between women and the process of capitalist development in terms of the material conditions that contribute to their exploitation. Material conditions refer to the economic structures that underlie the social organization of capitalism, such as the mode of production, the primacy of private property, unequal interactions between classes, and the **international division of labour** characterized by unequal exchange between the core and the periphery.

In contrast to the liberal claims of WID, the WAD approach offers a critical analysis of the relationship between capitalism and patriarchy. This analysis asserts that women did not just 'appear' after 1970 but have always contributed to the economic development of society. Whether they are salaried workers or housewives tasked with domestic production (e.g., housework, food preparation, child care), they are already 'integrated' into development because they participate in the enrichment of the patriarchal capitalist system. Although WAD treats the family as a unit of production, wherein women are the property of men, it fails to delve deeper and consider the power relationships that occur at the centre of the family. This omission results from a blind spot typical of Marxism that considers women as a social class subordinated to the capitalist mode of production and to unequal international relations. According to this notion, it would be necessary to abolish capitalism in order to make the patriarchal organization of society (including the family), which dominates women, disappear. Only then would a fair international economy be possible. According to Parini (2006, 77), however, 'On the one hand, non-capitalist societies can be organized in patriarchal fashion, as anthropologists have demonstrated, and on the other hand, communist countries have failed to break with patriarchy' (translation).

Furthermore, the WAD approach has turned a blind eye to the way that different power systems have interacted and contributed to the oppression experienced by women. Similar to its rival theory (WID), it pushes aside the problems of forming alliances and the divisions of age, class, caste, race, or ethnicity, which cut across the female population and influence the social status of women. A typical example of the interaction between different structures of power is the conflictive relationship between a black housekeeper and her white employer under the old apartheid regime in South Africa. Another is the dominance traditionally exerted by the first wife (the eldest) over the fifth (the youngest) in a polygamous household in Africa—a situation that is, interestingly, in the process of being undermined by the embrace of Western values like youth and beauty. Finally, materialist feminism can be criticized for its emphasis on production in the public sphere (the wage-labour market) at the expense of other fundamental aspects of the exploitation of women's time and unpaid labour. This latter point is a weakness that it shares with liberal feminism.

Gender and development (GAD)

Inspired by socialist feminism, the *gender and development* (GAD) approach was developed in the 1980s as a holistic analytical tool. In other words, it offered a comprehensive overview of the social, economic, and political realities of development. Its origins coincide with, but are not identical to, those of the Development Alternatives with Women for a New Era (DAWN) network, whose work—initiated in New Delhi, India—marks a turning point in the way in which feminists have understood development.

Bringing together activists, researchers, and development practitioners at the national and international level, DAWN was officially inaugurated in Rio de Janeiro in 1986 at the end of the activities of the Third United Nations Conference on Women in Nairobi the preceding year. It should be remembered that the goal of the Nairobi conference was to take stock of the achievements of the previous decade. Whereas the second conference (Copenhagen, 1980) was limited to evaluating the three areas deemed as priorities for promoting equality of the sexes (education, employment, and health), the Nairobi conference examined the full scope of the obstacles limiting women's advancement. In particular, the conference addressed the deteriorating situation in developing countries—in a context marked by the debt crisis and the adoption of structural adjustment policies (see chapter 14) promoted by the World Bank and the IMF—and sought to create awareness of the effects of neo-liberalism on the marginalization and impoverishment of women.

For the first time in an international forum, feminists of the South made their presence felt in international debates through, in particular, a devastating analysis of the macroeconomic foundations of the oppression of women. In a document that shaped the discussions in Nairobi, *Development, Crises and Alternative Visions*, DAWN denounced the links between the indebtedness of developing countries, the spread of neo-liberal economic policies, and the increase in religious fundamentalism that disproportionately affected women. This document became the reference point for the parallel development of the gender and development approach, which identified the social relations between the sexes as a development issue.

Open to the diversity of experiences and needs of women from the Third World (Aboriginal women, women of colour, women belonging to the officially abolished caste of 'untouchables', for example), the GAD approach fills the gaps left by earlier theoretical perspectives by linking relations of production with relations of reproduction. Its goal is twofold: on the one hand, it demonstrates that unequal gender relations hinders development and female participation in it; on the other, it seeks to transform the structures of power with the long-term goal of an equal partnership between the sexes in which both become participants in decision-making and beneficiaries of development.

To this end, GAD calls into question the dominant images of what is considered feminine and masculine as well as the structures of power that result from these assumptions (or social constructs). The distinction between biological sex and gender demonstrates that the inequalities between men and women are based on psychological, social, and cultural roles (which change with time and place) assigned since childhood following the dichotomy of nature/culture. Since social roles are assigned, they can also be modified.

This attribution of sexual characteristics—feminine and masculine—is based on a principle of social organization, which imposes different and hierarchically defined roles on women and men (also known as the sexual division of labour). The power differences between men and women that result from this sexual division interact with other relations of dominance such as class, race or ethnicity, sexual identities, and so on. Consequently, racial or class-based discrimination as well as **homophobia** can combine with discrimination based on gender and sometimes even override it in importance.

According to the GAD approach, three types of roles result from the socialization process instituted by the family, school, religion, the media, political parties, and the job market: (1) the reproductive role, which guarantees the perpetuation of society via procreation and the education and

Figure 5.2   The reproductive role of an Amazonian indigenous girl

Source: Caroline Heringer

care of children and vulnerable members of society (such as the elderly and the infirm); (2) the economic role, which assures the production of marketable goods and services and even subsistence production for direct consumption; and (3) the social role, which permits society to function for its collective well-being and assures the maintenance of the rules and rituals necessary for its **social cohesion** (see Box 5.3).

One of the most visible determinants of gender is the legal or customary institutional environment (illustrated by marriage practices, property rights, and the rules governing inheritance), which influences the inequality of access to endowments (economic, technological, social, and human, including education and health). In order to improve this situation and promote greater gender equality, GAD focuses on the **empowerment** of

BOX 5.3   THE THREE-FOLD ROLE OF WILLICHE WOMEN

The case of the rural Williche women, an ethnic group related to the indigenous Mapuche who live in the archipelago of Chiloé (in the south of Chile), illustrates the realities of a three-fold role: productive, reproductive, and social. In addition to taking part in agricultural work (subsistence production in which most of the production is allocated towards family consumption) and the sale of surplus vegetables or medicinal herbs, women also look after animals, weave baskets, collect water, maintain the hearth with wood, take care of the children and the elderly, do other domestic tasks (reproductive work), all the while finding energy to organize celebrations and traditional ceremonies, participate in various community meetings (of parents, neighbours, the association of Williche women, and municipal meetings) and contribute to collective initiatives such as community child care (social work).

Liberated from these tasks, the Williche men devote themselves to productive activities, which while not well remunerated financially at least provide social recognition. They have access to the most prestigious jobs in the community: they may be *lonkos*, the inherited role of political chief, or *werkenes*, men who are educated and trained to become spokesmen for the Williche people to the 'dominant power' (the state and employers) or representatives on the Williche council.

This comparative analysis of gender-based activities demonstrates that the work performed by women generally involves unremunerated and unappreciated tasks. Although they have access to fewer resources than men, their workload is about 20 per cent higher, a burden similar to that faced by women across the developing world. According to the FAO, a typical workday for poor women of the South is four to six hours longer than that of a man. For example, in numerous villages in Bangladesh, 'women work more than twelve hours per day—as compared to the eight to ten hours worked by men.' In numerous other regions in Asia and Africa, 'women devote up to five hours per day to the collection of firewood and water and up to four hours to the preparation of food' (FAO 2007). Not only do they work more, but women are more vulnerable and affected by unequal access to resources and lack of control over their earnings. They are particularly vulnerable because they lack property rights and must depend on men in this respect. Consequently, divorce and abandonment can leave them in a state of extreme poverty.

women. This concept and strategy has been borrowed from the economist Amartya Sen (see chapters 1 and 13). 'Empowerment' emphasizes that people who are victimized by poverty and discrimination need be given the tools that will allow them to lift themselves out of this situation. It can be applied to concrete socio-political situations (promotion of female participation and decision-making in the family and community), economic rights (better access to and control of financial resources inside and outside the home), and individual abilities (increased female literacy and access to education, health, employment, legal rights, leadership, and solidarity associations).

The GAD approach also lends itself to the analysis of issue areas such as the environment. Sometimes presented as a separate theoretical current, the *gender and environment* approach follows in the footsteps of eco-feminism, which links feminism and ecology. However, this theoretical approach is quite distinct from eco-feminism in that the latter is based on the essentialist positions of scholars such as Mies and Shiva (1993). In short, these scholars tend to reduce the exploitation of women to the degradation of their reproductive nature (women are seen as 'wombs', which is a symbol of their sexual essence) whose survival is threatened by the domination of men. In the meantime, the Brundtland Report on environment and development, published in 1987, provided the basis for integrating gender with 'sustainable development' (see chapter 17). The green belt movement in Kenya against desertification, deforestation, erosion, and the consequent shortage of firewood is a good example of a struggle based on the strategy of 'empowering' women.

The GAD approach is intended as a political project that transforms gendered relationships of power with the goal of instituting fair and equitable development. To do this, the project requires replacing the capitalist market model with an alternative model conferring more power on women and based on cooperation and equality between the sexes in terms of access, management, and control of resources and earnings. Experience shows, however, that public develop-

ment agencies and most NGOs view GAD as a toolbox: useful for taking inventory of the activities of each sex, targeting certain practical needs in the short- and medium-term, and developing strategies (particularly using technology) to alleviate the domestic burden of women, without addressing the underlying sexual division of labour. At the same time, the political component of 'empowerment' is pushed aside because it requires more radical structural changes unlikely to be endorsed by bilateral and multilateral institutions. As Rathgeber suggests (1994, 85), the tendency is rather to 'identify problems in the context of existing socio-economic structures'. In fact, most international institutions assume that all Third World women (Asian, Latin American, Arab, Caribbean, and African) constitute a homogeneous group and thus share similar problems and needs that can be solved through neo-liberal development policies. In their quest for gender equality, such policies emphasize the need for Third World women to gain financial autonomy and control over their lives, bypassing the tensions and contradictions of capitalist relations of production. For instance, highly technical debates about the positive effects of globalization tend to ignore the domestication/exploitation of the female labour force.

However, beyond the more traditional liberal analysis of labour market hierarchies related to gender discrimination and occupational segregation, post-colonial feminist economists have highlighted that the feminization of employment does not affect all women in the same way. The intersections of class, caste, race, ethnicity, and sexuality are particularly important, not only to understand the harmful effects of global restructuring on women in both paid (mainly at the low-wage level of the labour market) and unpaid work but also to re-envision forms of collective resistance. As pointed out by Mohanty (2004, 245–6), 'Women are not only the preferred candidates for particular jobs, but particular kinds of women—poor, Third and Two-Thirds World, working-class, and immigrant/migrant women—are the preferred workers in these global, "flexible", temporary job markets.' Examples of this pattern can be found in manufacturing export processing zones (mostly drawing on unskilled and cheap labour, often seasonal and unstable), in informal activities ranging from homework (through subcontracting industrial piecework for the garment or toy sectors) to preparing and selling street foods, to self-employment and work in micro-enterprises (all performed without legal protection such as minimum wage, paid leave, or health benefits) and in *pink-collar offices* (such as data entry or data processing in mail order businesses, telemarketing, or financial services). Other examples include the increasing migration of women from low-income countries to high-income countries to supply their workforce with domestic and daycare workers (in spite of harsh or precarious conditions and sometimes at the price of leaving their own children behind) and the internationalization of networks linked to prostitution or related services (Benería 2003).

Similarly, the struggles of Third World female workers to challenge the 'women-as-victims approach' through innovative strategies of survival and resistance are also dismissed by policy-makers. In documenting women's daily life experiences in free trade zones in Malaysia, the Philippines, and Sri Lanka, Rosa (1994, 86) has shown their 'habits of resistance': besides organizing themselves for sharing resources (such as child care, women's banks, producers' cooperatives), poor working women fight for their human rights through empowering initiatives such as providing mutual aid in the street or on the assembly line (from systematically lowering the production targets to helping slow workers meet those targets), engaging in strikes, creating women's unions, and developing transnational links between local grassroots organizations. Despite such political solidarities aimed at developing alternative economic strategies, policy-makers continue to push for increasing Third World women's participation in labour-intensive jobs for the global market. This narrowly defined construction of gender economics is underlined by the theoretical approach discussed in the next section.

The effectiveness approach (EA)

Over the course of the 1980s, the *effectiveness approach* (EA) took up the ideas of WID by making the point that the inequalities between the sexes can be traced to the fact that those who plan development failed to recognize the key role played by women in production. Conceived in the offices of the international financial institutions at the same time that structural adjustment policies were taking shape, EA aimed at including women in development projects in such a way as to make them more efficient and competitive. In light of the demands imposed by globalization, women's role in economic restructuring was viewed as essential, particularly because they were the linchpins of agricultural and industrial production. The World Bank (2003) estimates that female productivity could be increased by 22 per cent if women had access to the same inputs (capital and technology), training programs, and credit as men. Various programs were put into place to increase female output in the context of reduced social services, massive privatization, and trade liberalization. This period also saw the blossoming of micro-credit (or micro-financing) for women (see Box 5.4).

Other international agencies and NGOs have followed the example of the World Bank by developing infrastructure and equipment that allow women to increase their income-earning activities. Similar methods are used across the board: expand female participation in the decision-making process by improving their skills; improve their access to credit; increase their access to appropriate technology and more productive employment; and focus programs on rural women.

Mainstreaming gender equality (MGE)

The most recent arrival on the landscape of development policy focused on women is termed *mainstreaming gender equality* (MGE) and emerged in the second half of the 1990s. This initiative focuses on the efforts by local, national, and international

Figure 5.3   Celebrating a micro-credit project in Cameroon

Source: Andrea Martinez

women's movements to systematically integrate gender into all levels of society, politics, and programs and in all facets of development. During the Fourth UN World Conference on Women (Beijing, 1995), the 189 state representatives recognized that equality between women and men was 'the only way to build a society that is sustainable, fair and developed'. The adoption of an action plan asserting the universality and indivisibility of women's rights supported a shift in the institutional strategies of aid and developmental organizations: approaching women as a target group isolated from other development issues was abandoned in favour of a comprehensive and transversal approach to gender. For example, CIDA abolished its WID programs and replaced them with the 'transversal theme' of equality between men and women. However, in the absence of in-

depth studies on MGE, it is difficult to evaluate its repercussions on the lives of Third World women. Fundamentally, the literature highlights its 'anti-masculinist' virtues and thereby recognizes that, in comparison to 'women's projects' that triggered jealousy and tension among men, MGE promotes the full participation of both women and men through various strategies. In this respect, MGE proposes the establishment of guiding principles, planned objectives over a several-year period, coordination frameworks, and mechanisms for periodic evaluation of progress—in the form of annual reports or 'performance indicators'—in order to identify and overcome the obstacles that gender inequality poses for development. For example, these reports must record spending allocated to education, training, and health care of women and men and even specify the mechanisms put in place

BOX 5.4   DOES MICRO-CREDIT HELP WOMEN?

Conceived in 1967 by Muhammad Yunus, founder of the Grameen Bank in Bangladesh, micro-credit is a lending formula focused on the poor who, because of their lack of 'financial solvency', are generally denied loans by commercial banks. To be eligible for a loan, each applicant must belong to a 'solidarity group' (of five to ten people) who are responsible for monitoring and respecting the conditions of the loan. Operating in more than 45 countries, micro-credit mainly targets women, who have, over the years, become its principle 'beneficiaries'. While the interest rates are not significantly different from those of local moneylenders, the repayment rate is generally superior (97 per cent) to that of traditional banks. The 'discipline' that women have demonstrated in loan repayment is such that at the 1997 global summit at Washington, micro-credit was identified as a major tool in the fight against poverty.

Feminist analyses suggest, however, that micro-credit fails to generate sufficient benefits to lift women permanently out of poverty. Integrating poor women into the market encourages them to contribute to the global economy but at the cost of a pernicious accumulation of debt. They may, therefore, turn to informal sources of financing, such as the *tontines* (informal solidarity groups) in Africa, which offer community-based credit with less stringent conditions. By targeting women, micro-credit reduces male responsibility while placing increased social and economic pressure on women. For example, those who dare to neglect their reproductive functions can fall victim to various forms of physical abuse by husbands who are unsatisfied by their domestic 'productivity'. And this is without considering those single women who are forced to abandon their children in order to repay their debts, or those who are forced to go without food or other goods in order to fulfill their financial responsibilities. It is estimated that fewer than 37 per cent of female recipients of micro-credit actually have control over their loan. Instead, the majority of the debtors are under the control of men who use them either to obtain access to credit, thus creating debts registered in the woman's name, or to finance their own spending (Mayoux 2001).

However, such critiques do not necessarily apply to all micro-credit experiences. For example, the 'Thermometer' project, a Cameroon-based initiative to combat poverty that brought 4,217 women together under the aegis of the Parliamentary Secretariat of East Lékié, demonstrated that micro-credit can contribute to the economic and political autonomy of women when accompanied by measures seeking to balance public and domestic responsibilities.

to address the inequalities found in production, reproduction, and access to resources.

While the MGE approach was underscored at the Beijing +5 Conference (2000), its applicability remains nonetheless limited by the availability of statistics disaggregated by sex. Almost without exception, these statistics are hard to come by and unreliable in developing countries. Moreover, the reliance on management techniques meant to assure follow-up and co-ordination among the various parties involved creates the risk of bureaucratizing equality between the sexes. On this point, Jules Falquet (2003) worries about what she calls the 'NGO-ization of feminist movements': sucked up by the institutional logic of MGE, these movements would be 'not only neutralized, but contribute to the implementation of a new global order opposed to the interests of the population that was

Figure 5.4   Policewomen on parade in Chile: Gender equality or gender stereotyping?

Source: Paul Haslam

initially mobilized'. Specifically, MGE could benefit certain large NGOs that specialize in the transversal approach and would capture the major part of the available international funding in this issue area. Simultaneously, the emergence of a globalized elite of women responsible for implementing MGE could replace the spaces for conversation, reflection, and action by women at the grassroots, such as street-level activism or female-only trade union commit-tees. Such criticism does not, however, apply to all feminist organizations, as the vitality of the World March of Women attests (see Box 5.5).

Although cross-border feminist alliances unit-ing grassroots groups and organizations on a global scale may help the general public and social move-ments to support and institute changes necessary for improving the status and conditions of women around the world, they do not necessarily guaran-tee that these changes will encompass the particu-larized (i.e., the gendered, classed, and racialized) experiences of poor and marginalized women. As pointed out by Chandra Talpade Mohanty,

> While feminists have been involved in the antiglobalization movement from the start, . . . this has not been a major organizing locus for women's movements nationally in the West/North. It has, however, always been a locus of struggle for women of the Third World/South because of their location. Again, this contextual specificity should constitute the larger vision. Women of the Two-Third Worlds have always organized against the devastations of globalized capital, just as they have always historically organized anticolo-nial and antiracist movements. In this sense, they have always spoken for the humanity as a whole (2004, 237).

Furthermore, one may note that the United Nations Millennium Development Goals (MDGS)

BOX 5.5   BUILDING UP SOLIDARITY THROUGH
THE WORLD MARCH OF WOMEN

The World March of Women is an international feminist action movement connecting grassroots groups and organizations working to eliminate the root causes of women's oppression. Centred on the globalization of solidarity between women from all regions of the world, this movement organizes actions (mainly popular education activities, resistance, and national, regional, and world-wide mobilizations) directed at making political, economic, and social change.

Born out of the successful experience of the Women's March against Poverty, which took place in Quebec, Canada, in 1995, the World March of Women was officially launched during a news conference held in Montreal on 8 March 2000, with satellite links to women in New York City and Geneva. The same year (2000), its organizers collected five million signatures demanding the end of poverty and violence against women. On 10 December 2004, on the occasion of its fifth inter-national meeting in Kigali (Rwanda), the organization adopted a Women's Global Charter for Humanity promoting a non-hierarchical, democratic participation, based on five core values: equal-ity, freedom, solidarity, justice, and peace. Agreed to by some 6,000 women's organizations world-wide, the charter's preamble reads as follows:

> We women have been marching a long time to denounce and demand an end to the oppres-sion of women and end the domination, exploitation, egotism and unbridled quest for profit breeding injustice, war, conquest and violence.
>
> Our feminist struggles and those of our foremothers on every continent have forged new freedoms for us, our daughters and sons, and all the young girls and boys who will walk the earth after us.
>
> We are building a world where diversity is considered an asset and individuality a source of richness; where dialogue flourishes and where writing, song and dreams can flower. In this world, human beings are considered one of the most precious sources of wealth. Equality, freedom, solidarity, justice and peace are its driving force. We have the power to create this world.

On 25 November 2007—International Day for the Elimination of Violence against Women—the World March of Women mobilized around the world to reassert the values of the charter and reaf-firm four pathways to this end: (1) women's economic autonomy and the redistribution of wealth; (2) for food sovereignty and against the privatization of nature; (3) no to violence against women; (4) peace and demilitarization.

Source: http://www.worldmarchofwomen.org/index_html/en?set_language=en.

adopted in 2000 (see chapter 13) do not seem to have drawn lessons from the Beijing Conference, also sponsored by the UN. Of the eight key goals, two emphasize the needs of women and children in the areas of health and education, while a third refers to the equality of the sexes and the empowerment of women. In this respect, not only does the gender dimension remain modest and restricted, but once again, it is disconnected from macroeconomic structures (Kabeer 2005). In particular, the fight against poverty, which affects women and men differently, is addressed using the dominant economic indicators: income, variable poverty index, minimum caloric intake, and weight of children under the age of five. While this example certainly does not invalidate the international community's efforts to address inequality between the sexes, it does raise questions about the extent to which the social relations of gender are integrated into anti-poverty projects.

THREE LESSONS TO BETTER ORIENT YOURSELF

In reflecting on the maze of concepts and debates that characterizes the field 'women, gender, and development' as well as, broadly speaking, the 'discipline' of development, the reader may well ask, how should I orient myself in this complicated landscape? Three major lessons can help shape this reflection. The first is to recognize that no theory, policy, or development activity can be neutral in terms of its effects on the power relationships between women and men. Failing to take account of the sexual division of labour can lead to development strategies—such as modernization, basic needs, and more recently, poverty alleviation—that only serve to reinforce inequality between the sexes. In that the sexual division of labour operates both within and outside the home, one should be suspicious of projects that neglect the gender dimension or consider it purely in terms of a hindrance on women's productivity.

The second lesson is that the social construction of gender intersects with other power systems (e.g., class divisions, race or ethnicity, religion, nationality) that can, in their own right, hinder the recognition of women as key actors and negotiators of the development processes. Thus, acknowledging women as full citizens requires more than policies aimed at increasing their educational attainment, improving their employment possibilities, and bettering their health. Such policies are necessary but insufficient to realize women's emancipation. It is still necessary for women to be able to determine their own destiny—to make choices that enable them to exert this power. This is why projects that emphasize 'empowerment' must be pursued at all levels: individual, relational, socio-political, and economic.

The third and final lesson entails breaking free from the idea that theory must be developed in isolation from practice. Unlike fields of knowledge considered 'objective' because they are abstract and even detached from the object of analysis, feminism has demonstrated that theoretical reflection and socio-political engagement (addressing grassroots needs) can be mutually beneficial and promote the rights of women seen as subjects. Because rights gained are reversible and because development is a long-term process, the co-ordinated efforts, on a local and global scale, of men and women to construct a more just and equitable world remains the best antidote to the debilitating cynicism of disillusioned planners and intellectuals.

QUESTIONS FOR DISCUSSION

1. Why is it claimed that development can no longer ignore women?

2. To what extent have Southern/feminist movements influenced the policies and the programs of development agencies?

3. How do gender relations influence the feminization of poverty?

4. How could the mainstreaming gender equality approach improve power-sharing between the sexes in a sustainable development project?

FURTHER READING

Antrobus, Peggy. 2004. *The Global Women's Movement: Origins, Issues and Strategies*. London: Zed Books.

Boserup, Ester. 1970. *Women's Role in Economic Development*. New York: St Martin's Press.

Fraser, Arvonne S., and Irene Tinker. 2004. *Developing Power: How Women Transformed International Development*. New York: The Feminist Press.

Henshall Momsen, Janet. 2006. *Gender and Development*. London and New York: Routledge.

Oakley, Ann. 1972. *Sex, Gender and Society*. London: Temple Smith.

Rathgeber, Eva. 'Gender and development as a fugitive concept'. *Canadian Journal of Development Studies* 26 (special issue).

Tinker, Irene, and Bo Bramsen, Eds. 1980. *Women and World Development*. New York: Praeger.

INTERNET RESOURCES

Development Alternatives with Women for a New Era (DAWN): http://www.dawnnet.org.

United Nations Children's Fund (UNICEF): http://www.unicef.org.

World March of Women: http://www.marchemondialedesfemmes.org/index_html/en?set_language=en&cl=en.

Food and Agriculture Organization (FAO), Gender and Food Security: http://www.fao.org/Gender.

World Health Organization (WHO) on female genital mutilation: http://www.who.int/topics/female_genital_mutilation/en/index.html.

CHAPTER 6

GLOBALIZATION AND DEVELOPMENT

PIERRE BEAUDET

LEARNING OBJECTIVES

• To acquire a critical understanding of globalization in relation to development theories.
• To understand how globalization changes developing countries.
• To examine the impact that alternative globalization approaches have on development theories and practices.

INTRODUCTION

Over the past decade, the concept of globalization has invaded public space as well as the social sciences, including development studies. In many ways, the internationalization of the world economy has changed the way our societies and our states are structured and governed, simultaneously with the contraction of **time and space**, as explained by geographer David Harvey (2005). Scholars, practitioners, and experts debate the scope, depth, and impact of globalization through the reach of its tentacles into economics, politics, culture, the environment, and so on. There is an abundance of excellent analysis on this 'hot' topic (see the recommended reading at the end of this chapter).

Changing paradigms?

This chapter focuses on the impact of globalization on development and developing countries. It aims at triggering new debates and interrogations, especially for those who are working on and studying development. The development 'community', indeed, faces many questions:

• Is globalization really transforming the architecture of the world we live in?

• How can we understand the contradictory patterns of economic growth, as evidenced by growing social gaps in many parts of the world?
• Is it possible to talk about 'development' in the same terms as previously, now that China and other 'emerging' developing countries are becoming economic leaders?
• Is the pattern of globalization forcing development scholars and practitioners to revise their perspectives and theories?

These questions are theoretical and at the same time very practical. On the one hand, they relate to the way concepts are constructed in development studies. On the other, they are translated into actions, programs, and projects by many development agents, governmental and non-governmental.

GLOBALIZATION AND DEVELOPING COUNTRIES

Fernando Henrique Cardoso, one of the founders of the famous dependency school that had such great influence on thinking in development studies in the 1970s (see chapter 3), has given this globalization-and-development debate a rather provocative spin. After becoming the president of Brazil in 1994, Cardoso (2007) argued that past development theories were dead and buried and that everything he himself had said about development was wrong! Development, he proposed, requires full integration into the world system, which implies, in turn, accepting the terms of current macroeconomic policies as they are formulated by the World Bank, the International Monetary Fund (IMF) and the powerful G-8 (the group of eight countries that represent the bulk of the world's economy and military might): Canada, France, Germany, Italy, Japan, Russia, the United Kingdom, and the United States. Under his presidency, the social and economic priorities of Brazil were refocused to adjust to the needs and requirements of international markets. Yet a few decades previously, Cardoso and many of his colleagues in development studies had been arguing that the only path to development was to 'delink' from international capitalism!

'Success stories'?

For former president Cardoso, there is simply no alternative. His argument is fairly simple: the

Figure 6.1   World Social Forum, Brazil

Source: Alternatives/Dominic Morrissette and Catherine Pappas

world has changed. Capitalism has triumphed worldwide with the end of the Cold War. Developing countries have to conform, and if they do not, they will be left out. The World Bank (2004a) in particular has produced an enormous volume of analysis, arguing that developing countries can and should prosper and progress through (and not against) fully 'globalizing' and integrating into the world economy. The Bank has specifically documented what it presents as the 'East Asian miracle'. The idea is that East Asia is *the* 'model' whereby developing countries opening their borders find competitive niches and attract foreign capital, thereby triggering economic growth. According to the Bank, the evidence for that thesis is fairly strong, as exemplified by countries like China, South Korea, and smaller 'tigers'[1] that have indeed come out as big players in the global economy and improved the lives of their citizens.

Time and space contracting

Put simply, globalization translates into new sets of relations; activities, mostly in the economic arena, are taking place irrespective of the geographical location of participants. Globalization underpins a transformation in the organization of human affairs by linking together and expanding human activity across regions and continents (Held and McGrew 2003). Territory as a geographic reality no longer constitutes the whole of the 'social space' in which human activity takes place. Because of these major changes, social geographer David Harvey (2005) believes that modern capitalism has integrated the world much more profoundly, like different links in a chain, than ever before. Time and space are no longer insurmountable, as they were in the past, because with modern communication and transportation, everything moves everywhere, including goods, services, and human beings. Therefore, it appears that the geographic divide between the 'North' and the 'South' has become blurred.[2] This is not to say that the gap has disappeared. Rather, globalization is generating a new pattern whereby poverty and wealth are redistributed through a reconstituted structure of exclusion. For Harvey, current patterns of development under globalization lead to

BOX 6.1   CHANGING PATTERNS?

In popular discourse, globalization functions as a synonym for one or more of the following phenomena: the pursuit of liberal policies in the world economy ('economic liberalization'), the growing dominance of Western forms of political, economic, and cultural life, the proliferation of new information technologies, as well as the notion that humanity stands at the threshold of realizing one single unified community. Most contemporary social theorists endorse the view that globalization refers to fundamental changes in the spatial and temporal contours of social existence. As the time necessary to connect distinct geographical locations is reduced, distance or space undergoes compression or 'annihilation'. Theorists of globalization agree that alterations in humanity's experiences of space and time are working to undermine the importance of local and even national boundaries in many arenas of human endeavour.

William Scheuerman. 2006. 'Globalization'. In *Stanford Encyclopedia of Philosophy*. http://plato.stanford.edu/archives/sum2006/entries/globalization.

'shifts in the patterning of uneven development, both between sectors and between geographical regions' (1990, 147).

Trade and growth

No one could deny that in the past two decades, enormous changes have taken place in developing countries and at a broader level as well. World trade in particular has reached an unprecedented level. In 2005, for example, exports and imports of goods and services exceeded $26 trillion dollars (World Bank 2007b). From 1980 to 2001, the percentage of international exports coming from developing countries shot up from 25.8 per cent to 35.7 per cent, while the proportion coming from developed countries stagnated at around 20 per cent (UNCTAD 2004a). Daily international financial transactions, which stood at $2.3 billion dollars in 1983, reached the incredible level of $130 billion in 2001.

A lot of this has to do with the fact that developing countries are encouraged to open their economy, liberalize trade, and increase exports. Under the pressure of the G-8 countries and the powerful agencies promoting globalization, trade is expanding faster than production. The theory is that under the soothing influence of the market (the 'invisible hand' of Adam Smith), every country will find its 'niche' selling and buying where its comparative advantage dominates. Everyone wins in the end, so the story goes. Most

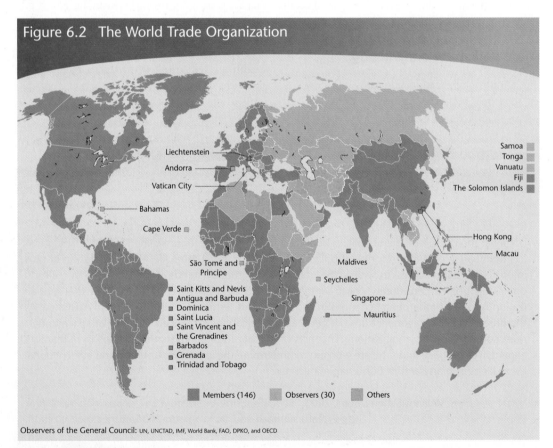

Figure 6.2   The World Trade Organization

Liechtenstein
Andorra
Vatican City
Bahamas
Cape Verde
São Tomé and Principe
Saint Kitts and Nevis
Antigua and Barbuda
Dominica
Saint Lucia
Saint Vincent and the Grenadines
Barbados
Grenada
Trinidad and Tobago

Samoa
Tonga
Vanuatu
Fiji
The Solomon Islands

Hong Kong
Macau

Maldives
Seychelles
Singapore
Mauritius

Members (146)   Observers (30)   Others

Observers of the General Council: UN, UNCTAD, IMF, World Bank, FAO, DPKO, and OECD

Source: World Trade Organization

countries of the world are now members of the World Trade Organization (WTO), the champion of international globalization, liberalization, and economic integration.

The World Bank is convinced that globalization—i.e., integration into the world market—is 'working' for the poor and the developing world. For David Dollar, an economist working for the Bank (2004), the simple proof that globalization works is that poor-country growth rates are higher than rich-country growth rates for the first time in modern history. The result, he argues, is that the proportion of the developing world population living on less than $1 per day is half what it was in 1981. These positive trends toward faster growth and poverty reduction are strongest in developing countries that have integrated most rapidly into the global economy. The World Bank is also encouraged by the fact that the growth of exports from developing countries is mostly in manufactured products.

In the meantime, **foreign direct investment** (FDI) in developing countries has increased from $3.4 billion in 1970 to $162.4 billion in 2002. This flow still lags behind FDI going to developed countries ($460 billion), but nevertheless the gap is narrowing.

Who is benefiting?

When we look at the details, however, the picture is more complex. Sub-Saharan Africa, for example, has a high ratio of exports to GDP (30 per cent) yet remains poor because its products are cheap. By contrast, rich and powerful countries concentrate their productive capacities and exports on high-value products. At the same time, only 12 developing countries are really participating in this expansion of trade, with one or two (such as China) taking most of the FDI flows. For the United Nations Conference on Trade and Development (UNCTAD 2006), the growth of exports in many poor countries does *not* necessarily lead to poverty reduction. Indeed, the incidence of poverty did not decline during the 1990s. And in the meantime, the gap in income between rich countries and poor countries has widened considerably (see Figure 6.2).

According to Oxfam International, the contrasting experiences of Latin America and eastern Asia illustrate the fact that globalization-induced growth and poverty can coexist. Even when the market expands, 'poor people are often excluded from opportunities by a lack of productive assets, weak infrastructure, poor education and ill-health' (Oxfam International 2000).

BOX 6.2   'THINGS ARE GETTING BETTER, BUT . . .'

The developing-country share of the global economy could rise from 23 per cent of world GDP today to 31 per cent in 2030, and developing-country average incomes could increase from 16 to 24 per cent of those of high-income countries. But the income gap between developing and high-income economies will remain substantial, and the absolute difference in per capita incomes will continue to widen.

World Bank. *World Development Indicators 2007.*
http://go.worldbank.org/3JU2HA6ODO

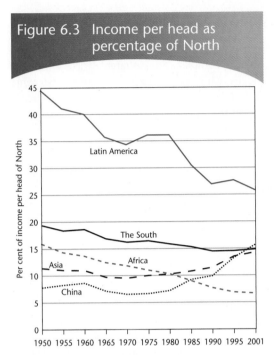

Figure 6.3 Income per head as percentage of North

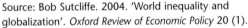

Source: Bob Sutcliffe. 2004. 'World inequality and globalization'. *Oxford Review of Economic Policy* 20 (1).

doubled since 1980 (African Development Bank 2004). Currently, most African countries appear to be trapped in a vicious circle of interlocking handicaps, including poverty and illiteracy, civil strife, environmental pressures, poor governance, and inflexible economies largely dependent on a single commodity. Many countries are also burdened by the steady decline in the world price of primary commodities. Although higher prices for oil and minerals have somewhat improved trade performance in the most recent period, Africa does not account for much of the extraordinary explosion of trade and investments worldwide. Less than 1.5 per cent of total international capital is invested in Africa.

In the meantime, Africa accounts for less than 1 per cent of the world's GDP. To add to the catastrophe, external debt has exploded—from $60 billion to $206 billion between 1980 and 2000. In 2002, while aid flows into Africa represented $3.2 billion, financial outflows from Africa were almost $10 billion (Bond 2005).

China: Exception or trend?

If Africa is in decline, other countries such as China seem to be profiting from globalization. Indeed, China has now surpassed Japan as the third biggest economy in the world. Most of the FDI to the Global South is absorbed by China, creating hundreds of thousands of jobs, mostly in coastal areas (Sung 2005). The result cannot be denied: the number of people living in poverty has declined in China, from 361 million to 204 million. Vast masses of rural people have moved to the cities where they have better access to food, health, and education. According to mainstream institutions such as the World Bank, most of that success can be attributed to the integration of China into the world economy (China joined the WTO in 2001).

But not everyone agrees. Some analysts argue that changes in China (such as land reform and nationalization of productive assets) after the 1948 revolution but before globalization have had more of a lasting impact on the economy and society.[4]

Amartya Sen (2002), a well-known economist originally from India who is critical of the World Bank and IMF policies, believes that the main issue is not globalization itself but inequity in the sharing of its benefits. According to the World Commission on the Social Dimension of Globalization set up by the International Labour Organization, 'Wealth is being created, but too many countries and people are not sharing in its benefits.'[3]

Sub-Saharan Africa under the shadow

Even the most ardent promoters of globalization will admit that Africa is not only stagnating but declining. Exclusion of the poorest countries, defined by the UN as the 'least developed countries' (LDCs) (see chapter 1), from the benefits of globalization remains a dreadful reality. Forty per cent of Africans 'live' on less than a dollar a day, and the number of extremely poor people has

BOX 6.3   IS GLOBALIZATION REDUCING OR INCREASING POVERTY AND INEQUALITY?

Vandana Shiva, a well-known ecologist and advocate of peoples' movements in India, puts globalization under trial using the example of peasants in India:

'Globalization is leading to a concentration of the seed industry, the increased use of pesticides, and, finally, increased debt. Capital-intensive, corporate-controlled agriculture is being spread into regions where peasants are poor but, until now, have been self-sufficient in food. In the regions where industrial agriculture has been introduced through globalization, higher costs are making it virtually impossible for small farmers to survive. The globalization of non-sustainable industrial agriculture is evaporating the incomes of Third World farmers through a combination of devaluation of currencies, increase in costs of production and a collapse in commodity prices' (*Resurgence* issue 202, 2002).

For Robert I. Lerman (*Globalization and the Fight Against Poverty*), on the other hand, globalization is benefiting the poor:

'It has helped the poor countries that adopted sound policies and contributed to income convergence among the countries participating in the global system. In principle, allowing trade, investment and migration should reduce global poverty. Less clearly, it should also shrink the gap between rich and poor. As firms move from high to low-wage areas, the demand for workers should grow in low-wage areas and decrease in high-wage areas, again lowering inequality' (http://www.urban.org/publications/410612.html).

Other China experts focus on the 'flipside' of the miracle in terms of class polarization, environmental degradation, and deteriorating governance. According to Wen and Li (2006), China's growth is not sustainable. It is triggering an immense energy crisis coupled with declining food and water resources. They predict that the current trend, if not reoriented, could create an uncontrollable public health crisis as well as many natural disasters.

What is new?

Once we have an idea of the global picture, we can come to a simple question: what is new? Are we not seeing the same thing, under new conditions perhaps, that has restructured the world since the expansion of Western capitalism? Is it not the same pattern observed by Karl Marx 160 years ago?

The bourgeoisie has, through its exploitation of the world market, given a cosmopolitan character to production and consumption in every country. Instead of the old local and national seclusion and self-sufficiency, we have intercourse in every direction, the universal interdependence of nations. National one-sidedness and narrow-mindedness become less and less possible, and from the numerous national and local literatures, there arises a world literature. (Marx and Engels 1967 [1848]).

What does appear to be new, however, is the speed and intensity of interconnected entities across the world. Around the world, 24 hours per day, financial markets are imposing immediate economic decisions. New technologies have, at least partially, created another reality—namely the 'world factory', managed by the world firm,

BOX 6.4   WINNERS AND LOSERS IN GLOBALIZED INDIA

Recently, India has become the site of rapid economic growth. Per capita GDP, foreign exchange reserves, and investments are increasing. In addition, Indian scientists and technicians are breaking down the Western monopoly on software in the Indian 'Silicon Valley' of Bangalore. However, 'shining India' is still facing development problems such as access to housing, transportation, education, and public health. In the countryside where small farmers were somewhat protected because of the system of public procurement and distribution, agro-industrial exports are growing, changing patterns of cultivation (away from food crops). At the same time, hikes in prices of electricity and fertilizers, limited access to credit, and other external factors are making life hard for peasants.[5]

under a world label, where everything from production to marketing and design is integrated throughout continents and communities. For Anthony McGrew (Held and McGrew 2003), what is more important is the 'intensification of interconnectedness, i.e., flows of trade, investment, finance, migration, culture. In this sense, the boundaries between domestic matters and global affairs become increasingly blurred.'

Manuel Castells (2000), a sociologist from Spain, has suggested another term to define this process: **informational capitalism**. World economics are no longer led by production as much as they are by control of the flow of strategic information, processes, and patents.

Who makes the decisions?

Globalization has a profound impact on politics. The nation-state, at the centre of the political architecture of the modern world, is losing parts of its sovereignty as an economic actor as large **multinational corporations** and financial institutions move freely across borders (see chapter 7). Kenichi Ohmae, in a provocative book *The End of the Nation State* (1995), affirms that

[a]s the workings of genuinely global capital markets dwarf their ability to control

exchange rates or protect their currency, nation states have become inescapably vulnerable to the discipline imposed by economic choices made elsewhere by people and institutions over which they have no practical control (1995, 12).

For Ohmae and other writers, political structures inherited from the nation-state are becoming obsolete. Susan Strange (1996) explains that markets, not states, are calling the shots. Fundamental policies governing macroeconomics are discussed and determined by agencies far removed from the public arena. While the powerful have influence, most developing countries are left out of the process. For example, the IMF is directed by a small group of countries because the institution, unlike the United Nations, is governed by shareholders and not by states on an equal footing (see chapter 9).

The governments of weaker states are therefore losing their influence in the international arena—but also at their own national level. At worst, this process ends up in a total breakdown, as we have seen in several sub-Saharan countries (as well as in the Balkans and elsewhere). This disjuncture between the economic/private and the political/public spaces is creating a vacuum. It remains to be seen, for example, whether the United Nations will be able to recover from its current semi-marginalization, considering that the rich and powerful do not want it to do so.

Along with nation-states, the international institutions that were built in the aftermath of the Second World War are also becoming more fragile. The United Nations, for example, is frequently bypassed by multilateral and bilateral structures (such as the WTO) and economic and trade accords (such as NAFTA, the North American Free Trade Agreement) that make decisions over a wide range of matters, including the maintenance of world peace. Most countries have now joined the WTO and are negotiating their place on the ladder within a new institution that is proposing to set new rules.

David Held and Anthony McGrew (2003) affirm that globalization has indeed changed the scale, magnitude, and impact of interregional flows and patterns: 'the locus of political power can no longer be assumed to be simply national governments.'

ANOTHER GLOBALIZATION?

Clearly, globalization appears set to remain at the centre of hot debates. The Global South is 're' and 'de' composing itself into a myriad of contradictory processes.

The new face of imperialism?

Some analysts believe that globalization is basically just 'another face' of imperialism, allowing the powerful, mostly in the Global North, to extend their reach and widen the net of international capitalism (Sklair 2002). Paul Hirst and Grahame Thompson (1996) argue that the world economy is becoming genuinely 'global'. The core, not to say the bulk, of key economic, commercial, and financial transactions remains concentrated in the 'triad', the traditional centre of power composed of western Europe, Japan, and North America.[6]

These critics contend that even the 'success stories' of eastern Asia, including China, represent a set of 'arrangements' with the triad, delocalizing some of the (labour-intensive) activities in countries that remain dependent, peripheral, and under the dominating influence of the rich countries. This situation is compounded by the fact that in many respects, China and the East Asian 'tigers' are still dependent on the Global North in key sectors such as finance and high technology.

'Global South'?

Walden Bello, a political economist from the Philippines, believes that the new globalizing

BOX 6.5 GOVERNANCE

Unfortunately, we have no world government, accountable to the people of every country, to oversee the globalization process. Instead, we have a system that might be called global governance without global government, one in which a few institutions, the World Bank, the IMF, the WTO, and a few players—the finance, commerce, and trade ministries, closely linked to certain financial and commercial interests—dominate the scene, but in which many of those affected by their decisions are left almost voiceless.

Joseph E. Stiglitz. 2002. *Globalization and Its Discontents*. New York: W.W. Norton.

structure does not erase the traditional geopolitics of power. He reminds us that the income gap continues to grow between 'rich' and 'poor' countries even if within rich countries, similar patterns are at play between social groups. According to the United Nations Development Programme (UNDP), the ratio of incomes between poor and rich nations has gone from 30:1 in 1960 to a staggering 78:1 in the mid-1990s!

Bello summarizes the process as the reconfiguration of a Global South (2006), which is no longer just a simple geographic definition but a reflection of new relations unfolding in the world, 'North' and 'South'.

Other scholars explain that this 'deterritorialization' is by no means confined to the delocalization of economic activities (for example, industrial plants moving to China or Mexico). It also implies the adoption of common policies on major issues governing the economy and society. Every country has to accept the rules established by the WTO and the IMF in order to maintain their 'macroeconomic stability', as it is usually worded. This implies cutting down on social expenses such as education and health and providing more incentives to investors and financial institutions.

Pursuing that line of thinking, Samir Amin (2004), a well-known radical economist from Egypt, thinks that globalization sets the stage for a new offensive from the United States to protect its imperial interests. The empire relies on unlimited military might and the overwhelming influence of **transnational corporations** (TNCs), compelling nations and states to submit.

Multiple facets

Obviously, enthusiasm for globalization has been challenged by many, such as the Indian scientist and ecologist Vandana Shiva:

> Globalization is not a natural, evolutionary or inevitable phenomenon [but rather] a political process that has been forced on the weak by the powerful. . . . 'Global' in the dominant discourse is the political space in which the dominant seeks control, freeing itself from local, regional, and global sources of accountability arising from the imperatives of ecological sustainability and social justice (2000, 92).

Within this context, there is a growing body of research and policy arguing that current globalization needs to be 'fixed' or eventually replaced.

Beyond the G-8

Clearly, globalization remains a process led by a few countries, mostly in the 'triad' (North America, Japan, and the European Union). Although representing less than 15 per cent of the world's population, the triad accounts for 75 per cent of economic output. It has been noted, however, that a small number of Southern countries are now important economic actors. According to the World Bank, three of these countries (China, Brazil, and India) are now among the 'top 10' economies of the world. But even if this is the case, the triad continues to play a dominant role in international forums such as the UN or through multilateral agencies such as the World Bank and the IMF. The powerful countries can also depend on their own instruments of co-ordination such as the G-8. This situation has prompted a drive within the Global South to challenge that hegemony.

Until recently, China was very quiet if not invisible in international forums. But China's role is changing, as one can see in the United Nations concerning controversial matters such as Sudan, Iran, and North Korea.[7] In the Doha round of the WTO, China sided with countries such as Brazil and India to oppose an accord that excessively favoured Northern countries on issues such as agricultural protectionism and liberalization of trade and services. Like previous Southern-led initiatives such as the 'Group of 77' and platforms such as UNCTAD where the call for a 'new economic order' was launched in the 1970s, these efforts are not intended as much to oppose globalization as to rebalance its impact. In addition to seeking the opening of Northern markets and protection of Southern assets, China and other countries are also critical of the liberalization of the financial sector: they want to keep control over the flow of speculative monies. Despite many demands from the US and the international financial institutions (IFIs), China has so far not allowed its currency to be put on the market.

In this context, China is trying to promote an alternative integration process in Asia, known as the Shanghai Cooperation Organization (SCO). The idea is to bring together China, Russia, Kazakhstan, Kyrgyzstan, Tajikistan, and Uzbekistan and eventually India, Iran, Pakistan, and Mongolia around a program of regional integration and security that would *not* be controlled by the G-8 countries. In reality, the SCO is very far from being anything but a discussion platform. But it might represent the beginning of an important process.

In substance, China and the other 'BRICS' countries (Brazil, Russia, India, China, South Africa) want to renegotiate (not destroy) international economic integration and trade. They want to reform agencies and processes such as the WTO so that Southern interests are integrated into the mainstream. The opening of these still underdeveloped economies, as BRICS see it, needs to be done gradually, protecting vulnerable and strategic sectors and enlarging access to Northern markets. In the meantime, China, India, Brazil, and other emerging countries want to further regionalize economic links, not necessarily against global integration but as a platform to gain strength and access to the global market on an equal footing. Through growing 'South–South' linkages, the general idea is to diversify (or reduce the dependency on northern markets and investments) and enlarge the economy.

'Rebels' with a cause

Other countries are relatively more radical in their demands for a new world order. In South America, the rise of centre-left governments in the past decade has changed the tone and to a certain extent the content of debates. The Free Trade Area of the Americas (FTAA), which the US and Canada had been hoping to push since the Miami Summit in 1994, is now stalled (some say it is dead) because Brazil, Argentina, and several other countries have refused to enter into what they perceive as a structure of subordination to the United States.

In the Mar del Plata Summit of the Americas in 2005, most countries affirmed that the FTAA was not in their national interest. For some of these countries, the alternative is to beef up the Mercosur, a loose regional grouping promoting trade integration within the region.

Venezuela, Bolivia, and Ecuador go even further, demanding a reversal of the policies of trade

BOX 6.6   SHANGHAI COOPERATION ORGANIZATION

Created in 2001, the alliance aims to form a comprehensive network of cooperation among member states, including military security, economic development, trade, and cultural exchange. In geopolitical terms, however, the SCO translates a convergent perspective primarily from China and Russia, with the implicit goal of curbing Washington's influence in central Asia. Both Russia and China want to have the dominant influence over the rich energy resources of Central Asia and also to link up with Middle Eastern countries such as Iran and others concerned with the Washington policy of 'regime change' in the region.

BOX 6.7   MERCOSUR IN/FTAA OUT

The Free Trade Area of the Americas (FTAA), a hemispheric trade initiative pushed by the Bush administration, is on the way out, says Carlos Alvarez, a high-level official in the Southern Cone Common Market (Mercosur): 'The FTAA is dead because it implies an asymmetrical model of negotiations between North and South.' Mercosur's full members are Argentina, Brazil, Paraguay, Uruguay, and Venezuela. Chile and Colombia are among the associate members of the trade bloc.

'Unlike other times when there was a greater dependency on the dominant power, the current period is one of having development strategies that will allow the South American trade bloc to operate with greater autonomy,' Alvarez said.

Since the founding in 1991 of Mercosur in the central Argentine city of Cordoba, trade within the bloc has surged from $4.12 billion to nearly $21.11 billion, while the region's gross domestic product, or GDP, climbed from $650 billion to $990 billion, and direct foreign investment soared from $2.6 billion to $20.24 billion. Brazil and Argentina, the two largest economies in the trade bloc, account for some 97 per cent of the regional GDP, according to economists.

MercoPress, Uruguay, 22 August 2006.

liberalization and privatization and openly challenging the **Washington Consensus**. They sometimes clash with Brazil, which as an 'emerging' country seems to be willing to negotiate the terms of engagement with the powerful nations rather than disconnecting. They are even afraid that Brazil as an emerging giant will duplicate some of the dominating practices of the big powers and establish itself as some sort of a sub-empire in South America.

Faced with that prospect, the government of Venezuela led by Hugo Chavez is proposing the creation of a new Southern alliance called the Bolivarian Alternative for the Americas (ALBA) in which economic and even political integration would be shaped around a different perspective based on social development, equality, and access for the poorest of the population. ALBA is still an abstract concept, although Venezuela, Cuba, Bolivia, and Ecuador are engaged in several programs to support one another in such areas as health, education, oil,

and the media. It remains to be seen whether these projects will last, given the vulnerabilities of the main actors.[8]

Movement from below

Beyond the recent phenomenon of states challenging neo-liberal globalization, of course, is the ascendancy of a **global civil society** expressing itself through a myriad of demands, demonstrations, movements, and networks. And beyond the image of 'anti-globalization' protests and riots, there is a 'movement of movements' which seems to be in the process of becoming a significant factor in world politics. Radical authors such as Michael Hardt and Antonio Negri (2000) think that the new alternative 'alter-globalist' movements and demands could eventually turn globalization 'upside down'. Thus, just as the empire appears to be expanding, an alternative political organization of global flows and exchanges is growing alongside it.

Figure 6.4   Massive street demonstration in Venezuela

Source: Alternatives/Dominic Morrisette and Catherine Pappas

BOX 6.8   ALBA

Preliminary meetings on the trade agreement known as the Bolivarian Alternative for the Americas (ALBA) have been proposed by President Chavez as a strategy for integrating Latin American markets in a mutually beneficial manner. ALBA has gained support in Bolivia, Nicaragua, Ecuador, Cuba, and Haiti. ALBA presents an alternative to the stalled Free Trade Area of the Americas (FTAA) and lies at the center of Chavez's regional policy, an umbrella under which he hopes to foster increasing cooperation between Latin American nations mostly in energy, banking, and agricultural matters. ALBA proposes to extend social programs in health and education, as well, and could involve the replication abroad of Venezuelan programs that have led to improvements in these areas.

Miami Herald. 28 April 2007.

From Chiapas to Seattle

In 1994 in southern Mexico, indigenous communities represented by a group known as Zapatistas appeared on the world stage, apparently out of the blue, to express their rejection of NAFTA and the neo-liberal globalization policies attached to that process. The movement captured the imagination of media around the world, partly because of the symbolism attached to Emiliano Zapata (a leader of the Mexican revolution in the early twentieth century) and also, more substantially, because the revolt was led by farmers and indigenous people who had traditionally been left out of the political arena, even among anti-systemic movements. In a rather unique poetic language, Zapatistas were demanding the end of neo-liberal policies.[9] They became widely known through their audacious use of modern communications at a time when use of the Internet was still embryonic for social movements and radical projects. Moreover, Zapatistas were capable of creating and deploying new codes and modes of social interaction and communication, different from the traditional leftist approaches. They clearly asserted, for example, that their rebellion was not about 'taking' power

but about 'changing' it. It might have been just a brilliant formula, but it has indeed changed the paradigm for many social movements. Anti- or alter-globalization perspectives are not caught up in the idea of replacing a 'system' with another but in articulating a new perspective that proposes to break down the structures of domination and exclusion that marginalize the poor.

In Seattle in 1999, that cry was taken up by a wide coalition of US and international NGOs and social movements that was later defined as the alliance of 'teamsters' (trade unions) and 'turtles' (environmentalists). The occasion was the ministerial meeting of the newly formed World Trade Organization. A large 'movement of movements' became visible after Seattle, with its adherents demonstrating in the streets of many cities in different parts of the world.

The spirit of Porto Alegre

The demand for 'another' globalization was captured by important national and international movements and social forces. In Brazil, a counter-hegemonic project had been building from the bottom up since the 1980s. By the year 2000, that

BOX 6.9   HUMANITY NEEDS CHANGE

The global corporation, the WTO, the IMF, and the World Bank are structured to concentrate power in the hands of ruling elites shielded from public accountability. They represent an outmoded, undemocratic, inefficient, and destructive way of organizing human affairs that is as out of step with the needs and values of healthy, sustainable, and democratic societies as the institution of monarchy. The current and future well-being of humanity depends on transforming the relationships of power within and between human societies toward more democratic and mutually accountable modes of managing human affairs that are self-organizing, power-sharing, and minimize the need for coercive central authority.

A Better World Is Possible. International Forum on Globalization, 2002

movement had established its capacities not only as an 'anti-globalist' or 'anti-neo-liberal' process but also as a real contender in the political arena. Out of this came the idea to convene a world meeting of civil society groups, not so much to protest (as was in the case with so many 'counter' popular and anti-globalization summits) but to define alternatives to the current system. This idea grew to become the World Social Forum (WSF), initiated in 2001 in the city of Porto Alegre, where alternative social and political movements had been ruling municipal affairs quite successfully for more than 10 years. The WSF called for a fair trading system that guaranteed full employment, food security, fair terms of trade, and local prosperity. Currently, more than 500,000 small and large social movements in the world participate in the WSF process, now decentralized into a myriad of local, national, and thematic forums and widely using the most advanced information technologies to stage permanent and complex debates.

The economics of alter-globalization

Critiques of the current model of globalization insist on the non-sustainability of the process. 'Hyper growth' and the unrestricted exploitation of the planet's resources are seen as challenges that social movements need to face and surmount. The International Forum on Globalization (IFG) (2002), an independent think tank based in Washington whose mandate is to nourish social movements with alternative perspectives, argues that the economy should first and foremost be geared to 'meet human genuine needs in the present without compromising the ability of future generations to meet theirs, and without diminishing the natural diversity of life on Earth'.

Alter-globalists promote slowing or diverting the homogenization process and especially the new rules imposed by neo-liberal globalization to reduce (if not eliminate) the principle of the 'common good'. They propose to insulate the provision of basic goods such as education, health, clean water, and the like from the law of profit—which does not necessarily imply a state monopoly in these sectors.

Overall, the key component of the alter-globalization approach is democratization of economic development, which is only possible, according to the IFG (2002), through a 'return to the local': 'Most economic, cultural, and political decisions should not be international. They should be made at the national, regional, or local levels. Power should be encouraged to evolve downward, not upward.'

BOX 6.10   PEASANTS NEED LAND REFORM

Neo-liberal globalization has led to the concentration of land ownership and favored corporate agricultural systems environmentally and socially destructive. It is based on export-oriented growth backed by large-scale infrastructure development such as dams, which destroys their livelihood. We call for democratic agrarian reform. Land, water, and seeds must be in the hands of peasants. We promote sustainable agricultural processes. Seeds and genetic stocks are the heritage of humanity.

Porto Alegre Call for Mobilization, 2001

CONCLUDING OBSERVATIONS

For more than 50 years, the development debate has been dominated by the issue of economic growth. In the 'golden era' of development, a variety of Keynesian-inspired policies did indeed allow some (not all) developing countries to build their infrastructures. As the US and the Soviet Union were competing to win allies, a limited number of states, mostly in Asia, were able to use these processes to their benefit. But the reality is that for most Southern countries, the development project ended in disaster. Some experts, such as Samuel Huntington (1993a), say that this failure reflects a 'civilization' issue. He argues that for a variety of reasons, a handful of mostly Northern countries can actually build the appropriate 'chemistry' of liberal democracy, market policies, and peace. Others oppose such arguments, maintaining that the Global South was unable to 'succeed' in globalization because of historical and contemporary barriers imposed by the Global North (Sklair 2002).

As this debate continues, macro and meta changes are taking place. In many countries, an astonishing number of social movements have indeed mobilized broad sectors of society. They are doing so (at least partially) by reinventing the language of protest while seeking more inclusionary politics. While political issues of power remain important, social movements increasingly do not focus exclusively on the state.

The strengths of this vast alter-globalist movement are obviously impressive—such as the capacity to create immediate coalitions to resist policies and propose alternatives, sometimes to the extent of changing the political leadership, as happened recently in Argentina and Bolivia.

At the same time, the weaknesses of these movements are apparent as mirror images of their assets—i.e., their dispersion, their fragmentation, their inability to propose coherent and long-term programs because such proposals could jeopardize the narrow limits of the alliances on which the movements are built.

Transnationalization of alternatives

As these experiments continue, it appears that another face of globalization is surfacing 'from below', based on vast networks operating at national and international levels. Many of these networks are 'glocal', meshing local issues with global perspectives. The old saying 'act locally, think globally' no longer applies, because alter-globalists are indeed acting globally.

A striking example of this phenomenon concerns the devastating HIV/AIDS epidemic. It was first 'discovered' and addressed by gay communities in northern California, later afflicting poor communities (mostly women) in sub-Saharan Africa with terrible consequences, and then confronted by large-scale coalitions in such places as South Africa. That led to the creation of an extraordinary 'rainbow coalition' of movements and movements of movements intervening at the very heart of international processes: in the UN, with powerful agencies like the World Bank, as well as directly with large pharmaceutical corporations.

During the 2005 Doha Summit of the WTO, rich countries were formally forced to concede that the worst affected countries could have access to generic medication, bypassing the usual system of patents and protection for the giant TNCs to provide basic services to HIV/AIDS communities and people. In practical terms, however, the struggle continues. The same countries that had indicated their willingness to concede later backtracked. But now, governments and agencies are being challenged by well-organized and structured movements operating across borders, able to share information and elaborate strategies across the planet.

QUESTIONS FOR DISCUSSION

1. How does globalization affect development?
2. Does the 'positive' side of globalization outweigh its negative aspects?
3. How are developing countries coping? Who are the winners? Who are the losers?
4. Is China changing the way we perceived development?
5. What will stop the decline of Africa?
6. Can alternatives to neo-liberal globalization prevail?

FURTHER READING

Held, David, Anthony McGrew, David Goldblatt, and Jonathan Perraton. 1999. *Global Transformations: Politics, Economics and Culture*. Stanford, CA: Stanford University Press.

Lechner, Frank J., and John Boli. 2006. *The Globalization Reader*. London: Blackwell.

Roberts, J. Timmons, and Amy Bellonte Hite. 2007. *The Globalization and Development Reader: Perspectives on Development and Global Change*. London: Blackwell.

INTERNET RESOURCES

Focus on the Global South: http://www.focusweb.org.

Global transformations: http://www.polity.co.uk/global/research.asp.

The globalization website: http://www.sociology.emory.edu/globalization.

Social Watch: http://www.socialwatch.org/en/portada.htm.

The World Bank: http://www.worldbank.org.

NOTES

1. The term 'tiger' usually refers to Asian economic powerhouses such as South Korea, Hong Kong, Taiwan, and Singapore that went through spectacular economic growth rates from the 1970s onward. Recently, the literature has focused on other 'emerging' tigers such as Thailand, Indonesia, Malaysia, and even Vietnam, also known for their economic progress. Because of its size and centrality, China is considered a special case that cannot be completely equated with the 'tigers'.
2. Traditionally, the 'North' meant the industrialized countries of North America and western Europe and Japan. The 'South' meant Africa, Asia, and South America.
3. http://www.ilo.org/public/english/fairglobalization/report/index.htm.
4. At the world level, there is controversy because, as some economists point out, the growth rates of the 1960s (3.5 per cent) and the 1970s (2.4 per cent) were much higher than those achieved under neo-liberal policies dominant in the 1980s (1.4 per cent) and the 1990s (1.1 per cent). Source: World Commission on the Social Dimension of Globalization 2004.

5. See Himanshu Jha. 2006. *Balancing Goals, Commitments and Means*. Social Watch India. http://www. socialwatch.org/en/portada.htm.
6. The 'triad' is sometimes referred to as the 'quad', a trade negotiation term for the United States, Japan, and Canada, plus the European Union.
7. Basically, China has opposed Western-led muscular interventions in these countries, where the United States in particular wanted to impose regime change.
8. There is controversy within and outside Venezuela over the presidency of Hugo Chavez. In South America, Chavez is very well-liked among the popular sectors but much less among the left-centre political elites.
9. See Subcommandante Marcos. 2001. *Our World Is Our Weapon*. New York: Seven Stories Press.

PART TWO

INTERNATIONAL DEVELOPMENT ACTORS

CHAPTER 7

STATE OF THE STATE: DOES THE STATE HAVE A ROLE IN DEVELOPMENT?

ANIL HIRA

LEARNING OBJECTIVES

- To gain familiarity with the historical context of debates about the role of states in development.
- To understand the differences between Northern and Southern states and why simple policy prescriptions do not seem to gain traction in the South.
- To be able to explain the differences between the market versus state-led views of development and related debates.

INTRODUCTION: WHAT IS THE STATE? THE LEGACY OF COLONIALISM

Before we get to the role of the state, we should first define it. The most prominent approaches—international relations and Weberian theory—rely on simple criteria to define the **state**: it is an entity with monopoly over the means of force within a designated territory that it controls, enjoying legitimate support for that monopoly from the majority of the population residing in the territory and recognition of its control by other states and is empowered by the population with making public decisions.

While this definition may seem straightforward, it is problematic in a developing country context and has been accused of being **Eurocentric**—that is, based on European experience. The most obvious problem is that states in the European context, such as the United Kingdom, developed a historical identity over thousands of years, along with slow political centralization, and in part reflect natural geographic communities (Poggi 1978). For example, the UK's physical separation from the European continent has and continues to have consequences for its view of itself as a force independent of Europe,

demonstrated by its policies towards Iraq and European integration. Even relatively new states such as Germany and Italy, formed in the 1870s, share a common language and cultural and religious identity as well as historical experiences, including civil wars and wars fought as a **nation**.

In the developing world, there was generally no such historical evolution. Rather, states were carved out through European conquest and division, and national identities and states were forged over short periods in response to European imperialism. In some cases, nations such as Brazil had no centralized entity that would resemble a modern state at the time of conquest. In others, genocide through direct means and through disease imported from Europe, as happened in many of the countries of the Americas, wiped out large portions of the indigenous population, opening the way for the transplantation of completely new populations, including slaves from Africa and cultivators from South Asia. In Africa, the Middle East, and India, colonial states were created with the express purpose of mixing different populations together, a divide and conquer strategy that allowed colonial masters to impose a relatively privileged minority's control over a large resistant native population in spite of the relatively low numbers of colonizers in relation to local populations. In several colonies, the imposition of a new colonial **elite** made up of a different group from another area was added to local divide-and-conquer strategies, such as administrators from South Asia imported as bureaucrats and military officers in South Africa. In yet others (as in Japan's control over Korea or the British favouring the Sunnis over the Sh'ia in Iraq), the colonial masters simply chose a local minority to be their surrogates. Thus, a relatively small external power could control a vast empire through its local allies, who then had a vested interest in the continuation of the system (see chapter 2).

While 'artificial' in the sense of not representing the natural evolution of historical and cultural identity forces over prolonged periods, the states set up by colonizers nonetheless enjoy the other aspects of statehood: control of the means of force (e.g., the army and police) and the ability to make public decisions. What they seem to lack in many cases is a strong sense of **legitimacy** in terms of support among the population. This does not diminish their central role in development, but it does begin to shed light on the myriad additional difficulties that developing states face above and beyond those of Western states.

Even in states without a system of direct colonial control, the colonial economic system created incentives for compliance. Colonial economies were set up under a system called mercantilism to serve the interests of the colonizing or 'mother' country. They provided raw materials or slaves to the colonizing country, receiving the home country's finished goods in return. They were generally banned from selling directly to other countries, including colonies within the same system, thus ensuring a profit for the home country acting as a middleman. The system also stifled or shut down existing industries; in India, a budding textile industry collapsed under British pressure. For colonial elites, many of whom had nobility status and had been given large mineral and land rights from the colonizing or metropolitan country during colonization, their well-being depended on the system's continuation. As colonies grew, local administrations relied almost exclusively on taxes on exports of their products, so the colonial state was very much tied into the commodity trade of the mercantilist system. This was also true in countries not directly colonized, such as China, where control by European imperial powers over trade and investment, extending at one point to dividing up control over various ports, led to a strongly dependent relationship between local Chinese administrations and European states. In many cases, outside investors controlled large and key strategic assets of the state, such as the British building and owning Argentina's railway. This system of economic control extended even after many colonies achieved independence in the post–World War II period. Thus, even though the formal mercantilist system broke down long ago, economies continue to exhibit many of the patterns of the colonial era.

Some analysts see this neo-colonial system as one in which there are both pressures and opportunities for state leadership. During the Cold War, for instance, the rivalry between the United States and the Soviet Union allowed some smaller states, such as Cuba, to play off the two superpowers, gaining independence from the US and receiving large amounts of aid from the Soviets. Mainstream economists also point to the rapid expansion of the world economy during the 1960s and large US expenditures and imports as an environment that allowed for the development of the East Asian economies of Japan, South Korea, and Taiwan, the 'miracle' economies of Brazil and Mexico, and rapid growth in states such as Kenya. On the other side of the debate, critics suggest that there is far less leeway for states to break away from neo-colonialism. The continuing reliance of many countries on commodity exports (such as Ghana's on coffee and cocoa), reliance on external technology, investment, and imports (highlighted by the debt crisis throughout the developing world in the 1980s—see chapter 14), and the 'brain drain' of the best and brightest to the West are all signs of the persistent difficulty that developing states face in engendering economic development. A further difficulty is the link between mil-

Figure 7.1   Tobacco growing, Pinar del Rio province, Cuba

Source: N. Kumar, IDRC

itary rule in much of the developing world over extended periods and the influence of outside powers, such as US support of a variety of dictators and strongmen during the Cold War.

DEFINING THE STATE'S ROLE IN DEVELOPMENT

Given this historical context, we can now turn to the task of analyzing the role of the state in fostering development. At the most general level, the debate revolves around whether a state should be an active leader or a responsive follower. Part of the answer to this question depends on whether you see the nature of the state as 'compradorial' or as Weberian. The term compradorial was coined by radical (Marxist-influenced) development analysts to describe the ties of the developing state to external interests, whether they be foreign governments, investors, or military, and to the local

resource-owning and internationally oriented capitalist class. Thus, this line of thinking sees the post-colonial state as continuing to be colonial in nature, run by an elite who is 'bought out' by and/or in alliance with foreign interests. In contrast, a Weberian view highlights the rational-purposeful nationalism of a modern state, regardless of its origin. Thus, in this view, even though India (for example) was created by colonial fiat, that does not prevent it from developing a government that is purposeful, rational, and legitimate.

Political economists such as Merilee Grindle (1996) have long pointed out that developing states struggle in several areas. The term 'state capacity' is often used to suggest that developing states may not be as capable of weighing technical decisions as their counterparts in the North. Their personnel may not be as well-trained; they may not have as up-to-date equipment; and their budgets are likely to be considerably smaller. The term 'state autonomy' is also often used in this context to mean the degree of 'insulation' that a state enjoys from social and, we could add, external forces. The governments of states that are overrun with political pressures are more apt to make politically rather than merit-based decisions. They may, in short, make decisions that favour a small group and themselves rather than the nation as a whole. For example, many developing-country civil services appear to lack meritocratic hiring and promotion practices. States that are insulated may be better able to resist pressures to escalate spending as a means of gaining political support. On other hand, insulation could mean greater opportunity either for enlightened leadership or for corrupt and incompetent administration. Scholars such as Peter Evans (1995) point out that the situation is much more complex in practice. Evans uses the term 'embedded autonomy' to refer to states that develop strong network ties with foreign and domestic elites yet manage to retain some degree of autonomy for the pursuit of national interest.

CENTRAL DEBATES ABOUT THE ROLE OF THE STATE IN ECONOMIC DEVELOPMENT

Early industrialization push

Considering the role of the state in terms of economic development takes the debate to a more detailed level of analysis. Over the course of the twentieth century, a debate about the role of the state raged throughout the field of economics between Keynesianism and free market theorists (see chapter 3).

Scholars such as Sir Arthur Lewis (1955) had posited that as previous colonies' agricultural sectors were modernized, the natural labour surplus of agricultural workers would be freed to move to cities. In fact, this movement of urbanization did happen and continues today. However, Lewis also expected that the labour surplus would lower wages to the point where the natural comparative advantage of abundant labour would begin to

attract industries, creating a positive cycle of growth and employment and thus no need for state leadership. In the aftermath of World War II, when many of the independent states of Africa and Asia were created, the lack of evidence for 'natural' industrialization à la Lewis led to the adoption of Keynesian-oriented policies, favoured for obvious reasons by states (because it required their leadership) and by organizations such as the International Monetary Fund (IMF), the World Bank, and the regional development banks (who two decades later would change their advice to promote the 'free market' approach) (see chapter 9).

In the early 1960s, the push for industrialization became one of the central goals of developing states in order to 'modernize'. Industrialization would help to diversify exports, reduce the commodity and other dependency aspects of post-colonial economies, and help to create a middle-class domestic market of highly skilled workers. However, a second basic axis of debate about the role of the state then became front-and-centre: how was industrialization to be accomplished? At one extreme, many saw the Soviet Union at the time as a paradigm of efficient and rapid industrialization, accomplishing large and rapid increases in basic industries production (such as steel and coal) as a result of successful five-year plans. Countries as diverse as India, Ghana, Cuba, and Egypt had begun to emulate the state planning model by the late 1950s and early 1960s. The Soviet, and later the Chinese, model was also attractive in terms of socialism—an example of state leadership in creating a more equitable nation, a nation that would correct the inequities rooted in colonialism and exacerbated by capitalism's privileging of elite classes. However, scepticism gradually emerged regarding the ability of the model to create either viable industries or improved equity. In terms of the former, the standard of living in the Soviet bloc appeared to be well below that of the West, and the gap was increasing over time. Large amounts of steel did not translate into the same price for or quality of middle-class consumer goods such as automobiles. With regard to equity, the image of socialism as a benign policy for the bet-

BOX 7.1   THE CENTURY-LONG DEBATE BETWEEN KEYNESIANISM AND MARKETS

While many of the pioneering works of economics are based on markets and free trade, such as the work of Adam Smith and David Ricardo, the belief in markets was severely shaken by the world-wide depression marked at the outset by the 1929 New York stock market crash. The crash led to a ratcheting up of tariff walls, and as unemployment rates soared throughout the US and Europe, the beginnings of the welfare state were constructed. John Maynard Keynes (1936) gained the attention of the Roosevelt administration and various European governments by creating a new set of theories about why the market might fail, including the possibility of a liquidity trap of low inter-est rates and high unemployment (Hall 1989). Keynesianism also reflected massive popular and social uprisings and demands (Polanyi 1944). In such cases, the state should step in to 'prime the pump' by spending in order to re-activate the economy. The state's role in addressing 'market fail-ures' then extended to many of the aspects of life we take for granted in the West: subsidized edu-cation and health care, unemployment insurance and pensions, and public aid for those who are not able to work. Around the same time, scholars such as Friedrich Von Hayek (1944) suggested that it was states, rather than markets, that were more likely to fail. This story resonated during the Cold War with fears of totalitarianism spreading from the Soviet Union and also following the diag-nosis that the increase in tariffs had choked off international trade, leading to the Great Depression. As we discuss below, Milton Friedman, a University of Chicago economist, became the new cham-pion of markets and helped to win this 'battle of ideas' by the 1980s.

Source: PBS. 'The commanding heights'. http://www.pbs.org/wgbh/commandingheights.

terment of people everywhere took a hit with Soviet repression of rebellions in the areas it con-trolled, such as East Germany, Hungary, and Czechoslovakia and Chinese repression of internal dissent. There was also growing awareness that the 'communist' states were creating their own privi-leged elite within the state party and the bureau-cracy, people who enjoyed a far more privileged life than the majority of the population. Finally, it is now well documented that the cost of militariza-tion and global conflict by proxy imposed a heavy burden on the communist, and particularly the Soviet, economies.

Industrialization in other areas began to occupy a middle ground between market and state. In Latin America, a school of thought called 'structuralism' began to emerge (Hira 1998).

Structuralist thinkers led by Raúl Prebisch (1950) suggested that the state was needed, at least ini-tially, to destroy the 'bottlenecks' that prevented a market-based industrialized economy from devel-oping naturally as expected. Prebisch, who later went on to become the head of the UNCTAD (UN Conference on Trade and Development), was highly influential throughout the world. One of his basic ideas was termed the Prebisch–Singer hypothesis. It suggested that over time, commod-ity prices were more volatile and earned less than industrial goods as manufactured goods became more sophisticated (while coffee remained cof-fee). Therefore, developing economies needed industry to reach the same standard of living as Northern economies; the policies adopted became known as 'import substituting industrialization' (ISI). Prebisch's ideas about bottlenecks refer to the basic aspects of an economy: its productive, financial, and labour systems. In terms of productive systems, for example, too many developing states rely on outside technology and know-how. They need to develop their own technology to avoid being left behind and having to pay for it and adapt it to local conditions: as Gerschenkron (1962) pointed out, protectionism was part of the industrialization experience for Northern states. Most developing states have poorly functioning financial systems. Because local populations do not trust their banking systems, for which regulatory oversight is generally poor (such as a lack of government-backed deposit insurance), those who can do so place their money in foreign accounts, while others have little formal means of saving or borrowing. In terms of labour systems, the poor educational systems in developing countries means that only a small number of people are well-trained, and lacking opportunities at home, they tend to emigrate. Thus, large-scale access to higher education is needed to create viable middle-class-based economies that can function as a domestic market for goods. Prebisch also added the importance of integrating Southern economies to achieve more efficient industries that can sell to each other until they can compete with well-established Western industries.

While Prebisch's ideas have been highly influential, they still leave a great deal of ambiguity in terms of how the industrialization process could best be pushed forward: where precisely does the state's role lie in the spectrum of possibilities between state planning and laissez-faire markets as a means of eliminating bottlenecks? On this foggy ground, a secondary level of debate has emerged. Many of the World Bank projects in the early 1960s centred around large infrastructure projects, such as airports and hydroelectric dams, which were expected to create the foundation for a modern economy. At the same time, argument ensued over whether a 'big push' or a targeted industrialization strategy would work best. Scholars such as Rosenstein-Rodan (1961) argued that a 'big push' of capital investment

across a variety of industries would be needed to sustain industrialization. This idea was reinforced to some extent by Albert O. Hirschman's idea of 'linkages'. Hirschman (1971) noted that an industry such as automotive relies on a series of other industries for production of its final product. It relies on mining and smelting to provide the steel, rubber and tire manufacturers, and a variety of other producers for inputs, and it also relies on a retail network to sell the product. However, for a developing country to pursue all industrial and infrastructure avenues simultaneously might not only be impossible in terms of its financial means but also might overwhelm the technical and managerial capacity of the state. As an alternative, the state could start by targeting specific industries and then extend the effort to other industries. Japan, for example, initiated advanced industrialization with electronics, with now well-known brands such as Sony and Toshiba leading the way under state guidance. Later, the Japanese began pushing into the more sophisticated and challenging auto industry.

By the early 1970s, economists and policymakers had become disillusioned about the state's role in development. In 1973, when a number of oil-exporting countries used OPEC (Organization of Petroleum Exporting Countries) to ramp up the price of petroleum, the world economy went through a tailspin of low growth and high inflation ('stagflation'), which Keynesian theory seemed inadequate to explain. In the short term, the situation created a large increase in liquidity in the form of petrodollars lent by newly wealthy oil sheiks to other developing countries via New York and London banks, which then used the free-floating dollar as the currency franca. Yet in the long run, this rash of increased borrowing for state projects created an extremely high level of indebtedness that continues to haunt the developing world today (see chapter 14). Determination to end inflation led the US Federal Reserve to raise interest rates precipitously in 1982. Along with a drop in oil prices, this action ended the period of easy borrowing and created a major debt crisis for developing states that had borrowed on adjustable interest rate terms in dollar denominations. With limited international borrowing and no mechanism of default (declaring bankruptcy), developing nations began to embrace or were forced into a new set of policies: neo-liberalism.

The rise of and justification for neo-liberalism

A number of factors lay behind the international wave of conservatism that swept the world in the 1980s. Stagflation was one factor, but on the political side, the sense of loss of power in the US and Europe also played a role. For example, the US under president Jimmy Carter had suffered a prolonged humiliation when its embassy was stormed and hostages were taken during the 1979 revolution in Iran, followed by a rescue attempt that failed miserably. These events resonated deeply with the earlier defeat in Vietnam and other historic 'losses' on the part of US allies in China, Nicaragua, and Iran itself. Conservatives pushed for a return to the 'good old days' of power and security in the North. The market-based economics they promoted was particularly appealing to many Southern economists and policy-makers because it seemed to offer a solution to the new constraints on spending created by the debt crisis. Moreover, the idea that the state was the problem with—not the solution to—economic development resonated with many people who had seen colonial states transformed into patronage-heavy and highly inefficient public projects and enterprises. Scholars such as Anne O. Krueger (1974) coined the term 'rent-seeking' to describe how states, even in the North, could become 'captured' by special interest groups in the private sector, leading to policies that benefited a privileged minority. The charge of state corruption had broad appeal in the South and led initially to the success of neo-liberal populists such as Carlos Salina in Mexico, Alberto Fujimori in Peru, Fernando Collor de Melo in Brazil, Carlos Andres Pérez in Venezuela, and Carlos Menem in Argentina. The fact that all these leaders themselves were later pushed out on corruption

charges helped to sour the popular appeal of neo-liberalism but did not eliminate the central problem of state capture.

Indeed, challenges to neo-liberalism sprang up almost immediately. While poverty has diminished in some areas, income inequality, by most measures, has increased in most of the world (and between the North and South) outside of the 'miracle' economies of East Asia. But are the gains sustainable in terms of the environment? Moreover, efforts to create textbook free-market models à la Chile (allegedly)—for example, in Ghana and Jamaica—led to short-term monetary stability but long-term stagnation and worsening equity. The most serious challenge to neo-liberalism probably comes from a wave of literature that sought to explain the precipitous rise of East Asian states and what lay behind their achievements in both growth and equity. Authors such as Chalmers Johnson (1982) led the charge that it was the state—not markets—that were responsible for these achievements. Johnson coined the term 'developmentalist' state to suggest that a state could target particular sectors for successful promotion, which would lead to improvements in equity through job creation. This concept raised the question as to why such efforts had apparently failed in the rest of the developing world. The answer is complicated, but Johnson et al. suggest that it is the ability of the state to 'govern' the market, or to guide the domestic private sector through incentives, that distinguishes the path followed in East Asia from that of other states (Wade 1990). For example, the developmentalist state provides subsidies and/or protection only if certain performance targets are achieved and requires competition among domestic companies in a bid for state help. Arguably, it is the level of autonomy of the East Asian state that enables it to provide greater leadership to the private sector than other regions are able to do (Hira 2007). Moreover, other authors (Haggard 1990; Gereffi and Wyman 1990) who have compared East Asian and Latin American industrialization conclude that East Asia's export orientation represents another key difference. Export orientation means

BOX 7.2   'THE CHILEAN MIRACLE'

In 1973, General Pinochet led a coup that took over Chile. By 1975, he had adopted economic policies that followed his largely University of Chicago–trained economic advisory team, nicknamed 'the Chicago Boys'. Chile's monetary stability, despite a crisis in 1982 and relatively high growth rates, acted as a demonstration effect for the ability of markets, rather than states, to lead to economic development. In the case of Chile, the state reduced legislation and regulation regarding labour unions and strikes, which the economists claimed made the Chilean labour market more flexible and adaptable (though it clearly also served political purposes). That was made possible by the extreme repression that was put in place after 1973, which left thousands dead or in exile. The Chilean government also reduced many import barriers that had been set up under the ISI (import substituting industrialization) system to protect domestic producers and unified and then floated, at least initially, the exchange rate. While maintaining some requirements for how long capital should stay in the country, the state also invited in foreign capital and investment. Chile went through a second wave of reforms in the 1980s, featuring the privatization of many state-owned companies (though not the copper company), including the state energy companies, to foreign interests, which would have been unthinkable in the 1960s when anti-imperialist sentiments surged. Another major reform, also previously unthinkable, was to privatize the social security system, allowing individuals to choose their own pension funds, overseen by government regulation. Similar market-friendly reforms were carried out in education and health. Though Chile is now a democracy, the same neo-liberal policies have been continued. Yet the success of new exports such as fish, wood, and fruit, based on previous state policies, have not reduced income inequalities. Therefore, the Chilean case remains highly controversial, both in its accomplishments and its 'lessons' for other developing states (Hira 1998).

that domestic producers have to produce goods and services that can compete in world markets. Export earnings offer a new source of revenue that the state can then funnel into new investments, including new industries, and reduce pressure to borrow from abroad, as well as decreasing exchange rate and interest rate volatility. However, mainstream economic institutions have not taken such challenges to market supremacy lying down. In 1993, the World Bank produced a rejoinder entitled *The East Asian Miracle*, suggesting that markets and macroeconomic balance were responsible for growth, although they grudgingly conceded some role for the efficient Asian institutions that allowed markets to function well (World Bank 1993a).

From neo-liberalism to governance

Mainstream economists, the vast majority of whom continue to support neo-liberal policies because they are in line with mainstream economic theories, have begun to consider institutions an important variable for economic growth as they seek to explain the disappointing results of market reforms (Stiglitz 2002). Economists such as Anne O. Krueger (2000), who went on to become head of the IMF, suggest that a second generation of neo-liberal reforms is needed for markets to function well. The state must become an efficient market regulator, ensuring that there is adequate contract enforcement and market-based information (such as price information); it

Figure 7.2   Worker preparing small ornamental fig trees for export, Las Palmas, Gran Canaria

Source: Jean-Marc Fleury, IDRC

quarters, critiques not that far removed in principle from the ideas within the new governance paradigm. In short, some New Left analysts are also sceptical of the role of the state in the developing world. They see the state not only as a vestige of colonialism but also as lacking in popular support. Even in states that hold elections, such as those in Iraq, New Left critics argue that this does not translate into the existence of a legitimate government that has the best interests of its population in mind. Scepticism towards the state and its allegedly illegitimate nature leads some to suggest that more autonomous social movements, such as the Zapatistas in Mexico, are needed to resolve long-standing problems of lack of equity and political accountability and transparency on the part of a repressive state. They suggest, therefore, that the state is the problem, not the solution. However, they differ from neo-liberals in that they see non-state local actors as better decision-makers than markets (see chapter 12). Along the same lines, other critics call for a massive reform of the state and international organizations to make them more participatory and accountable.

Globalization and the role of the state

Concern about representative accountable states that are engaged with equity as well as growth has only increased in a globalizing world. By globalization, authors such as Manuel Castells (1996) refer to increasing economic and social transactions and ease of communication across states. The explosive power of the Internet demonstrates the way that states may be losing some aspects of their control—in this case, the ability to control information and the means of communication within a state territory.

In addition, the movement towards foreign investment-friendly policies has been paralleled by the increasing dominance of large global companies such as Microsoft and Daimler-Chrysler. Some argue that these companies have no real national identity, provide few benefits to their home country, and drive hard bargains with the

must be capable in terms of taxing and restricting spending; and it must be free of corruption in its decision-making. The World Bank has picked up on this theme, using the term **governance** to refer to its new-found concern with how well states function in managing markets. It is interesting to note that this new tack still allows economists to avoid overtly political analyses (see chapter 9).

The collapse of the Soviet Union in 1989 seemed to signal an end to the model of state planning. With the continuing debt crisis reducing state budgets, the option of advocating a state leadership position, even its East Asian variant, seems to have fallen off the table as well. At the same time, it is interesting to note that renewed critiques of the state have emerged from radical

BOX 7.3   DEBATES OVER THE EAST ASIAN MIRACLE

Many scholars juxtapose East Asia with Latin America as a model for developing states (Hira 2007). In contrast to Chile, states across the region, from Singapore to Malaysia, South Korea, and Taiwan, have achieved both sustained growth and high levels of equity. Key to the early achievements was land reform in Japan, South Korea, and Taiwan. East Asian states have invested heavily in improving the educational and health levels of their populations across the board. They have also focused on 'moving up the ladder' (Chang 2002)—that is, starting out by exporting labour-intensive goods such as textiles and moving gradually towards more sophisticated goods such as computers. Alice Amsden (1989) suggests that East Asian states have created a system of learning new technologies and improving production processes in order to enter into new and more sophisticated industries over time. Other scholars, such as Frederic Deyo (1987), are more critical of the record, citing repression of labour as one of the key features of East Asian growth. The latest case, China, is also controversial, exhibiting miraculous growth and poverty reduction over short periods of time but, unlike its neighbours, with high levels of regional and class inequalities and increasing environmental concerns.

developing states that want to attract their activities. Meanwhile, their headquarters and sales offices remain concentrated in a few key areas—namely, the 'quad' (Canada, the US, Europe, and Japan) (see chapter 11).

There is even greater fluidity in financial transactions. Much of the world's financial transactions now take place 'offshore' in small tax havens, such as the Cayman Islands, where terrorists, drug traffickers, and corporations share accounts. While most financial activity continues to occur in New York and London, the offshore centres serve as important routes to tax evasion. During the 1980s, part of the neo-liberal reforms involved setting up stock exchanges in much of the developing world. The expectation was that these emerging markets would be able to attract increasing amounts of capital for their cash-starved growing businesses; markets, not the state, would provide leadership, taking on the risks and the analysis required to develop new businesses. However, the experience with emerging financial markets has been less than stellar. For example, there has been some 'contagion', meaning that the collapse of one stock market, such

as Russia's in 1997, creates a domino effect leading to the collapse of other developing markets.

Questions have also been raised about the international trade agreements that have multiplied during the neo-liberal period (see chapter 15). For example, NAFTA, signed by Canada, the US, and Mexico in 1994, was supposed to lead to an age of prosperity for Mexico because its comparative advantage—cheap labour—would be soaked up in US production chains. However, the effects of NAFTA on Mexico have been highly controversial. Critics suggest that only a limited number of low-paying jobs have been created and that many sectors, such as sugar cane production, have been adversely affected. They also note that with China's emergence, many of the labour-intensive industries have left Mexico and relocated in a lower-wage environment. Moreover, products such as computers are manufactured in a modular fashion, with components that can be sourced and assembled in many different locations. All of this has led some to suggest that the state has weakened in the face of globalization (Strange 1996). Some critics even suggest that the state is dying, not only in the developing world but also in the developed world, and point to diminishing social welfare protection in many states as evidence.

Yet other analysts, such as Linda Weiss (1998), argue that such ideas are 'greatly exaggerated' and that the state is more important than ever. The state still determines the rules for foreign investment and trade within its own territory. The state is still the dominant actor that chooses whether to trade and fixes the terms of signing international trade and investment agreements. The state can still proactively improve the nation's capability to compete in global markets through strategic investment in infrastructure and its own people. We could argue that, as in the story of blind men describing different parts of an elephant, both perspectives are correct. Globalization has weakened labour protections and labour power across the North as labour-intensive manufacturing has been 'outsourced'—

i.e., replaced by cheaper imports from overseas, where labour regulations are minimally enforced. This does not mean that developing states that capture new production are in control, because production can move from one country to another fairly quickly in response to global business supply decisions. For example, textile production has moved from Mexico and South Korea to China and Central America. At the same time, several analysts argue that it is strategic state intervention, not markets, that explains the ability of states such as China and India to attract new global industries and services (Hira and Hira 2005). Certainly, the state may still choose to create forms of insulation from and adjustment to global forces—Malaysia, for example, imposed controls over the movement of capital from outside the country for many years. Thus, the role of the state remains front-and-centre in the development debate.

BOX 7.4   GLOBAL CHAINS OF PRODUCTION

In 2005, *New York Times* journalist Thomas L. Friedman released a blockbuster book entitled *The World Is Flat*. Friedman suggests that the development of global chains of production creates a 'level playing field' through which developing countries will start to participate fully in the world economy. The book builds on the recent experience of Chinese and Indian companies springing up to compete in world markets. Friedman uses as an example the production of a computer: programming may be done in one place, while the manufacture of components, the assembly, and the testing are done in several other locations. This modularization of production is what some scholars had long ago signalled as global commodity chain production. Friedman sees the rapid development of global production chains as largely beneficial, leading to greater participation and reduced poverty as well as reducing prices for consumers. Expansion of this participation means larger world markets, so employment does not have to decline in the West. Some scholars (Gereffi and Korzeniewicz 1994) point out that the nature of the product and what parts of the production chain one is able to capture will determine the earnings that countries will receive. For example, we pay some $4 for a fancy coffee at Starbucks, but coffee farmers in developing states receive a tiny fraction of that amount. This discrepancy has led to the current fair trade movement, but arguably, it is the responsibility of states to find ways of making their economies more competitive and capturing more of the revenue and jobs.

QUESTIONS FOR DISCUSSION

1. Is the traditional international relations theory view of a state adequate to understand the types of states we find in the developing world? Does it vary by region?

2. Select a developing state, and identify the major issues it faces by examining current news reports. Now take a quick look at its history (a basic on-line encyclopedia will do). To what extent can you see ties between its colonial origins and current problems?

3. What are the advantages and disadvantages of market-based as opposed to state leadership? Consider efficiency and equity outcomes, economic stability, and employment.

4. If you were a state planner, what arguments could you see for and against a big push versus a targeted strategy for development? What kinds of blockages can you see in a typical developing economy, and to what extent are they related?

5. Take an industry that you would want to develop, such as automobile manufacture, and map out some of the linked industries, inputs, outputs, and accompanying infrastructure that you would need to make the industry viable. What other factors, such as timing and market power, would you have to consider?

6. Do you agree that there may be a disadvantage to producing commodities instead of manufactured goods? Why or why not?

7. Debate the meaning of globalization and whether it makes the state less relevant and powerful. What is your position on the state's role in development?

8. Do you believe that state leadership in 'embedded autonomy' is possible? What might affect the levels of embedded autonomy?

FURTHER READING

Evans, Peter. 1995. *Embedded Autonomy: States and Industrial Transformation*. Princeton, NJ: Princeton University Press.

Gerschenkron, Alexander. 1962. *Economic Backwardness in Historical Perspective*. Cambridge, MA: Belknap Press.

Hira, Anil. 2007. *An East Asian Model for Latin American Success: The New Path*. Burlington, VT: Ashgate.

Polanyi, Karl. 1944, 1957. *The Great Transformation: The Political and Economic Origins of Our Time*. Boston: Beacon Press by arrangement with Rinehart and Co.

Wade, Robert. 1990. *Governing the Market: Economic Theory and the Role of Government in East Asian Industrialization*. Princeton, NJ: Princeton University Press.

INTERNET RESOURCES

Eldis (great gateway for development documents): http://www.eldis.org.

Development Gateway: http://www.developmentgateway.org.

United Nations Industrial Development Organization (UNIDO): http://www.unido.org.

The World Bank: http://worldbank.org.

World Economic Forum annual competitiveness report: http://www.weforum.org/en/index.htm.

PBS. 'The commanding heights': http://www.pbs.org/wgbh/commandingheights.

CHAPTER 8

NATIONAL DEVELOPMENT AGENCIES AND BILATERAL AID

STEPHEN BROWN

LEARNING OBJECTIVES

- To understand the main terms and concepts applicable to bilateral foreign aid.
- To understand the reasons why donors provide assistance and how their priorities can vary.
- To understand current trends in and debates surrounding foreign aid.

This chapter provides an overview of the main actors, modalities, and resource flows involved in the aid that countries in the North provide to **recipients** in the South. It begins by explaining some key terms in what is known as **bilateral aid**. It then examines global aid flows, highlighting the differences among donors and analyzing the issue of their underlying motivations. Finally, it explores which regions and countries receive the most aid, before turning to an overview of current trends and controversies in foreign aid.

CLARIFYING THE TERMINOLOGY

The providers of development assistance are usually referred to as **donors**, although lenders may be a more appropriate term in cases where the aid is in the form of loans. Donors give part of their aid directly to developing countries (known as **bilateral** or government-to-government aid) and channel some of their funds through multilateral organizations such as the World Bank or UN agencies like UNICEF (**multilateral** aid). This chapter limits its discussion to bilateral aid and donors. Multilateral institutions and development assistance are discussed in chapters 9 and 10.

The expression *foreign aid* is often used interchangeably with the more technical term *official*

development assistance (ODA), as we do in this chapter. The two, however, are not quite synonymous. While foreign aid can include a wide range of assistance, what can technically be counted as ODA is more restricted. According to its official definition, ODA refers to 'flows of official financing administered with the promotion of the economic development and welfare of developing countries as the main objective, and which are concessional in character with a grant element of at least 25 per cent' (OECD 2003, n.p.). This means that in order to qualify as ODA, funding must be provided by governments and its main purpose must be improving economic or social well-being in developing countries. Thus, donations from individuals, foundations, or private corporations, whether directly to developing countries or through the intermediary of Northern **non-governmental organizations** (NGOs), do not count as ODA, nor do military assistance or export credits meant primarily to promote the sale of goods from the donor country. Aid to countries that are not classified as developing, such as Russia, does not qualify as ODA and is usually referred to as *official assistance* (OA). ODA financing can be provided in the form of a grant (a non-reimbursable donation) or a loan (to be repaid), but the terms of the loan would have to be significantly better than what is available on the commercial market (with a lower interest rate, an extended period of repayment, and/or a 'grace period' before the first repayment falls due) in order to be counted as ODA. For this reason, private investment or commercial loans are excluded as well. However, ODA does include administrative costs, such as the costs of maintaining aid agency offices and the salaries of staff both at home and abroad.

There is some controversy over what should be included as ODA. For instance, donor governments have agreed to count as ODA the expenses incurred during the first year of resettling refugees in their countries. In this case, it is not clear that this fulfills the requirement that the main objective be 'economic development and welfare of developing countries', and moreover, the period of one year is rather arbitrary. Some accounting measures are also contentious. For example, when debt is cancelled, the full outstanding amount is counted for the year in which the loan was forgiven, even if the scheduled repayment would not have been completed for decades. This allows donors to boost their ODA for a given year without actually spending any additional funds, which produces a temporary 'blip' that distorts true aid trends. Furthermore, as development assistance becomes more closely integrated with military and diplomatic initiatives—in Iraq and Afghanistan, for instance—it becomes harder to determine exactly what constitutes ODA and what does not. A few countries are trying to revise the guidelines to include the cost of peacekeeping operations as ODA, even if the funds are spent on the donor country's troops. (Currently, this only counts as ODA if the donor country is funding the participation of personnel from a developing country.) Critics object to the expansion of the definition of ODA, arguing that it leads to the militarization or securitization of aid and can prioritize the interests of donor countries rather than those of the recipients.

OVERVIEW OF AID DONORS

Most countries that provide foreign aid belong to a donors' club known as the Development Assistance Committee (DAC) of the Organisation for Economic Co-operation and Development (OECD), whose headquarters are in Paris. DAC members regularly provide the OECD with a breakdown of their aid figures, and the OECD in turn compiles the information, making it publicly available. Not all donors, however, are members of the DAC. Some smaller OECD members have foreign aid programs but do not belong to the DAC, such as the Czech Republic, Iceland, and Turkey. Several Arab states, including

BOX 8.1   THE MANY USES OF FOREIGN AID

Foreign aid can be spent in numerous sectors and ways, including:

- to purchase technology;
- to promote the building of local capacity or infrastructure, such as roads, bridges, dams, railways, and airports;
- to support policy reform;
- to promote agriculture, including improved crop techniques or improving pricing policy;
- to promote industry, such as food processing, training, or import/export regulations;
- to promote services, including transportation, technical training, education, and health care;
- to provide humanitarian assistance, notably emergency housing, food, or health care, especially in cases of war or natural disaster.

Figure 8.1   A patient proudly displays his insurance plan membership after visiting the Mulindi health centre in Byumba, Rwanda

Source: Phara Georges Rodrigue, USAID

In 2005, donors contributed US $107 billion in ODA. Of this, $83 billion was in bilateral assistance and $25 billion in contributions to multilateral institutions. Debt relief accounted for $25 billion of these amounts, $9 billion was spent on humanitarian aid, and another $2 billion went to refugee resettlement. Total ODA was significantly less than private flows to developing countries (including direct and portfolio investment), which totalled $182 billion for that year. In contrast, NGOs contributed about $15 billion (OECD 2007e, Tables 2 and 13).

The total volume of foreign aid has followed various trends over the decades. As Figure 8.2 illustrates (using constant 2005 dollars to facilitate comparison), total aid increased slowly in the 1960s and then much more rapidly in the 1970s. In fact, total aid flows increased by about 85 per cent between 1970 and 1980, even when adjusted for inflation. Aid growth rates slowed

Table 8.1 ODA from non-DAC donors, 2005	
Donors	**US$ millions**
OECD non-DAC	
Czech Republic	135
Hungary	100
Iceland	27
South Korea	752
Poland	205
Slovak Republic	56
Turkey	601
Arab countries	
Kuwait	218
United Arab Emirates	141
Saudi Arabia	1,005
Other donors	
Taiwan	483
Israel	95
Others	86
TOTAL	**3,905**

Note: Does not include China.
Source: OECD. 2007e. Table 33.

oil-producing Kuwait, Libya, Saudi Arabia, and the United Arab Emirates, also provide assistance, as do some developing countries themselves, such as Cuba, Taiwan, and Venezuela (see Table 8.1). China has in recent years gained much attention for its foreign aid, especially to Africa. However, most of it is in the form of loans or investments that do not generally qualify as ODA. Moreover, it does not disclose full information on its aid. This chapter concentrates on the ODA provided by the 22 member nations of the DAC, which constitutes some 97 per cent of global ODA.

again in the 1980s, increasing by less than 10 per cent between 1980 and 1990. Donors cut their aid in the early and mid-1990s, a period of 'aid fatigue'. Between 1991 and 1997, total aid dropped by one quarter. After remaining relatively steady for the rest of the decade, contributions rose again quite dramatically after 2000, reaching an all-time high to date in 2005, about 70 per cent higher than in 2000. The amount for 2005, however, the latest year for which figures are available, was inflated by exceptionally high debt relief, which as explained above provides a one-time boost that is reflected in accounting but not in actual spending on development activities. Although the ODA figures for 2006 might therefore be lower, the upward trend is expected to last until at least 2010 as many donors meet recent pledges to increase aid. Box 8.2 describes these aid cycles in greater detail.

The most generous donor by far in dollar terms was the United States, whose ODA totalled almost $23 billion in 2006 (see Figure 8.3). The next four largest donors were the United Kingdom, Japan, France, and Germany, each of which contributed between $10 and $13 billion, roughly half the disbursements of the US. Smaller countries, such as New Zealand, Luxembourg, Greece, and Portugal, each contributed less than $500 million dollars in that year.

The largest non-DAC donor in 2005 was Saudi Arabia, which contributed $1 billion. Though more than what each of the five smallest DAC donors contributed, this amount and indeed the total $4 billion that non-DAC countries contributed are dwarfed by the total amount disbursed by DAC donors.

Although absolute figures in US dollars immediately reveal who the most—and least—

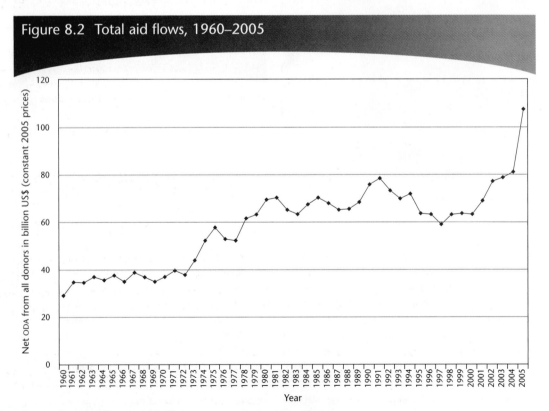

Figure 8.2 Total aid flows, 1960–2005

Source: Extracted from OECD. n.d.

BOX 8.2   FOREIGN AID CYCLES

The 1970s was a period of great optimism regarding the use of foreign aid to promote development. Donors agreed at the United Nations in 1970 to steadily increase their ODA to reach a minimum of 0.7 per cent of their Gross National Product within five years. Although they failed to meet the target, discussed below and in Box 8.3, donors did provide far more aid than ever before. In the 1980s, a period of slower growth in donor countries and severe economic crises in most recipient countries, new aid was often made conditional on major changes in economic policy. This slowed the growth of aid somewhat. In the 1990s, after the end of the Cold War and the collapse of the Soviet Union as a rival patron to many developing countries, Western donors cut their own foreign aid budgets, justifying it mainly by invoking a need to trim their budget deficits. At the same time, donors were growing increasingly disenchanted with what they considered a lack of concrete results and unacceptably high levels of corruption in recipient countries. In 2000, the pendulum began to swing back the other way. A new consensus emerged on the urgent need to fight poverty, especially in Africa, leading among other things to an agreement on the Millennium Development Goals (MDGs, discussed below and in chapter 13) to be reached by 2015. Total aid increased at a rate not seen since the 1970s.

significant players are in the area of foreign aid, they tell us little about how generous the countries actually are when measured against their capacity to provide assistance. Relative generosity is normally calculated by dividing ODA by Gross National Income (GNI), Gross National Product (GNP), or Gross Domestic Product (GDP), which provide almost identical figures.

In 1970, the UN General Assembly passed a resolution whereby donors would provide at least 0.7 per cent of their GNP in ODA by 1975 (see Box 8.3). Donors as a whole failed miserably to reach that target. In 2005, 30 years after the deadline, they collectively provided 0.33 per cent of their GNI, less than half the amount to which they had committed. Nonetheless, this was significantly higher than the 0.22 per cent provided in 2001 (OECD 2007e, Table 4). According to OECD projections, the ratio in 2010 will be 0.36 per cent, still a long way from the objective (OECD 2007b, 6).

Individual donors' relative generosity actually varies greatly from the average. In 2006, as illustrated in Figure 8.4, five countries contributed more than the UN target of 0.7 per cent: Sweden (1.03 per cent), Luxembourg (0.89 per cent), Norway (0.89 per cent), Netherlands (0.81 per cent), and Denmark (0.80 per cent). At the other end of the scale, Greece contributed 0.16 per cent of GNI in 2006. Paradoxically, the world's most generous donor in absolute terms is also the second least generous in relative terms: the United States' ratio was only 0.17 per cent for that year, less than one-sixth of Sweden's.

DONOR MOTIVATIONS

There are numerous reasons why donors provide development assistance. One of them—and for many, the most important one—is simply to help the less fortunate abroad. Thus, a primary justification is that just as social programs provide assistance to poor people at home, ODA should focus on helping people in other countries have access to food, housing, health care, education, and other

Figure 8.3   Total foreign aid by donor, 2006

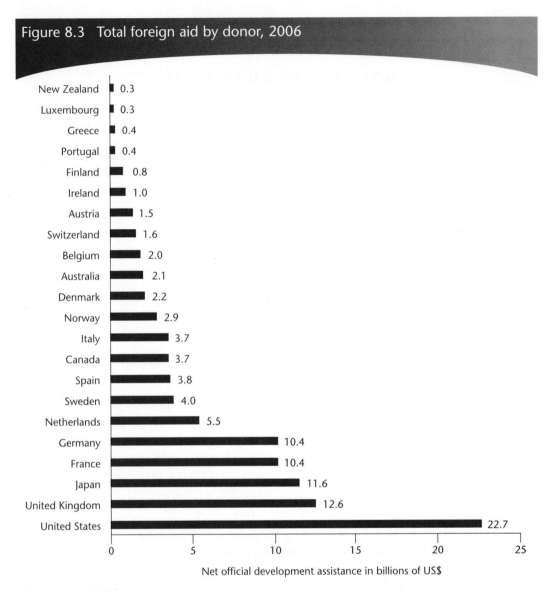

Net official development assistance in billions of US$

Source: OECD. 2007d.

basic necessities and opportunities. The best means of providing development assistance is often contested (as discussed below), but the goal from this perspective should not be related to self-interest. This motivation is most often shared by Northern NGOs and citizens of donor countries, if not all development officials. There are different forms of this mentality: a donor can be motivated by charity, often inspired by religious beliefs (and sometimes viewed as paternalism), or by solidarity, a more left-wing concept that frames actors in the recipient country as equal partners. The latter is criticized by some as being naively idealistic and wilfully ignorant of the need to pursue the donor's own national interest and of the realities of important struggles on the international level.

BOX 8.3   THE 0.7 PER CENT AID TARGET

In recognition of the special importance of the role which can be fulfilled only by official development assistance, a major part of financial resource transfers to the developing countries should be provided in the form of official development assistance. Each economically advanced country will progressively increase its official development assistance to the developing countries and will exert its best efforts to reach a minimum net amount of 0.7 per cent of its gross national product at market prices by the middle of the Decade.

International Development Strategy for the Second United Nations Development Decade,
UN General Assembly Resolution 2626 (XXV), 24 October 1970, para. 43.

At the same time, a more self-interested motivation is widely shared, especially among government officials not directly involved in aid delivery, including those working in national defence, foreign affairs, and international trade. From their perspective, aid is primarily a means to pursue other foreign policy objectives, including diplomatic, commercial, and security interests. Under this logic, aid should be used to promote diplomatic initiatives, including assisting 'friendly' countries, pursuing security objectives (for instance, rewarding countries that take part in the 'war on terror' or winning hearts and minds in a country where the donor country's troops are deployed), or facilitating trade relations, including the sale of donor nation goods and services in the recipient country. Aid programs can also serve to raise the donor's profile internationally, providing it with prestige among its peers as a country that makes an important contribution on the global level. The basic principle from this perspective is that foreign aid can be used to help people abroad but that the selection of recipients and aid modalities should prioritize instances where it maximizes the direct and indirect benefits to the donor country. Increasingly, donors are adopting a 'whole-of-government approach' that integrates foreign aid more closely with other for-

eign policy objectives. This mentality is often criticized for using aid as a fig leaf, hiding the pursuit of naked self-interest behind claims that it is designed to help others.

Since its origin at the end of the Second World War, foreign aid has simultaneously manifested both of these characteristics. Most donor aid programs are a compromise between these two perspectives, weighted differently from donor to donor. On the one hand, much foreign aid has been blatantly used as an instrument of foreign policy, most clearly during the Cold War when foreign aid from the West was often explicitly targeted to prevent the expansion of communism. Currently, ODA is more often linked to political and economic liberalization, including strengthening democracy, **good governance**, and the private sector in recipient countries. **Tied aid** (discussed in Box 8.4) is a clear manifestation of the principle that the donor's economy should also benefit from the aid it provides, although most donors are phasing out the practice. On the other hand, many billions of dollars have been spent with no clear benefit to the donor. Emergency-related humanitarian assistance best embodies the principle of selflessness.

There are other justifications for the provision of foreign aid, although they are not as widely

Figure 8.4   Relative generosity of donors, 2006

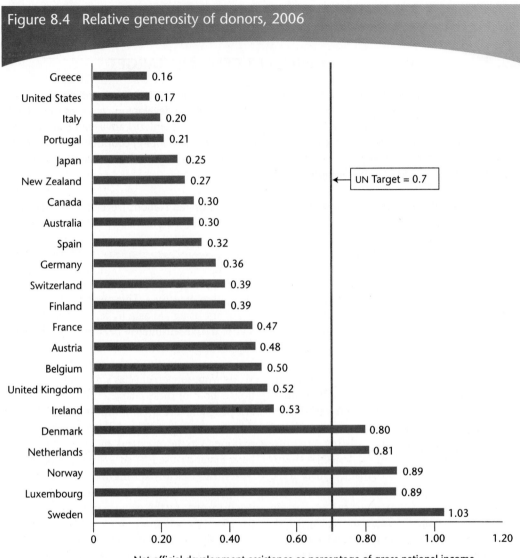

Net official development assistance as percentage of gross national income

Source: OECD. 2007d.

held. Some, especially in developing countries themselves, view ODA as a form of compensation for past or present injustices, be they colonial exploitation or an unjust international system. From this perspective, Northern countries have enriched themselves from their unequal relationships with Southern countries, either under colonialism in the past or currently under a global trading system that still disproportionately benefits wealthier countries and an ongoing debt crisis that has many developing countries paying more to service their debt than they receive in foreign aid. Under this logic, if the net transfer of wealth is from South to North, donors have a duty to increase their ODA to at least balance out the flow of resources.

BOX 8.4   TIED AID

Some ODA is conditional on the purchase of goods and services from the donor country, even if they are not the cheapest or the best value for money, a practice known as 'tied aid'. Tying aid increases costs by an average of 15 to 30 per cent, although in some instances the figure can be much higher (Jepma 1991, 15). Sometimes the additional costs can be incurred for a decade or more. For instance, Canadian aid to Mongolia's agricultural sector might require that equipment such as tractors be purchased from Canadian companies. Not only might those tractors cost more and be no better than, say, Japanese ones, but Mongolia will have to buy Canadian replacement parts for as long as the tractors are in use.

Aid that can be spent regardless of the country of origin of the goods and services is referred to as 'untied'. Donors have committed themselves to progressively untying aid, although they have not specified a deadline for eliminating the practice altogether (Paris Declaration on Aid Effectiveness 2005, 6, 9). Some countries, such as Sweden and the United Kingdom, have abolished tied aid altogether. Canada and the United States, however, continue to tie a sizeable proportion of their ODA.

Under some interpretations of international human rights law, foreign aid can also be considered an obligation. For instance, under the International Covenant on Economic, Social and Cultural Rights, which was adopted at the United Nations in 1966 and became legally binding in 1976, everyone has the right to a free primary education and to earn a livelihood. In cases in which developing countries do not have the necessary resources to provide adequate opportunities for schooling and employment, they cannot be held responsible, and donors, one could argue, therefore must assume the obligation to ensure these rights. From this perspective, no distinction can be made among recipients based on donor interests—these rights are universal. Some would claim, however, that many developing countries have the means to meet these basic rights but fail to do so because of waste, corruption, or emphasis on other priorities. In such cases, they feel, governments should be held accountable for their own failings, and donors should not be obligated to assume their responsibilities.

CHARACTERISTICS OF DONORS

Individual donor countries often choose to focus on a particular region, often on the basis of geography, security interests, or former colonial ties. For instance, in 2004–5, Australia and New Zealand gave more than two-thirds of their ODA to Asia and Oceania, their 'neighbourhood'. Seven other donors—Belgium, Denmark, France, Ireland, Netherlands, Portugal, and the United Kingdom—gave most of theirs to sub-Saharan Africa. The United States and Austria prioritized the Middle East and North Africa, while Spain placed far more emphasis on Latin America than any other donor (OECD 2007e, Table 28).

Some countries transfer a much larger proportion of their aid to multilateral institutions than they disburse directly to developing countries (see chapter 10). By doing so, they reduce their administrative costs but also some of their control over where and how their funds are spent. Figures from 2005 range from Italy, which spent 55 per cent of its aid through multilateral channels, to the United States, which disbursed only 8 per cent multilaterally (OECD 2007e, Table 13). Donors also have varying institutional set-ups, priorities, and preferred aid modalities.

The United States, for instance, the world's largest aid donor, has two main governmental aid agencies. The first, the United States Agency for International Development (USAID), has been since its creation in 1961 the principal government body for providing development assistance. A second government agency, the Millennium Challenge Corporation (MCC), was launched in 2004 with a more narrow focus than USAID's. The MCC aims to foster economic growth in a smaller number of countries that meet specific criteria regarding free markets, democracy, and good governance. In 2007, it provided assistance to 32 countries.

The US government openly acknowledges the simultaneously selfless and selfish motivations of its ODA. For example, the USAID website states that 'US foreign assistance has always had the twofold purpose of furthering America's foreign policy interests in expanding democracy and free markets while improving the lives of the citizens of the developing world' (USAID 2007, n.p.). The links between US security interests and development assistance are not difficult to trace. In 2004–5, the top recipient of American ODA by far was Iraq ($7 billion a year, or 28 per cent of total US assistance to all developing countries), followed by Afghanistan ($1 billion or 4 per cent) (OECD 2007a; 2007e, Table 32)—both countries with a significant US military presence.

The Canadian International Development Agency (CIDA) is responsible for disbursing most of Canada's ODA. Founded in 1968, it operates in more than 100 countries. Its two main recipients in 2004–5 were the same as those of the United States: Iraq and Afghanistan (OECD 2007a; 2007e, Table 32).

France emphasizes aid to sub-Saharan Africa, as mentioned above, as well as North Africa. The top recipients of French aid in 2004–5 were Nigeria, the Republic of Congo, Senegal, and Morocco. With the exception of Nigeria and Iraq, former French colonies occupied eight of the ten

top places in France's list of recipients for those years (OECD 2007a). Most of France's aid is managed by the French Development Agency, which provides assistance to more than 60 countries (Agence française de développement 2007).

Sweden, the world's most generous aid donor in relation to the size of its economy, channels its aid mainly through the Swedish International Development Cooperation Agency (SIDA), which works under the authority of the Ministry of Foreign Affairs (an institutional set-up parallel to those of Denmark and the Netherlands). It provides aid to more than 120 countries, with most of the top five recipients in 2004–5 (Tanzania, Mozambique, Ethiopia, Afghanistan, and Uganda) in Africa (OECD 2007a; 2007e, Table 32).

Most British aid is administered by the Department for International Development (DFID). Unlike its counterparts in most other countries, DFID is a full government department and is headed by a minister who sits at the cabinet table (see Box 8.5). Like France, the UK focuses its ODA mainly on its former colonies and—like Canada and the United States—Iraq and Afghanistan. Its top recipients in 2004–5 were Nigeria, Iraq, India, Bangladesh, and Zambia (OECD 2007a; 2007e, Table 32).

Although one can easily compare budgets and relative generosity, it is difficult to rank the overall performance of bilateral aid agencies. Some donors might be strong in one area, such as support to community development, but weak in another, like being overly bureaucratic. Nonetheless, there have been a few attempts to compare the main bilateral donors systematically. For instance, the Center for Global Development, a US-based think tank, annually assesses and ranks 21 donor countries' commitment to development in a number of areas, including the quantity and quality of foreign aid. The aid component of the index considers each country's relative generosity and adds points for policies like providing aid to the poorest recipients and allowing tax deductions for private donations. Points are deducted for tying aid, for providing aid to corrupt countries, and for splitting aid into a large number of

BOX 8.5   WHAT MAKES A GOOD DEVELOPMENT AGENCY?

Lessons from the United Kingdom

In recent years, the UK's Department for International Development (DFID) has gained the reputation of being one of the world's best bilateral development agencies. According to one study (Barder 2007, 300–13), DFID's success can be attributed to a combination of factors, including:

- DFID has focused its aid policy on achieving outcomes, basing it on concrete evidence rather than ideological preferences.
- DFID has built strong in-house technical expertise but also consults widely with outside experts.
- DFID resists short-term pressures, including promoting British commercial interests, and focuses on long-term strategies centred primarily on poverty reduction in low-income countries.
- DFID is responsible for all British foreign aid, rather than it being split among various government departments.
- DFID has been represented at cabinet by ministers with strong leadership skills and important political profiles.
- DFID has enjoyed key support from the prime minister and the chancellor of the exchequer (finance minister).

small projects (Center for Global Development 2007, 5). Table 8.2 summarizes the results for 2007, with three Nordic countries and the Netherlands ranked highest and the United States, Greece, and Japan at the bottom of the list. This ranking is provided as just one example of a comparison of donors' aid policies. Other criteria and calculations, of course, could produce quite different results. For instance, the UK is ranked eighth by this index and has an average score, but its development agency is actually widely recognized for its excellence (see Box 8.5).

AID RECIPIENTS

The OECD's Development Assistance Committee maintains a list of countries and territories that qualify as recipients of ODA. The main goal is to be able to compile comparable statistics. Donors can still provide assistance to countries not on the list; they cannot, however, count it as ODA. The DAC periodically revises the list. For example, since 1989, following the collapse of the Soviet bloc, it has added a number of poorer European countries, including Albania, as well as a number of new countries, including Belarus, Moldova, Ukraine, and the former Soviet republics in central Asia. The Palestinian Administered Areas, though not a country, have been eligible for ODA since 1994.

Countries are sometimes removed from the list when they 'graduate' to a higher income level. In the 1990s, these countries included Portugal, Greece, Singapore, Israel, some Caribbean nations, and a few oil-producing countries. As of 2005, Bahrain and numerous eastern and central European countries were deemed no longer eligible for ODA, notably Russia and countries that had recently joined the European Union or were negotiating accession.

Table 8.2	Commitment to development index, aid component, 2007	

Rank	Country	Score
1	Denmark	12.0
2	Sweden	11.6
3	Netherlands	10.7
4	Norway	10.5
5	Ireland	6.9
6	Belgium	5.7
7	Finland	4.9
8	United Kingdom	4.8
9	Switzerland	4.5
10	Canada	4.1
11	France	4.0
12	New Zealand	3.6
13	Australia	3.1
14	Austria	2.9
15	Spain	2.9
16	Italy	2.7
17	Germany	2.6
18	Portugal	2.4
19	United States	2.2
20	Greece	2.0
21	Japan	1.2

Source: Center for Global Development. 2007, 6.

Overall, sub-Saharan Africa receives more foreign aid than any other region. In 2004–5, it received almost 40 per cent of ODA. As can be seen in Table 8.3, the second largest recipient regions were the Middle East and North Africa and the rest of Asia and Oceania at almost 25 per cent each. At the bottom of the list were Latin America and the Caribbean (slightly under 10 per cent) and Europe (almost 5 per cent).

Almost all increases in ODA between 2000 and 2005, mentioned above, have been in the form of debt relief or in aid to Afghanistan and Iraq rather than increased spending in other developing countries. The proportion of aid to Africa has increased quite steadily from a low of about 20 per cent in 1999 to a projected 50 per cent in 2010, although most of the increase

between 2000 and 2005 was in humanitarian aid and debt relief rather than funding for core development programs (OECD 2007b, 1, 2, 6). The need to increase aid to Africa was an important focus of successive G-8 summits beginning in 2001 and was further underlined by the 2005 report of the Commission for Africa, composed of 17 prominent members from donor and African countries, appointed by British prime minister Tony Blair.

The top recipients of foreign aid often vary from year to year, depending more on international politics than on anything else. For instance, as indicated in Table 8.4, Iraq was the top recipient in 2005, obtaining about $21.7 billion. This was almost three and a half times more than the second-ranked country, Nigeria, which received $6.4 billion, much of which was in the form of debt forgiveness and thus not actual spending on development. The third largest recipient of ODA, Afghanistan, has—like Iraq—benefited from a surge in foreign aid that followed the US-led invasion in 2001 and has gone hand-in-hand with the continued presence of foreign troops. Indonesia's high ranking can be attributed in large part to humanitarian assistance in response to the 2004 tsunami that caused great devastation there.

Because of great variations in the sizes of their economy, the top recipients of aid are not necessarily the most dependent on aid. In a few countries, mainly in sub-Saharan Africa, ODA accounts

Table 8.3	Proportion of total ODA by region, 2004–5

Region	Share (%)
Sub-Saharan Africa	38.0
Middle East and North Africa	24.5
South and Central Asia	13.2
Other Asia and Oceania	10.7
Latin America and Caribbean	8.8
Europe	4.9

Source: OECD. 2007e. Table 28.

Table 8.4 Largest ODA recipients, 2005	
Country	**Billion US$**
Iraq	21.7
Nigeria	6.4
Afghanistan	2.8
Indonesia	2.5
Ethiopia	1.9

Source: OECD. 2007e. Table 25.

for more than one-third of the total size of the economy. In 2005, two small African countries, São Tomé and Liberia, depended on donors for more than half their Gross National Income (GNI). The six most aid-dependent countries in 2005, of which five are in sub-Saharan Africa, can be found in Table 8.5. In these countries, donors potentially have tremendous leverage to influence domestic policy. Such dependence, however, is relatively rare. The average for sub-Saharan Africa was 5.5 per cent, and for all developing countries it was only 1.3 per cent (OECD 2007e, Table 25).

Different countries receive aid from different donors and for widely varying purposes. In other words, the structure and purposes of ODA can vary tremendously. Bangladesh, for instance, has for many decades been a top recipient of foreign aid. Its top bilateral donors by far in 2004–5 were Japan (a fellow Asian country) and the United Kingdom (the former colonial ruler), distantly followed by the United States and the Netherlands (OECD 2007c). A densely and highly populated country, Bangladesh is characterized by widespread poverty and is particularly prone to natural disasters that include cyclones and flooding. It is also known as the home of the Grameen Bank, one of the world's most successful and innovative micro-credit initiatives.

During the 1970s and 1980s, the Soviet Union and many social democratic European donors provided a high level of assistance to Mozambique. The former was motivated mainly by geo-strategic interests related to a Cold War struggle for dominance in the developing world, the latter by solidarity with a socialist country in Africa on the frontline of the fight against apartheid in South Africa. The Mozambican civil war, however, prevented this aid from translating into economic development. Since the end of the civil war in 1992 and the country's renouncement of socialism, a wide range of donors have disbursed huge amounts of aid to Mozambique, and the country has achieve a consistently high rate of growth, admittedly from a low starting point. In 2004–5, the country's top bilateral aid donor was the United States (its former ideological opponent), followed by Sweden, the UK, Denmark, Norway, and the Netherlands, many of which were continuing historical ties (OECD 2007c).

Haiti, the poorest country in the western hemisphere, has long been plagued with social and political instability, notably since the Duvalier dictatorship was overthrown in the mid-1980s. Since then, the country has experienced a succession of democratic elections, military coups, and instances of violent unrest. It is widely hoped that the elections held in 2006 will mark the beginning of a new era of reconstruction and development. In 2004–5, the top donors by far were the United States and Canada, both of which are in the same 'neighbourhood' as Haiti and have large Haitian populations, followed by France, the former colonial ruler (OECD 2007c).

Table 8.5 Most ODA-dependent countries, 2005	
Country	**ODA/GNI (%)**
São Tomé and Príncipe	58.5
Liberia	54.1
Burundi	46.8
Afghanistan	38.5
Congo, Republic of	36.8
Eritrea	36.3

Source: OECD. 2007e. Table 25.

CURRENT TRENDS
AND CONTROVERSIES

This section reviews a few current trends and controversies in the design and delivery of foreign aid. Some trends are relatively uncontroversial. For instance, almost all donors are taking measures to greatly reduce or eliminate tied aid. Likewise, bilateral donors have, for the most part, phased out loans, preferring to provide grants. In 2004–5, only 2.8 per cent of ODA was in the form of loans, while 100 per cent of the aid from many countries, such as Canada, the Netherlands, the United Kingdom, and the United States, was in the form of grants (OECD 2007e, Table 20). Multilateral institutions, however, continue to provide a high proportion of loans.

A long standing debate in foreign aid is whether the focus of assistance should be primarily on fighting poverty or on promoting economic growth. For a long time, especially in the 1950s and 1960s, the argument was made that economic growth would eventually 'trickle down' to help the poor—that 'a rising tide lifts all boats'. Faced with a lack of evidence to support that assumption, the pendulum swung the other way in the 1970s, and donors put a higher priority on meeting the more immediate basic needs of the poor. By the late 1980s, donors turned to macroeconomic reform as a prerequisite for growth, encouraging—some would say forcing—recipient countries to implement programs that actually weakened the social safety net for the poor. A decade later, it became increasingly harder to credibly argue that poverty was being reduced at an adequate rate. A new consensus emerged on the centrality of more immediate action to alleviate poverty, culminating in the United Nations Millennium Declaration in 2000. The accompanying Millennium Development Goals (MDGs) set eight targets to be met by 2015, requiring urgent action to improve the lives of billions of people in all regions of the developing world (see chapter 13). Although the MDGs signalled that the pendulum had swung back to placing priority on fighting poverty in the short run, many other donor policies and activities still favoured an emphasis on longer-term economic growth. For instance, debt relief and assistance from international financial institutions and many bilateral agencies, notably the US's Millennium Challenge Corporation, depends on the presence of a broadly defined 'enabling environment' deemed amenable to economic growth. These conditions are often in addition to, rather than instead of, the components of 1980s-style **structural adjustment** programs (see chapter 9). Donors are thus currently supporting policies that place a greater priority on poverty reduction while simultaneously implementing others that tend to reduce government spending on the poor.

BOX 8.6   RESULTS-BASED MANAGEMENT

Donors currently favour an approach known as results-based management (RBM). Although its goal of improving aid effectiveness is widely lauded, its requirement for measurable and verifiable results introduces distortions and biases in development assistance that, some believe, could outweigh its benefits. Not all goals can be easily or accurately quantified—for example, the rule of law, good governance, or independence of the judiciary. Setting indicators means that efforts will be deployed to improve those possibly arbitrarily chosen figures rather than meeting less tangible or undefined development objectives that could be of equal or greater utility, especially in the long term.

BOX 8.7   HOW EFFECTIVE IS FOREIGN AID?

ODA's contribution to development success stories is hotly debated. In instances where rapid economic growth and poverty reduction have occurred, notably in East Asia, there is no consensus on what role, if any, foreign aid played. In fact, some students of foreign aid have long argued that aid cannot help bring about development. Some claim that it distorts economies and is actually detrimental to long-term economic growth. A recent book by former World Bank staff member William Easterly (2006), *The White Man's Burden: Why the West's Efforts to Aid the Rest Have Done So Much Ill and So Little Good*, epitomizes the belief, shared by many, that most aid is at best wasted and at worst counterproductive. By way of contrast, celebrity economist Jeffrey Sachs's (2005) optimistic book, *The End of Poverty: Economic Possibilities for Our Time*, argues that aid can be extremely effective and that in particular, a 'big push' of well-designed development assistance would help billions of people escape the 'poverty trap'.

A related debate addresses the question of which countries aid should be focused on. As mentioned above, many donors are making sub-Saharan Africa a priority because of its higher rate of poverty, although a couple of them concentrate their resources mainly on the Middle East and North Africa because of security concerns. But even within a given region, which countries are more 'deserving' of aid? Should resources go to the poorest countries, since they need it the most? Or should donors focus on well-governed countries, where they believe it will be used more effectively? Those who are pessimistic about aid's impact tend to favour the latter choice, which usually implies concentrating on middle-income countries, arguing that aid in poorly governed countries is all too often wasted. Critics respond that well-governed wealthier countries are more able to attract investment or borrow money on financial markets and therefore do not need ODA as much. Low-income countries require aid, they argue, precisely so that they can improve governance and reach a stage at which they no longer need aid. Cutting them off, critics warn, would lead to 'aid orphans' and great suffering, possibly even political or economic collapse, which could

in turn threaten regional and international stability (and perhaps require costlier interventions later). Thus, those who believe that aid contributes to social or human development—which is a goal in and of itself, even if it does not quickly translate into economic growth—favour a greater emphasis on the poorest countries.

Similarly, there is no consensus on to whom ODA funds should be given. Most disbursements are made directly to recipient governments, but many worry that such modalities only feed bloated bureaucracies and lead to graft, especially in non-democracies. Left-leaning proponents of foreign aid are more likely to advocate providing funds to Northern or Southern NGOs, which they consider more likely to involve communities and meet people's actual needs. Critics respond that using voluntary organizations to deliver services actually undermines the state and deprives it of resources necessary to ensure national standards and coverage. From a more right-leaning perspective, it is better for funds to be channelled through and promote the growth of the private sector, which is considered the key to long-term development. This approach, however, is criticized as inadequate, because a business's motivation is to make a profit, not to meet people's needs.

Increasingly, donors are co-ordinating their aid, channelling funds through joint programs and working more closely with recipient governments. The Paris Declaration on Aid Effectiveness (2005) epitomizes this trend, attributing to recipient countries the lead role in the design and implementation of their national development strategy, to be supported by donors in an integrated and transparent manner. Advantages include the elimination of duplication—or even contradictory programs—and of the onerous requirement of reporting separately to each of the donors. Harmonization, however, also carries some risks. It could be described as 'putting all eggs in one basket' when past experience has shown that development plans do not always produce the desired results. Moreover, it places a tremendous amount of power in the planning and administrative capabilities of the recipient government, ignoring problems of lack of capacity or corruption. It also assumes that the government has consulted its population, represents it, or has its best interest at heart, which is not necessarily the case. Paradoxically, when donors act together, they are in a position of great power over the recipient country, which can hardly reject their opinions or pick and choose the advice it wishes to follow. After the aid funds have been transferred to the recipient government, however, donors generally lose control over how it is spent. Still, provisions for transparency may compensate for that, allowing donors to suspend further contributions if the funds are not used according to agreement or do not produce the expected results.

QUESTIONS FOR DISCUSSION

1. Why should countries give foreign aid?

2. What kind of conditions, if any, should donors attach to their aid?

3. On what types of countries should donors concentrate their assistance?

4. To which kind(s) of actors in a recipient country should donors give their assistance?

5. What are the responsibilities of recipient countries, if any, in using foreign aid?

FURTHER READING

Collier, Paul. 2007. *The Bottom Billion: Why the Poorest Countries Are Failing and What Can Be Done about It.* Oxford and New York: Oxford University Press.

Easterly, William, ed. 2008. *Reinventing Foreign Aid.* Cambridge, MA: MIT Press.

Lancaster, Carol. 2007. *Foreign Aid: Diplomacy, Development, Domestic Politics.* Chicago: University of Chicago Press.

Lumsdaine, David Halloren. 1993. *Moral Vision in International Politics: The Foreign Aid Regime, 1949–89.* Princeton, NJ: Princeton University Press.

Riddell, Roger. 2007. *Does Foreign Aid Really Work?* New York: Oxford University Press.

INTERNET RESOURCES

French Development Agency: http://www.afd.fr.

Canadian International Development Agency: http://www.cida.gc.ca.

Center for Global Development (United States): http://www.cgdev.org.

Department for International Development (United Kingdom): http://www.dfid.gov.uk.

Development Assistance Committee, Organisation for Economic Co-operation and Development: http://www.oecd.org/dac.

Millennium Challenge Corporation (United States): http://www.mcc.gov.

Overseas Development Institute (United Kingdom): http://www.odi.org.uk.

Reality of Aid (Philippines): http://www.realityofaid.org.

Swedish International Development Cooperation Agency: http://www.sida.se.

United States Agency for International Development: http://www.usaid.gov.

CHAPTER 9

THE INTERNATIONAL FINANCIAL INSTITUTIONS

MARCUS TAYLOR

LEARNING OBJECTIVES

- To understand why the IMF and the World Bank were created and how their operations changed over the following decades.
- To comprehend their role in the process of structural adjustment and the controversy it created.
- To examine responses from the IMF and World Bank to criticism and to overview the new directions they have taken.

OVERVIEW

Few actors in international development have fuelled controversy to the same degree as the leading international financial institutions: the International Monetary Fund (IMF) and the World Bank. In spite of their official objectives of ensuring global economic stability and promoting poverty reduction, these institutions have attracted considerable criticism from a wide range of social movements and political groups. Opponents from the left of the political spectrum have claimed that IMF and World Bank policies have served to entrench global poverty and exacerbate inequalities. As a consequence, the annual meetings of the institutions are routinely confronted with large-scale organized protests from varied civil society groups. Conversely, conservative voices have argued that the institutions are overly bureaucratic and increasingly irrelevant in today's globalized world. Editorials in the *Wall Street Journal*, for example, have repeatedly claimed that the expanding role of private institutions such as multinational corporations and global financial markets have lessened the need for the IMF and World Bank and therefore, they should be either streamlined or simply disbanded.

To help to understand these debates, this chapter examines how and why the IMF and World Bank were established and outlines the subsequent evolution of their roles. We begin with the Bretton Woods Conference of 1944 at which these international financial institutions (IFIs) were designed and examine their original functions within the world economy after the Second World War. Subsequently, we focus on how both institutions assumed a growing influence on developing countries in the context of a deep social and economic crisis during the 1970s and 1980s and used their financial influence to promote structural adjustment policies. These policies involve a series of economic and social reforms designed to promote the role of market forces within the developing world and have provoked much controversy. While the IMF and World Bank suggest that structural adjustment reforms promote strong and stable economic growth, critics claim that their effects have been counterproductive and have led to increased poverty and growing inequality. In examining this debate, we look at the ways in which the IFIs have reformed their own practices in response to criticism. In this vein, current policies promoted by the institutions focus not just on economic reforms but on a wider set of policy changes that incorporate such diverse features as 'good governance', 'building institutions for markets', and 'empowering the poor'. We overview each of these in turn and ask whether they mark a change in direction from structural adjustment or are merely an adaptation of it. Finally, we turn to the controversy surrounding the IMF over its interventions in the East Asian financial crisis in the late 1990s before reflecting on the current relevance of both institutions in a world of globalized capitalism.

THE ORIGINS OF THE IMF AND WORLD BANK

The formation of the IMF and World Bank goes back to the Bretton Woods Conference held in New Hampshire in 1944. With the Second World War drawing to a close, the United States and Britain began to plan a new international order for the postwar era. At the forefront of their concerns was the creation of an international economic system that promoted trade and provided rules to guide economic relations between countries. This goal stemmed from events in the 1930s when economic conflicts between major European powers contributed to the outbreak of war. During this earlier period, the international monetary order was characterized by a system of flexible exchange rates, which allowed countries to manipulate their currency in order to gain economic advantages. When faced with economic stagnation, for example, countries could respond by devaluing their currency as a way to cheapen—and therefore boost—their exports. Although this strategy tended to provide short-term gain, it did so at the expense of other countries, which tended to follow suit, thereby leading to a spiral of currency devaluations that greatly interrupted the stability of international trade and investment.

The 44 allied powers that met at the Bretton Woods Conference agreed that the economic anarchy of the previous decade needed to be avoided. A clear consensus did not exist, however, regarding the precise character of the new international economic order that should be estab-

lished. Owing to the overwhelming economic and military power of the US, the American delegation was able to ensure that a blueprint proposal designed by Harold Dexter White set the basis for conference discussions.

Ultimately, this American proposal laid the basis for the articles of agreement that bound countries to the Bretton Woods System (Peet 2003). The American delegates had been quite forward about the type of international order they envisioned. Given the overwhelming superiority of the US's industrial base, they sought a system in which international trade could proceed relatively unhindered. This would not only help America to meet its goal of economic expansion,

Figure 9.1 John Maynard Keynes (right) and Harry Dexter White at the Bretton Woods Conference, 1944

Source: Wikipedia

the US delegates claimed, but would also fuel global prosperity and mutual development.

Given that monetary instability was blamed for the disintegration of international trade in the preceding era, the **Bretton Woods System** was founded upon the establishment of fixed exchange rates between national currencies. Each currency would be pegged at an agreed amount of US dollars, which in turn were redeemable for gold at a fixed rate. Only small variations to these exchange rates were permitted. Ensuring that currencies remained fixed was intended to provide the stable monetary conditions necessary for expanding world trade.

Once the articles of agreement were ratified by member countries at the end of 1945, the International Monetary Fund (IMF) was set up to oversee the workings of the system and to manage any potential disruptions. Each member country paid into the IMF a quota of its own currency, as well as some gold or dollar holdings based on the size of its economy. When facing severe economic problems, such as a balance of payments crisis in which a country was importing more than export earnings could pay for, countries would be permitted to draw temporarily on the reserves of the IMF in order to pay international debts. Usage of these funds, therefore, was intended to provide countries with sufficient time to stabilize their economy without resorting to measures such as currency devaluation that would cause international monetary instability. Thus, at this point, the IMF functioned as an important yet modest instrument to maintain international currency stability. This initial role gave no hint of the Fund's later emergence as a powerful agent within international development.

Along with the establishment of the IMF came the creation of the International Bank for Reconstruction and Development (IBRD), which later became known as the World Bank. In the immediate postwar period, the IBRD was designed to make loans at preferential rates of interest to the countries of western Europe that had been devastated by war. Nonetheless, the role of the IBRD in Europe was greatly diminished when the US government unveiled the Marshall Plan in 1947 under which it unilaterally lent large sums of money to European nations to accelerate the reconstruction process. Although this forced the Bank to refocus its activities away from Europe, the accelerating process of decolonization created a new and expanding clientele. US President Harry Truman is widely considered to have launched the project of international development in 1949 when he suggested that decolonization was creating a new 'underdeveloped world' that was in need of a 'program of development'

BOX 9.1   THE US AIMS FOR BRETTON WOODS

The purpose of the conference is . . . wholly within the American tradition, and completely outside political consideration. The United State wants, after this war, full utilization of its industries, its factories and its farms; full and steady employment for its citizens, particularly its ex-servicemen; and full prosperity and peace. It can have them only in a world with a vigorous trade. But it can have such trade only if currencies are stable, if money keeps its value, and if people can buy and sell with the certainty that the money they receive on the due date will have the value contracted for.

US Department of State press release (Peet 2003, 47).

BOX 9.2   IMF: INITIAL FUNCTION

To provide financial resources to allow countries to solve the balance of payments crises without devaluing their currencies. This would help to maintain the system of stable exchange rates established at Bretton Woods that facilitated stable international trade.

based on 'democratic fair dealing'. By serving as a conduit of development finance into the under-developed world, the IBRD was viewed as an important element of this development project.

The initial function of the IBRD was to act as a source of financing for state-organized development projects in the post-colonial countries. From the then-prevailing perspective of modernization theory, the new countries that emerged from the collapse of colonialism were considered to be on a natural path towards development, advancing through a sequence of structural transformations from traditional, agrarian societies to modern, industrial ones. Development economists, however, suggested that the rate of development was limited by the stock of capital a country could draw upon for productive investment. In the post-colonial period, capital was scarce for most developing-world countries. Domestic savings rates were low, and many private international banks would not lend to developing-world countries because they were viewed as too great a risk. In this context, the IBRD offered a partial solution by

acting as an intermediary between private international banks and developing-world governments. Backed by the financial and political support of the leading Western countries, the IBRD was able to finance itself through loans from private international banks at low interest rates. In turn, the IBRD could then lend money to developing-world governments to finance development projects at rates of interest that such governments would not be able to obtain dealing directly with private banks.

Initially, the Bank tended to fund very specific types of projects. In the first two decades of its existence, more than 60 per cent of its loans funded projects to build physical infrastructure, such as highways, airports, electricity grids, and hydroelectric dams. To receive such funding, applications from developing countries needed to meet the criteria established by the Bank to ensure that the project was technically sound and would generate sufficient revenue to repay the loan. These criteria tended to exclude many of the poorer nations because they could not guarantee a significant rate of return.

BOX 9.3   WORLD BANK: INITIAL FUNCTION

To provide financing for postwar reconstruction and development projects. From 1950, the Bank focused on providing loans to developing-world countries at lower rates of interest than those of private international banks. These loans were directed mainly towards building infrastructure for development.

To address this issue, the International Development Agency (IDA) was formed in 1960 as a new organization within the World Bank. Like the IBRD, IDA loans also funded large-scale development projects, such as dams, roads, and other projects that laid the infrastructural basis for capitalist development. However, these loans were provided at a virtually interest-free status over long periods of repayment, which allowed the IDA to fund a range of projects that would not qualify under the IBRD conditions of profitability and repayment. In this manner, a division of labour was created between the IBRD, which provided subsidized credit to middle-income countries, and the IDA, which provided zero-interest loans to poorer developing countries. In providing finance for development projects in which private banks would not invest and for which governments lacked the ability to guarantee repayment, the IDA sought to give impetus to processes of industrial development in the poorest of the new post-colonial nations.

GOVERNANCE STRUCTURES

Before tracing the evolution of the IMF and the World Bank, it is useful to examine their governance structures and the exercise of power within them. Unlike the United Nations General Assembly, where each country has one vote, voting rights in the IMF and World Bank are weighted according to quota subscriptions. These are based loosely on the size of a country's economy, meaning that advanced industrial countries have consistently held the majority of the voting power. At present, they hold approximately 60 per cent of the voting rights within the institutions, whereas the poorest 165 countries together have only 28 per cent. The US currently holds close to 17 per cent of the voting rights which, given that constitutional amendments need more than 85 per cent of the votes to pass, provides it with a unilateral veto over such proposals.

Voting power, moreover, translates into direct representation at board meetings. While the IMF

BOX 9.4   IMF QUOTAS AND WORLD BANK SUBSCRIPTIONS

On joining the IMF, each member country must pay a subscription quota that is based loosely on the size of its economy and measured in SDRs (Special Drawing Rights), the IMF's unit of account. These quotas form the financial holdings of the IMF, and a member's quota determines both its financial commitment to the IMF and its voting power within the institution. Moreover, they also determine how much a country can borrow from the IMF in times of crisis. Technically, a country can borrow 100 per cent of its quota annually, to a limit of 300 per cent cumulatively. In special circumstances, however, these limits can be waived. Quota sizes are reviewed every five years, and the current levels can be viewed on the IMF's website (http://www.imf.org).

World Bank 'subscriptions' also define voting rights. Upon joining the IBRD, member governments must 'subscribe' to a portion of the Bank's capital stock by pledging to purchase a specified number of shares according to their financial capacity. Members are required to purchase only a small portion of their subscription ('paid-in capital'), while the remaining portion ('callable capital') remains outstanding. Given that the IBRD raises the vast majority of its capital through bond issues, it has never had to request 'callable capital' from its members.

and World Bank are run on a day-to-day basis by an internal management structure, the board of executive directors oversees these actions, including approving loans and guarantees, setting the administrative budget, vetting country assistance strategies, and making borrowing and financial decisions. There are 24 seats on the board, and the representatives are chosen through vote shares. As a consequence, the 46 sub-Saharan African countries together have only two representatives on the executive boards, while the five richest countries each have one, as do China, Saudi Arabia, and Russia. Additionally, the US and the European Union both have the unilateral power to choose presidents: the US appoints the president of the World Bank, and Europe designates the president of the IMF. This caused controversy in 2005 when the government of George W. Bush insisted on placing Paul Wolfowitz at the head of the World Bank despite significant opposition from the developing world, European countries, and within the Bank itself.

Indeed, the role of the US in influencing IMF and World Bank decisions has been much debated. Although authors differ on the degree of power they ascribe to the US, there are numerous historical examples of US influence over decision-making. For example, in the Cold War period of the 1960s and 1970s, US governments used their ability to withhold IDA quotas to ensure that a disproportionate amount of financing was channelled to strategically crucial US allies and, following the Cuban revolution of 1959, to governments that were seen as bulkheads against communist revolutions (Caufield 1996). This often involved funding dictatorial regimes with dubious human rights records. Similarly, in the 1970s, the IMF made loans with abnormally flexible conditions to key US allies such as Egypt.

More recently, the record of US influence has been one of mixed success. For example, the US executive was successful in pressuring the World Bank's president to have controversial chief economist Joseph Stiglitz removed from his position at the Bank in 1999. However, it subsequently failed to significantly change the content of the Bank's *World Development Report 2000/2001* despite its considerable opposition to the anti-poverty strategy that the report advanced (Wade 2001). In a more constructive way, the US Congress, under pressure from non-governmental organizations such as the Sierra Club, lobbied the US Treasury in 1989 to instruct the US director to vote against all Bank projects that did not have an environmental impact assessment available 120 days before the board of governors' vote. Two years later, this practice became incorporated into standard Bank policy. The relationship between the US and the IFIs is therefore quite complex, and both institutions have at times needed to follow a delicate balancing act in order to maintain their multilateral credentials while appeasing the interests of their primary shareholder.

THE TURBULENT DECADE OF THE 1970S

During the first two decades of the IFIs' existence, their activities were relatively modest and did not provoke the controversy that currently envelops them. The decade of the 1970s, however, was a period of notable instability and crisis in the global economy, which prompted a dramatic transformation of both the IMF and the World Bank. First, the decision of the United States to withdraw its support for the Bretton Woods System in the early 1970s created a fundamental rupture within the IMF. Concerned with an escalating trade deficit and the growing amount of dollars held by countries abroad, President Nixon effectively abolished the system in 1971 by suspending the convertibility of dollars into gold. This unilateral action broke the key tenet of the Bretton Woods System and undermined the stability of exchange rates. Eighteen months later, the currencies of industrial countries were allowed to float freely, and the global economy entered an uncertain post–Bretton Woods period.

Since exchange rates were no longer fixed, the official role of the IMF to provide temporary loans to maintain currency stability had been undermined. In adapting to the new circumstances, the IMF did two things. First, it shed the aims of the Bretton Woods System from its constitution in order to recast itself as an international lender of last resort. Countries that needed short-term injections of money to pay international debts could turn to the IMF without the imposition of maintaining the value of their exchange rate. Indeed, the IMF frequently recommended that countries devalue their currencies as a means of strengthening their exporting sectors, which was the exact opposite of its original purpose.

Simultaneously, the IMF also began to increase surveillance of the policies pursued by borrowing countries and expanded the number of conditions attached to its loans. This trend would become increasingly important in the years that followed. In accepting financing from the IMF, countries were increasingly forced to accept the implementation of an IMF-sanctioned reform program to re-establish economic stability. Through what were known as 'stand-by arrangements', the standard IMF package involved austerity measures aimed at reducing government spending and lowering consumption within the economy so as to decrease imports and increase funds available for repaying international debts. As we shall see below, in the 1970s and beyond, growing numbers of developing-world countries found it necessary to resort to the IMF as a lender of last resort, and this entrenched the power of the institution within the developing world. Nonetheless, the austerity programs that the IMF insisted on were widely critiqued for their adverse effects on the poorer segments of society. In many countries, the financial solvency of the state was often restored through cutting subsidies on basic consumption goods and reducing expenditures on social services (Körner 1986).

The 1970s was also a period of notable transformation within the World Bank. Under the presidency of Robert McNamara (1968–81), the institution dramatically expanded its operations. McNamara viewed the Bank as an underutilized instrument in a fight against global poverty and communism. On assuming office in 1968, McNamara challenged his staff to find ways to increase lending, including making loans to countries hitherto untouched by the World Bank. Lending activity swelled from $2 billion in 1970 to over $11 billion in 1980, a more than five-fold increase over the decade. At the same time, the Bank's lending profile shifted away from large-scale infrastructural projects to target a wider range of development objectives. In particular, McNamara emphasized the need for the Bank to fund direct anti-poverty efforts through social programs and projects aimed at modernizing the agricultural sector. Indeed, McNamara saw the agricultural sector as neglected in the rush to industrialize and there-

BOX 9.5   McNAMARA'S CALL FOR A 'BASIC NEEDS' APPROACH

Nations need to give greater priority to establishing growth targets in terms of essential human needs: in terms of nutrition, housing, health, literacy and employment—even if it be at the cost of some reduction in the pace of advance in certain narrow and highly privileged sectors whose benefits accrue to the few.

Annual Speech, Washington, Fall 1972.

fore remaining a reservoir of poverty. By focusing on health and education programs, McNamara's approach became known as the 'basic needs' approach. Lending for infrastructure fell to about 30 per cent of total Bank funding, whereas loans for anti-poverty projects (including an emphasis on helping small-scale farmers increase productivity) rose to almost 30 per cent.

Two important factors stem from McNamara's period. First, the Bank became considerably more active and powerful on a global level. No longer was it content to lend cautiously to a limited number of developing-world countries, but rather it was prepared to actively propagate projects in the developing world as part of a broader mission to spread capitalist development. Second, in emphasizing the need to focus on social objectives rather than simply promoting industrialization and economic growth, the Bank opened up a debate about its own purpose and that of development finance in general. While McNamara's approach was well received by some members of the international development community, there was also a powerful conservative reaction that suggested the Bank should focus simply on promoting economic growth.

THE DEBT CRISIS, STRUCTURAL ADJUSTMENT, AND CONDITIONALITY

As the decade of the 1970s drew to a close, many developing-world countries were faced with the dual burden of high oil prices and falling prices for their primary exports and began to borrow heavily from private international banks to overcome expenditure shortfalls. These banks, moreover, had accumulated surplus holdings of dollars and were actively seeking to make loans to the developing world, often without regard for long-term sustainability. The orgy of borrowing that followed left countries across the developing world heavily indebted to Northern banks. In Latin America, for example, the total external debt (private and public) leapt from $100,000 million in 1976 to $336,230 million in 1983.

Events were brought to a head in 1982 when the US made a unilateral decision to raise interest rates. This action quickly and considerably deepened the debt burden of many developing-world countries. Mexico was the first to threaten default when, on 12 August 1982, it announced to the IMF and US government that it could not meet payments on an outstanding $80-billion debt. By October 1983, some 30 countries owing a total of $239 billion had or were attempting to reschedule debt payments of which 16 Latin American countries accounted for 74 per cent. Given the magnitude of the loans that hovered on the verge of default, a number of major US and international banks faced collapse, and this raised the spectre of a financial crash engulfing the entire Western financial system.

In direct response to the crisis, the IMF and World Bank began to pipeline billions of dollars to debt-stricken countries in order to facilitate continued payments on their old debt. In becoming the major funnel for emergency credit to the South, the IMF and World Bank became proponents of dramatic social and economic reforms in the South. The basic premise of their operations was that development policy in the preceding decades had become profoundly misguided. In the postwar period, it was generally accepted that the institutions of the state had a major role to play in promoting modernization through industrialization, and this was reflected in policies such as credits to industry and trade protectionism to block foreign competition. For the IMF and World Bank, these policies had created both inefficient industrial sectors that were a drain on national resources and an over-inflated state bureaucracy that distorted markets while breeding corruption.

To overcome the crisis, they claimed, it was not enough merely to stabilize the economies of the developing world through standard austerity programs. Rather, a much more profound process of transformation was also necessary through which economies would become more open to foreign trade and more focused on producing for export. At the same time, the state would decrease its interventions and allow market forces a greater role in distributing resources across the economy. This transformation was captured in the notion of **structural adjustment**. To pursue this new mission of promoting structural adjustment, the IMF and World Bank introduced sweeping changes to the nature and extent of their operations. McNamara had coined the term 'structural adjustment' in 1979 to describe a shift from 'project lending'—i.e., funding a specific project such as building a dam—to 'program lending'. This involved giving less funding to support specific projects, such as building dams and roads, and placing more emphasis on countries adopting structural adjustment programs. The first specific structural adjustment loan of US $200 million was granted to Turkey in March 1980, and many others followed during the debt crisis.

To ensure that countries undertook these difficult measures, numerous conditions were attached to World Bank and IMF loans, and the release of further portions of structural adjustment loans was made dependent upon the successful implementation of prior requirements, as decided by the IMF and the Bank. Surveillance functions were therefore greatly heightened, and both institutions took a much stronger role in setting the fundamental parameters of client-country policy. With both the Bank and the IMF seeking to impose mutually reinforcing cross-conditionality restrictions on lending, the two became embroiled in a far closer association than at any previous time. This rapprochement gave rise to the notion of the **Washington Consensus** as both leading financial institutions wielded their considerable influence in order to propagate a common development doctrine on a global scale.

The immediate phase of adjustment, usually managed by the IMF, consisted of the imposition of severe austerity measures to restore macroeconomic balances, particularly the suppression of inflation. Through a shock therapy program of rapid liberalization of prices, currency devaluation, and fiscal discipline, a deflationary period could be engineered within which 'excessive demand' was curtailed and inefficient producers

would go out of business. In the medium term, structural adjustment pursued the rapid liberalization of trade, deregulation of markets, privatization of state-owned industries, and the introduction of the private sector into providing public goods such as health care. This was meant to encourage new and dynamic export-oriented industries to form and target global markets. At the same time, market forces would play a greater role in distributing goods and services across the domestic economy.

While the emphasis of structural adjustment was on long-term economic growth, these reforms were also intended to ensure debt repayment and thereby re-establish the integrity of the international credit system. Thus, the IMF and World Bank were widely perceived as assuming the role of debt collectors for private banks. At no point did the institutions question the morality of the burden of debt crisis being placed on the developing world rather than being shared with the international banks that had lent money irresponsibly. As an answer to the debt crisis, therefore, structural adjustment appealed greatly to the Western shareholders of the IMF and World Bank, because new loans served to shore up the financial systems of the North while structural adjustment opened new avenues for investment in the South and refocused the productive apparatus in the South towards low-cost primary and secondary exports that lowered commodity costs in the West. The question remained, however, of whether structural adjustment would also provide a route towards long-term economic stability and growth within the developing world.

BEYOND STRUCTURAL ADJUSTMENT?

In the 1990s, the IMF and World Bank came under growing pressure because structural adjustment was widely critiqued as being unable to deliver on its primary promises of stable growth and poverty reduction. Whereas the severe austerity programs put in place following the debt crisis often achieved their goals of reducing inflation, lowering government deficits, and ameliorating balance of payments imbalances, the broader reforms of liberalization, privatization, and deregulation did not appear to be producing a period of rapid and sustained economic growth across the developing world. On the contrary, many countries in Latin America and Africa faced relative economic stagnation, while the social costs of adjustment were unequally distributed (SAPRIN 2004). Although the IMF and World Bank frequently challenged negative interpretations of economic performance and social dislocation under structural adjustment—often placing blame on countries unwilling to follow their prescriptions sufficiently—they nonetheless began to re-evaluate their primary goals and their policy prescriptions. Three factors in particular (described below) were important in forcing this rethinking.

1. The East Asian 'miracle'

The countries of South Korea, Taiwan, Hong Kong, and Singapore did not follow the structural adjustment model. While they embraced the premise of export-oriented growth, they achieved it through the sustained involvement of the state in nurturing selected industrial sectors to compete on international markets. The successes of the East Asian countries were encapsulated in the notion of an 'East Asian miracle', which seemed to contrast greatly with the experiences of countries in Latin America and Africa that had followed the orthodox structural adjustment model.

2. African stagnation?

Owing to high levels of debt during the 1980s, the IMF and World Bank wielded considerable influence over numerous countries in sub-Saharan Africa. As a result, these countries often undertook significant structural adjustment programs. The results, however, were profoundly disappointing. With only a few exceptions, the region was characterized by stagnant economies and worsening social indicators during much of the 1980s and 1990s. Critics also claimed that the increase in armed conflict in the region and the escalating HIV/AIDS crisis were strongly related to the impact of structural adjustment in cutting back state capacity.

3. The Mexican peso crisis

In the late 1980s and early 1990s, Mexico was heralded as a 'success story' that many advocates of structural adjustment used to justify the validity of the reforms. The structural adjustment programs pursued in the 1980s in Mexico had initially imposed a great deal of economic and social dislocation. However, with inflation tamed and market liberalization encouraging a stream of US investment in export-oriented industry, Mexico in the early 1990s appeared to be booming. Proponents suggested that rapid economic growth would remedy ongoing problems of stagnant wages and high poverty levels. In the latter part of 1994, however, the flows of investment turned into capital flight as investors became afraid that the Mexican boom was built on tenuous social and political foundations. Mexico was thrown into a deep recession, with wages falling and unemployment increasing, and the economic turmoil was resolved only when the US sponsored a massive IMF bailout package and the Mexican government socialized the debts of private banks.

In view of East Asian successes and the failures of structural adjustment in Africa and Latin America, the financial institutions faced growing criticism. In response, both institutions—but especially the World Bank—have sought to reinvent themselves by making changes to their policy prescriptions and the ways in which they engage client countries.

One of the important questions that arises is whether the changes have been superficial—aimed primarily at improving public image—or whether they reflect substantive changes in the way that the IFIs conceptualize development issues and orient their policy.

BOX 9.6   THE BANK REFLECTS ON STRUCTURAL ADJUSTMENT

In 2001, the World Bank published a report containing what it had learned from engaging with civil society over the successes and failures of structural adjustment:

- Adjustment should come 'from within', based on local analysis, local knowledge, local perceptions of political 'room for manoeuvre'.
- Institutions are essential to making adjustment succeed by generating new prosperity.
- In some cases, a step-by-step approach to adjustment is appropriate to allow complex reforms to be closely linked with the development of institutions.
- It is important to provide adequate safety nets to help mitigate potentially adverse effects of adjustment on the poor.
- Special attention should be paid to safeguarding social expenditures and maintaining access to health care and education.

World Bank. 2001. *Adjustment from Within: Lessons from the Structural Adjustment Participatory Review Initiative.* http://www.worldbank.org/research/sapri/index.htm.

THE WORLD BANK, GOOD GOVERNANCE, AND INSTITUTION-BUILDING

Introducing the concept of **good governance** was the first major move by the World Bank to explain the poor record of structural adjustment in many countries in the developing world. In addressing the reason for the failure of reforms in sub-Saharan Africa, the Bank suggested that '[f]undamental in many countries is the deteriorating quality of government, epitomized by bureaucratic obstruction, rent seeking, weak judicial systems and arbitrary decision making' (World Bank 1989, 3). In short, free markets were not failing the developing world, but political and legal systems—ridden by corruption and inequalities—were failing the markets. While it insisted that structural adjustment remained the only correct long-term solution to the problems of developing-world countries, the Bank argued that the gains from reform were often lost because the institutions of the state were not

enabling markets to work efficiently. Systemic failures of government and other state institutions therefore served to undermine the reforms.

The goal of 'good governance' is to craft a political architecture that supports market economies, with an emphasis on stable property rights and accountable decision-making. Corruption is seen as a key problem that distorts markets and hampers their ability to efficiently distribute resources across the economy. For the World Bank, corrupt government officials make decisions favourable to certain groups in return for monetary reward, and this skews the playing field and reduces the efficiency of the market. For 'good governance' to prevail, the Bank argued, it was necessary to find mechanisms that would enforce transparency and accountability. The former would ensure that citizens could see how decisions were made and therefore could force state officials to make decisions that benefited the common good, not special interests. Simultaneously, if the rule of law is not applied freely and fairly, the legal basis for a market system can falter. As Adam Smith argued some 200 years earlier, market actors must be certain that their private property is secure and their contracts will be upheld. If the law is not applied equally, a lack of confidence in the rules of the game will restrain market activity and frustrate development. As a consequence, good governance must also include judicial independence from both governmental influence and private actors and requires an accountable police force to implement the rule of law with an even hand.

The notion of 'good governance' offered a useful concept by which the Bank could explain the failures of structural adjustment and justify further reforms in developing countries. For market-oriented development strategies to be effective, the political systems that surround them must be made accountable, transparent, responsive, efficient, and inclusive. Critics, however, have delivered sharp responses. While few doubt that limiting corruption is an important goal in and of itself, they suggest that good governance has not been a necessary factor in the development of many countries, including those in the West where corruption was often rife during their early development. In a more contemporary setting, China—which has seen the most rapid expansion of any developing economy in recent decades—would fail on many counts of good governance. By blaming the political environment for the failure of structural adjustment, the 'good governance' doctrine denies that there may be weaknesses in the structural adjustment strategy itself. Moreover, for the World Bank and the IMF—whose governing boards operate in secrecy and in which Western countries have considerable influence over decision-making—to demand transparency and accountability from client countries seemed profoundly hypocritical.

The response from the World Bank to such critiques has been to broaden the scope of the debate by highlighting a wider spectrum of social and political institutions that are conducive to successful reform. Not only must accountability and transparency be present in all political and legal processes, but the state must play a proactive role in fashioning other social institutions to help markets work efficiently and fairly. Drawing on new theoretical trends in economics, such as the 'new institutional economics' represented by such authors as Douglas North (cf. Harriss, Hunter, and Lewis 1995), the World Bank places greater emphasis on the institutional context in which development occurs. Along with good governance, governments are expected to enforce a clear, fair, and consistent set of rules by which all market actors must operate.

In emphasizing the role of institutions in development, the Bank is arguing that states need to facilitate and regulate the conditions for free economic exchange and to correct potential market failures caused by unequally distributed information among market agents. These situations are viewed to be particularly common in the developing world because of the underdeveloped nature of market institutions. This means that there is a role for the state in establishing institutions that channel information about market conditions, goods, and participants, a role greater than the anti-state bias of initial restructuring models suggested. It would include such tasks as preventing the establishment of monopolies that would strangle competition and ensuring the efficient operation of labour markets by constructing institutions that would maintain a suitably flexible labour force.

Consequently, in the late 1990s, the Bank moved to what it called a comprehensive approach to development that encompassed not just economic policies but also the institutional, human, and physical dimensions of development strategy. These areas range from good governance and the rule of law, through to social safety nets, education, health, rural and urban strategies, and environmental and cultural dimensions (Wolfensohn 1999, 5–10). Together, they form an ambitious policy agenda covering a holistic range of issues that broadens the scope of policy and institutional reform well beyond the original confines of structural adjustment. Critics, however, suggest that this expansion has drawn the World Bank into policy areas that far exceed its expertise. Others suggest that solidifying structural adjustment in this manner is unlikely to have a profound developmental effect. Instead, they advocate a move away from the market-centric model to one that acknowledges the central importance of the role played by the state in development, as evidenced by the experiences of countries as diverse as the United States, Norway, Japan, and South Korea (Chang and Grabel 2004).

THE IMF AND THE ASIAN CRISIS

Whereas the World Bank in the 1990s was expanding its range of policy advice, the IMF maintained a more consistent focus on macroeconomic

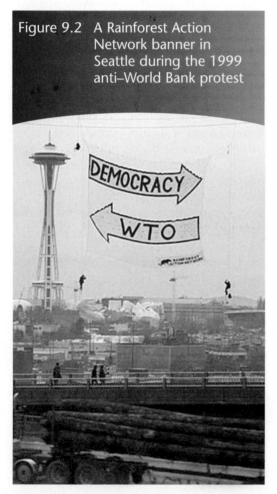

Figure 9.2   A Rainforest Action Network banner in Seattle during the 1999 anti–World Bank protest

Source: Touhig Sion/Corbis Sygma

policy. During the 1990s, the IMF placed further emphasis on the need for developing countries to open themselves to foreign investment. By removing restrictions on the entry of foreign capital, the IMF suggested, developing countries could tap into a large source of finance for development. In particular, during the 1990s, the IMF strongly argued that it was necessary for developing countries to attract **foreign portfolio investment** (FPI) by opening up their stock markets to foreign investors. This process is called 'capital account liberalization', and the IMF suggests that it complements other forms of liberalization and enhances the ability of developing countries to attract capital. Using these arguments, the IMF attempted to have the goal of furthering capital account liberalization written into its constitution.

The IMF's stance on capital account liberalization quickly came under pressure following the 1994 Mexican peso crash when investors panicked and rapidly withdrew their portfolio investment from the country, causing intense economic dislocation and social upheaval. Critics suggested that FPI is short-term, speculative, and prone to creating financial bubbles. Worse was to follow in 1997 when speculation on global financial markets against the Thai currency caused another crisis of confidence among investors, who quickly withdrew portfolio investments from across East Asia. Despite having been termed 'miracle economies' because of periods of sustained and relatively stable growth during the previous three decades, countries ranging from South Korea to Indonesia faced a crisis of immense proportions. The countries that were relatively least affected, moreover, were those that had either refrained from capital account liberalization or had quickly re-established controls on the movement of capital out of the country (Soederberg 2004). The crisis did not stop in Asia, however, and both Russia and Brazil faced capital flight and economic turmoil in 1998.

In response to the Asian crisis, the IMF claimed the crises were home-grown and placed the blame not on capital account liberalization but on 'crony capitalism'. According to the IMF, the murky relationships between East Asian governments and local businesses had made it impossible for foreign investors to judge the true conditions of the markets. This, according to the IMF, contributed to an overestimation of the strength of East Asian markets, leading to overinvestment and eventually financial panic once true market conditions were revealed. Good governance—i.e., openness, accountability, and transparency within East Asian governments—was prescribed as the solution, along with a series of new international institutions known collectively as the 'new international financial architecture'. These institutions were intended to promote financial transparency and co-ordinated actions among key nations at an international level.

Critics, however, lambasted the IMF's position. They pointed out that the Fund had praised the sound fundamentals of the East Asian countries just prior to the crash of 1997. The IMF, they claimed, had been cavalier in its approach to capital account liberalization, ignoring the potential risks by encouraging countries to liberalize rapidly without effective regulatory structures. This created the risk of rapid financial meltdown in countries with sound economies. Moreover, the immediate response of the IMF to the crisis was to make bailout loans conditional on reform measures similar to structural adjustment programs. The former World Bank chief economist Joseph Stiglitz, for example, is among those who argue that this

IMF intervention was entirely inappropriate for the East Asian countries and greatly exacerbated the severity of the crisis. Besides denting the image of the IMF, another consequence of the Asian debacle has been the build-up of large foreign reserve stockpiles by East Asian countries in order to avoid having to turn to the IMF in the future.

INTO THE NEW MILLENNIUM: POVERTY REDUCTION AND COUNTRY OWNERSHIP

Stung by criticism over the Asian financial crises and facing large protests at their annual meetings, the IFIs entered the new millennium under mounting pressure. Their response has been to re-emphasize their role as global poverty alleviators and to restructure the form of their relationships with client countries. The emphasis placed on poverty reduction reflected the need for the IMF and World Bank to anchor themselves to a cause with greater legitimacy than promoting the widely critiqued policies of structural adjustment. As one less-than-enchanted World Bank researcher put it, 'The poverty issue is so red-hot that IMF and World Bank staff began to feel that every action inside these organizations, from reviewing public expenditure to vacuuming the office carpet, should be justified by its effect on poverty reduction' (Easterly 2001).

BOX 9.7   IFIs EMBRACING ANTI-POVERTY

The ultimate systemic threat today is poverty.

Michel Camdessus, IMF managing director OECD forum speech, 15 May 2001.

Our dream is a world free of poverty.

World Bank mission statement (http://www.worldbank.org).

First and foremost, structural adjustment lending has been remodelled under the new motif of **Poverty Reduction Strategy Papers** (PRSPs). According to the IMF, these lending agreements have replaced the older 'structural adjustment facility' as the primary means of funding low-income countries to promote broad-based growth and reduce poverty. They formalize a clear division of labour between the IMF and World Bank, a relationship that World Bank president James Wolfensohn referred to as 'breathing in and breathing out'. While the IMF concentrates on a familiar range of macroeconomic policies and objectives, the World Bank is now responsible for overseeing the 'social and structural' policies of participating countries.

The first innovation in the PRSP model was the introduction of 'ownership'. According to James Wolfensohn (1999), president of the World Bank from 1995 to 2005, ownership means that '[c]ountries must be in the driving seat and set the course. They must determine the goals and the phasing, timing and sequencing of programmes.'

By applying the concept of ownership, the World Bank suggests that policies are no longer fashioned in a top-down manner by the IFIs but must find their initiative in the country itself. Moreover, when designing policies, governments must utilize participatory methods to ensure that all stakeholders—government, civil society, the private sector, and the international development community—are able to voice their opinions on what should be included within the PRSP. Reforms must not be centrally imposed, therefore, but must be designed by the borrowing country's government and require the support of all affected social groups.

Although it was introduced to counter criticism of conditionality as a neo-colonial form of governance, the notion of 'ownership' has itself caused controversy. The concept is taken from management theory, where it was developed to strengthen the commitment of employees to company projects. In that sense, the practices associated with 'ownership' are constituted within complex power relationships, in this case

between international finance providers and national governments. On the one hand, ownership aims at improving the viability and efficiency of program design by allowing national governments to take the lead in establishing social and structural reforms that respect local conditions that they would be in a privileged position to comprehend.

On the other hand, since both IMF and World Bank boards must approve all PRSPs before funding is granted, it is highly improbable that the broad trends of the development strategy will be allowed to diverge far from Bank and Fund orthodoxy. On the contrary, given the wide propagation of what the World Bank considers 'best development practice', national governments are expected to internalize these lessons if they are to receive funding. Thus, ownership could also feasibly be viewed as a modification and extension of conditionality. Indeed, some critics have suggested that the ownership concept resembles the situation of a taxicab. The developing country is in the driver's seat, yet it goes nowhere until the World Bank gets in, announces where to go, and pays the fare (Pincus and Winters 2002).

Beyond the notion of 'country ownership', the World Bank widely championed a new approach to poverty reduction in 2001. Poverty, it suggested, represents not just a lack of income but is also manifested in the conditions of 'voicelessness' and 'vulnerability'. Poor people suffer from an inability to influence political processes (voicelessness) and, because of a lack of assets, are also unable to adapt to sudden shocks, such as the illness or unemployment of a primary wage earner (vulnerability). The Bank saw these three dimensions of poverty interacting and reinforcing each other. Despite the new emphasis, however, the approach remains a market-centred one. For the IFIs, only markets provide opportunities for poor people to find employment, and the efficient provision of health and education better equips them to make use of those opportunities. The persistence of poverty within countries undergoing market reform, therefore, is explained by institutional and social barriers that prevent poor people from participating in market relations. In the words of the World Bank (2000, 61), 'Societies have to help poor people overcome the obstacles that prevent them from freely and fairly participating in markets.'

In the first place, to combat vulnerability, the World Bank has lauded the concept of 'social capital' as a 'missing link' in development theory. Social capital is a concept used to identify the networks and linkages an individual or household can use to gain access to resources. A household with high levels of social capital has greater support networks through family, friends, and the local community. These linkages facilitate access to extra assets—for example, money to help pay medical bills or to counter a sudden loss of employment. For the World Bank, the theory of social capital helps to explain the social dimensions of why some individuals and groups are more successful in gaining the assets to effectively participate in markets and are also less vulnerable to market fluctuations and other unforeseen events, such as ill-health. As a consequence, the institution now funds programs designed to build up the social capital of the poor.

Second, to combat voicelessness, the Bank suggests that it needs to 'empower the poor'. It presents **empowerment** as a process through which the poor are mobilized to assist in generating reforms that reduce constraints on their economic activities and upward mobility. Corruption, such as officials demanding bribes in return for letting people sell their goods, is seen as blocking market access. A similar example is unaccountable officials frustrating the growth of market activity by failing to provide poor people with the physical (roads, electricity) or social (health, education) infrastructure necessary for market activities. The solution, according to the Bank, is to empower poor people by giving them voice: first, by promoting democracy and the rule of law; second, by promoting education; and third, through technical assistance to civil society groups in forming 'pro-poor coalitions' that can enforce good governance.

In many respects, however, this is a very limited notion of 'empowerment', one that is con-strained by its ultimate goal: facilitating markets. Forms of empowerment that are not seen as market-facilitating—such as the creation of trade unions or movements aimed at the redistribution of wealth within society—are given short shrift within the World Bank's framework despite the important role they played in poverty alleviation in some Western countries. Most important for the critics, the Bank refuses to acknowledge that in some cases, participation in markets can also perpetuate or even deepen poverty. For example, jobs in the global textile industry are often characterized by extremely low wages, no job security, and repressive working conditions.

CONCLUSION: TOWARDS REFORM OR IRRELEVANCE?

More than six decades have passed since the creation of the IMF and the World Bank. Despite the constant evolution of their roles, they have not been able to shake controversy and debate. At present, their very relevance is being questioned. With ever-larger flows of private investment circulating within the global capitalist economy, it has been suggested that the need for the World Bank is minimal and that it should be limited only to aiding the poorest countries. Analysts have questioned why the Bank still makes loans to middle-income countries such as China and India, which have seen no shortage of private investment over the past decade. Moreover, the recent scandal over its president Paul Wolfowitz, who resigned amid claims that he had broken internal regulations by negotiating a lucrative transfer for his partner, further weakened the institution's prestige and its legitimacy in preaching 'good governance'.

Similarly, with the IMF widely criticized for mishandling the East Asian crisis, countries have been increasingly unwilling to draw on its resources. In 2007, the Fund had few active loans of any significance, and many countries have built up large foreign reserves to use should another financial crisis break out. In this context, Dominique Strauss-Kahn, the new managing director of the IMF, suggested that the institution could no longer act as the 'gendarme' of the global economy and must reform itself to restore its relevance and legitimacy. In particular, he claimed, it needed to become more responsive to the needs of poorer countries. Whether this will happen depends greatly on the outcome of negotiations among shareholders regarding the reform of the institution's governance structure and voting rights. Ultimately, however, only the outbreak of a new and severe bout of economic crisis could create the conditions under which the IMF would be able to reassert its global power.

QUESTIONS FOR DISCUSSION

1. Do you agree or disagree that the power that the IMF and World Bank exercise over many developing countries is a positive force for ensuring good policies?

2. Have the reforms that the World Bank introduced to its policy prescription since the 1990s solved the problems identified in structural adjustment?

3. Are the IMF and World Bank still relevant in today's global capitalist society?

FURTHER READING

The World Bank publishes the *World Development Report* on an annual basis. This report is the Bank's flagship publication, indicating what it considers to be the best-practice policy prescription on a wide range of development issues. All issues, past and present, can be accessed freely online at http://econ.worldbank.org/wdr.

For a general history of the IMF, refer to Harold James's *International Monetary Cooperation since Bretton Woods* (Washington: IMF; New York: Oxford University Press, 1996).

The semi-official history of the World Bank—*The World Bank: Its First Half Century*, written by John Lewis, Richard Webb, and Devesh Kapur—has been published in two volumes by the Brookings Institution (1997).

For critical discussion, see a probing set of articles that challenge the new directions taken by the World Bank over the past decade: David Moore, ed. 2007. *The World Bank: Development, Poverty, Hegemony*. Scottsville, South Africa: University of KwaZulu-Natal Press. Another excellent discussion of the present and possible futures of the World Bank can be found in: James Pincus and Jeffrey Winters, eds. 2002. *Reinventing the World Bank*. Ithaca, NY: Cornell University Press. Joseph Stiglitz, former chief economist for the World Bank, has been unabashed in his criticism of the IMF. This heavily influential critique is most clearly articulated in his 2002 book *Globalization and Its Discontents* (New York: W.W. Norton).

INTERNET RESOURCES

The International Monetary Fund: http://www.imf.org.

The World Bank: http://www.worldbank.org.

The Bretton Woods Project (a networker, information-provider, media informant, and watchdog to scrutinize and influence the World Bank and the International Monetary Fund): http://www.brettonwoodsproject.org.

CHAPTER 10

THE UNITED NATIONS AND MULTILATERAL ACTORS IN DEVELOPMENT

DAVID SOGGE

LEARNING OBJECTIVES

- To identify some of the most important multilateral organizations beyond the financial and trade institutions introduced in previous chapters.
- To see these organizations amid geopolitics, where interest blocs and policy ideas clash, rather than as immaculately conceived products reflecting harmony and consensus.
- To be able to debate the significance and coherence of different kinds of multilateral actors.

As the world becomes one place, many problems are showing no respect for national borders. These problems range from killer viruses to regional wars. Fuelling them are inequalities born of maldevelopment and the inflammable politics of injustice and humiliation. To cope with such threats, and to promote their own national interests, governments are choosing to act collectively: they have drawn up joint conventions, signed mutual defence pacts, set up international agencies, and formed economic blocs. As a result, today there are close to 70 major **multilateral** organizations and more than 2,300 international agreements.

'Development' has long been a common cause for multilateral action. Rich-country governments have rallied together under the banner of foreign aid, where multilateralism means singing from the same policy song sheets and contributing to the same collection boxes. Multilateral aid accounts for about 35 to 40 per cent of all aid originating from Western governments. Multilateral agencies design and transmit most of the policy formulas about how non-Western economies and governments should be run. Some observers claim that multilateral arrangements are intrinsically better than bilateral (one-to-one) arrangements. But others are less convinced. This chapter offers an overview of some of the main multilateral actors in development and the claims and counter-claims made about them.

Multilateralism refers to arrangements among three or more states, commonly for peaceful purposes over extended periods. Such arrangements can help governments improve their standing, influence, security, or economic advantage. In matters of international trade and investment, multilateral rules and means of enforcing them are well developed. Thanks to these rules, powerful players in global capitalism have gained and consolidated their advantages, including their means of influencing economic and political change in non-Western areas. So-called middle powers like Canada and the Netherlands usually favour multilateral approaches because they bring more benefits, at less cost and risk, than going it alone. Big powers like the United States, on the other hand, tend to pursue multilateralism 'à la carte', cooperating only when it suits them. In the twenty-first century, unilateral and bilateral approaches have become more common. Nevertheless, mounting problems that transcend borders, and a growing sense of interdependence, continue to draw states towards creating treaties, consultation systems, and agencies on a multilateral basis. Many of the large multilateral institutions that emerged after the Second World War have mandates to help steer economic and social development.

This chapter discusses multilateral agencies as clustered according to the source of their oversight, as follows :

1. the **United Nations** system;
2. Western industrialized governments;
3. governments of non-Western countries.

We focus both on their structures and functions and on their evolution as ideological currents and power balances have shifted. This two-sided perspective helps to bring out the distinction between international organizations (the products) and international organization (the process) as a means of grasping their roles and significance.

THE UNITED NATIONS SYSTEM

The United Nations was conceived in the closing months of the Second World War. The triumphant great powers—Britain, the Soviet Union, and the United States—negotiated and eventually agreed on a design for a new world body, the United Nations Organisation. It would be open to all but would reflect the strategic preferences of the one country then possessing the overwhelming military, diplomatic, and financial means to bring about such a global project: the United States. The US may have called the shots, but it could not act alone. Other nations' cooperation and consent were needed if the US was to steer postwar reconstruction of Europe and Japan successfully and indeed to shape a new global order according to its interests.

During its first phase up to the late 1950s, the United Nations was the main launching pad for ideas and institutions, with ambitions to promote a peace and prosperity-seeking world. It was the 'mother church' of developmental optimism. At the same time, the UN was sometimes used as a geo-strategic instrument for a few countries. It provided legitimacy and foot soldiers in support

Figure 10.1   UN troops in Africa

Source: Chr. Michelsen Institute/Ingrid Samset

of Western and especially US foreign policy, such as for the war in Korea in the early 1950s and the upheaval in the Congo in the early 1960s. As home base and key funder for the United Nations system, the US still retains decisive influence over the organization. However, the UN did not always behave as an obedient servant to American global political and economic ambitions; indeed, it has often been a forum for non-Western countries to resist Western pressures.

The 1960s ushered in a second and more tumultuous phase for the UN. On the economic and social cooperation front, the postwar emphasis on reconstruction in Europe was overtaken by a new, longer-term challenge: development in non-Western countries, particularly those emerging from decades of colonial rule. At its founding in 1945, the United Nations comprised 51 states; 15 years later, new sovereign nations in Africa and Asia had pushed its membership to 99. The Soviet Union promoted and tried to influence national **self-determination**, but so did the United States. Yet decolonization did not occur in all of these nations according to the wishes of the Western 'First World' or the 'Second World' of the communist bloc. A 'Third World' emerged with the legacy of the colonial period, including a vibrant tradition of resistance. As UN membership grew and tilted the General Assembly's one-state-one-vote balance towards the non-Western world, new issues emerged on the UN's agenda and expanded the scope of its agencies' work.

By the 1990s, a third and far more troubled phase had begun, ushered in by the collapse of the Soviet Union and the active propagation of a particularly raw, intractable brand of capitalism. In a shift of strategy, Western nations supported sending UN 'blue helmet' troops to try to restore order where conflict was at its worst. But in general, Western countries systematically bypassed the UN, choosing instead to pursue their interests in bilateral and unilateral ways. By the early twenty-first century, Anglo-Saxon coalitions under US leadership had begun to flout some of the most fundamental rules of conduct in international politics, including UN rules about the use

of armed force. In terms of development ideas and action, the United Nations and its agencies had fallen to a fourth- or fifth-ranked status, well below the International Monetary Fund (IMF), the World Bank, the World Trade Organization (WTO), and related trade and investment institutions. Multilateral agreements, such as the agreement on the UN's Millennium Development Goals and the Kyoto Accord, as well as multilateral cooperation, such as the campaign against HIV/AIDS, continue to arise. But current prospects for multilateralism along democratic lines appear to be dim.

Origin and oversight of UN agencies

The twentieth century saw international organizations grow and diversify, especially after the Second World War. Those emerging under UN auspices are among the best known. The United Nations Children's Fund (UNICEF), for example, became a household word because of its inherently appealing role in meeting the basic needs of children and those caring for them.

Giving rise to these organizations were certain ideas or assumptions. One was a widespread optimism, in both capitalist and communist nations, about what modern science and management methods could accomplish. In the 1940s and 1950s, terms like 'modernization', 'planning', 'big push', and 'population control' entered the discourse. Guiding the creation of UN agencies was a view of development as essentially a set of technical problems. They could be solved if they received sufficient attention from professionals such as medical specialists, engineers, crop scientists, nutritionists, and economists skilled in cost-benefit analysis. Thus, development agencies grew according to a logic of technical functionalism. Each professional group's know-how would be best applied through distinct, large-scale organizations guided by technicians and managed from the top down. In that sense, development was something to be supplied to or induced among those deemed 'underdeveloped'. There was no question of imposing anything, since it was assumed that each nation participated in UN processes with full understanding and without coercion. Further legitimizing such arrangements were rules and aspirations for international cooperation and fellowship. These norms helped to insulate multilateral agencies from left/right ideologies and international politics. The idea was to allow 'neutral' professionals to define the problems and get on with the job of solving them.

According to the first article of its Charter, a main purpose of the United Nations is 'to achieve international co-operation in solving international problems of an economic, social, cultural, or humanitarian character, and in promoting and encouraging respect for human rights and for fundamental freedoms for all'. The Charter's ninth chapter describes the UN's powers regarding economic and social issues. It defined the specialized agencies and mandated creation of its Economic and Social Council (ECOSOC), today composed of representatives of 54 states elected for three-year terms by members of the General Assembly. As defined in the Charter, the ECOSOC might seem to be the world's supreme forum for development policy. But not long after its creation, it became clear than ECOSOC had little authority, even over the specialized agencies formally answerable to it.

The UN categorizes its organizations mainly according their lines of accountability and funding. The first main category comprises *specialized agencies*. These are distinct organizations, established by **intergovernmental** treaties. They have their own charters and governing bodies; they appoint their own chief executives. States may join or withdraw as they wish. Each has a relationship agreement with the UN, although not all of these agreements involve close, subordinate ties. The World Bank and the IMF are in a formal sense specialized UN agencies, but they operate in complete independence of the United Nations. Funds for most specialized agencies come from assessed, obligatory contributions from governments, based on each country's capacity to pay.[1]

The second main category is that of UN *organs,* also termed *programs* or *funds.* They are direct arms of the United Nations itself and are

thus answerable ultimately to the General Assembly. The UN's secretary-general has formal powers to appoint the chief executive. Unlike that of the specialized agencies, their funding is through voluntary contributions, chiefly from governments. They therefore face financial incentives to perform well, or at least to develop the means to advertise and 'sell' themselves effectively. A third category comprises agencies, such as for peacekeeping and humanitarian action, that operate under the direct supervision of the secretary-general's office. Major UN bodies carrying out development and humanitarian tasks are depicted in Figure 10.1.

The agencies

The UN's family tree has grown many branches over several generations. Its development-related agencies, programs, funds, commissions, and other institutions number several dozen. This section discusses only a limited number of the most prominent or representative of them, grouped according to their fields of responsibility.

Food, agriculture, and rural development

Established in 1945 following preparatory meetings in the US and Canada, the Food and Agriculture Organization (FAO) is a UN specialized agency. Its headquarters are in Rome, where an earlier world body, the International Institute of Agriculture, had been based. The FAO's chief mandate is to provide governments with information and policy advice on nutrition, food, agriculture, and rural development. Its work also includes running development projects and providing emergency assistance in response to droughts and insect plagues. Together with crop research institutes financed by the Rockefeller and Ford foundations, it has promoted controversial 'green revolution' technologies designed for farmers and agri-businesses with substantial land, skills, and financial assets (see chapter 18). In the 1980s, the FAO promoted notions of food security and drew attention to nutritional issues. But despite these kinds of initiatives in pursuit of fairer rural development, the

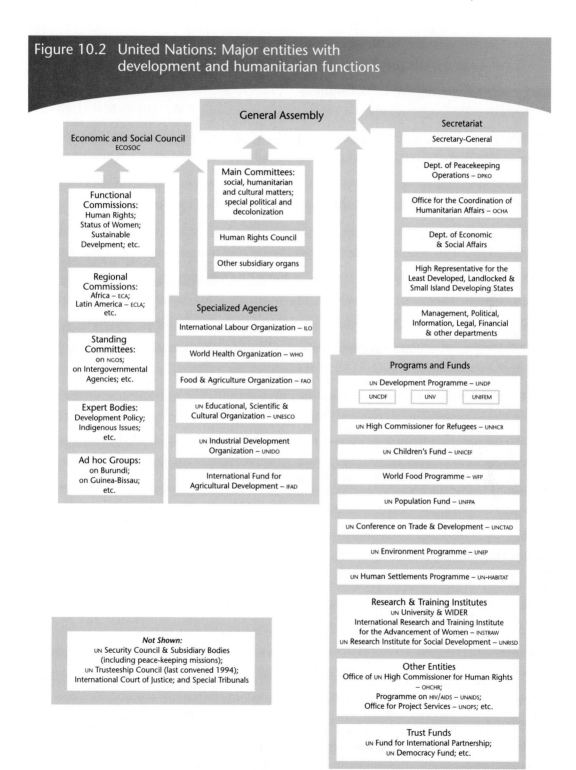

Figure 10.2   United Nations: Major entities with development and humanitarian functions

FAO continues to meet criticism. Donors and even former board members have expressed concerns about the organization's mediocre performance and management. Many **non-governmental organizations** (NGOs) have criticized the FAO's increasingly close accommodation of global agri-businesses, including its ties to trade associations represented in the International Agri-Food Network, a group set up in 1996 with the participation of the International Chamber of Commerce.

In 1961, the FAO set up the World Food Programme (WFP), a UN organ tasked initially with channelling Western food surpluses for use both in development efforts, such as for labour-intensive public works, and in humanitarian relief efforts. As both the WFP and FAO find themselves responding to complex emergencies and seeking support from the same donors, rivalry between them has grown.

Following the 1974 World Food Conference, a group of non-Western governments led by the Organization of Petroleum Exporting Countries (OPEC) established the International Fund for Agricultural Development (IFAD). Unlike the FAO, the IFAD operates as a small international bank for member governments. It channels most of its loans through other UN bodies to support rural development projects. A decline in OPEC funding by the early 1990s left IFAD dependent on Western donor governments, with whom relations have been rocky.

Health, children, and women

In 1948, ECOSOC created the World Health Organization (WHO), a UN specialized agency based in Geneva. It replaced an earlier intergovernmental body, the Office international d'hygiène publique (OIHP). Having defined health as more than merely the absence of disease or infirmity, WHO's constitution mandates promotion of all-round physical, mental, and social well-being. Its tasks range widely across health services and training, the prevention of endemic diseases and epidemics, as well as better nutrition, occupational health, and environmental conditions. Among its functions are the promotion of research

and knowledge-sharing and the setting of standards for health practices and biological and pharmaceutical products. By promoting inclusive, pro-poor approaches such as basic health care, essential drugs, and measures to deal with the causes of ill-health and premature death (including smoking and road accidents), it has been a progressive influence. But it has met criticism for its lack of transparency and responsiveness and for its readiness to accommodate big pharmaceutical corporations, whose lack of commitment to tackling the health problems of the poor continues to provoke intense dispute. The WHO has sometimes been willing to go along with 'Big Pharma's' efforts to improve their corporate image by making modest donations and, more seriously, to block low-income nations' production and use of low-cost generic drugs.

Set up in 1946 by the General Assembly to help feed, clothe, and vaccinate children in post-war Europe, the New York-based UN Children's Fund (UNICEF) today pursues a broad mandate focused on child survival and development, chiefly through community-based and national programs for preventive health, nutrition, and education. For this kind of work it was awarded the 1965 Nobel Peace Prize. UNICEF also promotes legislation for child protection consistent with the 1990 International Child Rights Convention. In the 1980s, it stood out among aid agencies for its dissent against orthodox macroeconomic austerity policies promoted by the IMF, the World Bank, and most other official donors. In the past, it was one of the few agencies to join activist NGOs in challenging corporations—for example, on the deadly effects of infant formula foods in low-income countries. UNICEF's data and analyses, much of them produced at its Innocenti Research Centre in Florence, Italy, focus on poverty, inequality, and powerlessness.

In 1946, ECOSOC established its Population Commission to draw attention to population issues. Then in 1966, the General Assembly set up a Trust Fund for Population Activities, which later became the UN Population Fund (UNFPA), with a mandate to disseminate information and promote policies for better access to family planning knowledge and services. In Cairo in 1994, the UN convened its third decennial world gathering, the International Conference on Population and Development. Here governments reached a more unified view of the linkages between population, development, and women's rights. Reinforced by this political consensus, and in the teeth of conservative religious and political opposition, the UNFPA has been able to advance thinking and action on reproductive rights and reproductive health, which have largely displaced the discourse of family planning or population control.

Helping to drive these achievements was the much larger global movement for women's rights and gender equity. That movement has gained momentum and effectiveness by helping to create and steer four kinds of UN institutions: commissions, conferences, agencies, and research/training bodies.

In 1946, building on earlier non-governmental and intergovernmental efforts, the UN's Commission on the Status of Women started work. Along with other organizations, it promoted a series of international conventions on such matters as women's rights in political participation, working life, human trafficking, marriage, and property. For governments adhering to these conventions, and even some that do not, these global policy commitments stand as points of reference for national legislation, legal systems, and budgets.

UN conferences related to women have helped to consolidate consensus and build global networks of persons and institutions. The World Conference of the International Women's Year, held in Mexico in 1975, was unprecedented in scope and importance. Among its results was the establishment of the United Nations Development Fund for Women (UNIFEM), a UN organ located within the UN Development Programme. As of 2007, its focus is on feminized poverty, violence against women, HIV/AIDS, and gender equality in democratic governance.

Extending and reinforcing the impact of these agencies and commissions are **knowledge-based** institutes. Among the most important is the International Research and Training Institute for the Advancement of Women (INSTRAW), a UN organ headquartered since 1983 in Santo Domingo, Dominican Republic. Its work involves the economic, political, and domestic challenges to women's rights as human rights.

Education, science, culture, and media

Established in 1946, the United Nations Educational, Scientific and Cultural Organization (UNESCO) is a specialized agency headquartered in Paris, where an intergovernmental forum to promote intellectual and cultural life had previously existed. UNESCO's mandate is to promote national systems of education, especially at basic levels, natural and social science education and knowledge-exchange, cultural policies and the preservation of cultural heritage, and communications technology and media policy. A large number of institutes, projects, and conferences operate under UNESCO auspices. Many of them follow equitable development paths, such as training and research in educational planning and lifelong learning systems.

In world conferences such as the one held in Jomtien, Thailand, in 1990, UNESCO has tried to forge intergovernmental consensus around education as a public good that should be available to all (see chapter 20). Such principles are not easy to promote. They collide with today's globalization axioms, which hold that scientific knowledge and education are not public goods but commodities in the marketplace.

Internal management failures have sometimes limited UNESCO's effectiveness. But external challenges have been more serious. In the 1970s, UNESCO's relations with Western donor governments turned sour because it sponsored an initiative by non-Western governments to eliminate biases against them in the world's media (see Box 10.1). The World Bank, which exercises major influence over education policy in low-income countries, has become a serious competitor.

Environment and shelter

Following citizen initiatives in Europe and North America, the 1972 United Nations Conference on

BOX 10.1   NEW WORLD INFORMATION AND COMMUNICATION ORDER (NWICO)

In the late 1970s, officials, journalists, and activists mainly from non-Western countries launched a debate about the dominance of Western media in the world and the lack of adequate access to unbiased information among people around the world. They challenged the way that Western media stereotyped non-Western societies and politics by simplifying, exaggerating, and generally biasing coverage while at the same time crowding out alternative, non-Western sources of news and analysis. Concentrated in the hands of a small number of Western corporations, ownership and control over news and information gathering, interpretation, and dissemination also drew criticism.

UNESCO was at the centre of this debate. In 1980, its International Commission for the Study of Communication Problems, chaired by the Nobel Peace laureate Seán MacBride, published its report *Many Voices, One World*. The commission made the case for what came to be called a New World Information and Communication Order—NWICO. In essence, this meant democratization of information production and consumption by enlarging, diversifying, and strengthening media, particularly in non-Western countries. To achieve such democratization, inequalities of access to communication infrastructure and technology would have to be redressed.

The United States, the UK, and a few other governments, strongly backed by mainstream media and right-wing think tanks in the West, argued that the NWICO was a stratagem to curb press freedoms and free markets. The US withdrew from UNESCO in 1984, rejoining only in 2003. Arguably, this opposition merely deflected the emergence of a new media order. The spread of the Internet and other communication technologies, and the rise of powerful media corporations in Asia, Latin America, and the Middle East, have furnished a response, though perhaps not wholly according what the UNESCO commission had envisioned in 1980.

(For an overview of the controversy, see Brown-Syed 1993.)

the Human Environment, held in Stockholm, Sweden, is seen as a major breakthrough in advancing global environmental issues on public and political agendas throughout the world. That UN initiative helped to spawn further citizen action, national legislation, and environment ministries. It led the General Assembly to create the United Nations Environment Programme (UNEP) in 1972. Headquartered in Nairobi, Kenya, it has regional and specialized offices around the world. UNEP's chief tasks are to monitor and assess global and regional environmental conditions, to facilitate negotiations of global environmental

agreements and supervise their enforcement, to raise awareness about environmental challenges, and to manage specific projects on issues ranging from climate change, weather early warning, and biodiversity. Some UNEP initiatives include anti-poverty dimensions, such as combating the pollution of urban water supplies (see chapter 17).

The United Nations Human Settlements Programme (UN-HABITAT), also headquartered in Nairobi, focuses on immediate development and poverty issues. Founded in 1978, it was an outcome of the first Conference on Human Settlements, known as Habitat I, convened by the

UN in 1976 in Vancouver, Canada. A second conference, Habitat II, in 1996 in Istanbul, Turkey, drew up a broad agenda for governments and others to tackle the massive and fast-growing problems of cities in low-income countries. That agenda poses an implicit challenge to market-led development in asserting that adequate shelter is a right. Working with member governments and specialized NGOs, UN-HABITAT promotes policies, laws, and planning methods around housing, land use, water and sanitation, security, and urban governance. It also promotes research and knowledge-sharing (see Box 10.2).

Employment and working life

The International Labour Organization (ILO), a UN specialized agency headquartered in Geneva, emerged in 1919 out of the settlement of the First World War. A product of civil society, it took shape after many decades of labour organizing and the advance of social democratic parties in industrialized countries. It is unique among world organizations in that representatives of civil society—namely, organized labour and employers' organizations—participate in its governance along with governments. The ILO's chief function historically has been to define and promote standards for working and social conditions, chiefly through intergovernmental conventions. In overwhelming numbers, national governments have ratified ILO conventions to advance four core human rights—freedom of association, collective bargaining and the elimination of forced labour, non-discrimination, and the elimination of child labour—as well as many other ILO conventions and recommendations.

Yet some of these universal statutes face opposition, not least from the United States. Their enforcement is therefore far from guaranteed. The ILO has tried to counter the harmful effects of globalization through studies, conferences, and thematic campaigns on 'decent work'. With few concrete results, it persists in trying to influence policies of the World Bank, IMF, and WTO. For most people in most countries, a decent job is the highest development priority. Yet the ILO is the only UN body regularly paying attention to job creation and decent livelihoods. Originally focused on formal sectors in industrialized countries, the ILO supports development and post-conflict rehabilitation efforts in non-Western places. Through training and technical assistance projects, such as labour-intensive public works, the ILO has contributed to thinking and action on

BOX 10.2   SLUMS: A UNITED NATIONS ALERT

The astonishing prevalence of slums is the chief theme of *The Challenge of Slums*, a historic and sombre report in October 2003 by the United National Human Settlements Programme (UN-HABITAT). This first truly global audit of urban poverty, which follows in the famous footsteps of Friedrich Engels, Henry Mayhew, Charles Booth, and Jacob Riis, culminates two centuries of scientific reconnaissance of slum life that began with James Whitelaw's 1805 *Survey of Poverty in Dublin*.

. . . If the reports of the Intergovernmental Panel on Climate Change represent an unprecedented scientific consensus on the dangers of global warming, then *The Challenge of Slums* sounds an equally authoritative warning about the worldwide catastrophe of urban poverty.

Mike Davis. 2006. *Planet of Slums*, pp. 20–1. London: Verso.

employment and labour relations in many non-Western settings.

Trade, investment, and corporate accountability

In 1964, at the initiative of African, Asian, and Latin American governments concerned about their disadvantaged status in the world economic system, the General Assembly created the UN Conference on Trade and Development (UNCTAD), with headquarters in Geneva. For nearly 30 years, UNCTAD tried to forge new policies in international trade, serve as a forum for negotiating trade agreements, and steer UN development thinking. Its campaign for a fairer world trade system was heavily influenced by concepts of dependency (see chapters 3 and 15) and Keynesian social democracy as articulated by its first secretary-general, the Argentine economist Raúl Prebisch (1901–86). The Group of 77 (see the third section of this chapter) had internal differences but were united in the view that no single development path was best. They used UNCTAD to try to preserve what little economic sovereignty they had and to gain occasional trade concessions that would favour non-Western exporters, such as a 1970 agreement on a 'generalized system of preferences'.

Rich countries generally disliked UNCTAD because they saw it as a forum for promoting new ideas and negotiations favouring non-Western countries. Their strategy was to deny its legitimacy and insist on the primacy of the Bretton Woods Institutions and the General Agreement on Tariffs and Trade (GATT) negotiations, which were not under UN auspices (see chapter 9). By the early 1990s, after a decade of concerted effort by the US under Ronald Reagan and the UK under Margaret Thatcher, the West finally forced a change. At the eighth conference in 1992, the rich countries decisively sidelined UNCTAD as a forum for negotiating trade rules. It was obliged to shift its attention from the global stage, where it had campaigned for systemic change, to domestic arenas, where each government was expected to 'reform' its economy along neo-liberal lines. This meant privatizing public assets, lowering taxes on

external trade and investment, and radically reducing control over inward and especially outward flows of capital. Attention to domestic markets could wait; the task was to orient national economies in an outward direction. UNCTAD's role became one of helping non-Western countries to integrate themselves into the new world economic system, not of bargaining for better deals in that system.

Today, UNCTAD's work comprises policy formulation, mainly through its intergovernmental conferences every four years; research and analysis, including the compilation of statistics on trade and investment; and technical assistance to governments on their trade and investment policies. It promotes private foreign investment through such programs as the Investment Deliverables Initiatives, a joint venture with the International Chamber of Commerce, and the Geneva-based International Trade Centre, a joint venture with the WTO chiefly serving exporting companies. In the UN system, UNCTAD has particular roles regarding the so-called least developed countries (LDCs). It runs programs to speed their repayment of their international debts, to develop small-scale enterprise, and to attract foreign investment.

In 1973, ECOSOC set up the UN Commission on Transnational Corporations and a research program managed by a New York–based Centre on Transnational Corporations (UNCTC). The centre gathered data, commissioned studies, held workshops, and prepared a draft code of conduct for **transnational corporations**—a code that Western business interests fought and UN members never ratified. In 1994, following concerted pressure by business lobbies, the UN abolished the UNCTC and placed its residual responsibilities under UNCTAD's Commission on Investment, Technology and Enterprise Development—whose role is not that of a watchdog but mainly that of a *promoter* of global corporations (see chapter 11).

Humanitarian and peacekeeping action

The United Nations was confronted with humanitarian emergencies from an early date. The forced expatriation of people from Palestine in 1948 led the UN to set up its Relief and Works Agency for Palestine Refugees in the Near East (UNRWA); 50 years later, it is still a vital UN program. In 1950, the General Assembly created the office of the High Commissioner for Refugees (UNHCR) to co-ordinate action and raise money to help refugees; in the early Cold War years, this meant people seeking asylum from communist eastern Europe. In 1967, the UN broadened the UNHCR's mandate to include future as well as past refugee flows and to cover the entire world. These measures effec-tively shifted its focus to non-Western settings.

Complex political emergencies, many of them arising from Cold War conflicts, have produced enormous human suffering, and the UN has established multilateral means to co-ordinate its response. Today, this effort is centred

in the Office for the Coordination of Humanitarian Affairs (OCHA), headquartered in New York. Its director has the status of a UN under-secretary-general. OCHA's main tasks are needs assessment, fundraising from govern-ments, humanitarian policy development, and field co-ordination involving UN agencies, Red Cross organizations, and NGOs. It supports a number of specialized organizations, including a news network, IRIN, set up in 1995 in recogni-tion of the power of media to mobilize political and financial backing for humanitarian causes.

The UN's humanitarian response is often linked with its conflict intervention efforts (60 were undertaken between 1945 and 2007). The UN Department of Peacekeeping Operations (DPKO), headquartered in New York, has become

Figure 10.3   UNHCR engages in a repatriation operation for displaced refugees

Source: Chr. Michelsen Institute/Jean-Christophe Goussand

a significant actor in attempts to create pre-conditions for reconstruction and development in politically fragile countries. With increasing frequency since the end of the Cold War, troops under United Nations auspices have been placed in zones of conflict. As of 2007, some 73,000 'blue helmets' and many thousands of police and civilian staff were on active duty in 18 countries; only the United States places more military personnel abroad. Yet in 2005, UN peacekeeping accounted for only about 0.5 per cent of total military spending across the globe.

Among the immediate causes of setbacks to economic, social, and political progress in low-income countries, armed conflicts have been the most devastating. Yet academic and civil society groups seeking to reduce the causes of conflict through equitable development and political compromise have expressed unease about the 'securitization' or 'militarization' of international responses to crises—and decisions to deploy UN blue helmets is a major example of that trend (see chapter 21).

Steering action, influencing thinking

In 1965, the General Assembly established the United Nations Development Programme (UNDP) under ECOSOC. Unlike other UN bodies, it has no specific mandate or formal charter. Yet it has high standing in the UN system; its chief executive officer, the administrator, ranks third after the secretary-general and deputy secretary-general. Set up originally to co-ordinate aid efforts, the UNDP has assumed strategic positions high on aid chains as a promoter of policy. Today, it describes itself as a network and advocacy organization for development.

Headquartered in New York, the UNDP has liaison offices in Geneva, Brussels, Copenhagen, Tokyo, and Washington. In non-Western countries where it operates, its resident representative usually serves as resident co-ordinator for the entire United Nations system. As of 2007, the UNDP operated in 166 countries, giving it more extensive field presence than the World Bank. Yet with an annual budget of about US $1 billion, the UNDP in financial terms is little more than one-twentieth the size of the World Bank, which in 2006 lent about US $19 billion and spent US $1.5 billion merely on its operating expenses. Because it is answerable to the UN General Assembly and to recipient governments (for example, through in-country 'roundtables'), the UNDP should be among the most accountable and responsive agencies in the aid and development industry. Yet its dependence on annual voluntary contributions from rich donor countries limits its responsiveness to recipients.

As of 2007, the UNDP was focusing efforts on five main issues:

- governance, with emphasis on participation and accountability;
- poverty reduction, as oriented by the Millennium Development Goals;
- crisis prevention and recovery;
- combating environmental degradation and promoting clean energy for the poor;
- preventing HIV/AIDS and reducing its impact.

In all five issue areas, the UNDP emphasizes human rights and women's empowerment. UN agencies under UNDP co-ordination follow a prescribed planning cycle, beginning with a country-level assessment and leading to a UN Development Assistance Framework (UNDAF) and a UNDP country program and action plan. Such plans may be technically competent and formulated through consultative processes. But their usefulness can be limited by adherence to a view that poverty and governance problems are mainly domestic matters to be resolved by authorities within a given national territory. Yet the origins of, and likely solutions to, development problems will not be found at the level of the national territory. Rather, they stem from *global* flows of money, information, people, and weapons and other commodities. Thus, a severe constraint on this new UN approach, or any development and aid framework and plan confined to the country level, is that it will neglect the spaces where various flows take place, with decisive consequences.

Several development agencies operate under the UNDP. Among them are the UN Capital

Development Fund (UNCDF), which has developed a model in which citizens co-determine where and how aid should be used in local development; the UN Volunteers (UNV), which as of 2007 supported about 5,600 persons working in development or rehabilitation projects, most of them linked with UN agencies; and the Special Unit for Technical Cooperation among Developing Countries (SU/TCDC), a small unit that originated in the 1970s at the initiative of non-Western governments seeking more 'South–South' interchange.

Together with the ILO, UNICEF, and UNCTAD, the UNDP has allowed alternative views to be voiced in policy debates dominated by organizations based in Washington. Since its first issue in 1990, the UNDP's *Human Development Report* has put forward a social democratic view of development. Together with its country-by-country reports, the publication has created intellectual competition for the World Bank's *World Development Report*, which despite occasional editorial flip-flops (for example, on poverty and on the role of the state in development), follows an orthodox neo-liberal line.

Other units of the United Nations system also engage in policy research, thus helping to draw attention to issues and shape understandings of problems that aid agencies purport to address. Europe is home to two of the more productive and innovative centres. Founded in 1963, the Geneva-based UN Research Institute for Social Development (UNRISD) generates multi-disciplinary research, informed by both mainstream and unorthodox perspectives, on issues of governance, market forces, social policy, and other development topics. In 1984, the UN University (jointly held by the UN and UNESCO) set up the World Institute for Development Economics Research (WIDER) in Helsinki, Finland. It manages research, trains young scholars, and holds seminars on issues of political economy.

During the late 1940s and the 1950s, the UN set up economic commissions in most world regions. They are: the United Nations Economic Commission for Europe (UNECE), based in Geneva; the Economic Commission for Latin America and the Caribbean (ECLAC) in Santiago, Chile; the Economic and Social Commission for Asia and the Pacific (ESCAP) in Bangkok, Thailand; the Economic Commission for Africa (ECA) in Addis Ababa, Ethiopia; and the Economic and Social Commission for Western Asia (ESCWA), in Beirut, Lebanon. Under active leadership in the 1950s, the commission for Latin America provided non-Western governments with intellectual ammunition in wars of ideas, especially about world trade and investment. ECLAC is still active and influential today, but the other regional commissions have low profiles. They gather statistics, monitor (macro) economic trends, serve as forums for setting standards and developing trade arrangements, and in many cases since the 1990s, promote wider roles for private enterprise.

Trends and prospects for UN agencies

The foregoing shapshots of the main UN actors involved in development and emergency assistance have highlighted some of their accomplishments. The UN was established in the name of peace, but it was also meant to afford space for vigorous debate. As Winston Churchill put it in 1954, 'Talking jaw-jaw is always better than war-war.' In that spirit, the UN has seen numerous concerted attempts, mainly by non-Western governments, to resist domination and advocate alternatives. In the 1960s and 1970s in particular, they tried to use the UN as a place where different ideas about development could compete and where issues of fairness and unequal power could gain a place on world agendas. In most instances, those efforts were deflected if not stopped dead in their tracks. Powerful interests based in Western countries have insisted that 'there is no alternative' to neo-liberal orthodoxies, reflecting the 'global intellectual hegemony' of our times (Gosovic 2000). Increasingly harnessed to one school of thought, the UN has seen one of its fundamental mandates—enabling contestation and debate about development—set aside. Nevertheless, for a few development questions, the UN has served as a platform and vehicle for **emancipatory ideas**. It has helped to propel improvements in the status of women and their access to reproductive health and reproductive rights. It has helped move such issues as the environment and slums higher on national and world agendas. Where these initiatives have seen real success (and such cases are as yet few), the active presence of forceful social movements has been a major factor.

UN agencies have many shortcomings: technocratic ways of defining problems and solutions, non-transparency, high overhead costs, and unproductive working cultures involving low staff morale. But such problems are by no means confined to UN agencies. Others in the aid and development industry also suffer from them. Further shortcomings stem from waste and duplication generated by the model of technical functionalism—agrarian/rural issues for the FAO, children's issues for UNICEF, and so on. The problem is that the lifeworlds of the people targeted for development interventions are not easily compartmentalized. Thus, the complexities that the agencies meet force them to add new fields of practice and new objectives, leading to 'mission creep'. For example, as many as 20 UN agencies are concerned with water in one way or another. With this kind of deficiency in mind, UN reform on the development front emphasizes a 'One UN' approach, with a single framework for each country. One example of the move towards 'joined up' management was the creation in 1997 of the UN Development Group, a consultative body of more than 25 UN agencies, funds, and commissions. As of 2006, it was pursuing priorities under the slogans 'One Programme/ Framework', 'One Leader', 'One Team'.

This approach may indeed streamline aid delivery and allow the UN to better satisfy the public authorities who receive aid and those who donate the money for it. Donors prefer prompt, streamlined spending. If they cannot 'move the money', they may face political and career problems. But will the approach address other sources of difficulty? At a deeper level, the effectiveness of UN agencies depends on who pays and thus on who makes the rules and sets the agenda. Even though the UN's one-country-one-vote system

favours poor countries because of their numbers, the power of money is decisive. Research has shown that the United States successfully uses its foreign aid, or the threat of withdrawing it, to get its way in the United Nations (Kuziemko and Werker 2006). Top-level UN jobs are held in disproportionate numbers by Americans and citizens of other big powers. In short, there is little room for 'good governance' and transparency at the United Nations unless some means are found to insulate members from the coercive power of rich nations like the United States.

Another challenge to the integrity and transparency of the United Nations, and to the development purposes it seeks to pursue, is the rising influence of large Western corporations. That influence has led to a wholesale re-orientation of UNCTAD and the weakening of other UN agencies.

A formal demonstration of this trend is the UN's 'Global Compact'. In 1999, at a gathering of world elites, the Global Economic Forum in Davos, Switzerland, the UN secretary-general invited corporations to acquire valuable goodwill and market opportunities with UN agencies. To do so, they were asked to endorse guidelines on corporate behaviour—an offer they found easy to accept, since the guidelines were not binding and involved no independent monitoring. The 'partnerships' between UN agencies and businesses take various forms. In specific projects, McDonalds and Microsoft have teamed up with UNESCO, Novartis with the WHO, Citigroup and ChevronTexaco with the UNDP, and so forth. The Global Compact has sponsored conferences and publications with titles like *Fighting Poverty: A Business Opportunity*. The strategy has required the UN to add new staff and entire departments to manage it, such as the UNDP Division for Business Partnerships. Engagements between UN agencies and big business are no longer merely experimental and short-lived but becoming structural and long-term. Recent assessments of Global Compact outcomes suggest that many corporations have gained public standing (they have been 'bluewashed') through their association with UN agencies; some UN agencies have gained a few more resources. Yet there have been serious net losses, chiefly in UN capacities to think and act critically on fundamental issues of development and global governance (Utting and Zammit 2006; Gasser 2007).

Well before their alliances with corporations, most UN agencies had developed ties with non-governmental organizations, both international and domestic. In 1946, the first year of its existence, ECOSOC granted 'consultative status' to 41 NGOs; today the number of NGOs with such status is close to 3,000. For development projects and humanitarian action, UN agencies routinely recruit NGOs to manage projects and deliver humanitarian aid on their behalf. These arrangements amount to simple subcontracting, but both parties prefer the term 'partnerships'. Under a large formal system it calls Partnership in Action, the UNHCR today has contracts with about 800 NGOs. Indeed, a former UNHCR director referred to NGOs as 'our right arm'.

MULTILATERAL AGENCIES OF WESTERN GOVERNMENTS

Some multilateral arrangements with great influence over development are clubs open only to rich countries. Apart from wealth, membership criteria include locale and adherence to certain economic and political norms and preferences. Because they commonly express the collective will of rich-country interest blocs—economic, military, geo-strategic—these intergovernmental agencies routinely shape the ways that interventions in non-Western places are talked about, planned, and carried out.

Development policy

Established in 1961 to succeed a European steering committee for American Marshall Plan postwar reconstruction aid, the Organisation for Economic Co-operation and Development (OECD) is today a club of 30 rich-country governments. Guided from the outset by US-led designs for economic globalization, it defines agendas and promotes consensus on macroeconomics, trade, investment, taxation, and public service reform along lines of 'new public management'—in short, almost everything of concern to member governments except military and security issues. The OECD's influence works through its vast linkages with governments and private sector actors. It applies a sophisticated communication strategy to make its findings virtually gospel among business and political classes. Every year an estimated 40,000 senior officials attend policy workshops and large formal gatherings at its Paris headquarters. Member nations together assign to the OECD almost 400 residential delegates, most with ambassadorial rank. Rivalled only by the World Bank as an official think tank, the OECD produces large streams of analytical reports, data, technical standards, and policy proposals. Some of this work takes place through open, public processes, but many policies are prepared behind closed doors.

The OECD makes no loans, grants, or other direct interventions. Its importance for development is in the realm of concepts, knowledge, and discourse. Since 1961, its Development Assistance Committee (DAC) has served as a platform to legitimate basic terms, norms, and 'talk' in the aid industry. Topics covered range from such things as aid 'tying' to aid evaluation. Under American leadership for most of its existence, the DAC was an active promoter of **Washington Consensus** policies (see chapter 8). However, since the late 1990s, the OECD has, together with the rest of the aid and development industry, emphasized poverty reduction.

European organizations

The European Commission (EC) is the executive branch of the European Union, which today consists of 27 western and eastern European countries. Only Norway, Switzerland, and most nations of the former Yugoslavia are not members. The EC headquarters is in Brussels, Belgium. In the 1980s, the EC emerged as the world's largest single multilateral aid donor, accounting for about one-third of all multilateral aid spending and for about 10 to 12 per cent of total world official aid.

As with the US and other donors, however, EC aid spending figures are often padded to demonstrate generosity levels pledged at summit meetings.

The EC's Directorate General for Development (DG Dev) formulates European policies towards low-income countries—in particular, Europe's ex-colonies, formally referred to as the ACP (Africa-Caribbean-Pacific) countries—regarding trade, macroeconomics, regional integration, food security, rural development, and so forth. Some of the EC aid budget is approved by the European Parliament. However, Europe's largest funding pool for Africa, the European Development Fund (EDF), falls outside the EC budget and is thus less transparent for citizens and their elected representatives. Also active is the European Community Humanitarian Aid Department (ECHO), accounting for about 30 per cent of world humanitarian spending. In the period 1999 to 2001, the EC overhauled its aid system but with only mixed success. Not one but two EC commissioners were assigned foreign aid portfolios. The creation of a new agency for implementation, the EuropeAid Co-operation Office (AIDCO), remedied the resulting incoherence only partially, and DG Dev was weakened.

In principle, multilateral aid like that of the EC should be able to benefit from economies of scale, as well as lowered overhead and procurement costs, and therefore should be more efficient than bilateral aid. Yet EC aid continues to be plagued by poor management, infighting over bureaucratic turf, above-average overhead costs, slow delivery, non-transparency, an overload of objectives, lack of priorities, and spending biases towards better-off countries in its near-abroad— that is, North Africa and southeast Europe (see Maxwell and Engel 2003). Even more serious are charges of incoherence. The EC has a much tighter hold over European commercial policy than over Europe's aid and foreign policies, which member states control. What the EC gives in aid is usually exceeded by what it takes through trade deals, natural resource extraction (fish from west African waters, for example), and capital flight to tax havens under the jurisdiction of EU member countries. However, such criticisms may apply just as much, if not more, to the US, Japan, and others. These kinds of problems underscore the critique that multilateralism helps to conceal old predatory relationships and re-invent them as neutral, market-based 'partnerships'.

In 1949, well before the European Union was formed, 10 European governments signed a treaty creating the Council of Europe (COE). Headquartered in Strasbourg, France, its mandate is to promote human rights, democracy, and the rule of law throughout Europe. Its founding strategic purpose was socio-political cohesion and thus stability at a time of vulnerability to political and trade union movements seeking greater social justice. Today, the COE has 47 members, including such low-income countries as Armenia and Macedonia, formerly in the Soviet sphere of influence. Canada is among several countries with COE observer status.

By pioneering intergovernmental conventions on human rights in 1950 and socio-economic rights in 1961, the COE has set important standards for domestic legislation to combat discrimination and social exclusion. Under COE auspices in 1959, the European Court of Human Rights was set up to enforce obligations inherent in the European Convention for the Protection of Human Rights and Fundamental Freedoms. Signed in Rome in 1950, the convention was the first international legal instrument safeguarding human rights. The COE's work is particularly relevant for anti-poverty policy in countries on Europe's eastern periphery. Its research, workshops, and conferences regularly draw attention to gaps between formal rights (enshrined in the European Social Charter) and actual performance.

Founded in 1956 and based in Paris, the COE Development Bank (CEB) is Europe's oldest multilateral financial institution and the only one with a mandate to promote social solidarity. Its loans go to public sector bodies for purposes of social integration (housing, rehabilitation of poverty-hit zones), environmental protection, and human services in health and education.

The COE is mandated to follow fundamental societal principles rather than conventional 'development' objectives. Perhaps for that reason it is often overlooked among multilateral organizations. Yet its mandates and activities pre-dated by 40 years the themes of human rights, **social cohesion**, and democracy that are the talk of today's multilateral development organizations.

The Organization for Security and Co-operation in Europe (OSCE) emerged in 1973 at a moment of détente in the Cold War as a means of lowering tensions between the West and the communist East bloc. When it was founded, dictators still ruled Portugal and Spain. Hence, neither bloc could crow loudly about human rights and democracy. However, in 1975, the US, west European states, and the Soviet Union with its east European allies signed the Helsinki Accords, a nonbinding agreement basically acknowledging the geopolitical status quo in Europe. These accords mention human rights, and the OSCE was tasked with monitoring observance of them, among other things. Headquartered in Vienna, Austria, the organization today includes all countries of the former Soviet Union, western Europe, the United States, and Canada. With improved politico-military stability as a main objective, the OSCE promotes arms control, police and military reform, and border management. It has also assumed tasks on 'developmental' terrains. Drawing on broader concepts of security, these tasks include governance (such as election monitoring), minority rights and reduction of ethnic conflict, promotion of media diversity, and curbing the small arms trade and human trafficking.

Multilateral 'sphere of influence' organizations

After recognizing the formal sovereignty of states in Africa, Asia, and Latin America, Western powers have sought to maintain ties with their former colonies or dependencies. To this end, they set up multilateral organizations with active secretariats mandated to promote policy dialogue, cultural ties, and even development efforts. The major Western **sphere of influence** bodies include the Organization of American States, the Organisation internationale de la Francophonie, and the Commonwealth of Nations.

The Organization of American States (OAS) originated from US efforts in the 1880s to advance its commercial interests in Latin America. As the Cold War began, amid fears of left-leaning movements in civil society, the US began aligning its security and intelligence-gathering policies with its development and aid policies. In 1948, 20 Latin American governments and the United States signed the charter of the OAS; in later decades, 13 Caribbean countries and Canada also joined. Cuba was expelled in 1962. Headquartered in Washington, the OAS cultivates consensus among governmental and business elites in the Western hemisphere on issues of development, women's status, drug trafficking, and human rights. It does so by way of special committees and intergovernmental conferences. Following on its success in creating the highly contested North American Free Trade Agreement (NAFTA) with Canada and Mexico, the United States has today enlisted the OAS to help create a Free Trade Area of the Americas (FTAA). As of 2007, however, this and other US-driven initiatives appear to be losing ground to multilateral arrangements driven by Latin American governments, some of which are noted later in this chapter.

The Organisation internationale de la Francophonie (OIF) comprises 55 member states in which French culture and the French language play at least some role in national identity. Canada is a member, and Quebec has the status of 'participating government'. Founded in 1970 as the Agence de coopération culturelle et technique, la Francophonie is headquartered in Paris, with branch offices in Gabon, Togo, and Vietnam. Promotion of the French language and cultural diversity is its chief purpose. As with comparable bodies, it also supports activities to foster respect for human rights and democracy, including encouragement for civil society organizations, and to improve education, media, information technology, the environment, and the economy—

in particular, the integration of member nations in the world economy. France's decline as an imperial power, and weaknesses and divisions among most members of the club, have cumulatively weakened la Francophonie, despite some efforts by Canada to shore it up.

The Commonwealth of Nations, known before 1950 as the British Commonwealth, consists of 53 countries, all but one of them (Mozambique) ex-colonies, including Canada. A number of countries eligible for membership, mainly Middle Eastern and African countries such as Sudan, have declined to join. With a secretariat in London since 1965, the Commonwealth organizes large and small gatherings of public officials and business people for a variety of political, cultural, and commercial purposes. In its early decades, the Commonwealth afforded member countries with trade preferences and other privileges. Today, they have been eclipsed by larger multilateral and bilateral arrangements. The Commonwealth has tried to promote consensus on governance, seen chiefly in conference declarations and the occasional expulsion of member states. Its Commonwealth Foundation facilitates interchange among and support to professional associations and non-governmental organizations. In 1997, the Commonwealth Business Council was set up to promote trade, investment, corporate social responsibility, and public–private partnerships.

MULTILATERAL ORGANIZATIONS ANCHORED IN NON-WESTERN GOVERNMENTS

In non-Western countries, the triumph of nationalist parties and armies over the colonial powers created optimism about collective action. After the Second World War, there sprang up among governments of the South a number of multilateral arrangements independent of the rich North. These arrangements included regional political alliances (for example, the League of Arab States, 1945) and trading arrangements (for example, the East African Community from 1967 to 1977, then revived in 1999). Created on crests of enthusiasm, many of these associations later became dormant or died altogether, the victims of internal difficulties or external opposition.

Lobbying blocs

A 1955 conference in Bandung, Indonesia, was the first multilateral forum in which leaders of the South could voice their collective demands for an end to colonialism. They also denounced their countries' adverse integration in the world economic system—something they saw as a main factor keeping their countries poor. Six years later, the same group, now reinforced by newly independent African countries, set up the Non-Aligned Movement (NAM), an intergovernmental association without a charter or secretariat. Today, the NAM comprises 118 countries, 61 per cent of all UN members. It seeks to uphold 'the right of independent judgement, the struggle against imperialism and neo-colonialism, and the use of moderation in relations with all big powers'. Despite the ending of the Cold War and resulting loss of its bipolar geopolitical compass, the NAM convenes heads of state meetings every three years and maintains working groups that analyze world politics.

Concerned about forming a coherent front in negotiations with rich countries on trade issues, most of the non-Western countries attending the 1964 UNCTAD conference formed the Group of 77 (G-77). Today enlarged to 133 members including China, the G-77 continues as an informal caucus at the UN. Its representatives gather at each year's UN General Assembly meeting and sometimes at UNCTAD assemblies. Its chief accomplishment was to have placed the demand for the New International Economic Order (NIEO) on the world's agenda. Led by Iran, Venezuela, Mexico, and Algeria (countries whose income was rising, thanks to sharp increases in world oil prices in 1973), the G-77 pursued three main objectives: faster economic growth, greater integration in the world trading system, and more foreign aid. These were hardly radical or new claims; indeed, they posed little threat to the global status quo. Yet Western powers rejected them and in many cases pursued policies, such as reduced supervision of transnational corporations, that were utterly contrary to what Southern governments were demanding. Northern powers have reduced the clout of G-77 and NAM by shifting most North–South economic negotiations to the World Trade Organization (see chapter 15), thus sidelining the UNCTAD and other UN forums.

The largest single sub-group in the NAM and the G-77 is the Organization of the Islamic Conference (OIC). Founded in 1969 at Rabat and headquartered in Saudi Arabia, it consists today of 56 governments. Financed largely through oil revenues, it promotes solidarity and cooperation among Islamic states. Its work is both cultural (protection of holy sites, broadcasting) and developmental (the Islamic Development Bank and various institutes of education and research).

To provide members with analyses of the deteriorating situation facing most of its members, the NAM summit of 1986 set up a commission under leadership of Tanzanian president Julius Nyerere. Following publication of its 1990 report, *The Challenge to the South*, the NAM put the commission's secretariat, the South Centre, on a permanent footing as a think tank. Despite internal difficulties, it has emerged today as an important source of critical analyses on global governance, trade, and South–South cooperation.

While most of the older Third World blocs have suffered marginalization and decline, there are emerging new groupings among Southern countries. Among them is the Group of 21, an informal alliance founded in 2003 at the WTO meetings in Cancun, Mexico. It is led by the strongest members of the Southern bloc: Brazil, Russia, India, China, and South Africa—collectively known as BRICS. At Cancun, these rising regional powers frustrated the negotiating stance of the rich-country bloc. The Group of 21 suggests a revival of the non-Western campaign for a New International Economic Order—something the rich countries hoped they would never see again.

Regional blocs

Governments in many parts of the world have sought to improve their economic prospects through economic pacts or *regional trading arrangements* (RTAS) with their neighbours. Sometimes termed developmental regionalism, this strategy has been gaining ground as an alternative to dominant neo-liberal strategies, emphasizing economic openness towards the rich countries of the North—strategies that have exposed many to predatory globalization.

Among Asian nations, there is a veritable 'noodle bowl' of RTAS of which the most important is the Association of Southeast Asian Nations (ASEAN). Founded in 1967 by the leaders of Indonesia, Malaysia, the Philippines, Singapore, and Thailand out of shared fear of communist advances in Vietnam, ASEAN has since admitted Vietnam along with Brunei, Burma, Cambodia, and Laos. Its regional trade promotion efforts began only in the 1990s but have not curbed trade with the rest of the world, contrary to the fears of business interests in Northern countries. However, in 2002, ASEAN signed a major pact with China—a move that may have far-reaching politico-economic consequences.

In Latin America, a major RTA is the Mercado Común del Sur (Mercosur), or Southern Common Market, founded in 1991 by Brazil, Argentina, Uruguay, and Paraguay and joined by Venezuela in 2006. Since 2004, steps have been taken towards something much more ambitious, a Unión de Naciones Suramericanas (UNASUR), or Union of South American Nations, an intergovernmental arrangement modelled on the European Union. As of 2007, its backers were planning to begin by merging Mercosur with its older counterpart, the Comunidad Andina, or Andean Community, composed of Bolivia, Colombia, Ecuador, and Peru. Thereafter, UNASUR would seek to lower barriers to trade and travel, to issue a common South American currency, and ultimately to set up a South American parliament.

Africa is home to a number of RTAS, many of them dormant. The forerunner to today's Southern

African Development Community (SADC) was established in 1980 by Angola, Botswana, Lesotho, Malawi, Mozambique, Swaziland, Tanzania, Zambia, and Zimbabwe—then all on the 'frontline' against an aggressive apartheid-ruled South Africa. SADC now consists of 14 governments, including that of South Africa. In its early years, SADC served as a vehicle to drive aid projects that reinforced southern Africa's outward economic orientation rather than its internal market. However, low purchasing power, huge differences in economic, political, and military power among states, and uneasy political relationships have set limits to real integration.

The impact of regional blocs on equitable development and responsive government has been modest at best. Trading arrangements may have contributed to faster growth, but such growth remains uneven, even polarized, as stronger economies tend to reap most benefits. Nevertheless, moves towards more active forms of regional multilateral action informed by principles of equity, as in Latin America, may well be creating genuine alternative pathways in development.

CONCLUSIONS

This chapter has noted the rise (and in many cases, the decline) of three categories of multilateral organizations. A red thread running through the stories of those in the UN community—and many of those anchored in Western states—is the role of a **hegemonic power**, the United States. Together with several other 'Anglo-Saxon' states,

it has usually managed to set development agendas and to determine whether or not the issues are to be managed multilaterally and, if so, within which multilateral forum. At the same time, the bloc of Western nations has successfully led others (though not without resistance) to enlist multilateral bodies in spreading a homogenized set of views about development and governance in non-Western places. Whereas the words 'equity', 'non-alignment', and 'self-determination' once inspired multilateralism, we now hear corporate capitalist terms like 'global competitiveness' and 'public–private partnerships'. Many multilateral bodies now reflect—and propagate—a new 'common sense' about development. Thus, global governance over development and the humanitarian response has been constrained. As a result, many UN and other multilateral institutions have lost legitimacy, especially in the eyes of many in the Global South.

However, as this chapter has noted and as other chapters explore in much greater depth, there are other emerging forms of multilateralism: alliances of states within regions and networks of social and political movements transcending national boundaries. Some of this 'bottom-up multilateralism' in global civil society has shown, as in the cases of women's rights and environmental sanity, important leverage for positive change. Whether and how much public action by citizens' groups can contribute to **emancipatory outcomes**—or to global backlash born of humiliation and anger—is central to today's unfolding drama of the world becoming one place.

QUESTIONS FOR DISCUSSION

1. Given grossly unequal distributions of power and wealth, how can multilateral initiatives produce more equitable development outcomes?

2. Why should some countries prefer to engage in multilateral arrangements 'à la carte' rather than accepting comprehensive ones?

3. How might multilateral arrangements among countries of a specific region, or among countries sharing cultural affinities, lead to positive development outcomes?

BOX 10.3   RETROSPECTIVE OPTIMISM

The twentieth century will be chiefly remembered . . . not as an age of political conflicts or technical inventions, but as an age in which human society dared to think of the welfare of the whole human race as a practical objective.

Arnold Toynbee, British historian

4. The historian Arnold Toynbee (see Box 10.3 above) wrote that the twentieth century would be remembered as an age when 'human society dared to think of the welfare of the whole human race'. In light of this chapter's contents, how valid is that observation ?

5. The political analyst Jens Martens (see Box 10.4 below) writes that world politics today faces a choice between elite multilateralism and a multilateralism of solidarity. What forces have created this choice? Which would you bet on in the long run and why?

6. The UN and its agencies have been criticized for serving unilateral political interests under the guise of multilateral politics. How valid are such criticisms?

BOX 10.4   MULTILATERALISM: WHICH WAY FORWARD?

International politics is at a crossroads. On the one hand, the path towards an elite multilateralism, which shifts decisions on global policy increasingly into exclusive clubs and political circles while excluding democratic control and participation; on the other, the path to a multilateralism of solidarity, which emphasises and strengthens the responsibility of democratically legitimate public institutions and complements this through a comprehensive involvement of civil society organisations and the well regulated interaction with the private sector. In the spirit of the UN Charter, one can only hope that over time, this model of a multilateralism of solidarity will prevail over the elite club model of global politics.

Jens Martens. 2007. *Multistakeholder Partnerships—Future Models of Multilateralism?*
Berlin: Friedrich Ebert Stiftung.
Dialogue on Globalization, Occasional Paper 29, p. 6.

FURTHER READING

Bøås, M., and D. McNeill. 2003. *Multilateral Institutions: A Critical Introduction*. London: Pluto Press.

Cox, R.W., ed. 1997. *The New Realism: Perspectives on Multilateralism and World Order*. London: Macmillan.

De Feyter, K. 2001. *World Development Law: Sharing Responsibility for Development*. Antwerp: Intersentia.

Gowan, P. 2003. 'US:UN'. *New Left Review* 24: 5–28.

Hildebrand, Robert. 1990. *Dumbarton Oaks: The origins of the UN and the Search for Postwar Security*. Chapel Hill: University of North Carolina Press.

Kennedy, P. 2007. *The Parliament of Man: The Past, Present, and Future of the United Nations*. New York: Vintage.

Rist, G. 2002. *The History of Development: From Western Origins to Global Faith*. Revised edn. London: Zed Books.

Schechter, M.G., ed. 1999. *Innovation in Multilateralism*. London: Macmillan.

Schlesinger, Stephen. 2003. *Act of Creation: The Founding of the United Nations*. Boulder, CO: Westview.

INTERNET RESOURCES

Note: Almost all of the multilateral organizations discussed in this chapter maintain websites. They can be easily found through Internet search engines.

Global Policy Forum (monitoring policy-making at the United Nations): http://www.globalpolicy.org.

One World Trust *Global Accountability Report*: http://www.oneworldtrust.org.

DFID's multilateral effectiveness framework (MEFF): http://www.dfid.gov.uk/news/files/meff-faq.asp.

Encyclopedia of the Nations, United Nations–related agencies: http://www.nationsencyclopedia.com/United-Nations-Related-Agencies/index.html.

World Campaign for In-Depth Reform of the System of International Institutions: http://www.reformcampaign.net.

World Economy and Development—In Brief: UN Reform: http://www.wdev.eu.

NOTES

1. The minimum contribution is 0.001 per cent of the UN's budget, an amount paid by 48 countries in 2006. Currently, the US pays about 22 per cent of the UN's budget. If assessments were based purely on each country's share of the world's Gross Domestic Product, the US would pay about 30 per cent and many poor countries less than the 0.001 per cent (CRS 2006, 2).

CHAPTER 11

MULTINATIONAL CORPORATIONS

PAUL ALEXANDER HASLAM

LEARNING OBJECTIVES

- To distinguish between different kinds of multinationals and their strategies.
- To identify the theoretical approaches that explicitly or implicitly underlie different accounts or analyses of multinational corporations.
- To understand the factors that affect how multinational corporations relate to host country governments.
- To identify the factors that determine whether a multinational's effects on a developing country are beneficial or not.

Multinational corporations are perhaps the most contentious, maligned, and misunderstood actors in international development. When thinking about multinationals, it is easy to come up with a list of companies and activities that have attracted negative media attention in the past: Nestlé's marketing of breast milk substitutes; Talisman Energy's oil project in conflict-ridden Sudan; Union Carbide and the Bhopal disaster; Exxon and the Exxon Valdez oil spill; Nike and sweatshop labour conditions. At the same time, we can point to major multinationals, often the same ones listed above, who act constructively to support local communities and economic development.

More than many other areas of development studies, multinationals tend to be polarizing, characterized as either heroes or scoundrels. This chapter aims to steer between these dichotomous positions in order to present a balanced picture of what motivates multinational corporations to invest abroad and their impact on developing societies. Although there is much disagreement about those effects, it cannot be disputed that as a result of their size, economic importance, role in trade, and global production chains, multinational corporations are drivers of globalization and important actors with real consequences in

the developing world. Multinationals are major players in many of the issue areas discussed elsewhere in this book.

WHAT IS A MULTINATIONAL CORPORATION?

A variety of terms are used to describe multinational corporations (MNCs), including **transnational corporations** (TNCs), **multinational enterprise** (MNE), and **foreign direct investment** (FDI). Overall, these terms can be and are used interchangeably. Differences between them stem principally from disciplinary and institutional divides and practices: MNC is the most widely used term, employed by political scientists, sociologists, and the media; TNC is the preferred terminology of the United Nations system; and MNE is used in international business studies. FDI is a catch-all phrase, often preferred by economists, which refers to investment that is made across borders. The word 'direct' in foreign direct investment indicates that the investment has a physical presence or corporate form (such as a branch plant) and differentiates this mode of investment from indirect investment, also known as **foreign portfolio investment**, or 'hot capital' flows. These kinds of

Figure 11.1   Coca-Cola™ at the end of the world, Patagonia, Chile

Source: Paul Haslam

investment are not made in an enterprise form and include the purchase of foreign debt, loans, and stock market investments. As discussed in chapter 9, foreign portfolio investment may rapidly flow into or out of a developing country, leading to financial instability and balance of payments crises. Foreign direct investment is much more stable than portfolio investment, since it involves an investment in physical and productive assets such as buildings, technology, and labour, which are more costly to abandon.

John Dunning, the pre-eminent authority on the multinational corporation, defines it as an 'enterprise that engages in foreign direct investment (FDI) and owns or controls value-adding activities in more than one country' (Dunning 1993, 3). According to Dunning, the two key distinctive features of the MNC that distinguish it from other enterprises are that it 'coordinates value-adding activities' across national borders (that is, it creates some kind of product based on bringing together productive assets from different

places in the world, including capital, labour, technology, management expertise, and know-how) and it internalizes the cross-border transfer of inputs used in the production process (in other words, these transfers take place within the firm and do not occur on the 'open' market) (Dunning 1993, 4). In this respect, the MNC is a 'hierarchy', or organizational structure based on command and control, and is distinct from a market, in which the price mechanism, not management fiat, co-ordinates relationships.

Although the two principles identified by Dunning apply to all multinationals, the reality of the universe of 77,000 MNCs with 770,000 foreign affiliates is that there is a great variation in their size and the degree to which they are internationalized (Dunning 1993, 3; UNCTAD 2006a, 10). Furthermore, the top 100 of these corporations are highly concentrated, in 2004 controlling a significant proportion of the total foreign assets (11 per cent), sales (16 per cent), and employment (12 per cent) of all multinationals. Their proportion of

Table 11.1 Number of MNCs by region

	Number of domestically based MNCs	Number of foreign affiliates in domestic economy
Developed countries	55,490	256,155
Europe	44,922	218,651
United States and Canada	3,857	28,332
Other developed	6,711	9,172
Developing countries	20,238	407,001
Africa	630	6,359
Latin America and Caribbean	3,006	36,448
Asia and Oceania	16,602	364,194
Southeast Europe and CIS	1,447	109,863

Source: UNCTAD 2006a, 270–1.

sales and assets has increased significantly over recent years, illustrating that the world's largest multinational corporations are growing relative to the rest of the pack. Furthermore, the world's 100 largest TNCs are also disproportionately from the developed countries: 85 come from the US, Japan, and the EU, and only 5 are from developing countries (UNCTAD 2006a, 30–1).

Developing countries as a group receive much less FDI than developed countries. In 2005, there was a record level of foreign investment inflows to the developing world, but these flows accounted for only 36 per cent of global inflows. In the same year, the United Kingdom was the largest destination for FDI, ahead of major emerging market economies such as China and India (UNCTAD 2006a, 3). Foreign direct investment constitutes the single most important source of new money for developing countries, with the possible exception of remittances from migrant workers, about which there are few reliable figures (see chapter 22). If we compare the net inflows of different sources of capital to developing countries, FDI accounted for just under US $250 billion, as compared to less than $140 billion in commercial bank loans, some $115 billion in foreign portfolio investment, and a net outflow of foreign aid. These figures for 2005 are in marked contrast to the

beginning of the 1990s when official development assistance (ODA), at just over $50 billion of net inflows, was twice as large as FDI and commercial loans and portfolio flows were at a similar level as direct investment by MNCs (UNCTAD 2006a, 5). In this respect, foreign direct investment and the activities of multinational corporations have become relatively more important to developing countries than other sources of capital over the past two decades.

However, it must be stressed that most of the FDI inflows to the developing world are concentrated in a handful of the more dynamic and industrialized developing countries. Five countries—Brazil, China, Hong Kong (considered separately from China in FDI figures), Mexico, and Singapore—attracted almost 50 per cent of all inflows to the developing world in 2005 and have consistently done so for a decade. Furthermore, FDI figures do not always indicate new productive investments, known as 'greenfield' investments, and thus should be viewed with caution. Mergers and acquisitions (M&As), in which a foreign company buys out a local company, involve only a transfer of funds, not an investment in the building of new facilities or employment of more people. In 2005, cross-border M&As made up 78 per cent of world FDI inflows (UNCTAD 2006a, 9).

Table 11.2 Selected multinational corporations ranked by foreign assets, including those from developing countries, 2004

Rank	Corporation	Home country	Industry	Foreign assets (US$ millions)	% of total assets
1	General Electric	US	Electric and electronic equipment	448,901	60
2	Vodaphone Group	UK	Telecommunications	247,850	96
3	Ford Motor Company	US	Automotive	179,856	59
4	General Motors	US	Automotive	173,690	36
5	British Petroleum (BP)	UK	Petroleum	154,513	80
6	ExxonMobil	US	Petroleum	134,923	69
7	Royal Dutch/Shell	UK/Netherlands	Petroleum	129,939	67
8	Toyota Motor Co.	Japan	Automotive	122,967	53
9	Total	France	Petroleum	98,719	86
10	France Telecom	France	Telecommunications	85,669	65
11	Volkswagen	Germany	Automotive	84,042	49
12	Sanofi-Aventis	France	Pharmaceuticals	82,612	79
13	Deutsche-Telekom AG	Germany	Telecommunications	79,654	54
14	RWE Group	Germany	Electricity, gas, water	78,728	62
15	Suez Group	France	Electricity, gas, water	74,051	86
16	E.on	Germany	Electricity, gas, water	72,726	47
17	**Hutchinson Whampoa**	**Hong Kong**	**Diversified**	**67,638**	**80**
18	Siemens AG	Germany	Electric and electronic equipment	65,830	61
19	Nestlé SA	Switzerland	Food and beverage	65,396	85
20	Electricité de France	France	Electricity, gas, water	65,365	33
59	**Petronas**	**Malaysia**	**Petroleum**	**22,647**	**36**
73	**Singtel**	**Singapore**	**Telecommunications**	**18,641**	**86**
86	**Samsung**	**South Korea**	**Electric and electronic equipment**	**15,399**	**23**
94	**CITIC Group**	**China**	**Diversified**	**14,452**	**17**

Source: UNCTAD 2006a, 280–2.

Foreign investment figures may also erroneously include domestic investment that has been routed through organizations located abroad (known as 'round-tripping') in order to benefit from preferential incentives and protection offered by some governments to foreign investors (UNCTAD 2006a, 12). In this respect, the geographic concentration and the mode of entry of massive inflows of money indicated by global figures can be somewhat misleading as to their developmental impact. Such caveats about the available figures and their meaning point to the difficulty of evaluating the effect of FDI on host economies.

WHAT MOTIVATES MULTINATIONALS TO GO ABROAD?

Why firms internalize by establishing branch plants or subsidiaries abroad, instead of by trade, is probably the most important question in the study of multinational corporations. A second

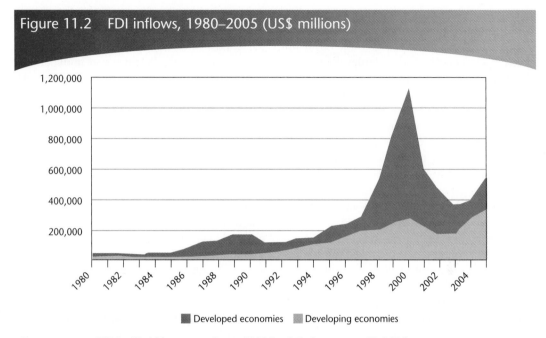

Figure 11.2   FDI inflows, 1980–2005 (US$ millions)

Source: UNCTAD. 2006a. *World Investment Report 2006* (statistical annex on CD-ROM).

and related question is what effect this internationalization has on the politics, economy, and society of the host country. As in most areas of the social sciences, the answers to these questions vary according to the theoretical and ideological frameworks used to analyze them. At the risk of some simplification, we can point to three main approaches to understanding the internationalization of the multinational corporation: a critical approach inspired by Marxism; the mercantile or nationalist approach; and the liberal or international business approach. Each approach reveals different facets of the MNC and its activities.

Dependency and critical approaches

Generally speaking, authors in the Marxist-inspired or critical tradition have tended to view multinational corporations as representatives of the global capitalist system and therefore negative for the developing countries in which they invest. The dominant current in this approach has been dependency theory, although to be fair, depend-

ency exhibits a wide range of attitudes towards foreign capital, some of which are quite ambivalent as to its beneficial or destructive effects (see chapter 3). Much recent writing by activist-scholars critical of the exploitation of workers and the environment by multinational corporations, although no longer embedded in neo-Marxism, continues to be inspired by the vision if not by the letter of this perspective and its critique of global capitalism (see Klein 2000).

The pioneers of dependency theory attributed an important role to multinational corporations in the maintenance of underdevelopment in the periphery. The structuralist critique in its original formulation by Raúl Prebisch was a trade-based explanation of underdevelopment (see chapter 3). Later variations, drawing more explicitly on Marxism, focused on the role of multinational corporations in organizing this trading relationship and their impact on the productive structure of developing countries. Paul Baran argued that multinational corporations, through the international division of labour (IDL) in which high-value manufacturing remained in the core countries and commodity and resource extraction was conducted in developing countries, maintained and deepened the underdevelopment of the periphery. Profits that were made in the periphery were sent back to the head offices in the North. Subsequent versions of this idea, known as the *new* international division of labour (NIDL), argued that manufacturing MNCs sought out Third World locations for their low-cost labour while maintaining high-value-added manufacturing in the developed countries with similar exploitative effects. Baran also pointed to the political alliances formed between multinational corporations and local elites uninterested in the social welfare of the poor in their countries. He described this alliance as a 'political and social coalition of wealthy compradores, powerful monopolists [MNCs] and large landowners dedicated to the defense of the existing social order' (as cited in Evans 1979, 20).

In this respect, multinational corporations change how countries (or rather, elites in those countries) perceive their interests. When multinational corporations control the major industries and a national bourgeoisie is absent, weak, or co-opted by MNCs, 'autonomous' local development is impossible. That is, the logic of industrialization follows the needs of external agents, not internal ones (Amin 1990, 11). This may lead to business choices that are dysfunctional for local development. For example, foreign export-oriented multinationals will not be interested in expanding local markets or buying-power (beyond sales to elites), use capital-intensive productive processes that create few jobs, have few links with local firms, and bring with them a cultural demonstration effect that encourages conspicuous consumption by elites.

But it would be inaccurate to view all *dependentistas* as arguing, as did André Gunder Frank (1991), that development in the North causes underdevelopment in the South. More sophisticated analyses point out that a specific kind of development and industrialization can occur under the aegis of multinational corporations in the larger Third World economies—what

Cardoso and Faletto called 'associated dependent development'. Peter Evans (1979) made this argument most forcefully by pointing to the 'triple alliance' between the Brazilian state, multinational corporations, and locally owned firms. He pointed out that the state can act as an autonomous 'class' actor or 'state bourgeoisie' by creating its own state-owed firms and joint ventures involving both multinational corporations and local firms. In this way, the state pushes industrialization forward by benefiting from the technology, management skills, and capital contributed by foreign firms. Evans argued, however, that this industrialization has its limits, since it is oriented towards production for upper-class consumption needs. It is therefore inevitably elitist and exclusionary of the popular masses (Evans 1979, 38).

The mercantile approach and the national interest

Another common approach to the multinational corporation is to see it as a representative of the political and economic interests of its home country. This approach has been particularly important in the study of US-based multinationals by both advocates of US hegemony and its detractors. But it is also seen elsewhere in the nationalist literature of all countries (particularly in Japan and South Korea) that advocates the formation of large domestic firms or 'national champions' capable of internationalizing and competing at the world level. Robert Gilpin argued that the era of multinationals corresponds with the era of American hegemony. The US actively promoted the expansion of its firms, particularly oil companies, for a number of reasons: to establish a safe supply of natural resources (a strategy currently being copied by India and China); to supply cheap petroleum to fund its politico-military Western alliance during the Cold War; to create a worldwide liberal and business-friendly culture; to improve its balance of payments and fund its military spending by means of repatriated profits (Gilpin 1975).

Beyond these general goals, there is evidence that during the Cold War, US administrations used their connections with certain multinational corporations to pursue specific foreign policy objectives in the developing world, including US attempts to undermine or overthrow 'unfriendly' governments. Two cases in particular reinforced this opinion, the CIA-sponsored coup d'état in Guatemala (1954) and the contacts between the CIA and International Telephone and Telegraph (ITT) in Chile in the period 1968 to 1970, which preceded the overthrow of socialist president Salvadore Allende. In the contemporary period, this perspective remains relevant. Close ties between large multinationals and their home countries continue to exist, and many governments seek to support the activities of their firms internationally. Most countries continue to build 'national champions', subsidize them through various means, and defend their companies at the World Trade Organization—well illustrated in the aircraft industry where Airbus, Boeing, Bombardier, and Embraer have become the national champions, respectively, of the EU, the United States, Canada, and Brazil. Multinationals in extractive industries continue to play an important role in guaranteeing supplies of needed raw materials for resource-poor countries, as illustrated by the internationalization of Brazil's Petrobrás, Chile's ENAP, Malaysia's Petronas, and China's China National Petroleum Company.

International business perspective

Whereas the mercantile and dependency approaches tend to view multinationals as homogeneous actors that are structurally determined by the global distribution of power and wealth, the international business perspective views them as differentiated actors with diverse strategies. From this perspective, the dominant explanation for the characteristics and internationalization of multinational corporations is the 'eclectic' or OLI **paradigm** developed by John H. Dunning. This approach turns around two questions: (1) Is there a common nature or feature of the multinational that distinguishes it from other kinds of firms? (2)

What explains the myriad forms of internationalization chosen by multinationals (subsidiary, joint-venture, equity participation, licensing)? One question gets at the multinational as institution and the other as actor.

According to the OLI paradigm, the multinational corporation is distinguished by ownership (O), location-specific (L), and internalization (I) advantages. *Ownership advantages* are those elements that are unique to the firm in question and generally not available to other firms, such as patents, processes, organizational abilities, marketing and management, and access to capital, resources, and markets. *Location-specific advantages* are those factors in a country where the investment takes place that work with the firm's other advantages and may include political (stability, political access and coverage, investment regime and protection), social (cultural, linguistic, ethnic commonalities), and economic (market size, market access, resources, workforce) factors. When location-specific assets abroad add something truly important to the firm's activities, then it will internationalize (become multinational) instead of simply trading with that country.

Internalization advantages are the advantages of co-ordinating production within the hierarchical governance structure of the firm instead of buying and selling the parts needed to produce any given product through arm's length market relationships. Indeed, one of the key reasons why multinationals invest in production across borders is because international markets are overwhelmed by a vast number of market imperfections (known as transaction costs). By organizing production inside the multinational, selling and buying from itself through administratively determined 'transfer prices', it benefits from lower transaction costs and is able to fully exploit ownership advantages without losing control of them on the open market. Open market relationships are much more likely to allow competitors to copy key ownership advantages like product design, technology, and industrial processes and are thus avoided (Dunning 1993, 76–9; Eden 1991, 204–7). Although the multinational corporation is often represented as the paragon of free markets, in fact the very existence of the multinational proves that 'free' markets are imperfect and inefficient!

The other very important contribution of international business studies is the recognition that multinational corporations can have four very different strategies when they go abroad to seek location-specific assets:

- *Resource-seeking strategy*: MNCs require specific resources that are only available abroad. Typically, these resources may include natural resources or agricultural goods, desirable services that can only be accessed locally, and specific managerial or technical skills.
- *Market-seeking strategy*: MNCs establish a subsidiary to serve the consumer demand of a local market directly instead of by trade. FDI is chosen over trade because it is required by law to enter the new markets, permits the product to be adapted to local conditions, is less expensive, or is a strategic response to competing firms. Direct investment in small market-seeking factories was a common response to import substituting industrialization (ISI) policies, which tended to restrict trade through high tariff barriers.
- *Efficiency (or cost-reducing)-seeking strategy*: MNCs plan to make their global operations more efficient through exploiting differences in the availability and cost of labour, capital, and resources. The location of light manufacturing and assembly plants in low-wage countries is an example of this strategy.
- *Strategic asset-seeking strategy*: MNCs buy up assets of other corporations as part of a global strategy to improve their competitiveness. Such a strategy may generate benefits such as 'opening up new markets, creating R&D synergies or production economies, buying market power, lower transaction costs, spreading administrative overheads, advancing strategic flexibility, and enabling risks to be better spread' (Dunning 1993, 57–61).

This more nuanced view of the structure and strategies employed by multinational corpora-

tions is essential for understanding the reasons that multinationals internationalize as well as the appropriate policies to regulate them.

RELATIONSHIP BETWEEN STATES AND MULTINATIONALS

The strategies of multinationals alone do not determine their effect on development. Governments play an important role by channelling FDI according to their developmental objectives. In this respect, a crucial part of the impact of MNCs on development is how governments mediate this relationship. The theories that explain the internationalization of multinational corporations tend to be too static, either assuming that the relationship is always beneficial or assuming that it is always negative. The reality is much more complicated, and the historical record is full of small states that have succeeded in getting important concessions from big firms—as well as big firms that appear to have had their way with small states. The **obsolescing bargaining model** offers a dynamic and flexible approach to state–firm relations in that it allows for the reality that both firm and state strength (and ability to get what they want) varies by country, firm, sector of activity, and the specific conjuncture (Vernon 1971). The obsolescing bargain approach assumes that each actor—state and firm—wants to capture a greater share of the benefits of the foreign investment. That is, the firm wants more profits, and the government wants to increase the developmental spillovers of the investment. Thus, there is a wide range of issues over which multinationals and governments can bargain.

The outcome of this bargaining is affected by their relative bargaining power (the resources each controls that are desired by the other party and not available elsewhere), strategy (how the investment fits into the firm's and the country's economic strategy), and constraints (the existence of alternatives and pressure from domestic and international actors). The model generally assumes that firms hold the upper hand when they first invest because governments try to out-

BOX 11.1   WOMEN AND EXPORT PROCESSING ZONES

Export processing zones (EPZs) are specially designated manufacturing-for-export areas in developing countries that attract efficiency-seeking FDI through offering a regulatory regime favourable to multinational corporations. Typically, EPZs allow duty-free imports and exports, have lower corporate taxation rates, may be exempt from minimum wage legislation, and do not permit unionization of the labour force. The EPZ labour force is 27 million worldwide, 60 to 90 per cent of whom are women (1998 figures). In this respect, female labour is the backbone of the light manufacturing export industry based in developing countries (particularly in electronics, garments, and footwear). There is a significant and unresolved debate about whether the employment of women under these conditions is liberating or exploitative. On the one hand, entry into the wage labour force may allow women to escape the restrictive moral code of traditional households and cultures, form friendship and political networks, increase their power relative to men because of their contribution to household income, and provide a nest-egg that increases their individual opportunities for advancement and education later on. On the other hand, EPZ jobs involve low wages, long hours, and frequently poor working conditions. Light manufacturing firms may also reinforce gender stereotypes by selecting employees based on racialized or gendered characteristics, such as the 'nimble fingers' that facilitate detail work, docility, youth, and marital status. Young women are also considered 'secondary wage earners' and therefore paid less than men. Furthermore, the literature has recorded cases of factories using gender to control women: male floor managers; a paternalistic discourse to convince families that their daughters are being well looked after (and controlled); allocating less 'skilled' jobs (like sewing) to women while other 'skilled' jobs (like cutting) go to men; and beauty contests to reinforce traditional female norms. Evaluating whether EPZs liberate or exploit women is therefore a difficult question to resolve.

compete other potential locations by offering attractive conditions. Once the investment is sunk, however, and the company cannot easily leave, the bargaining power begins to shift towards the government. At this point, the government may change the rules of the game and try to extract more benefits from the firm. The classic example of the obsolescing bargain can be found in the mining industry, which is a nationalist lightning rod for those who decry multinational investment as exploiting the 'national patrimony' belonging to all citizens. For example, in Theodore Moran's analysis of the nationalization of US-owned copper mines in Chile in 1970, he described how, after the MNCs' initial investment, Chilean policy-makers put pressure on the mines over a 15-year period: they increased taxation on the industry, created institutions to monitor and regulate it, and eventually developed the technical capacity to take it over (Moran 1974).

But firms have proved that they are able to defend themselves from state regulation, particularly in manufacturing. Manufacturing companies are capable of keeping up a constant stream of innovation and product mixes that governments could not replace. Some low-wage manufacturing operations (such as basic assembly and textile operations) require relatively low levels of start-up investment, permitting firms to move elsewhere if they are threatened by regulation—a phenomenon known as 'footloose' investment (Kobrin 1987). But in all industries, including the extractive sector, multinational corporations have been able to limit obsolescence by structuring their financing to include home countries and international financial institutions (IFIs) as financiers (thus ensuring that nationalization would 'damage' organizations that could hit back) and by developing 'political cover' through close relations with prominent local political and economic actors (Moran 1998). Another method, discussed below, has been to encourage home governments to promote international investment protection through bilateral agreements and at the World Trade Organization.

During the 1990s, analysts increasingly questioned the relevance of the obsolescing bargaining model because it appeared that states, under the influence of neo-liberal ideology, were giving a lot away to attract multinational corporations and doing very little to bargain with them once

they were established (Haslam 2007). Gone were the battles over ownership and performance requirements typical of the 1960s and 1970s. Some even suggested that the obsolescing bargaining model had itself obsolesced as the overall mood in the 1990s became a cooperative one and governments and foreign corporations sought to complement each other in order to improve their ability to compete in world markets (Stopford and Strange 1991)!

Not only was state–firm bargaining not in vogue during the 1990s, but some authors even claimed that it was counterproductive and that policies to encourage firms to integrate 'backwards' with local suppliers had failed. Theodore Moran (2005) argues that the greatest spillovers on the local economy occur when the MNC is the most free to take the productive decisions that make sense in terms of the company's global strat-

BOX 11.2   BACKLASH: THE LATIN AMERICAN NEW LEFT

For much of the 1990s, many observers concluded that MNCs and governments had entered a cooperative period that had definitively put an end to the nationalization and aggressive regulation of foreign investors that had characterized the 1960s and 1970s. This triumphalism proved to be short-lived. In Latin America, the perceived failure of **Washington Consensus**-style economic reforms (including investment liberalization) during the 1980s and 1990s brought to power a wave of new left-leaning governments, beginning with the election of Hugo Chávez in Venezuela (elected 1998). Chávez and his counterparts Evo Morales in Bolivia (elected 2005) and Rafael Caldera in Ecuador (elected 2006) have adopted a nationalist attitude towards foreign investors, particularly in the oil, gas, and mining sectors. The high prices of commodities since 2003 (including oil, gas, gold, and copper) has been a key factor encouraging governments to try and capture more of the 'windfall' profits generated by foreign investors. It also appears that this newest wave of nationalizations confirms some of the predictions of the obsolescing bargaining model: after big improvements in productive capacity were made by MNCs under very profitable conditions, the state stepped in to appropriate more of the surplus.

Source: Haslam 2008.

egy. Companies that are not regulated by government are more likely to be larger (up to 10 times larger than import-substituting plants), to use more advanced technology, to develop and 'coach' local suppliers to improve their product and production processes, and to use professional management techniques. Simply put, when MNCs integrate their local plants into their global strategy, there are more beneficial spillovers for both the firm and the country (Moran 2005). Moran's thesis is a contentious one and may be most relevant to high-tech sectors like automobiles. Certainly, in the early years of the twenty-first century, the pendulum seems to be swinging towards more state regulation of MNCs. Indeed, the question 'to bargain or not to bargain?' may itself be too simplistic. Most of the literature on the successful developmental states of Southeast Asia points to the need for a close and supportive working relationship between foreign and domestic firms and governments (see chapter 7).

INTERNATIONAL REGULATION OF MNCs

The state-firm relationship is no longer determined simply by the willingness of states to pursue either a cooperative or a bargaining strategy. Increasingly, international agreements limit the range of policy choices open to governments in their relationship with multinational corporations. In the 1960s and 1970s, developing countries organized themselves in the United Nations General Assembly and the Group of 77 (G-77) to demand changes to the world trade regime that would be 'fairer' for developing countries (see chapter 15). These demands, inspired by nationalist and mercantile ideas, included controls on the activities of multinational corporations. The major projects of this period that reflected these concerns were the Charter of Economic Rights and Duties of States (1974) and the Draft Code of Conduct on Transnational Corporations. The draft code negotiations dragged out into the mid-1980s before being abandoned (UNCTAD 2004b,

9–11). Its importance, however, was the counter-offensive it provoked from the rich countries to protect the rights of foreign investors in the developing world.

This counter-offensive took place on several fronts: (1) a campaign was launched to sign bilateral investment protection agreements with developing countries; (2) investment issues were included in the GATT negotiations; and (3) corporate social responsibility was promoted as a way to improve corporate behaviour in lieu of state regulation. The first two offensives sought to build a body of international law based on the principle of protection for foreign direct investors.

The first efforts in this direction involved the negotiation of **bilateral investment treaties** (or BITs) between developed and developing countries. Such agreements typically enunciated principles of treatment that foreign investors were entitled to receive from host governments, such as most-favoured nation and national treatment (the same treatment as that accorded to the firms of any third country or locally owned firms), just and equitable treatment, full protection and security (from expropriation), and the right to sue host governments in international arbitral tribunals for breach of obligations. The first BIT was signed between Germany and Pakistan in 1959, but since that time the web of agreements has expanded to approximately 2,500 worldwide by 2006. Few developing countries are not caught in this web, and many signed such agreements in the hope that demonstrating the 'right' attitude towards foreign investors would encourage increased FDI inflows. Thus far, there is little evidence that international investment agreements do contribute to increased investment.

At the global and regional levels, rules to protect foreign investors were included in trade agreements. The Uruguay Round (concluded in 1994) of trade negotiations added agreements protecting the rights of foreign investors, the most notable of which are the TRIPS (Trade-Related Aspects of Intellectual Property Rights) agreement requiring respect for intellectual property and the TRIMS (Trade

Related Investment Measures) agreement forbidding the use of certain performance requirements (policies that imposed 'developmental' obligations on MNCs). Since that time, a number of regional **free trade** agreements, such as the North American Free Trade Agreement have included investment disciplines. The Doha Development Round (2001) also had investment on the agenda, although it was dropped in 2005 because of opposition from developing countries concerned about its effect on their policy space. As a result of this 'legalization' of the rights of foreign investors, multinational corporations now enjoy more protection from governments and civil society groups than at any other time in history.

CORPORATE SOCIAL RESPONSIBILITY

The third element of this counter-offensive is the promotion of **corporate social responsibility** (CSR) as a way of forestalling or deflecting calls for government regulation of the activities of MNCs. Corporate social responsibility, broadly speaking, is the idea that corporations have a responsibility beyond their shareholders to a broader set of 'stakeholders'. Such stakeholders include any group that is affected by the activities of the firm, including employees, local communities, other companies sharing the same resources (such as water), indigenous communities, and people

BOX 11.3   INVESTOR–STATE DISPUTE SETTLEMENT

A major question related to international investment agreements [(IIAs)] is whether they restrict the 'policy space' or the policy options open to governments in their dealings with multinational corporations. Most IIAs include investor-state dispute settlement provisions. These provisions permit a foreign corporation (but not domestically owned ones) that believes its rights under an investment agreement have been violated to take the host government to 'court' in binding international arbitration. Frequently, multinational corporations will claim that they have not received 'fair and equitable treatment' or that a particular governmental measure has affected their profitability to the extent that it may be considered 'tantamount to expropriation'. Known arbitration cases have skyrocketed from a total of 14 in April 1998 to 219 by November 2005, with some resulting in major damage awards such as the $US 834-million award against Slovakia in 2004. Argentina, as of late 2005, faced 42 known cases, most of which were related to its financial crisis and currency devaluation of 2002. This may represent the tip of the iceberg, since several of the arbitration venues open to investors conduct the proceedings in secret. Environmental and social activists have been particularly concerned that such investment protection could limit the ability of governments to make policy in the public interest if the interests of multinational corporations were damaged in the process. Or that a **regulatory chill** could result in which a government never implements good public policy for fear of being sued by affected foreign investors. For example, most developing countries have private health care delivery, but it might be too expensive to move to a universal public system if that damages the profits of multinational corporations and causes them to sue. Governments may also be sued if they enact environmental regulations that damage corporate profitability, as has occurred in several cases under the investment chapter protection of NAFTA.

Source: UNCTAD 2006b, 4–7.

involved in nearby economic activities (such as farming). CSR is a *voluntary* commitment of firms to improve the quality of their relationship with stakeholders. It is presented as both a moral argument that companies should behave ethically and good business because it reduces operational risk, improves worker commitment, increases efficiency, and promotes profitability. The inequity of arms should be immediately apparent: on the one hand, corporate rights have been enhanced through international law and binding dispute settlement; on the other, corporate responsibilities remain purely voluntary.

The immediate response of the OECD club of rich countries to the Draft Code of Conduct on Transnational Corporations was the *Guidelines for Multinational Enterprise* (1976). To this day, these guidelines constitute the most significant corporate social responsibility effort by developed countries, requiring all OECD countries to establish an institution, the National Contact Point, to promote the guidelines and mediate disputes involving investors from that country. Another prominent international code is the Global Compact, an initiative of former UN secretary-general Kofi Annan. Each set of codes advocates different principles, implies obligations for different actors, and involves different standards of verification and compliance. The Global Compact, for example, requires companies to voluntarily adhere to a set of 10 principles on human rights, labour standards, environmental stewardship, and anti-corruption. However, there is no independent audit or verification of company efforts, unlike codes that require 'triple bottom line accounting' (quantification of economic, social, and environmental impacts).

Most multinationals have developed their own codes of conduct, as well as adhering to global codes promoted by international organizations. Yet there is considerable doubt as to whether CSR is appropriate for the developing world. Much of the thought on CSR was created in developed countries where a strong legal and social framework already forces high standards of responsible behaviour by corporations. In the Third World,

where this framework is often either absent or not enforced, the appropriateness of putting the accent on 'voluntary' efforts may well be questioned. Furthermore, there is little systematic evidence on the consequences of corporate social responsibility for development in poor areas. The argument for its value has mostly progressed through advocacy and case study examples of good citizenship. Nonetheless, most world surveys of MNCs do show an increasing uptake of CSR norms and practices by firms operating in the developing world. In this respect, the contribution of CSR to development may improve with time.

MNCs, POVERTY, AND DEVELOPMENT

We have yet to specifically address the question of whether multinationals are good or bad for poor and developing countries in general. This question is extremely difficult to answer for two principal reasons: first, FDI is extremely heterogeneous (different MNC strategies and firms have different effects on host countries), and second, the policy regime and bargaining outcomes vary greatly among states. In other words, some MNCs are better for development than others, and some states are simply better at getting the most out of multinationals. Andrew Sumner (2005) provides a useful framework for evaluating the economic effects of multinational corporations. He suggests that for FDI to be beneficial overall, it must meet five conditions: net beneficial effects on the capital account, the current account, government revenue, local spillovers, and poverty (and inequality) reduction.

The capital account. In order to be beneficial, foreign direct investment inflows must be greater than outflows to the multinational's home office from such sources as repatriated profits and capital, licensing fees, royalties, and intra-firm financial transfers. Multinationals usually go through phases in which there are significant capital inflows during the initial establishment phase (either as a result of M&As or the construction and operation of new facilities). As the plant matures, however, the MNC must decide either to re-invest its profits and other sources of revenue locally or to repatriate them to the home country. Over a long period of time, therefore, capital flows from a given investment may turn negative. The problem that profit and capital remittances pose for capital account is exacerbated when countries are economically or politically unstable. For example, multinationals in African countries are much more likely to repatriate profits, presumably because of greater political risk (outflows averaged well above 50 per cent of inflows during the 1990s and peaked at close to 100 per cent in several years) than in Latin America, East Asia, or South Asia (Sumner 2005, 279). Once again, the countries most in need of the developmental push of FDI (the poorest and least stable) are the least likely to benefit.

The current account. In order to be beneficial, the sum total of trade generated by the multinational must result in a greater value of exports than imports. It is very difficult to know the real value of trade conducted by multinational corporations, since a third of world trade is intra-firm trade (the firm trades between different parts of its internal structure, using administratively determined 'transfer prices' instead of the free market). Multinational investment is often extremely import-intensive because much of the high-quality machinery it needs to start operations is unavailable locally. MNC performance on this point varies mostly by firm strategy. Investment designed to serve the consumer demands of Third World countries (market-seeking strategy) is almost always import-intensive. This pattern of FDI was typical during the import-substitution era in the larger Latin American economies. In contrast, both extractive industries (resource-seeking) and manufacturing for export (efficiency-seeking) are more likely to generate trade surpluses. The export of manufactures was more common in East Asia and China (Sumner 2005, 279–80). MNCs following these latter strategies may provide new access to foreign markets for local suppliers within their global distribution and production networks (UNCTAD 1999, xxxi), which can be beneficial.

Government revenue. Governments frequently provide massive incentives to encourage multinationals to invest, re-invest, and stay in the country, such as tax holidays, subsidies, promotional and training regimes, and the construction of road, airport, and port infrastructure. In order to be beneficial, the multinational should generate more government revenue than that paid out in incentives. A key debate in this area is whether multinationals seek to deliberately reduce their tax burden via the transfer prices used to organize their global production chains. Since transfer prices are set by administrative fiat, they can also be used to shift the profits made in a given intermediate product to countries where corporate tax rates are lower (by undervaluing the product in the high-tax jurisdiction and overvaluing it in the low-tax jurisdiction). In recent years, however, the incentives and tax deductions used by governments to attract foreign firms appear to be a bigger problem, because these sources can directly reduce the governmental funding for social welfare spending. Unfortunately, it is almost impossible to evaluate these effects, since transfer pricing information is not made available by corporations (for obvious reasons), nor is much of the deal-by-deal incentives granted by governments made public (Sumner 2005, 280).

Spillovers and poverty reduction. The central issue regarding the impact of MNCs on development is whether multinationals *crowd in* (provide opportunities for new firms to develop and improve their competitiveness) or *crowd out* local firms (push them out of business). This issue turns principally around the question of whether multinationals develop links with local suppliers that improve their efficiency, product quality, and management skills, transfer technology, and encourage exports. As with the other effects discussed above, the mode of entry and strategy of the MNC is very important. M&As (in comparison to 'greenfield' investments), for example, are particularly problematic because of their potential to trigger employment reductions and scaling down of local research and development (R&D) and the

Figure 11.3   Multinationals, such as this one in Mozambique, are present in most developing countries

Source: Jessica Schafer

introduction of imported inputs (UNCTAD 1999, xxx). Natural resource-seeking investment is likely to have weak links with local suppliers because of its need for capital-intensive machinery that is not available locally. In comparison, market and efficiency-seeking investment offer more potential for spillovers, but this also depends on whether the MNC employs a 'static' or a 'dynamic' strategy—whether it wants to exploit (static) low-cost labour before moving on to another location as costs go up (footloose) or to build and upgrade (dynamic) a supplier network to feed its global strategy (UNCTAD 1999, xxxi).

Another key spillover with a major impact on poverty is the extent to which MNCs contribute to quality employment, a glaring deficiency in the neo-liberal model (Stallings and Peres 2000). Multinational corporations are part of the equa-

tion here for a number of reasons: the acquisition of privatized firms may lead to lay-offs as foreign owners seek to improve the productivity of the firm; multinationals are generally more capital-intensive and employ fewer workers per output than local firms; and their employees are more skilled and are paid better than those of local firms, contributing, ironically, to growing income inequality. As discussed above, the key issue is whether MNCs crowd out or crowd in employment. But the answer cannot be known a priori, because it depends not only on firm strategy but also on the policy environment and state–firm bargaining (Moran 2005; Sumner 2005, 277–81; UNCTAD 1999, 279–83). Certainly, it seems that East Asian economies have been more successful than those of Latin America or Africa, and most economists believe that crowding in predominates overall. However, a recent OECD report on FDI concludes that policies that harness FDI for development are the same policies required to spur economic growth domestically, and such policies are frequently absent in poor countries (OECD, 2002). The irony is that the poorest countries are the least likely to be able to implement a framework that generates spillovers and therefore the least likely to benefit from foreign direct investment.

THE PEOPLE STRIKE BACK: CONTENTIOUS ISSUES IN THE COMMUNITY–MNC RELATIONSHIP

Beyond the issue of how governments bargain with multinational corporations about economic spillovers, there is the issue of how communities engage with and, in some cases, organize against multinational corporations because of concerns over their non-economic effects. This brings us to a related difficulty in evaluating the developmental effects of multinationals: when the political, social, and cultural impact may be negative even when economic spillovers are advantageous. It is possible to group the non-economic effects of multinationals into four broad categories: political, health and environment, human rights, and culture and lifestyle. Many of these impacts are discussed in other chapters, so we will not go into a great deal of detail but instead outline the characteristics of each problem area.

Political. As predicted by both dependency and mercantile approaches, multinational corporations often cultivate political ties in both their home and host countries. Their economic and symbolic importance gives them privileged access to policymakers. In many poor developing countries, such revenues supply the resources necessary to maintain and build **patron–client networks** that provide politicians with political support.

Health and environment. Industrial accidents, normal production processes, and marketing strategies may negatively affect human health and

the natural environment. Some of these are the consequence of lower safety or environmental standards in the developing world and in this respect may be considered deliberate firm policy (to the extent that they are a reason behind the internationalization of the firm, as in the case of so-called 'polluters' havens' attracting dirty heavy industry). Normal marketing strategies may also have a deleterious effect on human health, such as the marketing of breast milk substitutes by Nestlé in the 1970s and early 1980s, as may the withholding of products that can save lives, such as essential medicines that are priced out of reach for many in developing countries (Richter 2001).

Human rights abuses. Companies may also have an impact on human rights through deliberate decisions about how to organize their global production process or as a consequence of operating in a country whose government abuses human rights. The former usually involves labour standards that fail to meet developed world standards or that may deny certain rights such as unionization—often in order to lower prices for Northern consumers. The latter issue bears on the responsibility a firm may have when operating in a country known to violate human rights. In some cases, a company may be complicit when it permits the government or paramilitaries to use its installations or commit abuses in the name of protecting the company. In other cases, a firm's complicity is less evident, as when its normal activities and compliance with the law provide an unsavoury government with revenue and economic support.

Culture and lifestyle. The activities of multinationals also may affect local cultures and lifestyles. A long-standing critique has been that MNCs encourage, via a demonstration effect, conspicuous consumption and adoption of (sometimes unhealthy) Western lifestyles and values, such as individualism over communitarianism.

In the absence of adequate governmental or international action, local people have spontaneously organized to protect their interests, and in this respect, it is important to recognize the

BOX 11.4   MINING MULTINATIONALS AND COMMUNITY OPPOSITION

In 1999, the mining company Manhattan Minerals Corporation acquired the exploration rights to a 10,000 ha. mining concession including the urban area of the town of Tambogrande, Peru. The company formed a joint-venture with the Peruvian state to exploit the gold deposits found near and under the town. The project involved an open-pit gold mine that would have required the relocation of some 8,000 residents. However, Tambogrande residents opposed the mine, largely based on lifestyle concerns, particularly fears that the environmental fallout from the mine could damage livelihoods in the predominantly agricultural region. Residents of the area organized the Tambogrande Defence Front to protest the development of the mine and were joined by a good number of national and international NGOs such as Oxfam. This opposition culminated in the municipal government's decision to hold a non-binding plebiscite on the proposed mine, a significant milestone since it was the first time a community had been consulted in Peru on mining development in its midst. The plebiscite was held on 2 June 2002, financed in part by Oxfam Great Britain. In a tense climate, the participation rate was high (73 per cent of registered voters), and the 'no' campaign won a decisive victory of almost 94 per cent. The legality of the plebiscite was disputed by the national government, which argued that the existing legal framework for public consultations was adequate. Nonetheless, the domestic and international publicity associated with the campaign prompted the government to revoke Manhattan Minerals' concession in December 2003, alleging the failue to fulfill its concession obligations.

Source: Rousseau and Meloche 2002

potential of individuals and non-governmental organizations (NGOs) to put effective pressure on multinational corporations. A key element of many successful campaigns has been the mobilization of consumer and citizen pressure in the developed countries against MNCs trying to sell to these same consumers. Where local community groups do not have much influence with MNCs or their own governments, mobilization may occur through networks involving both local and foreign NGOs. In this context, international NGOs can help to generate a **boomerang pattern** in which they pick up the concerns of the local group, then put pressure on actors external to the country like international organizations or the home government of the multinational, which in turn directly pressure the host government and MNC. International NGOs are also particularly good at framing disputes in a way that makes them easy-to-understand moral issues, allocates clear blame, and proposes a credible way to change the situation (Keck and Sikkink 1998, 12–17). The power of civil society organization is explored more fully in chapters 6 and 12.

CONCLUSION

This chapter has sought to analyze the importance of multinational corporations for development by presenting an overview of MNCs in the world, different theoretical approaches to the firm and its relationship with governments, the

BOX 11.5   THE CHANGING FACE OF FDI:
THE THIRD WORLD MULTINATIONAL

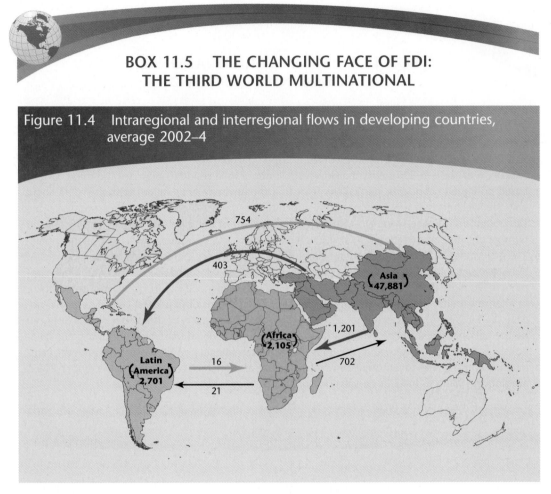

Figure 11.4   Intraregional and interregional flows in developing countries, average 2002–4

Source: UNCTAD 2006a, 119

In recent years, some developing countries themselves have developed home-grown multinationals that invest in other developing countries and the OECD countries. This change may prompt us to re-imagine some of the more simplistic approaches to the relationship between multinationals and developing countries. At the very least, it makes it harder to see multinationals as simply the North exploiting the South. Since some multinationals now call developing countries their 'home', the issue of the impact of FDI on development is not just an issue of its impact on host countries but also on home countries. FDI from developing countries offers a number of potential benefits for the home country, such as increased profitability and competitiveness, access to foreign financing (on developed country markets), technology transfer (especially if internationalization occurs through M&A of developed-country firms), integration into global production and distribution networks, secure supplies of natural resources, and spillovers for local firms. Indeed, one of the unique characteristics of Third World multinationals is that they seek to absorb First World technology and managerial practices, unlike First World MNCs, who seek to protect their ownership advantages from competitors (UNCTAD 2006a, 169–83). In addition, Third World MNCs frequently internationalize to poorer countries in their immediate regional environment. As a result, investment from developing countries is particularly important to nearby economies that are relatively unattractive to First World MNCs. In this way, South Africa is a source of more than 50 per cent of investment inflows in neighbouring southern Africa (UNCTAD 2006a, 120). The relatively recent emergence of South–South FDI flows means that it is hard to judge whether this new phenomenon will have different developmental effects from those of North–South flows. Some possible benefits have been noted above. On the other hand, FDI from larger economies like China and India has shown little interest in the direct or indirect human rights violations (such as in Sudan) that might accompany their investments and little permeability to pressure from domestic and transnational NGOs and civil society groups. This may represent a setback for activists who have successfully pushed Western MNCs to act more seriously regarding their responsibilities of corporate citizenship.

international regulation of FDI, and a discussion of its economic, political, social, and cultural effects on developing countries. Above all, the chapter has sought to demonstrate that the multinational corporation is not a monolithic, homogeneous actor whose effects are structurally determined and easily characterized as good or bad. Instead, MNCs are diverse and complicated actors applying a wide range of strategies and whose developmental effects depend on the particular nature of their engagement with governments, international organizations, and civil society actors. Multinationals are neither entirely responsible for the successes of development nor for its failures. UNCTAD puts it as follows: multinational corporations 'do not substitute for domestic effort: they can only provide access to tangible and intangible assets and catalyse domestic investment and capabilities. In a world of intensifying competition and accelerating technological change, this complementary and catalytic role can be very valuable' (UNCTAD 1999, 149).

QUESTIONS FOR DISCUSSION

1. If some multinationals do not adequately contribute to development, is it their fault or the fault of host governments that fail to regulate them?

2. Why do both the divergence in government policy and the divergence in multinational strategies make it difficult to evaluate the effect of TNCs in development?

3. Can corporate social responsibility contribute to good developmental outcomes? Why; why not; what are its limits?

4. Which theoretical approach to the multinational corporation (mercantile, Marxist, international business perspective) do you find most appealing, and why?

5. Why would the emergence of Third World multinationals change how we evaluate MNCs' effects on developing countries?

FURTHER READING

Dunning, John. H. 1993. *Multinational Enterprises and the Global Economy*. Reading, MA: Addison-Wesley.

Eden, Lorraine. 1991. 'Bringing the firm back in: Multinationals in international political economy'. *Millennium: Journal of International Studies* 20 (2): 197–224.

Grosse, Robert. 2005. *International Business and Government Relations in the 21st Century*. Cambridge: Cambridge University Press.

Richter, Judith. 2001. *Holding Corporations Accountable: Corporate Conduct, International Codes and Citizen Action*. London: Zed Books and UNICEF.

United Nations Conference on Trade and Development (UNCTAD). *World Investment Report* [various years]. Geneva: UNCTAD.

INTERNET RESOURCES

UNCTAD World Investment Report: http://www.unctad.org/Templates/Page.asp?intItemID=1485&lang=1.

Multinational Monitor: http://multinationalmonitor.org.

United Nations Global Compact: http://www.globalcompact.org.

CHAPTER 12

CIVIL SOCIETY AND DEVELOPMENT

HENRY VELTMEYER

LEARNING OBJECTIVES

- To be able to identify the agencies of change and development in the context of local and community-based development—i.e., in the localities and communities in need.
- To understand the role of civil society organizations in the process of alleviating poverty and facilitating self-development for the poor.

The idea of **civil society** has achieved prominence over the past two decades, particularly in connection with successive waves of democratization, beginning in Latin America and eastern Europe and spreading across the developing world. In normative terms, civil society has been widely seen as an agent for limiting authoritarian government, empowering a popular movement, reducing the atomizing and unsettling effects of market forces, enforcing political accountability, and improving the quality and inclusiveness of **governance**, a term that denotes a particular set of interactions between civil society and governments.[1]

Reconsideration of the limits of government intervention in economic affairs and a related neo-conservative attack on the welfare—and developmental—*state* (see chapter 7) have also led to an increased awareness of the potential role of civic organizations in the provision of public goods and social services, either separately or in a synergistic relationship with state institutions. Indeed, it is possible to view the turn towards civil society in the provision of hitherto public goods and services as a form of *privatization*: turning over the economy to the 'private sector' (profit-oriented or capitalist enterprises) and responsibility for economic and political development to 'civil society'.[2]

Recourse to the notion of civil society, and the construction of a civil society *discourse*, take dif-ferent forms. There are three different traditions in the use of the term, each associated with a particular conception of civil society. One of these, associated with a mainstream form of political science and economics in which politics and economics are treated as analytically distinct systems, can be labelled *liberal*.[3]

The liberal tradition is fundamentally concerned with 'political development'—establishing a participatory form of politics and 'good', i.e., 'democratic', governance. Here civil society is rooted in the Anglo-American tradition of liberal democratic theory in which civic institutions and political activity are essential components of 'political society' based on the principles of citizenship, rights, democratic representation, and the rule of law. On the ideological spectrum (left, centre, right), liberals see civil society as a countervailing force against an unresponsive, corrupt state and exploitative corporations that disregard environmental issues and human rights abuses (Kamat 2003).

The second tradition, rooted in a more sociological view of the state–society relation and the ideas of Antonio Gramsci, is similarly concerned with the form of politics but sees civil society as a repository of popular resistance to government policies and the basis of a 'counter-hegemonic' bloc of social forces engaged in a process of contesting state and other forms of class power. It is based on a radical ideology—a shared belief in the need for radical change. Civil society is thus seen as a repository of the forces of resistance and opposition, forces than can be mobilized into a counter-hegemonic bloc.

The third tradition is associated with international cooperation for development. In this tradition, civil society is viewed as an array of social organizations representing 'stakeholders' in a process of economic development, a strategic partner in the war against global poverty waged by the World Bank and other international development associations and agencies. Here civil society is viewed as an agency for a *participatory* and *empowering* form of *development*. Proponents of this view share a liberal ideology in terms of seeing in civil society the beneficial effects of globalization for democracy and economic progress. On the other hand, conservatives who hold this view of civil society view non-governmental organizations (NGOs) as 'false saviours of international development' (Kamat 2003). Here the entire project of cooperation for international development (technical and financial assistance to poor developing countries) is seen as misbegotten, more likely to result in a stifling of initiative than to work as a catalyst for an improvement in the physical quality of people's lives.

The purpose of this chapter is to deconstruct this civil society discourse. First, we review the origins and contemporary uses of the term. Then we turn towards the development dynamics associated with the contemporary discourse on civil society. This discourse is of two types, one associated with the dynamics of political development and the search for 'democratic governance', the other with the search for alternative forms of development initiated from below and within 'civil society'—forms that are socially inclusive, equitable, participatory, and empowering. The chapter ends with a brief review of the role of different types of civil society organizations in the development process. The central focus of this review is on **non-governmental organizations** and social move-

ments, elements of civil society conceptualized as agencies of anti-globalization—repositories of the forces of resistance against global capitalism in its current neo-liberal form.

CIVIL SOCIETY: THE ITINERARY OF A CONCEPT

Definitions of 'civil society' are bewilderingly diverse, rooted in alternative social and political philosophies that are hard to reconcile. However, for our purpose it is important to come to some agreement about what it means in the context of current development discourse.

One definition is that of an intermediate realm between the state and the family, populated by organized groups or associations that have some autonomy in relation to the state and are formed voluntarily by members of society to advance their interests, values, or identities. This definition excludes most highly informal associations of the personal network kind as well as families, since they operate in the private sphere. Civil society, by contrast, operates in the public, albeit non-state, sphere. But some kinship organizations above the level of the nuclear or extended family may constitute elements of civil society. Civil society here generally excludes profit-oriented or capitalist corporations, although several caveats are in order. Certain types of firms, such as the media and non-profit enterprises, are often important elements of civil society. And when corporations and their CEOs combine in the form of business associations, these associations can also be regarded as part of civil society.

Civil society includes all manner of social organizations ranging between the family and the state—the state being an apparatus composed of institutions such as governments, the judiciary, the legislature, the armed forces, and any other institution used to determine 'who gets what'. The United Nations Development Programme (UNDP), the World Bank, and other such agencies of international development adopted the term 'civil society' in their discourse precisely because it was so inclusive, containing within its scope the 'private sector' (basically, capitalist or multi-national corporations governed by the logic of capital accumulation or profit-making). The incorporation of the 'private sector' into the development process has been a fundamental aim of these international organizations since 1989 (Mitlin 1998).

Another consideration is that civil society or non-governmental organizations are generally issue-oriented in their actions rather than class-based, raising questions about whether or not to include social movements. *Social movements* are generally concerned with disputing state power—with bringing about a change in government poli-cies or, like political parties, in governments themselves (albeit in a different way—mobilizing the forces of opposition and resistance rather than participating in elections). In contrast to social movements (see discussion below), civil society in the form of NGOs (or in the voluntary sector) are generally concerned with more specific interest group issues, such as the environment, the empowerment of women, human rights, develop-ment education, disaster and other forms of relief or emergency aid, or poverty alleviation. Some analysts see in NGOs a very different form of organization from social movements, which are not as much issue-oriented as concerned with bringing about a change in government policy or in the class system behind it.

The type of organization encompassed by 'civil society' is not the only issue. Social organi-zations generally take one of three basic forms: (1) *associations* or *associational* (sharing an orga-nizational objective); (2) *communities* or *commu-nity-based* (held together by social bonds and a culture of solidarity, a shared sense of belonging); and (3) interest groups or *class-based organiza-tions* (defined by a pursuit of economic interest or political power), such as capitalist enterprises, multinational corporations within the 'private sector' of the economy, and labour unions.

The size and strength of 'civil society' in this organizational context is usually measured in terms of the number of 'active' formally consti-tuted social organizations, the density of the resulting social fabric, and the networks that bring people together to act collectively to achieve or in pursuit of their shared goals and common objectives. A major factor here is the degree to which people rely on governments as opposed to their own social organizations and networks to achieve their goals and objectives. Thus, from the 1940s to the 1970s, with the growth of the wel-fare and development state (in which govern-ments assumed primary responsibility for both welfare and development), many societies increased their reliance on the government, with a corresponding weakening of 'civil society'. In the 1980s, in a new context involving the inser-tion of many countries into the system of global capitalism (see discussion below on this 'seismic shift'), there was a general retreat of the state, resulting in a corresponding growth and strength-ening of civil society.

We discuss the emergence, strengthening, and role of civil society organizations in this con-text below.

CIVIL SOCIETY IN CONTEXT: SETTING THE STAGE

Social change can be analyzed in terms of three dynamic factors: *agency* (the strategies pursued and actions taken by diverse organizations and individuals), *structure* (the institutionalized prac-tices that shape or limit action), and *context* (the specific 'situation' or historical conjuncture of objectively given and subjectively experienced 'conditions' of social or political action). In regard to the emergence, growth, and strengthening of civil society in the 1980s, there are at least five contextual elements, each taking the form of a variable but persistent trend that can be analyzed in terms of three critical dimensions: (1) the actions or policies that provide the driving forces of social change; (2) the social, economic, and political impacts of these actions and policies; and (3) the strategic and political responses to these impacts by different social groups and classes according to their location in the social structure and the broader system of global capitalism.

- *Globalization.* The integration of countries across the world into a new world order in which the forces of economic and political 'freedom' are allowed to flourish has had an ambiguous impact on civil society organizations. On the one hand, the invasive pressures of global markets often compromise their autonomy or sovereignty. On the other, globalization—particularly in terms of freer flows of information and communication across national boundaries—has fostered the spread of 'transnational communities' (see also chapter 22) and an incipient **global civil society**.
- *Democratization.* The spread of democracy, as an idea and value, has in recent years changed the political and institutional environment in which civil society organizations operate. In some cases (see Box 12.1), civil society has been the locus of active opposition to authoritarian governments, providing a breeding ground for alternative, participatory, or 'democratic' forms of political organization—and governance. In other cases, civil society is marginalized or weakened through state repression or withdrawal from active engagement in politics. Civil society in this context may constitute a locus in which civic values and norms of democratic engagement are nurtured, although greater political freedom can be exploited to advance narrow, self-interested agendas that can exacerbate political conflict and undermine **good governance**.[4]
- *Privatization.* The rapid economic growth experienced by many developing countries from the 1950s on was fuelled in large measure by growth of the public sector and a policy of nationalization—taking over from the 'private sector' (the multinational corporations, that is) and buying out firms in the strategic sectors of the economy (oil production, for example). In the 1980s, this policy was reversed with a privatization policy: turning over state firms to private enterprise under the guise of a presumed 'efficiency'. This new policy allowed capitalist corporations—often multinational in form and foreign-owned—to acquire these enterprises at bargain-basement prices, greatly enriching their new owners.
- *Decentralization.* Until 1980 or so, many political scientists (and economists, for that matter) in both liberal and conservative traditions subscribed to the notion that democracy was not necessarily conducive to economic development—that authoritarianism provided a better agency (see chapter 16). In the 1980s, however, there was a sea change in this idea, leading to widespread calls for 'democracy' and 'good governance' in the form of a more participatory form of politics and development. To establish an appropriate institutional framework for these developments (also to reduce fiscal pressures on governments), the World Bank argued for the need for a policy of administrative decentralization, with a partnership approach to both local governments and civil society (Rondinelli, McCullough, and Johnson 1989; World Bank 2004b).
- *Economic liberalization.* The improvement in socio-economic conditions in the 1950s and 1960s was based on the active agency of governments in redistributing market-generated wealth and incomes for the common benefit. In the developing countries of the Global South, it was also based on protectionism, a policy designed to protect fledgling industries from the forces of the world market, to give domestic companies a chance to grow by placing restrictions on foreign investment and the operations of multinational corporations in their countries. Under the 'new economic model' of free-market capitalism and **neo-liberal globalization**, this policy was reversed.

Liberalization has had a number of contradictory consequences for civil society. In some contexts, it weakened predatory state structures and limited the scope for 'rent-seeking behaviour' by political and bureaucratic elites. Some groups are better placed than others to exploit the opportunities created by liberalization for advancing their own economic agendas, and organizations representing their interests can wield considerable influence over decision-making. The removal of price controls and other restrictions on economic activity are often accompanied by growth of the informal economy and the emergence of a dense network of groups and associations geared towards the advancement of collective economic interests. The removal of safety nets and reduction in government welfare spending gives rise to a proliferation of self-help groups and development associations with a mandate to provide relief and services to people marginalized or impoverished by market reforms.

- *Deregulation*. State-led development is predicated on government regulation of private economic activity and markets in the public interest. However, from the perspective of firms concerned with maximizing profit-making opportunities, this policy is viewed as an intolerable attack on freedom, resulting in 'inefficiency', a distortion of market forces that, if left unhindered, produce an optimal distribution of society's productive resources, wealth, and income. In the 1980s, the perceived 'failure' of the state—in the form of a widespread fiscal crisis (an inability to finance costly social and development programs out of government revenues)—created political conditions for a reversal of this regulatory approach.

BOX 12.1   APPO: POPULAR ASSEMBLY OF THE PEOPLE OF OAXACA

All the Power to the People (website logo)
When a woman advances there is no man who will retreat. (on a placard in a political march)

Oaxaca is the name of both a state in Mexico and that state's capital city. APPO (the Spanish acronym for an organizing body of diverse protest groups) is a coalition of organized social and political groups. APPO is nothing if not popular, bringing together broad sectors of the community and civil society organizations, including COMO, an organization of women—the Women of Oaxaca the First of August—formed in the wake of state repression of the teachers' struggle. With the march of COMO on the radio and TV broadcasting facilities, the struggle was elevated to an entirely different level, broadened into a social movement for democratic transformation (see John Gibler's report below).

John Gibler. 'Scenes from the Oaxaca Rebellion'
ZNet, 4 August 2006

On Tuesday, August 1, about 3,000 women marched through downtown Oaxaca City banging metal pots and pans in an oddly melodious cacophony that served as the background for their chants demanding the ousting of governor Ulises Ruiz. . . .

Once gathered in the central town square—where teachers and other protestors have been camping out since May 22—the women decided to take over the statewide television and radio

(continued)

company. . . . Some women walked, others hopped on buses. Thousands of them met at CORTV's broadcasting headquarters outside the colonial town center, where they walked right in and took it over. Not a shot was fired. Not a punch was thrown. While the station's director had fled, the women gathered the station's employees and demanded that they hook up the cameras for a live broadcast. Outside the building, about 50 women and a handful of men with clubs . . . guarded the entrance. They would not let any men enter the building (with a few exceptions of well-known reporters who were escorted in by groups of women). When reporters from the national television station Televisa arrived on the scene, the men and women gathered at the gates marched them right back to their cars shouting: 'Get them out!' and 'Liars!'. . .

It took several hours of negotiation before the women were able to fix a live broadcast, during which—still clutching their pots and wooden spoons, dressed in aprons and work clothes—they set out to correct the mistakes in the station's reporting on the violent June 14 attempt by state police to lift the teachers' encampment and demand on the air that the press 'tell the truth' about the social movement that is taking over Oaxaca.

The women are all part of the Popular Assembly of the People of Oaxaca, or APPO, an organizing body that was created after the June 14 police raid with the objective of concentrating local residents' outrage over the violence into the single demand that the governor step down, or get the boot, and the TV station take-over was only the latest in a series of in-your-face civil resistance tactics aimed at shutting down the state government.

On June 16, just two days after the raid, some 500,000 people marched to demand the governor's resignation. . . . APPO also organized a boycott of the state's largest tourist event, the Guelaguetza, and convoked an alternative, and free of charge . . . that drew a crowd of 20,000. Throughout July . . . APPO took over the coordination of the town square encampment and began to organize sit-ins at government buildings, which became permanent encampments on July 26.

THE ECONOMIC AND POLITICAL DYNAMICS OF DEVELOPMENT AND CIVIL SOCIETY

Development means a combination of improvements in the quality of people's lives—marked by a reduction in or alleviation of poverty, an increased capacity to meet the basic needs of society's members, **sustainable livelihoods**, and empowerment—and the changes in institutionalized practices or 'structures' needed to bring about these improvements. The idea of development can be traced back to an eighteenth-century idea of progress—of the possibility of and necessity for a better form of society characterized by freedom from tyranny, superstition, and poverty (see chapter 2) and social equality. But it was reinvented in 1948 in the context of: (1) a postwar world order based on the International Monetary Fund (IMF), the World Bank, and the General Agreement on Tariffs and Trade (GATT), a free trade negotiating forum; (2) an emerging East–West conflict and Cold War; and (3) a national independence struggle by countries seeking to escape the yoke of colonialism—Pax Britannica in the pre-war, Pax Americana in the postwar period.

In this context, international cooperation for development—foreign aid, in official parlance—nation-building, capitalist industrialization, and modernization were designed as a means of ensuring that those countries emerging from colonialism would not fall prey to the lure of communism. The active agent in this process was the state in the form of policies and programs designed to: (1) increase the rate of savings and productive investment (capital accumulation); (2) invest these savings in new technology and industrial expansion (modernization); (3) redistribute market-generated incomes via progressive taxation and social and development programs; and (4) provide technical and financial assistance to developing countries in the South.

From the outset of this development process in 1948, signalled by Harry Truman's Point 4 program (of development assistance), to the early 1970s, when the world capitalist system ran out of steam and entered a period of prolonged crisis, these policies and this state-led form of development generated an unprecedented period of economic growth and societal transformation. Growth rates, fuelled by rising wages and a rapid growth of the domestic market as well as international trade, exceeded by a factor of two the economic growth rates of previous decades, resulting in an incremental but steady improvement in the physical quality of life and the social conditions of health, education, and welfare. Historians have dubbed these advances the 'golden age of capitalism'.

In 1973, at the height of an apparent crisis of overproduction, characterized by cutthroat competition, saturated markets and stagflation, sluggish productivity, and falling profits, the capitalist class in the rich countries, the CEOs of its multinational corporations, and governments in their employ or service abandoned the system that had served them so well. Or, to be more precise, they sought to renovate this system to resolve the crisis of capitalist production by: (1) changing the relationship of capital to labour, favouring the former and weakening the latter; (2) incorporating new production technologies and constructing a new regime of accumulation and labour regulation (post-Fordism); (3) relocating labour-intensive industrial production overseas, thereby unwittingly creating a **new international division of labour**; and, above all, (4) bringing about a 'new world order' in which the forces of 'economic freedom' were liberated from the regulatory apparatus of the welfare-developmental state. The policies that facilitated this process generated epoch-defining changes, a seismic shift in international relations—a new world order in which it

was thought that the forces of freedom and democracy could prevail.

By 1990, most countries were aligned to this 'new world order' of 'globalization' and free market capitalism. In the 1970s, in the first phase of neo-liberal experiments, the implementing agency was a series of military regimes in the southern cone of South America—in Chile, Argentina, and Uruguay (Veltmeyer and Petras 1997; 2000). When these neo-liberal policy experiments crashed in the early 1980s, a new crop of liberal democratic regimes, forced into line by the realities of a region-wide debt crisis of historic proportions, initiated a second round of 'structural reform'. They did so with the assistance of an emerging civil society in the so-called 'third sector' of non-profit, voluntary associations and non-governmental organizations. These organizations, formed in response to the retreat of the state from its erstwhile responsibility for economic development, were enlisted by international financial institutions (IFIs) such as the World Bank and the international community of development associations and aid donors to mediate with the poor— to assist them in their self-development efforts in return for acceptance of their policy advice (market-friendly 'reforms' and 'good governance').

The literature on these issues is divided. Some see the development NGOs as 'false saviours of democracy', enlisted to help rescue capitalism from itself (Hayden 2002; Kamat, 2003). These authors do not see the role of NGOs as one of delivering economic assistance (through micro-development projects or poverty alleviation funds) but as one of promoting democracy, which, Ottaway (2003, vi) notes, was a 'new activity which the aid agencies and NGOs [originally] embarked [upon] with some trepidation and misgivings' but that in the early 1990s '[came] of age'. But others see them as agents of global capitalism—a 'Trojan horse of neo-liberal globalization' (Wallace 2003)—to facilitate the entry of foreign investment and the domestic operations of multinational corporations and, in the process, to help some achieve their imperial dream of world domination.

Figure 12.1   An informal street monument to protesters killed during political demonstrations in Argentina, 2001

Source: Paul Haslam

THE EMERGENCE OF A GLOBAL CIVIL SOCIETY: THE POLITICAL DYNAMICS OF ANTI-GLOBALIZATION

The measures associated with neo-liberal policies in the 1990s led to a dramatic increase in social inequalities—disparities in the global and North–South distribution of wealth and poverty, marked by an extension and deepening of existing poverty and a social polarization between the rich and the poor. In the 1990s, this 'inequality predicament' (as the United Nations, in a 2005 study, defines it) assumed grotesque proportions. In a world of spreading poverty, neo-liberal policies produced a new class of multi-billionaires, the clear 'winners' of globalization. In 1996, according to *Forbes* magazine, there were 793 of them, but within a year the number of multi-billionaires had grown to 946. In the US, there were just 13 billionaires in 1985. Today, according to *Forbes*, there are 415, representing the top .01 per cent of the US population, a group that has managed to appropriate at least 25 per cent of the wealth produced over the past two decades. By 2005, neo-liberal policies had created 227,000 millionaires across the world. The wealth of these millionaires amounted to $30 trillion, more than the combined GDP of China, Brazil, Russia, and the EU.[5]

The UNDP (1996; 2001) estimates that a roomful of these super-rich, some 358 people, dispose of the equivalent income of 45 per cent of the world's poorest (3.5 billion), who have to subsist on less than $2 a day, a statistic that the UNDP understandably finds 'grotesque' and others criminal. The total wealth of the world's richest individuals (*Forbes*'s list of billionaires), representing a one-hundred-millionth of the population, increased their wealth by 35 per cent to $3.5 trillion in 2007—more than the total wealth of the world's poor. In other words, poverty is the product of the same policies and the same system that generated a very unevenly distributed wealth: wealth for the few, the 'winners' of globalization, and poverty for the many, the 'losers'.

Neo-liberal policies that the World Bank describes as 'pro-growth' and 'pro-poor' not only produced mass poverty but made some individuals incredibly rich. However, the 'losers' in the global competition for wealth—or the victims, to be more precise—have not been passive in their response to neo-liberal globalization. They have responded by forming social movements in opposition to these policies, in resistance against the dynamics of globalizing capital. These movements have taken different forms in the North and the South. In the Global South, they have been generally led by indigenous communities, peasant farmers, and rural landless workers who have been the major targets and victims of 'globalization'. The working class, in both its waged/formal and its unwaged/informal forms, is also its victim. But the capacity of the workers to wage either a defensive or an offensive struggle has dramatically diminished over the past two decades, which has meant that the leadership of the popular movement in the Global South now rests with landless rural workers, peasant farmers, and indigenous communities.

As for the North (the rich industrial societies, mostly in Europe and North America), the anti-globalization movement has been centred in the urban centres, based in the middle class, and has taken the form of opposition to the agenda of corporate capital. Unlike the South, where anti-globalization is directed against the neo-liberal policies of governments, the anti-globalization movement in the North is most visible in counter-summits to G-8 summits, protests at the periodic gatherings of the World Trade Organization (WTO) and other such organizations of global capital, and, perhaps more importantly, at the World

Social Forum, which annually brings together thousands of anti-globalization activists, representing hundreds of civil society organizations, to discuss problems and debate strategy. This anti-globalization movement is not against globalization as such but against its neo-liberal form (see chapter 6). In this context, anti-globalization can be seen as a movement formed in the search for 'another world', a more ethical form of globalization, a more equitable and socially inclusive and participatory form of development—an alternative to neo-liberal globalization, capitalism, and imperialism.

In the spring of 2007, the UK Ministry of Defence published a report (*Global Strategic Trends 2007–2036*) warning that the whole system of global capitalism, and with it the new world order, could well be brought down by the mounting forces of resistance. The report argues that excessive inequalities will likely lead to a 'resurgence of not only anti-capitalist ideologies . . . but also populism and the revival of Marxism' (2007, 3). It expresses particular concern that the widening global divide in wealth and income has spawned a mass global justice movement, a broad movement that threatens to unite the most diverse forces of resistance and opposition to neo-liberal globalization.

The meaning of this anti-globalization movement, and the growth of a transnational or global civil society committed to the search for 'another world', is subject to continuing debate. Some see it as a palliative. Others see it as the salvation of humanity on a fast road to self-destruction. But there is no question that it might very well scuttle the best-laid plans of the new world order architects for imperial rule.

CIVIL SOCIETY AND LOCAL DEVELOPMENT

The search for a new development paradigm acquired a particular vigour in the 1980s with the turn towards a 'new economic model' prioritizing the free market. Proponents of the new paradigm visualize development as community-based

Figure 12.2   Street demonstration in Mexico

Source: Jennifer Rogers

and localized, reaching beyond the state and the market into the localities and communities of the rural poor. The goal in this context is to advance development that is human in form, sustainable in terms of the environment and livelihoods, socially inclusive and equitable, participatory—and initiated 'from below', from within civil society as opposed to 'from above' or 'from outside'.

To some extent, this paradigm shift has to do with a long-standing concern with giving development a *social* dimension. From the beginning, the study of development was dominated by economics, in which the 'social' and the 'political' are often abstracted from analysis, treated as 'externalities' in a process viewed in strictly economic terms. But in the 'new paradigm', the 'social' is given more weight, even with regard to 'capital', the sum total of society's wealth (or income-generating assets). Economists had formulated the theory that economic development was based

on capital accumulation and advanced by increasing the rate of savings and productive investment. However, 'capital' in this theory was defined purely in economic terms—money invested in the design of new technology, the purchase of labour power, and the transformation of natural resources into commodities or tradable goods. Within the framework of the new paradigm, however, society's productive assets ('capital') are also conceived in social terms—that is, as the norms, institutions, and organizations that promote trust and cooperation among persons in communities and in the wider society. Initially advanced by several sociologists (notably James Coleman and Pierre Bourdieu), this notion of 'social capital' was elaborated by leading development scholars such as Robert Chambers and Robert Putnam.

This was the thinking in the 1980s. In the 1990s, the concept of 'social capital' took on a new life, supported and advanced by all manner of scholars, international organizations, and policy-makers in their development discourse. At issue in this discourse was an alternative way of conceiving 'development' and fighting the war against world poverty (Durstan 1999, 104). More specifically, the proponents of this approach claim that the accumulation of social capital based on norms of trust and reciprocal exchange, and a culture of social solidarity, can produce public goods, facilitate the 'constitution of sound civil societies', and constitute the poor as 'social actors', empowering them to act on their own behalf. As an asset that the poor have in abundance (their only asset, one could add, besides their capacity to labour), social capital promotes self-development of the poor in their localities and communities, alleviating the socio-economic (and psychological) conditions of their poverty.

Robert Putnam's book, *Making Democracy Work* (1993), served as the catalyst for this interest in social capital as a research and policy tool. But the rapid spread and ubiquity of the notion in academe, and its wide-ranging applications in research, policy formulation, and practice, has been followed by serious questioning and several concerns. First, what is striking about the concept of social capital is not only the extent of its influence but its enthusiastic acceptance by both scholars and policy-makers. This is evident in the World Bank's notion of social capital as 'the glue that holds society together', as the 'missing link' in an analysis of the development process (Solow 2000).

Second, despite the plethora of survey articles that litter the intellectual landscape, the concept is notoriously difficult to define. Most recent contributions to the literature acknowledge this before adding a definition of their own to suit their purpose. The ambiguity of 'social capital' is reflected in the suggestion that it is merely a metaphor or a heuristic device and, with regard to the World Bank's formulation, based on 'a vicious circle of tautological reasoning without any basis in empirical fact (Portes 1998).

Third, the concept of social capital is used to describe and explain virtually anything and everything, from the networks formed by the poor, the sick, the criminal, and the corrupt to the social dynamics of the (dys)functional family, schooling, community development, work and organization, democracy and governance, collective action, the intangible assets of the social economy, 'the analysis and promotion of peasant-level development', or, indeed, any aspect of social, cultural, and economic activity across time and place—everything, it would seem, except the norms, institutions, and social networks formed by those that constitute what the Australian documentary filmmaker and award-winning journalist John Pilger (2003) terms 'the new rulers of the world', the class that runs the global economy and makes its rules.

The final concern about social capital has to do with ideology and politics. What is missing in the analysis informed by the notion of social capital is any concern for the structure of economic and political power. The concept of social capital appears to serve analysts and policy-makers in the same way that post-modern social theory serves analysis: as a means of eluding in thought what for most people is all too real—the dynamic workings of the world capitalist system. The power relations that determine life for most people are inverted: what is essentially a class struggle over the allocation of society's productive resources, a matter of state and economic power, is transmuted into empowerment—a feeling of power gained by individuals through participating in decisions (such as how to spend the poverty alleviation funds that come their way) that affect their livelihoods and an improvement in the physical quality of their lives. The point is that empowerment means changing oneself (how one feels about one's self) rather than changing the system.

Another criticism is that the concept of social capital is ideologically all too convenient for the powerful and that it is politically demobilizing. In this connection, Harriss (2001) and others argue that making people responsible for their own development falsely implies that they themselves were responsible for their problems, such as poverty, which draws attention away from the operating structures of the economic and social system. With its focus on 'civil society', social capital ignores the dynamics associated with the formal structures and institutions of society's political economy, particularly that of state power.

Critics argue that the way in which the concept of social capital is used has a demobilizing effect on dynamics of radical change. Local development built on the basis of social capital brings limited improvements, with even more limited or no changes in the existing distribution of 'capital' in the form of land and related resources or money in the form of investment capital or credit. Access to these 'resources'—arguably the major factors of economic development—remains in the hands (and institutions) of the rich and powerful, while the poor and powerless are encouraged to exploit their own rather limited resources and to do so without challenging the structures of economic and political power. Some critics regard social capital and empowerment as illusory—not that they are false assumptions but rather a trick used by the rich and powerful to preserve their wealth and keep the have-nots at bay.

NGOs: CATALYSTS FOR DEVELOPMENT OR AGENTS OF OUTSIDE INTERESTS?

The major expression of civil society in the 1980s was the 'voluntary private association' or 'non-governmental organization', formed in what at the time was defined as the 'third sector' (as opposed to the 'private sector', composed of

Figure 12.3   Civil society can cross borders: A chieftaincy on the Mozambique–Zimbabwe border participates in community consultations with government and non-government development actors

Source: Jessica Schafer

profit-making economic enterprises, and the 'public sector', organizations and enterprises set up by the government).

At the beginning of the decade, there were relatively few such organizations, most of them voluntary associations to provide poverty relief or to assist communities in their adaptation to the forces of change. By the end of the decade, however, these non-governmental organizations had mushroomed, responding to the vacuum left by the retreating state, assuming responsibilities that it had hitherto fulfilled. While in 1970 there were barely 250 development NGOs working in Latin America, it is estimated that by the end of the 1990s, the number had grown to tens of thousands, organized to assist poor communities in the quest for self-development as well as assisting citizens in the struggle to prevent the violation of human rights, advance women's equality, protect the environment, and take on other such concerns of the urban middle class. Political sociologists, armed with a post-modern political imagination, saw this development as the emergence of 'new social movements' (Escobar and Alvarez 1992) concerned with a multitude of issues, not just with state power or transformative social change.

NGOs were enlisted by international organizations such as the World Bank as strategic partners in the war on poverty to act as intermediaries between the providers of financial and technical assistance and the poor communities ravaged by the forces of modernization and abandoned by their governments (at the behest of these same international organizations, it could be added). 'Development' here is conceived within the optics of a new paradigm that valorizes 'popular participation' and grassroots self-development initiated 'from below' with the support of civil society.

To create an appropriate institutional framework for an 'alternative' form of development, the development associations involved in 'international cooperation' promoted a policy of administrative decentralization in developing nations. This policy was incorporated into a new economic model, together with the structural reforms mandated as the cost of admission into the new world

order: privatization, financial and trade liberalization, deregulation of markets and private economic activity, democratization, and good governance.

The NGOs were recruited not only to mediate between the aid donors and the poor communities but to promote the virtues of private enterprise and reform. By the 1990s, the marriage between capitalism (the free market) and democracy (free elections) had been consummated, with the NGOs preparing the bridal chamber. In the process, the NGOs helped to dampen the fires of revolutionary ferment among the rural poor, who were encouraged to turn away from the confrontational class politics of the social movements.

There are two fundamental theoretical perspectives on the NGOs in this context. One is to see them as catalysts of an alternative form of development that is participatory, empowering of women and the poor, equitable and socially inclusive, human in form, and sustainable in terms of both the environment and livelihoods. Other scholars, however, take a less sanguine view of these development NGOs, viewing many of them not as change agents but as the stalking horse of neo-liberal globalization—a Trojan Horse for global capitalism—the paid if at times unwitting agents of US imperialism (Wallace 2003). Proponents of this view argue that NGOs do not serve the interests of the rural poor as much as the interests of their masters, the new 'rulers of the world', a *transnational capitalist class* composed of corporate CEOs, financiers, and major investors—the guardians of the new world order and its billionaire beneficiaries.

The argument of these scholars is that NGOs are enlisted as frontline soldiers in the war on poverty, in the localities and communities of the poor, to provide what assistance (poverty alleviation funds) might be available and, in the process, instil respect for the virtues of capitalism and democracy. The war on poverty, it is argued, is simply a charade to mask the real agenda: to create a world safe for capital—to facilitate the entry of foreign investment and the multinational corporations. The implicit mandate of these NGOs, it is further argued, is to help turn the rural poor away from joining social movements and engaging in the confrontational politics of direct action against government policy: to encourage them to seek change and improvements in their lives not by challenging the power structure but by turning inwards—to change not the system but themselves (by 'empowering' them to act on their own behalf)—and to seek improvements and change in the local spaces of the power structure rather than challenging the power itself. That is, NGOs are seen as unwitting agents of outside forces and interests, helping to depoliticize the poor in their struggle for change.

DEVELOPMENT BEYOND NEO-LIBERALISM: CIVIL SOCIETY AND THE STATE

The problem with the term 'civil society' is that it is so nebulous as to make analysis and prescriptions for action difficult. It includes all manner of social organizations, whose role in the development process must be carefully assessed. For the sake of this assessment, and to facilitate analysis, it is possible to break down 'civil society' into three sectors:

1. A complex of associational-type organizations ('associations' formed for a common purpose, such as environmental protection, to advance the status of women, or to promote development or respect for human rights). The 'anti-globalization movement' in the North is an amalgam of such organizations. For the most part, they are located in the cities and middle-class-based.
2. Community or grassroots organizations, making up the 'popular sector' of civil society. The Landless Workers Movement (MST) in Brazil is an example of this type of 'civil society organization' (CSO).
3. 'Interest groups' or profit-oriented organizations constituting the 'private sector'. This sector includes the capitalist economic enterprises and multinational corporations that until the 1990s were excluded because they

were seen as a large part of the problem.

This chapter has already discussed the role of the first sector, Northern development NGOs, the main component of the middle-class sector of civil society activism (in some contexts, as in India and Latin America, for example, 'the new politics' or the politics of the 'New Left'). As for the third, these private-sector organizations are normally excluded from the discourse on development, primarily because as a rule they do not have a development agenda. But in 1989, the UNDP launched a campaign to incorporate the private sector into the development process. For this effort, they used the ideological cover of a more inclusive 'civil society' discourse (Mitlin 1998).

This leaves open for discussion the role of the second sector, or what might well be regarded as the most relevant sector of development CSOs— namely, grassroots social organizations formed in the localities and communities of the poor. CSOs in this sector arguably have the greatest potential for constituting themselves as 'actors'. They consist of organizations targeted by international donors and Northern NGOs as the object of aid policies and poverty alleviation funding (micro projects). They include social movements, a more politically oriented form of popular organization concerned with bringing about social change through social mobilization and direct action.

MST is a good example of this type of organization. It is dedicated to improving the access of its members to the land, using the politically confrontational tactic of 'occupation', as well as organizing for agricultural production on the land, a concern that requires a working relationship with the state. Of course, there are less political, more social forms of grassroots organizations as well, such as Via Campesina, a transnational grouping of some 88 peasant and indigenous organizations from at least 25 developing countries (Desmarais 2007). For such organizations, some closely linked to the anti-globalization movement, their relationship with the state is critical, although it is characterized more by dialogue and cooperation than by the conflict that defines

Figure 12.4   Diverse forms of civil society in developing countries: Syncretic religious movements are growing rapidly

Source: Jessica Schafer

the relationship between most social movements and the state.

The relationship between the state and organizations such as MST is characterized as much by conflict as by cooperation because it tends to be marked by dispute and pressure rather than partnership and dialogue. To push for change and to increase pressure on the state, social movements—and MST represents an excellent case study of this point—often form alliances with groups and organizations in other sectors of civil society. In the 1990s, for example, MST expanded its ties to diverse solidarity and advocacy networks, such as the World Social Forum and Via Campesina, that make up what many regard as an emerging 'global civil society'.

As for the relationship between the state and grassroots CSOs, whether non-governmental or social movement in form and action, it is difficult to generalize. One pattern is for social movement-type grassroots organizations—such as MST, Latin America's largest and most dynamic social movement—to take on the central government in the demand for social change. Other grassroots social organizations, in contrast, tend to work with the state at the level of local governments. At this level, one can find many cases of 'good practice' as well as 'local development theory' (see Box 12.2 for an example).

CONCLUSION

A conclusion reached by some analysts of development is that neo-liberal globalization is dysfunctional, unethical, and unsustainable (see chapter 6). The benefits of neo-liberal globalization are appropriated by the few—a small group of super-billionaires—while its social costs are borne by the vast majority, many of whom are dispossessed, excluded, or impoverished in the process. In the neo-liberal theory of globalization, the benefits of the economic growth generated by the free

BOX 12.2   A CASE OF GOOD PRACTICE
(AND 'MARKET-DRIVEN SOCIAL JUSTICE')
IN ALTERNATIVE DEVELOPMENT

Civil society encompasses a wide gamut of social and political organizations in both the Global North and the South. An important example of a more 'political' CSO is the Council of Canadians headed by Maude Barlow. It has played a critically important role in challenging the corporate agenda of neo-liberal globalization, particularly with regard to the Multilateral Agreement on Investment (MAI) negotiated behind closed doors by the powerful and rich countries to advance the interests of their corporate capitalists. An example of a less political and more social CSO would be Just Us!, a Nova Scotia–based organization committed to promoting fair trade (versus neo-liberal free trade) and sustainable livelihoods for coffee-growing indigenous peasants in Mexico and Central America. Just Us! has been hailed as a model of 'good practice' in development. It is a profitable business, but its profitability is not based on economic exploitation of vulnerable peasant and indigenous groups but rather on ensuring that coffee producers are organized cooperatively without middlemen (or capitalist corporations) taking an undue share of their social product, trading with them on an equal playing field.

The Just Us! Development

Fair Trade was initiated by a cooperative of small producers in Mexico in the late 80s. It has had unbelievable success gaining market access all over the world for hundreds of thousands of small Third World farmers with sales now in the billions of dollars. . . . Fair Trade producers in Latin America with very limited resources have organized over 100 thousand families of small producers in 16 Latin American countries into a very strong organization bent on keeping the Fair Trade system true to its original mission—better prices and improved standards of living for the small farmers. It is called CLAC. Just Us! agreed to help sponsor a recent CLAC meeting in Santo Domingo, in November 2006, to develop strategies to keep the system honest. . . . It was so well organized and was truly a landmark meeting in the history of Fair Trade. Producers in Africa and Asia are following their lead and these strong producers' organizations will play a major role in keeping Fair Trade healthy . . . well into the future (http://www.justuscoffee.com).

market will eventually trickle down to the poor. But this is evidently not the case. Apart from the super-rich, the only apparent beneficiaries of the globalization process are members of the 'global middle class', who because of a higher level of education can position themselves favourably in the world market and thus improve their 'life chances'. Most of the world's urban and rural poor do not have either the opportunities or the education of this middle class and are thus socially excluded from any benefits of economic globalization.

Another conclusion, more directly related to the topic of this chapter, is the need for a better balance between the market and the state—to restore the capacity and the authority of the state to regulate private economic activity and restrict the power of big property as well as the freedom of private interests and to do so for the public good (O'Campo and Khan 2007). This does not necessarily mean a return to the welfare and development state. Although the government and regulatory apparatus of the state needs to be reinstituted, it is evident that it must have an entirely new form (see chapter 7).

What is needed is that people assert their 'right to development' and to organize—both to empower themselves to act in their collective interest and to advance the local, regional, and national development of society as a whole. This means that the rights of private property need to be restricted, particularly regarding the appropriation of an excessive share of wealth and income. These resources should be shared and distributed more equitably. It also means the abolition of class rule—i.e., reducing the capacity and power of one class, by virtue of its property entitlement (ownership of the means of social production), to set the rules and control who gets what. Above all, it means that civil society

QUESTIONS FOR DISCUSSION

1. How is civil society constituted—in response to objective changing conditions and trends or as a means of bringing about these conditions?

2. What is the role of civil society in the social change and development process in mediating between donors (and outside forces) and the localities/communities of the poor? As a facilitator or catalyst of a participatory form of economic or social development? Or to contribute to the establishment of 'democracy' and 'good governance'?

3. Are NGOs a positive factor in the development process? Whose interests do they primarily represent—those of the donors and the guardians of the new world order? Or the groups that are socially excluded, marginalized, and poor?

4. What is the best way to advance the interests of the socially excluded, marginalized, and poor—by joining (and encouraging the poor to join) anti-systemic (anti-globalization) movements for social change or to serve as strategic partners of overseas development associations and their so-called 'war on poverty'?

5. Is it possible for development NGOs to support or facilitate the self-development of the poor outside the program of international cooperation—without serving as a strategic partner of the development associations and without any funding from them?

FURTHER READING

International Development Research Centre (IDRC). 1997. *Civil (Dis)Obedience and Social Development in the New Policy Agenda: Research Priorities for Analyzing the Role of Civil Society Organizations in Social Policy Reform, with Particular Attention to Sub-Saharan Africa and Latin America*. Ottawa: IDRC.

International Institute for Environment and Development (IIED). 1998. *What Does Strengthening NGO Capacity Mean for Civil Society and Governance?* Winnipeg: IIED.

Loxley, J., ed. 2006. *Towards a Theory of Community Economic Development*. Halifax: Fernwood.

North-South Institute (NSI). 1998. *Civil Society and the Aid Industry*. Ottawa: NSI.

Rice, J., and M. Prince. 2000. 'Civil society and community capacity: Links between social policy and social capital'. In J. Rice and M. Prince, *Changing Politics of Canadian Social Policy*, 207–31. Toronto: University of Toronto Press.

Veltmeyer, H. 2007. *Civil Society and the Quest for Social Change*. Halifax: Fernwood.

INTERNET RESOURCES

Association for Research on Nonprofit Organizations and Voluntary Action: http://www.arnova.org.

Council of Canadians: http://www.canadians.org.

Union of International Associations (for web resources on civil society): http://www.uia.org/civilsoc/links.php.

Eldis: http://www.eldis.org.

Institute of Development Studies, University of Sussex, Brighton, UK: http://www.ids.ac.uk.

Documentation flowing from the World Summit on Sustainable Development: http://www.wssd-and-civil-society.org.

NOTES

1. 'Good governance' is generally understood to mean an array of practices that maximize the common/public good. More specifically, it denotes a relation between social organizations and government that conforms to the following 'democratic' principles: transparency, effectiveness, openness, responsiveness, and accountability; the rule of law, acceptance of diversity and pluralism, and social inclusiveness

2. The term 'civil society' dates back to the eighteenth-century 'Enlightenment' when moral philosophers like Adam Ferguson invented the term to distinguish more clearly between 'society' and 'government' in their writings about 'progress'. But the term 'civil society' disappeared from the map of social scientific discourse until it was resurrected in the 1980s by a generation of social scientists concerned once again with creating a new and better form of society—this time liberated from Soviet authoritarianism as opposed to the class-based and elitist monarchy of the *ancien régime* (characterized by a ruling landowning aristocracy, serfdom, monarchy, and an all-powerful church).

3. 'Liberal' in academic discourse has both an ideological and theoretical meaning. As 'ideology' (belief in ideas used to promote action), liberalism concerns a belief in the need for progress (slow incremental change or reform) in the direction of individual freedom. As 'theory', it is associated with the notion that economic interactions among individuals are based on a rational calculus of self-interest by each individual.

4. 'Good governance' implies a democratic regime in which the responsibility for human security and political order is not restricted to the government and other institutions of the state but is widely shared by different civil society organizations (UNDP 1996; World Bank 1994).

5. A study by Petras (2007) argues that Bill Gates and others who made their fortunes via technical innovations or wealth/job-generating industries or services are in a distinct minority. The vast majority of the world's billionaires used the money of others and speculation to build their fortunes. Many, as in Russia, built their fortune by looting public assets, pillaging the state's accumulated assets, stealing, and speculative investment and commodity trading—in construction, telecommunications, chemicals, real estate, agriculture, vodka, foods, land, media, automobiles, and airlines.

PART THREE

ISSUES IN INTERNATIONAL DEVELOPMENT

CHAPTER 13

POVERTY AND EXCLUSION: FROM BASIC NEEDS TO THE MILLENNIUM DEVELOPMENT GOALS

DAVID R. MORRISON

LEARNING OBJECTIVES

- To examine the ethical and practical arguments that have been advanced for poverty reduction.
- To understand the assumptions underlying changes in approaches towards aid and how they relate to poverty reduction. (The dominant approach of the aid regime, after flirting with redistribution with growth and basic human needs in the 1970s, reverted in the 1980s to 'trickle down' but an even more radical version that saw the market rather than the state as the key to economic development. The discourse was subsequently modified by the promotion of 'good governance' and challenged by the notion of human development.)
- To examine the major assumptions, strengths, and weaknesses of approaches to defining poverty framed in terms of income/consumption, capabilities, social exclusion, and participatory assessment.

Most students of international development would agree that tackling poverty and global inequality must be high priorities for action. Poverty is often seen as the antithesis of development, but they are not exact opposites. As O'Connor (2002, 37) observes, 'poverty is a condition while development is a process or set of processes.' Moreover, while 'development' is contested and there is intense debate about whether it should be supported however it is defined, few see poverty as something to be welcomed and preserved. All member countries of the United Nations have declared their support for Millennium Development Goals (MDGs) that set 2015 as a target date for the eradication of extreme poverty and hunger, the achievement of universal primary education, the elimination of gender discrimination at all educational levels, a large reduction in child and maternal mortality, a halt to and reversal of the spread of HIV/AIDS, malaria, and other major diseases, and

a more determined pursuit of environmental sustainability. Goal 8 calls for a global partnership for development and sets several targets relating to trade, debt, and the needs of the poorest countries and populations. Multilateral and bilateral development agencies are now rhetorically committed to assessing their policies in terms of their impact on poverty alleviation. Bono and other celebrities have associated themselves with the campaign 'to make poverty history'. There are, however, huge obstacles standing in the way of this achievement, not least sharp clashes among scholars and practitioners about how to pursue it.

This chapter surveys perspectives on poverty reduction, in particular as they have evolved within the **international aid regime** and among people who study and criticize foreign aid. After asking the question 'why be concerned?', we sketch in broad brush strokes changes in the dominant discourse on poverty

Figure 13.1   An elderly musician earns his keep by performing on the street, Rosario, Argentina

Source: Paul Haslam

and development. We then examine differing conceptions of poverty and how they relate to policy debates. Proposals for action in turn raise questions about how to align domestic and global forces and institutions in ways that could reduce poverty. The chapter concludes with a recent imaginative attempt to move beyond the **neo-liberal orthodoxy** that has defined and constricted official discourse during the past quarter century.

WHY BE CONCERNED ABOUT POVERTY REDUCTION?

Alan Thomas (2000, 11) reminds us that just 200 years ago, most people were poor. This situation was widely understood as natural, or at least was portrayed that way by rich and powerful elites. Current ideas about poverty and the gap between rich and poor have been shaped in the context of 'a unique era' during which 'both population and per capita income came unstuck, soaring at rates

never before seen or even imagined' (Sachs 2005, 27). But dramatically rising per capita income, as an average, masks staggering disparities. Branko Milanovic captures this reality poignantly:

> Even as large numbers of Indians and Chinese were joining the consumer society, many in the two countries were left behind. . . . While a part of the rich world was discussing techniques that would prolong the human life-span to over 100 years, millions were dying from easily preventable diseases, lack of safe water, or infections . . . for those who found themselves born in wrong countries, in wrong social groups, and of a wrong race or sex, a large part of the promise went unfulfilled (2005, 2).

Milanovic and most other authors cited in this chapter express a deep ethical concern about poverty, together with a determination to find ways of reducing both its severity and the number of people afflicted by it. Among them is Paul Streeten (1998, 2–4), who also offers four practical reasons for pursuing these objectives: (1) poverty reduction can be a means of achieving higher productivity by contributing to 'a well-nourished, healthy, educated, skilled and alert labor force'; (2) it would lower fertility rates; (3) it is good for the physical environment (the poor are both a cause—though less than the rich—and the main victims of environmental degradation); and (4) it can contribute to a healthy civil society, democracy, and greater social stability, at least in the long run. 'Although the very poor, being too weak, are not a source of rebellion, gross inequalities can contribute to social conflict and possibly to civil war.' With respect to this last point, Jeffrey Sachs, director of the UN Millennium Project from 2002 to 2006, strongly criticizes the one-sidedness of the American strategy of fighting terrorism. 'Almost three thousand people died needlessly and tragically at the World Trade Center on September 11; ten thousand Africans die needlessly and tragically *every single* day—and have died every single day since September 11—of AIDS, TB, and malaria. We need to keep September 11 in perspective, especially since ten thousand daily deaths *are* preventable. To fight terrorism, there is a need to fight poverty and deprivation as well' (Sachs 2005, 215).

There are dissenting voices. From the right, we hear that the rich have no responsibility for the poor because poor countries have only themselves to blame for wrong-headed economic policies and civil wars or that they are doomed by unfavourable geography and climate. Milanovic (2005, 157) answers one of these dissenters—Leszek Balcerowicz, former head of the Bank of Poland—by asking, 'can one seriously argue that colonization, or, more recently, the Cold War had nothing to do with furthering civil wars and adding to the misery of the poor countries?' From the post-development left, Majid Rahnema argues that poverty as a global construct is new, arising from the economization of life and the forced integration of vernacular societies into the world economy:

Following a consensus reached among the world elites on the diagnosis of the disease (underdevelopment and lack of income), as well as its cure (economic and technological development), armies of experts, politicians, planners, bureaucrats, socio-economists, and even anthropologists started acting as pauperologists . . . [who pursue] a universalist, one-track, income-based, and totally acultural recipe for abstract 'patients' (Rahnema 1992, 161–2).

There is substance to this critique, although as we shall see, thinking and action about poverty have become increasingly multi-dimensional. Moreover, as with much post-development analysis, a powerful indictment such as this can be a recipe for disempowering paralysis.

THE INTERNATIONAL AID REGIME AND POVERTY REDUCTION: A BRIEF HISTORY[1]

Economic growth and 'trickle down'

In the shadow of the Cold War after World War II, Western states agreed to channel small proportions of their public expenditures into foreign aid for developing countries in Africa, Asia, and the Americas. Each donor pursued its own mix of mainly geopolitical and commercial objectives, although relief of poverty was always cited as a central reason for what came to be known as **official development assistance** (ODA). Development economists were supremely optimistic that poverty would decline in the wake of economic growth. Simon Kuznets was a major contributor to this confidence, producing in 1955 his famous Inverted-U Hypothesis on the relationship between growth and income inequality. Based more on speculation than empirical evidence, the 'Kuznets Curve' predicted that as primarily agricultural economies moved towards industrialization, inequality would initially increase. As more of the population moved out of agriculture, however, inequality would eventually decrease (Kanbur and Squire 1999, 7). The ripple effects of economic growth would result in a 'trickle down' of benefits, the relative share of the income of the poor would rise, and people would be lifted out of poverty.

Foreign aid was seen as one means of catalyzing growth in what were first described as backward areas and later as developing or less developed countries. While capital assistance captured most aid resources in the 1950s, the wonders wrought by the Marshall Plan in the reconstruction of postwar Europe did not occur in the developing world. The amounts transferred were of course tiny by comparison (except in South Korea, Taiwan, and other areas of strategic interest to the US). Growing numbers of practitioners and academic observers argued that technology and human capital were also needed to change methods of production. What emerged was a new aid paradigm. Rondinelli summarizes its major assumptions:

> (1) all societies could modernize and grow economically in a sequence of historically verified stages that had occurred in Western nations over the previous two centuries; (2) this [process] could be accelerated in poor countries through the transfer of resources and technologies from the industrialized nations; . . . [and (3)] leaders of developing countries, eager for growth and modernization, would sacrifice other values and—with the help of Western advisors—would provide the political and moral support necessary to achieve these goals (1987, 22).

Within this ahistorical conception of the experience of the already industrialized countries, belief in trickle down obviated any need for explicit consideration of poverty and inequality in aid programming.

In the late 1960s, growing debate about non-aid issues culminated in demands by many developing countries for a New International Economic Order (NIEO) that would rein in multinational corporations and foster beneficial changes in the rules of international trade. Meanwhile, academic and popular commentaries were questioning the value

of development assistance—from the right as a wasteful intervention in the marketplace that was undermining dynamism and from the left as a tool for capitalism to exploit the Third World (see Riddell 1987). 'Horror stories' about inappropriate projects and corruption began to appear in the media, and foreign aid became highly controversial within the US Congress. The failure of trickle down was apparent everywhere. Within newly established multilateral and bilateral aid agencies, doubts were increasing about the efficacy of pursuing economic growth as *the* pathway to development, especially if development implied such goals as a more equitable income distribution and poverty reduction.

Redistribution with growth (RWG)

Official discourse on development assistance began to shift during the 1970s. Increasing attention had already been devoted to devising employment-generating and rural development schemes, but the big push for change came in the wake of a speech by World Bank president Robert McNamara to his board of governors in Nairobi in 1973:

> The basic problem of poverty and growth in the developing world can be stated very simply. The growth is not equitably reaching the poor. . . . The data suggest that the decade of rapid growth has been accompanied by greater maldistribution of income in many developing countries and that the problem is most severe in the countryside. . . . One can conclude that policies aimed primarily at accelerating economic growth . . . have benefited mainly the upper 40 per cent of the population (cited in Wood 1986, 196–7).

Also in 1973, Congress mandated the US Agency for International Development (USAID) to concentrate on the needs of the 'poor majority'.

The World Bank under McNamara sponsored a major study, *Redistribution with Growth* (Chenery et al. 1974). As Wood (1987, 201) comments, it 'did not actually advocate redistribution of income or wealth' but rather envisioned generating new income increments to increase the absolute incomes of the poor. Essentially, 'redistribution with growth' (RWG) was tacked on to the prevailing ideology without altering its fundamental slant. There was a clear preference for market over governmental mechanisms. Moreover, it paid insufficient attention to factors that generate poverty and operated within an idealist conception of the need for a coalition of interests that would capture power and see some advantage in directing more investment to the poor. As a result, there were contradictions and ambiguities in work at the project level (Ayres 1983, 79–80, 89).

Basic human needs (BHN)

The World Employment Conference of the International Labour Organization in 1976 attempted to push RWG in a more concrete direction by popularizing the **basic human needs** (BHN) approach. Shortly thereafter, the Development Assistance Committee (DAC) of the Organisation for Economic Co-operation and Development (OECD) (the club of rich-country donors) adopted a statement that recognized 'the plight of one billion people in the world who, largely for want of productive employment, remain unable even to meet the most urgent needs for food, decent drinking water, shelter, health care and education'. It saw efforts to satisfy BHN as 'not primarily welfare or charity but productivity-oriented, aiming at increasing the productive income of the poor' (OECD 1977, 149–51). In many cases, BHN was simply appropriated to re-label ongoing activities; in others, it spawned narrowly technocratic programming that viewed the poor as target groups rather than participants in development. Nonetheless, it further legitimated poverty reduction as an ODA goal separate from growth. Moreover, the donor establishment came to respect as developmental, rather than as mere welfare, small-scale community-based projects in the spheres of basic education and literacy, primary health care, and water purification.

Although portrayed by Western development agencies as complementary to aspirations for an NIEO, BHN was generally not well received by governments in aid-recipient countries. Efforts to make ODA conditional on meeting basic needs were resented and seen as distracting 'attention from the problems connected with underdevelopment and . . . the industrialised countries' joint responsibility for them' (Netherlands Ministry of Foreign Affairs 1991, 18–19). Meanwhile, within the World Bank, there was interest in BHN as a more thoroughgoing alternative to RWG but also scepticism from McNamara and other senior managers, who saw it as potentially too radical (Ayres 1983, 83, 89). Nevertheless, the new approach influenced the Bank's *World Development Report 1980*, which focused heavily on poverty and 'human development issues' (defined as education, health, nutrition, and fertility).

The Washington Consensus

As it turned out, that report symbolized the end of a brief era in official development discourse. A paradigm shift, but to the right of existing orthodoxy, occurred with the presidential election victory of Ronald Reagan and McNamara's replacement by A.W. Clausen, a former CEO of the Bank of America (see Ayres 1983, 229). As the US—until 1980 a major capital exporter—became a huge capital importer to finance its massive current account and budget deficits, loans to most developing countries dried up, and interest rates and debt skyrocketed (see chapter 14). Along with the Conservative government of Margaret Thatcher in the UK, the new American administration questioned the utility of both the World Bank and poverty-oriented programming. The North–South dialogue then faded into scarcely audible whispers after Mexico announced in August 1982 that it could not meet payments on its foreign debt. While the developing countries had been overestimating their bargaining strength, any hope for a NIEO evaporated 'in the wake of the worst global recession in 50 years, the collapse of oil and other commodity prices, an enormous debt overhang in Africa and Latin America, growing trade protectionism among governments in the North, and, within many of the latter, a neo-conservatism interested in international development only if state interventionism yields to the magic "of the marketplace'" (Morrison 1998, 187).

Neo-liberal **structural adjustment** became the order of the day, albeit asymmetrically, in what came to be known as the **Washington Consensus**. The South was told to grow out of debt by exporting, yet OECD countries continued to shield themselves from developing-country competition in agriculture, textiles, and other sectors through tariffs, quotas, and subsidies. Western aid agencies were just beginning to gear up for BHN-oriented programming when the World Bank and the International Monetary Fund (IMF) decreed that poverty reduction should take a back seat to debt service and adjustment. What Ferguson (1992, 11–12) characterized as 'scientific capitalism', every bit as doctrinaire as 'scientific socialism', called for policy reforms aimed at 'getting the prices right', reducing external and fiscal imbalances, privatizing public enterprises, downsizing the state, and promoting the private sector as *the* engine of development. Aid was granted with tighter strings than ever before as the rest of the donor establishment began to make project-specific and budget assistance conditional upon IMF and World Bank prescriptions.

There were some global success stories in the 1980s, in the sphere of disease immunization, for example, but the decade is remembered mostly for bad news—the debt crisis and the virtual derailment of development in Latin America, the Caribbean, and Africa. Human conditions deteriorated and poverty deepened most severely in sub-Saharan Africa, where debt was compounded by drought, famine, violent conflict, corrosion of the economic infrastructure, and intense pressures on ill-equipped public institutions. Food security, nutrition, health, and education all suffered reverses. As subsidies for essential foodstuffs were removed and prices shot up, the purchasing power of the poorest weakened dramatically. Women, children, and the elderly were hit hardest, and rural producers suffered from the collapse of extension services and concessional credit schemes. The alarming spread of HIV/AIDS added a new dimension to human insecurity.

Human development, but aid retreats

UNICEF took the lead in studying the social impact of structural adjustment and called for 'adjustment with a human face'—special measures to alleviate the impact on the people most severely affected (Cornia, Jolly, and Stewart 1987). The World Bank remained resolute that its formula for reform was the key to development. However, it appeared to rediscover poverty, which was the theme of its *World Development Report* in 1990. Echoes of RWG and BHN resurfaced in calls for investment in the productive capacity of the poor and greater access to health care, primary education, nutrition, and safety nets for those excluded from the benefits of growth.

That same year, the United Nations Development Programme (UNDP) began annual publication of a *Human Development Report*. Building on earlier efforts to develop indices of comparative development that went beyond aggregate growth and per capita income data, the UNDP constructed a **Human Development Index** (HDI) based on life expectancy, adult literacy, and purchasing power to buy commodities for meeting basic needs. The agency also tried to secure acceptance for a reconceptualization of the development problematic: 'human development is a process of enlarging people's choices . . . at all levels of development, the three essential ones are for people to lead a long and healthy life, to acquire knowledge and to have access to resources needed for a decent standard of living (UNDP 1990, 11).

The end of the Cold War brought hope for a peace dividend that would free up more funds for ODA now that it was no longer tied to East–West security concerns. That prospect soon evaporated as Western industrial countries became more tight-fisted in response to both the diminished geopolitical impetus for aid and a preoccupation with their own fiscal and foreign deficits. Meanwhile, ethnic and regional conflicts diverted potential development assistance into military operations and emergency relief, and eastern Europe and the former Soviet Union became competitors for declining resource transfers. Rather than moving upward towards aid budgets that would meet the long-sought UN target of 0.7 per cent of the Gross National Incomes (GNI) of donor countries, OECD ODA fell during the 1990s from 0.33 to 0.22 per cent.

While there was no peace dividend for development assistance, the collapse of communism brought politics out of the closet and into official aid discourse. A new buzzword—**good governance**—entered the lexicon of the international aid regime. It has been appropriated to mean many different, often contradictory, things. There may be a broad consensus about the desirability of strengthening human security or reducing public expenditures on armaments or curbing corruption, but understandings differ radically on what is needed to make governments more accountable to the people they supposedly serve. Ideologically and practically, there is a wide gap between, on the one hand, those who seek widespread popular participation in public life, empowerment of the poor, and a state capable of counteracting the polarizing effects of market forces and, on the other, a revamped Washington Consensus with governance as a surrogate for economic liberalization, minimal state intervention, and low-intensity democracy.

Millennium Development Goals (MDGs)

Meanwhile, stung by falling budgets, criticisms of waste and duplication, and weakening public enthusiasm for ODA, bilateral donor agencies began to focus on rebuilding support and improving the quality of their declining resources. *Shaping the 21st Century: The Contribution of Development Co-operation* was endorsed by the OECD Council in May 1996. It called for a global effort to achieve goals that 'seek to give real meaning to the improved quality of life that is the ultimate aim of sustainable development': reduction by at least one-half the proportion of people living in extreme poverty by 2015; universal primary education in all countries by 2015; elimination of gender disparity in primary and

secondary education by 2005; reduction of infant and child mortality rates by two-thirds the 1990 level and of maternal mortality by three-fourths that level by 2015; access through the primary health care system to reproductive health services for all individuals of appropriate ages no later than 2015; and creation of operational national strategies for sustainable development in all countries in 2005. The agenda claimed to place 'stronger emphasis than ever on the developing country itself as the starting point for development co-operation efforts' (OECD 1996, 5, 12–28).

While still grafted onto the Washington Consensus and ironically—in view of this last statement—devised without the active participation of developing countries, these goals reaffirmed at least rhetorically the centrality of poverty reduction in ODA programming. They were incorporated into *We the Peoples: The Role of the United Nations in the 21st Century* (United Nations 2000), which UN secretary-general Kofi Annan presented to the General Assembly in September 2000. It was soon followed by the Millennium Development Goals, which modified the OECD's proposals by adding a specific goal to combat HIV/AIDS, malaria, and other diseases and—at the insistence of the Bush administration—by dropping the reference to reproductive health services. The eighth goal, calling for global partnership, was also new (see Mehrotra and Delamonica 2007, 321–2). The MDGs and 18 associated targets were approved by the General Assembly in 2002 (see Box 13.1).

The structural adjustment programs of the 1980s and 1990s have been replaced since 1999 by Poverty Reduction Strategy Papers (PRSPs) as the key documents that outline the conditions under which donors transfer much of their aid to recipient countries (particularly budget support and debt relief). PRSPs represent two rhetorical shifts—poverty reduction is conceived as the main objective, and the plans are supposedly negotiated jointly by donors and recipients so that the latter will take effective ownership of them. While PRSPs have resulted in more effective donor co-ordination, as Smillie comments:

BOX 13.1   THE UN MILLENNIUM DEVELOPMENT GOALS (MDGs)

Goal 1: Eradicate extreme poverty and hunger

Target 1:   Halve, between 1990 and 2015, the proportion of people whose income is less than one dollar a day.

Target 2:   Halve, between 1990 and 2015, the proportion of people who suffer from hunger.

Goal 2: Achieve universal primary education

Target 3:   Ensure that, by 2015, children everywhere, boys and girls alike, will be able to complete a full course of primary schooling.

Goal 3: Promote gender equality and empower women

Target 4:   Eliminate gender disparity in primary and secondary education, preferably by 2005, and in all levels of education no later than 2015.

Goal 4: Reduce child mortality

Target 5:   Reduce by two-thirds, between 1990 and 2015, the under-five mortality rate.

Goal 5: Improve maternal health

Target 6:   Reduce by three-quarters, between 1990 and 2015, the maternal mortality ratio.

Goal 6: Combat HIV/AIDS, malaria and other diseases

Target 7:   Have halted by 2015 and begun to reverse the spread of HIV/AIDS.

Target 8:   Have halted by 2015 and begun to reverse the incidence of malaria and other major diseases.

Goal 7: Ensure environmental sustainability

Target 9:   Integrate the principles of sustainable development into country policies and pro-grammes to reverse the loss of environmental resources.

Target 10: Halve, by 2015, the proportion of people without sustainable access to safe drinking water.

Target 11: By 2020, to have achieved a significant improvement in the lives of at least 100 million slum dwellers.

Goal 8: Develop a Global Partnership for Development

Target 12: Develop further an open, rule-based, predictable, non-discriminatory trading and finan-cial system (includes a commitment to good governance, development, and poverty reduction—both nationally and internationally).

Target 13: Address the Special Needs of the Least Developed Countries (includes tariff and quota free access for LDC exports; enhanced program of debt relief for HIPC and cancellation of offi-cial bilateral debt; and more generous ODA for countries committed to poverty reduction).

Target 14: Address the Special Needs of landlocked countries and small island developing states.

Target 15: Deal comprehensively with the debt problems of developing countries through national and international measures in order to make debt sustainable in the long term.

Target 16: In co-operation with developing countries, develop and implement strategies for decent and productive work for youth.

Target 17: In co-operation with pharmaceutical companies, provide access to affordable, essential drugs in developing countries.

Target 18: In co-operation with the private sector, make available the benefits of new technologies, especially information and communications.

Source: http://www.un.org/millenniumgoals.

Many . . . have been rushed; much of the content has been designed offshore; the participation of civil society has been weak . . .; and the commitment of donors . . . is patchy. . . . The approach could . . . be described as a 'babysitter model' rather than one genuinely based on ownership. Donors, usually in the form of the World Bank, hold the government's hand while it creates a suitable PRSP (2004, 14).

Even an external consultation for the IMF concluded that 'the PRSP is a compulsory process wherein the people with money tell the people who want the money what they need to do to get the money' (IMF 2001, 147, cited in Mehrotra and Delamonica 2007, 88). Moreover, conditions continue to reflect a neo-liberal 'one size fits all' approach that still sees economic growth and open markets as the main solutions to poverty.

Aside from the question of whether much current aid programming is appropriate for poverty reduction (a question to which we return in the last section), donors have not been prepared to come forward with sufficient ODA to fund their shares of the MDG agenda. There were encouraging signs at the 2002 Monterrey Conference on Financing for Development when several European Union countries pledged to reach 0.7 per cent by 2014 (a level that historically only Sweden, Norway, the Netherlands, Denmark, and Luxembourg have attained). Canada, Switzerland, and Japan also promised substantial increases, and so did the laggard United States. There was still an air of optimism at the 2005 G-8 meeting in Gleneagles, Scotland, held during the height of the 'make poverty history' campaign.

The actual record shows that many donors are failing to meet commitments and that total DAC aid is falling far short of the trajectory needed to achieve the MDGs. Sachs (2005, 291–301) approaches the question of resource requirements by assessing both needs and the investments in infrastructure and human capital that are essential if the poor are to become more productive. Estimating an annual cost of $110 per person, he suggests that this be shared in the poorest countries on the basis of $10 from households, $35 from developing country governments, and $65 from donors. (A different calculus would apply in middle-income countries.) Assuming that ODA spending continues more or less in its current configuration (which includes large transfers to middle-income recipients and substantial expenditures on technical cooperation, emergency assistance, and donor operating costs), Sachs calls for an annual top-up in net ODA from a base of $58.3 billion in 2002 to $135 billion in 2006 and $195 billion in 2015. (The calculation excludes additional resources needed to help the poorest countries adapt to climate change). He notes that the targets require an increase in the proportionate aid effort of DAC donors from 0.23 per cent of GNI in 2002 to 0.44 in 2006 and 0.54 in 2015, still well below the target of 0.7 per cent.

As it turned out, the actual figure for DAC ODA was just under $104 billion in 2006, down 5.1 per cent from the previous year (the record high, reflecting emergency relief in the wake of the Asian tsunami). The European Union reached 0.44 per cent in 2006, but the average for all DAC members was only 0.30 per cent, dragged down by the US (0.17) and Japan (0.25). While $104 billion represents an impressive increase of $43 billion per annum between 2002 and 2006 (albeit much below what Sachs calls for), not much has become available for poverty reduction. The 2006 total includes $19 billion in debt relief (up from $4.5 billion in 2002)—welcome but not involving any new resource transfers. Moreover, much of the increase has gone into Iraq and Afghanistan and is related more to war and security than anti-poverty agendas. Excluding debt relief for Nigeria, non-emergency ODA to sub-Saharan Africa barely rose in constant dollar terms from 2002 to 2006 (see OECD 2006; 2007b; 2007f).

WHO ARE THE POOR? DEFINITIONS AND CONCEPTIONS OF POVERTY

If poverty reduction is a priority requiring more resources, an effective response necessitates clarity about who the poor are. The distinction between relative and absolute poverty is important. Relative poverty is measured against societal standards, which vary considerably across countries, regions, and demographic groups and which also change over time. Absolute poverty involves some measurement against a benchmark, such as food costs, caloric intake, or being able to write one's name (see White 2002, 33). Sachs makes a further distinction between moderate and extreme poverty: whereas people living in moderate poverty are able to meet their basic needs, but only just,

> . . . [e]xtreme poverty means that households cannot meet basic needs for survival. They are chronically hungry, unable to access health care, lack the amenities of safe drinking water and sanitation, cannot afford education for some or all of the children, and perhaps lack rudimentary shelter—a roof to keep the rain out of the hut, a chimney to remove the smoke from a cook stove—and basic articles of clothing such as shoes (2005, 20).

The very poor tend to be inarticulate, isolated, non-mobile, and powerless. They are suspicious of change, because pursuing bad risks can lead to disaster. Disproportionate numbers are women, children, and the elderly (Chambers 1983, 109–10; Riddell 2007, 280–1).

The benchmarks long used by the World Bank (and incorporated in the MDG target of halving extreme poverty by 2015) are below $1 a day for extreme poverty and $1 to $2 a day for moderate poverty (as measured in terms of **purchasing power parity** [PPP], an exchange rate that equates the price of a basket of identical traded goods and services in two countries). According to estimates based on household surveys, the number of people falling below the dollar-a-day threshold fell from 1.5 billion in 1981 to 1.1 billion in 2001. Extreme poverty is found in almost half of Africa, a slight increase during this period. In contrast, it fell from 58 to 15 per cent and from 52 to 31 per cent in East and South Asia, respec-

tively. The incidence remained stuck in Latin America at about 10 per cent; in eastern Europe it was 4 per cent in 2001 (Sachs 2005, 20–1). As a proportion of global population, the extreme poor dropped from 29 to 23 per cent in the 1990s. However, most of the decline occurred in China, India, Vietnam, and other Asian countries. There was little progress in reducing extreme poverty elsewhere (Mehrotra and Delamonica 2007, 8).

As White (2002, 33) notes, while 'poverty' in everyday usage is synonymous with income shortage, the development literature stresses multi-dimensionality. Other non-income data have been used to reflect the depth and persistence of extreme poverty. There has hardly been a dent since the early 1990s in the number of people whose daily caloric intake is below that of 1960. In 50 countries with almost 40 per cent of the world's population, more than one-fifth of children suffer from protein energy malnutrition. About 11 million children die each year from preventable causes, usually for want of simple improvements in nutrition, sanitation, and maternal health and education. At the turn of the century, a sixth of humanity lacked safe water. More children were in school than a decade earlier, but the number not enrolled increased as well. The number of illiterates, some 900 million, was still rising (Mehrotra and Delamonica 2007, 9).

More broadly, White (2002, 33) argues that deprivation in any of these spheres and others that are harder to quantify (environmental quality, spiritual and political freedom) 'can be called poverty'. Kanbur and Squire (1999, 1) highlight a progressive expansion of definitions from a focus on command over market-purchased goods (income) to other dimensions such as longevity, literacy, and healthiness and most recently to concerns with risk, vulnerability, powerlessness, and lack of voice. The most prominent approaches are income/consumption (the basis of the dollar-a-day benchmark), capabilities, social exclusion, and participatory assessment (for a detailed discussion, see Stewart, Saith, and Harriss-White 2007).

Figure 13.2   Local women collect water at the borehole, Mozambique

Source: Chr. Michelsen Institute/John Barnes

Income/consumption (I/C)

The most common indicator for comparing the economic standing of countries—Gross National Income per capita—tells us nothing about poverty. As an average of incomes—poor and rich, women and men, children and adults, rural and urban—it takes no account of how equally or unequally those incomes are distributed (see White 2002, 33). Rather, the notion of a 'poverty line' is the key concept in the I/C approach to determining relative and absolute poverty. B.S. Rowntree (1910) first developed the methodology in a study undertaken in York, England, early in the twentieth century. Seeking to ascertain the minimum budget

required to maintain physical efficiency, he found that a family of four needed 15 shillings a week for food and 11 shillings for other necessities, yielding a poverty line of 26 shillings. From pioneering household surveys, he estimated that the poverty rate in York (the proportion of the population falling below the line) was 10 per cent. Although the conception of bare necessities has changed over time and differs from country to country, this approach is still used today. It informs Indian and American poverty lines, although when the lines are expressed in PPP dollars, the latter is 20 times the former (Kanbur and Squire 1999, 23).

This approach is called income/consumption because surveys have variously sought information on how much money comes into a household and how much is actually spent. Generally, consumption is preferred because it is easier for people to grasp when they are questioned. Because a head-count to determine the poverty rate takes no account of how far people fall below the poverty line, there have been further refinements. One is the notion of a poverty gap—the distance below the line—and another is poverty severity—the implications for those who are well below it (White 2002, 34).

The use of I/C to measure poverty has been criticized on several grounds, some focused on what it fails to capture and others related to technical complexities inherent in the construction of poverty lines (see Streeten 1998, 13–16; Kanbur and Squire 1999, 4–5; White 2002, 34–6; Sender 2003, 412; and Milanovic 2005, 12–17). Country-wide poverty lines do not allow for cost of living differences within a country or region. There are also problems associated with how to impute income from self-employment and sub-sistence production within the household. As Streeten (1998, 8) notes, neither income nor consumption exhausts the sources of material benefits to the poor. One must add goods and services provided by the state (which again vary by location) and access to common property resources. Moreover, the World Bank's dollar-a-day standard is based on household surveys that miss intra-household distribution. Adult males, women, children, the elderly, and the disabled—besides having differing needs—may consume quite unequal shares. More generally, I/C can be criticized because income and spending measure only one dimension of human well-being.

Capabilities approach (CA)

Nobel Prize–winning economist Amartya Sen has criticized the dominance of I/C measures and, more generally, the utilitarian assumptions of mainstream economics. He argues that development should be seen as an expansion of human capabilities and freedom, not a maximization of utility or its proxy, money income:

A person's 'capability' refers to the alternative combinations of functionings that are feasible for her to achieve. Capability is thus a kind of freedom: the substantive freedom to achieve . . . various lifestyles. For example, an affluent person who fasts may have the same functioning achievement in terms of eating . . . as a destitute person who is forced to starve, but the first person does have a different 'capability set' than the second (the first can choose to eat well and be well nourished in a way the second cannot) (1999, 75).

Sen offers several 'good reasons' for seeing poverty not merely as low income but as a deprivation of basic capabilities—or, as Streeten (1998, 17) puts it, the incapacity to obtain and convert resources into well-being. Deprivation of elementary capabilities can be reflected in premature mortality, significant under-nourishment, persistent morbidity, widespread illiteracy, and the terrible phenomenon of 'missing women'. All of these must be analyzed with demographic, medical, and social information, rather than simply income data. Low income may be an instrumental factor, but capability deprivation can also result from endemic diseases, biases based on social difference, and location (potential for drought, flooding, ethnic and religious discrimination, and violence) (Sen 1999, 20–1, 87–90).

A major advantage of CA is that the 'shift from the private resources to which individuals have access to the type of life they can lead addresses the neglect of social goods in the monetary approach and its narrow vision of human well-being' (Laderchi, Saith, and Stewart 2003, 257). The approach also highlights the way in which various factors that contribute to a lack of functionings are interrelated. The poor are often excluded from economic growth because their major asset, their labour power, is curtailed by a lack of education and poor nutrition and health (Kanbur and Squire 1999, 13). The perspective is relevant in more affluent as well as developing countries: for example, high unemployment in Europe is not simply a deficiency in income (which can in part be made up by state transfers) but also a source of debilitating effects on individual freedom, initiative, skills, self-reliance, and health (Sen 1999, 20–1, 87–90).

Sen's analysis contributed conceptually to the UNDP's Human Development Index. By making international comparisons with reference to literacy rates, mean years of schooling, and life expectancy at birth, as well as purchasing power, the HDI highlights the inadequacies of other indexes, especially those based just on income. Critics have argued, however, that decisions on what to include and how to assign weights are arbitrary. Moreover, just as average income per head masks great inequalities, life expectancy and literacy are also averages that conceal vast differences between men and women, boys and girls, rich and poor, urban and rural, and different ethnic or religious groups. HDI does not include any measure of what Sen himself agrees are basic needs (such as leisure, security, justice, freedom, and human rights) or of morbidity. At best, the index is useful for ranking countries (Kanbur and Squire 1999, 10).

The same reservations apply to the UNDP's Human Poverty Index (HPI). It estimates the percentages of a population expected to die before age 40 and adults who are illiterate and combines them with proxies for inadequate living standards (see Box 13.2). As the UNDP recognizes, the HPI suffers from being a composite and from the exclusion of critical dimensions of human poverty such as lack of political freedom, inability to participate in community life, lack of security, and threats to sustainability and intergenerational equity (UNDP 1997, 17–18). Laderchi, Saith, and Stewart (2003, 256) are also critical, but 'aggregation can be desirable for political purposes and to reduce a large amount of information to manageable proportions.' In addition, the HPI, like the HDI, has the heuristic value of highlighting the need to examine poverty indicators other than income, and although practicalities abound, it suggests ways in which data from household surveys can be disaggregated both at the country level (as the UNDP has done for gender) and at sub-national levels.

Laderchi, Saith, and Stewart (2003, 257) draw attention to additional defects in both I/C and CA: they are individualistic—that is, both utility deprivation and capability failure are characteristics of individuals—but these characteristics are shaped by household and community dynamics, which yield differential outcomes based on gender, age, and other social differences. Neither focuses on the fundamental causes or dynamics of poverty, and both capture just a moment in time.

Social exclusion (SE)

The social exclusion approach addresses these deficiencies. Unlike I/C and CA, social and political perspectives are central in SE, and issues of inequality and redistribution are necessarily involved. Laderchi, Saith, and Stewart (2003, 257–8) suggest that SE exists if a person is excluded when he/she (a) is resident in society but (b) for reasons beyond his/her control cannot participate in normal activities and (c) would like to do so. These reasons may be rooted in cultural and social structures or based on the actions of agent(s). SE focuses on women, the aged, the handicapped, and racial or ethnic minorities rather than on individuals. It highlights the precariousness of work, physical weakness, powerlessness, humiliation, psychological factors, and other issues not reflected in low incomes. For example, women may have adequate incomes and food but be deprived as a result of excessive workloads, social subordination, and reduced life expectancy (Streeten 1998, 24).

SE points towards policies for eliminating discrimination and promoting affirmative action. Although there is cultural complexity involved in defining 'normal' and 'desirable', UN system agencies and civil society organizations have argued that efforts to eliminate poverty and social exclusion are justified on human rights grounds. In a linkage of CA and SE, 'the language of human rights adds to the expanded *conceptualisation* of poverty the notion that poverty is the denial of an entitlement, a right which is unfulfilled.' It directs attention to legal and juridical tools for struggles to

BOX 13.2   THE HUMAN POVERTY INDEX (HPI)

If human development is about enlarging choices, poverty means that opportunities and choices most basic to human development are denied. Thus, a person is not free to lead a long, healthy, and creative life and is denied access to a decent standard of living, freedom, dignity, self-respect, and the respect of others. From a human development perspective, poverty means more than the lack of what is necessary for material well-being.

For policy-makers, the poverty of choices and opportunities is often more relevant than the poverty of income. The poverty of choices focuses on the causes of poverty and leads directly to strategies of empowerment and other actions to enhance opportunities for everyone. Recognizing the poverty of choices and opportunities implies that poverty must be addressed in all its dimensions, not income alone.

The *Human Development Report 1997* introduced a human poverty index (HPI) in an attempt to bring together in a composite index the different features of deprivation in the quality of life to arrive at an aggregate judgment on the extent of poverty in a community.

The three indicators of the human poverty index (HPI)

Rather than measure poverty by income, the HPI uses indicators of the most basic dimensions of deprivation: a short life, lack of basic education, and lack of access to public and private resources. The HPI concentrates on the deprivation in the three essential elements of human life already reflected in the HDI: longevity, knowledge, and a decent standard of living. The HPI is derived separately for developing countries (HPI-1) and a group of select high-income OECD countries (HPI-2) to better reflect socio-economic differences and also the widely different measures of deprivation in the two groups.

- The first deprivation relates to *survival*: the likelihood of death at a relatively early age, represented by the probability of not surviving to ages 40 and 60 respectively for the HPI-1 and HPI-2.
- The second dimension relates to *knowledge*: being excluded from the world of reading and communication, measured by the percentage of adults who are illiterate.
- The third aspect relates to a *decent standard of living*: in particular, overall economic provisioning. For HPI-1 countries, the specific indicators are the percentage of people without access to health services and safe water and the percentage of malnourished children under five. It is measured by the unweighted average of the percentage of the population without access to safe water and the percentage of children who are underweight for their age. For the HPI-2, it is measured by the percentage of the population below the income poverty line (50 per cent of median household disposable income).

In addition to these three indicators, the HPI-2 also includes social exclusion, which is the fourth dimension of the HPI-2. It is represented by the rate of long-term unemployment.

Source: http://hdr.undp.org/en/statistics/indices/hpi.

reduce poverty (Shaffer 2002, 8). Unfortunately, as Tomlinson (2005, 3) laments, the commitment to 'the right to development' voiced in the Millennium Declaration was not explicitly incorporated in the MDGs.

Participatory assessment (PA)

While other approaches are criticized for being externally imposed, participatory poverty assessment (PA), pioneered by Robert Chambers, seeks to remedy this by getting people to participate themselves in decisions about what it means to be poor. PA involves a variety of techniques, including social mapping, participatory diagramming, modelling and scoring, and public meetings that encourage active participation (Streeten 1998, 23). Chambers (1997b, xvii) expresses astonishment about 'the

analytical abilities of poor people. Whether literate or not, whether children, women or men, they showed that they could map, list, rank, score and diagram often better than professionals.'

As Shaffer (2002, 6) notes, PA is not so much a way of conceptualizing poverty and deprivation as a means of determining who should do the conceptualizing.

Many problems identified by the poor point towards social exclusion and political isolation. They report rude and arrogant behaviour on the part of officials, hospital workers, and so on, and offer evidence of their sense of powerlessness when caught up in the web of clientelistic relationships. Two aspects of poverty that emerge from participatory assessments that are not well captured in other methods concern risk and volatility of incomes: 'we come to understand poverty not

Figure 13.3   Reconstruction in Mymane, Afghanistan

Source: Chr. Michelsen Institute/Arne Strand

just as state of having little, but also of being vulnerable to losing the little one has' as a result of natural disasters, epidemics, violence, or forced migration (Kanbur and Squire 1999, 16–17).

Everyone in the development industry now lauds participatory approaches, but success requires patience to work in a labour-intensive way at a micro level. The skills needed are not necessarily those of aid workers who are under pressure to move money and achieve quick fixes (Burnell 1997, 245). The World Bank has been criticized for being instrumental, 'adopting PA primarily so that the poor would cooperate. . . . There is little of self-determination and empowerment in most of this work' (Laderchi, Saith, and Stewart 2003, 260). In any case, to the extent that outsiders conduct the assessments and interpret the results, the impact of the poor on projects and policies is limited. There is also the question of whose voices are being heard, especially when there are conflicts within a community and when some people are structurally excluded or fear reprisal if they stand up to local elites. Moreover, all parties to participatory assessments may overlook objective conditions and can be biased as a result of limited information and social conditioning.

HOW THE DIFFERENT APPROACHES FRAME POLICY

In surveying these approaches, Laderchi, Saith, and Stewart (2003, 268) conclude that there is no unique or objective way of defining and measuring poverty. There is in each a large element of 'construction' based on a conception of what constitutes a good life and a just society. As Kanbur and Squire (1999, 23) argue, the main contribution lies in the insights that are derived for pro-poor policies. I/C suggests that the solution lies in increasing money incomes. CA emphasizes a wider range of mechanisms, such as social provision of goods to improve health, nutrition, and education. Conceptually, the approach can be extended to other spheres, such as political or cultural life, which is not the case with the monetary approach. Laderchi, Saith, and Stewart (2003, 269, 264–5)

report that the different approaches do not lead to the same groups being identified. For example, India has emerged much worse in capability than in monetary poverty, while the reverse has been the case for Peru. Asking whether this outcome may be an artifact of the particular ways in which poverty lines are drawn, they argue that it is important to draw upon all of the approaches when undertaking in-depth empirical assessments of the underlying causes of poverty.

Both I/C and CA are concerned with absolute and especially extreme poverty, and neither makes distributional issues a central priority. In contrast, the relative element in poverty is at the forefront in SE. As a result, it draws attention to the need for redistributive and structural policies aimed at overcoming racial and ethnic discrimination, class barriers, inequities based on gender, age, and disabilities, and restrictions on full citizenship (Laderchi, Saith, and Stewart 2003, 262–3). A report of a Canadian civil society conference on the MDGs criticized 'simplistic assumptions advanced for the goals by Sachs and other advocates', such as the notion that

> . . . poverty is like dirt that can be sucked up by the 'vacuum cleaner' of more aid. While aid is an important catalyst, making poverty history is much more complicated. The history of poverty demonstrates that highly unequal structures at all levels perpetuate and continue to create poverty (CCIC 2005, 3).

A stronger focus on causation has been one of the significant changes in official thinking since 1990. Comparing the 1990 and 2000 versions of the *World Development Report*, Shaffer (2002, 1–4) identifies three significant changes in mainstream discourse (all based on ideas that are not themselves new). First, the concept of poverty has been broadened from a physiological model of deprivation to a social one that pays increasing attention to powerlessness, vulnerability, inequality, and human rights. Second, the causal structure has been broadened to include a range of variables that previously received little attention—social, political, coercive (reflecting the use or the threat of violence), cultural, and environmental. Third, the causal structure has been deepened to focus on flows of individuals into and out of poverty, rather than just on changes in the stock of poverty. As with the participatory approach, Robert Chambers has been enormously influential, in this instance in promoting the dynamic concept of **sustainable livelihoods**.

BEYOND NEO-LIBERALISM: A NEW APPROACH TO POVERTY REDUCTION?

There is considerable evidence that the aid regime's new, more radical version of 'trickle down' has been a colossal failure on its own terms and has had a disastrous impact on the world's poor and disadvantaged. Many critiques of neo-liberal orthodoxy have come from non-economists, NGOs, social movements, and alter-globalization activists. But some have emerged from efforts to re-energize development economics (see Chang 2003) and yet others from development agencies, even the IMF and the World Bank (see Milanovic 2005). The UNDP and UNICEF have been significant incubators for spearheading a rethinking. Two scholars who have done considerable work for these latter agencies—Santosh Mehotra and Enrique Delamonica—recently published *Eliminating Human Poverty* (2007), a book that is refreshing for the way it moves beyond criticism to a policy agenda for poverty reduction.

Mehrotra and Delamonica contrast the views of defenders and critics of the Washington Consensus:

> The first group typically takes a competitive view of market structure, while the second group believes that there are strong elements of monopolistic power, especially in the corporate sector. . . . When the former group worries about poverty, it is only at the national level . . . , while those in the second group are concerned with the disaggregated outcomes of economic policy (by region, income-group, gender and age). . . . The first group has a strong belief in the power of eco-

nomic growth to transform the lives of the poor; while the second, although not opposed to growth, is far from convinced of market power being able to deliver the poor from poverty (2007, 14–15).

They agree that neo-liberal reform has yielded a meagre harvest. India and China stand out in terms of economic growth, making the past two decades a developmental success on a population-weighted basis; however, both cases are an awkward fit with orthodoxy, and other Asian high-growth economies also flouted mainstream advice. Apart from these exceptions, a dismal picture emerges of greater economic instability, lower per capita income growth, and imperceptible declines in poverty when compared to the situation in previous decades (2007, 26).

Dismissing arguments for privatization, free trade, and lower taxes as means of promoting growth and efficiency, Mehrotra and Delamonica (2007, 19) reaffirm the earlier wisdom in economic discourse that prolonged growth stems from innovation and productivity increases. Moreover, to the extent that income inequality declined historically, growth was only one factor alongside critical changes in education, organization, and the political power of workers (25). Sender (2003, 419) offers a reminder of the bias of the aid regime in this last respect, noting that the focus on 'capacity building' ignores any organization that has a realistic prospect of increasing the political and economic bargaining power of the lowest-paid workers. Trade unions and labour legislation are dismissed as potentially 'market distorting' and, ipso facto, harmful to the poor.

In advancing an alternative model, Mehrotra and Delamonica (2007, 358) reject the assumptions that underpin orthodox policy advice—the 'abstract separation of economics from its institutional foundations in politics and society; . . . super-rational individuals who maximize their own (and only their own) utility; money-metric . . . measures as main indicators of efficiency, or well-being; . . . and simplistic causal mechanisms'. Conceiving economic and social policy as integrally related, they reject the conventional hierarchical model 'where macroeconomic policy is determined first, while social policy is left to address the social consequences' (13–14). Drawing upon Sen and CA, they argue for placing capabilities and functionings at the centre of the analysis, because economic growth will be more effective in reducing income poverty when the capabilities of citizens are enhanced. While greater provision of basic social services can lead to a reduction of the non-income dimensions of poverty, in the absence of this investment, 'economic growth may not reduce the income or non-income dimensions of poverty, primarily because the poor may be unable to take advantage of market opportunities on account of ill health or poor education or limited skills' (4, 31).

Actions on several fronts can be put into play through two kinds of synergy:

> One takes place at the macro-level among income-poverty reduction, expansion of human functionings and economic growth. The other . . . at the micro-level, occurs as a result of interventions to provide the basic services that are the foundation of the expansion of functionings. These two synergies are linked by the synergies among good health, nutrition and education—which are ends in themselves, but also means to other ends at the macro-societal level, and hence common to both sets of synergies (Mehrotra and Delamonica 2007, 5).

Mehrotra and Delamonica claim that their model erases the separation of the economic and the social because macroeconomic and social policies are balanced and integrated in a non-hierarchical way. They also emphasize that gender equality and women's functionings are critical at the micro level and not simply—as in much mainstream analysis—one among several important variables. 'Hastening the demographic transition and reducing the fertility rate is the flip side of increasing per capita income; and greater gender equality is an instrument of reduced fertility' (2007, 5, 361).

KEY ELEMENTS OF THE MEHROTRA–DELAMONICA AGENDA

Macroeconomic policies and institutions for pro-poor growth

Mehrotra and Delamonica effectively capture and distil the wisdom of several scholars and practitioners within their model. They call for 'pro-poor growth', defined (following van der Hoeven and Shorrocks 2003) as growth that benefits the poor proportionately more than the non-poor (2007, 31), 'both in terms of income, and in terms of financing social services, improving working conditions and protecting the environment (especially the areas where the lowest socioeconomic strata live' (59–60). They advocate several measures for reducing income poverty and managing distributional conflict focused on land ownership, tenancy, landlessness, and public investment in rural infrastructure (61–6). On land reform, which they note remains outside the purview of the dominant discourse on 'reform', they review the familiar evidence about the differing but special circumstances that permitted redistribution in Japan, South Korea, Taiwan, China, Vietnam, and the Indian states of Kerala and West Bengal (63). They say that substantive redistribution with growth would also involve policies that influence the structure of production in favour of commodities largely consumed by lower-income and poor people (66; see also Cassen 1994, 42–3).

Mehrotra and Delamonica (2007, 67–8, 86) push for an active state-led industrial policy for technological and structural change that seeks 'strategic' rather than close integration with the international economy. While the very notion of 'industrial policy' is anathema in the orthodox paradigm, they stress how important this factor was in the Southeast and East Asian successes, as well as in the older industrial countries that picked 'winners' and protected infant industries (see chapter 7). They see a positive role for foreign direct investment in restructuring the economy, suggesting (perhaps too soon?) that the

Chinese experience offers a lesson on how it can be harnessed by a strategic vision and effective regulation. They recognize that the global context is not as propitious for most poor developing countries as it was for earlier industrializers, that demographic pressures are much greater, and that World Trade Organization (WTO) rules restrict freedom of action (75–6). (Nonetheless, they say that WTO rules still allow more room for manoeuvre than is commonly supposed [363]). For these reasons, diversification into new labour-intensive manufacturing is a priority (75–7). 'We suggest that the growth and the development of informal and formal micro-, small, and medium enterprises and . . . local systems of development can be considered a direct approach to poverty reduction and human development. . . . informal activities need not be perceived as a symptom of economic dysfunction . . . but as an opportunity.' They urge as well the introduction of limited forms of social protection in the informal sector (78–9).

Public expenditure on basic social services

Much of *Eliminating Human Poverty* explores how to make effective interventions in basic social services (BSS) and achieve synergy between these interventions and macro-level policies for pro-poor growth. It documents how important *public* and somewhat equitable spending has been in the experience of industrial and high-achieving developing countries (364–5). State provision lowers unit costs and, importantly, promotes social integration when provision does not depend on political favours or ability to pay (272). Mehrotra and Delamonica accept that poor countries lack sufficient resources and that there is a 'need for greater efficiency . . . in the provision of BSS'. No matter how inadequate spending may be, however, it is essential to make provision for health, education, and safe water and sanitation. As none is 'sufficient by itself, . . . low expenditure levels in one sector (reproductive health, for instance) have an overall effect on other sectors (e.g., education)' (132–3).

They take a strong stand against those who see privatization as a solution (see chapter 9)—citizenship is debased and an important shared value is lost when these basic services are rationed through the market (273). They then come to the challenge of how the state can become a more effective instrument for the delivery of BSS—only, they say, through 'a deep democratic decentralization of social service delivery' (208).

Deep democratic decentralization

The policies advocated by Mehrotra and Delamonica require extraordinary political and fiscal changes. The authors advance a familiar analysis of the post-colonial state superimposed on an authoritarian colonial predecessor that was organized for maintaining order and extracting surplus. Though generally 'low on corruption, especially at the top echelons', it was not concerned with accountability or transparency. This structure was replaced by a varying mix of formally democratic, populist, authoritarian, and military regimes 'reliant upon rent-seeking for personal enrichment'. That situation will not change, and accountability will not improve, unless there is 'deep democratic decentralization' involving:

1. democracy at the national level;
2. decentralization of key functions related to service delivery to local governments;
3. institutions and mechanisms to enable the collective voice of the community in the jurisdiction of the local government (233).

There has been an increasing movement towards the first two in the past two decades (although much decentralization has been shallow and has avoided a transfer of taxing authority); however, 'the last prerequisite is almost entirely missing.'

A critical ingredient in empowering people at the local level and challenging social exclusion is the right to information, especially 'about the use of funds allocated for various services . . . —whether it is for a health centre, a school or a water facility' (234). In his review of pro-poor governance reforms, Shaffer (2002, 18–19) adds an issue missing from much of the poverty literature—the further need to promote lawfulness through such measures as legal and judicial reform, police reform, domestic violence awareness campaigns, and human rights legislation and support. He also responds to those who argue that interventions are unlikely to work because they will not generate or maintain requisite political support from powerful social groups who do not reap direct benefits. This tendency does not hold if powerful social groups view poverty targeting to be in their own interest or when the state is ideologically committed to poverty reduction (Shaffer 2002, 13). These conditions have been present in what Mehrotra and Delamonica (2007, 366) flag as successful cases of deep democratic decentralization in Brazil, Kerala, and West Bengal (see also Fung and Wright 2003).

Several scholars have focused on the question of how to circumvent or lessen the influence of elites, particularly those at the local level who tend to 'act as a net to trap the goods that are aimed at the poor' (Chambers 1978, cited in Riddell 1987, 221). As Chambers (1983, 163) argues, ignoring the power and interests of local elites possibly accounts more than any other factor for the failure of aid projects designed to benefit the poor. In 'some situations it is not possible to target the poor without paying a significant price in terms of buying off the non-poor, whose cooperation or acquiescence could prove indispensable' (Burnell 1997, 32). In any case, even when there is empowerment from below, if the provision of BSS is perceived as a zero-sum in which the non-poor are losers, there is little likelihood of success (Mehrotra and Delamonica 2007, 314). For this reason, increased revenues are essential.

Mobilizing increased domestic resources

Mehrotra and Delamonica (2007, 277) estimate that (at 1995 prices) $206 to $216 billion per annum is needed to provide basic social services to all citizens in developing countries. This compares to actual expenditures of $136 billion, yielding a shortfall of $70 to $80 billion. Once more, they stress the crucial role of the state. The main challenge—again, dependent on a deepening of democracy—is to shift the 'reform' agenda from cutting government expenditures to mobilizing higher tax revenues, with some earmarking for BSS. Longer-term advance requires inter-sectoral reallocation, especially away from defence, debt repayment, and subsidies to production or consumption that have no positive impact on the well-being of the poor (81, 367).

Increasing external resources

Eliminating Human Poverty summarizes various proposals that have been advanced for international taxation to help fund investments in poverty reduction—levies on cross-border financial transactions (the 'Tobin tax'), the brain drain, international air travel, ocean fishing, arms exports, luxury goods, remittances, and the global environment (carbon taxes)—and for creating new IMF Special Drawing Rights and an International Finance Facility. Although Mehrotra and Delamonica (2007, 315–17) encourage movement on several of these fronts, they also review the formidable obstacles, not least the inertia and inequity within the governance structures of international bodies.

The unlikelihood of imminent global action on these measures takes us back to the aid regime. Mehrotra and Delamonica (2007, 322) ask, 'should we have high expectations of a poverty focus . . . when the past history of aid tells a different story?' They are not sanguine. They report the critical findings of Stephen Browne—that the relationship between aid and human development is entirely random (Browne did correlations at 10-year intervals); that low-income countries (below $745 per capita) account for three-quarters of the people who live in poverty yet receive only 40 per cent of aid; that aid is volatile and unpredictable; that volume depends on short-term donor concerns of affordability; and, as has always been the case, that aid mostly

Figure 13.4   Afghanistan

Source: Alternatives/Catherine Pappas

tracks the non-developmental concerns of donors (Browne 2006; see also Riddell 2007). Mehrotra and Delamonica (2007, 358) welcome the focus of the 2006 *World Development Report* on equity and development, especially the land access issue. They ask, however, whether 'this "nuanced" analysis' will become part of the 'policymaking toolkit on a daily basis'.

While concerned about the failure of aid flows even to keep pace with growth in donor countries, unstable funding, and aid dependency, Mehrotra and Delamonica (2007, 321–6) nonetheless see ODA as an essential source of transitional funding for social services in the poorest and most highly indebted countries. They lament that support for BSS, though up slightly, remains stuck at not much more than 10 per cent of total ODA a decade after the UNDP challenged donors and recipients to accept jointly a '20:20 compact for human devel-

opment' to raise public expenditures in developing countries on essential human goals from 13 per cent to 20 per cent of national budgets and the proportion of ODA devoted to basic human development from a mere 7 per cent to 20 per cent (UNDP 1994, 7–8).

They note that falling aid for education has been accompanied by a higher share for basic education (though perhaps as a result of expenditure reclassification), a continuing bias towards bricks and mortar rather than improvements in the learning experience, and huge expenditures on technical cooperation—that is, mostly the remuneration of expatriates (Mehrotra and Delamonica 2007, 329, 334). Technical cooperation eats up 25 per cent of aid spending and as much as 40 per cent in some countries (340). Collier (2007, 112) makes a provocative counter-point to critics of reliance on Western experts: 'remember the skilled people have already left. They are in London, New York, and Paris, not Bangui.'

Foreign aid and private donations for health have gone up with the welcome emphasis on HIV/AIDS, tuberculosis, and malaria, but this has left underfunded acute respiratory infections, maternal mortality, and nearly all non-communicable diseases. Health delivery systems remain endemically under-resourced (Mehrotra and Delamonica 2007, 335). Water and sanitation remain the best supported of BSS, but half of these allocations go to just 10 countries, and many with the worst access receive little (330).

Mehrotra and Delamonica laud policies to achieve greater donor harmonization and to bring ODA into national budget processes through the shift from project to program support. They see as a step in the right direction a pooling of 'resources that could be disbursed by the recipient according to a general development strategy, including a poverty reduction plan, discussed in advance by donors and the country' (2007, 339). There is a long way to go, however, in convincing donors to take cooperation and partnership seriously. Typically, it is 'not the case that ODA passes through a recipient government system. . . . Large shares of . . . expenditures are made directly to . . . private firms, NGOs, and individuals—more often to donor-country nationals than to those of the recipient country.' Corruption is a two-way street:

> . . . to discourage corruption fed by aid, donors should provide, on a public basis, access to specific figures on aid flows, mech-

anisms and intended target recipients so that independent monitors . . . can provide effective scrutiny. Also, donors have to ensure that corruption is not aided and abetted by their own private sector, and that the earnings from corruption are not laundered through their own financial markets' (2007, 340).

Donors are also enjoined to take more seriously their rhetorical commitment to overcome the inconsistencies between their aid and trade policies, particularly the ways in which their policies on market access, intellectual property rights, and liberalization of social services run counter to the realization of MDGs. The most glaring examples are, of course, in the spheres of agriculture (dominant-country subsidies and protectionism that undermine prospects for expanding rural incomes in developing countries) and access to essential drugs (Mehrotra and Delamonica 2007, 342–50).

The logic of their agenda calls for a deepening of democracy beyond the nation-state. Milanovic (2005, 149–50) decries 'plutocracy at the global level' and notes that arguments against global inequality and in favour of some redistribution or help for the world's poorest are inextricably linked with the need for supra-national democratization. But probably the best one can hope for is some redress of the current imbalance of power between and within rich and poor countries. This will not come about without continuing political struggle—manifested in a variety of ways—on the part of all those who seek to make poverty history.

QUESTIONS FOR DISCUSSION

1. Should the case for poverty reduction stand on moral grounds alone? How do you respond to critics who say that the poor should be left to their own devices? To those who claim that efforts to define poverty and devise anti-poverty policies are culturally and socially destructive?

2. What do the Millennium Development Goals (MDGs) imply in terms of the responsibilities of governments of developing countries and aid donor countries? Should aid for poverty reduction be restricted to only those countries where the government has demonstrated a pro-poor commitment convincingly?

3. How does the model advanced by Mehrotra and Delamonica challenge the orthodox neo-liberal recipe for poverty reduction? What are their major recommendations for poverty reduction? How do these recommendations differ from the approach embodied in the MDGs? To what extent do Mehrotra and Delamonica address, or fail to address, what you consider the key questions for understanding poverty? For devising pro-poor policies?

4. Do you believe that it is possible to eradicate poverty—or at least extreme poverty—within a global capitalist political economy?

FURTHER READING

Canadian Council for International Co-operation (CCIC). 2005. *A Summary Report of a CCIC-NSI Conference on 'The Politics of the Millennium Development Goals'*. Ottawa: CCIC. http://www.ccic.ca.

Laderchi, C.R., R. Saith, and F. Stewart. 2003. 'Does it matter that we do not agree on the definition of poverty? A comparison of four approaches'. *Oxford Development Studies* 31 (3): 243–73.

Mehrotra, S., and E. Delamonica. 2007. *Eliminating Human Poverty: Macroeconomic and Social Policies for Equitable Growth*. London: Zed Books.

Sachs, J.D. 2005. *The End of Poverty: Economic Possibilities for Our Time*. New York: Penguin.

Streeten, P. 1998. 'Beyond the six veils: Conceptualizing and measuring poverty'. *Journal of International Affairs* 52 (1): 1–31.

INTERNET RESOURCES

End Poverty 2015: http://www.endpoverty2015.org.

Make Poverty History: http://www.makepovertyhistory.ca.

United Nations Development Programme: http://www.undp.org/poverty.

United Nations Millennium Development Goals: http://www.un.org/millenniumgoals.

World Bank: http://www.worldbank.org (search using 'poverty' as keyword).

NOTE

1. Parts of this section are drawn from Morrison 1998.

CHAPTER 14

DEBT AND DEVELOPMENT

JOSEPH HANLON

LEARNING OBJECTIVES

- To learn that lending has a long history and that even lending to developing countries goes back 500 years.
- To recognize that lending to developing countries is linked to economic cycles and capital surpluses, to 'loan pushing' and default, and to the political interests of lenders.
- To understand the roots of the 1980s debt crisis.
- To recognize the role of the South as lender to the North and as a contributor to solving a Northern financial crisis.
- To take cognizance of the growing understanding of the liability of lenders and of the concepts of illegitimate and odious debt.

Borrowing and lending is often sensible and necessary. Borrowing to cover unexpected expenses or loss of income, such as through sickness or a bad crop, has been common for millennia. Capitalism is based on borrowing for productive investment—a piece of machinery or an irrigation system or simply more stock that will produce increased income to more than repay the initial loan. Most large companies and many countries grow with borrowed money. Many people live in mortgaged houses—rather than save over many years to build a house, they borrow money and repay it over many years, and during that period the borrower can live in a better house.

Banking originated in Babylonia before 2000 BCE, when temples and palaces provided safe places for the storage of valuables—initially deposits of grain and later other goods, including cattle, agricultural implements, and precious metals. By the reign of Hammurabi in Babylon (c. 1792–50 BCE), lending had become common, and his famous code—the first public written code of laws—covers banking and debt.

Initially, people would borrow from relatives, temples, or merchants who might provide goods on credit. Credit-based banking had developed in the Mediterranean world by the fourth century BCE. The Roman Empire developed banking that took deposits and lent money at interest, but this ended with the decline of Rome. Modern banking began to develop in the Mediterranean in the twelfth to fourteenth centuries CE. As banking systems developed, individuals, kings, companies, and even countries borrowed.

But from the first, three issues have dominated. First, what happens when the borrower cannot repay? Can the lender take property from the borrower? Can the lender force the borrower to work for him or her? Can the loan become a liability of spouses or children? The Hammurabi code contains two important restrictions. Article 48 says that if a person owes on a loan and the crop fails because of lack of water or a storm, not only does the person not have to make debt payments in that year, but no interest is paid for that year as well. Article 119 says that a man in debt can give himself or his wife, son, or daughter in forced labour to the creditor but only for three years, after which the debt is considered paid and the person freed.

Second, what can the lender charge the borrower? **Interest** payments are most common, usually a percentage of the outstanding loan each year. The borrower pays back part of the money borrowed—the **principal**—plus interest. The basis of modern commercial banking is to take deposits and pay interest on those deposits and then lend out the money at a higher interest rate, with the difference between the two interest rates covering risk of losses for non-repayment and allowing some profit for the bank. This remains controversial, and **usury**—excessive interest rates—has been an issue down through the ages; most religions allow interest but ban usury. But the Greek philosopher Plato (427–347 BCE) opposed lending at interest. The Koran also opposes lending at interest but permits trading profits and profit from investment, which means that banks should invest in businesses, sharing risk and profit, rather than lending to them. The early Christian church also banned lending at interest, but this was later eased to a ban on usury.

The third issue has become more important only with the growth of capitalism: what happens if an individual, company, or country borrows money for an investment that proves not to be profitable and the loan cannot be repaid? Until the mid-nineteenth century in both the United States and Britain, debtors who failed to repay were thrown into prison. This regime was replaced by liberal bankruptcy laws that allowed most of the assets of the debtor to be distributed to creditors, thus ending the debt, even if the assets were insufficient to cover full repayment. This proved to be one of the most important provisions of modern capitalism, because it encouraged business people to take risks without the fear of being thrown in debtors' prison. Over the twentieth century, bankruptcy laws became even more liberal, allowing individuals to keep their homes and giving more rights to workers in a company facing bankruptcy—even finding ways

to keep a company operating rather than liquidating it to sell its assets. Thus, lenders have come to take an increasing share of the risks of modern capitalism.

LENDING TO DEVELOPING COUNTRIES

Private banks in developed countries have been lending to poorer developing-country governments and businesses for centuries, and the record has often been one of default and political intervention.

'After King Edward I expelled the Jews in 1290 he needed the Italians to finance his wars. . . . To these Italian bankers England was a wild developing country on the edge of the world, a kind of medieval Zaire. Its exports of wool offered prospects of big profits; but with its despotic monarchs, its tribal wars and corrupt courtiers, it had a high country risk,' wrote Anthony Sampson (1981, 29–31, 54–6) in his prescient book *The Money Lenders*. 'But after King Edward III came to the throne in 1327 he was confident that he could compel his own English merchants to finance his wars; he defaulted on his Italian debts, and the [Florentine] banks of Bardi and Peruzzi collapsed.'

A century later, King Edward IV's War of the Roses took him deeper into debt. 'After trying to reschedule their debts with the King, the Medici Bank had to write off 52,000 florins and close their London office. "Rather than refuse deposits," concludes the historian of the bank', the Medicis succumbed to the temptation of seeking an outlet for surplus cash in making dangerous loans to princes. 'It was a warning relevant to more modern bankers,' commented Sampson.

Four centuries later, London was lending to the new United States. 'London saw it as a very unreliable developing country, with a black record of embezzlement, fraudulent prospectuses and default,' noted Sampson. But the bankers made loans in any case. In 1842, 11 states, including Maryland, Pennsylvania, Mississippi, and Louisiana, defaulted. Setting a precedent that would be used often in later years, Barings Bank simply intervened in local politics. In Maryland, Barings helped to finance candidates in the next election who were willing to repay. 'In the elections in 1846 the "resumptionists" narrowly won, and soon afterwards Maryland raised new taxes which enabled it to repay its debts. The campaign had cost Barings about $15,000; it was worth it,' wrote Sampson. Mississippi held out. By 1929, the unpaid debt was estimated at $32 million, and as recently as 1980, London banks were still trying to get Mississippi to repay on the loans it defaulted on 138 years earlier.

Sometimes there was military action in response. After Mexico defaulted in 1861, Britain, France, and Spain invaded. France installed Ferdinand Maximilian as emperor; he lasted only four years and failed to repay the debts (Eichengreen and Lindert 1989).

But why do banks lend to foreign governments when it is too easy for them to default? In part, they do so because many of these loans are profitable for both parties and are repaid. In his book *Manias, Panics and Crashes*, the eminent economist Charles Kindleberger (1978; 1996), details his view of economic cycles and international lending. He argues that each cycle starts with a period of real growth involving a rise in profits, often coming from the use of new technologies or new transportation/communication systems such as railways. This growth is linked to a rapid expansion of bank credit. Eventually, money growth outstrips possible productive investments while investors look for ever higher rates of profit. Increasingly, money goes into speculation, and this is often linked to fraud and swindles. This is the period of 'bubbles', or what Kindleberger calls 'manias'. It usually involves international lending as banks run out of domestic borrowers and become more desperate to lend and make higher-risk foreign loans—just as the Medicis did with Edward IV in the fifteenth century. Eventually, the bubble bursts, prices fall, and investors try to sell or to collect on their loans. This is the period of 'panic' as investors all rush for the exit. The panic feeds on itself, leading to the 'crash'. Kindleberger points to the tulip mania

of 1634, the South Sea bubble of 1720, the cotton and railway booms of the 1830s, and so on.

The past 250 years have seen four of these cycles:

1. growth 1780–1820, mania 1820s, crisis 1830s and 1840s;
2. growth 1850s, mania 1860s, crisis 1870s and 1880s;
3. growth 1893–1913, mania 1920s, crisis 1930s;
4. growth 1948–67, mania 1967–79, crisis since then.

Both the 1870s and the 1930s saw crises triggering major international depressions.

After each cycle, there have been retrospective complaints of reckless lending and of **loan pushing**—banks and lending agencies so desperate to lend money that they encourage foreign governments to take loans they do not need and encourage borrowers to live beyond their means. Towards the end of the mania, borrowers are encouraged to take new loans simply to repay old ones. With the panic, lending suddenly stops, borrowers cannot repay, and they default. Francis White, the US assistant secretary of state for Latin American affairs in the early 1930s, commented that 'in the carnival days from 1922 to 1929, when money was easy, many American bankers forsook the dignified, aloof attitude traditional of bankers and became, in reality, high pressure salesmen of money, carrying on a cut-throat competition against their fellow bankers, and once they obtained the business, endeavoured to urge larger loans on the borrowing countries' (Drake 1989, 43). During the 1920s, according to evidence before the Senate Committee on Finance, there were 29 representatives of US financial houses in Colombia alone trying to negotiate loans with the government.

In 1973, the US Federal Reserve governor Andrew Brimmer noted that 'the main explanation' for the sharp rise in lending to less developed countries was the 'failure of demand for loans from borrowers in developed countries to keep pace with the expansion of credit availability' (Darity and Horn 1988, 8). Brimmer cited a particular form of loan pushing, which involves a drastic softening of terms—similar to a drug pusher offering cheap heroin in order to create addiction. In the mid-1970s, international loans had a negative real interest rate—that is, in real terms (taking inflation into account), poor countries had to repay less than they borrowed. Loan pushers in the mania phase stressed that they were literally giving money away. But these loans were on variable interest rates, and in the early 1980s, those rates jumped dramatically, setting off the threat of default and fuelling the panic.

International development lending has two phases. In the growth period, lending can be profitable and promote productive investment and growth; indeed, careful borrowing by poorer countries has accelerated industrialization and development by allowing investment in infrastructure and equipment that could not have been afforded otherwise. But in the mania and loan pushing phase, when bankers are 'high pressure salesmen of money', poor countries take unproductive loans that they cannot repay.

GOVERNMENTS, POLITICS, THE COLD WAR, AND THE DEBT CRISIS

Initially, most lending was by banks, but increasingly in the late nineteenth and early twentieth centuries, loans were in the form of bonds, which could be sold to individuals and other investors (and which were often highly speculative or fraudulent). During the First World War, the United States government became a substantial lender to the countries fighting against Germany. In 1923, it extended the repayment period until 1983 and reduced the interest rate, but in 1934, in the depths of the Depression, Britain and five other European countries defaulted. No further payments were ever made, except by Finland. The debts are still on the books, and the US Treasury revealed that as of 30 June 1997, they stood at $33.5 billion. Outstanding First World War debts to the US include: $14.6 billion for the UK, $11 billion for France, and $3.2 billion for Italy.

The Second World War was even more expensive, and in 1945 Britain became the world's largest debtor. John Maynard Keynes was sent to Washington, and in December 1945 he negotiated the best deal he could get for Britain—a loan of $3.75 billion at 2 per cent interest. The final repayment was made only in 2006.

The end of the Second World War brought about four major changes in global politics and economics (some of which had their roots in earlier decades):

- Decolonization began, and many countries became independent.
- The Depression of the 1930s and then the war had made clear that there was a need for new international institutions, leading to the creation of the United Nations and the two **Bretton Woods Institutions** (BWIS)—the World Bank and the International Monetary Fund (IMF). The World Bank first lent for European reconstruction and then to newly independent countries (see chapter 9).
- Major corporations began to arise, increasingly international and linked to international trade and often backed by 'export credits' (loans given to government and companies to import goods from the lending country).
- The advent of nuclear weapons changed the nature of war and of empire. Military power and brute force were no longer the means to conquest, replaced instead by three options. The first was so-called 'low-intensity warfare' in which unacceptable governments were undermined or overthrown by security services backed by limited military force. For example, the United States created or backed opposition movements in Nicaragua, Angola, and Mozambique. The second involved larger wars but limited to single countries such as Vietnam. The third, and most important for this chapter, was the growing use of non-military means—economic power in particular. Thus, loans became an important way of wielding power.

One of the first developments in postwar economic conditions was US lending to Britain in 1945 for which the United States required Britain to move quickly to free trade and to make the pound convertible to the dollar within 15 months. The outflow of money from Britain was so great that much of the loan was dissipated, and convertibility was abandoned within weeks. But this was an early example of the kind of package of conditions that in the 1970s became known as structural adjustment.

John Perkins (2004), in a book titled *Confessions of an Economic Hit Man*, describes working for one of the largest international consulting firms and, indirectly, for the US National Security Agency from 1971 to 1981. He was one of a group of people, he wrote, whose job was to produce hugely exaggerated economic growth forecasts (in some cases, greater than any country had ever reached) for developing countries. These forecasts would justify vastly oversized electricity, railway, and other infrastructure projects that would be financed by international loans (both from commercial banks and the World Bank). Some money was siphoned off into the foreign bank accounts of the these countries' leaders to ensure they would not 'notice' that the projects were indeed white elephants. This strategy had two goals. First, contracts would go to US engineering companies (and often the money never left the US). But second, and much more sinister, was a conscious effort to burden the developing country with unpayable debts 'so they would present easy targets when we needed favors, including military bases, UN votes, or access to oil and other natural resources' (Perkins 2004, 15). It was a particularly political form of loan pushing.

The Cold War led to quite extensive lending in order to prop up and tie Western client dictators. One study (Hanlon 2006) estimated that one-quarter of developing-country debt consisted of Cold War loans to Western-backed dictators. Box 14.1 gives the example of the Congo/Zaire.

THE 1980s DEBT CRISIS

In 1970, developing-country debt was $70 billion, which may seem like a lot of money, but it proved to be quite small in comparison to what was to come in the following years. The 1970s was one of Kindleberger's mania periods, with a surplus of capital. There was a sharp increase in loan pushing; in the mid-1970s, global interest rates were 3 per cent lower than global inflation, which meant that real interest rates were negative—countries were being told, in effect, that they could repay *less* than they borrowed. Over the decade, developing-country debt increased seven-fold to $537 billion in 1980. Figure 14.1 shows both total debt stock and what is called 'net transfer on debt'—that is, new loans minus interest payments and principal repayments on old debts—which is thus the actual cash flow into or out of the borrowing country. The top graph shows the sharp increase in debt, while the bottom graph shows that there was a real transfer of money to developing countries in the 1970s.

But by 1984, **real interest rates** had reached a peak of 12 per cent. In 1982, Mexico could not pay the interest on its $60-billion debt and defaulted, setting off a massive debt crisis. Throughout the remainder of the 1980s, debt was constantly renegotiated, and new loans and bonds were issued to repay old loans. Most commonly, the new bonds or loans allowed a longer time to pay and sometimes lower interest rates. Money was borrowed to pay even the unpaid interest on old loans, which meant interest was charged on the interest. By 1990, developing-country debt had reached $1,330 billion, yet as the second graph shows, the poor countries received no benefit from these new loans—indeed, in the period 1983–90, developing countries transferred $154 billion to the rich countries, but their total debt increased by $550 billion.

Initially, it was hoped that the crisis was temporary and that if debt was rescheduled or refinanced, it could be paid off eventually. The main idea in the mid-1980s was simply to lend more money to debtor countries to allow them

BOX 14.1 CONGO, KLEPTOCRACY, AND THE COLD WAR

General Joseph Mobutu took power in the Congo in 1965, changing the country's name to Zaire. Mobutu may have been on the West's side in the Cold War, but he was also one of the world's most corrupt dictators, and his government was widely described as a 'kleptocracy'. In 1978, the IMF appointed its own man, Irwin Blumenthal, to a key post in the central bank of Zaire. He resigned in less than a year, writing a memo in which he said that 'the corruptive system in Zaire with all its wicked manifestations is so serious that there is no (repeat no) prospect for Zaire's creditors to get their money back.' When Blumenthal wrote his report, Zaire's debt was $4.6 billion. When Mobutu was overthrown and died in 1998, the debt was $12.9 billion, and Mobutu had luxury estates in France and elsewhere and probably billions of dollars stashed abroad. For once, the private sector saw that they had no chance of getting their money back and stopped lending after 1981. But shortly after the Blumenthal memo, the IMF granted Zaire the largest loan it had ever given an African country. The World Bank was hardly involved in Zaire when Blumenthal wrote his memo, but during the next 15 years it lent $2 billion to Zaire—and was still giving new money to Mobutu as late as 1993. Western governments were the biggest lenders and continued to pour in new money until 1990—even though Zaire had virtually stopped repaying its debts in 1982. As part of his loyalty to the United States, Mobutu provided a home for the US-backed Unita forces in Angola; in 1987, when he permitted US covert action against neighbouring Angola, the US pushed through yet another IMF loan to Zaire, this time over the objections of some IMF officials.

After the overthrow of Mobutu, Zaire was renamed the Democratic Republic of the Congo (DRC), and donors were anxious to help the new government. But the IMF pointed out that the DRC was in arrears because it was not repaying the debt of the old Mobutu regime. This had the effect of blocking other aid, since donors will not help a country that has no IMF program. Four countries—France, Belgium, South Africa, and Sweden—gave the DRC a bridging loan of $522 million in 2002 to repay the money the IMF should never have lent to Mobutu in the first place. The IMF immediately gave DRC a new loan of $543 million, of which $522 million went directly back to the four countries to repay the bridging loan.

---

to at least pay the interest on their debts. But it was becoming clear that the crisis was systemic. (See, for example, George 1988, Payer 1991, and Pineda-Ofreneo 1991.)

Since loans could not be repaid, some private lenders wanted to be able to sell the debts. Selling debt goes back to at least the fifteenth century: typically a bank or investor gives cash to the original lender, usually for less than the actual face value of the loan, and takes on the responsibility of collecting the debt. Factoring or invoice selling became a common method of industrial finance in the twentieth century. For example, a company sells goods and sends an invoice requiring a promise of payment in 90 days but then immediately sells the invoice to a finance company; the company is thus paid immediately, which reduces its need for working capital. Bonds are explicitly

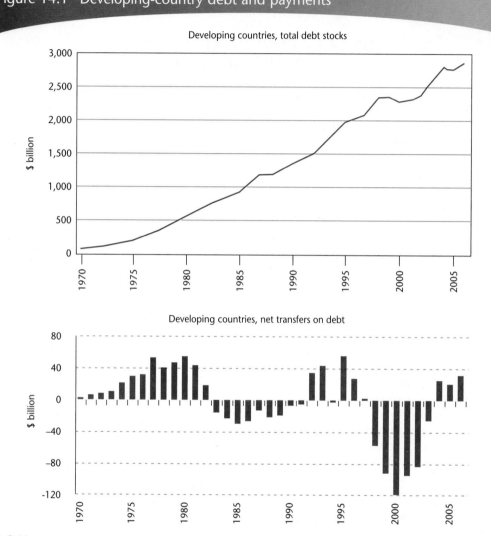

Figure 14.1   Developing-country debt and payments

Developing countries, total debt stocks

Developing countries, net transfers on debt

Definitions:
'Stock' is the total amount owed.
'Net transfer' is the amount of new lending minus interest payments and principal repayments. It is thus the total
   amount developing countries received from (above the 0 line) or paid to (below the 0 line) all creditors.
Source: World Bank. *Global Development Finance.* April 2007.

a form of tradable debt, because the original bondholder, who actually lent the money, can sell the bond to other investors.

A market grew up in which developing-country debt was traded, and some countries bought their own debt back at a discount. Debt was used for privatizations, and there were debt-for-nature and debt-for-development swaps in which small amounts of debt were cancelled if the money was used for environment or development purposes. But as Figure 14.1 shows, that debt was still rising inexorably.

Table 14.1 External debt, $ billion

	1970	1980	1990	2000	2006
All developing countries	70	537	1,330	2,266	2,851
Low-income countries	19	93	310	347	352

Notes: All developing countries are those with a GNI of less than $11,115 per capita per year in 2006, calculated by the World Bank atlas method.
Low-income countries are those with a GNI of less than $905 per capita per year in 2006, calculated by the World Bank atlas method.
Source: World Bank. *Global Development Finance.* April 2007.

Industrialized-country finance ministers became increasingly worried in the 1980s that the debt crisis would lead to the collapse of major banks because they had to write down developing-country debt on their books and not treat them as assets. So ministers looked for ways to help the banks, and they settled on bond issues to refinance the debt, because such bonds could be sold by banks to investors. Thus, because they had a value, they could be treated as assets if they were not sold.

In 1989, US Treasury Secretary Nicholas Brady launched a scheme for middle-income creditors that came to be named after him. Countries would issue new 20-year bonds, effectively guaranteed by the US, and these bonds would be exchanged for outstanding bank debt—usually at a discount so that the total debt was reduced by 30 per cent or more. Nearly $200 billion in such bonds were eventually issued.

Many of the bond issues, new loans, and refinancings had conditions attached, especially conditions linked to free market and neo-liberal economic policies. Another issue was that many of the loans in the 1970s had been made to private companies rather than to governments, and as part of efforts to save industrialized-country banks, developing-country governments came under huge pressure to take over these private loans—in effect, the North demanded that the South nationalize private debt.

By the mid-1990s, the World Bank and the IMF had accepted that the poorest countries could not sensibly repay their debt, and they were approving poor-country budgets in which only a small portion of debt was being repaid. In 1996, they finally launched the **Heavily Indebted Poor Countries** (HIPC) initiative, which broke new ground by accepting for the first time that some loans made by the two institutions would have to be cancelled. This was to be done in parallel with proportionate debt cancellation by government (bilateral) and private creditors.

Debt cancellation involved three groups of creditors—the **Paris Club**, which comprises most government (bilateral) lenders; the 'London Club' of banks and commercial creditors; and the IMF, World Bank, and other development banks. The IMF and World Bank handled the negotiations and demanded that developing countries follow strict neo-liberal structural adjustment. The process was very complex, and in the first two years there was no debt cancellation.

Meanwhile, Jubilee 2000, an international campaign launched in 1997, called for the 'cancellation of the unpayable debt of the world's poorest countries by the year 2000 under a fair and transparent process'. The campaign was highly successful in three ways. First, it took what had been considered an arcane and technical issue, which supposedly could only be understood by economists, and turned it into an easy-to-understand campaigning issue. Second, it joined together local debt campaigns in numerous countries, North and South. Third, it gained

Figure 14.2   IMF Headquarters, Washington DC

Source: Wikipedia

unexpected support—24 million people from 166 countries signed a petition—and successfully brought pressure on Northern governments. At the 1999 meeting of the finance ministers of the Group of Eight (G-8) in Köln, Germany, it was agreed that HIPC debt cancellation would be increased from $55 billion to $100 billion. At that time, 41 countries were considered eligible for HIPC, and they had $207 billion in debt. But of that, $100 billion was not being serviced anyway—mainly with the agreement of the IMF and the World Bank, since most of those countries had Bank and IMF programs. This meant that

the Bank and the IMF were admitting that the money would in effect never be paid out. The $100 billion would just go to writing off debt that the institutions knew would never be repaid—not a particularly generous move. In 2006, after 10 years of HIPC and six years after Köln, the World Bank admitted that debt cancellation under HIPC had only reached $62 billion for 30 countries. The failure of HIPC led to increased pressure from the G-8, and in 2006, the IMF, World Bank, and the African Development Fund (ADF) introduced the Multilateral Debt Relief Initiative (MDRI) under which they agreed to cancel another $38 billion in debt for countries that had already completed the HIPC process—thus finally reaching the level promised seven years earlier. Although most debt cancelled was not being repaid in any case, for a few very poor countries such as Mozambique, the process did substantially reduce actual debt service payments.

The World Bank estimates that between 1989 and 2005 (inclusive), $251 billion of developing-country debt was cancelled under HIPC and other negotiations. That may seem like a lot of money until one looks more closely at Figure 14.1. As the second graph shows, in just four years during the mid-1990s was there a transfer of money from North to South. In most other years, the poor have continued to subsidize the rich. Between 1989 and 2005, the net transfer on debt from South to North was $302 billion. The World Bank estimates that total aid (grants less technical assistance) in the same period was $543 billion, so two-thirds of aid went back to the North as debt servicing. Middle-income countries were hardest hit because they did not receive much aid. And in the same period, despite the large repayments and debt cancellation, total developing-country debt increased by $1.5 trillion. So the debt cancellation was like using a bucket to try and empty an ever-deeper ocean.

The key point is that in the 1970s, developing countries did gain money through international borrowing, but in the years since the crisis of the 1980s, they gained nothing. Struggling to repay and sending more and more money to rich countries, they fell deeper and deeper into debt.

In the earlier crisis phase of the 1930s, many international borrowers simply defaulted. Europe stopped paying its First World War debt to the US in 1934; most Latin American borrowers also stopped paying. The major difference between the 1930s and the 1980s was the existence of the Bretton Woods Institutions, which enforced continued repayments (as is clear from Figure 14.1). Many poor countries became increasingly dependent on international aid from the industrialized countries, and these 'donors' in turn made their aid conditional on recipient countries hav-

ing World Bank and IMF programs. One condition of these programs was continued debt repayment. Little concession was made for economic problems such as bad crops, and the debt bondage has lasted indefinitely. Indeed, with respect to the BWIs, developing countries have fewer rights than the citizens of Hammurabi's Babylon did nearly 4,000 years ago.

Another highly controversial condition was that poor countries adopt neo-liberal economic policies and what were known as 'structural adjustment programs', which we will explore in the next section (also discussed in chapter 9).

THE SOUTH PAYS TO SOLVE THE NORTHERN CRISIS

The 1930s Depression largely affected the United States and Europe, while developing countries, notably in Latin America, continued to grow. The response of the industrialized countries, and mainly the United States, to the most recent Kindleberger cycle—growth 1948–67, mania 1967–79, crisis since then—has been to ensure that the situation of the 1930s is not repeated. The crisis was to be exported to the South, and money was to be extracted from the developing countries in order to prevent depression in the industrialized countries. The US pursued four strategies: imposing a neo-liberal economic model, raising interest rates in the early 1980s, borrowing to fuel consumption, and forcing countries to keep dollars as reserves. The following discussion elaborates these strategies.

The development model that originated in the 1930s Depression, continued through the Second World War, and then supported the 1960s and 1970s growth phase had been state-led—not just in the then-socialist countries but also in European and Asian capitalist countries and in developing countries following either model. But the crisis beginning in the late 1970s was marked by stagnation in the US economy and led to the introduction of an entirely new economic model—neo-liberalism. First introduced by Augusto Pinochet after he took power in a

US-backed coup in Chile in 1974, it was later adopted by the British government of Margaret Thatcher beginning in 1979 and the US administration of Ronald Reagan from 1981. Linked to right-wing libertarian political philosophies, this policy called for smaller government, **privatization** and the withdrawal of the government from the economy, sharply reduced regulation and reduced power for trade unions, and lower taxes on the rich to encourage them to invest (usually accompanied by lower spending on health and education, on the grounds that the poor should take more responsibility for looking after themselves). A key part of the package was free movement of goods and capital (but not people), so customs barriers and capital controls were removed. In the 1980s, the World Bank and the IMF began to impose neo-liberal economic policies on developing countries (see chapters 3 and 9). The poorest countries had to accept, because aid was dependent on having programs the BWIs imposed, which included three key policies:

1. They enforced debt repayment.
2. They forced poor countries to open their borders to manufactured goods from the industrialized countries. This put an end to import substitution industrialization, which had been the model followed by the now-industrialized countries and was the model being followed by the developing world.
3. They forced the developing countries to instead follow a model of export-led growth, which led to many countries rapidly expanding the production of agricultural and mineral exports. That meant increased competition and a drop in the prices paid by the rich countries to the poor countries. Cocoa sold for $2,604 a tonne in 1980, less than half that ($1,267) in 1990, and even less in 2000 ($906). Coffee similarly fell from $3,243 per tonne in 1980 to $1,182 in 1990 and $913 in 2000. For many countries, the loss in income was far greater than the aid they received or their debt service payments. The result was little growth and an increase in poverty in

most developing countries in the 1980s and 1990s—except for China, which did not follow the new model, had the highest growth rates, and became a major industrial country (see epilogue).

So the impact of neo-liberalism was to lower the prices of raw materials for the industrialized countries, thus reducing the impact of the crisis on them and forcing the developing countries to bear the brunt of it. The second step came in the early 1980s when US President Ronald Reagan sharply raised interest rates, which did initially create a flow of money from South to North (as shown in Figure 14.1) but which also triggered the debt crisis.

The third response to the crisis was simply to borrow money. The United States' public debt in 1940 was $43 billion, and the cost of the Second World War pushed it up to $260 billion. By 1970, it had only risen to $390 billion. But as stagnation set in, the US started to borrow at an unprecedented rate, pushing the debt to $930 billion in 1980, $3.2 trillion ($3,200 billion) in 1990, $5.7 trillion in 2000, and $8.5 trillion by 2006.

At the same time, the US was increasingly consuming a great deal more than it produced. The trade deficit (goods and services) increased from $40 billion in 1994 to $100 billion in 1995, $420 billion in 2002, and $760 billion in 2006. Increasingly, the US was importing goods instead of producing them, and it had to borrow money to pay the bills.

The United States had already made a fourth change, the impact of which only became clear later. From 1934, the price of gold had been fixed at $35 per ounce; gold was used as financial reserves by most countries. But the US was having trouble paying for the Vietnam War, and in 1971, president Richard Nixon announced that there would be a free market in gold; the price rose to $140 within two years. As well as helping to pay for the war, this move had a much more subtle effect—instead of gold, US dollars became the world's reserves. Each dollar that a country holds as a reserve (usually deposited in a US bank) is a promise by the US government to eventually provide one dollar in goods. Indeed, reserves are mostly held in US government bonds. Thus, in effect, countries holding reserves were lending money to the United States.

Two very different factors have led to a sharp increase in foreign holdings of US bonds in the early years of the twenty-first century. An East Asian financial crisis from 1997 to 1999 was triggered in part by excessive and speculative international and domestic borrowing, causing the collapse of banks and currencies. With a sudden outflow of speculative capital, Thailand, Malaysia, Indonesia, the Philippines, and South Korea all found themselves unable to pay short-term debt. The IMF and the US offered to 'help' but imposed neo-liberal conditions requiring that the economies become even more open. This was exactly the wrong response and made the crisis worse. One result was that East Asian countries built up their reserves sharply so that when the next cyclic monetary problem occurred, they would not need to turn to the IMF.

But in one way, this suited the United States, because middle-income East Asian countries were holding large amounts of dollars—in effect giving a big loan to the US. Meanwhile, the IMF insisted that poor countries substantially increase their reserves. They were too poor to use these reserves to gain independence from the IMF, and many thought that the reserves were excessive and that the money would be better spent on development. But it meant sharply increasing their holding of US dollars or bonds. Roughly $2 trillion, one-quarter of US public debt, was held by foreign governments as reserves in 2006.

Figure 14.3 shows foreign reserves held by developing countries and makes clear the dramatic rise from 2003 when the US and its allies needed money to pay for the Iraq war. Approximately half of these reserves are in US dollars or US government bonds.

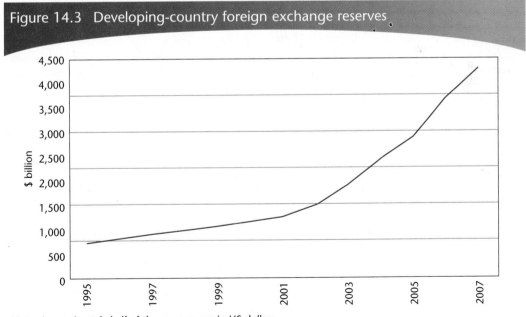

Figure 14.3   Developing-country foreign exchange reserves

Note: Approximately half of the reserves are in US dollars.
Source: International Monetary Fund. *Currency Composition of Official Foreign Exchange Reserves (COFER).* 28 September 2007.

The net result is that since developing country debt is $2.9 trillion but developing countries are holding $4.3 trillion, the poor countries are currently lending $1.4 trillion to the rich countries. These loans have been preventing a 1930s-style depression in the industrialized countries while creating just such a depression in the developing countries.

TWO FINAL QUESTIONS

First, why borrow?

The changing nature of international debt in the second half of the twentieth century and the way that post-1980 debt has mounted astronomically without any apparent benefit to developing countries raises two key questions: Is borrowing worth it? And what is the liability of the lenders?

Poor people well understand the debt trap, constantly borrowing to survive and sinking ever deeper into debt, with debt service payments becoming greater than any benefit gained from the initial borrowing. And yet the other side of borrowing is also obvious. Borrowing to buy a car and having the use of the car while paying off the loan over three years, or taking a mortgage on a house and being able to live in it for the 20-year repayment period, means that because of interest, we pay far more than the actual cost of the car or house but we consider it reasonable because we have the use of the car or house during that period. And large parts of modern industrial development are based on borrowing money to construct a building or buy a piece of machinery that will make a company more productive and thus sufficiently profitable to pay off the loan. This is exactly the argument used by the World Bank and developing countries alike for foreign borrowing as a way of stimulating more rapid growth.

But economists distinguish between foreign and domestic borrowing. Does a country borrow from its own banks and citizens—say, by issuing bonds—or does it borrow from foreign banks and the World Bank? Economists such as Cheryl Payer (1991) have argued that few countries have suc-cessfully developed on the basis of foreign loans, or at least not for very long periods. Borrowing for economic development requires that the economy and productivity grow rapidly enough to generate the extra income to repay the loan. Foreign borrowing makes very different repayment demands from those of domestic borrowing, and the imposed policies of the Bretton Woods Institutions become very important.

Traditionally, countries developed by protecting their infant industries from foreign competition so that these companies could sell their goods locally, become profitable, and repay their loans. The imposed neo-liberal model requires that economies be open, which gives no space for local industry to grow and become profitable. Further, foreign borrowing is in currencies of the industrialized world—US dollars or euros. Therefore, the BWIs pushed countries to produce exports that they could sell for hard currency. But as we have seen, this strategy was undermined by what is known as the 'fallacy of composition'—if everyone is producing more of the same exports, the price falls. So countries had to produce still more exports to pay for their loans. At the same time, structural adjustment policies often demanded devaluation of the local currency. All of this made foreign loans much more expensive than domestic ones, and as it turned out, economies simply did not grow rapidly enough to pay the much higher cost of foreign borrowing. Economies also did not grow because the imposed BWI policies did not promote growth. So foreign borrowing not only was more expensive but came with policies that retarded growth.

Second, what is the responsibility of the lender?

Boxes 14.2 and 14.3 help to explain the final question. Is it acceptable to lend to a government that the United Nations says is committing a crime against humanity? Do lenders and contractors have a responsibility to point out that a nuclear power station should not be built on an earthquake fault?

BOX 14.2   LENDING TO APARTHEID SOUTH AFRICA

When Nelson Mandela walked out of prison in 1990, the international banks handed him a bill for $21 billion. In effect, the bankers told Mandela, 'In 1985, we told the white government that we understood that they had financial problems and that it was expensive to keep you in jail and maintain white minority rule, and thus debt payments could be deferred. But now that you are out of jail, and South Africa has majority rule, it is time for you to pay the cost of keeping you in jail.' Mandela was told by the international community to pay up, so he did. In 1997, South Africa paid an incredible $6.5 billion in debt service—more than four times what the banks demanded of the apartheid state.

Yet because of apartheid, South Africa had been forced to leave the Commonwealth in 1961. In 1973, the United Nations began to describe apartheid as a 'crime against humanity', and in 1977, the UN imposed a mandatory arms embargo on the country. In 1982, an article by two lawyers from the First National Bank of Chicago in the *University of Illinois Law Review* warned their employer and other banks of the consequences of a change of sovereignty in South Africa for loan agreements. They noted that in loan documents, the description of the intended use of the money was often too general to ensure that the loan benefited the people and thus to ensure repayment. The banks did not listen, however, and South Africa's debt jumped to $16.9 billion.

Was the new South African government liable for repayment of the apartheid debt?

In international law, it is widely accepted that when a government changes, the successor government assumes the laws, contracts, and debts of the previous government. The United States exemplified one of the few exception to this convention after it seized Cuba from Spain in 1898. Spain demanded that the US pay Cuba's debts, but the US refused on the grounds that the debt had been 'imposed upon the people of Cuba without their consent and by force of arms'. Furthermore, the US argued that in such circumstances, 'the creditors, from the beginning, took the chances of the investment. The very pledge of the national credit, while it demonstrates on the one hand the national character of the debt, on the other hand proclaims the notorious risk that attended the debt in its origin, and has attended it ever since' (Adams 1991, 164). In the intervening century, the US has never revised its view that Cuban debt was not the liability of the new gov-

ernment. It held a similar view in 2003 after the invasion of Iraq to overthrow the government of Saddam Hussein, when US Treasury secretary John Snow said, 'Certainly the people of Iraq shouldn't be saddled with those debts incurred through the regime of the dictator who is now gone' (Hanlon 2006, 211).

The name and doctrine of **odious debt** was formalized by Alexander Sack, who wrote:

If a despotic power incurs a debt not for the needs or in the interest of the state, but to strengthen its despotic regime, to repress the population that fights against it, etc., this debt is odious to the population of all the state. This debt is not an obligation for the nation; it is a regime's debt, a personal debt of the power that has incurred it, consequently it falls with [the] fall of this power (Adams 1991, 165).

BOX 14.3   PHILIPPINES AND NUCLEAR POWER

The Philippine dictator Ferdinand Marcos was finally overthrown in 1986 and fled into exile with his wife Imelda. He had an estimated $5 to $13 billion stashed away in foreign banks, suggesting that up to one-third of the Philippines' foreign borrowing had passed into his very deep pockets. Most of Marcos's borrowing took place during the loan-pushing boom of the 1970s, and by 1983 there was a net outflow of money, which continued during more than a decade of democratic government.

The largest single debt of the Philippines is for the Bataan nuclear power station. Completed in 1984 at a cost of $2.3 billion, it was never used because it was built on an earthquake fault at the foot of a volcano. It was built by the US multinational Westinghouse despite a much lower bid by General Electric that was favoured by a technical committee. Marcos overruled his own advisors, and Westinghouse later admitted that it paid a commission to a Marcos associate, which the *New York Times* estimated at $80 million. Much of the construction was done by companies in which Marcos had an interest. Bribes were paid in Switzerland. The International Atomic Energy Authority noted that attempting to build a nuclear power station in an area of such high seismic activity was 'unique in the atomic industry'. We can all be grateful that the plant was never put into operation and never became an Asian Chernobyl.

The nuclear power station was financed by the US export credit agency Ex-Im Bank, the Union Bank of Switzerland (which is accused of holding some of the Marcos billions), Bank of Tokyo, and Mitsui and Company, all of which are still being repaid. The Philippines still pays $170,000 per day for a power station that has never been used, and the debt will not be repaid until 2018.

Surely the same rule should have been applied to the apartheid regime in South Africa and the Mobutu regime in Zaire (Boxes 14.1 and 14.2), but lenders, including the World Bank and the IMF, refused to accept that their original lending had been improper.

Although the Jubilee 2000 campaign focused simply on 'unpayable debt', campaigners increasingly took up the issue of lenders' co-responsibility and of what came to be defined as the broader areas of 'illegitimate debt'—loans that were improperly made and should be the liability of the lender, not the borrower. This would include the Philippines Bataan nuclear power station on the grounds that the lenders and builders had a fiduciary duty—not just to the Philippines but to the safety of all of East Asia—not to support a nuclear power station on an earthquake fault.

Rapidly growing consumer protection in the second half of the twentieth century applies also to lending. That principle would require that lenders take due care to see that a loan is reasonable, that the borrower is competent to borrow, and that the borrower can reasonably be expected to repay. The British Consumer Credit Act 2006, for example, defines 'unfair relationships between creditors and debtors': if a borrower refuses to pay and alleges that the relationship was unfair, then 'it is for the creditor to prove the contrary.'

Similarly, modern civil and commercial law has broadened contractual obligations in complex business transactions beyond the strict delivery of goods to include dissemination of professional advice, discovery of special risks, and so forth, especially if one party is less knowledgeable than the other and therefore must trust the other's superior skills. Neglecting these accessory obligations may be considered a breach of contract.

In domestic law, greater responsibilities have been imposed on lenders. This means that loans like those to apartheid South Africa and Mobutu or for Bataan would simply not be acceptable under domestic law in most industrialized countries. Yet concepts of unfairness and the broader obligations in domestic law are only now being brought into international lending. For example, the United Nations Institute for Training and Research argues that in developing countries, the lender is often connected with the project design, while the borrower must rely on external expertise, typically from the lender, because they lack the technical know-how to plan infrastructure policies and to implement projects. Therefore, the lender must bear some responsibility for improperly designed, badly implemented, or environmentally damaging projects.

The first move by a government in this direction came in 2005 when the new governing coalition in Norway said that 'the UN must establish criteria for what can be characterised as **illegitimate debt**, and such debt must be cancelled.' The following year, Norway unilaterally cancelled export credit debt for ships that had been used to promote Norwegian shipyards rather than for developmental purposes.

It is clear that lender–borrower co-responsibility, as well as odious and illegitimate lending, are now becoming recognized as concepts in international law and that domestic lending concepts such as unfairness and broader obligations of lenders are being taken into account. However, it may take several more years before the principle becomes established.

Illegitimate debt is not just an issue for developing countries. Indeed, the 2007–8 financial crisis in the United States was triggered by trading in illegitimate debt. Mortgage companies gave home loans to people who were manifestly unable to pay, then sold on the loans to gullible bankers. The crisis came when banks realized that poor people could not repay the outstanding billions of dollars in loans and that the original lenders were taking no responsibility for what was clearly illegitimate lending. Thus, even in the US, questions have been raised about the right of the initial lender to shirk all responsibility for manifestly bad loans.

SUMMARY AND CONCLUSION

Lending and borrowing, and regulations to control loans and loan collections, go back some 4,000 years. International borrowing goes back at least 800 years, but it remains controversial. Charles Kindleberger proposed that the economy runs in cycles of growth, mania, and crisis and that during the mania phase, there is a surplus of capital that leads to increasingly risky and speculative lending, particularly loan pushing to developing countries. During the crisis period, borrowers often cannot repay and therefore default.

Lending in the 1970s, both commercial loan pushing and lending to Cold War allies, led to a loan crisis in the early 1980s when interest rates were suddenly driven up. During the 1970s, lending did provide new money for developing countries, but since then there has been a net transfer of wealth from poor countries to rich ones. Developing-country debt has increased dramatically—from $537 billion in 1980 to $2,851 billion in 2006—but with no discernable benefit to borrowing countries. Meanwhile, however, the United States and other industrialized countries have been net borrowers, with developing countries holding $4,300 billion in Northern bonds and other debts. Thus, the period since 1982 has seen a huge transfer of wealth from poor countries to rich ones, and developing countries have become major lenders to the rich industrialized countries.

QUESTIONS FOR DISCUSSION

1. Should lenders take more responsibility for improper lending?
2. How would one define 'illegitimate lending'?
3. Are developing countries building up excessive reserves in US dollars and thus lending too much to the United States? What are the alternatives?
4. Do developing countries need to borrow internationally?

FURTHER READING

Adams, P. 1991. *Odious Debts*. London: Earthscan.

George, S. 1989. *A Fate Worse than Debt*. London: Penguin.

Hanlon, J. 2006. '"Illegitimate" loans: Lenders, not borrowers, are responsible'. *Third World Quarterly* 27(2): 211–26.

Jochnick, C., and F. Preston, eds. 2006. *Sovereign Debt at the Crossroads*. Oxford: Oxford University Press.

Kindleberger, C. 1978. *Manias, Panics and Crashes*. 1st edn, London: Basic Books-Macmillan; 3rd edn (1996), New York: John Wiley.

Perkins, J. 2004. *Confessions of an Economic Hit Man*. San Francisco: Berrett-Koehler.

INTERNET RESOURCES

World Bank Heavily Indebted Poor Countries (HIPC) initiative: http://www.worldbank.org/hipc.

IMF on HIPC: http://www.imf.org/external/np/exr/facts/hipc.htm.

European Network on Debt and Development (EURODAD): http:// www.eurodad.org.

For up-to-date discussion on illegitimate and odious debt, Probe International: http://www.probeinternational.org/catalog/odious.php.

Jubilee Debt Campaign: http://www.jubileedebtcampaign.org.uk.

For archive of Jubilee 2000 campaign: http://www.jubileeresearch.org.

CHAPTER 15

FREE TRADE AND FAIR TRADE

GAVIN FRIDELL

LEARNING OBJECTIVES

- To recognize the difference between a 'free trade' and a 'fair trade' perspective and be able to assess whether a given author would better represent one perspective over the other.
- To understand the general history of international trade since 1945 and the differences between the past and today.
- To be able to discuss and assess cultural and political critiques of the notion of 'free trade'.

INTRODUCTION

International trade is an important topic that poses major challenges for development practitioners and academics. Over the past half century, the total amount of world trade has grown substantially, with the value of world exports of merchandise trade increasing from $130 billion in 1960 to more than $6,414 billion in 2002. During this period, the share of expanding world trade held by advanced industrialized countries in the North has remained relatively the same, while several booming Asian economies have significantly increased their share and the majority of remaining Southern developing countries have experienced a diminishing percentage—Africa's share of world merchandise exports declined from 7.5 per cent in 1960 to 5.4 per cent in 2002! (UNCTAD 2004a, 48–53) These statistics offer a snapshot of the current world system and the importance of international trade in shaping its social, economic, and political contours. Because of its significance, international trade seems to find its way into most key debates, making it difficult to talk about 'development' without reference, either directly or indirectly, to trade. The seemingly unavoidable connection between trade and development is made even stronger by the growing number of international 'free trade' agreements which, as many commentators have pointed out, go well beyond trade to include a wide range of rules that intrude on the broader social and economic policies of states (Harvey 2005; Gill 2003; Hoogvelt 2001; McNally 2002). Consequently, it becomes difficult to discuss perspectives on international trade without getting lost in a conversation around the general theories of development discussed in Part I of this book.

Nonetheless, at the risk of oversimplification, it is possible to speak broadly about two overarching perspectives on trade that are generally apparent, in varying ways, in most development works. I will refer to these as a **free trade** perspective and a **fair trade** perspective, the latter of which is less commonly known and should not be confused with the specific project of 'fair trade' certification (discussed near the end of the chapter) whose proponents represent only part of a broader fair trade movement. Neither of the two perspectives can be precisely defined, since they represent a wide range of sometimes vastly different development approaches. Some development thinkers might fit very well into one of the two groups, whereas others might fit only partially into a group or present ideas compatible with both. The notion of a free trade and a fair trade perspective is thus a reference not to two cohesive approaches to development but rather to two general overarching assumptions. While these groupings might lack a bit of precision, they are also highly instructive, because they allow us to talk about general trends in development theory and practice—to focus on the forest and not get lost in the trees—and can offer us a great deal of insight into the past and present of international trade debates.

The first of these perspectives, that of *free trade*, is premised on the notion that the removal of barriers to trade and the limitation of state intervention in economic and social interactions at the national and international level will provide the greatest social gains in the North and the South. This is the dominant view today among most official international organizations, such as the World Bank, the International Monetary Fund (IMF), and the World Trade Organization (WTO), as well as within many national governments and non-governmental development organizations (although certainly not all). The free trade perspective has not always been dominant in international affairs in the postwar era. It was not until the 1970s that free trade moved to the centre of current policy debates on development, spurred on by the growing influence of neo-liberal thinkers such as economist Milton Friedman (1962) and his disciples at the University of Chicago, nicknamed the 'Chicago Boys'. Drawing on neoclassical economic ideals from the second half of the nineteenth century, neo-liberals were deeply opposed to state intervention in the economy, which they felt was bound to be inefficient and inaccurate because of state officials' limited access to information and their tendency to be biased towards the demands of specific interest groups, such as unions or trade lobbies. In contrast, they argued that the unregulated market served as a 'hidden hand' that responded efficiently and accurately to the 'rational', self-interested actions of countless individuals through the undistorted market signals of supply and demand. Thus, while the state was depicted as choking individual liberty and initiative, caus-

ing economic waste and stagnation, the market, as summarized by David Harvey, was presented as 'the best device for mobilizing even the basest of human instincts such as gluttony, greed, and the desire for wealth and power for the benefit of all' (Harvey 2005, 20–1).

In terms of international trade and development, neo-liberal thinkers have been central to advancing a free trade vision based on a particular understanding of the histories of highly industrialized countries in the North, such as the United States and the United Kingdom. They argue that one of the key driving forces behind the pattern of rapid, modern economic growth experienced by these countries beginning in the eighteenth and nineteenth centuries was a devotion to the principles of free trade (Sachs 2005). Free trade, they assert, sparks competition, which leads to technological innovation and specialization as nations seek to enhance their **comparative advantage**—a concept formulated by British millionaire stockbroker David Ricardo in the nineteenth century. Ricardo's theory held that each nation had an economic advantage relative to other nations for the production of some goods. Thus, Country A might produce both iron and wheat more efficiently than Country B, which also produced the same goods. But Country A might be most efficient at producing iron. Consequently, it would be in the relative interest of both nations if Country A focused on producing iron and Country B focused on producing wheat, and the two countries could then trade iron and wheat to their mutual benefit. Based on these historical and theoretical assumptions, free traders argue that developing countries need to remove their barriers to trade to gain access to Northern technology, products, and investment, while at the same time producing and trading those goods for which they have or can develop a comparative economic advantage relative to other nations (Bhagwati 2002; Sachs 2005). If each nation were to specialize in those products for which it has a comparative advantage, all of the nations in the world would benefit in relative terms. The conclusion, according to Earth Institute Director Jeffrey Sachs, is that international trade and development is not a zero-sum game but 'one that everybody can win' (Sachs 2005, 31).

Some free market proponents are less optimistic about the overall benefits of global free trade. 'New trade theory' advocates Paul Krugman and Anthony Venables (1995) argue that new transportation and communication technologies have significantly reduced the historical need for industries to cluster together in regions close to consumer markets in order to minimize transportation costs. Corporations can now locate themselves where labour is cheapest, regardless of proximity to specific national markets. This fact has opened the possibility that Southern states, which have the competitive advantage of low wages, may one day become the new industrialized core of the global economy. Krugman and Venables argue that this possibility will not occur overnight; the North will continue to benefit the most from world trade, since industry is already clustered there for historical reasons. Over time, however, transportation costs will become so low that industry will increasingly move to the South. Real wages between the North and South will converge, resulting in a situation 'in which the peripheral nations definitely gain and the core nations may well lose' (Krugman and Venables 1995, 859). While not the rosiest outcome for Northern workers, Krugman and Venables argue that a revival of protectionist policies in the North would only wreck the North's competitiveness and unjustly suppress industrialization in the South. In their view, free trade may not bring about a strictly win-win scenario, but it represents the best choice of the available options.

In contrast, the *fair trade* perspective is even less optimistic about the possibilities of a win-win situation emerging in international trade—unless the terms of North–South trade are readjusted and market interventionist mechanisms are employed to support development efforts in the South. Fair trade proponents challenge free traders' historical understanding of trade and assert that national and international markets have always been regulated to some extent, generally in the interests of

the rich and powerful. They argue that the rich nations in the North, as well as the Newly Industrialized Countries (NICs) in East Asia and Latin America, all emerged historically behind a protective wall of import controls, tariffs, levies, quotas, and preferences designed to protect domestic industry and enhance export industry (Baer 1972, 95–122; Stiglitz 2003, 7–37). Market regulation has, in particular, been employed by powerful nations to ensure their dominant position in the global division of labour: they demand relatively easy access to raw materials and markets in the South while erecting trade barriers to protect key industries in the North from Southern competition. To counter this historical legacy, fair traders argue that it is necessary to use market regulation to protect the weak, not the strong, and to create a more equal international trading system (Barratt Brown 1993).

The strongest proponents of the fair trade perspective tend to be located within a broad and diverse school of thought on underdevelopment and dependency theory, which moved to the fore of critical development during the 1960s and 1970s. As discussed in chapter 3, these theorists have argued that the history of colonialism has led to the formation of a world system divided into First World imperialist nations in the North and Third World neo-colonial nations in the South. Rather than Southern countries being in a position to enhance their comparative advantage through international trade, their national development is restricted and distorted by the **unequal exchange** of lower-priced primary commodities (such as coffee, tea, cocoa, and bananas) for higher-priced industrial goods, technology, and services from the First World (Frank 1972; Prebisch 1950; Wallerstein 1974b). While a select group of NICs have been able to attain rapid industrialization since the 1970s, many of these countries have in fact moved into the low-waged manufacturing stage of production while still remaining dependent on the North for advanced technology, services, investment capital, and core markets (Hoogvelt 2001, 43–6). In this context, international trade does not bring about a win-win scenario for all but, as famously stated by Andre Gunder Frank (1972), the 'development of underdevelopment' for the South.

Fair traders criticize free trade proponents for focusing too much on abstract trade models while neglecting the actual political conditions under which the battle for comparative advantage is carried out and the human impact of this competitive struggle. Without active government support and protection, free trade policies often present Southern producers with a double-edged sword. On the one hand, they result in domestic markets in the South being flooded with high-technology, industrial goods produced by Northern-based transnational corporations (TNCs) that employ their comparative advantages (including enormous economies of scale) to beat out potential domestic competitors. On the other hand, they unleash an overwhelming amount of competition from both the North and South for agricultural and low-waged industrial goods around which poor Southern regions hope to eke out their own comparative advantage. This is exemplified by the intense competition in the global textile industry. A widely celebrated blue jeans industry dominated by small producers in Ecuador has been devastated in recent years by free trade reforms that have opened domestic markets to fierce competition from other low-waged jeans producers (North 2003) (see Box 15.1). Similarly, most of Africa's domestic textile industries have been wrecked in recent years as a result of heavy competition from Asia combined with Northern charities dumping second-hand clothes on African markets at unmatchable prices (Bunting 2005). While textile producers in Ecuador and Africa have lost out in this competitive environment, low-waged Asian producers have gained (see Box 15.1), along with giant US retail stores like Wal-Mart that have profited significantly from enhanced access to cheap textile supplies (Gill 2003, 210). Win-lose outcomes such as this lead fair traders to argue that the poorest regions in the South cannot develop economically, socially, and environmentally viable industries without active government support at the national and international level to protect them

from overpowering global market forces (North and Cameron 2003; Stiglitz 2002).

The ideas of fair trade proponents had a significant influence on international trade policy, especially during the 1960s and 1970s when many Southern governments and international organizations pursued policies based on economic nationalism, self-reliance, and autonomous development (Fridell 2007). But the popularity of the fair trade perspective has waned significantly since the 1980s as free trade policies have moved to centre stage in most international and national governing bodies. Some key non-governmental organizations (NGOs), however, like Oxfam International (2002), have continued to promote policies based on the fair trade vision, and in recent years there has been somewhat of a revival of fair trade thinking among development specialists and some state policy-makers. Thus, while free trade thinking is currently entrenched as the dominant paradigm in international affairs, the tug-of-war with fair trade is ongoing, and both have had significant impacts on concrete development policies over the past 50 years.

FREE TRADE AND FAIR TRADE SINCE 1945

The debate on free trade versus fair trade in both the mainstream media and academic and policy circles frequently focuses on whether or not the 'state' should or should not intervene in the 'market'. While debating trade issues in these terms might serve as useful shorthand for public discussion, it can also give an erroneous impression of the nature of the relationship of the state with the market. Whether one adopts a free trade or a fair trade perspective, the state remains the essential player in constructing the rules around which markets operate and ensuring that they are followed. While neo-liberal free traders, for example, might oppose the state intervening in the market for social and environmental reasons, they do not oppose the need for a strong state to protect private property rights and to create powerful, bureaucratic organizations, like the WTO, to

Figure 15.1   Low-priced clothing in a Wal-Mart store

Source: Gavin Fridell

regulate and enforce free trade policies (Harvey 2005, 21; McNally 2002). Consequently, the core issue of debate between free and fair traders is less about the *extent* to which the state should regulate the market and more about the *manner* in which the state should regulate the market.

In the wake of the Second World War, state leaders created regulations for an international trade and development regime that contained a variety of mechanisms designed to enforce both free and fair trade policies. The process through which these mechanisms were created was by no means an equal one but was dominated by rich countries in the North, in particular the United States, who met in Bretton Woods, New

Hampshire, in 1944 to initiate negotiations for agreements that would lay the basis for the post-war order. In free trade terms, most of the participants at the negotiations viewed the international system prior to the war, driven by protectionism and commercial warfare, as having been responsible for the economic chaos of the 1930s, along with the rise of fascism and militarism. Consequently, they sought to create a liberal international trading system. To this end, the General Agreement on Tariffs and Trade (GATT) was established to achieve the reduction of trade barriers through a series of negotiated rounds.

Along with this free trade mechanism, however, was the establishment of a regulated inter-

BOX 15.1   NEO-LIBERALISM AND 'ENDOGENOUS' DEVELOPMENT: THE JEANS INDUSTRY IN PELILEO, ECUADOR

The town of Pelileo in Tungurahua, Ecuador, has long had a reputation in the country for its successful blue jeans industry, constructed on the basis of small-scale, family-run textile enterprises. A 1995 World Bank report on Ecuador even held up Pelileo's jeans industry as an example of the possibility for small-producers to attain social progress and rural diversification in a neo-liberal world order. Research conducted by Liisa North (2003), however, has revealed that Pelileo is far from a neo-liberal success story. The core aspects of Pelileo's development lie in a variety of 'endogenous' (internal) factors, including the absence of large estates and servile social relations; the existence of a broad class of efficient, small-scale agriculture producers; Pelileo's long history as a strategic point of commercial exchange; and the early construction of transportation and communication infrastructure in the region. These endogenous factors formed the basis for a boom in the jeans industry in the 1980s, which then declined significantly by the end of the millennium *after* the introduction of neo-liberal reforms. Neo-liberal structural adjustment programs (SAPs) and the dollarization of Ecuador's currency in the 1990s caused a national economic crisis, which reduced domestic demand for jeans, while trade liberalization policies opened the region up to overwhelming competition from jeans producers in other Southern countries. From 1999 to 2000, anywhere from 25 to 50 per cent of Pelileo's jeans establishments disappeared. Rather than promoting human development in Pelileo, North argues that neo-liberal reforms have been 'overwhelmingly destructive' to the town's previously successful endogenous development pattern (North 2003, 224).

national monetary system, dominated by the US, designed to provide stability for the new trading system. This entailed an exchange rate system pegged to the American dollar, a fixed American dollar–gold convertibility, and international cooperation to control short-term financial flows (Helleiner 1994; Gowan 1999). Two key public institutions were formed to oversee the system: the International Monetary Fund (IMF), designed to provide short-term loans for countries with balance of payment difficulties; and the International Bank for Reconstruction and Development (IBRD, commonly referred to as the World Bank), designed to provide long-term financing for development projects (see chapter 8). The international trade regime that emerged out of Bretton Woods is frequently referred to as one of **embedded liberalism** because it combined a mixture of state intervention to con-

trol capital and investment flows with liberal trade objectives (Helleiner 1994).

Despite the official goal of attaining more liberal trade, the Bretton Woods System allowed for the formation of some significant mechanisms for regulating international trade to ensure a degree of stability for Southern economies. Among the most noteworthy were **commodity control schemes**, which under the terms of the Havana Charter (1948) were managed internationally by the newly formed United Nations (UN). These commodity control schemes entailed the use of buffer stocks that could be built up in times of surplus production and run down in times of shortage. When prices were low, participating countries agreed to withhold a specified amount of their products from the market until prices were forced up. In the 1950s, new international agreements under the terms of the charter were signed for nearly all major commodities, including coffee, cocoa, cotton, sugar, wheat, tin, rubber, wool, and zinc. Over time, most of them collapsed for a variety of political-economic reasons. For example, a sugar agreement failed in the 1960s after the United States unilaterally boycotted Cuban sugar amid the tensions of the Cold War, and a tin agreement fell apart in the 1980s because of a global decline in demand for tin (Barratt Brown 1993, 89–92; Furtado 1976, 215–21).

Some commodity control schemes succeeded in providing important price supports to small producers, especially in the case of coffee (Talbot 2004) (see Box 15.2). In general, however, it was widely perceived by the 1960s that most commodity schemes had failed to bring the anticipated increase in export earnings to the South (Furtado 1976, 221). This disenchantment led to the organizing of the first United Nations Conference on Trade and Development (UNCTAD) in 1964 (see chapter 10). At the conference, resolutions were passed by a substantial majority of mostly Southern nations in favour of a greater transfer of wealth from the North to the South through aid, compensation, and most importantly, 'fairer trade'. The strategy for attaining fairer trade focused on two key demands. First, Southern nations demanded that UNCTAD members replace financial aid provisions with expanded efforts to ensure fairer prices for Southern commodities through a system of direct subsidies for poor producers. The slogan that accompanied this demand was 'trade not aid' (Barratt Brown 1993, 92; Furtado 1976, 221–4).

Second, Southern nations demanded that Northern states eliminate 'unfair' protectionist policies towards Southern agricultural goods. These policies included a variety of tariffs, import controls, and levies, which Southern representatives asserted prevented primary commodity producers from developing the value-added, processing stages of primary production (Barratt Brown 1993, 92). A particularly glaring instance of this was the system of escalating tariff rates in the North, which were and continue to be applied

unequally to processed and unprocessed primary products. For example, the tariff rate for coffee beans entering the European Union from 2001 to 2003 was zero for unprocessed green beans, 7.5 per cent for roasted beans, 8.3 per cent for decaffeinated green beans, 9 per cent for decaffeinated roasted beans, and 11.5 per cent for substitutes containing coffee, such as instant coffee (UNCTAD and IISD 2003, 4). This means that Southern coffee countries are in effect punished by the European Union with an 11.5 per cent export tax if they attain the technological capacity to process their own green beans into instant coffee.

As the above example suggests, the first UNCTAD failed to address the demands made by Southern nations for fairer trade. The conference was required to work by consensus, and representatives from the North voted against or abstained from every key resolution. UNCTAD itself, however, was established as an important forum and research body for information and ideas on fairer trade for Southern nations (Bello 2004, 34–5). Along with other UN bodies, UNCTAD served as a negotiating forum in which Southern nations demanded more secure prices for primary commodities, preferential access to Northern markets for infant industries in the South, reforms to the international monetary system, new aid flows, and codes of conduct for TNCs. These demands became enshrined in the UN Programme of Action for the Establishment of a New International Economic Order (NIEO) (1974) and the UN Charter of Economic Rights and Duties of States (1976) (Bello 2004, 38–41; Hoogvelt 2001, 41–2).

One of UNCTAD's more successful efforts was the promotion of compensatory finance schemes in which rural producers receive financial compensation when commodity prices drop below agreed-upon levels. The most notable example of this was the export earnings stabilization system (STABEX) agreement adopted by the European Community in the early 1970s and designed to compensate its ex-colonies—known as the African, Caribbean and Pacific Group of States (ACP Group). Under the terms of the agreement, target prices were established for more than 50

BOX 15.2   REGULATING MARKETS: THE INTERNATIONAL COFFEE AGREEMENT

One of the most successful examples of regulating international prices is the International Coffee Agreement (ICA). It was formed in 1963 under pressure from coffee-producing states and was renewed several times until 1989 when major participants, in particular the United States, withdrew their support as part of the movement towards free trade reforms. The ICA was a quota system signed by all major coffee-producing and consuming countries designed to stabilize and increase coffee prices by holding a certain amount of coffee beans off the global market to avoid oversupply. John Talbot (2004) has calculated that the ICA resulted in higher coffee bean prices, which translated into a significantly greater retention of coffee income in the South. At the same time, the agreement was plagued by many difficulties, including the inability to deal with the structural causes of oversupply, the failure to do little more than dampen the swings of the coffee cycle, which continued to be unpredictable and chaotic, and the persistence of constant conflict among signatory nations over the quota system. Moreover, the ICA proved to have a minimal effect on how the extra wealth retained in the South was distributed. Countries that pursued social reformist projects that distributed greater resources to small farmers and workers, such as Costa Rica and Colombia, attained significantly better development gains than countries with highly unequal distributions of land and resources, such as El Salvador, Guatemala, and Brazil (Fridell 2007, 135–72). Yet, as Talbot (2004, 163–95) has noted, overall, ICA-supported prices provided varying degrees of 'trickle down' improvements to the living standards of broad sectors in the South. In contrast, the decade and a half since the end of the ICA has been characterized by a widely documented crisis in the Southern coffee industry, entailing extremely low prices, mass layoffs, bankruptcy, migration, and hunger for tens of thousands of poor coffee farmers and workers worldwide (Fridell 2007; Jaffee 2007; Talbot 2004). In this light, would the ICA not appear to be a more successful model for promoting human development than an unregulated, free trade coffee market?

products, and the European Community pledged to make up the difference when prices fell below the target. In practice, European nations frequently resisted providing sufficient funds to support STABEX and in some years failed to meet even 40 per cent of the agreed-upon obligations. Nonetheless, despite its shortcomings, it did provide much-needed price subsidies to poor producers in the South (LeClair 2002). Perceptions about its relative benefits led to the adoption in 1980 of a similar agreement for mining products called the system for stabilization of export earnings for mining products (SYSMIN).

The 1970s proved to be the pinnacle of the political influence of fair trade ideas. By the end of the decade, the pendulum had swung significantly in the direction of free trade. States and international financial organizations abandoned embedded liberal policies that had allowed for state regulations on capital, investment, and in some instances trade. Instead, they turned towards neo-liberal policies devoted to significantly reducing or eliminating as much state intervention as possible (Bello 2004, 42–4). Declining national economic growth rates in the North compelled more powerful nation-states—

in particular the United States with its burgeoning trade deficit—to seek to pry open Southern economies in search of new markets and cheap labour (Helleiner 1994; Gowan 1999). The result was a renewed interest in existing political agreements designed to regulate and enforce free trade policies, such as the GATT, as well as the development of new mechanisms to expand the construction of an international free trade order.

One of the most powerful mechanisms for the expansion of free trade policies were neo-liberal structural adjustment policies (SAPs), which were imposed on highly indebted nations as a condition for the refinancing and rescheduling of loan repayments. While fair traders were pushing for 'trade not aid', a crisis had emerged in the South in the form of unserviceable amounts of foreign debt acquired as development 'aid', culminating in many Southern nations defaulting on their debt repayments beginning in the early 1980s (Cobridge 1993, 123–39; Gowan 1999, 48–51; Stiglitz 2003, 7–37) (see chapter 14). In response to the defaults, the IMF moved in and offered highly indebted nations a 'rescue package', which included refinancing and rescheduling some loan payments on the condition that they agreed to implement a series of neo-liberal SAPs. These programs included severe cuts to public spending, reducing or eliminating trade barriers and capital controls, and devaluing local currencies to make exports more competitive. By the early 1990s, more than 100 highly indebted Southern nations had initiated SAPs. They proved to be ineffective in solving the debt crisis, and indebted countries had an estimated net outflow of resources to the North of more than $200 billion in the 1980s (Cobridge 1993, 123–39; Stiglitz 2003, 7–37).

Figure 15.2 Fair Trade co-founder Francisco VanderHoff examines coffee plants in Buena Vista, Oaxaca

Source: Jeff Moore

What SAPs did accomplish was to usher in a new era of free trade in the South. The political support upon which many fair trade mechanisms had been constructed dissolved, and most of them declined or disappeared. At the end of 1994, the GATT agreements were ratified at the Uruguay Round, and the World Trade Organization was formed. The WTO is charged with policing and promoting free trade and deregulation among its more than 120 member states. Its formation was accompanied by moves on the part of Northern countries to successfully oppose any linkages between the WTO and UNCTAD, essentially rendering the latter 'impotent' (Bello 2004, 51). In 2000, the WTO succeeded in pressuring the European Union and the ACP Group to gradually phase out all preferential trade arrangements, including STABEX and SYSMIN, by 2008. Negotiations for future free trade agreements between and among Northern and Southern countries are ongoing, including negotiations for a 34-member Free Trade Area of the Americas (FTAA).

The 'scorecard' on free versus fair trade

As the world nears the end of the first decade of the twenty-first century, the final tally on the impact of free trade versus fair trade policies remains to be seen. Free trade policies continue to dominate the international trade regime, and their effects continue to spread, with diverse results in different regions in the South. Some general assessments, however, can be made on the basis of past performances. In a report by the Center for Economic and Policy Research (CEPR), *The Scorecard on Globalization*, the authors compare 20 years of embedded liberalism from 1960 to 1980, during which time fair trade policies were on the rise, to 20 years of neo-liberalism from 1980 to 2000, when free trade policies emerged as the dominant trade paradigm. They determine that despite some of the shortcomings of embedded liberal policies, the 1960s to the 1980s was a period of previously unprecedented overall progress in the South for most major indi-

cators of human development, including life expectancy at birth, GDP per capita, infant and child mortality rates, education, and literacy. In contrast, the decades of neo-liberal policies since the 1980s have been accompanied by a decline in progress for most of these indicators (Weisbrot et al. 2001). Included among these statistics is economic growth, which has slowed significantly since the 1980s, even while free traders claim it to be a central goal of their policy objectives—GDP per capita in Latin America grew by 75 per cent from 1960 to 1980 compared to only 6 per cent from 1980 to 1998 (Stiglitz 2003, 7–37; Weisbrot et al. 2001). If the 'scorecard' reads like this, why do free trade policies continue to dominate the international trade agenda?

THE LIMITS OF A TRADE PERSPECTIVE

'It's not about free trade'

One reason put forward for the apparent expansion of free trade policies despite their shortcomings in practice is that the many official free trade organizations are, in the provocative words of political scientist David McNally (2002), 'not about free trade'. McNally and others have pointed out that, while 'globalization' is frequently considered to be synonymous with expanded and freer trade, most nations' international exports as a percentage of their GDP is similar today to what it was nearly a century ago. Moreover, while total world trade has certainly increased since the nineteenth century, much of this increased trade has occurred between rich Northern nations and a handful of NICs, while the majority of Southern nations have garnered a *declining* share of world trade. In terms of trade policy, while official tariffs on exports and imports have declined over the past 20 years, quotas and non-tariff trade barriers have increased substantially over the same period (Hoogvelt 2001, 67–93; McNally 2002, 29–59). Despite countless rounds of negotiations, the WTO has failed to address these trade barriers, many of which are applied unevenly by powerful countries to the detriment of poorer ones—developing countries face unfair trade barriers for their exports to the North that are four times those encountered by rich countries (Oxfam International 2002; Stiglitz 2002, 59–64; 2003, 7–37) (see Box 15.3).

If 'free trade' mechanisms are not effective at evenly eliminating trade barriers, McNally argues, this is because they are primarily concerned not with trade but with the goal of protecting the property rights of transnational corporations and limiting the rights of states to intervene in their operations for the sake of social, environmental, or developmental concerns. For example, the North American Free Trade Agreement (NAFTA) contains a chapter 11 provision that allows foreign investors to sue governments if they believe that their company has suffered a loss because of a breach of 'free trade'. In the mid-1990s, when the governor of the Mexican state of San Luis Potosi blocked attempts by US-based Metalclad Corporation to build a toxic waste landfill site in the state, the company filed a chapter 11 complaint. In 2000, the NAFTA tribunal ruled in favour of the company and ordered the Mexican government to pay $16.7 million in damages to the company (McNally 2002, 40–2). A case such as this suggests that NAFTA is less about promoting free trade than about formulating a 'new constitutionalist framework' that elevates the rights of transnational corporations above the social and environmental concerns of communities and citizens (Gill 2003).

The hegemony of 'free trade'

If we accept McNally's premise that the array of agreements and organizations that regulate the international trade regime are not primarily concerned with free trade, why do global institutions, national governments, and NGOs persist in discussing and debating trade issues along free trade lines? Some current thinkers, drawing on the work of political and cultural theorists like Antonio Gramsci and Michel Foucault, have argued that the concept of 'free trade' is most powerfully understood as an ideological tool designed to ensure the 'hegemonic' dominance of the world system by the elite in Northern countries. Free trade is more than a mere policy proposal but is a discursive component of a **power/knowledge regime** designed to naturalize and legitimize the current world order (Goldman 2005; Harvey 2005).

According to sociologist Michael Goldman, this regime is in part maintained by international organizations such as the World Bank, which produces mountains of reports and policy frameworks that construct 'knowledge' about development and what it should or should not entail. The knowledge the Bank produces is not value-neutral but rather is designed to promote the idea that 'there is no connection between increased poverty in the South and increased wealth accumulation in the North, and that such global institutions as the World Bank are composed of mere technocratic experts offering transhistorical truths to those who lack know-how, experience, and skills' (Goldman 2005, 21). Consequently, while neo-liberal policies over the past 25 years may not have proved very effective at promoting actual free trade or combating poverty in the South, the World Bank has spent tens of millions of dollars per year developing reports, working papers, data analysis, seminars, journals, and policy prescriptions to advance exactly the opposite claims. Many of these sources are self-referential, lack the scholarly requirements of independent research, and are produced by officials who tend to share a 'scientific esprit de corps that is rare among research institutions' (Goldman 2005, 101). The result, states Goldman, is that '[k]nowledge is indeed power for the World Bank' (Goldman 2005, 103).

Fair trade concepts are not immune to the above political and cultural critique, and many have suggested that fair trade ideas remain largely within the discourse of neo-liberal hegemony. They assert that despite their differences in approach, both free traders and fair traders currently tend to aspire ultimately to competitive markets, free trade, export competitiveness, and a reliance on foreign investment (Bello 2002; Fridell 2007; Hart-Landsberg and Burkett 2005, 13–25; McNally 2002). Indeed, one of the

BOX 15.3   THE WTO VERSUS FREE AND FAIR TRADE?

The WTO began operations in 1995, officially designed to promote and regulate free trade and cre-ate a somewhat level playing field for its member states. Many have argued, however, that the WTO's rules are inherently structured in favour of rich and powerful nations, which has undermined its man-date from the very beginning. It is commonly accepted that during the negotiations leading up to the formation of the WTO, Southern nations abandoned their opposition to Trade-Related Aspects of Intellectual Property Rights (TRIPS) in order to gain concessions on greater access to Northern mar-kets for their agriculture and textile products. Yet while this may have been the case on paper, in practice Northern countries have employed a variety of exemptions and selective liberalization poli-cies to ensure that increased market access for most Southern countries has been minimal or non-existent. At the same time, poor countries have been hit hard by increasing rent payments for Northern technology as a result of TRIPS (Mendoza and Bahadur 2002; Rosset 2006). Moreover, TRIPS has raised the growing prospect of Southern countries having to pay rents for *their own* technology, as giant Northern TNCs use their wealth and power to patent technology originally developed in the South. For example, much controversy was raised in 1997 when the US-based Rice Tec company was granted several patents for basmati rice, the product of centuries of indigenous breeding and cultivation in India. This has sparked concerns that Indian farmers might have to pay a royalty fee to an American company in order to grow their own basmati rice (Shiva 2001). Taken together, the economic impact of the WTO's unfair trade rules and their implementation, according to Ronald Mendoza and Chandrika Bahadur, analysts for the United Nations Development Programme, has not been a win-win scenario for the North and the South but one in which 'developing countries suffer annual losses of US $20.8 billion' (Mendoza and Bahadur 2002).

criticisms of neo-liberal reforms most frequently made by fair traders is that they do not do enough to promote *true free trade*, which they posit would work in the best interest of the poor and the rich as long as the proper institutional sup-ports are provided (Oxfam International 2002; Stiglitz 2002). An Oxfam trade report produced in 2002 has raised considerable controversy by suggesting that 'insufficient liberalisation' was a major barrier preventing trade from being able to 'work for the poor' (Oxfam International 2002, 122, 239). Critics have charged that Oxfam is moving too close to the free trade camp by maintaining that market access is the primary 'evil to be flayed' in combating global poverty (Bello 2002). The effect, they argue, is to narrow the development debate down to what is and is

not the most effective way to integrate into global markets, while neglecting and obscuring alternative visions of development and trade.

THE FUTURE OF INTERNATIONAL TRADE

Free trade continues to remain the dominant dis-course on international trade in most official development institutions and government agen-cies. This will likely remain the case in the near future, although free trade has faced considerable challenges over the past decade that have signifi-cantly dented its image. Throughout the globe, an array of labour, environmental, indigenous, human rights, and women's groups have actively protested against free trade policies and their destructive impacts on local communities (see chapter 12). These groups have put intense pressure on Southern governments, some of which have grown increasingly resistant to the trade agenda advanced by rich Northern governments and international financial institutions (McNally 2002; Rosset 2006). One of the most notable examples of this has been the emergence of a coalition of developing countries, the Group of 20 (G-20), headed by India, Brazil, China, and South Africa, which derailed the fifth ministerial meetings of the WTO in Cancún, Mexico, in September 2003 and has since slowed negotiations at the WTO. The G-20 has made some demands compatible with fair trade ideas but only when they have also been consistent with an overarching free trade framework—such as the elimination of Northern agricultural export subsidies and protectionist barriers blocking Southern commodities (Rosset 2006).

In academic and policy circles, the debate on free versus fair trade continues. Many free traders have sought to defend the record of the policies of the past 30 years while acknowledging that a greater need exists for international financial institutions, governments, and charitable organizations to make basic investments in health care and education (Bhagwati 2002; Sachs 2005). They depict the negative social and environmental impacts of free trade as necessary outcomes of the development process. As Jeffrey Sachs has stated, 'sweatshops are the first rung on the ladder out of extreme poverty' (Sachs 2005, 11). Countering these arguments, fair traders, such as former senior vice-president and chief economist of the World Bank Joseph Stiglitz, have called for reforms to international financial institutions and agreements that would allow nation-states a greater role in regulating capital and trade flows and protecting social and environmental standards (Stiglitz 2002; 2003). More radical proponents of fair trade, such as Walden Bello, have insisted on the need to 'deglobalize' by eliminating the power of the World Bank, IMF, and WTO and creating a new system of global economic governance devoted to empowering local and national bodies to determine their own trade and development priorities (Bello 2004).

Fair trade ideas also continue to have an influence on a wide variety of social movements and non-governmental organizations. Some of these movements have focused on stemming the tide of global market integration, seeking to prioritize production for local and national markets over international trade. This is exemplified by 'food sovereignty' groups like the Landless Workers Movement (MST) in Brazil, a country with one of the most unequal patterns of land ownership in the world. Since 1984, the MST has seized more than 50,000 square kilometres of land upon which they have settled hundreds of thousands of families and constructed cooperative enterprises (as well as 1,200 public schools) designed to produce goods for local, national, and global consumption—in that order (Rosset 2006).

Other movements have sought to attain the integration of poor workers and farmers into global markets under better conditions. One such movement is the **fair trade network**, which connects small farmers, workers, and craftspeople in the South with organizations and consumers in the North through a system of 'fair trade' rules and principles, including democratic organization (of cooperatives or unions), no exploitation of child labour, environmental sustainability, a minimum guaranteed price, and social premiums paid to producer communities to build community infrastructure (Fridell 2007; Jaffee 2007). Some critics have expressed concern that fair trade certification promotes continued dependence on tropical commodities characterized by long-term oversupply and declining prices. In response, fair traders argue that most small producers in the South do not have viable alternatives to tropical commodity production and that those who do still require the support of fair trade standards to assist them in their transition to other economic activities (LeClair 2002). Other commentators have pointed out the limited reach of fair trade because of its dependence on relatively small niche markets in the North. For example, the network's more than 670,000 certified fair trade coffee producers represent less than 3 per cent of the 25 million coffee farmer families worldwide. Concerns have also been raised that the growth of the fair trade network over the past decade has been driven by the increasing participation of corporations and international institutions that are using token support for fair trade to mask their broader devotion to a free trade agenda. Thus, corporations such as Starbucks gain positive publicity for selling 6 per cent of their coffee beans fair-trade-certified, even though 94 per cent of its Southern suppliers remain without fair trade standards. The World Bank has given increasing support to fair trade—including serving fair trade tea and coffee at its headquarters in Washington—while continuing to push ahead in international affairs with the very same free trade agenda that the fair trade network was created to counteract (Fridell, Hudson, and Hudson 2008; Fridell 2007; Jaffee 2007). Fair trade author and activist Daniel Jaffee has expressed concern that unless the principles of the fair trade network can be adopted by national and international governing bodies as a matter of state policy, 'it might indeed become irrelevant in the face of the larger effects of corporate-led economic globalization' (Jaffee 2007, 266) (see Box 15.4).

At the level of the state, alternatives to the dominant free trade agenda have also emerged in recent years, most notably the Bolivarian Alternative for the Americas (ALBA). Promoted by President Hugo Chávez in Venezuela as an international component of the government's vision of 'twenty-first-century socialism', ALBA has been designed as a conscious alternative to the US-backed FTAA (the Spanish acronym of which is ALCA). Whereas the FTAA/ALCA proposes the further integration of Latin America into the global economy through deregulation, privatization, and liberalization, ALBA proposes a socially oriented regional trade bloc in which wealth would be redistributed to poorer countries through a special fund, social issues such as local food sovereignty or access to generic drugs would take precedence over international trade agreements, and social, environmental, and indigenous rights would be protected and promoted. One of ALBA's

most successful projects has been a unique agreement between Venezuela and Cuba in which the former has traded tens of thousands of barrels of oil a day in exchange for the latter sending thousands of doctors and medical supplies to poor and rural communities in Venezuela, making medical services and training available to 17 million people (Arreaza 2004; Gibbs 2006, 265–79).

ALBA is still in its infancy, and as of 2007 its members consisted of Venezuela, Cuba, Nicaragua, and Bolivia, with Haiti and Ecuador sending signals that they might soon join. Critics have charged that ALBA represents less a coherent alternative to free trade than an attempt by the Venezuelan government to extend its sphere of influence in Latin America through massive spending of the state's oil revenues. Indeed, the Chávez government has emerged in recent years as the single largest foreign aid donor in Latin America and in one case lent Argentina $2.5 billion, which it used to pay off its debts to the IMF (Forero and Goodman 2007). While the development of ALBA may in part be driven by the geostrategic interests of the Venezuelan government, a similar critique can also be levelled at international free trade agreements, a great many of which have been adopted by elite-dominated autocratic states under intense pressure from Northern powers, the World Bank, the IMF, and the WTO. 'Power politics' has always played a central, if unfortunate, role in shaping the nature of modern international trade regimes (Gill 2003; Gowan 1999). Consequently, the particular free trade agenda of the richest and most powerful nations in the North will likely continue to pervade international trade policy, while ALBA and other non-governmental fair trade projects, such as the fair trade network and food sovereignty movements, driven by significantly less powerful supporters, will face an uphill political battle. For development thinkers, the ultimate measure of the success of these projects, both free and fair trade, should be the extent to which they promote and enhance human development for the poorest people in the South. International trade should be merely a means to this end.

BOX 15.4   FAIR TRADE COFFEE IN AN UNFAIR WORLD?

Figure 15.3   Canadian coffee roasters meet with Fair Trade partner UCIRI in Ixtepec, Oaxaca

Source: Jeff Moore

Research conducted on fair trade groups in the South suggests that fair trade provides important social and economic benefits to certified producers, although with important qualifications (see Jaffee 2007). This can been seen in the case of the Union of Indigenous Communities of the Isthmus Region (UCIRI), one of the most successful fair trade coffee cooperatives in the world, located in Oaxaca, Mexico (Fridell 2007). Through their participation in fair trade, UCIRI members have attained higher incomes and significantly better access to social services through cooperative projects in health care, education, and training. UCIRI has also constructed its own economic infrastructure, such as coffee processing and transportation facilities, and provided its members with enhanced access to credit, technology, and marketing skills. Yet its developmental project has not been without limitations. In one instance, an attempt to diversify UCIRI's efforts into producing clothing for local markets met with bankruptcy, in part as a result of the high costs of providing 'fair' social security provisions to employees and tough competition from low-wage textile factories in China. In broader terms, despite the cooperative's success in combating extreme misery, UCIRI members still report the persistence of general poverty. Fair trade prices are inadequately low because they must remain somewhat competitive with lower conventional coffee bean prices dragged down by a saturated, highly competitive global market. How effective can the **fair trade network** be at the local level as long as free trade agreements dominate the international agenda and impose a fierce, global market discipline on poor farmers in the South (Fridell 2007)?

QUESTIONS FOR DISCUSSION

1. What are the core differences between the 'free trade' and 'fair trade' perspectives? Are there similarities?

2. To what extent can the different policies inspired by free trade and fair trade ideals be understood as a difference of 'market versus state'?

3. What have been the relative impacts on human development of free trade and fair trade policies?

4. Explain the meaning of the concept of free trade 'hegemony'? Do you think this concept is instructive?

5. What are some alternatives to free trade policies? Do you think they represent effective alternatives that are feasible in the long term?

FURTHER READING

Bello, W. 2004. *Deglobalization: Ideas for a New World Economy*. London: Zed Books.

Bhagwati, J. 2002. *Free Trade Today*. Princeton, NJ: Princeton University Press.

Fridell, G. 2007. *Fair Trade Coffee: The Prospects and Pitfalls of Market-Driven Social Justice*. Toronto: University of Toronto Press.

Goldman, M. 2005. *Imperial Nature: The World Bank and Struggles for Social Justice in the Age of Globalization*. New Haven, CT: Yale University Press.

Jaffee, D. 2007. *Brewing Justice: Fair Trade Coffee, Sustainability, and Survival*. Berkeley: University of California Press.

McNally, D. 2002. *Another World Is Possible: Globalization and Anti-capitalism*. Winnipeg: Arbeiter Ring Publishing.

North, L., and J.D. Cameron. 2003. *Rural Progress, Rural Decay: Neoliberal Adjustment Policies and Local Initiatives*. Bloomfield, CT: Kumarian Press.

Rosset, P. 2006. *Food Is Different: Why We Must Get the WTO out of Agriculture*. London: Zed Books.

Sachs, J. 2005. *The End of Poverty: Economic Possibilities for Our Time*. London: Penguin.

Stiglitz, J. 2002. *Globalization and Its Discontents*. New York: W.W. Norton.

INTERNET RESOURCES

Center for Economic and Policy Research: http://www.cepr.net.

Earth Institute: http://www.earthinstitute.columbia.edu.

Fairtrade Labelling Organizations International: http://www.fairtrade.net.

Focus on the Global South: http://www.focusweb.org.

Global Exchange: http://www.globalexchange.org.

Make Trade Fair (Oxfam Campaign): http://www.oxfam.org/en/campaigns/trade.

United Nations Conference on Trade and Development: http://www.unctad.org.

CHAPTER 16

DEMOCRACY

CÉDRIC JOURDE

LEARNING OBJECTIVES

- To understand the different definitions of democracy.
- To know the different theoretical approaches that explain democratization and to be able to apply them concretely to a specific country.
- To know the constituent factors of democratic consolidation and to be able to apply them to specific countries. To know the obstacles, dangers, and risks that could pull a democratizing country back towards authoritarianism.
- To understand the debate surrounding the causal weight of democracy in relation to the challenges of economic and social development.

The concept of democracy is the source of much debate among researchers studying the politics of developing countries. We will explore four of these debates in this chapter. The first relates to the meaning of democracy: neither scholars nor political actors can agree on a common definition. Democracy is a polysemic concept—that is, it is a word with many different meanings. The differences can be very large, not only between countries but also within countries. The second debate concerns the pathways that lead to democracy. Specialists do not agree on the causes or the factors that trigger democratic transitions. For example, can we say that the level of economic development is a factor that favours the emergence of democracy? Some believe that this is the case, whereas others emphasize entirely different factors. Third, researchers disagree with respect to the factors that hinder (and favour) the consolidation of democratic institutions. Once a country establishes its first democratic institutions, how can we ensure that they will develop fully and not disintegrate a few years after the transition? Finally, the fourth debate revolves around the causal role of democracy: what is the effect of democracy and

democratization on social and economic dynamics? Some researchers believe that democracy hinders the economic and social development of the world's poorest countries because it promotes constant competition and political one-upmanship. In contrast, others believe that democracy is the only type of government capable of establishing firm foundations upon which to build a functioning economy and legitimate and just social relations. These are the four main debates explored in this chapter.

CLARIFYING THE CONCEPTS: A DIFFICULT TASK

The first task is to clarify our concepts, since terms in common usage are often ambiguous and admit of multiple definitions. Yet even if we try to be as clear as possible with the terms we use, it is impossible to come to a universally accepted definition. Indeed, researchers do not share a common vision of political reality, as we see in their choice of terms and the meanings that they attribute to those terms.

However, let us begin with the least problematic concepts. When scholars consider political institutions in developing countries, their first step is to determine the type of political regime in place. **Political regime** refers to the set of principles and rules that govern power relations between society and the state (Przeworski et al. 2000, 18–19). More simply, what are the rules of the political game, written and unwritten, that connect rulers and citizens? Thus, when we refer to a regime as 'democratic', this implies in a very broad sense (and without entering into debates for the moment) that there are principles and rules that govern relations between the representatives of the state and society, which render the state the instrument, or the representative, of society. In other words, the state must answer to society. Society is the ultimate source of political power, and the state makes decisions according to society's wishes. This is more or less what is

meant by the phrase 'political power is exercised by and for the people'. But as we will see below, the concept of democracy is open to divergent interpretations.

It is often easiest to understand a concept by comparing it to its opposite: democratic regimes are distinguished from **authoritarian regimes**. These are regimes in which state officials actively prevent society from participating in the decision-making process; frequently resort to arbitrary violence against their population; extract, use, and distribute economic resources in an arbitrary and often violent fashion; and finally, are rarely held accountable for their actions and decisions (Médard 1991).

Increasingly, researchers also differentiate democracies and authoritarian regimes from a third type of system. Its name and definition are,

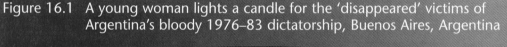

Figure 16.1   A young woman lights a candle for the 'disappeared' victims of Argentina's bloody 1976–83 dictatorship, Buenos Aires, Argentina

Source: Paul Haslam

once again, the subject of debate: it is usually called a **semi-authoritarian regime** (or a **hybrid regime**). Here we are referring mainly to countries that undertook democratic reforms at the beginning of the 1990s. Although they officially abolished the one-party system and/or removed the military from political office, elites of the old regime still perpetuated (sometimes informally, sometimes in a more formal fashion) a plethora of heavily authoritative political practices. These practices ranged from the repression of opposition to massive electoral fraud or even to the systematic use of public administration for their personal gain (Brownlee 2002; Levitsky and Way 2005; Ottaway 2003; Schedler 2006).

In addition, scholars often differentiate between two phases in the process of democratization—namely, **democratic transition** and **democratic consolidation**. Democratic transition refers to the phase during which authoritarian institutions and practices are in the process of being reformed and replaced by institutions and practices that are more democratic (or that are less authoritarian). This transitional phase is characterized by a degree of *uncertainty*; as during all transitions, no one is completely certain about the outcome of the process. It is not clear whether democracy will be achieved, because the actors or forces pushing for democracy are struggling with those attempting to maintain the authoritarian status quo. This phase is distinct from a more stable phase, democratic consolidation, which is characterized by a solidification of the democratic foundations. During this phase, political actors are no longer in debate over *whether* they should conserve the authoritarian regime or adopt a democracy but rather over how they should go about reinforcing the democratic system (Schedler 2001).

The concepts of democratic transition, democratic consolidation, or even authoritarianism remain, nonetheless, relatively vague unless we clarify the most central concept of this chapter, *democracy*. This concept is the subject of intense debate among researchers, and it is clear that a single and universal definition does not exist. To generalize somewhat, one of the debates reveals a division between two main camps: those who advance a 'procedural' definition of democracy and those who propose a 'substantive' definition of democracy (Collier and Levitsky 1997).

Researchers who adopt the procedural approach, which is sometimes labelled 'minimalist', argue that a country is democratic as long as certain political procedures are enforced. First, citizens regularly and uninterruptedly choose political representatives who govern in their name. This choice is made through free and fair elections in which any citizen can stand as a candidate as well as being able to participate as a voter, regardless of gender, ethnicity, language, race, religion, social class, or disability. Second, the state must guarantee the fundamental freedoms of all its citizens, in particular rights of participation, assembly, expression, and information. As mentioned above, this definition is sometimes characterized as 'minimalist' in the sense that it requires only a minimum number of elements to be present in order to determine whether a state is democratic or not. This will become increasingly clear when we expand on the 'substantive' approach.

Using the procedural approach, certain specialists seek to classify different countries of the world, either by distinguishing democracies from non-democracies (a binary distinction) or by classifying them according to their degree of democracy and observing the changes that take place from year to year. For example, Larry Diamond (2002, 26) has created a typology in which he classifies governments into six different categories. The most democratic countries are found in the first two categories: 'liberal democracies' and 'electoral democracies'. They are followed by less democratic regimes: either 'ambiguous regimes', 'competitive authoritarian', or 'hegemonic electoral authoritarian', and finally, the 'politically closed authoritarian' regime. Other researchers, like those who work for Freedom House or the Polity IV[1] Project, quantify the degree of democracy of each political system in the world by giving them a grade. Freedom House distinguishes between three types of countries: 'free', which is the equivalent of democracy, 'partly free', and 'not free'. Table 16.1 gives us an overview of the evolution of democracy in the world since 1974 (the year that Freedom House started to collect its data). We see, for example, that the number of democracies—grouped together under the 'free' category—has significantly increased since 1974. Democracies represented 28 per cent of all the regimes of the world in 1974, increasing to 34 per cent in 1985. Today, at 47 per cent, they represent nearly half of the countries of the world. In contrast, authoritarian regimes—classified under the 'not free' category—represented 41 per cent of the regimes in the world in 1974 and represent merely 23 per cent today.

The procedural approach has provoked significant reactions from many scholars who find it too reductionist and minimalist. They propose what is known as the 'substantive approach' to emphasize that it is important to look at the 'substance' of a democracy, not only its procedures. While they do not challenge the components of the procedural definition, they consider them insufficient. This substantive approach has three principal components, 'cultural', 'socio-economic', and 'citizenship'.

The cultural-substantive definition is based on the idea that the concept of democracy, while having a certain universal dimension that is understood worldwide, should nevertheless incorporate *local meanings* of the term. According to these researchers, the meaning of the word democracy varies from one society to another and even varies strongly within a given society (something often forgotten). Frederic Schaffer (1998) gave a good summary of the problem when he demonstrated that the American understanding of the concept of democracy was not necessarily the same as a Senegalese view. In the United States, according to Schaffer, democracy evokes the notions that were previously highlighted in the 'procedural' definition. In Senegal, however, the concept evokes notions of solidarity, consensus, and equal treatment among people. He also observed that in Senegal, an election does not have the same meaning that it does in the United States. The act of putting a slip of paper into a ballot box is not seen as 'democracy in action'; rather, it is perceived in Senegal as an economic transaction between a 'politician-businessperson' and a 'voter-client'. It is not necessary to judge whether Schaffer has accurately understood the meaning of democracy as expressed by the Senegalese (or whether he has accurately understood the American conception of democracy, or even if he is right to talk about *an* American conception of democracy). What is important to understand here is that Schaffer, like other researchers, conceives the concept of democracy as being very variable between one national (and sub-national) culture and another. Moreover, these local con-

Table 16.1 Evolution of political regimes, according to Freedom House

Type of regime	1974		1985		1991		2006	
	Absolute #	%	Absolute #	%	Absolute #	%	Absolute #	%
Free	42	28	57	34	76	41	91	47
Partly free	47	31	56	34	66	36	58	30
Not free	63	41	53	32	42	23	45	23

Note: The total number of countries in the survey increased from 1991 onwards with the independence of the ex-Soviet republics, the disintegration of Yugoslavia and Czechoslovakia, and the independence of countries such as East Timor and Eritrea.

Source: http://www.freedomhouse.org.

BOX 16.1   MALI

The case of Mali, one of the poorest countries in the world, provides an illustration of the global tendency that Freedom House has documented. During the 1970s and 1980s, the military regime of Moussa Traoré reigned over Mali, placing this African nation within the category of a 'not free regime'. After Traoré's regime was toppled in 1991, however, political actors began to construct a multi-party system and to design a constitution that guaranteed fundamental liberties. As a result, Mali started to receive much higher grades. It moved up into the category of 'partly free' countries in 1991–2, then into the category of 'free' countries the following year. Interestingly, the victorious candidate in the 2002 and 2007 presidential elections was Amadou Toumani Touré, who in 1991 was the young officer who led the putsch that toppled the military regime of Moussa Traoré.

ceptions—in all of their diversity—must be integrated into any study of democracy.

Indeed, not only can the basic meaning of democracy vary from one country to another or from one social group to another, but the concept can also refer to political actors and political dynamics that are unique to a particular society. For example, when Romain Bertrand (2002) conducted research in Java—the most populous island of Indonesia, an archipelago with around 200 million inhabitants—he realized that if he wanted to understand fully their democratic process, he could not limit himself to analyzing the actors that are normally studied in the West. Based on his findings, Bertrand entitled his book *Invisible Democracy*. According to him, it was not that democracy does not exist in Indonesia but rather that political actors think about and practise democracy through a cultural lens that is 'omnipresent': the dimension of the invisible world. Of course, political parties, journalists, non-governmental organizations (NGOs), the central government, and women's movements are democratic actors in Indonesia in exactly the same way that they are in a country such as Germany. In Indonesia, however, one must also study the role of 'supernatural experts', 'forces of the night', and religious leaders who—in the eyes of Indonesians—play a critical role in politics. For Romain, as for other researchers, it is not a matter of drawing a car-

icature of an 'exotic' political system but rather simply saying that we cannot understand democratization if we focus our analysis only on electoral results and parliamentary reforms.

The second aspect of the substantive approach is socio-economic in nature. The argument put forth here is that the procedural approach is too minimalist and that it ignores one of the fundamental characteristics of any political system: the distribution of wealth and economic well-being. Whereas supporters of the procedural approach might classify a country as 'democratic' once the electoral cycle is put in place correctly and political freedoms are respected, supporters of the substantive approach might hold that this same country is hardly democratic if it exhibits profound socio-economic inequalities. For procedural approach supporters, distribution of wealth has nothing to do with democracy; for advocates of the substantive approach, this issue is at the very heart of democracy. Thus, those who support the substantive approach would paint a very different picture of countries such as South Africa and Brazil. In these countries, there are free elections, and most political liberties are either respected or in the process of being implemented (freedom of expression, right of assembly, and so on). Yet the level of inequality is so high—with the richest 20 per cent enjoying more than 65 per cent of national wealth, while 80 per cent of the population have to make do with 35 per cent—that we cannot consider these countries as true democracies (UNDP 2006). Thus, according to this approach, democracy is not merely a matter of electoral cycles and individual rights; it also presumes a more equitable distribution of wealth within a country.

Finally, the third component of the substantive definition, directly related to the previous one, raises the question of **citizenship**. For supporters of this approach, a democratic regime is one in which all adult citizens are granted a wide range of social and political rights. Moreover, in order for the regime to be truly democratic, these rights must be applied universally, equally, and systematically. In a number of countries, unfortunately, citizenship is often heterogeneous in that political rights are not respected in a systematic and universal way. For example, in a number of Latin American countries, access to justice, social services, security, or any other public service is unequally distributed and depends on whether a person lives in a city or in the country or even in certain neighbourhoods over others. There are zones of 'complete citizenship' but also a number of 'brown areas', as

Guillermo O'Donnell called them (2004). Impunity, arbitrariness, violence, and identity-based discrimination (according to ethnicity, race, social class, and gender) are the norm in these brown areas. So while officially everyone is an equal citizen, carrying the same social and political rights, individuals within these countries do not hold equal citizenship in practice. De facto citizenship can vary according to whether one is a native peasant woman, a doctor in a gated community in Rio, or a young Afro-Brazilian living in one of the *favelas* that surround the big cities (Calderia and Holston 1999). In such cases, the officials who represent the state (i.e., judges, the police, cadastral officers, or, more generally, civil servants) cannot or do not want (the difference is important) to guarantee equal citizenship for all. This infringes upon the most fundamental principles of citizenship and constitutes a significant limit to the democratic nature of the regime.

The issue of citizenship also arises in relation to the question of upon whom it is conferred. The answer to the question 'who is a citizen?' varies greatly from one country to another. In countries such as the Democratic Republic of the Congo,

BOX 16.2   INDIA

During the debates surrounding the drafting of India's first constitution as an independent nation in 1949, Bhim Rao Ambedkar, the leader of the Untouchable (or *Dalit*) Movement (the most disadvantaged caste in India), argued that India's democratic political institutions were not enough to make India a true democracy. According to Ambedkar, the Indian constitution lacked democratic substance because it did not take into account the massive socio-economic gap that separated the different social groups of Indian society, notably between the untouchables and the so-called 'noble' castes. According to him, limiting 'democracy' to elected assemblies, elections, and political parties was not only insufficient, it was dangerous. Here is what he said in 1949: 'On January 26, 1950 [the date when the new Indian constitution would be enacted], we will enter into a life of contradiction. In politics we will have equality and in social and economic life we will have inequality. . . . We must remove this contradiction as quickly as possible, or else those who suffer from inequality will blow up the structures of political democracy this Assembly has so laboriously built up' (in Keer 2005, 415).

Ivory Coast, and Malaysia, the formal distinction between citizens and non-citizens who reside on national territory has even been the source of conflict. Some politicians have campaigned for the state to distinguish and discriminate between the 'real sons and daughters of the country' (*bumiputri* in Malay, for example) and 'foreigners'. They argue that foreigners should not be granted the status of citizens (Bayart, Geschiere, and Nyamnjoh 2001). The Chinese in Malaysia and in Indonesia, the Indians in Malaysia, the Malinkés in Ivory Coast, and the Tutsis in the Democratic Republic of the Congo have all seen their citizenship brought into question in recent years; occasionally granted citizenship, occasionally having it revoked, their position is always precarious. People who were born in the country, or who had migrated and worked there for many years, find themselves stripped of their citizenship and therefore of their rights. They can no longer buy land, enter the civil service, or even vote. In sum, a state is not worthy of being called democratic if it does not grant full and complete political and social citizenship.

As we can see, although democracy might seem like a simple concept, it is in fact the source of numerous debates among scholars. Thus, it is not easy to answer the question 'what is democracy?' The main point is that it is not necessary to agree upon a universally accepted definition—an apparently impossible endeavour—but rather to realize that we must indicate clearly the approach we have chosen and that we must be as clear and precise as possible when we use the concept of democracy.

'WAVES' OF DEMOCRATIZATION

Similarly, explaining the process of democratization is also a matter of debate among researchers. In fact, a number of explanations have been offered to try to understand why and how a number of developing countries have gradually democratized their political regimes. This section will present the different approaches researchers use to explain and understand these transitions to democracy.

Before we examine them, we should say a few words about the *historical sequence* of these democratic transitions to better understand the different contexts in which democratization has taken place. Samuel Huntington's metaphor of the 'wave' (1993b) is interesting, despite some limitations, in that it clearly evokes the idea that the process of democratization has often affected a large number of countries simultaneously and within a relatively short period of time.

With respect to developing countries, we can divide these transitions into three main historical periods. The first started in the middle of the nineteenth century and lasted until the beginning of the twentieth. During this period, many European, North American, and Latin American countries (such as Chile and Argentina) established representative institutions, such as parliaments and heads of state elected by the people, and independent judicial systems (Valenzuela 2000).

The second historical wave began immediately after the Second World War and ended towards the beginning of the 1960s. As chapter 2 outlined, this was a period during which a number of colonies obtained their independence. These newly independent countries often inherited democratic institutions that the colonial powers had set up in the final years of colonization. However, a number of them soon abandoned these institutions and replaced them with some form of authoritarian rule, ranging from single-party systems to military regimes. An important exceptions was India, which has maintained and developed its democratic institutions ever since independence in 1947 (although this claim should be put in perspective, because depending on the definition of democracy we use, Ambedkar's concerns about social inequalities [see Box 16.2] might lead us to arrive at different conclusions).

Finally, Huntington's 'third wave of democratization' (1993b) started in 1974 with the democratization of Portugal, gained pace at the end of the 1980s, and continues to the present day, to the point that the number of developing-country regimes undertaking democratic reform has attained unprecedented heights. Clearly, the size of this number depends on how we choose to define democracy and democratization. Again, although numerous authoritarian regimes are indisputably reformed in the initial phases of democratic transition, there is no guarantee that many of them will not later adopt political practices and institutions that deviate from the democratic model and find themselves transformed into more neo-authoritarian regimes.

HOW CAN WE EXPLAIN DEMOCRATIZATION? STRUCTURE OR ACTORS? THE NATIONAL OR INTERNATIONAL ARENA?

Let us now examine the main theoretical approaches that researchers have proposed to explain and understand these waves of democratic transition. As we will see, scholars have offered a number of different (and sometimes incompatible) answers to the question of why political regimes choose to democratize. To simplify, there are two key questions that all studies have to address. Note that although we present these theoretical approaches separately, in reality they are not mutually exclusive. Indeed, researchers often mix and combine approaches.

First, we can distinguish between the approaches in terms of their *level of analysis*. For some specialists, the fundamental causes that explain democratization are to be found at the *international* level (or exogenous), while for others, these causes are mainly situated at a *national* level (i.e., within the borders of a country, or 'endogenous'). Thus, when a scholar states that the end of the Cold War was the principal cause of the third wave of democratization in Africa and Asia, she is suggesting that the most important level of analysis to understand democratization is the exogenous or international. Conversely, if a researcher argues that the role played by women's movements and labour unions in a given country explains the democratization of that country's political regime, then she privileges the national or endogenous level of analysis.

Next, researchers have to take a position on a question that has endured since the beginning of the social sciences concerning the fundamental source of social, economic, and political change. To simplify, we can say that those who identify with Émile Durkheim—a French scholar who was one of the founders of the social sciences—propose an approach according to which the fundamental causes of democratic transitions are *structural* or *systemic* in nature. The starting premise is that major social and political phenomena—such as revolutions, ethnic conflict, or democratization—are the result of changes that take place within political, economic, institutional, cultural, or social structures. In other words, they are not the product of individual decisions and actions.

Conversely, those who identify with another father of the social sciences, the German Max Weber, assert that the source of social and political change—such as democratic transitions—lies with individuals and their relationships with other people. This approach is an *agency-based explanation*. In this framework, we explain democratization based on the preferences, identities, interests, and strategies of political actors, the information at their disposal and what they choose to do with it, and, of course, the relationships these actors develop with each other (including negotiations, conflicts, tricks, and pacts). Ultimately, it is the decisions of political actors (and not structural forces over which these actors have no control) that explain important political change, such as democratization.

Thus, if we combine each of the possible answers to these two questions (international or national; structures or agency), we have four principal approaches: democratic transitions are caused by either international structures, national structures, international actors, or national actors. We will now use concrete examples to illustrate each of these four cases.

National structural approach

This approach involves explaining the causes of a democratic transition by examining the political, social, and economic structures within the borders of a nation-state. Those who use this approach often argue that changes within a country's social and economic structures are one of the principal causes of democratization (Lipset 1959; Moore 1966; Rueschemeyer, Stephens, and Stephens 1992). Note that the modernization approach that we saw in chapter 3 has had a direct influence on this theory. In fact, researchers have demonstrated that when the economic structures of an authoritarian state begin to develop—especially when the economy is experiencing rapid industrialization and a high rate of urbanization—the social structures of the country are in turn transformed, notably an accelerated growth of the working and middle classes. These classes are concentrated in the major cities and close to the centres of political power. Once they attain a certain size and level of education, they become powerful forces that challenge authoritarian leaders to an unprecedented degree. The authoritarian regime is thus unable to maintain the status quo—namely, a political regime that excludes the majority of the population from the political game. It was easy to deny democratic reform when the majority of the population was scattered in rural areas, without basic education and with barely enough income to pay heed to anything other than daily survival. The situation completely changed, however, when urbanization and industrialization transformed the social structure, increasing levels of education and income for large groups of people who were previously disadvantaged. Supporters of this approach point to a quasi 'automatic' effect (a characteristic of structural approaches) in hypothesizing that these economic and social transformations increase the probability of democratic transition.

Not all researchers agree on the causal role of structural economic transformations in the process of democratization. Carles Boix (2003), for example, introduced an important nuance, demonstrating that an increase in the level of economic development is not sufficient in and of itself to generate a transition towards democracy. According to Boix, this transition is statistically more likely to occur if economic development is accompanied by a redistribution of national wealth. To simplify, imagine two countries that are administered by similar authoritarian regimes. Suppose that both countries experience economic growth but that severe inequalities persist in one country, while growth in the other country is accompanied by a relatively equal distribution of the fruits of development. It turns out that the statistical probability of a democratic transition is much stronger in the second case than in the first.

Other researchers entirely refute the hypothesis of a causal link between the development of socio-economic structures and democratic transition. One of the best known examples is the work of Adam Przeworski and his colleagues (1997; 2000), who demonstrate that there is practically no statistically significant connection between the level of economic development and the likelihood of democratization. In other words, the fact that an authoritarian regime experiences economic growth has no effect on the probability that this regime will eventually transform itself into a democracy. The thesis of Przeworski and his colleagues is illustrated by the cases of China, Vietnam, and Singapore. While these countries have experienced significant economic and social transformation (economic growth, industrialization, urbanization, and so on), these changes have not led to the democratization of their political regimes. The only signification relationship that these authors found was that the higher the level of economic development, the smaller the chance a democratic regime will collapse and be replaced by an authoritarian regime.

International structural approach

For some researchers, structural changes are clearly the cause of democratic transitions, but it is *international* structural change that is most important rather than change on a national level. To demonstrate their hypothesis, these researchers take a close look at the two most recent waves of democratization, one that began at the end of the 1940s and the other that started at the end of the 1980s. What was particular about these two periods? The answer, according to these researchers, lies in major transformations of the international system. With respect to the wave that began towards the end of the 1980s, there was a massive change in the international system as the world moved from a bipolar configuration—dominated by the two superpowers of the Cold War—to a unipolar configuration with one sole superpower. This change in the international system generated a significant amount of pressure on authoritarian regimes, forcing many of them to undertake democratic reforms. In fact, the dissolution of the Soviet bloc signalled the victory of the model of liberal democracy. Liberal democracy became the norm in the international arena, a norm to which most countries had to adapt. Moreover, the end of the Cold War signalled the end of authoritarian regimes that owed their survival (and very existence) to the structural rivalry between the American and Soviet superpowers. This rivalry, in effect, had served to subordinate questions about whether a particular country was democratic or not: as long as the authoritarian regime aligned itself with one of the two camps, its survival was guaranteed. Loyalty towards either of the two poles allowed the state to crush any pro-democracy movement within its borders. Once the superpower rivalry disappeared, the authoritarian regime's survival was no longer guaranteed. Faced with this structural transformation, the international system began to exert more pressure on the authoritarian regimes of the developing world, which in turn increased the likelihood of democratization.

If we apply this hypothesis to the case of South Africa and Indonesia, for example, the reasoning would be as follows: the only reason that these authoritarian regimes were capable of crushing opposition movements was that they held key positions in the international alliance system of the Cold War. The international East-West bipolarity created a system of 'international clientelism' in which client-states offered their loyalty to one of the two superpowers in return for military, political, economic, and diplomatic support (Clapham 1996; Afoaku 2000). Thus, being a geo-strategic link between the Atlantic and Indian oceans and surrounded

by self-proclaimed communist regimes, the authoritarian and apartheid regime of South Africa was the recipient of unfailing Western support. As for the Southeast Asian country of Indonesia, it was located in one of the 'hottest' regions of the Cold War, right next to the frontlines of Vietnam and the Indochinese peninsula and fairly close to the two Koreas and the regional superpower, China. Whether in southern Africa or Southeast Asia, the question of authoritarianism was 'structurally' subordinate to or relegated beneath the sole priority of the day: the East-West rivalry. Once the international system was transformed at the end of the 1980s, these regimes could no longer use the logic of the Cold War to garner international support. Thus, they found themselves vulnerable to the challenge of pro-democracy movements. Democratization was the logical consequence in these two countries. However, it is important to note that a number of critics challenge this argument. In the current context in which the fight against terrorism dominates the international political agenda, this logic can favour support for authoritarian regimes—such as Egypt, Tunisia, Pakistan, and Ethiopia—that position themselves as allies in the 'war on terror'.

National actor approach

As explained above, agency-based approaches are based on a very different standpoint from that of the two we have just discussed. First, supporters of this approach criticize their counterparts for having an overly mechanistic vision, giving the impression that democratization is an automatic process without the possibility of deviation, diversion, mistakes, or surprises. Moreover, their vision is seen as 'teleological' in the sense that it gives an impression—a false and misleading one, according to these critics—that we can know in advance whether a country will democratize (the end point of that process) and how it will go about the transition. According to the supporters of the agency-based approach, reality shows that transitions are full of surprises, uncertainties, failures, and contingencies. They go on to underline that these transitions produce political regimes, institutions, and political practices that are vastly different when compared from country to country. For example, Benin and Togo have similar underdeveloped economic structures that evolved within the same international structures, yet Benin democratized in 1991 while Togo remains trapped in authoritarianism. Thus, the factors that really count must be found elsewhere. This 'elsewhere'—what makes the difference in democratization—is the role of political *actors*.

Just as with the structural approach, however, the supporters of an agency-based approach are differentiated according to whether they focus on national (endogenous) actors or international (exogenous) actors. Studies that explain democratization by analyzing the struggles between the governing faction of the authoritarian regime and the faction spearheading pro-democracy movements (and the alliances and divisions within each respective faction) are examples of the *national actors* approach. This type of approach has been used to study the case of South Africa, for example. The argument is that South African democratization was made possible because the ruling bloc of the apartheid regime split into two rival factions near the end of the 1980s. One group was known as the 'securocrats' and the other as the 'technocrats'. The first group was composed of military officers who took a hard line against the democratic and anti-apartheid movements. They were also insensitive to the risks entailed by a frontal confrontation with the anti-apartheid movement. The technocrat group, however, was composed of high-level bureaucrats and businesspeople who were more pragmatic (soft-liners) and open to negotiation with their opponents. At the time, this group was led by the newly elected president Frederik W. de Klerk. This split in the authoritarian regime developed in parallel with a split among opponents of the apartheid regime. On one side was the African National Congress (ANC) led by Nelson Mandela, which was more open to dialogue and envisioned a democratic and multiracial South Africa. On the other side were groups such as the Pan Africanist Congress that were completely opposed to the presence of a white population on South African territory and the idea of negotiating with the leaders of apartheid. The agency-based approach analyzed the strengths and weaknesses of each of these actors, including the demographic weight and legitimacy of the ANC, the military and economic strength of the apartheid government, and negotiations between the 'moderates' of both camps who sought dialogue rather than an absolute confrontation. The argument was that the 'moderates' (of both respective camps) made a political calculation: knowing that their first preference was unattainable (i.e., to avoid giving into their adversary), they had to fall back on their second-best option, that being 'collusion' or a willingness to play the game of negotiation (Darbon 1995).

Continuing with the national actor approach, some researchers have conducted in-depth studies of the role of social movements in the process of democratization. They emphasize an often neglected aspect of politics—namely, the capacity to garner support by drawing on symbols, rhetoric (in the true sense of the term), and representations. Often, these social movements spearhead the process of democratization in developing countries, especially since they cannot rely on coercive measures or financial resources. Their main strength is their ability to mobilize a large number of people by way of persuasion and moral arguments, presenting alternative ways of interpreting the political situation and moving people into action. For example, studies have followed with interest the case of a women's movement in Argentina—the Madres (mothers) of the Plaza de Mayo—that emerged in Buenos Aires at the end of the 1970s and the beginning of the 1980s. Argentina had a military dictatorship at the time, and the women were demanding the truth about the disappearance of thousands of youth abducted by the military. These women, without financial or (obviously) military power, managed to create a movement that enjoyed widespread support among the population by presenting themselves as mothers and grandmothers—that is, legitimate actors in Argentinean society—rather than, for example, 'revolutionaries'. The military dictatorship was trapped by its own rhetoric: it was accustomed to confronting and repressing 'revolutionaries', 'communists', 'terrorists', and even 'feminists' (the expressions they used at the time), but in this case it found itself confronted by a segment of Argentinean society representing tradition—grandmothers, mothers, sisters. Given that the regime had always promoted a traditional conception of Argentinean society, it could not repress the movement. The Madres of the Plaza de Mayo thus dealt a powerful blow to the military junta through the use of symbols and representations that served to de-legitimize the regime. The military regime finally stepped down from power in 1983 (Oxhorn 2001).

International actor approach

Some analysts accept that actors (and their interactions with each other) provoke a number of democratic transitions but hold that the most important actors are those operating in the international arena. Such international actors include the state, international organizations, international non-governmental organizations, and other transnational networks (formed around a diaspora or around a particular ideal, such as human rights or women's rights). Authors such as Levitsky and Way (2005), for example, affirm that many processes of democratization were caused by the leverage that democratic states used against authoritarian regimes. Examples of leverage include military pressure and economic sanctions (i.e., 'conditionalities'). Levitsky and Way add, however, that these tactics have a relatively modest impact and that there are many factors that undermine their effectiveness, both at the level of the country employing the tactics and of the country that is subject to them. With regard to a powerful democratic country, its willingness to apply leverage is often weakened by competing strategic interests. In a targeted country, authoritarian regimes that have considerable military or economic power (or both, as in the case of Iran and China) are more able to resist the democratic pressures exerted by third-party states.

Instead of concentrating solely on relations between states, other researchers prefer to analyze the critical role played by non-state actors, such as international institutions, non-governmental organizations, and transnational networks. The latter are conglomerations of people from several countries who come together around common principles such as human rights or democracy. These groups have been able to exert relatively strong pressure on certain authoritarian regimes. Their strength lies in their capacity to bridge the gap between individuals living in democratic countries and those living in authoritarian regimes. These networks also facilitate the exchange of information and ideas, drawing the attention of the international public to the injustices, atrocities, and repression that exist under an authoritarian regime. They can put pressure on other international actors, including industrialized democracies and international organizations, which in turn exert pressure on the authoritarian regime identified in the activists' campaigns. Keck and Sikkink (1999) have called this technique the **boomerang effect** in which activists solicit international actors that are better placed to 'hit' the authoritarian regime in question. While it is true that these actions are not *sufficient* in and of themselves, they are nonetheless *necessary* in explaining many processes of democratization.

It is important to understand that these four distinct approaches are not necessarily mutually exclusive. They are presented separately here both for the sake of clarity and because researchers often do not agree on the virtues and defects of each approach. Certainly, when we wish to analyze a democratic transition in a given country, we are not obliged to choose only one approach. On the contrary, researchers often combine and use several approaches at once.

AFTER THE TRANSITION? CONSOLIDATION OR A RETURN TOWARDS AUTHORITARIANISM?

After exploring the different approaches that seek to explain and understand democratic transitions, we now turn to another question. What are the factors that serve to consolidate democratic gains in developing countries, and conversely, what are the factors that might pull a regime back to authoritarianism or semi-authoritarianism?

Among the factors that can contribute to democratic consolidation, *popular support* is one of the most fundamental that has drawn scholarly attention. Research groups connected to the 'barometer' institutes (present in every region of the developing world) have carried out opinion polls in many countries to gauge popular support for democratic governments. Although reservations exist with respect to these opinion polls—in particular, that they assume a procedural conception of democracy—they nonetheless provide very interesting indicators. For example, researchers working for the Afrobarometer conducted 18 opinion polls in Africa in 2005 and 2006, asking the same questions to each respondent (Afrobarometer 2006, 1). The results were revealing: on average across the 18 countries, 62 per cent of those polled thought that 'democracy is preferable to any other kind of government' and only 9 per cent supported the claim that 'in some circumstances, a non-democratic government would be preferable.' In Latin America, the Latinobarometro conducted a survey in 2006 that showed approval rates for a similar statement—'democracy may have problems, but it is the best system of government'—averaging at 74 per cent. In some countries, such as Uruguay, Venezuela, and Argentina, support was upwards of 80 per cent (Latinobarometro 2006, 65–6). Clearly, in and of itself, popular support is not a guarantee of democratic consolidation. However, it is certainly a fundamental factor. A country cannot consolidate democracy if the population does not perceive the system as being necessary in the first place.

A second factor of importance for democratic consolidation is the *institutionalization of defeat*. Indeed, one of the fundamental characteristics of political life in any democracy is that it is normal and legitimate for a government to lose power. Political actors accept defeat in democratic regimes because they know that they can run for office again during the next election. Learning to lose and accepting defeat mean that politicians

will not seek to use other non-democratic means to regain power, nor will they seek to hold onto power at all costs. Thus, in many countries that are democratizing, the politicians who led authoritarian regimes for years or even decades (whose willingness to hand over the power that they had monopolized for so long was in doubt) have finally accepted stepping down. We can also think of countries where the military or a single-party regime (on both the right and the left sides of the political spectrum) formerly monopolized political power. A few years ago, for instance, it was still doubted whether the right-wing parties in Brazil and the military that backed them would concede defeat to centre-left candidates, such as president Fernando Henrique Cardoso (who was elected in 1994 and in 1998), or later to Luiz Inácio 'Lula' da Silva, a candidate from the popular left (elected president first in 2002 and again in 2006). Likewise, the Institutional Revolutionary Party (PRI) of Mexico, which had held power without interruption since the 1930s, lost the presidential election for the first time in 2000 and again in 2006. The end of this lengthy reign signalled to other political actors that the PRI had finally accepted the idea that voters could shift political power through the ballot box. Similarly, in Africa, many political parties that had governed their respective countries from independence (dating back to the 1960s in most cases) have also recently succumbed to defeat. For example, the Socialist Party of Senegal lost the presidential election in 2000 and parliamentary elections in 2001, and in Kenya, the Kenya African National Union party was dislodged from power in 2004. Of course, admitting defeat is not a guarantee that a country is entering the phase of consolidation. But while the institutionalization of defeat is not a sufficient condition for speaking of democratic consolidation, it is nonetheless necessary, just as the other indicators are.

Nevertheless, a number of significant obstacles may surface during the process of democratization, which can weaken democratic consolidation and can even turn the regime into a situation of semi-authoritarianism. A complete list of obstacles

Figure 16.2   Chileans spontaneously react to a ruling by the British House of Lords that former dictator Augusto Pinochet could be prosecuted for human rights abuses, Santiago, Chile, 1998

Source: Paul Haslam

would be too long to elaborate, so we will just look at a few here. First, as supporters of the 'substantive' approach often claim, the problem of *socio-economic inequality* is an important factor. This phenomenon is particularly critical in countries where the process of democratization takes place simultaneously with drastic economic reforms. As Marcus Kurtz (2004) explains in his study of Latin America, the application of neo-liberal economic reforms promoted under the **Washington Consensus** had disastrous effects on the quality of democracy in the region. The economic difficulties these reforms produced seem to have resulted in a lack of political motivation among Latin Americans, which reduced the capacity of the most marginalized social classes to undertake sustained collective action.

Another important factor that can derail a country from democratic consolidation is *political violence*, especially when it pertains to identity. In a number of countries, democratization has been concomitant with the development of ethnic, religious, linguistic, or racial violence. In many cases, the authoritarian regime created—or at the very least played up—identity tensions as a means of averting calls for democracy. This has been the case notably in a number of African and Asian countries, where regimes have created and encouraged violence between ethnic or religious communities. For example, in Indonesia, violence between militant Muslims and militant Christians in the Moluccas—and violence between ethnic militias of Sulawesi—were in part produced by political actors close to Suharto's regime. These actors, both military officials and civilians, wanted to show that the iron-fisted regime of General Suharto was the only government capable of managing the country's cultural diversity. This was an attempt to associate democratization with instability and ethno-religious tensions. Uncertainty about democratic transition allowed certain political actors to take advantage of the situation to build institutions that were favourable for their particular community (Bertrand 2002).

THE CAUSAL WEIGHT OF DEMOCRATIZATION: IS IT AN OBSTACLE TO OR CATALYST FOR ECONOMIC AND SOCIAL DEVELOPMENT?

The last debate that we examine in this chapter takes the discussion to a level beyond the question we explored in the previous three sections. Instead of looking to understand the factors that may lead to democratization and democratic consolidation, we ask what effects democracy itself can generate.

In fact, this debate has been raging ever since a number of developing countries gained independence in the middle of the twentieth century. Many observers believed that it was ill-advised for the newly independent states to adopt a demo-

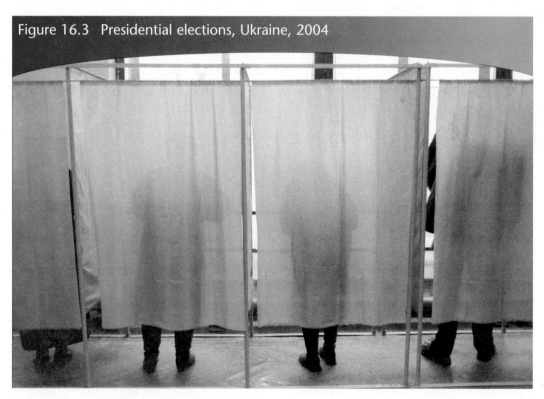

Figure 16.3   Presidential elections, Ukraine, 2004

Source: Alternatives/Dominic Morrissette

cratic regime, claiming that democratic governance could undermine economic and social development. While each observer offered slightly different arguments, the general idea can be summarized as follows: if a poor country opts for democracy, this type of regime would trigger a political cycle that would have a devastating effect on the economy. For these researchers, democracies are fundamentally based on short electoral cycles. This encourages politicians to think only of the short term and base their decisions solely on the goal of being re-elected. As a result, these politicians will be inclined to overspend their country's meagre resources on showering the electorate with 'gifts', thereby undermining the foundations of an already fragile economy. Politicians might also seek to borrow funds internationally, which would put the country further into debt. Moreover, according to this school of thought, in a democracy, political decision-makers rarely make decisions that are politically difficult but economically necessary (for example, to abolish generous subsidies for an industrial sector that is running a deficit or to sell a failing public enterprise). For these researchers, the logic is that it is preferable for a poor country to *initially* set up an authoritarian regime. Then, *after* the authoritarian regime has brought the country to a certain level of development, the country should adopt democracy. Samuel Huntington (1968) advanced the argument that military regimes are the best placed to resist and repress excessive financial demands from the working class, middle class, peasants, and unions, to name but a few—demands that are impossible for a poor country to meet. The examples these researchers cite most often are those of Chile, Taiwan, and South Korea, countries that would not have achieved such a high level of development without a strong authoritarian regime.

However, many researchers contest this argument. For example, Przeworski et al. (2000) found that statistically speaking, authoritarian regimes do not produce more wealth than democracies. Moreover, according to them, nothing indicates that leaders of an authoritarian regime are necessarily 'enlightened despots' who make sound decisions when it comes to economic or social matters. Can we not point to a number of authoritarian regimes that were governed by dictators or military officers whose sole preoccupation was to satisfy their own personal needs (and the needs of their entourage)? From Suharto's Indonesia, Marcos's Philippines, Mobutu's Zaire (now known as the Democratic Republic of the Congo), to Abacha's Nigeria, how many of these authoritarian regimes literally pillaged the resources of their country?

Thus, not only is there no reason to believe that authoritarian regimes are better placed to generate cycles of economic growth than their democratic counterparts, but democracies are much more appropriate in terms of establishing a sound economic base and, more generally, a society that looks after the well-being of its citizens. In democracies, the population holds decision-makers liable for their actions and accountable for their decisions. Clearly, democratic decision-makers cannot pillage the national resources of their country without paying the price at the next election! In contrast to authoritarian regimes, democracies create barriers that reduce the temptation to enrich oneself beyond the legitimate salary of a public servant. Democratic institutions, for example, would not allow a political leader to personally siphon off more than 25 per cent of the national budget, as President Mobutu did in Zaire. Democracy is founded on mechanisms of transparency, checks and balances, and controls that reduce the risks and magnitude of corruption and patronage, both of which have disastrous consequences for a country's economic development.

Moreover, to the extent that democracy is a system in which conflicts and tensions between political actors are managed in a peaceful, predictable, and legitimate way—not arbitrarily or through oppression—the risks of political instability and violence are significantly reduced. In the absence of such risks, it is much easier to achieve economic and social development. In addition, given the fact that a democracy is based on holding decision-makers accountable, politicians are institutionally conditioned to make decisions that are in the general public interest. In other words, they are more likely to adopt social and economic policies that are inclusive and that tend to reduce inequalities. The ability of the public to replace decision-makers who do not head in this direction is an inevitable constraint that all democratic politicians must face (Hubert et al. 2006).

CONCLUSION

As we have seen throughout this chapter, democracy and democratization are relatively complex issues. They are the source of continuous disagreement among researchers and social scientists, and the possibility of consensus is very slim indeed. We elaborated on four fundamental debates surrounding the issue of democracy. First, just as researchers disagree over what constitutes a democracy, they cannot reach a consensus on what the concept actually means in the political reality of developing countries. Is democracy universal and simply a collection of liberal electoral procedures? Or is it a variable and polysemic concept, one that is embedded in the specific realities of each society? Or is it a group of political practices surrounding the redistribution of wealth? Since the answers vary tremendously and it is impossible to arrive at a universally accepted definition, it is important that researchers clearly state which definition they adhere to in order to avoid ambiguity and misunderstanding.

The second debate concerned the different approaches that seek to explain why developing countries have undertaken, and continue to undertake, democratic reforms. Is socio-economic development the ultimate source of democratization for countries of the South? Or do the major structural transformations of the international system, such as the end of the Second World War and the end of the Cold War, count the most? And what about political actors? Are they simply passive entities, or do their actions actually effect political change? Can they be the true architects of democratization? Conversely, do they have the ability to sabotage a democratic transition? The answers to these questions vary tremendously as well.

Third, we looked at the factors that favour or hinder democratic consolidation in developing countries. Once again, the experts disagree. Beyond any doubt, however, democratic consolidation is not possible without two fundamental pillars of democracy: popular support and the acceptance of defeat on the part of elected officials. But are these pillars sufficient in the face of a number of other factors, such as ethnic violence or persistent socio-economic inequalities?

Finally, we looked at the causal weight of democracy in terms of the all-important issues of economic and social development. Should we believe that an iron-fisted authoritarian regime is the only type of government capable of making and imposing difficult (but necessary) decisions to institute economic and social reform? Or, knowing that an incalculable number of predatory dictators and military regimes have plundered national resources, is democracy—despite all of its faults—the only form of government that can generate the necessary conditions to improve social and economic welfare? Clearly, there are many questions that we need to examine more thoroughly by comparing the multiple political experiences of countries in the developing world.

QUESTIONS FOR DISCUSSION

1. Compare the different definitions of democracy. Which one seems most convincing to you, and more important, why? Beyond the elements that we presented in this chapter, what additional criteria would you add to arrive at your own personal understanding of democracy? What elements seem unimportant to you?

2. Using developing countries that you are familiar with, compare their experiences with democratization: which of the approaches seems to be the most convincing in explaining each of these cases? Make a list of the strengths and weaknesses of each approach with respect to the specific cases that interest you.

3. In your view, what factors—in addition to the ones that we presented in this chapter—are absolutely necessary for democratic consolidation? Using countries that are of interest to you, write a list of obstacles that prevent democratic consolidation. Which of these obstacles pose short-term risk, and which ones might be dangerous over the long term?

4. If you were the head of an international organization such as the United Nations and a country that wanted to establish democracy came to you for advice, what major reforms would you recommend? Are there certain reforms that could be useful for one country but not for another? Why?

FURTHER READING

Brownlee, Jason. 2002. '. . . And yet they persist: Explaining survival and transition in neopatrimonial regimes'. *Studies in Comparative International Development* 37 (3): 35–63.

Gandhi, Jennifer, and Adam Przeworski. 2007. 'Authoritarian institutions and the survival of autocrats'. *Comparative Political Studies* 40 (11): 1279–301.

Huntington, Samuel. 1993. *The Third Wave: Democratization in the Late Twentieth Century*. Norma: University of Oklahoma Press.

Karlstrom, Mikael. 1996. 'Imagining democracy: Political culture and democratisation in Buganda'. *Africa* 66 (4): 485–505.

Levitsky, Steven, and Lucan Way. 2005. 'International linkage and democratization'. *Journal of Democracy* 16 (3): 20–34.

O'Donnell, Guillermo. 2004. *The Quality of Democracy: Theory and Applications*. Notre Dame, IN: University of Notre Dame Press.

Posner, Daniel, and Daniel Young. 2007. 'The institutionalization of political power in Africa'. *Journal of Democracy* 18 (3): 126–40.

INTERNET RESOURCES

Afrobarometer: http://www.afrobarometer.org.

Latinobarometro: http://www.latinobarometro.org.

Asiabarometer: http://www.asiabarometer.org.

Freedom House: http://www.freedomhouse.org.

Polity IV Project: http://www.systemicpeace.org/polity/polity4.html.

Human Rights Watch: http://www.humanrightswatch.org.

International Crisis Group: http://www.crisisgroup.org.

NOTE

1. http://www.systemicpeace.org/polity/global2.htm.

CHAPTER 17

ENVIRONMENT AND DEVELOPMENT

DEBORAH SICK

LEARNING OBJECTIVES

- To understand the concept of sustainable development and competing perspectives on the relationship between poverty and environmental degradation.
- To become familiar with the role of national and international organizations, NGOs, corporate interests, and individuals at the local level in the use and management of environmental resources for human development.
- To understand how equity—in terms of property rights, participatory governance, and consumption practices—relates to issues of environmental degradation and sustainable development.

> There has been a growing realization in national governments and multilateral institutions that it is impossible to separate economic development issues from environment issues; many forms of development erode the environmental resources upon which they must be based, and environmental degradation can undermine economic development.
>
> Gro Harlem Brundtland. 1987.
> *Our Common Future*, p. 3.

The question of how best to preserve our natural environment while at the same time allowing human beings to pursue their livelihoods and improve standards of living has no easy answer. This chapter introduces some of the debates surrounding the impact of formal development efforts on the environment, the relationship between environmental degradation and poverty, and changing policies to reconcile the need to protect the productive capacity of the environment with peoples' livelihood needs.

Formal development efforts to boost productivity and economic growth worldwide appear to have contributed to overall increased life expectancies and better standards of living for many, but deforestation, drying rangelands, depleted fisheries, dwindling clean water supplies, and industrial pollution affect the health and livelihoods of millions of people worldwide. According to the 2005 Millennium Ecosystem Assessment report, 'over the past 50 years, humans have changed ecosystems more rapidly and extensively than in any comparable period of time in human history' (2). Today, water scarcity affects roughly one to two billion people worldwide; 10 to 20 per cent of the world's drylands have become so degraded that they cannot adequately support human populations living there; 20 per cent of the world's coral reefs have been lost and an additional 20 per cent degraded; reactive nitrogen in terrestrial ecosystems has doubled, and flows of phosphorous have tripled; and fisheries have seen a 90 per cent reduction in targeted food fish populations since the onset of industrial fishing in the last century (2–15). While temperate forest cover actually increased between 1990 and 2005, the annual deforestation rate in the tropics for that same period was 130,000 km^2 (UNEP 2007, 82). Some see economic development and globalization as the solution to these environmental problems; others argue that development is the cause of environmental degradation.

The impact of human endeavours on the natural environment is shaped by a variety of factors. State policies, national and international economic systems, cultural beliefs, social and political institutions, population pressures, available technologies, and the type of ecosystem itself all influence the ways in which people make their livings and the ways in which environmental resources are used. Within this complex context, national governments, international organizations and NGOs, private enterprises, and regionally and locally situated individuals have all contributed to the condition of the world's natural environment today.

POST–WORLD WAR II DEVELOPMENT POLICIES AND THE ENVIRONMENT

As discussed in chapter 3, early development policy and programs focused primarily on stimulating economic growth and industrialization in developing countries at the national level. While some states, such as the former Soviet Union, sponsored wide-scale industrialization, others did not have the means to industrialize immediately and turned to the production of cash crops and resource extraction, such as mining and lumbering, to raise capital to fund industrialization.

Not only has the production of agricultural exports such as coffee, cotton, cocoa, tea, and beef contributed to deforestation throughout the South, but the increased use of irrigation and chemical pesticides and fertilizers have resulted in the salinization of agricultural lands and the contamination of soils and water systems.

Transnational corporations (TNCs) were often brought in to set up factories and run resource-extraction operations. While developing states welcomed revenues from these operations, environmental regulations were often lax or nonexistent. In countries desperate for foreign exchange to fund development efforts and finance growing debt, corporations were often not held accountable for the adverse environmental impacts of their operations. Many critics contend

that TNCs were taking advantage of less stringent environmental regulations in the 'pollution havens' of the South, allowing them to increase their profit margins.

The Shell Oil Company in Nigeria is one of the more notable examples of how national economic development efforts and corporate irresponsibility can lead to environmental and social disaster. Oil has been one of the main sources of government revenue in Nigeria since independence in 1960, and Shell Petroleum Development Corporation was a partner in one of the country's largest joint oil development ventures. But from 1976 to 1991, a poorly maintained above-ground network of oil pipes resulted in 2,976 oil spills equalling 2.1 million barrels of oil throughout the Niger delta region, destroying vast stretches of farmland. Soot and air pollution were also big problems, and gas flaring was sending more than 35 million tons of CO_2 into the atmosphere (Cayford 1996, 184–5).

The private sector is not alone in creating environmental havoc. Development projects funded by international organizations such as the World Bank also have a long history of producing adverse environmental and social impacts. Many projects of this early era in particular focused on investments in large-scale, centrally designed infrastructural development programs, which were believed would help boost national productivity. Roads were built to provide easier access to natural resources, such as timber and ore deposits, and to facilitate the transportation of raw materials and agricultural produce to urban centres and world markets. They also paved the way, so to speak, for newcomers to migrate to previously inaccessible regions.

The construction of large hydroelectric dams throughout the world also illustrates many of the human and environmental problems that have arisen from large-scale, centrally managed development projects. Proponents argue that these dams not only provide an environmentally friendly (as compared to coal or nuclear-generated power) supply of badly needed electricity for both industrial and residential needs but also control flooding and provide freshwater supplies for urban populations and irrigation water to increase agricultural productivity.

By 2000, more than 45,000 large dams had been built, providing 30 to 40 per cent of irrigated lands worldwide with water and 19 per cent of the world's electricity (WCD 2000, xxix). Yet their construction has not been without human and environmental costs. As many as 40 to 80 million indigenous peoples and other poor rural dwellers have lost their lands, their homes, and their livelihoods to accommodate reservoirs and roads, and 60 per cent of the world's river ecosystems have been adversely affected (xxx).

According to Patrick McCully, more than 400,000 square kilometres of forest and wetland have been flooded by reservoirs created by hydroelectric dams (2001, 32). Not only have the flooded lands and associated resources been lost, but rivers have become fragmented, making it difficult for fish such as salmon to reach their spawning grounds. Surrounding ecosystems such as flood plains are also affected, and many plants and animals cannot adapt to the new conditions. Furthermore, decomposition of submerged vegetation has been shown to lead to increased levels of mercury in reservoir fish. In Quebec, for example, six years after the completion of Hydro Québec's La Grande 2 Dam, 64 per cent of the Cree living on the reservoir were found to have blood mercury levels exceeding the World Health Organization tolerance limit (McCully 2001, 40). In addition, deforestation of non-flooded areas increases as new roads to the dam sites are built to facilitate access by loggers and other developers.

Local people—typically poor rural peasant or indigenous communities—most directly affected by the construction of large dams were seldom

Figure 17.1   Making the desert bloom through irrigation, La Serena, Chile

Source: Paul Haslam

consulted about the process. For example, in the late 1980s, the Indian government began to implement plans to construct a series of dams along the Narmada River, which runs through western India. Funded in part by the World Bank and the Japanese government, these dams, the largest of which was the Sardar Sarovar dam, were going to submerge tens of thousands of hectares of land and disrupt the lives of millions of rural people. Yet the affected communities received little or no information about the loss of their lands or how they might be compensated (Baviskar 1995).

As the social and environmental impacts of large-scale dams became increasingly evident, displaced communities, together with environmentalists, human rights groups, and environmental NGOs (ENGOs), such as the International Rivers Network, began to pressure national governments and international organizations to halt the construction of these mega-dams. Like the Rubber Tappers Movement in Brazil and the Chipko Movement protesting deforestation in the Himalayas (see Box 17.1), grassroots organizations called the world's attention to the adverse impacts of mega-dam projects.

Along the Narmada River in India, word slowly spread about the potential impact of the dams both on rural communities and on upstream and downstream ecosystems. Grassroots movements—supported by urban-based NGOs in India as well as US-based organizations like the Environmental Defense Fund, the Environmental Policy Institute, and the National Wildlife Federation—began to take action. Thousands of inhabitants refused to move from their land, World Bank teams were mobbed and sent away, and hunger strikes were staged. With increased public pressure, the World Bank conducted a review of the project and in 1993 halted funding. Similar pressure from Friends of the Earth in Japan led to the suspension of Japanese aid for the dam (Baviskar 1995).

While the Indian government continues with its plans to build dams on the Narmada River, pressure worldwide from local community groups and NGOs opposing the creation of large-scale dams eventually led to the creation of the World Commission on Dams (WCD). Comprised of both pro- and anti-dam representatives and co-sponsored by the World Bank, the WCD in 2000 released its findings from a comprehensive examination of large-scale dam projects around the world. The findings of the WCD (2000) confirmed much of what dam critics had been saying.

The World Bank and other international funding agencies are now less keen to support large-scale dam projects and have developed stricter social and environmental guidelines for their construction. Nevertheless, despite these findings and increasing evidence that the reservoirs of large-scale dams (particularly shallow tropical reservoirs) are emitting greenhouse gases at levels sometimes higher than those from coal-fired power generators (McCully 2006), as world demand for energy continues to rise, large-scale dams continue to be built. For example, despite opposition from national and international ENGOs and the withdrawal of World Bank support, to meet rapidly rising energy demands, China has just recently completed the construction of what is now the world's largest hydroelectric dam on the Three Gorges River in central China. While hydroelectricity will help to reduce the air pollution produced by current coal-fired energy plants, millions of people have been displaced from their homes, and a vast ecosystem has been altered.

CHANGING PERSPECTIVES ON ENVIRONMENT AND DEVELOPMENT

The limits to growth debate

Throughout the latter part of the twentieth century, the adverse environmental impacts of hydroelectric dams and countless other programs designed to stimulate economic growth led many academics and environmental activists to question the sustainability of such economic development processes. In 1972, the so-called Club of Rome, a group of environmentally concerned academics and industrialists, published its report *The*

BOX 17.1   THE CHIPKO MOVEMENT

In the early 1970s, peasant women from the hill districts of Uttar Pradesh in northern India caught the world's attention when they brought the commercial forestry industry to a halt by wrapping their arms around trees and refusing to move as lumbermen moved in with their axes and saws. The image of women quietly protecting their beloved trees with their own bodies made the Chipko Movement (*chipko* means 'to hug') one of the most celebrated environmental movements in the world, but their actions were actually part of a more widespread grassroots movement among these hill peoples protesting the loss of rights to their forests. The roots of this discontent go back to the colonial era, when the British began to explore the region as a source of timber and other forest products. Rapid growth in forest industries and industrialization after Indian independence in 1947 led to a drastic increase in timber cut from Himalayan forests.

According to Ramachandra Guha, commercial forestry brought in much revenue for the state of Uttar Pradesh, but both colonial and post-colonial forest policies were 'at the expense of the hill peasantry and their life support systems' (1989, 143). While some villages were given rights to use small sections of forest, for the most part, local residents had little or no say in how to manage forests, and many people lost access to grazing land and other forest resources. Nor did local residents benefit from the new extractive industries. Timber contracts were awarded to outside firms, and because processing was done by large industry in the plains of India, little local employment was generated.

Local residents became increasingly frustrated by the loss of control over resources essential to their livelihoods and with having to bear the costs of increasing environmental degradation as well. In 1973, when a local co-op was refused permission to cut trees to make agricultural implements but an outside firm was granted permission to cut trees to make sporting goods, residents decided to take action. Local leader Chandi Prasad Bhatt came up with the idea of hugging the trees. As Chipko spread throughout the region, hundreds of similar local protests were organized. As the movement grew, it drew the attention of national and international ENGOs and the media and became a symbol of the power of local action to confront social and economic injustice and to heighten awareness of the ecological importance of forest systems.

Source: Guha 1989

Limits to Growth in which they argued that the world was reaching its limit of economic growth (Meadows, Randers, and Behrens 1972). Unless rates of population growth, production, and consumption were quickly constrained, we would soon face catastrophe and collapse; estimates varied, but the authors argued that **carrying capacity** would be exceeded by the middle of the twenty-first century (cf. Dryzek 2005, 30–1).

Not everyone agreed with these dire predictions. Many developing countries felt that they were being held to overly high standards. Industrialized countries were not held to these same standards while they were developing their economies. Thus, they argued, it would be unfair for the international community to place restrictions on how developing countries now use environmental resources in their efforts to raise standards of living.

Critics also argue that for the most part, the dire consequences of the limits to growth model have not come to pass. Overall, they say, standards of living around the world have improved, yet changes in technologies and price mechanisms ultimately have been able to minimize the impacts of production and to regulate consumption. According to economists such as Wilfred Beckerman (1974) and Julian Simon (1981), when a resource begins to show signs of scarcity (i.e., it begins to run out), human beings inevitably find either new supplies or a substitute, and as resources become more scarce, prices rise, thereby limiting overall consumption.

Further evidence relating environmental degradation with income levels in the industrialized world suggests that economic growth might cause environmental degradation in the short term but that as incomes rise, environmental conditions improve. That is, there may be increases in pollution and environmental degradation in the short term, but once people's standards of living rise and they feel more secure about their livelihoods, then they begin to put their energy into addressing environmental problems. This is known as the Environmental Kuznets Curve (EKC) and has been cited by those advocating liberal market policies as evidence of the need to continue to focus efforts on improving incomes in the developing world (Kuznetz 1955, cited in Grossman and Krueger 1995).

Sustainable development

In the midst of these debates, there was a growing recognition among scholars, policy-makers, and social and environmental activists from all points on the ideological spectrum of the need to examine more closely the relationship between efforts to improve standards of living worldwide and the environment. In 1983, the UN General Assembly established the World Commission on Environment and Development (WCED). In late 1984, this interdisciplinary, international body, headed by Gro Harlem Brundtland, met to discuss the impacts of various forms of development on

environmental resources as well as the ways in which environmental degradation itself can hinder people's ability to improve their standards of living. The commission's report, which was published in 1987 as *Our Common Future*, is often referred to as the Brundtland Report. The commission tried to balance the various perspectives on development and the environment and took the stance that with caution, economic growth and industrialization could be achieved without causing irrevocable damage to the environment but that poverty, as delegates from the developing world argued, was as responsible for much environmental degradation as was industrialization (Clapp and Dauvergne 2005, 61). The report was instrumental in bringing the notion of **sustainable development**—an idea that had its roots in the earlier environmentalist movement of the 1970s—into public discourse. Defined as development that 'meets the needs of the present without compromising the ability of future generations to meet their own needs' (WCED 1987, 8), sustainable development has become a central concept in development policy worldwide.

Poverty and the environment

Although the 1972 United Nations Conference on the Human Environment in Stockholm had raised the issue of poverty, injustice, and environmental degradation, it was at the 1992 United Nations Conference on Environment and Development (UNCED) held in Rio de Janeiro, Brazil, that the concept of sustainable development really gained new ground. One of the principal outcomes of the Earth Summit, as it came to be known, was Rio Agenda 21, a declaration of principles that clearly placed human beings at the centre of concerns for sustainable development and emphasized the relationship between poverty and environmental degradation (Carruthers 2001, 290) (see Box 17.2).

According to the 1992 *World Development Report*, alleviating poverty is not only morally imperative but 'a prerequisite for environmental sustainability' (World Bank 1992, 30). Most of the world's poor depend directly on the use of natural resources for their day-to-day survival: animals

BOX 17.2   RIO AGENDA 21

The largest conference of its kind, the Earth Summit brought together both state and non-governmental representatives from 179 countries, who created the Declaration on Environment and Development, also known as Rio Agenda 21. Though not without disagreement, negotiation, and criticism, Rio Agenda 21 provided a key set of guidelines and goals for policy-makers, planners, and activists interested in issues of environment and development.

Principle #1 states that 'Human beings are at the centre of concerns for sustainable development. They are entitled to a healthy and productive life in harmony with nature.' Other concerns embodied in the document include the need to:

- create accounting systems to account for the full value of natural resources and the full costs of environmental degradation;
- reduce consumption and pollution in the industrialized world;
- create integrated social and environmental policies at all levels of government;
- improve conditions of trade for poorer countries;
- encourage and facilitate broad public participation and greater accountability;
- facilitate technology transfers and training;
- make information for all decision-making widely available and accessible in both the developed and developing world.

Subsequent UN conferences have continued to address these issues. At the most recent, the World Summit on Sustainable Development (Rio+10)—held in Johannesburg, South Africa, in 2002—partnership initiatives between governments, businesses, and civil society were discussed as a practical means of achieving sustainable development objectives. Problems of unchecked global capitalism also were raised.

Source: http://www.un.org/esa/sustdev/documents/agenda21/index.htm;
http://www.worldsummit2002.org; http://www.iisd.org.

are raised and crops grown for both consumption and sale; water is drawn from rivers and wells; wood is collected for fuel for heating and cooking and for building shelters; plants are gathered for food and healing; fishing and hunting provide essential protein sources and cash incomes. As poor families struggle to feed and care for themselves, they often must resort to overexploitation of natural resources. Growing populations and attempts to increase incomes exacerbate demands on natural resources. Farmers reduce fallow periods, which leads to loss of soil fertility and erosion; forests and woodlands disappear for farming, heating, and cooking needs; fishing peoples fish more intensely and extensively as local stocks dwindle. For those who are struggling to survive from day to day, conserving resources for some distant future is seen as a luxury they cannot afford. As the environment becomes further degraded, there are fewer productive resources with which people can support themselves, and so they are required to further exploit what few resources they have or exploit new resources in new areas. Many scholars and policy-makers see poverty and environmental degradation related in an unending downward cycle.

The struggle to survive is itself directly related to conditions in the natural environments within which people live. Millions of the world's poorest peoples rely directly on common grazing lands, forests, and fisheries for their livelihoods, which some hope will 'provide a natural asset base that the rural poor can use to begin a process of wealth creation that will boost them beyond subsistence and into the mainstream of national economies' (UNDP et al. 2005, 4).

Yet in 1998, more than 500 million of the world's poorest people lived in ecologically marginal areas (UNDP 1998, 56–7)—i.e., regions that cannot support populations at more than a bare subsistence level. As noted below, this situation is often, in large part, the result of more productive lands being monopolized by political and economic elites.

Women often suffer the most from the impacts of environmental degradation. Throughout much of the developing world, women are responsible for providing for the domestic needs of their families. This includes fetching water and gathering wood for cooking and heating and fodder for animals. As wells and streams dry up and local supplies of wood disappear, women must go farther and farther each day to provide these basic necessities for their families. In parts of rural India, for example, women often travel up to five hours and more than 10 kilometres per day in search of firewood, and as women's time spent gathering increases, they have less time to spend on other productive activities (Agarwal 1997, 28).

SUSTAINABLE DEVELOPMENT IN PRACTICE

Although many development efforts have continued as 'business as usual', the adverse impacts of poorly regulated corporate practices, the poor track record of so many large-scale national development projects, and the more liberalized eco-

Figure 17.2   Coal barges ply the Yangtze, fuelling China's modernization

Source: Deborah Sick

nomic climate of the 1990s have led to a number of fundamental changes in the ways in which most international organizations, national governments, and NGOs now approach conservation and development issues. For the most part, sustainable development initiatives have focused on managing rural resources rather than on addressing 'brown' environmental problems: urban or industrial pollution, sanitation, and waste disposal problems (Forsyth 2002, 294).

Among the more prominent changes in policy and practice have been a focus on land tenure and property rights and on creating more effective resource management institutions at international, national, and local levels. Such efforts include the strengthening of old institutions and the creation of new ones 'to guide and channel' global economic processes so that they enhance 'environmental cooperation and better environmental management' (Clapp and Dauvergne 2005, 8). National governments continue to play a key role in environmental governance, but international institutions such as the UNEP (United Nations Environment Programme), the GEF (Global Environmental Facility), and the WHO (World Health Organization) are playing increasingly large roles, as are ENGOs, like Greenpeace and the WWF (World Wide Fund for Nature), and research institutes like the IISD (International Institute for Sustainable Development). More significantly, there has been a shift (at least on paper) from top-down, centralized conservation and development programs to a more decentralized, participatory approach in which local resource users themselves play a greater role in environmental protection and resource management.

Property rights

Many economists argue that one of the underlying causes of both poverty and environmental degradation is a lack of well-defined property rights. Property rights are claims to a resource that are allocated to a particular individual or groups of individuals by some larger authority—usually the state—which allow that person or group to reap the benefits of the resource and to exclude others from doing so. Secure property rights (e.g., holding title to a piece of land) means that the owner(s) can confidently make investments and improvements to the property without fear of others taking over and use the property as collateral for credit to do so (de Soto 2000). In addition to the economic benefits for individuals, many economists and ecologists argue that well-defined property rights are also necessary for environmental protection. After all, if you are certain that your farm cannot be taken away from you or used by others without your permission, then you will invest your time and resources into maintaining the productive capacity of that land.

In his classic work *The Tragedy of the Commons*, ecologist Garrett Hardin (1968) argued that the reason that forests, oceans, water systems, and rangelands are so often overexploited is that these resources typically are those to which no one seems to have clearly defined property rights. Anyone who wishes can use them at will, and each individual will try to extract the most value out of the resource until eventually it becomes degraded. For example, the more animals that a herder can put out to pasture, the better off she/he will be. But as each herder grazes more and more animals on the common rangelands, eventually pastures will become overgrazed. Individuals will be reluctant to invest in improving the pasture (limiting the number of animals, investing in irrigation, and so on), because there is no guarantee that the benefits of these improvements will not be appropriated by other herders.

The neo-liberal solution to the **tragedy of the commons** has been the privatization of state and common lands. But while private property rights have been shown to contribute to more sustainable management of intensively used resources like agricultural land (Netting 1993), privatization does not always serve the goals of sustainable development—particularly for extensive, difficult to delimit resources like forests, fisheries, rangelands, wildlife, and freshwater systems. In fact, the widespread privatization of forests and rangelands, for example, has been shown to lead to increasing social inequalities because some people are excluded from the use of resources upon which they had previously depended (Peters 1994).

In some cases, private property rights can actually exacerbate environmental degradation. For example, the **rule of capture**—whereby property rights are granted to individuals who can demonstrate presence or productive use of a resource—has led to rapid deforestation as thousands of people cut trees, farm, and build homes in order to claim title to land (Collins 1995). And in many places, where the ownership of land also grants right to water beneath that land, landowners are drilling wells and extracting groundwater as they please. Governments cannot adequately monitor pumping, and aquifers are shrinking at alarming rates (Postel 1999).

Furthermore, many forests, rangelands, and fisheries have long been sustainably managed as common property by local user groups. Unlike the 'open access' systems described by Hardin (1968)—in which there is no way to limit who uses a resource—in common property systems, only those who belong to the group have rights to use the resource. Individuals within the group hold clear rights to use resources within the commons, but overarching rights and management decisions are vested in the group as a whole (Ostrom 1990). Clearly defined boundaries, rights, and responsibilities involve users directly in resource management and provide them with a stake in protecting resources upon which they depend for their livelihoods (Berkes 1989).

PARTICIPATORY APPROACHES IN GOVERNANCE

States in both capitalist and socialist regimes have played a large role in managing national economies and environmental resources. Concerns for the environment began to make their way into formal public policies as early as the nineteenth century as citizens in the industrialized world worried about a loss of 'wilderness' as a result of expanding industrial economies. To protect natural resources from human exploitation, states and international organizations created national parks and conservation areas. Local people residing in these and surrounding areas were not only forbidden to use the resources within the boundaries of these newly created parks and conservation areas but were often forced to relocate. Typically, it has been the world's indigenous peoples who have suffered the most from the creation of national parks and protected areas, since lands considered vital by many biologists to enhancing ecosystem viability—and thus deemed essential to protect—are often located within or adjacent to areas used by indigenous peoples (Redford 1996).

Not surprisingly, these people frequently saw the preservation of natural resources as a threat to their ability to make a living (Wells and Brandon 1992). Monitoring and enforcing rules to protect the resources within such vast areas is extremely difficult, and in many cases, local people responded by ignoring prohibitions on resource use and sometimes even deliberately sabotaging conservation efforts.

Exclusionary, centrally managed parks and conservation areas have not been a good model for addressing the persistent problems of poverty and environmental degradation. As our understanding of property systems and poverty-degradation linkages has grown, policy-makers, planners, and environmental activists have begun to incorporate the needs of local peoples into conservation and development policies and programs. The International Union for the Conservation of Nature and Natural Resources (IUCN) was one of the first conservation organizations to do so when it formally announced in the early 1980s the need to include the concerns of local peoples in conservation efforts in its World Conservation Strategy (IUCN 1980). Today, most international organizations such as the World Bank and ENGOs such as the World Wide Fund for Nature recognize the need to 'involve local communities and indigenous peoples in the planning and execution' of their conservation programs while respecting local cultural and economic needs (WWF 2007).

There are a number of reasons why many analysts and policy-makers feel that participatory approaches are a necessary part of achieving sustainable development goals. First, as noted earlier, systems in which local users are actively involved in resource management are better suited to the management of many types of resources than are state control or privatization alone. Furthermore, those who directly depend on natural resources for their livelihoods have a direct stake in trying to protect the environment from overexploitation.

Second, local people usually have an intimate knowledge of the environment in which they live and in most cases live in communities that have been managing resources for many generations. While not every individual in a community has the same level of knowledge about all aspects of her or his environment, **traditional ecological knowledge** (TEK) can form an essential part of our understanding of ecosystems and help to plan for the protection of natural resources and biological diversity (Berkes and Davidson-Hunt 2006). Furthermore, living in close proximity to the natural resources they use allows local residents to more readily note changes in resource conditions than distant technocrats and bureaucrats working for government agencies. Environmental degradation can be more quickly spotted and action taken to alleviate the situation.

In the early 1990s, these ideas were put into practice in a number of innovative integrated conservation and development programs (ICDPs) that attempted to incorporate the livelihood needs of local human populations into the design of national parks and conservation areas. Among the best known is UNESCO's Man and the Biosphere (MAB) program in which significant ecological zones that have been targeted for conservation are managed by establishing a variety of multiple-use zones designed to meet both human development and conservation objectives (Kaiser 2001). Typically, a core area is designated as 'off limits' to human activities, while surrounding buffer and multiple-use zones allow for farming, hunting, and the collection of non-timber forest products but environmentally friendly practices are encouraged.

The Mesoamerican Biological Corridor (MBC), for example, is a cluster of more than 600 protected areas and a connecting corridor spanning eight countries from Chiapas, Mexico, to the Darien Gap in Panama. Mesoamerica is not only one of the world's most biologically diverse regions, it is also home to numerous human populations, so integrating conservation with rural development has become a primary concern. The program is ambitious, involving a wide range of actors: national agencies and NGOs in each of the countries involved; international organizations such as the UNDP, the World Bank, the Global Environment Fund, and the Central American Commission on Development and Environment (CCAD); German, Dutch, and US aid agencies and international NGOs; and a number of culturally diverse peoples living throughout the corridor.

An emphasis on participatory natural resource management has also led to an explosion of community-based natural resource management (CBNRM) and co-management initiatives (in which the state and local communities work as partners). In general, the goal of CBNRM and co-management schemes is not to protect the environment per se but to facilitate the sustainable use of productive resources like fisheries, forests, rangelands, and water resources. In essence, the people who live near and rely on particular resources for their livelihoods are given more decision-making power with respect to resource use and management. In many instances, the devolution of control over local resources has helped both local communities and the environment (see Box 17.3).

Zimbabwe's CAMPFIRE (Communal Areas Management Program for Indigenous Resources) is one of the most noted CBNRM initiatives. Initiated in 1989, the CAMPFIRE program was an attempt to break the 'culture of resistance' to wildlife conservation that had developed in response to decades of exclusionary wildlife conservation practices by giving local resource users a greater stake in wildlife conservation (Hill 1996). Hostility towards wildlife conservation has a long history in Zimbabwe, beginning in the British colonial era with the creation of wildlife preserves that alienated local peoples from their

BOX 17.3   MEXICO'S COMMUNITY-MANAGED FORESTS

Mexico, like many countries, has been grappling with the issue of how to stem rapid deforestation while at the same time dealing with high rates of rural poverty. As in many parts of the world, the Mexican state has a long history of claiming forests as national property, granting logging concessions to private enterprises and dispossessing the indigenous peoples who lived in the forests of their rights. But Mexico is also unique in that its land reforms following the Mexican revolution (1917) granted thousands of rural communities communal rights to forests and other lands. Although the state long continued to sell concessions to communal forests to outside enterprises, in the mid-1970s policies began to shift in favour of community forestry.

The Mexican case is unique as well in terms of the large number of communities that are managing their forests for the commercial production of timber and in some cases finished timber products. These community forest enterprises (CFEs) have created employment opportunities and brought in significant revenue, which is invested back into the enterprises and into creating potable water systems, schools, health clinics, and other public goods.

While there is a great deal of variation among CFEs, many seem to be conducting their operations in a sustainable manner. By 2002, the Forest Stewardship Council—which provides certification for sustainably managed forests—had certified more than 500,000 hectares in 25 Mexican communal forests. In addition, many communities are showing a greater commitment to preserving biodiversity by choosing to put aside parts of their forests for preservation. Satellite images in many areas show an increase in forest cover in communally managed forests. 'Today, Mexico's common-property, community-managed forests, in both temperate and tropical areas, appear to be at a scale and level of maturity unmatched anywhere in the world' (Bray et al. 2003, 673). The success of Mexico's CFEs seems to be tied to the long history of village-level democracy, communal governance, and experience in self-organizing. As more governments worldwide decentralize control of forests and place them in the hands of local communities, Mexico's CFEs may provide a model for communal forestry elsewhere.

Source: Bray et al. 2003.

lands and banned hunting—except by permit on game preserves, usually affordable only by rich European hunters—even when wildlife were destroying crops. Local farmers thus suffered the consequences of living with wildlife but were not able to reap any of the benefits.

Established in 55 districts throughout the country, the CAMPFIRE program was part of an overall shift in government policies in the mid-1970s to link the problems of local communities and wildlife conservation. By providing local communities greater involvement in management decisions and a percentage of any of the direct monetary benefits that might arise from commercial hunting and/or ecotourism enterprises that rely on wildlife preservation, it was hoped that the program would give people a greater stake in wildlife conservation (Hill 1996).

In both ICDPs and CBNRM programs, one of the main priorities has been to devise new strategies for resource use to meet the growing demands of expanding populations and production for markets and to encourage residents to adopt more biodiversity-friendly practices. These tactics may include the introduction of new techniques for traditional livelihoods like farming or fishing, encouraging the production of more environmentally friendly agricultural produce or forest products (such as coffee, tea, cotton, or tropical fruits) for sale in fair trade and other alternative trade markets (see chapter 15), or the creation of new income-earning enterprises, such as ecotourism.

Problems in participatory approaches

Despite being an improvement over previous top-down, exclusionary environmental and develop-ment policies, ICDPs, CBNRM, and co-management programs have not been without problems. Widespread use of the term 'sustainable development' suggests that everyone has a common perspective on what constitutes 'development' and 'sustainable' levels of resource use. But different cultural and social groups have different ideas about the relationship between humans and the natural environment, and frequently local people, CBNRM practitioners, and government officials disagree about the primary goals of these projects. For example, while protection of biodiversity is top among the goals of many conservation projects, it is not necessarily the primary objective of most indigenous groups and other local communities. Many indigenous groups are concerned with fostering economic security and, when given the opportunity, are often keen to use their resources more intensively (Whitesell 1996).

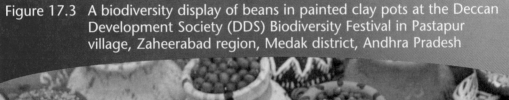

Figure 17.3   A biodiversity display of beans in painted clay pots at the Deccan Development Society (DDS) Biodiversity Festival in Pastapur village, Zaheerabad region, Medak district, Andhra Pradesh

Source: Daniel Buckles, IDRC

There is also the question of how to define the boundaries and membership of 'local' communities and what constitutes participation. Many critics argue that despite official rhetoric, in reality most local 'participation' has been passive at best (Redclift 1992). Participation can range from being cooks and park guards in conservation areas to full and effective control of management practices, but most often it is an outside government agency or NGO that is the effective decision-maker (Gray, Prellada, and Newing 1998). As Walley found in her research on the creation of the Mafia Island Marine Park in Tanzania, lack of effective participation and decision-making powers, as well as differences in perceptions of the goals of sustainable development, have led to conflict and renewed hostility on the part of local groups towards conservation efforts (see Box 17.4).

BOX 17.4   NATURE AND DEVELOPMENT IN A TANZANIAN MARINE PARK

In 1995, the Tanzanian government, with support of World Wide Fund for Nature, created the Mafia Island Marine Park (MIMP). Through the promotion of ecotourism, the MIMP was envisioned as a way to help preserve this unique ecosystem, improve the lives of local residents (among the poorest people in the country), and bring in much-needed foreign exchange to debt-ridden Tanzania. Not only was this the first national park in the country to focus on a marine environment, it was also the first to legally incorporate the local residents. Residents were at first sceptical about potential restrictions on their fishing practices. But they were also worried about their own inability to stop outsiders from depleting fish stocks and destroying the reefs through the practice of 'dynamite fishing'. A larger authority such as the MIMP, they reasoned, would be able to stop these destructive practices. Once assured of their participation in the planning and management of the MIMP and promised jobs and other economic opportunities within the park, residents agreed to support the project.

From the beginning, residents 'saw themselves as central actors in a park they perceived as their own' (Walley 2004, 35). But it soon became clear that residents' desires for 'development'—which included improving their standards of living through fishing and obtaining better schooling, heath care, and dependable transportation in their communities—were in direct conflict with conservationist goals of limiting use of marine resources and with the desire of tourists to vacation in a 'pristine' environment. In practice, residents were seldom consulted and played a very small role in the design and management of the park.

By 2000, new park management plans had eliminated earlier references to a park 'for the people and by the people'. Local residents complained that restrictions benefited park officials and rich tourists, not themselves; participation had brought not "rights" but rather oppression' (Walley 2004, 247–8). No longer seeing themselves as *stakeholders* in the resource, residents were no longer concerned with long-term sustainability of the coastal reefs. Thus, what seemed to be an innovative solution to both conservation and development problems was derailed through a lack of understanding of competing perspectives on what constitutes sustainable development and the failure to allow local residents to actively participate in decision-making.

Source: Walley 2004.

Integrated conservation and development programs also often fail to deliver significant economic benefits to local peoples. For example, many planners and environmental activists see ecotourism as an ideal means of achieving both conservation and development objectives: economic benefits accrue directly from protecting local environments and biodiversity. But while it can provide a means for local residents to make a living from the preservation of the environment, it does not always do so.

For example, in theory Zimbabwe's CAMPFIRE program (see above) granted local communities greater involvement in management decisions and a percentage of direct monetary benefits from commercial hunting and/or ecotourism enterprises. Yet one of the biggest complaints by communities involved was that most of the benefits of ecotourism were going to tour operators while the local communities were bearing most of the costs—such as the destruction of crops by elephants and other wildlife (Hill 1996).

In addition, there is growing evidence that in many cases, so-called ecotourism is actually contributing to environmental problems. For example, some scientists suggest that the rapid decline of some species of frogs in the world's rainforests may be due to the impact of human recreational activities, such as well-meaning ecotourists trekking through the woods (see, for example, Rodriquez-Prieto and Fernandez-Juricic 2005).

Finally, there is the issue of representation. Local communities are not homogenous groups but comprise a variety of interest groups defined by social status, gender, age, occupation, ethnicity, ideological orientation, and so on. These groups are often engaged in struggles over power and resources (Agarwal 2001; Gibson, McKean, and Ostrom 2000). Marginal groups, including women, ethnic minorities, and the poor, are rarely included in decision-making, since local elites and vested interest groups monopolize access to resources and co-opt decision-making at the local level (Kepe, Cousins, and Turner 2001).

EQUITY, CONSUMPTION, AND ENVIRONMENTAL JUSTICE

While the linkages between poverty and environmental degradation seem clear, political ecologists contend that we must pay more attention to the structural inequalities underlying both poverty and environmental degradation (see, for example, Peet and Watts 1996). From this perspective, to understand the root causes of the actions of the poor, we must examine the actions of a variety of other actors, such as national and international governments, corporations, and local elites. For example, the **desertification** of many rangelands and pastures as a result of overgrazing and over-cultivation is often attributed to growing populations and desperate measures on the part of the poor to survive by intensifying their farming practices and/or increasing the number of animals they graze. But as discussed earlier, other factors—such as government-sponsored dams and irrigation schemes, the expansion of elite-controlled commercial agriculture, or corporate logging practices—frequently force the poor and politically less powerful into smaller and less desirable areas, in essence forcing them to resort to unsustainable practices (see, for example, Igoe 2004). Unlike their counterparts in the North, environmental movements in the South have long focused on the inequities of development and questions of resource distribution (Dwivedi 2001).

For many, it is a pragmatic issue, because such inequities themselves contribute to the poverty and conflict that then result in resource degradation. For others, it is a question of **environmental justice**. The poor often are blamed for environmental degradation to which they actually have contributed the least. Delang (2005) shows how powerful interest groups have been able to influence government development policies in Thailand, some of which included extensive logging and deforestation in the highlands. Yet as the problems of deforestation (mudslides and water shortages) come to light, the small populations of hill tribes who practise shifting cultivation have been the ones blamed for deforestation.

Many rurally based subsistence groups in the developing world claim that they are expected to disproportionately bear the costs of ecosystem conservation while others (e.g., urban-based populations in the industrialized world) benefit from the environmental services provided by their conservation measures. Payments for environmental services (PES) have been proposed as a means of addressing this inequity. The idea is that those who conserve resources (e.g., landowners who preserve trees rather than cut them down) are compensated by those who share in the benefits of conservation (e.g., cleaner air, protection of watersheds).

Since the Millennium Ecosystem Assessment, the valuation of ecosystem services and the need to compensate land users for preserving those services has been gaining increasing attention. Costa Rica's *Pago por Servicios Ambientales* is one of the most elaborate PES programs, but PES programs have been developed throughout the world, in developed and developing countries alike, and have been hailed as a way to address issues of rural poverty while simultaneously preserving ecosystems.

While PES does hold promise as a means of spreading the costs of environmental protection among upstream and downstream users and beneficiaries, the approach is not without problems. In addition to the difficulties of assigning a value to ecosystem services, only those with secure rights to land are eligible for payment; lack of secure tenure often prevents the poor from benefiting and has been a significant obstacle for many PES programs (Pagiola, Arcenas, and Gunars 2005). In addition, some argue that by making some land more valuable, PES programs may in fact provide incentives for more powerful groups to push out more marginal residents who lack secure tenure (Landell-Mills and Porras 2002).

Post-development scholars argue that development itself is responsible for both poverty and environmental degradation. Many contend that the problem lies not with the developing world but in the high consumption rates of the industrialized countries. As Rees and Westra (2003) argue, not only have the benefits of economic growth gone to the world's wealthiest, but the burden of environmental decay falls disproportionately on the poor in both the North and the South, resulting in a situation of 'eco-apartheid' and prompting calls for environmental justice. The underlying causes of ecological decay, they argue, are 'contemporary "Western" values and consumer lifestyles' (Rees and Westra 2003, 101). The challenge, then, is not to raise consumption and limit population growth in the South but to drastically reduce consumption in the North (Sachs 1999) (see Box 17.5).

Thus, while sustainable development is hailed as a concept that addresses the need to protect both human livelihoods and the natural environment, not everyone sees it as a new hope for the future. According to Colombian anthropologist Arturo Escobar, the discourse of sustainable development does nothing to challenge the foundations of capitalist development and its inherent focus on economic growth but merely has been a way of incorporating 'nature' into the discourse of a world capitalist system. The preservation of the natural environment has now become an effort to conserve 'natural resources'—i.e., inputs into the production process that need to be used and managed in a 'rational' manner. Sustainable development creates 'the impression that only minor adjustments to the market system are needed to launch an era of environmentally sound development, hiding the fact that the economic framework itself cannot hope to accommodate environmental considerations without substantial reform' (Escobar 1995a, 197).

CONCLUSIONS

The problems of both poverty and environmental degradation are complex. Many early attempts to raise standards of living through large-scale economic development projects in fact only exacerbated human misery and environmental degradation. Questions remain concerning the underlying causes of both poverty and environmental degradation and hence the solutions to those problems. The notion of sustainable development has become a key concept both among

BOX 17.5   CONSUMPTION PATTERNS AND ENVIRONMENTAL JUSTICE

Population growth rates in the developing world have been pinpointed as a cause for concern, but a comparison of the *ecological footprint* of various societies around the world suggests that we need to look closer to home to find the biggest contributors to environmental degradation. The *ecological footprint* is an estimate of the area of land and water needed to produce the resources that a particular population consumes and to assimilate the waste it produces; it also takes into account resources that a population appropriates through trade (Rees 2001, in Rees and Westra 2003).

A comparison of eco-footprints is revealing. For example, at the end of the twentieth century, the wealthiest 25 per cent of the world's populations had an ecological footprint as large as the entire biologically productive surface area of the Earth. Canada and the US are among the world's biggest consumers, each requiring five to ten hectares of productive land/water per person to support their consumer lifestyles. In comparison, people in the world's poorer countries have an average eco-footprint of less than one hectare. The average child born in an industrial country today consumes and pollutes more in his/her lifetime than do 30 to 50 children born in some developing countries. From this perspective, consumers in the industrialized world—driven by a culture of consumption and reinforced by neo-liberal development policies—not burgeoning populations of the poor in the South, are primarily responsible for the collapse of fisheries, the decline of water tables, and the global warming we are witnessing today.

Some countries' ecological footprints exceed their national territories. This is possible because they are able to finance massive eco-deficits by buying unused productive capacity in other countries or appropriating it in global commons, such as open-sea fisheries. While the benefits of economic growth are enjoyed primarily by the world's richest peoples, the burden falls on the world's poor—in both low-income and high-income countries—who typically live in the most degraded and polluted environments. These ecological inequities raise the question of how to achieve environmental justice. Should citizens in the over-consuming world begin to take responsibility for their actions? Does the international community need to devise institutions that can ensure that they do so?

Source: Rees and Westra 2003.

---

conservationists and among those working on issues of human development, yet putting this concept into action has not been without problems. While some advocate secure property rights and the participation of local resource users as key ways of achieving goals of both improving human well-being and preserving the environment for future generations, others argue that existing social and economic inequalities must first be addressed. Still others contend that the notion of development itself is to blame for both poverty and environmental degradation and that the real problems lie with global capitalism and cultures of over-consumption in the industrialized world. There are no easy answers, but a better understanding of the complex interrelationship between social and economic contexts and the biophysical environment will aid in the formulation of more viable environmental policies in the future.

QUESTIONS FOR DISCUSSION

1. Do the benefits provided by large-scale development projects such as hydroelectric dams outweigh their adverse environmental and social costs? Why or why not?

2. Can market mechanisms like PES resolve the problems of achieving goals of sustainable development? What other mechanisms might be necessary?

3. Given the multitude of competing actors and their interests and knowledge bases (can you name them in any given situation?), who should decide how environmental resources should be used and managed?

4. How important are property rights for achieving goals of sustainable development? What should be done about extensive resources like oceans and the atmosphere?

5. In what ways does what you consume every day affect the environment and the lives of others in the world? What concrete ways can you think of to reduce that impact on a day-to-day basis?

FURTHER READING

Fratkin, Elliot. 1997. *Ariaal Pastoralists of Kenya: Surviving Drought and Development in Africa's Arid Lands*. Scarborough, ON: Prentice Hall Canada.

Stonich, S. 1993. *I Am Destroying the Land! The Political Ecology of Poverty and Environmental Destruction in Honduras*. Boulder, CO: Westview.

Vivanco, Luis A. 2006. *Green Encounters: Shaping and Contesting Environmentalism in Rural Costa Rica*. New York: Berghahn Books.

INTERNET RESOURCES

Millennium Ecosystem Assessment: http://www.millenniumassessment.org/en/Index.aspx.

Natural Resource Institute: http://www.nri.org.

UN Environment Programme: Dams and Development Project: http://www.unep.org/dams/WCD.

Earth Summit (UN Conference on Environment and Development, 1992): http://www.un.org/geninfo/bp/enviro.html.

Suzuki, David. *Amazonia: Road to the End of the Forest* (video).

International Institute for Sustainable Development: http://www.iisd.org.

Friends of River Narmada: http://www.narmada.org.

Interactive game on sustainable living: http://sustainability.publicradio.org/consumerconsequences.

CHAPTER 18

RURAL DEVELOPMENT

JOSHUA RAMISCH

LEARNING OBJECTIVES

- To identify and explain the key features of 'rurality'.
- To grasp the 'sustainable rural livelihoods' concept as a tool for understanding agriculture in context and use it critically to assess claims made about smallholder households (e.g., as 'rational', 'tradition bound', or 'multi-locational').
- To contrast the 'labour-rich' and 'land-rich' patterns of rural development and explain the importance of population pressure or other factors on innovation.
- To describe and evaluate the paradigm shifts in thinking about rural development.
- To identify the key challenges to rural development in the twenty-first century.

> Agricultural development polices are unduly affected by urban, roadside, dry-season, male-based perceptions of rural life and its problems.
> Paul Richards (1985, 156, drawing from Chambers 1983).

INTRODUCTION

For the first time in human history, more than half of us live in cities. It might therefore be tempting to conclude that this demographic shift proves that the development problems of rural poverty are being resolved, or at least now being outweighed by the new problems of urban poverty. And yet the vast majority of the world's poor is still 'rural': depending on definitions, somewhere between 68 and 75 per cent of those earning less than $1 per day (World Bank 2007d). This is a state of affairs that will persist for many decades even with the present rates of urbanization. Notwithstanding long histories of interconnection and migration between rural and urban areas, the persistent challenge of rural poverty has meant that 'rural development' remains a crucial element of the developmental agenda into the twenty-first century.

This chapter introduces the rural face of development in economic, social, and historical terms that reflect the incredible diversity and complexity of rural **livelihoods** and environments. It joins with other recent reviews of rural development (e.g., World Bank 2007d; Ashley and Maxwell 2001; IFAD 2001) that reaffirm its importance despite a history of failed goals or only ambiguous successes. Taking a global perspective on development processes that by definition differ according to their local contexts, we will begin by exploring the notion of 'rurality' and its relevance. We will explore the patterns of contemporary rural poverty and whether past histories of rural transformation can offer useful insights for current rural populations. The chapter then discusses the evolution of thought on rural development as a process to be managed. We will pay particular attention to the rise and fall of several key ideas, such as the emphasis on 'small farms' or agriculture as the engine of rural development, the benefits and challenges of taking an **integrated approach** to rural problems, and the merits and limitations of **participatory approaches** to rural development.

Perhaps more than most fields of development studies, the history of rural development is tangled with internal contradictions and frustrations at unmet targets. While agriculture has served as the basis for growth and has reduced poverty in many countries, it is also true that livelihoods based largely on subsistence agriculture remain quite vulnerable and are frequently caught in vicious circles or 'poverty traps', which are so widespread and enduring that rural poverty can appear inevitable (Ellis 2000; Barrett, Reardon, and Webb 2001).

Despite the persistence of rural poverty—or perhaps because of it—the response of most national governments (rich and poor) is to continue to debate both the relevance and necessity of rural development, even after decades of investment and planning. A caustic review more than 20 years ago at the height of interest in rural development noted that 'rural development does not usually achieve its objectives' and '[b]y any criteria, successful projects have been the exception rather than the rule' (Williams 1981, 16–17). While agriculture remains the primary livelihood source for the rural poor (and particularly rural women), the flows of overseas development assistance (ODA) targeting the rural sector continue to decline worldwide in both absolute and relative terms (World Bank 2007d, 41–2). Already stagnating in the early 1980s, worldwide ODA to agriculture declined after 1985 at an average annual rate of 7 per cent (far greater than any downward trend in ODA overall), falling from a 17 per cent share of ODA in the early 1980s to 8 per cent at the start of the new millennium (OECD 2001, 3). It is plausible that the exclusion of agriculture from the poverty reduction agenda of the 1990s explains some of the decline. Indeed, rural poverty is not even explicitly acknowledged in the Millennium Development Goal commitments, which therefore fail to recognize where the poor

live and how they make their living, only indirectly addressing rural poverty through targets relating to **food security**, 'natural resources', and the overall goal of halving poverty by 2015.

PUTTING THE 'RURAL' IN CONTEXT

> The village is the centre; you are peripheral.
> (Indian village leaders' comment to development visitors)
> Chambers 1983, 46.

To the development planner (or student), the twenty-first-century world of email and global interconnectivity seems inherently distinct from the world of the peasant. A vast range of places that might be recognizable as 'rural' includes farmlands, forests, savannas, pastoral rangelands, mountain villages, and mining or coastal communities. Yet the apparently 'obvious' categorical divisions between 'rural' and 'urban' (or 'local' and 'global') may actually be quite ambiguous.

Rural sociologist Michael Bell (2007) describes how the seemingly recognizable 'rural' exists in two inextricably linked forms. First, it has a fundamentally *material* form with a spatial identity: as an area of low population density, agricultural or resource-based in its livelihoods, defined forever in opposition to an 'urban' reality. Its second form is as an *ideal*: the romance (and terror?) of the 'village', of tight-knit communities, maternal hearths, and masculine, patriarchal power—or of 'nature', redolent of fresh air, dirt, hard work, and disease, the freedom of isolation and of desolation. The coexistence of this *material* reality and the *ideal* underpins the assumption that the 'rural' actually exists as a real entity to be 'developed'.

For national statistical services, urban populations are distinguished from rural ones by threshold levels: an urban area must typically contain a certain, non-agricultural production base and also a minimum population level. Within such frameworks, rural areas therefore become a catch-all defined in opposition to the urban—the 'not-urban'. However, the diversity of

Figure 18.1   A recognizably 'rural' landscape of Indonesia, featuring intensively managed rice fields, irrigation networks, family homes, and a reliance on an overwhelmingly female labour force.

Source: Joshua Ramisch

livelihoods found in rural areas (including petty commerce, 'cottage' industry or artisanal production, and seasonal or long-term migrations to urban or industrial areas such as mines or ports) blurs the notion that certain activities, or residential patterns, can actually or meaningfully distinguish the 'urban' from the 'not-urban' (McDowell and de Haan 1997).

Combining Bell's ideas with the logic of national statistical services, we can distinguish at least four enduring, material features of 'rurality'. These features are general enough to cover diverse rural contexts, such as the pampas of Argentina or the steppes of Mongolia, the widely spaced farms and clusters of villages in west Africa's Sahel, the densely settled smallholder farms of Indonesia or Rwanda, tenant farmers working on large estates in Colombia, landscapes of commer-

cial farmers interspersed among smallholders in India or Brazil, or even the hunter-gatherers of Papua New Guinea. These features are:

1. A *relative abundance of natural capital* (land, water, soil, trees, wildlife, and other natural resources) and therefore a dependence on (and vulnerability to) the unpredictable elements of the natural environment, including drought or flooding, pests and diseases, and global climate change.

2. A *relative abundance of labour*, which is often structured and negotiated at the household level on the basis of gender and age (e.g., household tasks and the care of crops are often conceptually divided into duties done only by men, by women, or by children). Seasonal or prolonged out-migration of the

fittest labourers is often widespread and may adversely affect the quality of the labour actually available in rural areas, particularly at 'bottlenecks' of high labour demand in the rural calendar, such as land cultivation, planting, weeding, and harvesting.

3. A *relative isolation* (because of remoteness, internal distances, or the general lack of infrastructure) that translates into a relatively high cost of movement and a relatively limited ability to participate in or influence national politics. As will be discussed, the urbanite's image of rural 'isolation' is often much stronger than the reality. Historic linkages within and between rural areas themselves, and between rural and urban ones, may be strong and long-standing.

4. A *relative importance of social factors* in stratifying or structuring access to resources that may be equal to or greater than the importance of market-based mechanisms (if these exist at all). Examples include the likely coexistence of multiple (formal and informal) land tenure regimes (e.g., governing access to farmland, water, fuel wood, pasture rights), the prevalence of reciprocity in social networks (based on kinship, ethnicity, religion, or other groupings), and obligations in hierarchical relationships (such as between elders and younger generations, 'native' and 'migrant' populations, men and women, 'big men' leaders and their 'clients', to name just a few).

Each of these features can be challenged and obviously may not be true in all rural places or in all time periods. Furthermore, they should not be accepted as politically neutral 'facts', unrelated to the urban characteristics against which they are defined. It is certainly true, for example, that the flow of capital and labour out of rural areas to urban ones sustains many of the features of isolation or perceived 'underdevelopment' assigned to rural areas. Ashley and Maxwell (2001, 407) also point out that rural areas, even ones of great poverty and apparent marginalization, often have much greater income

diversity, stronger rural–urban links, and longer-standing interactions with the world economy than they are normally given credit for. In many parts of the world considered 'remote' (e.g., much of rural sub-Saharan Africa), the penetration of global markets for labour or commodities is in fact centuries old and not something that has 'yet to happen' once rural development planners finally arrive on the scene (Ferguson 1994).

Worldwide, rural contexts can be distinguished on the basis of the relative importance of agriculture and the relative levels of rural poverty. The 2008 *World Development Report: Agriculture for Development* (World Bank 2007d) categorizes countries into three different 'rural worlds':

- **Agriculture-based countries**, where agriculture is a dominant component of overall GDP and of GDP growth and where most of the poor are in rural areas. Most countries in this category are found in sub-Saharan Africa.
- **Transforming countries**, where agriculture is no longer a major contributor to economic growth but rural poverty remains widespread. Most of the world's rural poor are actually now found in 'transforming' countries, including India, China, Indonesia, Morocco, and Thailand. This category includes most of East and South Asia, the Pacific, the Middle East, and North Africa.
- **Urbanized countries**, where poverty is predominantly urban but rural poverty still exists and agriculture or the food industry can represent up to one-third of GDP. This category includes most countries of Latin America, the Caribbean, eastern Europe, and Central Asia.

The *World Development Report* presents these categories as part of an evolutionary model, tracking the progress of countries such as China and India from 'agriculture-based' to 'transforming' or Indonesia from 'transforming' to 'urbanized' over the 1993–2005 study period. While such a model might obscure radically different processes of change in different parts of the world, or assume that processes of the past 15 years are similar to

Table 18.1 Characteristics of three country types

	Agriculture-based countries	Transforming countries	Urbanized countries
Rural population (millions), 2005	417	2,220	255
Rural share of population (%), 2005	68	63	26
GDP per capita (2000 US$)	379	1,068	3,489
Agriculture share of GDP (%)	29	13	6
Annual agricultural GDP growth (%), 1993–2005	4.0	2.9	2.2
Annual non-agricultural GDP growth (%), 1993–2005	3.5	7.0	2.7
Number of rural poor (millions), 2002[a]	170	592	32
Rural poverty rate (%), 2002[a]	51	28	13

[a]Poverty rate is $1.08/day.
Source: Adapted from World Bank 2007d.

those of other time periods, the report does acknowledge that heterogeneity exists within countries. For example, even in a strongly 'transforming' country like India or an 'urbanized' country like Mexico, sub-national regions like Bihar and Chiapas within each remain strongly agrarian in orientation. This internal heterogeneity has important implications for equity and future rural development and change.

Defining rural areas purely on the basis of spatial or economic features, of course, gives undue weight to the knowledge and priorities of urban-based elites. The rural that is 'recognizable' to rural inhabitants may in fact be based much more on social or cultural attributes: the types of communities and relationships, the crops or animals raised, and the foods consumed. Whereas hunger and food insecurity might be addressed in economic terms by strategies to increase crop production, the rural solutions might be social, calling on reciprocity within existing or potential social networks to gain access to food supplies in times of need. These strategies are often essential to rural livelihoods (see Box 18.1), but it would be unwise to romanticize the social solidarity or inherited wisdom of all rural communities, especially since the opportunities to effectively deploy this knowledge are often severely constrained by economic, political, and even environmental pressures.

'Peasant' societies, for example, are rural cultures highly reliant on local production, where the distribution of wealth and power at a local level is affected by contact with a nation-state. Such societies are typically highly structured and stratified as a result of that contact, especially on the basis of who owns or controls access to the fundamental resources (land and labour). These hierarchical structures (of landlords, chiefs, or local administrators) are in turn reinforced and amplified by cultural, economic, gendered, religious, or cosmological systems and technologies.

Despite such commonalities of structure, peasant societies are complex and varied and have adapted and evolved across centuries around the world as one of the dominant forms of human organization. The resilience of peasant societies (and smallholders more generally) has become increasingly understood in recent decades, and the contribution of that understanding to rural development theory and practice will be discussed in various forms below. Nonetheless, many of the inherited, structural constraints of unjust social orders are overlooked in the *ideal* image of the rural. As a result, the 'tradition-bound, conservative peasant' is an image still regularly

BOX 18.1   RURAL LIVELIHOODS
AND DIVERSIFICATION

As defined by Scoones (1998, 5), a 'livelihood' as a whole represents: 'the capabilities, assets (including both material and social resources) and activities required for a means of living. A livelihood is sustainable when it can cope with and recover from stresses and shocks, maintain or enhance its capabilities and assets, while not undermining the natural resource base.'

The concept of sustainable livelihoods is particularly relevant to the rural context where, for example, the seasonal fluctuations of climate drive the viability of different activities within an agricultural calendar and oblige individuals and households to consider multiple strategies if they are to exploit their environment and flourish.

Livelihood analysis is based on understanding how different types of *capital* (financial, natural, social, human, or physical) are combined in a particular *context* (of policy settings, politics, history, agro-ecology, or socio-economic conditions). Different *livelihood strategies* (agricultural intensification or extensification, diversification, or migration), therefore, can be pursued depending on the mediation of *institutional processes* (the matrix of formal or informal institutions or social organizations, such as land tenure or inheritance patterns).

For example, in rural western Kenya, a single household reported meeting its needs (for food security, school fees, medical services, or funeral expenses) over a six-month period by the following means: cultivating maize and beans (staple crops), cassava (long-term crop), or tea (cash crop) on their own farm; 'borrowing' food, fruit, and milk from relatives; growing and selling vegetables; selling firewood; pension money from a retired railway employee; working for day wages and a cooked lunch on neighbours' farms at planting, weeding, and harvest seasons; working as 'casual labour' for local woodcutters; selling handicrafts sewn at home; and searching for work as a watchman or bicycle taxi driver in a nearby town (Ramisch and Akech 2005, unpublished data).

Such strategies represent a combination of *coping* mechanisms to address immediate hardships as well as longer-term *adaptations* (e.g., migration of one or more family members to town in search of work) to adjust to changing conditions or crises and to reduce vulnerability or poverty. Population growth, urbanization, education, global climatic change, and structural adjustment have all called into play a multitude of diverse and dynamic activities geared towards making a secure livelihood.

---

invoked and looked down upon by leaders and planners or chastised by revolutionaries for not throwing off the yoke of their 'oppression' by landlords or village chiefs. To begin to get a sense of what potential local knowledge and experience can offer rural development, we will now consider how rural change has been shaped in various parts of the world.

RURAL TRANSFORMATIONS

Societal perspectives on rural transformation

Even before the developmental era of the twentieth century, most of the world had already lived (repeatedly) through vast restructurings of rural landscapes and communities. The industrial revolutions that spread across the temperate world, from England in the mid-eighteenth century to Japan in the late nineteenth century, were preceded and fuelled by agricultural growth. For many centuries before that, the lack of rural opportunities (lived as rural poverty and misery) had fuelled peasant rebellions and uprisings from the time of the Roman Empire, through medieval Europe and feudal Asia, colonial Latin America and the Caribbean, South and Southeast Asia, and Africa (see Box 18.2).

The vast colonial networks of resource exploitation that spanned the globe from the sixteenth to the twentieth century were also responsible for great socio-cultural and political upheavals in rural society, most notably reorienting far-flung communities to world markets for commodities and labour and leaving legacies of violence. In an economic slump, the colonial instinct (e.g., that of the French in west Africa in the 1930s or the English in India in the 1880s and during Ireland's potato famine) would not be to protect the peasant sector from market fluctuations but rather to put even greater pressure on it to maintain the revenue flow. Describing the colonial period in Southeast Asia, Scott (1976, 10) portrays 'an almost total absence of any provision for the maintenance of a minimal income while, at the same time, the commercialization of the agrarian economy was steadily stripping away most of the traditional forms of social insurance'. Colonial structures of commercialization became enmeshed with previously existing peasant society institutions that had once upheld the 'norm of reciprocity' and 'right to subsistence' even as they worked directly counter to them (Scott 1976).

Many development scholars have attempted to draw lessons for rural development in the tropics from the agricultural development histories of currently industrialized societies. We will leave aside for the moment the significant assumptions that such an approach to history might entail and look at two countries often chosen as opposite ends of a continuum—Japan (portrayed as 'labour-rich' but with limited land resources) and the United States (portrayed as 'land-rich' but with scarce

labour until the early twentieth century) (Hayami and Ruttan 1985; Tomich, Kilby, and Johnston 1995). The context of present-day rural poverty in many parts of the world is still framed by these two extremes of factor endowments, which explains the enduring popularity of using the US and Japan as potential rural development models.

Rural development in Japan ('intensification')

The experience of Japan during the Meiji restoration period (1868–1920) was indeed framed by a limited land base and an abundant rural population. New land could not be brought into production within the Japanese landmass, and so agricultural production and the rural economy grew over this period through **agricultural intensification**, increasing the overall crop output of the land by increasing inputs of labour, capital, knowledge, and other technological resources. Highlights of the Japanese experience include:

- Overall production was improved by the efforts of farmers on relatively small pieces of land (0.5–2.0 hectares), not by industrial agriculture. The smallholder-led strategy centred on improved varieties of the staple crop (rice), increasing reliance on inorganic fertilizers, and increased use of irrigation to manage and regulate water supply.
- As rice production increased, there was a significant expansion of non-farm income opportunities in the small urban centres that dot the countryside, meaning that there was only a low degree of inequality in income and lifestyle between rural and urban areas or within rural communities themselves.
- Success depended on the strong collaboration of the leadership and resources of the national government and a national research and extension system to promote the latest scientific knowledge.
- Meiji leaders were under intense pressure to 'modernize' their society by opening up to the outside world as producers and con-

BOX 18.2   LAND TENURE AND INEQUALITY

The importance of land to rural livelihoods cannot be overstated. Land 'tenure', or the security with which individuals, households, or communities have access to land, is regulated by custom (traditional 'laws', conventions, and practices), enshrined in national legal and administrative frameworks, or quite frequently both at the same time. The social and political institutions that regulate tenure often distinguish between specific rights to land, from 'usufruct' (use-rights such as cultivation, tree-planting or cutting, grazing, house-building, or drawing water) through to the rights of full 'ownership' (such as the rights to sell or transfer land, to subdivide, or to bequeath as an inheritance).

The basic assumption of many rural development programs—that the 'rural poor' are 'small farmers'—neglects the widespread and growing fact that the poorest of the poor are often landless. Without land of their own, members of such households are thus obliged to labour on the farms of others in exchange for wages or shares of the crop ('sharecropping').

The complexity of land tenure regimes often also means that the inequality in land ownership and use-rights is deeply entrenched. Land reform movements that attempt to redistribute land more equally have therefore been a dominant component of rural development, particularly in Latin America, where landlord and tenant farmer are effectively hereditary positions. Members of radical land redistribution movements have often forcibly occupied large farms or plantations, winning localized concessions and gaining access to land. However, large-scale land reform has been elusive in most of Latin America because of the persistence of deeply entrenched social, economic, and political barriers. Even in post-apartheid South Africa, many landless blacks are effectively excluded from land redistribution programs because they are unable to afford the up-front costs (including long-distance relocation), have less labour available for farming, and have less capacity to cope with agricultural risk (Zimmerman 2000).

Customary social arrangements that regulate conflicting use-rights have an important role to play in managing land in highly variable environments, such as grazing lands and seasonal watering points (see chapter 17). However, while such regimes may protect the rights of diverse groups to manage common property resources, they often rely on negotiation processes that are highly contested. As such, they may reinforce the social disadvantage of already subordinate groups, such as women who after marriage move away to live on the land of their husbands.

With the emphasis on the rationality of 'small farmers', many rural development projects have also assumed that granting formal legal title to land is essential to securing land rights and creating a land market. There is a vast literature showing that simply replacing customary regimes with legal title does not necessarily increase security or willingness to invest in agriculture. For example, in Honduras (Jansen and Roquas 1998), the land-titling process actually increased conflicts over land as holders of some customary rights were favoured over others, state intervention in the local community increased to solve conflicts, and conflicts effectively suppressed any potential land market.

sumers of global goods, a pressure similar to that experienced by contemporary developmental states.

It can be argued that there is too much that is unique about the Japanese success story to make it a useful model for rural development elsewhere. And it is certainly true that the economic and technological success of contemporary Japan has contributed to a mythology about the enlightened and progressive 'vision' of the Meiji leaders that obscures some of the challenges actually faced at that time. The Japanese people may share a common language, traditions, and ethnic heritage to an extent that many land-scarce developing nations today do not, but during the first decade of the Meiji restoration, the political climate was actually far from settled. More than 200 peasant uprisings, four samurai revolts, and significant internal discord within the government severely constrained the 'free hand' that the Meiji rulers supposedly used to reshape their nation (Tomich, Kilby, and Johnston 1995, 99). Their strongly nationalist desire to industrialize rapidly was matched by an awareness on the part of many leaders that a growing economy would enrich them too and not simply serve the public good. In other words, the adoption of policies that effectively stimulated agriculture and the rural non-farm economy appears to represent a happy convergence of factors that might just as easily have led to corruption, rent-seeking, and stagnation.

Rural development in the US ('extensification')

Compared to Japan, the United States had abundant and cheap land but relatively scarce and expensive labour. This meant overall output was increased through **agricultural extensification**—by expanding the areas cultivated. Highlights of the American experience include:

- Fertilizers were not a significant input in American agriculture until the 1930s. Before this point, the incentive to intensively manage soil fertility in a given piece of land was outweighed in nearly all locations by the ease with which new, fallow land could be put under cultivation.
- For most of the nineteenth century, agricultural policy was aimed at opening up 'virgin' land and creating new family farms, which relied heavily on the household labour (and draft animals) of the settlers themselves.
- Expanding the transportation network was the greatest stimulus to rural development in the interior. Navigable rivers and canals were important in the northeast and upper Mississippi, but railroads were the most crucial link between the expanding areas of settler agriculture and the growing urban markets back in the east.

Lessons drawn from the experience of the United States are typically considered most relevant to the African context. For example, Wood (2002) argues that an increasingly prosperous Africa could be 'more like America' than land-scarce regions such as Asia and Europe. Since Africa, like the Americas, is land-rich in relation to its population, its primary (rural, agricultural) sector will tend to predominate over its manufacturing sector. With the bulk of its landmass far from the sea and without major navigable waterways, internal transport costs are comparatively higher. This also leads Wood to conclude that a prosperous Africa will have urban, industrial concentrations along its coasts and a less densely settled interior, dominated by agriculture and mining.

Of course, such arguments synthesize patterns across a huge landmass with vast socio-economic and agro-ecological differences and inevitably take an incomplete view of the rural development experience in the United States. The American South—based on slavery and plantation agriculture until the latter part of the nineteenth century—was largely bypassed by the railways and the influx of immigrants (Tomich, Kilby, and Johnston 1995, 73). After slavery, most land in the South was cultivated by sharecroppers or tenant farmers, and low-wage agricultural labour remained abundant. New Deal legislation in the 1930s helped to raise wages for some unskilled workers and encourage greater land ownership among African Americans, but in many ways the legacy of the colonial plantation agriculture system is still deeply entrenched, such that social inequality and rural poverty in the United States remain at their highest levels in the South even today.

Cultural and technological perspectives on rural transformation

For an alternative perspective on rural transformation as opposed to examining the experiences of particular nations, it is illuminating to consider local patterns of rural technological change. The work of the Danish economist Ester Boserup (1965; 1981) is one of the most comprehensive and useful frameworks for understanding smallholder adaptations cross-culturally (see chapter 5). Before Boserup, models of rural transformation assumed that technology was the primary (if not the only) engine of agricultural change. Progress was the ability to command larger sources of energy, and the smallholder in such scenarios was inevitably doomed to obsolescence because human labour would eventually be replaced by draught animals, mechanical power, and fossil fuels (Netting 1993, 270). Boserup's emphasis on relationships between population density, technological change, agricultural intensification, and markets is of particular value, since these relationships are not presented as part of an evolutionary model of stages or 'progressive' change. As such, she breaks with the more rigid formulations suggested by Thomas Malthus and Karl Marx.

Boserup's hypothesis is that an increase in population density is an independent variable sufficient to trigger agricultural intensification and the technical innovations needed to support it. More labour-intensive technologies—such as replacing natural fallows with the spreading of animal manure as a means of improving soil fertility, or replacing digging sticks with hand hoes, ox ploughs, or tractors for cultivation and planting—

are only sensibly developed and adopted in the face of the scarcity induced by population pressure. This 'pressure' may be due to a population's natural increase, the influx of migrants, or land degradation that reduces the amount of useable land. This relationship between rural population density and agricultural intensification helps to explain why it is not some innate 'conservatism' on the part of rural-dwellers but rather an entirely rational choice that would keep farmers from adopting the ploughs or purchasing pesticides used by their neighbours in more densely settled landscapes or promoted by an 'enlightened' extension agent (Netting 1993, 263). It also explains why out-migration or other population decreases could lead to rational decisions to give up labour-intensive soil conservation methods or to return to 'older' methods of land clearance such as burning, even if farmers are aware of more 'modern' techniques.

Originally developed from observations of Asian and European smallholder farming systems, Boserup's expected patterns of agricultural intensification have since been validated when applied to population densities in a range of conditions and time periods (cf. Turner, Hyden, and Kates 1993 for Africa). It has also been demonstrated that successful intensification may be 'induced' by forces other than land shortage, such as policy changes or the improvement of infrastructure and better access to markets (Boserup 1981). These more sophisticated models show how intensification's benefits may be hindered or missed altogether if not supported by policy, credit and infrastructure development, or access to growing markets.

Malthus, Marx, and Boserup understood the systematic interaction of population, environment (land), and technology (agricultural methods) in different ways. For Malthus in early nineteenth-century Europe, land was the ultimate constraint against population growth. He acknowledged that exogenous technological changes could improve food production (and thus general welfare) but did not see any instances in which such innovations were anything more than random and certainly not in response to population pressures (Netting

1993, 278). Marx, on the other hand, saw economic growth as powered by exogenous technological change. He saw these changes as guided by the interests of landowners, not rural population density, with greater intensification supporting the extraction of surplus value from the labour of agricultural workers. In contrast, Boserup shows how population growth drives technological innovation and agricultural intensification that can significantly increase the productive potential of a fixed piece of land so that it keeps pace with (or even exceeds) population's growth.

MODELS

As the history of endogenous rural change suggests, there is no shortage of models or potential ideas about rural development. In the past half century, thinking about rural development has undergone two key 'paradigm shifts' (Ellis and Biggs 2001). The first was a switch in the mid-1960s from a belief that smallholder 'peasant' agriculture was inherently inefficient (and therefore doomed or destined to be replaced by more modern forms) to a set of beliefs that saw smallholders as 'inherently rational' and therefore the potential driving force of increased efficiency and productivity. The second was a switch in the late 1980s and early 1990s, from top-down rural development led by national-level policies and the 'blueprint' transfer of technologies, towards efforts to make rural development more 'participatory', led or at least more controlled by the rural communities themselves at the grassroots.

In the 1950s, a dual-economy theory of development held sway in which the small-farm subsistence sector was perceived to lack the vigour or capacity to raise national productivity. The 'traditional' sector would therefore passively support the 'modern' industrial agricultural sector of commercial plantations and ranches by supplying labour and land resources until the former sector was ultimately absorbed into the latter.

The catalyst for the first paradigm shift came with the publication of a book entitled *Transforming*

Traditional Agriculture (Schultz 1964). Schultz's central proposition was that 'traditional' small farmers in fact allocated their resources rationally and could lead rural development if given the right tools to improve their efficiency. This perspective led in turn to the proposition that agriculture had a key role to play in a country's overall economic growth in which an emerging industrial sector would be supported by the agricultural contributions of labour, capital, food, foreign exchange (from export crops), and markets for consumer goods. In effect, if it could be shown that the 'rural poor' were also 'small farmers', growth and equity concerns could be addressed in a single, pro-smallholder, pro-agriculture strategy of rural development—an apparent 'win-win'.

Such ideas have in fact been incredibly powerful, motivating practitioners of 'integrated' rural development and the Green Revolution's pioneers (as well as their successive generations of critics) to see their work as focused on improving the efficiency of smallholders with technologies 'appropriate' to their conditions. Schultz's ideas continue to hold sway, as in International Fund for Agricultural Development (IFAD) reviews of global data that show the agricultural productivity of 'small' farms to be at least twice that of 'large' farms in settings as diverse as Colombia, Brazil, India, and Malaysia (IFAD 2001, 79). The greater productivity of smallholder farmers is attributed to more intensive use of labour and land, particularly in growing higher-value mixes of crops, intercropping, and leaving less land fallow.

The second paradigm shift, towards more 'participatory' models of rural development, has also gained broad acceptance since the late 1980s to the extent that it is now voiced all the way from the offices of World Bank liberalizers to the most radical grassroots NGOs. This shift was fuelled in part by the perceived failures of large state-led 'integrated rural development' projects in the 1970s and 1980s, when NGOs with alternative models began to enter the spaces created by retreating states. Of course, the disengagement of states from 'top-down' rural development projects was itself further encouraged by international financial and donor actors through **structural adjustment**. It can also be argued that much of the present emphasis on rural development that is 'led' by communities themselves revives ideas of the original 1950s-era 'community development' approach.

Figure 18.2 presents a very simplified overview of the evolution of ideas and modes of thinking about rural development over the past half century. Majority discourses are given prominence in such a diagram. Dominant ideas of a given time period may have taken 10 to 15 years to fully spread from academic circles to policy arenas and practical action, while many minority or dissenting theories and orientations have simmered (or boiled) underneath, even up to the present.

Community development

The 'community development' approach of the 1950s derived from both British experience in 'preparing' India for independence in the 1940s and the domestic policy of the United States in the 1930s. Community development then became the guiding logic of the US's development assistance—primarily in Asia, where rural development was seen as a powerful antidote to communist agrarian movements—and the United Nations system.

Community development was defined as a process, method, program, institution, and/or movement involving communities in the solution of problems, teaching democratic processes, and activating and/or facilitating transfer of technol-

Figure 18.2   Timeline of dominant ideas in rural development

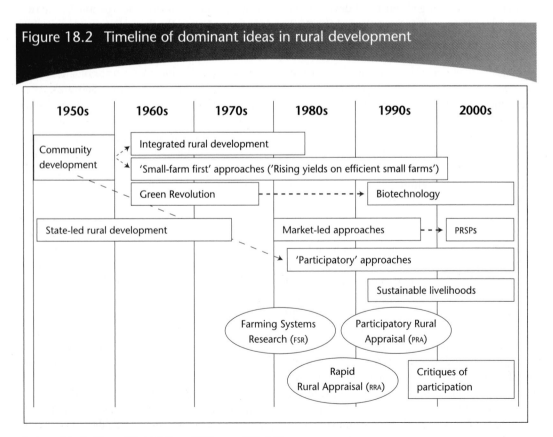

Source: Adapted from Ellis and Biggs 2001, pp. 439, 442.

ogy to a community for more effective solution of its problems (Holdcroft 1976, 1–3). The 'rural reconstruction' movement in pre-independence India had amassed a great body of experience in the early twentieth century, well-documented by Gandhi and Tagore, showing that rural people would respond and take initiative when they realized that they would benefit from community-wide efforts. From these roots, community development programs were assumed to have universal relevance and appeal as part of a democratic social movement embracing the idea of a balanced, integrated development of the whole of community life.

The approach flourished in the immediate post–World War II era through the 1950s, and (as we shall see) it has much in common with the present-day 'sustainable livelihoods' approaches that emphasize a holistic development that is locally 'owned' and responds to 'felt needs'. The approach relied heavily on specially trained civil servants (e.g., 'multipurpose village workers' in India) to facilitate the community development process, who would be accountable to and working on behalf of both the local communities and the national governments. This usually spawned a new and large bureaucracy at the national, regional, and local levels to support and co-ordinate the efforts of technical ministries such as agriculture, education, and health. Given the complexity of co-ordination, community development practitioners increasingly stressed the unique contribution of their own subject matter (e.g., agricultural production, cooperative development, local government, rural education, rural health, social welfare, development economics) while believing that any shortcomings arose from inadequate support from other subject matter areas.

By the mid-1950s, community development programs had become fairly institutionalized, standard 'models'. The price of this oversimplification and standardization was that by the 1960s, most programs were not reaching their stated targets for rural poverty alleviation or food security, and funding from the US and other donors declined sharply. As these supposedly universal

models contended with local realities, the (usually expatriate) community development specialists' ideals and social scientific perspectives often ran against the interests of the national technical specialists (particularly in agriculture). These tensions were resolved mainly in favour of the more bureaucratically established technical services personnel to the extent that by 1965, many host country 'development' ministries were absorbed into the more disciplinarily focused ministries of interior or of agriculture (Holdcroft 1976, 28).

Integrated rural development

The demise of the 'community development' approach fed into two contrasting strains of thought. On the one hand, it fed into the emerging emphasis on small-farm growth and agricultural improvement through Green Revolution technologies (see Box 18.3). On the other hand, its lingering influence fed into renewed efforts to promote 'balanced' rural development through even larger-scale 'integrated rural development' (IRD) projects, supported by multilateral institutions.

By the late 1960s, the context of rural development had evolved from the community era. Many more countries (particularly in Africa) were newly independent from colonialism, and the economic gulf was widening between rich and poor nations as well as within poor nations where the bulk of poverty remained 'rural'. The IRD approach attempted to revive and build on community development while incorporating the new ideas of small-farm efficiency, promoting 'balanced' development strategies that would target all regions of a country instead of relying on urban and industrial growth as the engine of the national economy. The comprehensive nature of IRD strategies also reflected free-market efforts to mirror the apparent successes that China was experiencing during the same period in improving overall production and consumption through rural collectivization.

The appeal of IRD to the World Bank, its greatest proponent, was that the results promised by projects 'integrated' with each other would theoretically outweigh the results of projects

BOX 18.3   THE 'GREEN REVOLUTION'

These and other developments in the field of agriculture contain the makings of a new revolution. It is not a violent Red Revolution like that of the Soviets, nor is it a White Revolution like that of the Shah of Iran. I call it the Green Revolution.

William Gaud, USAID director, 1968.

The so-called 'Green Revolution' of improved crop varieties, fertilizer, and irrigation technologies that transformed South Asia from a famine-prone, food-insecure region into a net exporter of food-stuffs between the mid-1960s and the 1980s is often presented as the greatest success of rural development, if not of agricultural research generally. Many of the plant breeders and agronomists who developed and promoted high-yielding varieties (HYV) of staple crops such as wheat and rice became household names, like Norman Borlaug, who won the Nobel Peace Prize in 1970. Innovation continues in plant breeding (and now biotechnological methods), broadening the range of crops for which HYVs have been developed and selected for improved drought or pest resistance or tolerance of salinity, soil acidity, or low fertility conditions.

HYVs significantly outperform traditional varieties in the presence of adequate irrigation, pesticides, and fertilizers. In the absence of these inputs (e.g., under the prevailing conditions of most resource-poor farmers), traditional varieties may outperform HYVs. A further criticism of HYVs is that they were developed as 'F1 hybrids', meaning they need to be purchased by a farmer every season rather than saved from previous seasons, thus increasing a farmer's cost of production.

Almost 40 years later, the Green Revolution remains a polarizing term and still faces many critics. For example, Vandana Shiva (1991) highlights 'red' issues, such as the negative socio-political implications of technologies that widen the wealth and power gap between landowners and landless farmers and shift the burden of labour for new crops onto women. As discussed in this chapter, simply raising the yields of a few key crops may not help to improve incomes or livelihoods in 'diverse, risk-prone, and resource-poor environments'. 'Green' issues include the negative environmental consequences of increased reliance on commercial fertilizers, the breakdown of soils under continuous cropping, contamination of groundwater, and the loss of biodiversity as exotic varieties and crops displace local varieties. While proponents often respond that higher rice productivity per unit area has 'spared' wetlands that might otherwise have been cleared and note that Asian farmers plant a greater variety of crops today than they did in 1970 (Djurfeldt et al. 2005, 13), claims of net positive or negative impacts can only truly be assessed at the local level.

implemented on a piecemeal basis. For example, investment in an irrigation system could be combined with improvement of local roads so that surplus agricultural produce could reach other markets. However, the large-scale nature of these projects and the consequently large budgets made them ripe targets for political manipulation as prizes to be shared among governments, donors, and contractors (cf. Ferguson 1994). Thus, the selection of target locations for IRD projects would become a seriously political act. Deferring to national governments to identify the regional targets most 'in need', or where the impact would be greatest, exposed the selection process to politicians and other leaders with ties to specific regions. Indeed, since government agencies are likely to be dominated by representatives of relatively wealthy regions, their influence would tend to divert development funds away from the areas most in need.

In general, despite strong donor support, the IRD of the 1970s and 1980s had only mixed expe-riences. The most common criticisms focused on their top-down nature, supply-driven approach, and excessive reliance on technical assistance and on heavy, non-sustainable, project-specific man-agement structures. While many IRD projects were intended as 'pilots', to be replicated elsewhere if successful, many obstacles prevented the realiza-tion of such goals, including fiscal constraints, the shortage of personnel with the appropriate inter-disciplinary expertise, and regional differences

Figure 18.3   Integrated rural development programs emphasized the export of cash crops as a means for 'agriculture-based' or 'transforming' countries to derive significant foreign currency earnings. Such dependence on cash crops is still widespread even as commodity prices have declined. Leading cash crops include tea (shown here in Kenya), coffee, cotton, sugar, tobacco, cut flowers, fruits (bananas, oranges), oil palm, spices, and vegetables such as French beans or snow peas.

Source: Joshua Ramisch

(e.g., cultural, social, organizational, and administrative) between the pilot and replication sites.

Participatory rural appraisal

Unlike the grand schemes for rural change promoted by community development or IRD, 'participatory rural appraisal' (PRA) is more of a conceptual framework for rural development in the South that stresses putting 'farmers first' and 'handing over the stick [of authority and control]' to local communities. An approach popularized by Robert Chambers (1983), it grew out of holistic research traditions such as farming systems research (FSR) and rapid rural appraisal (RRA) to reflect critically on the failure of most rural development programs in the 1970s and 1980s to substantially improve rural livelihoods in large parts of the South.

The assumption is that top-down planning without the adequate involvement of concerned stakeholders (particularly the local population) was one of the core reasons for the failure of previous approaches. The PRA paradigm seeks to incorporate local communities in analyzing, planning, and implementing their own development programs. The key to PRA, which Robert Chambers repeatedly emphasized and which stands in contrast to the earlier community development approach, is that 'experts' change their attitudes towards local people: facilitators should act as conveners and catalysts without dominating local processes. While not a strict method but rather a family of approaches, methods, and behaviours, PRA is now a standard tool for many development agencies that promote community development.

Development initiatives that put a stronger emphasis on rural people's voice and ways of supporting governments to respond to those voices have been the 1990s and 2000s answers to the large-scale IRD approach. Nonetheless, their success has been mixed. Weaknesses that have been identified in relation to these more recent approaches include inadequate ownership of the processes by government (e.g., too much has been devolved to isolated NGOs) and consequently weak links with the macro policy environment and the wider processes of governance. These rural development initiatives also have the tendency—usually because of the disciplinary focus of the implementing team or their limited resources—to see the 'rural poor' mainly as 'farmers'. Such a restricted perspective limits the opportunities to address wider aspects of rural livelihoods, such as the roles of the rural poor as labourers and consumers. Finally, there are also many problems related to sustaining such interventions once their external funding comes to an end.

'Participation' itself is now also criticized as having become a 'new tyranny' (Cooke and Kothari 2001) of suffocating rhetoric and routines that do not actually provide the tools or space for community empowerment. Translating the rhetoric of participation into practice has often proved much more complicated (or demanded considerably more resources and dedication) than proponents initially thought. This leads to a cynical view that many projects effectively dress up their top-down, blueprint activities in the current politically correct rhetoric of 'participation', thereby debasing the potential for 'truly' participatory work to develop. Critics would also argue that the language of participation has strayed far from its emancipatory roots and has essentially been co-opted for utilitarian and instrumental purposes: indeed the World Bank's online 'Participatory sourcebook' is now the largest repository of participatory writing and research.

Sustainable livelihoods

The 'sustainable livelihoods' approach (see Box 18.1) is the latest attempt to confront the issues of rural poverty in as holistic a manner as possible (Ellis 2000). Its greatest value, according to its backers, is that it challenges the 'farming first' mentality of previous approaches and considers instead the full range of livelihood strategies being pursued in rural areas. Even in agricultural countries, such as most of sub-Saharan Africa, where the persistent image is of subsistence farmers, non-farm (often non-rural) sources may already account for about half (40 to 60 per cent) of average household income and seem to be growing in importance (Barrett, Reardon, and Webb 2001, 316). This means that it is misleading to assume that just because the rural poor happen to be engaged in farming (even if fairly regularly), they are therefore 'farmers' or are automatically interested in investing in means to improve those farms with new agricultural technologies.

Clearly, this perspective draws heavily on Chambers's work (1983) on the multiple realities of rural poverty, which is shown to be not merely an outcome of financial or nutritional deprivation but, more important, of one's exclusion from political or institutional processes. Sen's definitive work on famines (1981) is also crucial: his argument is that famines occur not because of a lack of food but rather because of inequalities in people's rights (their 'entitlements') to access or distribute that food. Finally, we can see roots in the ideas of Boserup and the understanding that decisions about technology are rationally made with reference not only to environmental variables (population density, land quality and availability) but also to socio-economic ones (access to markets, policy or institutional settings).

The livelihoods framework does allow us to better describe and understand the processes occurring in the rural context (see Box 18.4). However, it is not yet clear whether the sustainable livelihoods approach will be better able to master the interdisciplinary complexity that ultimately limited the implementation of holistic approaches such as 'community development' or IRD in the past. Thus, while the sustainable livelihoods framework is currently de rigueur among rural development donors, such support may not be sustained if (as was the case with previous 'integrated' approaches in the 1950s and 1970s) 'interdisciplinary collaboration' means funding potentially critical (or at least sceptical) social research and disciplinary experts who are fundamentally working towards different agendas.

Finally, it is also worth noting that the sustainable livelihoods approach currently vies with a quite different stream of thinking about rural development—namely, the 're-branding' since 1999 of structural adjustment as Poverty Reduction Strategy Papers (PRSPs). These commitments by aid-receiving nations are typically structured quite explicitly on sectoral bases, meaning that their approach to rural poverty remains heavily centred on agriculture. Livelihoods research suggests, of course, that rural poverty reduction depends on inter-sector mobility and adaptability (Ellis 2000, 532). However, the PRSPs do not acknowledge this by, for example, encouraging rapid urban and non-farm growth in low-income agrarian economies but rather stick to liberal market orthodoxies, such as 'linking farmers to markets'.

CHALLENGES

To synthesize across the themes already discussed—the complex nature of 'rural' and 'local' livelihoods, the diverse histories of rural transformation, and the ever-changing approaches to rural development—we will consider three concluding issues. First, must rural development necessarily view the rural world in crisis? Second, what is the potential for agriculture-led development? And third, is the rural still important in a world of multi-locational households pursuing diverse livelihoods?

The 'rural' in crisis

We began by demonstrating the continuing importance of rural poverty, which remains widespread even in the vast majority of countries considered by the World Bank (2007d) to be 'transforming' from agrarian to urban and industrial foundations. This should be motivation enough to pursue a development agenda focused on 'rural' issues, even if there were not further evidence suggesting that rural communities in the Global South are likely to be among those most affected by climate change, HIV/AIDS, and deteriorating terms of trade for the commodities they produce (Ashley and Maxwell 2001).

However, as mentioned above, definitions of the 'rural' that cast it in a subordinate, victim's role relative to the power of urban, metropolitan

BOX 18.4   GENDER DIMENSIONS OF HOUSEHOLD LIVELIHOODS

While it is convenient to describe 'households' as if they were units, they are often fraught with internal dynamics and tensions. Often the most important divisions within households are gendered, although age differences may also intersect powerfully with gender in decision-making and power over household resources such as land and income. The livelihoods framework allows us to look inside the household and its multiple activities to see, for example, who has the power to decide about cropping patterns and labour allocation and who has the power to refuse such decisions. In processes of rural development, which involve the introduction of new resources or knowledge alongside the introduction of new labour demands or adaptations, decisions about allocating these benefits and burdens within the household involve significant internal bargaining and negotiation.

For example, even if household incomes are rising, the welfare of women and children can worsen. Consider that in many societies, women have the primary responsibility for food preparation, child care, and other domestic tasks such as cleaning and fetching water and fuel. In much of sub-Saharan Africa, women are the main agricultural workers and suppliers of food for the household (to the extent that it is often conceptually useful to refer to 'the farmer and her husband' rather than abiding by the patriarchal assumption that the household head is the farmer). If the labour demands of introducing new crops or agricultural activities fall mainly on women, they will either have to work much harder than they already do, reduce the time spent caring for children, or both (see chapter 5).

While some crops may be known culturally as 'women's' crops, we do not know in advance whether a new activity will also be considered 'women's'. Very often, cash crops that produce revenue (such as tea, coffee, or sugar cane) are considered 'men's'. However, even staple crops, such as maize, rice, or vegetables, might also become controlled by men if they are commercialized. 'Household' decisions to switch land from staple crops to marketed ones may therefore be hotly contested, affecting women's rights over land and its produce, which could in turn have implications for food consumption and allocation within the household. Likewise, intergenerational disputes about labour allocation and whether (or how) to subdivide the household's land can often be pivotal in decisions by the younger generation to migrate out of rural areas.

---

knowledge are inherently and dangerously partial. Consider, for example, how the Ukambani region of Kenya—a hilly, agro-pastoral territory just east of Nairobi that is home to the Akamba people—has been portrayed for more than a century as going through 'crisis' (see Table 18.2). Note that the interpretation of the external phenomena *as* crisis is heavily structured by the prevailing rural development preoccupation(s) of the time. Note also that the official response (of colonial or independent Kenyan governments) has also frequently acted not to resolve the 'crisis' but to further its own goals. The result of such overly simplistic solutions to single problems appears to be the creation of yet more crises (Rocheleau, Steinberg, and Benjamin 1995).

Against this image of constant 'crisis' in which rural people are forever doing something

Table 18.2 'Crisis' in Ukambani, Kenya, from 1890 to the present day

Years	External phenomena	Internalized definition of crisis	Official response
1890–World War I	Rivalry between colonial powers	Justifying English settlers' privileged access to land and control of commodity production	Disruption of Akamba land tenure system
	Equation of poverty, 'high' population densities, and 'primitive' cultivation with disease	Identification of 'irrational', disease-prone Akamba cattle-rearing practices on crowded reserves	Further land alienation and segregation of Akamba society
1920s and 1930s	Equation of 'poor agricultural practices' with soil erosion	Identification of 'destructive' Akamba agricultural practices	Forced terracing and Akamba crop production limited by quotas
1940s and 1950s	Wartime and post–World War II First World resource needs	Identification of 'under-production' on Akamba reserves; recognition of 'land hunger' as a source of political instability	Forced cash crop production; enclosure and privatization of land
1960s and 1970s	Competition among newly independent states in world commodity markets	Identification of 'low productivity' among Akamba farmers	Further promotion of cash cropping; concentration of land among 'efficient' producers
1980s and 1990s	Concern about declining soil quality	Identification of Akamba agricultural practices causing river and dam sedimentation	Promotion of intercropping and terracing techniques
	Concern about declining global energy resources	Identification of 'the other energy crisis' and Akamba 'over-cutting' of trees for fuel wood	Promotion of agro-forestry options (e.g., 'alley-cropping' trees with crops)
	Concern about declining global gene pool, endangered species, and endangered ecosystems	Identification of the 'threat' posed to national parks and wildlife by area residents	Increased efforts to separate parks from the rural population; conservation and agricultural policy pursued in separate spaces
2000s	Concern about global climate change	Identification of 'greenhouse gas-releasing' agricultural practices (tillage, manuring); identification of rural livelihoods 'vulnerable' to climate change	Promotion of conservation tillage, 'carbon sequestration'; livelihood diversification as 'adaptation' to changing climate?

Source: Adapted from Rocheleau et al. 1995, 1041.

'wrong' that demands immediate intervention, we can present a counter-narrative. This same region of Ukambani has also been celebrated for a seemingly remarkable recovery—from a landscape of ecological degradation and extreme soil erosion in the 1930s to a robustly populated, highly productive agricultural society in the 1990s (Tiffen, Mortimer, and Gichuki 1994). The portrayal of Machakos in *More People, Less Erosion* is entirely at odds with the crisis narrative, depicting resourceful rural people applying local knowledge and adapting social institutions to restore a degraded environment to productivity.

On the other hand, this analysis has been criticized as too simplistic, an attempt to generalize widely from a case study situated in a uniquely favoured economic context near the significant markets of Nairobi, glossing over other, still-dysfunctional elements of Akamba society. We must also be wary of accepting the myth that poor households always somehow manage to survive without resources and in the face of macroeconomic policies that foster unemployment and poverty, as if their capacity to work, draw on local knowledge, or call on networks of reciprocity were endless. However, the contrasting depictions of Ukambani highlight the need to consider the broader context of rural poverty before we insist that our latest rural development interventions represent the solutions that the rural poor urgently need.

Commodities and agriculture-led development

If the current global goals of reducing poverty— as embodied in the PRSPs and Millennium Development Goals—now depict rural development as nearly synonymous with agricultural development, there are at least three reasons to be concerned. First, despite occasional spikes (such as the current interest in using crops as 'biofuels'), the price of every agricultural commodity has fallen steadily over the long term, making the profitability of agriculture as a business questionable in the absence of subsidies (Ashley and Maxwell 2001). For example, world cereal prices have fallen in real terms by almost 50 per cent since 1970: advantageous for net food buyers but not likely to benefit food producers (the prices of inputs, such as fertilizers, have also fallen over this same time period but by only 10 per cent). Second, agriculture in many parts of the globe confronts environmental limitations, particularly in terms of soil and water (Scoones 1998). Third, diversification out of agriculture appears to be widespread and increasing, even in dynamic rural economies (Barrett, Reardon, and Webb 2001).

These observations have important implications, especially with the prevailing interest in linking farmers to markets (World Bank 2007d, chapter 5). Consider that if in many supposedly 'agricultural' countries, the current agricultural production per capita is insufficient to meet food security needs, then these needs are increasingly being met by food purchased from non-farm and non-rural sources (wage labour, remittances, reciprocity) (Barrett, Reardon, and Webb 2001; Rigg 2006). Describing rural Lesotho in the 1980s, where rural communities gained most of their livelihoods from working as migrant labour in South African mines, Ferguson (1994) points out that the conventional wisdom about farmers and markets was actually completely backwards: the rural areas of the country were not the 'suppliers' of food but rather the 'market' for it. As a result, any further penetration of markets and infrastructure (such as new roads) into Lesotho's rural areas would not raise the farm-gate prices paid to agricultural producers but rather make it even more feasible for residents of those areas to purchase food and even less attractive to grow food domestically.

Agricultural growth must certainly play a part in pathways out of poverty. Abundant evidence, most recently summarized in World Bank 2007d (cf. IFAD 2001; Ellis 2000), does show that improved or diversified agricultural production will benefit some segments of the rural poor and in some settings will stimulate the rural non-farm economy. However, we must bear in mind that targeting agriculture is necessary but not sufficient for improving the livelihoods of the 'rural poor' as a whole. Not only are non-farm activities becoming central to rural livelihoods, but there are also increasing numbers of households—in 'agricultural' countries, not just in 'transforming' ones—that have no commitment to farming whatsoever (Rigg 2006, 181).

The 'rural' and multi-locational households

A final comment addresses livelihood diversification and the supposed urban–rural divide. The importance of 'multi-locational' households, with members resident in or moving between various communities, economic sectors, and even nation-states is on the increase (McDowell and de Haan 1997). One outcome of this multi-locationality, besides blurring the boundaries between 'rural' and 'urban' identities, has been to boost the importance of remittance income from migrants as a force in rural development, equal to or surpassing that of national investment or international development assistance. In rural Mexico, Mali, or the Philippines, for example, these remittances support infrastructure development and

social services in a way that the government simply cannot, helping to build health clinics, schools, and even roads. This reality could be better supported by migration policy and financial systems to facilitate the direct transfer of funds back to rural areas.

On a deeper level, the increasing irrelevance of the artificial 'urban–rural' divide in terms of livelihoods, markets, and activities also needs to be addressed. Assumptions that productivity gains in agriculture will drive increased consumption of non-agricultural goods (e.g., Hayami and Ruttan 1985) now look flawed and incomplete. The rural non-farm economy today accounts for 40 to 45 per cent of average rural household income in sub-Saharan Africa and Latin America and 30 to 40 per cent in South Asia, with the majority of this coming from local 'rural' sources rather than resulting from urban (or transnational) migration (Start 2001, 491). The spatial designation of 'rural' may thus still be useful for locating the poor, but given the range of livelihood strategies now pursued in rural areas, 'rural' and 'urban' may not be so easily distinguished on the basis of economic activities. The non-farm opportunities in rural areas are very often of only limited viability—barely more productive than the agriculture that rural people and households may be struggling with—and deserve to be supported in their own right.

QUESTIONS FOR DISCUSSION

1. What are the core differences between 'rural' and 'urban' areas? In what ways is the distinction between them useful?

2. Explain Boserup's model of agricultural intensification and technological change and relate it to Malthus's or Marx's perspectives on rural development.

3. Discuss how the various rural development models of the past 50 years differ in terms of their conceptual approach and understanding of rural poverty. You should be able to contrast them on a number of levels: their reliance on specialist or generalist knowledge, their top-down or bottom-up orientation, the importance they ascribe to small farms or non-farm activities; and their changing emphases on technology, such as the Green Revolution or GMOs.

4. Discuss to what extent agriculture can or should lead rural development.

FURTHER READING

Boserup, E. 1965. *The Conditions of Agricultural Growth.* New York: Aldine.

Chambers, R. 1983. *Rural Development: Putting the Last First.* London: Longman.

Ellis, F. 2000. *Rural Livelihoods and Diversity in Developing Countries.* Oxford: Oxford University Press.

Hayami, Y., and V.W. Ruttan. 1985. *Agricultural Development: An International Perspective.* 2nd edn. Baltimore, MD: Johns Hopkins University Press.

Sen, A. 1981. *Poverty and Famines: An Essay on Entitlements and Deprivation.* Baltimore, MD: Johns Hopkins University Press.

World Bank. 2007. *World Development Report 2008: Agriculture for Development.* Washington: World Bank. http://go.worldbank.org/ZJIAOSUFU0 (accessed 19 October 2007).

INTERNET RESOURCES

Brazil's Landless Workers Movement: http://www.mstbrazil.org.

Centre for Information on Low External Input and Sustainable Agriculture: http://www.leisa.nl.

International Fund for Agricultural Development: http://www.ifad.org.

International Institute for Environment and Development: http://www.iied.org.

Sustainable Livelihoods: http://www.livelihoods.org.

World Bank 'Agriculture and rural development': http://www.worldbank.org/rural.

World Bank 'Participatory sourcebook': http://www.worldbank.org/wbi/sourcebook/sbhome.htm.

CHAPTER 19

DEVELOPMENT AND HEALTH

TED SCHRECKER

LEARNING OBJECTIVES

- To understand the relation between income/wealth and health and be able to critically evaluate claims about the relevance of this relation to development policy.
- To understand at a conceptual level the respective contribution of health care and social determinants of health to health status and socio-economic gradients and be able to provide a basic assessment of alternative policy directions based on this understanding.
- To be able to identify and assess the possible effects on health of development policy in areas that are superficially unrelated to health.
- To understand how globalization and the international political economy affect health in the developing world and be able to use this understanding to identify potential health impacts of policy choices made by industrialized countries and institutions like the World Bank and IMF.

INTRODUCTION: WEALTH, HEALTH, AND THE REST OF THE STORY

In the global frame of reference, most of us who live in high-income industrialized countries lead a charmed life when it comes to health. On average, Canadians can expect to live to the age of 80. Only 6 Canadian children out of every 1,000 die before the age of five. (Along with life expectancy and infant mortality, this measure—the under-five mortality rate, or U5MR—is one of the most common indicators of health status. These measures are useful for comparative purposes, even though they drastically understate differences in health status between rich and poor countries.) A Canadian woman's lifetime risk of dying from complications of pregnancy or childbirth is 1 in 8,700; for a Malawian woman, it is 1 in 7 (AbouZahra and Wardlaw 2000). Communicable diseases like tuberculosis that once were major killers are now almost unheard of, and routine immunization has either eliminated or all but eliminated scourges like pertussis and diphtheria.

Canada's health indicators, which are similar to those for most industrialized countries like Britain and the United States, stand in striking contrast to the situation in the so-called developing world. In countries classified by the World Bank as low-income, life expectancy averages 58.9 years, and U5MR is 114 per 1,000. In some poor countries, especially those in sub-Saharan Africa worst hit by the HIV/AIDS epidemic, average life expectancies are much lower (see Figure 19.6). Immunization rates in sub-Saharan Africa peaked in 1990, then plunged in some countries in the region during the decade that followed (Department of Vaccines and Biologicals 2002). These comparisons highlight one of the most basic facts about health and development: over the long term, and with important variations, health status improves in parallel with economic growth. This point can be seen from Figure 19.1, which is an updated version of a graph known as the Preston curve, named after the economist who first drew it. In the graph, most of the world's countries are represented by a circle, the area of which is proportional to the size of the country's population. The vertical axis shows life expectancy, and the horizontal axis shows the country's Gross Domestic Product (GDP) per capita, adjusted for purchasing power. The line on the graph, calculated on the basis of the country data, shows the national average life expectancy that would be anticipated at a given level of GDP per capita.

At low per capita incomes, up to about US $5,000, small increases in income tend to be associated with substantial gains in health status. Above that point, life expectancy increases con-siderably more slowly with income, although it does continue to rise. However, the relation between income and health status is not linear at any income level. Some countries do much bet-ter in terms of providing for the health of their populations than one would expect based on the averages. Mexico is one example, as suggested by its position above the line on the graph (mean-ing that life expectancy is higher than one would expect based on its statistical relation with GDP/capita); Costa Rica, which is not identified on the graph, is another example often cited in the literature. Other countries do less well in terms of the average life expectancy that they 'purchase' for their inhabitants with a given level

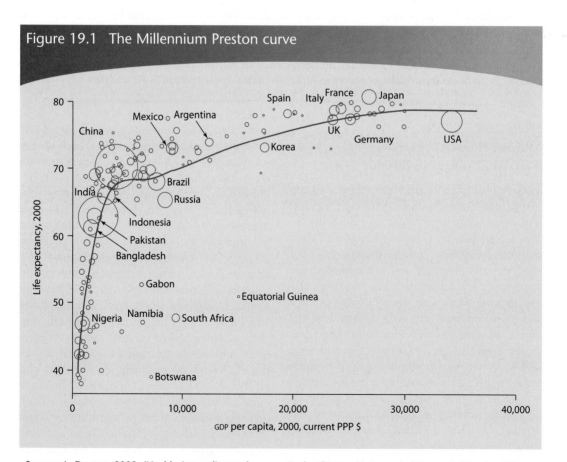

Figure 19.1   The Millennium Preston curve

Source: A. Deaton. 2003. 'Health, inequality, and economic development'. *Journal of Economic Literature XLI* (March): 116. Reproduced with permission.

Figure 19.2   Rural health care often relies on traditional healers in developing countries

Source: Jessica Schafer

of GDP per capita. Russia (see Box 19.1) and the United States are two examples—but for quite different reasons. Even more dramatic outliers are a number of southern African countries because of the ravages of the HIV/AIDS epidemic (see Box 19.3). However, the graph by itself sheds little light on *why* these differences occur or, for that matter, on the sources of the overall relation between income and health.

To oversimplify, two major lines of explanation exist. The first emphasizes access to health care, including not only treatment but also preventive interventions like immunization. Figure 19.3 shows the 100-fold difference in annual health spending per capita (from both public and private sources) between high- and low-income countries. Perspective is provided by the fact that 2.4 billion people live in low-income countries and 770 million in the least developed countries as classified by the United Nations Conference on Trade and Development (World Bank 2007c). The research literature contains numerous examples of packages of generally low-cost, low-technology interventions that, if delivered consistently, could save literally millions of lives per year (Jha et al. 2002; Bryce et al. 2005). These interventions include provision of skilled birth attendants for childbirth; oral rehydration therapy for diarrhoea; insecticide-treated bednets to reduce the transmission of malaria and anti-malarials for treatment; infant immunization; nutritional supplements; and antibiotics for such conditions as dysentery and pneumonia. Such interventions are either taken for granted in the industrialized world or else respond to conditions that are hardly ever encountered there.

The second line of explanation emphasizes **social determinants of health**: the conditions under which people live and work that affect their opportunities to lead healthy lives. Poverty, for instance, leads to inadequate nutrition: approximately 850 million people suffer from chronically insufficient caloric intake (FAO 2006). It may also create situations in which the daily routines of living are themselves hazardous: charcoal or dung smoke from cooking fires is a major contributor to respiratory disease among the world's poor. In another illustration, at least 150 residents of Manila who made their living as scavengers were killed in 2000 when a mountain of garbage at a refuse dump collapsed onto the surrounding settlement. The settlement was home to some 20,000 people—just a few of the more than four million people who live in metropolitan Manila's squatter settlements in conditions that will be experienced by a growing number of people as the developing world urbanizes. More than 850 million people now live in slums, with the number projected to rise to 1.4 billion by 2020 in the absence of effective policy interventions (UN Millennium Project Task Force 2005).

BOX 19.1   DEVELOPMENT IN REVERSE: RUSSIA

Perhaps for the first time since the influenza pandemic of 1918–19, substantial declines in the health status of national populations are now evident for reasons other than the direct consequences of war. The situation of the former Soviet Union, described by historian Stephen Cohen (2000, 41) as 'the unprecedented demodernization of a twentieth century country', is a case in point. Following the collapse of the Soviet system in 1991, the Russian Federation entered an economic depression more severe than that of the 1930s in the West. According to some authors, the promotion of market-oriented 'shock therapy' by US consultants and the IMF was an important contributor to this economic decline, which was accompanied by the accumulation of fabulous fortunes by a small number of the politically well-connected. GDP dropped by roughly 50 per cent in the course of the 1990s, and much of the existing health care system was privatized or simply fell apart. Effects included major increases in under-nutrition and in the incidence of communicable diseases like diphtheria and tuberculosis, but the most drastic increases were in non-communicable diseases (such as cardiovascular disease). These appear, in turn, related to a drastic increase in alcohol consumption (arguably in response to social disintegration). Male life expectancy dropped from 64.9 years in the mid-1980s to 57.6 years in 1994; it recovered somewhat up to the financial crisis of 1998, then dropped again to 58.5 years in 2002. In this case, as in others, trends in life expectancy almost certainly understate changes in health status. This is an oversimplified description of a complex situation, but it does suffice to show that (a) continuing improvements in population health cannot be taken for granted and (b) as in many other countries where impacts on national aggregate statistics have not been as dramatic, the uncritical application of market-oriented policies that lead to rapid social transformation and increases in insecurity can be hazardous to health (Wedel 1998; Field, Kotz, and Bukhman 2000; Sapir 2000; Field 2000; Shkolnikov et al. 2004).

These explanations are not mutually exclusive. Access to health care and social determinants of health tend to reflect similar distributions of social (dis)advantage—a point that has been made eloquently by physician/anthropologist Paul Farmer in describing clinical experience in Haiti, Mexico, and Russia (Farmer 2003). Together, access to health care and social determinants of health account for differences in health status not only among but also within nations (referred to as the **social gradient** or **socio-economic gradient**) which are often dramatic. Figure 19.4, one of many such graphs in the literature, shows a pronounced gradient in U5MR in Brazil, Egypt, India, and Kenya. Across the developing world, millions of lives could be saved each year (1.4 million in India alone) if the gradient could be eliminated—in other words, if U5MR for the entire population could be reduced to the level characteristic of the richest quintile today. This is not happening; indeed, in a number of countries, including Ghana, Nicaragua, Zambia, India, and Uganda, the gradient is becoming steeper as the health of the richest quintile of the population improves faster than that of the poor, which may be deteriorating (UNDP 2005, 62; Victora et al. 2003).

Socio-economic gradients exist worldwide. In Canada, for instance, life expectancy at birth for

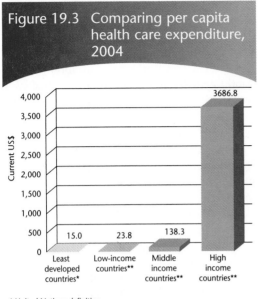

Figure 19.3 Comparing per capita health care expenditure, 2004

Current US$

| Least developed countries* | Low-income countries** | Middle income countries** | High income countries** |
| 15.0 | 23.8 | 138.3 | 3686.8 |

* United Nations definition
** World Bank definition

Source: World Bank Health 2007, accessed 31 December 2007.

Aboriginal men living on-reserve is 67.1 years as against 76 years for the Canadian male population as a whole. Diabetes is three to five times as prevalent among Aboriginal Canadians as among the rest of the population, and Aboriginal suicide rates are more than twice as high (Frohlich, Ross, and Richmond 2006). Apart from race and economics, research on health in cities indicates that socio-economic gradients have a spatial dimension as well. This reflects both the concentration of rich and poor households in certain areas and the fact that neighbourhood characteristics themselves may contribute to the gradient. Thus, the difference in average male life expectancy between some of the poorest of Montreal's 29 health districts, where almost half the population lives on an income below Canada's official low income cut-off (LICO), and the richest districts is 13 years (Agence de la santé et des services sociaux de Montréal 2007). This difference is comparable to the difference in national average life expectancy between Canada and El Salvador, Nicaragua, or Thailand.

Figure 19.4 Under-five mortality per 1,000 children by socio-economic quintile of household

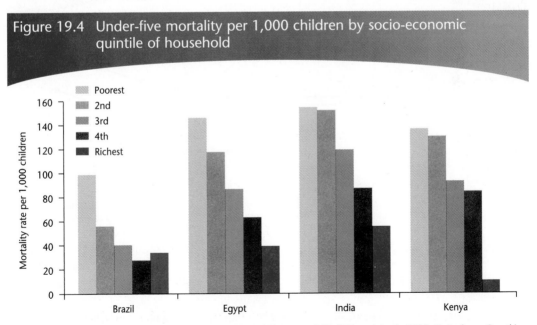

Legend:
- Poorest
- 2nd
- 3rd
- 4th
- Richest

Mortality rate per 1,000 children — Brazil, Egypt, India, Kenya

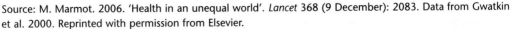

Source: M. Marmot. 2006. 'Health in an unequal world'. *Lancet* 368 (9 December): 2083. Data from Gwatkin et al. 2000. Reprinted with permission from Elsevier.

Comparable differences exist in Britain and in the United States: the difference in life expectancy between poor African-American men in downtown Washington and Chicago and white residents of the wealthy suburbs is 20 years (Dreier, Mollenkopf, and Swanstrom 2001, 72; Marmot 2006)—reflecting the interaction of high levels of economic inequality, a legacy of racial discrimination, local differences in homicide rates, and the absence of Canadian- or European-style universal health insurance.

Given the correlation between wealth and health, it is superficially plausible to argue that development policy should focus on maximizing the rate of economic growth in the expectation that health improvements will follow. Although growth is clearly important for improving population health, a single-minded policy focus on growth is inadequate and may even be counterproductive.

Improvements in health do not follow either automatically or rapidly from economic growth. Data compiled by historian Simon Szreter (Figure 19.5) show that during a period of rapid economic growth as a result of industrialization in nineteenth-century England and Wales, national average life expectancy remained constant (at 41 years) through most of the century, but in 'provincial cities' with more than 100,000 inhabitants—the crucibles of industrialization like Manchester and Birmingham—it plunged to 29 years by the 1830s and did not recover for several decades. To put the chronology into perspective, Friedrich Engels's *The Condition of the Working Class in England*, which graphically described the conditions that imperilled life and health, was published in 1845. Szreter explains the eventual improvement with reference to the provision of water and sanitation services by local governments, responding to

Figure 19.5   Life expectancy, England and Wales, nineteenth century

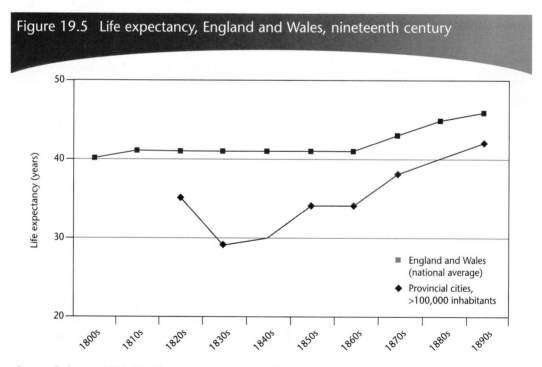

Source: S. Szreter. 1999. 'Rapid economic growth and "the four Ds" of disruption, deprivation, disease and death: Public health lessons from nineteenth-century Britain for twenty-first-century China?' *Tropical Medicine and International Health* (Wiley-Blackwell) 4 (no. 2, February): 150. Reproduced with permission from Blackwell Publishing.

demands from a 'cross-class political alliance' of the newly enfranchised working class and an industrial and mercantile bourgeoisie concerned about the health of its workforce. He concludes that '[t]he relationship between market-led, rapid economic growth and human health and welfare may be most accurately characterized as an antagonistic or, at best, a dialectical one, which is critically mediated by politics' and argues that the English experience offers important lessons for contemporary developing economies if they wish to avoid or minimize the 'four Ds' of disruption, deprivation, disease, and death (Szreter 1999). Angus Deaton, the economist who generated the updated Preston curve shown in Figure 19.1, has similarly warned that 'economic growth, by itself, will not be enough to improve population health, at least in any acceptable time' (Deaton 2006). This observation is especially important in view of the context provided by globalization.

GLOBALIZATION, DEVELOPMENT, AND HEALTH[1]

Many definitions of globalization can be found, but here it is identified as: 'A process of greater integration within the world economy through movements of goods and services, capital, technology and (to a lesser extent) labour, which lead increasingly to economic decisions being influenced by global conditions' (Jenkins 2004, 1). Globalization is partly explained by advances in technology, notably increases in computing power and drastic declines in the cost of information processing, telecommunications, and transportation. At the same time, globalization has also been promoted, facilitated, and (sometimes) enforced by political choices about such matters as trade liberalization, financial (de)regulation, and the conditions under which development assistance is provided. It did not 'just happen'.

Globalization affects health through its influence on development in several ways. It is sometimes claimed that 'globalization is good for your health, mostly' because countries that integrate into the global economy more rapidly (specifi-

cally, through trade liberalization) experience more rapid growth and are therefore better able to reduce poverty (Feachem 2001). Some countries, such as Vietnam and China, have achieved impressive growth rates and poverty reduction track records while at the same time opening their borders to imports and foreign investment and rapidly deregulating domestic markets. However, they and other fast-growing Asian economies normally have been quite selective about the process of economic integration and retain a considerable degree of state control over economic development. In Vietnam, growing economic inequality, the dismantling of a system of basic health care provision linked to agricultural production cooperatives, and the implementation of a series of market-oriented or neo-liberal health care reforms have drastically increased the cost of health care for much of the population. A similar pattern can be observed on a much larger scale in China. Indeed, Vietnam's progress in poverty reduction is markedly less impressive when one considers the irony demonstrated in research by economist Eddy van Doorslaer and his colleagues: because the World Bank's poverty estimates are based on surveys of the value of household consumption that include out-of-pocket health care costs, large numbers of households appear to have escaped poverty *because of* catastrophic medical expenses (van Doorslaer et al. 2006).

Globally, progress towards poverty reduction remains modest against a background of unprecedented abundance (Chen and Ravallion 2004; Kawachi and Wamala 2007). 'More than 40% of the world's population constitute, in effect, a global underclass, faced daily with the reality or the threat of extreme poverty' (UNDP 2005, 24). More than two decades after the **new international division of labour** was first identified (Fröbel, Heinrichs, and Kreye 1980), a genuinely global labour market is gradually emerging. The integration of India, China, and the former transition economies into the global marketplace will accelerate this process, since it roughly doubles the size of the global workforce. As national jurisdictions compete for foreign direct investment

(FDI) and outsourced production, the need to appear 'business-friendly' will almost certainly limit governments' ability to adopt and implement labour standards, health and safety regulations, or other redistributive social policy measures (Cerny, Menz, and Soederberg 2005). It is not clear where health fits into this equation, especially in a world where the workers whose health and productivity were (according to Szreter) of concern to the more enlightened industrialists of the nineteenth century now are located in multiple jurisdictions that compete against one another based at least in part on labour costs. Scholar-activist Patrick Bond argues that this abundance of labour partly explains the South African government's notorious intransigence with respect to providing antiretroviral therapy: AIDS is, after all, 'killing workers and low-income consumers at a time when South African elites in any case are adopting capital-intensive, export-oriented accumulation strategies' (Bond 2001, 179–82).

Further, one of the most widely noted effects of global economic integration is the sharp decline in the wages of, and demand for, so-called low-skilled workers that has been associated with deindustrialization in the rich countries. This pattern can be expected to repeat itself worldwide. International relations scholar Robert Cox has argued that globalization divides labour forces into a hierarchical structure of 'integrated, precarious, and excluded' workers (Cox 1999)—a pattern that clearly emerges from survey data from Brazil, Chile, Colombia, Costa Rica, El Salvador, Mexico, Panama, and Venezuela (ECLAC 2000). The World Bank, normally an enthusiast for globalization, conceded in 2006 that despite predictions for sustained global growth and the expansion of a global middle class, labour market changes will lead to increased economic inequality in countries accounting for 86 per cent of the developing world's population over the period until 2030, with the 'unskilled poor' being left farther behind (World Bank 2007b, 67–100), even before taking into account the shift of income shares from labour to capital that is evident in many national economies. The implications for health in view of what is known about socio-economic gradients and about the dynamics of public support for social provision—an issue briefly revisited at the end of the chapter—deserve careful consideration.

Workplace health is a related issue; an extensive review of studies published as of the late 1990s identified a clear preponderance of findings that precarious or contingent work is associated with deterioration in health and safety protection (Quinlan, Mayhew, and Bohle 2001a; Quinlan, Mayhew, and Bohle 2001b)—which is important, given the global increase in the prevalence of such work. At the same time, expansion of export production has been shown to create new opportunities for some workers, which despite low wages and poor working conditions offer an improvement relative to the options they would otherwise have. This point has been made with special eloquence with respect to women working in Asian **export processing zones** (Kabeer 2004; Kabeer and Mahmud 2004).

The transformation of food production and processing provides a valuable illustration of how globalization affects health and the social determinants of health. Trade liberalization has sometimes wiped out the livelihoods of small-scale agricultural producers. Food production is now often (re)organized in multinational commodity chains, with large processing firms and supermarket chains at the top and (for instance) workers at Costa Rican banana plantations or Mozambican cashew harvesters at the bottom. While the buyers engage in price competition, farmers and processing workers often pay the price in the form of low wages, insecure work, and hazardous working conditions. At the same time, far-reaching effects on diet in developing countries (sometimes referred to as the nutrition transition) are associated with rapid urbanization; the growth of foreign investment by transnational corporations in food processing, marketing, and fast food restaurants; and intensive advertising of such products as snack foods and soft drinks. (Mexicans drink more Coca-Cola per capita than people in the

BOX 19.2   THE DOUBLE BURDEN OF DISEASE

It has long been believed that countries would undergo a relatively standardized *epidemiological transition* as they grew richer: infectious or communicable diseases, many of which disproportionately affect children, would decline in importance as causes of death relative to non-communicable diseases like cardiovascular disease and cancer, which normally affect people later in life. Some of this effect is apparent from the change in slope of the Preston curve in Figure 19.1. The full picture is considerably more complicated. People outside the industrialized world are increasingly affected by a double burden of disease, as vulnerabilities to communicable disease that were (erroneously) supposed to be taken care of by economic growth coexist with exposure to industrial pollution and to risk factors for non-communicable diseases such as cardiovascular disease and diabetes, exemplified by the nutrition transition. In addition, road traffic accidents in developing countries kill more than a million people each year and injure many times that number.

Vietnam provides an illustration of the double burden. A report by the United Nations Country Team Viet Nam noted that its basic indicators of health status are high relative to its income level; in other words, it would be found above the line on the Preston curve in Figure 19.1. Nevertheless, the report warns about continuing problems with under-nutrition and communicable diseases such as acute respiratory infections and parasitic diseases in children. Furthermore, 'there has been a steady increase in non-communicable diseases such as cardiovascular diseases, cancers and diabetes; an increase in new or re-emerging diseases such as tuberculosis, HIV/AIDS, dengue fever and Japanese encephalitis; and an increase in lifestyle-related diseases and accidents (e.g., tobacco-related diseases, alcohol and drug abuse, injuries from road accidents, violence, suicide, mental health). Accidents are set to overtake infectious diseases as the most common cause of mortality—they already account for more than 20 per cent of total mortality and are the first cause of premature mortality' (United Nations Country Team Viet Nam 2003)—this in a country with a GDP per capita of just US $400 in 2000.

United States do.) Ironically, against a background of persistent under-nutrition, diets high in fat and caloric sweeteners are among the contributors to a rapid increase in overweight and obesity in many low- and middle-income countries, sometimes to levels approaching those in the industrialized world. The resulting increases in diabetes and cardiovascular disease form part of a pattern now recognized as the **double burden of disease** (see Box 19.2). Within such countries, as in much of the industrialized world, an inverse correlation often exists between overweight and education or income; in other words—and stereotypes to the contrary—it is the poor and those on limited incomes who are more likely to be overweight or obese. Some public health researchers are now calling for a co-ordinated, strategic response to the global food industry along the lines of tobacco control efforts that, at least in the industrialized world, have shown considerable success (Chopra and Darnton-Hill 2004; FAO 2004; Ezzati et al. 2005; Hawkes 2005, 2006; Popkin 2006; Rayner et al. 2007).

Financial markets offer another illustration of globalization's complex influence on social determinants of health. The debt crises that many developing countries experienced starting in the early 1980s reflected new forms of economic interconnectedness, rooted as they were in the global reach of the banking industry and in the volatility of commodity prices on international markets. (The destructive effects of the structural adjustment programs undertaken to secure loans that enabled debtor countries to reschedule their foreign debt are discussed elsewhere in this book, especially chapter 14.) The International Monetary Fund (IMF) remains an important presence in the social and economic policy choices of many developing countries, as noted in the next section of the chapter, but its demands have been supplemented and sometimes replaced by 'implicit conditionality' (Griffith-Jones and Stallings 1995) created by the hypermobility of private capital in global financial markets.

The effects of large-scale disinvestment and the resulting financial crises have been devastating, undermining the livelihoods of hundreds of millions of people. Hopkins (2006) shows that reductions in household income as a result of financial crises in Indonesia, Thailand, and Malaysia during the late 1990s led to reduced food intake, health care utilization, and education expenditure. Indicative of the potential health effects is a South Korean national survey that found substantial increases in morbidity and decreases in health service utilization following the 1997 currency crisis (Kim et al. 2003). Simultaneously, declining tax revenues led to lower public expenditure on health and education. The combined effect was to increase mortality and reduce longevity—a disturbing reprise of the findings from the original UNICEF study that documented the destructive effects of domestic austerity programs in the 1980s (Cornia, Jolly, and Stewart 1987). A comparison of the effects of financial crises in 10 countries showed that employment recovers much more slowly than GDP in the aftermath of financial crises (van der Hoeven and Lübker 2005), exacerbating their effects on economic inequality and insecurity. Predictably, given existing national and household-level distributions of power and access to resources, the impact of

financial crises is often felt first, and worst, by women (Floro and Dymski 2000; Parrado and Zenteno 2001)—one illustration among many of the need for a gender-specific approach to analyzing the health effects of globalization.

Globalization has affected health systems and access to health care in several ways apart from lender conditionalities, which are briefly addressed in the next section of the chapter. Commitments made under the General Agreement on Trade in Services (GATS) and bilateral and regional agreements that are an increasingly important element of the global trade regime have the potential to lock in privatization of health services, as well as privatization in other health-related areas, such as provision of water and sanitation, against future governments' efforts to expand public provision, although disagreement exists about the seriousness of this prospect (Pollock and Price 2003; Blouin, Drager, and Smith 2006). Driven by the US pharmaceutical and information technology industries (Sell 2003), the Agreement on Trade-Related Aspects of Intellectual Property Rights (TRIPS) was part of the package of agreements that concluded the Uruguay Round of multilateral trade negotiations and accompanied the establishment of the World Trade Organization (WTO). Harmonization of patent protection as required by TRIPS was widely viewed as creating formidable barriers to the affordability of medicines in developing countries, especially antiretroviral drugs for AIDS, and prompted a sustained and co-ordinated activist response ('t Hoen 2002). A 2001 WTO statement (the Doha Declaration on the TRIPS Agreement and Public Health) affirmed that patent harmonization under TRIPS would not always preclude compulsory licensing of patented drugs in order to protect public health—a provision of limited value to countries without their own pharmaceutical industries. A subsequent (2003) WTO interpretation specified that countries lacking their own manufacturing capacity could import generic copies of patented drugs produced elsewhere and that countries could issue compulsory licences for such export production. The availability of compulsory licensing as an option has been credited with enabling governments such as Brazil's to negotiate drastically lower prices for antiretrovirals, but the actual flexibilities provided as a result of the Doha Declaration and the 2003 interpretation had almost never been used as of mid-2007 (Haakonsson and Richey 2007; Kerry and Lee 2007).

Several factors combine to account for this. The procedures involved are complicated and cumbersome, and countries may lack the sophisticated legal expertise needed to complete them effectively. (This probably has always been understood by key industrialized-country governments and the pharmaceutical industry.) Meanwhile, the United States has successfully negotiated stronger intellectual property protection (TRIPS-plus) in bilateral and regional trade agreements (Malpani and Kamal-Yanni 2006; Fink 2006). Since an economic superpower will always have the upper hand in negotiating with most developing-country governments because of the value of even small improvements in access to its domestic markets, strong incentives exist to agree to such provisions. Finally, a minority view in the research community is that patents have never presented a substantial barrier to access to essential medicines in developing countries; on this view, the real issue is rather the overall impoverishment and fragility of health systems (Attaran 2004; 2007).

A more fundamental problem in access to medicines arises from how priorities for health research are set. Private for-profit firms, mainly pharmaceutical firms, now outspend governments worldwide on health research (Global Forum for Health Research 2004), but the objectives and accountabilities involved are quite different. The result is a continuing mismatch between health research directions and the illnesses of primary concern outside the industrialized world: the so-called **10/90 gap**, referring to the fact that 10 per cent or less of the world's health research spending is directed to the conditions that account for 90 per cent of the global burden of disease. Because they have almost no income, the poor do not constitute a market of sufficient size to attract research funding based on anticipation of commercializable products. Thus, of 1,556 new drugs

(new chemical entities) marketed between 1975 and 2004, just 21 were for tropical diseases of the poor, malaria, and tuberculosis (Chirac and Torreele 2006). '[I]t is more profitable to develop and market Viagra than to research a new drug to treat patients with visceral leishmaniasis, a fatal disease if left untreated. Such a drug is more likely to be developed through veterinary research if it has economic potential on the pet market' (Veeken and Pécoul 2000, 309). The problem is even more acute with respect to findings from research on social determinants of health: even when the effectiveness of interventions is clearly demonstrated across multiple settings, they are not amenable to packaging or patenting. It probably is, and certainly should be, impossible to obtain a patent on a method for improving the take-up of insecticide-treated bednets for preventing malarial infection or the health consequences of cash transfers to low-income households. Although the issue cannot be explored further here, new ways of matching research priorities with the health needs of those who do not have enough money to cast a meaningful vote in the global marketplace are critical to the future of health and development.

Finally, the 'brain-drain' of health professionals from developing countries, in particular those in sub-Saharan Africa, to industrialized countries such as Canada and the UK where they can earn far more is now recognized as one of the most serious problems confronting health systems. This is a special case of the globalization of labour markets, as rich countries outbid poor ones in order to save themselves the high costs of training health professionals domestically. It is further complicated by the existence of internal migration within and among developing countries, as health professionals are drawn to employment in a private sector that caters to a wealthy minority (and in some cases, to medical tourists from the industrialized world) and by a variety of 'push factors', especially intractable in terms of the policy instruments available to governments in sending countries, that lead those who have the opportunity to seek employment elsewhere (Schrecker and Labonte 2004; Chen et al. 2004; Grant 2006.

BOX 19.3   DEVELOPMENT IN REVERSE: HIV/AIDS IN SUB-SAHARAN AFRICA

No treatment of development and health would be complete without a discussion of HIV/AIDS. The AIDS epidemic has been responsible for unprecedented declines in life expectancy in much of sub-Saharan Africa over relatively short periods of time (Figure 19.6). The prevalence of HIV infection among adults is 6.1 per cent across the entire region but much higher in some countries: for instance, 18.8 per cent in South Africa and 24.1 per cent in Botswana. As many people die from AIDS every day in the region as died in the attacks on the World Trade Center and the Pentagon on 11 September 2001 (Fourie 2007). 'Today, someone living in Zambia has less chance of reaching age 30 than someone born in England in 1840—and the gap is widening' (UNDP 2005, 4). It is estimated that in sub-Saharan Africa, 12 million children have lost one or both parents to AIDS; in 2006, that figure was projected to rise to almost 16 million by 2010 (UNICEF 2006). Children 'orphaned by AIDS are at an especially heightened risk of malnourishment, illiteracy, lack of education, medical neglect, not being immunised, and being ostracised from society' (Sachs and Sachs 2004).

The destructive impacts on health and livelihoods at the household level, and the potential of AIDS to initiate a cycle of poverty and privation, are difficult to comprehend through statistics (Nolen 2007). AIDS may also undermine society-wide progress towards economic development. For instance, completion rates for primary education are already low across most of sub-Saharan Africa, and AIDS orphans clearly face special difficulties (Case, Paxson, and Ableidinger 2004; Hewett and

Figure 19.6   Effects of aids on life expectancy in five African countries, 1970–2020

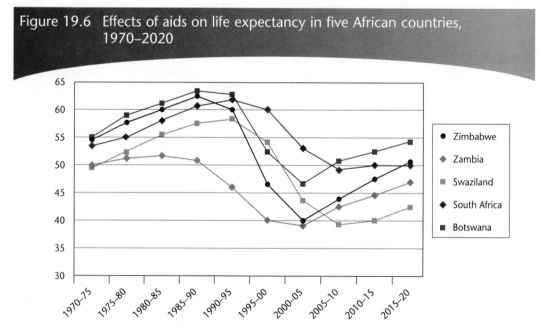

Source: United Nations World Population Prospects database, 2006 revision. Reproduced with the kind permission of UNAIDS (2006).

Lloyd 2005). South African political scientist Pieter Fourie noted in 2007 that the more apocalyptic predictions of societal collapse or state failure as a result of the epidemic have failed to materialize, that even the econometric evidence of its macroeconomic impact is equivocal, and that societies may be able to respond effectively. Warning against hasty generalizations about the epidemic's effects, he also emphasized that assessments of the epidemic's consequences need to adopt a far longer (i.e., multigenerational) time frame than is normally the case and that forms of collapse cannot be ruled out in the future.

It is clear that the AIDS epidemic underscores the need to examine how elements of the international political economy undermine health at the household and community level. According to medical anthropologist Brooke Grundfest Schoepf, by 1988 people in Zaire (now the Democratic Republic of the Congo) 'had another name for AIDS (SIDA in French) that encapsulated their understanding of its social epidemiology', which included rapid social change, endemic economic insecurity, and the subordination of women: '*Salaire Insuffisant Depuis des Années*' (Schoepf 1998, 110). More recently, De Vogli and Birbeck (2005) identified multiple pathways by which structural adjustment policies adopted by governments in response to demands from the World Bank and the IMF could increase the vulnerability of women and children in sub-Saharan Africa to HIV infection. The pathways included elimination of food subsidies, increases in economic insecurity as a result of privatization and trade liberalization, and reduced access to health care and education as a result of user charges. Similar pathways can be identified with respect to many effects of globalization more generally.

The claim is not that globalization or the IMF 'cause' HIV infection, which is far too simplistic, but rather that elements of contemporary neo-liberal social and economic policies as adopted by national governments and multilateral institutions may increase vulnerability to HIV infection—and arguably, to a variety of other communicable and non-communicable diseases as well. The need, then, is for comprehensive assessment of the possible health impacts of policies well outside the remit of health ministries—and sometimes, even outside the control of the national governments of countries within whose borders the effects will be felt. This is a formidable ethical, political, and institutional challenge for health and development studies professionals and for national governments and multilateral institutions.

OLD PLAYERS AND NEW IN DEVELOPMENT AND HEALTH

The World Health Organization (WHO) is the agency within the UN system with primary responsibility for health issues (see also chapter 10). Its 193 member-states meet annually as the World Health Assembly (WHA) to set policy, which is overseen by a 34-member executive board. It operates 147 country offices and six regional offices as well as its Geneva secretariat, staffed in all by 8,000 people. WHO operates on an annual budget of approximately US $3.3 billion. Of that amount, only a quarter is a 'core' budget from contributions assessed as part of members' UN obligations. For the balance, WHO must rely on voluntary additional contributions from member states; these contributions are not under the control of WHA, meaning that its programming and priorities are donor-driven to a degree that is often difficult to discover. By way of polemical comparison: US consumers spend approximately US $8 billion a year on cosmetics and on bathroom renovations and Europeans approximately $50 billion on cigarettes; the world's annual military spending approaches US $1 trillion.

WHO once sought leadership in promoting primary health care: a strategy for integrating prevention and treatment that was at the core of the goal of achieving 'Health for All in the Year 2000', which was endorsed by member states in 1978. However, it failed to defend this vision effectively against critics both within the medical and health communities, including WHO itself, and outside them (Brown, Cueto, and Fee 2006). Meanwhile, the much larger and richer World Bank and IMF emerged as decisive players in development policy, with major influence on health both directly and indirectly. The Bank's importance derives from its role as a source of financing—having created a Health, Nutrition and Population (HNP) department in 1970, by the end of the 1990s it was 'the single largest external source of HNP financing in low- and middle-income countries' (Preker, Feachem, and de Ferranti 2000, ix)—and from its authority as a source of technical advice, generated from a massive research budget and disseminated through transnational networks of professionals with common assumptions, training experiences, and career paths. The IMF's importance derives not only from its role as a source of last-resort financing for countries facing debt crises but also (and more significantly in the contemporary frame of reference) from the seal of approval it provides to private investors with respect to the soundness of national macroeconomic and social policy. Jeffrey Sachs, an economist with extensive experience in the field, wrote in 1998 that many developing-country governments 'rarely move without consulting the IMF staff, and when they do, they risk their lifelines to capital markets, foreign aid, and international respectability' (Sachs 1998).

The World Bank and IMF often acted in concert during the era of structural adjustment lending, demanding a relatively standard package of macroeconomic policies designed primarily to ensure that debt service payments to external creditors could be maintained. They continue to do so, albeit in somewhat different ways. For example, approval of country-generated Poverty Reduction Strategy Papers (PRSPs) by both the Bank and the Fund is required before debt relief can be obtained under the Multilateral Debt Relief Initiative (discussed elsewhere in this book and briefly in the last section of this chapter); PRSPs must then be updated periodically. This approval is also becoming a precondition for receipt of development assistance from many bilateral agencies. Consequently, as of September 2007, some 64 countries either had prepared PRSPs or were in the process of preparing them (World Bank 2007a). It is difficult to be against poverty reduction, but the nature of the exercise has raised concerns that the PRSPs process replicates earlier macroeconomic conditionalities and that its priority remains the incorporation of national economies into the global marketplace (Cheru 2001; Cammack 2004). In 2004, the leader of the team that produces the UN Conference on Trade and Development's annual least developed countries report described the PRSPs process as 'a compulsory process in which governments that need concessional assistance and debt relief from the World Bank and the IMF find out, through the endorsement process, the limits of what is acceptable policy. . . . [T]here is an inevitable tendency for Government officials to anticipate the endorsable' (Gore 2004, 282).

Now we turn to two specific topics related to the World Bank, the IMF, and health; they are relevant to the broader health impacts of neo-liberal development policies as well.

First, the World Bank and regional development banks have strongly promoted a market-oriented concept of health sector reform (HSR) that favours private provision and financing (Lister 2005), an approach viewed by some authors as contributing to the eventual demise of WHO's commitment to primary health care (Hall and Taylor 2003). Indeed, HSR was once defined as 'those activities undertaken cooperatively between the international development banks and a national government to alter in fundamental ways the nation's health financing and health provision policies' (Glassman et al. 1999). In 1987, the World

Bank endorsed a set of policy prescriptions including partial cost recovery through user charges for health services at the point of delivery, expansion of insurance as a financing mechanism, strengthening 'nongovernment [sic] provision of health services for which households are willing to pay', and decentralizing the delivery of health services (Akin, Birdsall, and de Ferranti 1987). In its widely cited *World Development Report 1993: Investing in Health*, the Bank was even clearer about its preference for markets as mechanisms for resource allocation: 'There must be a basis for believing that the government can achieve a better outcome than private markets can' in providing and financing health services (World Bank 1993b, 55); it recommended that public provision be limited to a package of low-cost interventions with demonstrated 'value for money' that could not be provided with private financing. Reinforcing this policy orientation, retrenchment in public sector health spending, along with user fees and other cost recovery measures as an alternative source of financing, were often required directly or indirectly by structural adjustment conditionalities. The Bank has recently moderated its enthusiasm for market-oriented HSR, but as the leaders of a team funded by Canada's International Development Research Centre (IDRC) to rebuild health systems in Tanzania put it: 'The era of structural adjustment may be over, but the effects of earlier damage continue to cast a long shadow' (de Savigny et al. 2004, 10).

Second, and more recently, controversy has arisen over the IMF's practice of setting public sector wage bill ceilings as part of its recipe for sound macroeconomic policies. Critics with extensive field and health sector experience, including the executive director of Médecins sans frontières (Belgium) and Kenya's assistant minister of health (Ooms and Schrecker 2005; Ambrose 2006), have argued that the effect is to prevent governments from hiring badly needed health personnel and teachers even when funds are available from development assistance. Initially, the IMF strongly disputed these claims. However, the Fund's own Independent Evaluation Office confirmed in 2007 that wage bill ceilings were often recommended, that projections of the aid that recipient governments could anticipate were consistently conservative (i.e., low), leading to excessive caution with respect to the public sector wage bill, and that in 29 sub-Saharan countries, IMF policy prescriptions meant that just 27 cents of every incremental dollar in development assistance was allocated to new programs, with the balance used for paying down domestic debt and accumulating foreign exchange reserves (Independent Evaluation Office 2007; see also Working Group on IMF Programs and Health Spending 2007). Perhaps most revealing is the Fund's consistent description of public spending on health care and education as 'fiscal expansion'. From the standpoint of textbook macroeconomics, this is entirely correct, but the effect for policy purposes is to classify health care and education together with military spending, roads (in countries where a large majority of the population do not own a vehicle), or for that matter pyramids.

WHO, the World Bank, and the IMF have been joined by various other high-profile institutions; just two of the most important are discussed here. The Global Fund to Fight HIV/AIDS, Tuberculosis and Malaria (the Global Fund) was established as a multilateral partnership by the G-8 countries in 2001 and hailed by the G-8 as promising 'a quantum leap in the fight against infectious diseases'. The Global Fund operates as a foundation with a board that includes representatives of donor and recipient governments, non-governmental organizations, and the private sector. Most of its funding comes from industrialized-country governments, and as of mid-2007, it had committed US $7.7 billion to projects that must be proposed by recipient-country applicants and approved by a scientific review panel. The Global Fund was established at least partly to circumvent what were seen as the excessively bureaucratic routines of WHO; it has been criticized for emphasizing 'vertical', disease-specific programs at the expense of efforts to support integrated primary health care, although much of this criticism remains corridor talk rather than research-based publication. Further, it can be argued that this problem is less serious than the Global Fund's severe lack of resources, relative to its own and others' estimates of the resources needed, and the fact that without any guarantee of stable long-term funding, it relies on periodic replenishment meetings where it in effect passes around a hat. Stephen Lewis, the former UN special envoy for AIDS in Africa, has also charged that 'African governments are being discouraged from asking for what they really need from the Global Fund. The word is out, and it's often reinforced by Western diplomats at country level—don't ask for too much, because the Global Fund just doesn't have the resources. . . . [G]overnments are reluctant to ask for what they really need, lest their whole proposal be turned down' (quoted in Cook 2006).

The Bill and Melinda Gates Foundation, established by one of the world's richest men, signals what may be a longer-term shift to supporting development and health through private wealth rather than public resources. Even before its windfall from the wealth of Warren Buffett, the Gates Foundation's resources enabled it to spend more annually than the core budget of the WHO; health promotion scholar and consultant Ilona Kickbusch has described this as 'a scandal of global health governance' (Kickbusch and Payne 2004). How, and how effectively, has the Gates Foundation spent its money? Systematic evaluations are not yet available, but one major initiative involves the Grand Challenges in Global Health program, launched in 2003 in collaboration with the US National Institutes of Health to address the lack of research on new interventions to address diseases of the poor. Despite the urgent need for such research, the University of Toronto's Anne-Emanuelle Birn, a specialist in the history of private support for public health, is highly critical of the initiative. She argues that its focus on developing new technologies (for example, genetic modifications to prevent disease-transmitting insects from reproducing and new therapies to address chronic infections) fails either to make use of what

is already well and widely known about the social determinants of health or to address the lack of resources that prevents more rapid diffusion of demonstrably effective, low-cost existing technologies (Birn 2005). This is symptomatic of a more fundamental tension between biomedically and socio-economically oriented perspectives on how best to improve population health in the developing world—a tension that is likely to be one of the key issues in health and development research and policy in the coming years. Against this background, opportunities for meaningful debate about global health priorities[2]—already constrained by the neo-liberal allegiances of key industrialized-country governments and financial market players—may be further limited.

INVESTING IN HEALTH, SECURITY, EQUITY, OR ???: CRITICAL CHOICES AHEAD

Until recently, if conventional development policy wisdom was concerned with health at all, it treated improvements in health status as a routine accompaniment of economic growth, with little special status or importance attached to spending on health care or social determinants of health. The Commission on Macroeconomics and Health, an ad hoc panel established by WHO in 2000 to examine the evidence linking health and development, turned conventional wisdom on its head by demonstrating that this approach might well be counterproductive. Ill-health not only results from poverty but also limits the ability of individuals, households, and entire societies to escape from poverty (Commission on Macroeconomics and Health 2001). Households faced with the choice between paying for medical care and selling off assets critical to their economic survival fall into a 'medical poverty trap' (Whitehead, Dahlgren, and Evans 2001), creating a vicious circle of poor nutrition, abandoned education, and still more illness that compromises the potential for future growth at the societal level. More than 90 per cent of the world's approxi-

Figure 19.7 Family collecting contaminated water in Dhaka, Bangladesh

Source: Shehzad Noorani/The Canadian Press

mately one million annual deaths from malaria, for instance, now occur in sub-Saharan Africa; the direct and indirect negative effects on economic growth can be estimated using a variety of methods, which yield different results but they are clearly substantial (Sachs and Malaney 2002).

The commission therefore promoted 'investing in health for economic development', which became a subsequent theme of WHO activity but appears to have had limited influence on development policy more generally. It estimated the cost of a package of basic, demonstrably effective interventions that could save 'at least 8 million lives *each year* by the end of this decade [i.e., by 2010], extending the life spans, productivity and economic wellbeing of the poor' at US $34 per capita per year (US $40 in 2007 dollars). The commission warned that this figure was 'on the

low end of the range of estimates' of the cost of providing basic health services. As noted earlier, the health budget in many countries is only a fraction of this amount; further, not all of that budget supports services for the poor or otherwise vulnerable—reflective of a general and ironic trend in which the poorer the country, the larger the proportion of health expenditure that comes out of the pockets of patients, who may have to compromise their households' economic futures to secure even minimal care today. The commission concluded that in order to address this problem, development assistance funding specifically for health care would need to rise to US $27 billion by 2007, with continuing increases thereafter. Despite substantial increases, as of 2004 (the most recent year for which figures are available) it stood at just $12 billion (Schieber, Fleisher, and

Gottret 2006). Consistently inadequate support for the Global Fund is just part of this picture.

Jeffrey Sachs, who chaired the commission, subsequently estimated that poor sub-Saharan countries might be capable of generating US $50 per capita in total annual public revenue. 'This tiny sum must be divided among all government functions. . . . [T]he health sector is lucky to claim $10 per person per year out of this, but even rudimentary health care requires roughly four times that amount. . . . Foreign aid is therefore not a luxury for African health. It is a life-and-death necessity' (Sachs 2007). The argument is not relevant only to sub-Saharan Africa—think, for example, of Haiti, the poorest country in the western hemisphere, or Vietnam, where public sector spending on health care was just US $4 per capita as recently as 2001—or to health systems. Rather, its savage arithmetic underscores the urgency of substantial and long-term redistribution of life-saving resources to the developing world.

A similar point was made in two high-profile syntheses of research evidence on development policy published in 2005: the reports of the Commission for Africa, set up by the British government in advance of the Gleneagles G-8 Summit, and the UN Millennium Project, established as an advisory body to the secretary-general on achieving the Millennium Development Goals (MDGs) endorsed by the General Assembly in 2000. Among other findings, each report called for an approximate doubling of the industrialized world's development assistance spending, including a several-fold increase in aid for health. The Commission for Africa was also explicit in recommending that the elimination of user fees—as noted earlier, a central element of earlier efforts to 'reform' health systems—be supported by long-term development assistance commitments. Indeed, such commitments of financial support are essential to ensure that the increased use of services that follows the elimination of financial barriers does not create demands that already overstressed public health systems cannot meet. Each report directly challenged fashionable scepticism about the value of

development assistance, crucially emphasizing *donor* policies and practices as constraints on aid effectiveness. The Millennium Project, in particular, further acknowledged the validity of two decades of critiques by development researchers and civil society organizations on the issue of external debt: '[D]ozens of heavily indebted poor and middle-income countries are forced by creditor governments to spend large parts of their limited tax receipts on debt service, undermining their ability to finance investments in human capital and infrastructure. In a pointless and debilitating churning of resources, the creditors provide development assistance with one hand and then withdraw it in debt servicing with the other' (UN Millennium Project 2005, 35). At the very least, then, these two reports should have shifted the burden of proof away from proponents of increased aid, assigning it instead to those who invoke the limited 'absorptive capacity' of recipient countries (which is, in large measure, itself a consequence of past resource scarcities) or insist that health systems and social provision must be 'sustainable' in the sense that they do not rely on external resources.

The preceding discussion, along with the analysis provided in chapter 14, suggests emerging agreement (consensus is too strong a term) on the need for substantial international redistribution of resources to support development and health care and specific commitments to improving social determinants of health. The international policy response has clearly been inadequate and incomplete (Schrecker, Labonte, and Sanders 2007): why have similar problems often characterized the domestic policies even of countries that have considerable autonomy in the context of the global economy? For example, in the 2001 Abuja Declaration and Plan of Action on HIV/AIDS, Tuberculosis and Other Related Infectious Diseases, the member states of the African Union (AU) established the goal of increasing their health spending to 15 per cent of the general government budget. As of 2005, most AU countries had not met this target; for many, health spending remained under 10 per cent of the budget (WHO data cited in Working Group on IMF Programs and Health Spending 2007, 19–20). The demands of the global economy and the IMF clearly provide just part of the explanation.

Only a first cut at answering these questions can be undertaken here. The logic of investing in health is entirely consistent with neo-liberal pre-occupation with markets and the idea that policies should 'pay for themselves'—for example, by improving a country's human capital stock and thereby contributing to economic growth. In the context provided by globalization, it may well be that only *some* people's health is a worthwhile investment, based on anticipated returns on investment in their 'human capital'. An especially dramatic illustration is provided by South African economist Nicoli Nattrass (2004), who argues that because '[t]wo of the three leading South African macroeconomic models predict that the [HIV/AIDS] pandemic will increase per capita income because the impact will be greater on population numbers than on economic growth', South African elites see little benefit to themselves in paying taxes to support either prevention or publicly financed treatment of HIV infection. They view themselves as being at minimal risk, and in any event have access to private care and insurance if they do become infected. This may, Nattrass suggests, help to explain the country's notorious reluctance to provide publicly financed antiretroviral treatment—a perspective that complements Bond's view of the relations between AIDS policy and integration into the global economy. In the absence of countervailing influences, politically decisive pluralities in the industrialized world and the policy-makers who respond to them will almost certainly undertake comparable calculations with respect to lives that might be saved half a world away by modest expenditures on health care and social determinants of health.

Since 11 September 2001, health (like everything else) has been viewed through a 'security lens' with increasing frequency, so one might expect some policy directions to follow. It is sometimes asserted that ill-health, in particular large-scale socially disruptive epidemics like HIV infection in some parts of the world, creates a hospitable political context for insurgency and terrorism. Such 'securitization' of disease (O'Manique 2005) is tactically appealing as a way of getting policy-makers' attention, but the underlying factual claims are difficult to verify. Further, the appeal to security is ethically troubling, because it is at least as likely to lead to appeals for new and more effective ways of containing the (actual or perceived) threat as to generate interest in ameliorating the conditions that lead to ill-health or in providing more effective treatment. Even in situations where poverty-related threats of social disintegration are considerably more immediate, as in some internal and regional conflicts in Africa, the international community's response has been minimal when measured in terms of new resources. Another security-related claim is exemplified by the effort to justify increased development assistance on the grounds that '[i]nfectious diseases, security threats, illicit weapons and drugs, and environmental problems cross the borders separating rich countries from poor countries as readily as diseases crossed between rich and poor areas of Britain's major industrial centres in the 1830s' (UNDP 2005, 78). Although superficially credible in the age of SARS and intensified planning for an influenza pandemic, the observation applies only to a limited number of cases (communicable diseases that can be transmitted through casual contact during a period before symptoms develop) and certainly not to the increasing burden of non-communicable disease and injury in low- and middle-income countries (see Box 19.2). As in the case of investing in health, political leaders and electorates usually seem well aware of who is at risk, and why, within their own borders. More diffuse efforts to incorporate the health of people half a world away into a 'human security agenda' (Chen and Narasimhan 2003) raise even more immediately the question of *whose* security, and against what kind of threats, should be considered a priority and command the necessary political support.

WHO's multinational Commission on Social Determinants of Health, established in 2005, addressed this question by way of a conceptual framework that adopts **health equity** as 'the explicit ethical foundation of the Commission's work' (Solar and Irwin 2007, 7). Building on a small but powerfully argued recent literature (see, for example, Braveman and Gruskin 2003a, 2003b; Braveman 2006), the framework defines health equity as 'the absence of unfair and avoidable or remediable differences in health among populations or groups defined socially, economically, demographically or geographically' (Solar and Irwin 2007, 7). It elaborates on the significance of social determinants of health with reference to a model for explaining disparities in health that emphasizes economic and political context, crucially including 'those central engines in society that generate and distribute power, wealth and risks' (Diderichsen, Evans, and Whitehead 2001, 16). Understood in this manner, health equity is a far-reaching, potentially subversive concept and therefore especially valuable. Unless the highly unequal distribution of income, wealth, and opportunities to lead a healthy life both within and across national borders is taken to be a fact of nature, *most* health disparities not associated with genetic vulnerabilities that are unaffected by alterable environmental factors are revealed as inequitable and demanding policy attention.

Two observations follow from this discussion. First, policy-makers have the option to organize policies around investing in health, health and security, or health equity—or, of course, to combine these organizing principles. Each one, however, implies distinct priorities, strategies, program delivery modalities, and (especially) beneficiaries. For example, health equity suggests the need to reduce the slope of socio-economic gradients or eliminate them altogether. Investing in health might prioritize improving the health of those who are already relatively healthy, young, comparatively well educated given the context, and (especially in regions of high HIV prevalence)

seronegative; based on their future economic productivity, they are likely (as Bond suggests) to yield the best return on investments of limited health budgets. It is more difficult reliably to describe the distributional implications of a security-based approach to development and health, partly because the factual claims on which this perspective rests are not especially robust. It is clear that in many situations, strategies of containment would receive priority, even when directed at populations that are already vulnerable or marginalized—in direct contrast to what might be expected from an equity-oriented approach.

Second, with rare exceptions *none* of these perspectives is clearly evident in the recent development policies of the industrialized world as they affect health (Schrecker, Labonte, and Sanders 2007). Exceptions include the Finnish government's role in hosting, jointly with the government of Tanzania, the Helsinki Process on Globalization and Democracy (2007) and the positions on development and equity taken by the Norwegian government elected in 2006. For instance, Norway's official policy as of 2007 was to oppose development conditionalities that promote privatization, support only trade policies that will not prevent poorer countries from developing into 'welfare societies' similar to Norway's own, and take a leadership role in seeking 'new global financing sources that can contribute to a redistribution of global wealth and the strengthening of the UN institutions' (Government of Norway 2006). Although Finland and Norway are high-income countries, they are at best 'semi-peripheral' with respect to centres of power such as the G-8, the World Bank, and the IMF, where policy continues to be driven by the economic and geopolitical interests of the powerful, nationally and globally. Thus, 'why care?' will remain a central ethical and political question in global health for some time to come and one that is logically prior to issues of program design, implementation, or evaluation.

QUESTIONS FOR DISCUSSION

1. What are the strengths and limitations of the argument that the best development policy for health is the one that maximizes economic growth?

2. Identify one common consumer product that you own and/or use regularly: for example an MP3 player, a cellphone, or an item of 'designer' clothing. Using the Internet, try in one hour to find out as much as possible about where the product was made, under what conditions, and how those conditions affect the health of the people manufacturing, processing, or assembling the product. (This is also an excellent starting point for group discussions on globalization.)

3. You are a senior official in the health ministry of a low- or middle-income country, and you are trying to help the health minister make the case for an increase in your ministry's budget to cabinet or parliamentary colleagues. Would you be most likely to use arguments based on investing in health, on health and security, or on health equity? Why?

4. You are a senior official in a Canadian department or agency with responsibilities for international development and health, and you are trying to help the cabinet minister in question make the case to cabinet and parliamentary caucus colleagues for new, long-term commitments of development assistance for health. Would you be most likely to use arguments based on investing in health, on health and security, or on health equity? Why?

FURTHER READING

Farmer, P. 2003. *Pathologies of Power: Health, Human Rights and the New War on the Poor.* Berkeley: University of California Press. A powerful description of how disparities in power and resources affect life and death 'on the ground' by a physician and medical anthropologist who spends much of his time in clinical practice.

Whitehead, M., T. Evans, F. Diderichsen, A. Bhuiya, and M. Wirth, eds. 2001. *Challenging Inequities in Health: From Ethics to Action.* New York: Oxford University Press. Although slightly dated, this book provides a valuable combination of theory, linking ethics with public policy, and carefully argued case studies, some of which will be useful models for students writing on health-related topics.

INTERNET RESOURCES

National Library of Medicine, PubMed: http://www.ncbi.nlm.nih.gov/sites/entrez. A searchable bibliographic database on medicine and health. Once confined almost exclusively to medical and scientific journals, it now indexes a growing number of journals in the social sciences and law. An indispensable first step for research on specific health topics.

People's Health Movement, Medact, and Global Equity Gauge Alliance. *Global Health Watch: An Alternative World Health Report*: http://www.ghwatch.org. A critical, equity-oriented perspective on health and development compiled by a consortium of academic researchers and NGOs. The first (2005–6) edition is available on-line, and the second is in preparation at this writing.

United Nations Development Programme. *Human Development Reports* (annual): http://hdr.undp.org. Although not exclusively concerned with health, the reports are probably the single most useful compendium of material on development and human needs, including social determinants of health.

Labonte, R., and T. Schrecker. 2007. 'Globalization and social determinants of health', parts 1–3, *Globalization and Health*: http://www.globalizationandhealth.com/content/3/1/5; http://www.globalizationandhealth.com/content/3/1/6; http://www.globalizationandhealth.com/content/3/1/7. A three-part open-access article based on work originally done for the WHO Commission on Social Determinants of Health.

World Health Organization: http://www.who.int. A valuable source of scientific and technical information as well as some critical perspectives on health and development; see in particular the *Bulletin of the World Health Organization* (http://www.who.int/bulletin/en/). Reports and background papers from its Commission on Social Determinants of Health are available at http://www.who.int/social_determinants/en.

NOTES

1. Some of this material is adapted from a longer discussion in three open-access journal articles (Labonte and Schrecker 2007a; 2007b; 2007c) in which more extensive documentation is provided.
2. For a discussion of how and why 'global health' has largely superseded 'international health' in policy discourse, see Brown, Cueto, and Fee 2006.

CHAPTER 20

EDUCATION AND DEVELOPMENT: THE PERENNIAL CONTRADICTIONS OF POLICY DISCOURSE

RICHARD MACLURE, REFAAT SABBAH, AND DANIEL LAVAN

LEARNING OBJECTIVES

- To understand different perspectives concerning the relation between education and development.
- To understand the rationales of diverse institutional actors—governments, international donor agencies, NGOs, and civil society organizations—in supporting the expansion of education in developing countries.
- To understand the inherent contradictions of education as essential for progressive social change while simultaneously serving to reinforce prevailing political and socio-economic relations.
- To appreciate the political, financial, and cultural dynamics of international aid to education.

EDUCATION FOR DEVELOPMENT: COMPETING PERSPECTIVES

Education and international development have long been regarded as interconnected and mutually reinforcing. As such, throughout the developing world, educational policies are replete with references to the critical role of education in ensuring the realization of national development strategies. Yet while few question the connection between education and development, for several decades there have been strikingly different views concerning the nature and purposes of education and its relationship to national and international strategies of development. This diversity of views can be encapsulated in two fundamentally contradictory perspectives that have never been satisfactorily reconciled and yet ironically have long been incorporated in educational policy discourse throughout the developing world.

One common view is that education entails the transmission of knowledge and skills deemed to be necessary in the world of work and for the broader purposes of economic growth and national unity. This essentially utilitarian perspective portrays education as a social investment designed to ensure that succeeding generations are able to assume their place as productive citizens within an established socio-economic order. Implicitly, therefore, through an elaborate system of sequential age-related classes, standardized curricula, quantifiable testing of student performances, and the subsequent certification of those who successfully complete specific stages of schooling, a key function of education is to legitimate a long-standing and still predominant view of development as primarily an economic phenomenon that best occurs in circumstances of political and social stability. This view of education adheres to an abiding structuralist position concerning the status quo as a basis of stability and continuity and the notion of development as a linear process of growth defined by governing elites and implemented by those with technical expertise. Not only is this utilitarian perspective strongly endorsed by governments and international aid agencies, but it is also entrenched ideologically and normatively among those who are involved as producers, deliverers, and consumers of education (Jones 2007; Ramirez and Boli 1987). From ministry officials, curriculum planners, and teachers to community leaders, parents, and pupils, there is a strong sense that education—and particularly formal schooling—is a competitive process with direct implications for the financial security and social status of individuals and families within the context of established political economies.

At the same time, however, as much of the public also recognizes, the economic and political status quo is never fully equitable but instead is generally skewed in favour of those endowed with wealth and power, often to the detriment of social groups that are poor and politically marginalized. In such circumstances, therefore, critics have long argued that national systems of educa-tion play a fundamentally hegemonic role by legit-imating the vested interests of those who benefit from prevailing political and socio-economic arrangements while simultaneously depoliticizing the frustrations and social difficulties experienced by those compelled to struggle in situations of structural disadvantage (Clayton 2006). Conse-quently, the utilitarian view of education must reg-ularly contend with an alternative perspective that conceives the main purpose of education as addressing the inequalities and injustices that are embedded in the larger society (Samoff 2007). In accordance with this transformation perspective, education should be a force for liberation, encour-aging learners to regard the world critically and to acquire the skills and aptitudes necessary for generating fundamental social change. This is a view of education as a form of counter-hegemony

Figure 20.1   School children in Nampula, Mozambique,1996

Source: Alternatives/Dominic Morissette

and highlights its role in empowering disenfranchised social groups to challenge and radically alter prevailing structures and processes that have reinforced their marginalized status (Maclure 2006; Mayo 2006).

Although these two contrasting perspectives of education are strikingly divergent, they have nonetheless for many years been intertwined in educational plans and programs throughout the developing world. That such opposing views of education can coexist is in part a consequence of the predominant educational policy discourse articulated by developing country states and by the international organizations that provide them with assistance. Given the profoundly institutionalized nature of post-colonial education in developing countries, governing authorities generally regard national systems of education as indispensable for ensuring the achievement of social and economic development as sanctioned by donor country states and international aid regimes. Simultaneously, however, governments and international donors are generally quite prepared to acknowledge the well-documented inequities and social injustices that exist. As a way of partially responding, national and international policy-makers routinely refer to the moral imperative of education to contribute to the development of more equitable and democratic societies. Thus, official policy discourse generally embraces the notion of education as an agent of social change and social justice. Yet this rhetorical reconciliation of utilitarian and transformative perspectives almost never leads to an upset of the established bureaucratic structures and the competitive, selection-oriented processes of national school systems. Instead, the incorporation of the ideal of education as a catalyst for societal transformation in official policy pronouncements has essentially served to depoliticize the concept of educational change and to render it in the popular imagination as a process that reinforces officially sanctioned development strategies.

In this chapter, we will discuss how, despite the major political, economic, and cultural changes that have swept the globe and caused major fluctuations in the fortunes of educational systems over the past half century, educational policy-making in developing countries has consistently embraced both the utilitarian and transformation perspectives, all the while ensuring that the transformation perspective is rendered subservient to the utilitarian view of education.

THE ERA OF EDUCATIONAL EXPANSION AND CONSENSUS

The merging of utilitarian and transformative perspectives in educational policy discourse began in the late 1950s with a set of assumptions concerning the relation between publicly funded school systems and strategies of national development. In the context of the Cold War and the demise of old imperial regimes, state-funded schooling came to be viewed as a critical investment in modernization and economic growth. A host of empirical studies were produced that demonstrated the significance of formal education in fostering individual modernity and in transmitting the skills and aptitudes necessary to ensure workforce diversity and productivity (Fuller 1991; Inkeles and Smith 1974). Similarly, the role of education as a form of human capital development was substantiated by cost-benefit analyses that repeatedly demonstrated the positive returns of ever-higher levels of schooling for individuals (as reflected in types of employment and earned incomes) and for nation-states (in terms of the correlation between numbers of school graduates and Gross Domestic Product) (for example, Schultz 1971; Psacharopoulous 1973). Although enrolment in school often entailed some opportunity costs for households, this was generally offset by state subsidies that covered most of the capital and recurrent costs of schooling and by widespread evidence of the personal rewards that accrued to individuals who were scholastically successful (Lewin 1998; Meyer 1992). Indeed, underlying popular demand for publicly funded education was a widely held assumption that schooling was a significant vehicle in reducing traditionally ascribed inequalities and opening opportunities for individual social and economic advancement (Farrell 1999). Such popular interest in education likewise had a feedback effect on public policy, since in financing the extension of schooling for the populace at large, governments were able to demonstrate their responsiveness to the needs and interests of their citizens. Education was thus not only a means towards achieving broadly defined objectives of economic and social development, but from the perspective of governing elites, it soon became very much a political end in itself. Explicitly mandated to foster national unity and common allegiance to the nation-state, education emerged as a bedrock of state legitimacy (Fuller and Rubinson 1992; Weiler 1984). As indicated in Table 20.1, with few exceptions, national school systems expanded steadily for approximately two decades. Overall, this unprecedented worldwide expansion of education reflected a broad consensus concerning the causal link between modern education and the notion of development as a linear trajectory of modernity and economic growth, which, through a myriad of 'trickle down' processes, would facilitate the achievement of the goals of increased equality and social justice.

THE TARNISHED PROMISE: EDUCATIONAL CRISIS AND THE EROSION OF CONSENSUAL DISCOURSE

By the early 1980s, however, the apparently seamless synergy of utilitarian and transformative perspectives of education as a basis of national development began to unravel. A sequence of interconnected circumstances in many developing countries—population increases, rising levels of migration and urbanization, economic recession, national indebtedness, and subsequent structural adjustment policies—set in motion a steady decline in the capacity of central states within these countries to manage national economies and to finance and administer social services. This in turn led to growing concerns about a looming world crisis in education (Coombs 1985) that appeared to be confirmed by a general slowdown in—and in some regions a reversal of—increases in primary school enrolment in the latter half of the 1980s (Table 20.1). Whereas schooling had previously been widely accepted as an invaluable social and economic investment for nation-states, in the wake of growing fiscal and monetary constraints, the potential economic and political

Table 20.1 Gross primary school male and female enrolment ratios, 1970–90

Year	Developing countries			Sub-Saharan Africa			Latin America and the Caribbean			Southern Asia		
	MF	M	F	MF	M	F	MF	M	F	MF	M	F
1970	81.2	90.3	71.7	52.5	62.3	42.8	105.9	107.4	104.3	69.8	86.0	52.4
1975	92.6	101.7	83.0	62.1	71.9	52.3	97.8	99.4	96.2	74.6	90.5	57.4
1980	94.9	103.7	85.7	79.5	88.7	70.2	104.1	105.6	102.7	75.9	90.5	60.1
1985	99.3	107.5	90.7	78.9	87.2	70.6	104.7	106.8	102.6	85.1	98.5	70.7
1990	98.8	105.6	91.7	74.8	81.9	67.6	105.0	106.2	103.7	90.3	102.6	77.1

Note: Gross enrolment ratios include the number of pupils (of any age) enrolled in school as a percentage of the total number of children of official school-age. This can include children who are repeating grades. Therefore, gross enrolment ratios can exceed 100 per cent.

Source: http://www.uis.unesco.org/en/stats/statistics/yearbook/tables/Table_II_S_5_Region(GER).html.

gains from the investment came to be viewed with growing scepticism (Weiler 1978). Weighed down by debt and structural adjustment measures, governments throughout the developing world, often at the behest of international lenders, were increasingly compelled to either reduce or cap their expenditures on education. For poor countries, the erstwhile policy objective of extending free access to education was generally abandoned, and in its stead, families and local communities had to assume responsibility for tuition fees, for purchase of items such as textbooks and school uniforms, and often for construction and maintenance of school infrastructure as well. Rarely, however, did the transfer of these educational costs to families and neighbourhoods offset reduced government expenditures on schooling, especially in many poor communities (Mehrotra and Delamonica 1998).

As the allocation of public resources for education went into decline, official policy discourse focused more and more on internal and external efficiency. Evidence of high rates of grade repetition, low achievement levels as indicated in examination scores, and early school dropout rates were cited as symptoms of the lack of 'internal efficiency' within national school systems (Lockheed 1988). Of equal concern were problems associated with the disconnection between school curricula and the local realities and occupational prospects of young school leavers. In contrast to earlier sentiments lauding education as a means of developing human capital, with rising youth unemployment and with national economies unable to accommodate the productive *use* of human capital, critics began to point to the weak 'external efficiency' of national education systems (Lockheed and Hanushek 1994).

In light of fiscal constraints and growing indications of poor educational 'efficiency' in many developing countries, questions were inevitably raised about the quality of education and its relevance for young people. Critical attention began to focus on the heavy 'academic' orientation of school curricula, with its emphasis on the transmission and memorization of textbook 'facts', and

on the use of standardized examinations to certify students when they 'regurgitated' the acquired information (Stephens 1991). Even more pointed was the barrage of rising criticisms directed at teachers. After two decades of steady educational expansion, the number of teachers had risen considerably throughout the developing world. Along with this rapid increase in educational personnel came the need for ongoing expenditures on the training and monitoring of teachers and for steady increases in budgetary allocations for teachers' salaries and operating costs. Yet when confronted by the demands of structural adjustment, governments in many developing countries were no longer able to adequately cover these costs. Inevitably, this had profound implications for the standards of teaching. With minimal pedagogical resources and little more than their own experience as former pupils to draw from, vast numbers of teachers conducted lessons in rote fashion, with classroom routines designed as much to ensure discipline among pupils as to give them new knowledge. Not surprisingly, therefore, although teachers had been regarded as moral and intellectual leaders in the early years of rapid educational expansion when there was abundant public faith in the promise of schooling, by the 1980s the profession had entered into a free fall of declining real incomes, low morale, absenteeism, and the exodus of some of the most qualified teachers from classroom practice and the profession as a whole (Davies 1993; Villegas-Reimers and Reimers 1996).

With governments caught in the squeeze of structural adjustment policies and a neo-liberal ethos championing market dynamics as more effective than state-directed approaches to development, the ideal of education as a force for progressive social transformation was rapidly overshadowed by the notion of education as a form of high-stakes competition from which no individual, community, or nation-state was immune. For affluent social groups, the central function of education was to sustain and legitimize their positions of socio-economic privilege. Thus, as state resources for schooling shrank or stagnated, well-heeled governing and entrepreneurial elites tended to view education as less of a public than a private good and so generally focused on the privatization of schools that were capable of offering good-quality education for their children. In contrast, impoverished families and communities continued to regard public schooling as a source of hope and potential mobility for their children. Yet by the late 1980s, it was apparent that for millions of the world's most needy children—notably girls, disabled children, indigent minority groups, and those living in rural areas and impoverished urban neighbourhoods—formal schooling was becoming less and less useful as a forum for learning and as a basis for attaining long-term social and economic security.

THE JOMTIEN CONFERENCE AND THE VISION OF EDUCATION FOR ALL (EFA)

In view of these indications of widening educational crisis in the developing world and the inability of governments to reverse its course, benign assumptions concerning the putative role of education in furthering diverse goals of modernization, economic growth, national unity, social equity, and democratization had given way to narrower preoccupations with the notion of education as subject to the imperatives of individualistic competition and the marketplace. Yet this shift to a predominantly utilitarian view of education, a result of the deepening educational crisis, was by no means a matter of consensus. In response to declining confidence in the relation between education and social development, and to corresponding indications of dwindling Northern support for education in developing countries, an array of international donor agencies, non-governmental organizations (NGOs), and education officials gathered in Jomtien, Thailand, in 1990 to map out a new vision of education (see Box 20.1).

A watershed of sorts, the Jomtien Conference focused specifically on basic education and reasserted the conflation of utilitarian and transformative perspectives. While reiterating the significance of education as a *sine qua non* for economic development, delegates to the conference also expounded on the indispensability of basic education for the full development of human potential and for improvements in the livelihoods of millions languishing in dependency and impoverishment. In line with the UN Convention on the Rights of the Child, which had been adopted a few months earlier, the Jomtien World Declaration on Education for All (EFA) espoused an ambitious goal of achieving EFA worldwide by 2000. This was a departure from earlier national policy objectives that had centred principally on investments in formal educational systems and on the goal of attaining universal primary education (UPE). As articulated at Jomtien, the vision of basic education encompassed six dimensions— early childhood education, universal access to and completion of primary education, improvements in learning achievement, reduction of adult illiteracy, vocational skills training for youth and adults, and a general increase in community-level knowledge and skills for improved livelihoods and sustainable development (*World Declaration on Education for All* 1990).

Besides an expanded vision of basic education beyond the relatively brief period of primary schooling, the EFA declaration specified the need for educational innovation and reforms and for substantial efforts to expand educational access to groups traditionally under-represented in schools. In acknowledgement of the limited effectiveness of ritualized authoritarian interactions that too-often passed for teaching in many school classrooms, attention was to be directed not only towards the local relevance of *what* was being taught but also towards *how* learning and teaching were taking place. Instead of the common expectation that all learners should adjust to a uniform system of education, the EFA declaration endorsed the view that education should adjust to and accommodate differences in culture, language, experience, and gender among learners. To this end, efforts were to be directed towards implementing reforms in school curricula and in teacher training that would help

BOX 20.1   THE JOMTIEN CONFERENCE AND THE WORLD DECLARATION ON EDUCATION FOR ALL

In March 1990 in Jomtien, Thailand, some 1,500 participants representing governments, multilateral and bilateral donor organizations, and various international NGOs met to address the critical importance of providing basic education for all. The impetus for the meeting was a recognition that school enrolments in several regions of the world were in decline and that there was an urgent need to draw international attention to the significance of education for development and to mobilize new partnerships and resources for basic education in the world's poor countries. The ensuing World Declaration on Education for All (EFA) highlighted the importance of meeting the basic learning needs of all people and set out a vision of basic education that encompassed six dimensions:

- expansion of early childhood care and development;
- universal access to and completion of primary education by the year 2000;
- improvement of learning achievement;
- reduction of adult illiteracy;
- expansion of basic education and training in essential skills required by young people and adults;
- increased acquisition by individuals and families of the knowledge, skills, and values required for better living and for sustainable development through all educational channels.

In accordance with the EFA declaration, governments in developing countries were asked to establish their own goals and objectives for achieving EFA within the next decade. An EFA forum comprised of major international donors and a broad representation of NGOs was established at the UNESCO headquarters in Paris with a mandate to monitor progress, to facilitate dialogue and partnerships focusing on EFA, and to ensure that EFA remained on the world's development agenda through advocacy and information dissemination.

Throughout the 1990s, significant achievements were documented. More than 100 countries had developed specific EFA goals and strategies, and by the end of the decade, an estimated 50 million more children were enrolled in primary school than in 1990. Yet there was disappointment as well. Some 100 million children aged 6 to 11 remained out of school, and it was evident that millions of adolescents had not completed primary school and were thus without basic literacy skills. Gender disparities and rural–urban differentiation in relation to educational access and quality persisted. Disbursements of international financial and technical assistance for basic education had fallen short of commitments made in the wake of the Jomtien Conference. Consequently, the first so-called 'EFA decade' ended with mixed results and with general acknowledgement that the broad goals set out in the 1990 EFA declaration had not yet been fulfilled.

to diminish rote-style teaching and foster more interactive 'child-friendly' schools and classrooms. The EFA declaration also emphasized the importance of educational programs for traditionally underserved populations, such as street and working children, the disabled, rural and remote populations, and those displaced by war and hostile occupation. Above all, urgent priority was to be placed on ensuring that girls and women had greater access to good-quality education and that gender stereotyping in education be eliminated. While there were utilitarian implications underlying these goals (e.g., lower fertility rates and improved levels of productivity and health care), there was clearly an orientation towards enhancing the role of education as a force for greater equity and social justice.

In adopting a broad conceptualization of basic education, the EFA declaration deliberately aimed to reduce conventional distinctions between 'formal' and 'non-formal' education and to emphasize the significance of extending educational opportunities regardless of contexts and personal circumstances. In doing so, it re-asserted the possibility of merging the utilitarian perspective of education, with its focus on human capital development and wealth creation, and the transformative perspective, with its orientation towards social justice and the well-being of traditionally marginalized and disadvantaged populations. In addition, it was clear that education could no longer be regarded as the responsibility of central governments alone. Henceforth, as outlined in the EFA declaration, it would be 'essential to mobilize existing and new financial and human resources, public, private and voluntary. All of society has a contribution to make' (Article IX, 1). In accordance with these precepts, governments and international aid agencies began to press for the decentralization of educational administration and for greater civil society participation in the delivery of both formal and non-formal education. Through this duality of decentralization and participation, the role of central governments was not to disengage from the provision of basic education but rather to undertake partnerships with 'non-governmental organizations, the private sector, local communities, religious groups, and families' (Article VII) so as to ensure more effective educational administration and greater responsiveness to the learning needs and situations of different regions and social groups.

The promulgation of the Jomtien EFA declaration, with its rhetorical emphasis on education

as a force for social transformation, went a long way towards shaping national and international policy discourse on education and development throughout the 1990s. Underlying formal commitments to achieve EFA by 2000 were explicit pronouncements about 'promoting equity' and the need to provide education for 'underserved groups' (Article III). In keeping with these commitments, many developing countries undertook to expand and diversify basic education. As indicated in Table 20.2, primary school enrolments steadily increased, and with financial subsidies and other in-kind incentives designed to encourage girls' attendance at school, the rate of increase in female enrolment generally outpaced that of males (although overall, boys still outnumbered girls in schools).

Alongside the intake of new teachers, ministries of education devoted substantial resources towards improvements in teacher training and in-service support. Similarly, many national and international NGOs, often with assistance from major international donors, introduced or greatly expanded various forms of community-managed schools and non-formal education programs. These programs ranged from internationally renowned modalities of innovative education, such as the BRAC schools and community programs in Bangladesh (Nath, Sylva, and Grimes 1999) and the network of *Escuela Neuva* community schools in Colombia (Kline 2002), to many small-scale vocational training and indigenous language literacy programs in neighbourhoods striving to overcome obstacles associated with illiteracy, unemployment, and poverty (DeStefano et al. 2006). Although mastery of metropolitan languages such as English, French, and Spanish was still widely valued, notably in established formal school systems, the use of mother tongue instruction was increasingly recognized as a legitimate means of strengthening the connection between education and the local realities of learners (Malone 2003). Gradually, as well, despite ambiguities and tensions associated with efforts to implement policies of educational decentralization, collaboration and partnership among central

Table 20.2 Primary school enrolment ratios, 1991–2005

| Region | Gross enrolment ratio (Total and Gender Parity Index) School year ending in | | | | | | Net enrolment ratio School year ending in | | |
| | 1991 | | 1999 | | 2005 | | 1991 | 1999 | 2005 |
	Total (%)	GPI F/M	Total (%)	GPI F/M	Total (%)	GPI F/M	(%)	(%)	(%)
World	99	0.89	100	0.92	107	0.95	81	83	87
Developing countries	98	0.87	100	0.91	108	0.94	79	81	86
Sub-Saharan Africa	72	0.84	80	0.86	97	0.89	54	57	70
Arab states	83	0.80	90	0.88	95	0.91	73	79	83
Central Asia	90	0.99	99	0.99	101	0.99	84	88	90
South and West Asia	92	0.76	94	0.82	113	0.93	72	77	86
Latin America/Caribbean	104	0.97	121	0.97	118	0.96	86	92	94
Caribbean	71	0.97	115	0.97	117	0.98	52	77	77
Latin America	104	0.97	121	0.97	118	0.96	87	93	95

Note: Net enrolment ratios comprise only the number of pupils whose ages are appropriate to the grade in which they are enrolled as a percentage of the total official school-age population. This is in contrast to gross enrolment ratios that include children enrolled in school regardless of their age or whether they are repeating grades. Differences in gross and net enrolment ratios are one indicator of educational efficiency: the higher the gross enrolment ratio in relation to the net ratio, the more pupil-years of resources are needed to educate a student.
Source: UNESCO. 2007. EFA *Global Monitoring Report 2008. Education for All by 2015: Will We Make It?* p. 362–3. Oxford: UNESCO and Oxford University Press. http://unesdoc.unesco.org/images/0015/001547/154743e.pdf.

governments, international donor agencies, and civil society organizations (CSOs) became widely accepted for purposes of educational expansion and reform (Johnson and Wilson 2000).

Nevertheless, despite official pronouncements articulating the juncture of transformative and utilitarian perspectives of education, the humanistic dimensions of EFA policy discourse continued to be overshadowed by a combination of political conservatism, resource scarcity, and the dependence of poor and often highly indebted countries on international lending agencies espousing principles of neo-liberalism and market-oriented development policies. Although formally embracing the rhetoric of education as a force for social equity and the reduc-

tion of poverty, governments generally shied away from undertaking the reforms needed to support these transformative goals. Similarly, despite the ideals underlying decentralization and civil society participation in education, rarely were these processes initiated in ways that were directed towards social transformation. Instead of generating a basis for democracy and greater social justice, civil society participation in educational administration was often encouraged as a means of permitting central governments to offload expenditures and day-to-day management responsibilities while still retaining direct control over the national education sector. Rather than signalling a genuine devolution of power and resources, decentralization and participation

BOX 20.2   EDUCATION AND THE STRUGGLE FOR SOCIAL TRANSFORMATION: THE TEACHER CREATIVITY CENTRE IN PALESTINE

The Teacher Creativity Centre (TCC) is a Palestinian non-profit, non-governmental organization established in May 1995 in Ramallah by a group of teachers working in schools run by the government, the private sector, and the United Nations Relief and Works Agency.

TCC's mission is to promote a democratic Palestinian civil society that believes in respect for human rights, the supremacy of law and justice for all, and freedom from violence, discrimination, and all types of oppression and marginalization. In addition, it aims to provide equal opportunities for citizens to develop and express themselves freely in safety and stability.

In the Palestinian Territories of the West Bank and Gaza, more than 20,000 teachers are active in primary and secondary education. There are also higher education institutions such as the University of Birzeit. Generally speaking, these institutions are in a very difficult situation, as are the people studying and working in them, because of the deteriorating social, economic, and political context.

Despite this arduous environment, TCC has succeeded in building a wide network of teachers, students, and even parents committed to eliminating violence from schools by means of encouraging human rights and civic education. TCC has been in the forefront of organizations calling for the integration of civic education and human rights concepts into the entire school curriculum, not only at the Palestinian level but also in the wider Arab world. It has successfully implemented a number of research and training programs in the fields of human rights, democracy, and civic education.

TCC works with the Palestinian Ministry of Education and Higher Education to deliver training programs to teachers, principals, supervisors, and senior managerial personnel. It is also an active member of the NGO community, grouped under the umbrella of the Palestinian Network of Nongovernmental Organizations (PNGO), as well as a founding member of the Arab Civic Education Network (Civitas) and a member of Alternatives-International, an international NGO network.

For further information, see http://www.teachercc.org/index.html.

---

were generally oriented towards enhancing educational efficiency within established systems of state schooling.

Overall, therefore, throughout the post-Jomtien decade, the principal characteristics of institutionalized school systems—established curricula, standardized methods of teaching, conventional modes of student assessment, and the alignment of school examination results with opportunities available either in higher levels of education or the job market—remained largely unchanged. Moreover, despite ringing declarations of international financial and technical support for EFA at the Jomtien Conference and for two or three years afterwards, external donor assistance fell far short of the commitments deemed necessary to achieve EFA by 2000. Indeed, throughout the post-Jomtien decade, external assistance generally accounted for less than 2 per cent of the educational budgets of recipient countries (UNESCO 2007). As the new millennium approached, it was clear that although the rhetoric of education as a force for social transformation was an integral feature of official policy pronouncements, and although it continued to colour many NGO and civil society interventions, structural changes in national systems of education had been minimal. In a context of neo-liberalism and incremental privatization of social services, education systems continued to largely replicate and reinforce the status quo of social and economic stratification throughout the developing world.

RE-ASSERTING TRANSFORMATIVE IDEALS

The Dakar Framework for Action and the Millennium Development Goals

The failure to achieve EFA by 2000 not only underscored the frequently ephemeral nature of transformative perspectives in educational policy discourse but also highlighted the tendency in official policy pronouncements to depoliticize the notion of education for social transformation. It was one thing for governments and Northern donor organizations to articulate the imperative of good-quality education as a fundamental human right and as a basis for furthering the goals of equity and social justice. It was another, however, to circumvent the convoluted norms of educational bureaucracies and global capital markets in order to undertake the radical changes implied by the transformative perspective. Nevertheless, despite structural constraints that generally overshadow transformative ideals when policies were translated into practice, the rhetorical appeal of education for equity and social justice has remained strong, especially among multilateral agencies such as UNICEF and UNESCO and the vast number of international NGOs and CSOs that became actively involved in education in the years following Jomtien. Indeed, if anything, by the end of the 1990s, the shortcomings of the first 'EFA decade' served as an incentive

Figure 20.2. School children in Mumbai

Source: Alternatives/Catherine Pappas

among proponents of transformative education to reinvigorate the potential of education as an agent of radical social change.

Consequently, with the turn of the century generating sentiments of fresh starts and the possibility of elaborating more effective global strategies (Mundy and Murphy 2001), two international protocols emerged that revived the vision of social transformation as a central feature of educational policy. In April 2000, a new EFA Framework of Action emanated from a global review of basic education in Dakar, Senegal (see Box 20.3). Essentially reiterating the transformative discourse of the earlier Jomtien declaration, the Dakar framework proclaimed 2015 as the new target year for universal primary school completion, a 50 per cent increase in rates of adult literacy, and gender equity at all educational levels. In emphasizing the idea of education as a 'fundamental human right' and as a key to 'poverty elimination', 'peace and stability', and the inherent capacity of learners 'to transform their societies', the Dakar framework articulated a more compelling transformative perspective than the earlier Jomtien declaration had.

Shortly afterwards, reflecting similar transformative ideals, the UN General Assembly adopted the Millennium Development Goals (MDGs) for reversing chronic world poverty. Of the eight MDGs, two focused specifically on education—universal primary school completion and elimination of gender disparity in primary and secondary education. Although the MDGs focused on a narrower view of education than the Dakar framework, both sets of goals maintained the ideal of education for transformation as a common inspirational threshold.

Galvanized by the Dakar framework and the MDGs, government signatories agreed to draft national EFA plans that were to relate significantly to Poverty Reduction Strategy Papers (PRSPs) and be annually assessed by a special UNESCO monitoring team. International donor agencies likewise committed themselves to a resurgence of assistance to education, with notable attention to be directed towards 'sector-wide approaches' (SWAs) in order to improve the effectiveness and co-ordination of external aid to education (Buchert 2002). The World Bank likewise proposed a Fast Track Initiative (FTI) that held out the promise of rapid infusions of assistance to countries with 'credible' national educational plans. The combination of these measures reflected a resurgence of international consensus concerning the significance of education for development.

Yet at the time of writing, as the first decade of the new millennium nears its end, there is once again a perceptible aura of *plus ça change, plus c'est la même chose*. Despite the rhetoric of a renewed EFA regime, basic education for millions of children still remains either non-existent or of minimal value. The poorest countries of the world, most in sub-Saharan Africa, are unlikely to achieve full primary school enrolments, let alone universal completion rates, by 2015, nor are they capable of adequately redressing problems related to educational quality and the often tenuous link between education and dubious employment prospects for many youth (UNESCO 2007). While official policy pronouncements routinely embrace the concept of education as a catalyst of societal transformation, the established bureaucratic structures and the competitive, selection-oriented processes of national school systems have changed little. Rather than a force for reducing or bringing an end to poverty, education for most learners and their families continues to represent a hopeful avenue of *escape* from pervasive conditions of poverty. Ironically, the international emphasis on targets such as enrolment levels and completion rates is itself viewed by some critics as symptomatic of a utilitarian preoccupation with quantification rather than with educational quality and relevance to local contexts (Jansen 2005). Globally defined conditionalities that have linked national EFA targets to PRSPs and donor largesse such as the World Bank's FTI have likewise raised questions about diminishing national 'ownership' of educational systems and the decontextualization of educational planning. As several critics have argued, strict adherence to the

BOX 20.3   THE DAKAR FRAMEWORK FOR ACTION

In recognition of the shortfalls in achieving the goals set out in the Jomtien EFA declaration, all the major international actors connected with the EFA agenda met in Dakar, Senegal, in April 2000 to re-assert the EFA vision and strengthen commitments to its attainment. This meeting led to the formulation of a Framework for Action that reiterated the goals of the Jomtien declaration and espoused seven major principles:

- expansion of early childhood care and development;
- an uncompromising commitment by governments, civil society, and the international community to ensure universal access to forums and processes of comprehensive good-quality learning;
- recognition of the need for a beneficial learning climate for the 'whole child';
- creation of more effective links between new technologies and basic learning;
- concrete goal-setting and explicit targets at national and local levels in accordance with internationally established criteria;
- a more prominent role for, and engagement with, civil society;
- improvements in collaboration, information-sharing, transparency, and accountability among all institutional partners.

Alongside these principles, notable goals and objectives to be achieved by 2015 included: (1) access to and completion of free primary education for all children; (2) measurable improvements in the quality of teaching and learning; (3) elimination of gender disparities in education among all children through to age 15; (4) increased mobilization of resources at all levels for EFA; and (5) tangible connections between educational policies and anti-poverty strategies.

Nevertheless, despite ostensible renewed commitment to EFA as articulated in the Dakar Framework for Action, indications are that once again results will be mixed. According to the EFA *Global Monitoring Report* for 2008 (http://www.unesco.org/education/gmr2008/highlights-en.pdf), primary school enrolments have continued to rise, increasing by 36 per cent in sub-Saharan Africa and 22 per cent in South and West Asia, and the number of out-of-school children has declined worldwide. Yet gender disparities, poor-quality learning environments, skewed emphasis on primary schooling to the detriment of early childhood education and adult literacy, and shortfalls in international aid to basic education are all troublesome. Reflecting growing concerns regarding the extent to which the goals of the Dakar Framework for Action will be achieved by 2015, the EFA *Global Monitoring Report* is subtitled *Will We Make It?*

MDGs and the EFA agenda is akin to relying on internationally standardized 'templates' or 'blueprints' that are essentially utilitarian in their focus and ignore the complexities of history and culture (Freeman and Faure 2003; Rose 2005).

Of equal concern is the continuing gap between stated aid commitments to EFA and the MDGs and the actual disbursements of technical and financial assistance to education in developing countries. Although support for basic education rose considerably in the immediate aftermath of the Dakar framework, from an estimated US $2.7 billion in 2000 to US $5.1 billion in 2004, aggregate aid to education in developing countries has since declined to levels that are 'at odds with the positive statements made by donors . . . about their intentions to increase support to education significantly' (UNESCO 2007, 155). In a pattern similar to that of the first EFA decade, annual international aid to basic education since 2000 has reached only about half the estimated level required to meet EFA goals by 2015 (UNESCO 2007). Overall, therefore, international pronouncements concerning the imperative of education for the social transformations required to reduce poverty and social injustice have not been matched by the political will and the resource transfers needed to ensure the realization of these pronouncements. As time passes, the consensus connecting the transformative and utilitarian perspectives of education once again appears to be fading.

CONCLUSION: THE CONTRADICTIONS OF EDUCATION FOR DEVELOPMENT

For the past half century, education and development have been conceptually and pragmatically interrelated, with education widely viewed as a linchpin for the long-term realization of development policies and programs. Yet as we have discussed in this chapter, perceptions regarding the purposes of education and its relationship to national and international strategies of development are diverse and can generally be encapsulated in two fundamentally contradictory positions.

On one side is what we have characterized as education for utilitarian purposes. From this perspective, regardless of time and context, the main function of education is to transmit knowledge and skills that enable learners to adapt and contribute to an established economic, political, and social order. In doing so, education helps to legitimate strategies of development that combine economic growth and stable forms of governance capable of facilitating this growth. Viewed in this

way, education can serve as an effective lightning rod for many social problems. In the current neoliberal era, for example, with systems of education linked to the dynamics of the market, success or disappointment among individuals is often regarded as a function of their education or the absence of it. Even in fragile political economies where the connection between education and prospective jobs is weak, the barriers that many young people from impoverished backgrounds face are often seen as a result of their lack of education or to the poor quality of the education they have received. In contrast, for those whose positions of power and relative affluence are generally entrenched, the status quo is frequently and conveniently attributed to the meritorious nature of school systems that the wealthy can afford.

On the other side, precisely because the status quo is inequitable and the utilitarian perspective is clearly open to criticism and contestation, the transformative view of education presents an attractive alternative. As exemplified by the Millennium Development Goals and by the EFA agendas of Jomtien and Dakar, this is a perception of education as facilitating 'an end to poverty' and reinforcing ideals of social justice, individual freedoms, and respect for human rights. From this perspective, the principal goals of education are to generate understanding and skills that will enable disadvantaged social groups to overcome the constraints of poverty and discrimination and undertake actions oriented towards broad societal reform. Given the destitution of many people throughout the developing world, this evident moral imperative has ensured the continuing appeal of the transformative view of education.

Despite being clearly divergent, these two broad perspectives have long coexisted in educational policy discourse and are generally regarded as compatible in the public imagination. In part, this is due to parallel divergence in conceptions and strategies of development—between those that are strongly oriented towards the reduction of poverty through economic growth and those that regard poverty as the result of inequitable

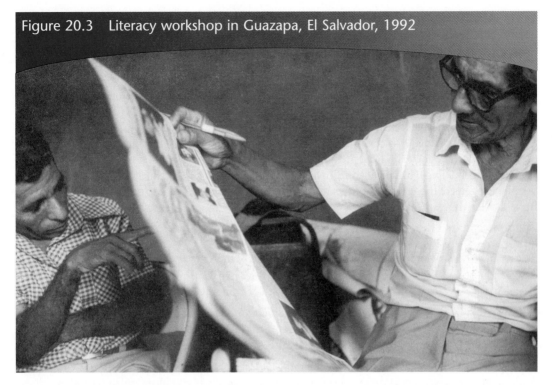

Figure 20.3   Literacy workshop in Guazapa, El Salvador, 1992

Source: Alternatives/Dominic Morissette

social structures that need to be transformed. Given the strong connection between education and development, these contradictory perspectives inevitably overlap. In part as well, however, just as concepts of *empowerment*, *participation*, and *social justice* are now routinely articulated in official development policy statements, so too have the goals of attaining equity and social justice in and through education been absorbed into mainstream educational policy discourse. The effect of this co-optation of the language of radical change by established political and bureaucratic authorities, however, has essentially been the depoliticization of the transformative agenda.

Of course, throughout much of the developing world, education *has* served as an agent of modest progressive change. Increased access to schooling among disadvantaged social groups, changes to curriculum and teacher training, the emergence of an array of innovative non-formal

and community education programs, and the engagement of NGOs and CSOs in educational planning and administration have all contributed to incremental improvements in education. Similarly, it is clear that education has been an integral facet of social movements and human rights advocacy; indeed, many activists for social justice have themselves been formally educated. Yet on the whole, it is the utilitarian orientation of education that has remained dominant throughout the developing world. Despite periodic surges in national and international rhetoric endorsing a transformative agenda for education, as demonstrated by the Jomtien and Dakar accords, and by the MDGs with their focus on primary school enrolments and completion, governments and international donor agencies, and indeed many NGOs, have consistently regarded education as a force for strengthening rather than radically altering prevailing political and economic arrangements. In effect, the fact that utilitarian and transformative perspectives have generally coexisted in mainstream educational policy discourse is largely because the transformative agenda has been superimposed on strongly entrenched policies and programs of national schooling. While accommodating the *idea* of education as a basis of social transformation, the language of radical change has consistently skated over the rigidities of formal school processes and structures. In doing so, it has failed to undo the peripheral status of those forms of education that strive to affect fundamental change.

Overall, therefore, the coexistence of utilitarian and transformative perspectives in educational policy discourse has served to legitimize the contradictions of education and to thwart the dimensions of political mobilization and change as implied by the transformative ideal. In the long term, the articulation of these two perspectives is likely to continue in education and development policy discourse, mirroring contradictory visions and struggles for influence that show no signs of diminishing. At the very least, this will ensure that the dynamics of education and development will remain subject to critical scrutiny and intense debate.

QUESTIONS FOR DISCUSSION

1. Can education systems be catalysts for social change, as the transformative perspective suggests, or must societies change first in order for educational reform to occur?

2. Investment in education as a means of strengthening human capital has been shown to have played a significant role in the rapid economic development of several small South Asian countries (e.g., South Korea, Taiwan, and Singapore) in the post–World War II era. Can these experiences serve as examples for still struggling countries? Why or why not?

3. What are the advantages and disadvantages of various mechanisms of international aid to education (e.g., direct collaboration on projects with local communities versus pooled donor support to central ministries of education)?

4. What are the problems associated with educational 'targeting' as reflected in the Dakar Framework for Action and the Millennium Development Goals?

5. Does formal schooling serve the interests of the poor, or should more resources be allocated to various forms of non-school education?

FURTHER READING

Arnove, R.F., and C.A. Torres, eds. 1999. *Comparative Education: The Dialectic of the Global and the Local*. Lanham, MD: Rowman and Littlefield.

Bray, M., ed. 2003. *Comparative Education: Continuing Traditions, New Challenges and New Paradigms*. London: Kluwer.

Chabbott, C. 2003. *Constructing Education for Development: International Organizations and Education for All*. New York: Falmer.

Crossley, M., and K. Watson. 2003. *Comparative and International Research in Education: Globalisation, Context and Difference*. New York: Routledge and Falmer.

Stromquist, N., and M. Basile, eds. 1999. *Politics of Educational Innovations in Developing Countries: An Analysis of Knowledge and Power*. New York: Falmer.

INTERNET RESOURCES

Association for the Development of Education in Africa: http://www.adeanet.org.

BRAC Education: http://www.brac.net/education.htm.

Consultative Group on Early Childhood Care and Development: http://www.ecdgroup.com.

Escuela Nueva: http://www.volvamos.org/english/fundamentos.php.

Global Campaign for Education: http://www.campaignforeducation.org.

UNICEF: http://www.unicef.org.

United Nations Convention on the Rights of the Child: http://www.crin.org/docs/resources/treaties/uncrc.asp.

World Declaration on Education for All: Meeting Basic Learning Needs (1990): http://www.unesco.org/education/wef/en-conf/Jomtien%20Declaration%20eng.shtm.

CHAPTER 21

CONFLICT AND DEVELOPMENT

ASTRI SUHRKE AND TORUNN WIMPELMANN CHAUDHARY

LEARNING OBJECTIVES

- To understand the liberal view of the relationship between conflict and development.
- To understand why and how this liberal theory of violence has been challenged and several alternative perspectives that have been proposed.
- To understand how policy measures to contain violent conflict have been conceived and implemented and how these measures are related to the liberal and alternative approaches to understanding the conflict–development nexus.

This chapter introduces students to ways in which the relationship between conflict and development has been understood and studied in the field of social science. Within this wide and controversial field of inquiry, the chapter identifies two main perspectives:

1. The liberal view, which sees underdevelopment as a cause of conflict and development as a way out of strife and towards peace.
2. A competing perspective, which sees conflict as integral to development. Development is therefore likely to produce conflict, although according to some, this can be contained by proper policy measures.

The first part of the chapter lays out these two perspectives and the different methods of approaching the question of whether conflict is part of development or outside it. The second part takes the reader to contemporary issues of development and peace, often called **peacebuilding**, in order to illustrate how these different theories play out in practice.

POSING THE QUESTION

Conflict is the opposite of development—war is development in reverse. This was the message of a recent major report on civil wars from World Bank researchers. The study concluded that '[w]hen development succeeds, countries become safer; when development fails, countries experience greater risk of being caught in a **conflict trap**' (Collier et al. 2003). At first glance, this seems persuasive. Wars destroy lives, property, and the environment. As such, it is 'development in reverse'. Most recent wars, moreover, have taken place in poor countries in Africa, Asia, and Latin America. Western Europe and North America—by most accounts the richest and most developed countries in the world—have experienced very little war since World War II. The Balkan wars in the 1990s appeared to many as a shock, a gust from a past it was assumed Europe had left behind.

On closer examination, however, the picture is not so simple. Violence may set back 'development', but it also may sweep away older structures and make way for change. Nor is national development necessarily a ticket to safety, either for self or for others. Countries considered as having 'succeeded' in development terms are still subject to violent civil strife, such as race riots in the United States, separatist violence in Spain, sectarian fighting in Northern Ireland, and terrorist attacks in London. If we add international violence, we find that NATO members in recent years have repeatedly attacked other states (as in Iraq in 1991 and 2003, Kosovo and Serbia in 1999, and Afghanistan in 2001). At the other end of the development spectrum there is also some variation. Among the 10 least developed countries according to the **Human Development Index** of the United Nations Development Programme (UNDP), some have escaped what seemed to be a conflict trap (e.g., Mozambique and Mali), while others have experienced recurrent conflict (e.g., Ethiopia and Burundi) (UNDP 2006). Perhaps some are poor and underdeveloped because of recurrent violence caused primarily by other factors.

Social scientists, philosophers, and historians have long tried to understand the relationship between violence and development. Among the many perspectives and interpretations, two main streams are notable. A **liberal theory of violence**, which approximates the World Bank report cited above, considers violence an aberration and as the opposite of development. The implication—sometimes spelled out—is that development is a way out of violence. In a very different perspective, violence is 'at the heart of societal transformations', as Christopher Cramer writes in a recent book, and also a frequent companion in the 'expansionary modernism' of Western states (Cramer 2006). If violence is at least potentially inherent in the very process of social change, there is little prospect for an exit from strife—unless we declare 'the end of history' (as some Western writers indeed did when the Soviet Union was defeated and collapsed (Fukuyama 1992).

These perspectives will be explored below. We will start with the proposition that underdevelopment leads to conflict and that development therefore is a way to reduce conflict. We will then examine the competing view that development is a conflictual process and must be understood and studied as such, although the violent manifestations may vary and arguably can be modified. Finally, we turn to a contemporary policy arena where these perspectives are being tested: that is, the growing international effort to help reconstruct societies emerging from violence, often

called 'peacebuilding'. But first, a brief note on definitions, approaches, and methods.

DEFINITIONS, APPROACHES, AND METHODS

Development

Development is a multidimensional concept, and the links and relative priority of its various dimensions are debated. In economic terms, development is often understood as sustained high growth rates or the transformation of agrarian economies into industrialized systems of production. Social development is typically taken to mean poverty reduction and improvement in education and health. The term political development was once widely used by Western political scientists to refer to a combined process of national integration, state-building, and social modernization thought to produce effective institutions and political stability. More recent studies have focused on democratization, either as a means to promote other aspects of development or as an end in itself.

A discussion of the relationship between development and conflict therefore obviously depends upon which meaning, or dimension, of development is being used. Empirical studies in the positivist tradition typically disaggregate development along these dimensions in order to assess its relationship to conflict. For instance, if development is understood primarily in terms of macroeconomic indicators such as Gross Domestic Product (GDP) growth, one can investigate the relationship between growth rates and the incidence of conflict. If the focus is on social development, some measure of education, health, and distribution of goods would be relevant. Ethnic diversity and the importance of ethnic divisions are classic indicators in studies of national integration. Elections and related political freedoms are typically used to indicate political dimensions of development. The relationship between such economic, social, and political dimensions of development and conflict can then be examined, either

Figure 21.1   Postwar social reconstruction:
An ex-combatant in rural Mozambique

Source: Jessica Schafer

individually or in combination. Many recent studies have analyzed the relationship statistically, using various indicators for development from generally accessible databanks.[1]

A very different approach is 'the grand narrative', which seeks to uncover the essence of the development process as it has unfolded historically. Among the classical scholars here are Karl Marx (1818–83) and Max Weber (1864–1920). Writing at the time of rapid change and much violence in Europe as well as beyond, both tried to understand 'development' and the processes and patterns of social change. For Marx, development cannot be separated from conflict or seen as independent of it. Rather, the two are interlinked: conflict is intrinsic to the development process itself, the motor that drives it forward as power and resources are redistributed to different classes and peoples. In a continuation of this grand narrative, Lenin argued that imperialism was the highest stage of capitalism before the imperialist nations, the 'most developed' in conventional terms, would succumb to war against each other. In Weber's grand narrative, by contrast, capitalism is peaceful, emerging through rationalization and efficiency. Industrial capitalism overcomes its own internal tensions through rational planning and orderly competition for power within an arena of secular politics. The rules of competition are guarded by a state that has a legitimate monopoly of force. 'Modernity', then, is associated with societies ruled primarily by reason as enshrined in predictable, efficient, and secular institutions, which suggests an exit from violence.

Conflict, violence, and war

So far, we have used the terms 'conflict', 'violence', and 'war' interchangeably, but the meaning of these words is a debate in itself. Conflict is generally understood to mean tension between opposing views, interests, or wills. Conflicts may or may not involve violence, even if we allow for the many meanings of 'violence'. The most obvious and common sense meaning is physical violence. But there is also 'structural violence', a concept launched by peace researcher Johan Galtung in the 1950s to denote extreme and systematic inequality, and 'symbolic violence', understood in the tradition of French sociologist Pierre Bourdieu as internalized humiliation and legitimation of inequality and hierarchy. In the following exploration, we will focus on physical violence, particularly of the kind political scientists call war.

War has long been considered a unique category of conflict. 'War' suggests that special attention is warranted: it signals extraordinary violence, a situation when normal rules do not apply but special rules have been developed (as in international law governing warfare). In the social sciences, war has usually been studied separately from other forms of violence. Typically, students of international relations and political science study 'war', while anthropologists and sociologists study 'violence'.

Within political science, one approach to the study of war in relation to development is to treat 'war' as a discrete event, the appearance of which can be examined statistically in relation to other factors that are believed to be its causes or (more rarely) consequences. Large databases have been established for this purpose since the 1960s, with data on events classified as internal and international wars, as well as some hybrid forms. Classification systems are controversial, particularly with regard to the definition of 'civil war'. The most widely used datasets have both quantitative measures (1,000 battle-related deaths per year or per duration of the conflict) and qualitative data such as organization of the belligerent parties (usually states or rebels with some organization) and the incompatibility of their aims.[2]

Using these databases to determine the links between war and development, such as the World Bank study cited above, is subject to some limitations. One problem is the unreliability of raw data from war zones where the parties sometimes are armed factions with no centralized organization and human rights monitors have poor access. Estimates of casualties during the 1989–97 war in Liberia, for instance, vary from 60,000 to 200,000. Use of different thresholds of casualties will produce different frequencies of war. No current datasets have indicators for intensity, although this clearly affects the impact of wars on society and hence on development in practically all its dimensions. For example, a thousand deaths in civil strife is much less significant for national development in a country of more than one billion people (India) than it is for a state with just under one million (Timor Leste). Moreover, what should be counted as battle-related deaths? In the classic image of warfare, war is fought on the battlefield between opposing armies. In many contemporary conflicts, violence is diverse, carried out by militias as well as state or rebel armies, and civilians are often the victims. It is unclear how massacres of unarmed people should be counted (most civil war datasets do not include the massacre of some 800,000 persons in Rwanda in 1994, since it was mostly a one-sided genocide). Likewise, current civil war datasets rarely include deaths related to famine and disease, which often outnumber battlefield deaths.

Another way to approach the question of 'war' is to place the violent event (whatever its name) in its historical and sociological setting. In this perspective, organized violence is examined as part of a social process of transformation, with causes and functions that cannot be abstracted from this context. This perspective also opens the way for a deeper inquiry about the causes of violence (external as well as internal) and its functions in relation to the formation of social capital and new institutions—both regarded as central ingredients of 'development'—as well as the more obvious destruction of life and material property. This approach is favoured by anthropologists but also by economists and political scientists working in the tradition of **political economy** (Cramer 2006; Richards 2005; Keen 2001).

Methods matter

The choice of definitions, approaches, and methods will influence the results and has important policy implications. On the issue of the relationship between economic growth, inequality, and conflict, for instance, different methods have produced very different conclusions. The World Bank study cited above used statistical analysis, which showed that social or economic inequality was not a significant cause of contemporary civil wars. Overall economic level and growth rates, by contrast, was significant: poorer countries were more likely than rich ones to experience civil war, and after a war, high economic growth rates meant less chance of experiencing another one. If general statistical trends were to guide policy, this would mean that policy-makers intent on preserving peace should emphasize economic growth over structural change to reduce socio-economic inequality, particularly in the aftermath of war.

BOX 21.1　WAR AS A COMPLEX 'EVENT'

If we were to plot 'the war in Afghanistan' as an event in a database, how would we do it? The first phase started in April 1978, when the Afghan communists seized power and the militant resistance formed. A year and a half later, the Soviets invaded, and the resistance started receiving international arms support and training. It was now an internationalized civil war. In 1988, the last Soviet soldiers withdrew, and after a brief peace, Afghan factions turned on each other in a full-scale civil war. That lasted roughly until 1996, when the Taliban seized Kabul, thereby completing their hold over some 90 per cent of the entire country. In October 2001, US-led forces invaded the country and, with the help of a local faction, defeated the Taliban. After a brief peace, violence resumed and by 2007 had grown into a serious insurgency in parts of the country.

If we plot this as a 30-year war, it is reasonable to assume that governing structures, social relations, and economic activity existed in this period. In some areas, warlords emerged; in other areas, traditional leaders or new political movements held sway. Many of them conducted 'foreign relations' with outside governments or agencies. Social and economic capital accumulated during periods of warfare was invested in times of (relative) peace for personal or community benefits. Thus, after the Taliban lost power, one of the first public acts of the 'warlord of Herat' in western Afghanistan, Ismail Khan, was to beautify public parks and restore the magnificent mosaic arcs that graced the entrance to the city.

But the most obvious impact of the long wars was destruction. Successive waves of fighting left a trail of death and disintegration, displaced families and communities, economic stagnation, near standstill in social services, and pervasive violence—not only regular warfare among fighting units but also alleged war crimes, crimes against humanity, and massive human rights violations. For those close to the event, it was difficult to see that this kind of destruction could be the foundation for new development.

Critics say that the limitations of the dataset and methods, such as those mentioned above, make such generalizations hazardous. The raw data on death counts are uncertain, little or no allowance is made for the significance and intensity of different wars, and researchers include many different kinds of conflicts in one category so as to get a sufficiently large number of cases to make the use of statistical methods worthwhile. In the search for average trends, important variations can easily be lost. For instance, historically informed studies of the recent civil wars in Central America and Nepal show that they revolved around issues of systemic inequality and oppression and that mitigating these conditions is important to preserving the future peace (Jones 2000; Wood 2003). Policy prescriptions must be careful here: recommendations based on general trends that emphasize growth rather than equality as

means of reducing internal violence would in this case be quite misleading. Analysis that takes into account the historical and social context of particular cases can do better justice to such varying situations. More fundamentally, historically based studies can address issues of underlying causality in ways that statistical analysis cannot.

CONFLICT AND DEVELOPMENT: PERSPECTIVES AND FINDINGS

When development theory became an academic field of study of its own after World War II, it was largely with the premise that development and conflict are separate phenomena and appear intermittently: development stops when conflict starts and can continue when conflict subsides. As a result, there was little effort to explore the relationship between development and conflict. Only

Figure 21.2   Rebuilding bridges in postwar Mozambique

Source: Jessica Schafer

in the past decade or so has this separation been challenged within mainstream development studies and practice. The result, as indicated above, is an affirmation of two classic perspectives. The probably dominant view, a liberal theory of violence, sees underdevelopment as a source of conflict and development as a prerequisite for peace. In the competing view, conflict and potential violence are both embedded in development *qua* social transformation.

Underdevelopment as a cause of conflict—development as the foundation for peace

A powerful theme within Western liberal thinking is that modernization and economic progress bring stability. Drawing on Weber's concept of modernity as secularism and rationalism, Western political scientists produced a huge 'modernization' literature in the 1960s (see chapter 3). Societies would develop and modernize by establishing effectively functioning bureaucracies, streamlining individual affinities away from primordial or ethnic identities towards larger national loyalties, incorporating modern technology, and putting foreign aid capital to good use. The political development component was usually understood as the establishment of representative and plural institutions that could aggregate interests and provide checks and balances on executive power.

In fact, progress along this path was uneven, sometimes abandoned, and often strewn with violence. The deviations became increasingly clear as the Cold War between the superpowers was played out in what was then called the Third World. The United States and the Soviet Union exploited local divisions in order to enhance their own interests, a process that in several cases turned into 'proxy wars'. In Mozambique, for instance, the long struggle for independence against the Portuguese that ended in 1975 was followed by renewed conflict. The post-colonial government policy of radical socialist change had alienated many traditional farmers, antagonized

the church, and sharpened divisions between the northern and southern regions of the country. When the government also denounced apartheid and colonialism, it alienated external forces as well. The neighbouring white-ruled Rhodesia sponsored a rebel force, the Mozambican National Resistance Movement (RENAMO), which was also backed by South Africa and, in the background, the United States. The main rationale for the US engagement was the active support given to the Mozambican government by the Soviet Union. More generally, the Cold War meant that Western states reshaped the modernization agenda to fit the anti-communist struggle. This often meant supporting military strongmen rather than democratic forces (as in Southeast Asia and South America) and promoting groups that in Weberian terms were distinctly 'unmodern'. The latter included patrimonial bureaucracies that served individual rulers, such as Joseph-Désiré Mobutu, president of Zaire from 1965 to 1997, as well as movements seeking unity between state and religion, such as the Afghan *mujahedin* who fought the Soviets in the 1980s.

The democratic peace
The idea that democracies and peace belong together nevertheless survived and was reborn in new research in the 1980s. This work was inspired by Immanuel Kant's *Perpetual Peace*, a small pamphlet written in 1795 in the shadow of the French Revolution and Napoleon's rising power. *Perpetual Peace* outlined the conditions for peace *among* states. Prominent among these conditions was a republican constitution (which did not mean democracy in the form of majority rule) and free trade encouraging economic interdependence. Prosperous burghers, Kant believed, would not want to send their sons into battle or pay for the national debt incurred by war. Economic interdependence would make it difficult in practice for states to fight each other. The 1980s version of this thesis launched by American political scientists held that 'democratic' states very seldom went to war against each other, with 'democratic' defined as periodic competitive elec-

tions and universal adult suffrage. Here, it seemed, was a clear link between one dimension of development (political democracy) and the absence of at least some kinds of violence (Rummel 1975–81; Doyle 1983). A flurry of further studies confirmed the link. These studies relied on statistical analysis and provided little explanation for *why* countries with regular elections and adult suffrage did not fight each other. Yet—as critics pointed out—these countries did not shy away from going to war against weaker states or entities, as demonstrated, for instance, by the history of US military interventions in Central America, France's war against the Algerian independence movement, and, just the decade before this literature developed, the enormously controversial US war in Vietnam. In an earlier period, European states with at least some democratic features had readily gone to war to establish and maintain empires. In other words, the democratic constitution of a state clearly produced only a selective peace.

The promises of political democracy held out by liberal theory seemed less ambiguous with respect to internal wars. Using statistical analysis of data to compare types and frequency of internal disturbances with indicators of democracy, one leading American scholar found a clear pattern (Rummel 1997). Non-democratic countries were much more likely than democratic ones to experience internal violence of almost all kinds, ranging from civil wars to political assassinations and terrorist bombings. Subsequent studies using statistical methods affirmed the point but added a significant elaboration. Countries defined as autocratic are as stable as democracies when it comes to internal conflict. It is the countries in between, the 'anocracies' with both autocratic and democratic features, that are statistically most likely to experience internal violence. (Hegre et al. 2001; Fearon and Laitin 2003)

The finding was not surprising, but it put a dent in the comfort of liberal theory. Even if democracies were stable and non-violent internally, the process of getting there, or being halfway there, was associated with violence and instability. This pattern was more in accord with the competing prism of development as a conflictual process, as we shall see below. More was to follow. Focusing specifically on the effects of democratization as a process of change—rather than an end product as in the democratic peace thesis—other scholars found that in the European experience, democratization had been associated with war. European states underwent what today we would call a period of rapid economic and political development in the 150 years between the French Revolution and World War II. The process fuelled nationalism and wars. 'States being dragged by social change into a transition to democracy,' Edward Mansfield and Jack Snyder concluded, 'have been more likely to participate in wars and more likely to start them than have states whose [political] regimes did not change [towards more democracy]' (Mansfield and Snyder, cited in Snyder 2000, 20). Elaborating the theme in a book called *From Voting to Violence*, Snyder found that opening up democratic competition is likely to stimulate appeals to ethnic identity and to be exploited by elites. Democratic transitions, therefore, tend to produce **ethnic conflict** within states and nationalistic conflicts among them.

Ethnicity

Modernization theory assumed that as societies made the transition to modernity, identities related to clan, tribe, village, or ethnic group would become less important and gradually be submerged by a higher national identity. The point was supported by scholars of nationalism, such as Ernest Gellner (1983), who argued that growth of national identities paralleled the growth of a modern market economy. By extension, 'ethnic conflict' would become less pronounced. World events in the 1990s, however, suggested otherwise. Did the rise of apparent ethnic conflict in the disintegration of the Soviet Union and Yugoslavia represent a slip back to an earlier stage, or was it a challenge to the idea that modernity would reduce ethnicity? Perhaps 'ethnic conflict' in itself was a problematic concept.

To many analysts, the conflicts were caused by collapse of Cold War constraints, which previously had kept ethnic animosities in check. Some suggested that the Balkans were trapped in ancient hatred that modernization had not quite neutralized. The view was popularized by widely read authors such as Robert Kaplan and the military historian John Keegan.[3] The wars in Yugoslavia and the Caucasus, Keegan argued in the newspaper the *Daily Telegraph* (15 April 1993, quoted in Cramer 2006), 'were a regression from the civilised order'; the fighting in Bosnia was 'a primitive tribal conflict only anthropologists can understand'. Similarly, conflicts in sub-Saharan Africa were often explained by referring to persistent tribal warfare, especially in the media but also by popular writers like Kaplan. His article

'The coming anarchy: How scarcity, crime, over-population, tribalism, and disease are rapidly destroying the social fabric of our planet' (Kaplan 1994) paints a gloomy picture of much of Africa. These are societies in decay, he argues, where environmental degradation, tribalism, and state disintegration prevail. Tribalism is also invoked to explain the genocide in Rwanda, where violence largely did follow ethnic lines.

However historians and political scientists have documented how ethnic identities have been profoundly shaped by processes of modernization, including the colonial experience. British colonial rulers, in particular, institutionalized and reified ethnic identities in subtle and not-so-subtle divide-and-rule strategies (see chapter 2). As constantly created and re-created, ethnic identity can-

Figure 21.3   A weapons cache, Southern Africa

Source: Chr. Michelsen Institute/Jan Isaksen

BOX 21.2   RWANDA: PRIMITIVE, ETHNIC VIOLENCE?

Some 800,000 persons were killed in Rwanda in 1994. The victims were mainly ethnic Tutsi, while the perpetrators were mainly Hutu. Many outside observers initially attributed the violence to long-standing tribal animosities between the Hutu and the Tutsi. Yet these ethnic identities were in part a product of Belgian colonial policy, which deliberately treated the two as separate peoples and issued ethnic identity cards to institutionalize the division. The 1994 massacres were triggered by conflicts over concrete issues (power-sharing in the government, distribution of economic aid) and an uneasy military stand-off between the (Hutu-led) government and (Tutsi) rebel forces. A radical Hutu faction that controlled the state had meticulously planned and organized the massacres. Machete was the weapon of choice—which seemed to symbolize the primitive nature of the society and the violence it produced—but modern guns bought on the international market or received through foreign military assistance agreements were used with decisive effect or deployed in the background.

not be understood simply as a feature of tradition. If ethnic identity is constructed and malleable, as numerous studies suggest, that makes the idea of 'ethnic conflict' more complex than the 'ancient hatreds' thesis claims (Horowitz 1985). Moreover, even conflicts that follow and are fuelled by ethnic divisions are frequently intertwined with economic and political interests in a very complex manner. To illustrate, consider the causes of the Balkan war in the early 1990s.

One common explanation is that the violent break-up of the Socialist Federal Republic of Yugoslavia was caused by ancient ethnic hatreds among Serbs, Croats, and Muslims, which were released after Tito's socialist regime came to an end. These hatreds further defined the war, characterized by ethnic cleansing and massacres of members of 'the other' ethnic group. But more careful consideration of the dynamic of the break-up suggests a different picture. Socialist Yugoslavia had consisted of six republics, each with mixed populations. The system was finely balanced by interlocking rights on the individual, republican, and federal level. After Tito's death in 1980, and with the encouragement of Western governments and the international

financial institutions, Yugoslavia moved towards a market economy and political reform. With both economic and political reform on the table, the political contest intensified. Leaders in the various republics started to make appeals in terms of 'national' (i.e., 'ethnic') interests. Then, as Susan Woodward writes, a vicious cycle of mutual insecurity and exclusion developed:

> [U]nder the budgetary austerities of macroeconomic stabilization, debt repayment, and economic reform in the 1980s . . . political nationalism began to take an exclusionary form. Individuals and politicians first claimed social and economic rights for their national group against others, as they faced worsening unemployment, frozen wages, and declining welfare funds, and then escalated those claims to political rights over capital assets and territory in moves towards exclusive states' rights for the republics, in the name of their majority nation . . . and, eventually independence (Woodward 1999, 81).

As national majorities in individual republics claimed independence—starting with Croatia in

1991—minorities in these republics felt threatened. An escalatory dynamic of intervention and attack developed, involving first established armed forces but soon also paramilitaries of many kinds. In this phase of the conflict, violence largely followed ethnic lines. Even so, the traditional value of 'good neighbourliness' (*komsiluk*) persisted for some time and was even cautiously reappearing after the war, as anthropologist Tone Bringa observed in a mixed Muslim-Croat village in war-ravaged Bosnia (Bringa 2003).

Inequality

Efforts to reduce systemic social, economic, and political inequalities have been at the heart of the development process in many countries. In a few, historically rare cases, this has taken the form of successful social revolutions (as in France, Russia, and China). At times, such struggles have been intertwined with the fight for independence from colonial rule (e.g., Algeria and Vietnam). Conflicts born of structural inequalities have also led to more recent civil wars. During the 1970s and 1980s, landless or poor peasants and workers fought the landed oligarchy that controlled the state and its armed forces in Central America. In Nepal, caste and class coincided to create highly unequal access to basic social services, economic opportunity, and political power. In both cases, radical movements mobilized the disenfranchised to challenge the structure of power. The wars ended in compromise peace settlements in Central America and, eventually, in Nepal as well in 2006.

Well-known cases such as these have raised questions as to whether sharp inequality stimulates violent social transformations as a rule. To some, it seems common sense. Revolutions, separatist movements, and peasant rebellions throughout history are widely seen to be 'about' inequality. Yet careful investigation again reveals more complexity. Statistical analysis shows no clear link between inequality and level of conflict, even if different indicators are used for both sets of variables. For instance, a simple measure of inequality is the Gini coefficient of income distribution at the national level. Studies using this measure of

inequality and various levels of violent conflict have failed to find clear, systematic links between the two (Cramer 2006). Nevertheless, stubborn evidence from historical cases of wars and revolutions suggests that inequality does matter.

The most obvious explanation is that systematic inequality is a necessary but not sufficient condition for violent social transformation. 'The mere existence of privations is not enough to cause an insurrection; if it were, the masses would always be in revolt,' Leon Trotsky observed in his *History of the Russian Revolution*. Dissatisfaction and despair is the raw material of violent change

Figure 21.4   Two boys on the streets of Iraq

Source: Alternatives/Josée Lambert

but not sufficient for a rebellion to materialize, let alone succeed. Organized revolt against the status quo requires mobilizing people (or solving what is often called 'the collective action' problem) and finding resources and support (consistent international support seems critical to success), and progress requires an accelerated weakening of the state that typically started as more powerful than the rebels. All these conditions help explain the three major revolutions in modern history—in France, Russia, and China (Skocpol 1979).

Some recent literature on inequality seeks to combine older concepts of socio-economic inequality and identity differences among groups. When people have unequal access to political, economic, and social resources, the divisions will deepen when they also coincide with cultural differences among groups, or what Frances Stewart (2000) calls horizontal inequalities. Coincidental boundaries among groups are more likely to produce political instability and conflict than cross-cutting divisions.

The greed/grievance debate

During the Cold War, many conflicts in the developing world were linked to the global strategic rivalry between the superpowers, which actively supported the local protagonists. While fought over many issues, these wars were generally framed in terms of broad ideological contests. In Mozambique, for instance, the Marxist movement Mozambican Liberation Front (FRELIMO) that had led the independence struggle seized power when the Portuguese left in 1975 but—as we have seen—immediately faced a rebel movement, RENAMO, established by outside powers for whom FRELIMO represented a dangerous 'socialist' and radical anti-colonial influence. The war lasted for almost 20 years, until the end of the Cold War itself.

The end of the Cold War did not, of course, bring an end to strife in the developing world, although the conflict dynamic now seemed more obscure. Many explanations focused on ethnicity, driven in part by the parallel conflicts in the Balkans. Another, economically oriented, theory was also launched, built around the question of

how rebel wars are financed. As noted above, deprivation alone is insufficient to produce a rebel movement. After the Cold War, continued warfare in Angola, west Africa, Afghanistan, and Cambodia was increasingly self-financed by the exploitation of locally available natural resources such as diamonds, timber, oil, or poppies. The observable importance of self-finance and the lack of recognizable ideology led some to argue that an economic agenda of individual gain had replaced political agendas as the motivating force of rebellions. War, in other words, had become a lucrative enterprise. The thesis was elaborated and tested by the economist Paul Collier and formulated in terms of 'greed' rather than 'grievance'. His argument that (individual, economic) greed rather than (collective, political) grievance was the cause of civil war triggered a large debate in the 1990s on the dynamic of civil wars and how best to study it.[4] As such, it deserves closer examination.

Collier's economic model was rooted in rational choice theory in which the self-interested cost-benefit-calculating individual is the starting point for explaining a social phenomenon. Since political change and the redressing of collective grievances could also be enjoyed by those who had not participated in the rebellion, cost-benefit-calculating individuals would not have incentives to join. Access to loot, however, counted as a direct individual gain from rebellion, only accessible through direct participation, and hence was a strong incentive to join. The existence of primary resources suggested high availability of lootable goods, which made rebellion a profitable undertaking. A large number of unemployed and uneducated young men meant a pool of likely soldier-entrepreneurs. Thus, the Collier model developed for statistical testing relied on indicators such as national dependence on primary resources, level of schooling, and proportion of young males.

The model made some important points about economic activities during war, but it was criticized on many accounts (Ballentine and Sherman 2003; Cramer 2002). First, there were methodological issues about the choice of indicators. A low level of education, for instance, might mean that young males were ready to join a rebel army in order to make a living ('greed') or that angry young males joined to claim their social rights ('grievance'). Second, building a theory around the motivations of individuals was hazardous when the researchers had no data from fieldwork or interviews with potential or actual rebel soldiers but merely national statistical indicators. Third, the rational choice approach was contradicted by anthropological field studies of rebels and their supporters in actual wartime situations. A study from El Salvador, for instance, found that ordinary people supported rebels out of anger and fear, justice and solidarity (Wood 2003). Finally, the policy implications of the economic model were decidedly conservative. If rebels are driven only by personal greed, they have no claim to legitimacy. Moreover, the model sees the sources of violence as entirely internal to the 'conflict trapped' countries themselves. One result of this is that international aspects of war economies—such as the Western demand for diamonds, timber, and coltan, and the profits brought home by international traders and private military companies, are overlooked.

Development as a conflictual process

Social change as a source of instability

Many social scientists hold that periods of change—be it economic growth or decline, political transitions, or social innovation—are associated with conflict. Existing institutions come under pressure and may be unable to control or integrate new forces, demands, and collective actors. Change is likely to be uneven and to create a sense of relative deprivation, injustice, and threat among the losers. The theme was explored on the micro-level by the political scientist Ted Gurr, who in a book entitled *Why Men Rebel* found the answer in the concept of relative deprivation (Gurr 1970). Men rebel, he concluded, when they feel they are worse off than their relevant reference groups, and change is likely to produce precisely such differences. Similarly, rapid cultural change tends to create individual anxiety, as the

sociologist Émile Durkheim noted some 150 years ago. When accompanied by rapid and uneven economic change, it may stimulate radical reactions. Contemporary versions of this argument often appear in relation to 'globalization', which has increased communication among societies but also accentuated the often unequal distribution of benefits (see chapter 6).

Given that social change is a source of instability and conflict, some writers focus on bottom-up violence by mobs, rebels, and revolutionaries and warn against the systemic upheavals this entails. A notable example of this genre among contemporary social scientists is Samuel Huntington, whose influential 1968 book warned against the dangers of rapid modernization and development (Huntington 1968). Countries undergoing modernization risked instability as new expectations were created and traditional mechanisms of social control eroded. The liberal theory of violence, which held that modernization would lead to more stability, was misguided. It was a fallacy to believe that 'the achievement of one desirable social good aids in the achievement of others' (Huntington 1968, 5). Instead, modernization and change had to proceed within carefully constructed institutions so as to preserve stability. The critical issue in development studies, he concluded in a faint echo of the classic conservative lament of Edmund Burke, was the question of order. To secure order, mobilization must not proceed ahead of institution-building.

Violence in development

The link between conflict and social change can also be conceived differently—namely, by considering the role of violence in social transformations. In this perspective, violence is regarded as internal to development rather than a consequence of development. The premise here is that development is a conflictual process because it involves redistribution of power and resources, which sometimes takes place through violence. An obvious example is the colonization of Asia, Africa, and the Americas. Often established and maintained through violence, European domination facilitated the flow of resources that underpinned the **Industrial Revolution** in the West. To what extent the colonial experience also paved the way for later development in the post-colonies is more controversial.

The great trail-blazer with regard to the role of conflict in development is Karl Marx. For Marx, violence played an important role in social change. He held that history could be understood through modes of production, characterized by the technical and material inputs into production as well as the social relations that men enter into when producing. As the transition from one mode of production entailed a complete change of the relations of production, it meant that property rights and hence the distribution of resources radically changed. Such processes were accentuated through the use of force, for in Marx's words, 'revolutions are not made through laws.'

In *Capital*, Marx described how he saw the transition to the capitalist mode of production as having emerged through a process he called primitive accumulation. His account of primitive accumulation was closely linked to his understanding of capitalism. Marx held that capitalism was historically distinct because capitalists owned the means of production, whereas workers had to sell their labour to survive because they had no other means (e.g., land) of subsistence. The state of affairs—in which capitalists owned all the means of production and workers none—had not come about naturally. Rather, it was a result of a process of primitive accumulation that entailed 'conquest, enslavement, robbery, murder, briefly force' (Marx. *Capital*, vol. I, ch. 26). A prominent example of primitive accumulation is the enclosure process in fifteenth- and sixteenth-century England when peasants were evicted, often forcibly, from land that had previously been treated as commons. Similar processes, Marx pointed out, took place in Scotland and Ireland as English soldiers were sent to enforce the claims of landlords. Often, whole villages were burned and destroyed.

Marx did not see the process of primitive accumulation as taking place only within Europe and the industrializing world at the time. The colonial system facilitated the accumulation of riches from Asia, Africa, and America to capitalists in Europe. Here, the methods of primitive accumulation were especially brutal. 'The treasures captured outside Europe by undisguised looting, enslavement, and murder floated back to the mother country and were there turned into capital' (*Capital*, vol. I, ch. 31).

While rebuking classical political economists for painting a rosy picture of the beginnings of capitalism, Marx concluded that capitalism represented technological and economic improvement that in turn would pave the way for socialism. The transition to socialism would likewise necessitate violence, he predicted, although less so than in the transition to capitalism.[5] After socialism, however, there would be social harmony. Marx can therefore be said to be a modernist thinker in that he envisaged human history as a matter of continual progress towards an emancipatory endpoint.

Several contemporary writers have likewise explored the role of violence in development. Drawing on Marx's historical analysis, the American scholar Barrington Moore produced a now-classic study of the origins of the industrial democracies in the United States, France, and England, which showed that they grew out of civil wars, slavery, physical violence, and structural violence in the form of systematic oppression. The critical transformations in the development of these democracies were violent. For instance, by destroying the conditions for a plantation economy based on slave labour, the civil war in the United States laid the foundation for the modern industrial development of the nation and the growth of the middle class (Moore 1966).

The development of the modern state in the European experience has also been a violent process. Charles Tilly famously described early European state-building as 'our largest example of organised crime' (Tilly 1985, 167). Tilly depicted heads of states-in-the-making as self-interested entrepreneurs in the business of producing organized violence. As they set about to eliminate internal and external rivals who threatened their monopoly of violence, these rulers entered into alliances with monied clients, merchants, landowners, and so on. These alliances functioned as a bargain. Rulers, needing funding for their war efforts, sold military protection to their clients. Their protection, however, was of a double nature. While the rulers sold their clients protection against enemies, both within and outside the rulers' territory, they also sold their clients protection against themselves. Clients who did not pay risked facing the rulers' coercive powers. In effect, it was a protection racket. Thus, Tilly argued, organized crime was at the heart of early state formation.

Much recent literature on 'war economies', sometimes referred to as the **political economy** **of war**, also belongs to a tradition that sees violence as intertwined with development. These scholars, while rejecting a rational-choice, 'greed'-based approach to conflict, nevertheless call for analysis of the *dynamics* of violent conflict in developing countries, including the economic transactions taking place through and during violence. Until now, such research has been inhibited by the tendency of researchers, particularly in the development tradition, to put violence in a 'black box', as David Keen (2001) argues. Whereas the causes of conflict are investigated, conflict itself has been seen as a breakdown of 'normal' life: more or less a nothingness

Figure 21.5   Peace process, Guazapa, El Salvador, 1992

Source: Alternatives/Dominic Morissette

or wholly negative condition not worth exploring in its own right. It follows that during violent conflict, there is no development; rather, violent conflict constitutes a pause or even a setback in the development process. The challengers assert, in contrast, that war is no such 'nothingness'. War also entails intense economic activity and often involves a significant transformation of power relations and the control of resources. Hence, violence and development do not always occupy separate spaces.

The perspective above opens up the possibility that violence has played a part in development and social change. However, this would leave us with a stark dilemma: does this mean that violence is *necessary* for development to take place? Do we defend suffering for the sake of progress? In a recent book, Christopher Cramer (2006) addresses this question, or what he calls the **tragic view of history**. The tragic view of history, he warns, can serve to justify cruel actions; at worst, it advocates war as a choice 'bound to

BOX 21.3   SIERRA LEONE'S 'BLOOD DIAMONDS'

In 1999, a Canadian NGO published a report on the ongoing war in Sierra Leone called *The Heart of the Matter: Sierra Leone, Diamonds and Human Security*. It began: 'This study is about how diamonds—small pieces of carbon with no great intrinsic value—have been the cause of widespread death, destruction and misery for almost a decade in the small West African country of Sierra Leone.' The authors argued that diamonds played a central and hitherto unacknowledged part in the brutal war. The levels of violence in Sierra Leone, the authors argued, could only have been sustained through diamond trafficking. Indeed, they said, 'The point of the war may not actually have been to win it, but to engage in profitable crime under the cover of warfare.' The report called for the international community to urgently address the issue. It received worldwide attention and contributed to an international momentum to stop the trade in 'conflict diamonds'. One result was the establishment of a global certification system to trace the origin of diamonds, designed to stop diamonds mined by rebels from reaching the world market.

However, some argued that the focus on diamonds risked reducing the war, and particularly the rebel movement Revolutionary United Front (RUF), to a simple greed for diamonds, thus obscuring the political dimension of the conflict. For instance, when the RUF leader Foday Sankoh was appointed head of the commission for mineral resources as part of a 1999 peace deal, this was seen by many merely as a confirmation that the movement had all along only been after control of the diamond fields. However, the conflict was deeply rooted in political exclusion and deteriorating living conditions, which had been a mobilizing factor for many rebel soldiers. Moreover, it was pointed out that the wartime diamond economy did not represent a radical departure from peacetime practices in trade and production. Rather, a regional network of illicit trade and production in diamonds had existed for decades before the war broke out. The RUF and other factions were able to tap into and sometimes alter these structures, but they did not replace them completely and often entered into alliances with established traders, miners, and exporters. Thus, many of the actors in the Sierra Leone diamond industry have remained the same through war and peace.

have progressive consequences' (Cramer 2006, 47). History is full of examples of large-scale violence undertaken in the name of progress, whether dressed in socialist, fascist, or other ideologies. The alternative, therefore, Cramer suggests, 'may be a *melancholy* perspective, one that accepts violence in the "human condition" the likely links between violence and progress, while accepting too that any and all progress simply raises new conflicts and problems, that no amount of progress will erase conflict and violence' (Cramer 2006, 47).

DEALING WITH THE DEVELOPMENT–CONFLICT NEXUS: INTERVENTION AND PEACEBUILDING

The end of the Cold War opened up space for new forms of international activism. In the Western industrialized world, there was renewed interest in ending conflicts and building peace in the developing world but also greater opportunities for military intervention regardless of motive (which ranged from humanitarian concerns to imperial

BOX 21.4   RESISTING VIOLENCE?
THE STRATEGIES OF NON-VIOLENT ACTORS

The political economy of war literature that considers violence as a strategy in accumulating power and resources, or a vehicle for 'greed', typically emphasizes the perpetrators and beneficiaries of violence. The focus is on warlords, faction leaders, and conflict entrepreneurs. Such perspectives sometimes extend into peacebuilding processes as well. For instance, power-sharing deals, amnesty, or concessions to natural resources are often offered to military leaders as incentives to give up violence.

In this landscape, 'ordinary people' often appear simply as victims, innocent civilians who are caught up in the mayhem. Some scholars, however, have stressed that people living in conflict zones must be recognized as active participants in the conflict setting. They are not merely victims but agents, adopting strategies of surviving and—resisting—conflict (Goodhand 2006). Gilgan (2001) calls for more research on why and how people choose *not* to fight. She suggests that people actively oppose violent domination through non-compliance, political dissidence, and flight and that it is important that outside intervention recognize such acts of resistance to violence.

This also means that peace processes must be careful not to further marginalize local communities vis-à-vis armed factions. Often, only those who have picked up guns are included in the peace negotiations. The numerous peace talks in southern Somalia were sometimes criticized for focusing too much on 'warlords' at the cost of traditional authorities and civil society, thereby conferring political legitimacy on anyone who had established military power:

> Outsiders' insistence on holding high profile, centralized peace conferences for Somalia gives warlords incentives to continue fighting. If they are disruptive enough to defeat peace proposals, they get included in talks, which subsequently increases their reputation and consolidates their position. If they 'only' represent legitimate interests of a local community, they have a tendency to be forced to concede powers. Thus, the international community empowers the violent warlords (Hansen 2003, 72).

interests). A reinvigorated UN engaged itself early in the 'peacebuilding' efforts to end wars that had been fuelled by the rivalry between the superpowers. Peace settlements and postwar reconstruction followed in short order in Central America (Nicaragua, El Salvador, Guatemala), Asia (Cambodia), and southern Africa (Mozambique). At the same time, the collapse of the bipolar international order created new forms of upheavals. Turbulent transitions occurred at the rim of the ex–Soviet Union (in the Caucasus and the Balkans). In the Horn of Africa, regimes that had been propped up by the superpowers collapsed (Somalia). Elsewhere in Africa, new violence developed as well, in Rwanda and Zaire, Sierra Leone and Liberia. To deal with these conflicts, the UN collectively honed its 'peacebuilding' skills.

The then-secretary-general Boutros-Boutros Ghali had defined the agenda in a 1992 document called *The Agenda for Peace*. A long decade later, the UN had massively expanded its peacebuilding capacities and established a new Peacebuilding Commission. More than 20 major operations had been undertaken, most with a military component of peacekeepers as well as an administrative structure to co-ordinate a myriad of social, economic, and political reconstruction activities. 'Peacebuilding' had by this time come to mean an increasingly standardized package of postwar aid, designed to provide security (by UN soldiers and police), promote demilitarization of the belligerent armies or factions, encourage refugees to return, restart or kick-start the economy, restore or reform political institutions, ensure the rule of law and respect for human rights, and—sometimes—establish accountability mechanisms for war crimes and massive human rights violations perpetrated during the conflict.

The package—and despite some variation, it should be understood as a package—was developed by the major donors and aid agencies, the international financial institutions (the World Bank, the International Monetary Fund, the regional development banks), and the UN specialized agencies (especially UNDP, the World Food Programme, and the UN High Commissioner for Refugees) as well as the UN secretariat. It was further streamlined by international organizations such as the Organisation for Economic Co-operation and Development (OECD), which started harmonizing guidelines for aid from the rich industrialized states to peacebuilding activities.[6]

The premise of this package is an expanded version of what we referred to earlier as 'the democratic peace'. In the peacebuilding context, it involved both economic and political reforms and became known as 'the liberal peace'. The essence was a package of reforms believed to constitute the foundation for peaceful reconstruction and development. Political reforms typically meant elections, with participation of political parties and the establishment of plural institutions. Civil society organizations and a free media were encouraged. On the economic side, reforms focused on market mechanisms, a minimalist but effective state, and macroeconomic stability. In addition, human rights monitoring was strengthened and legal reforms patterned on Western legal traditions initiated. The package was firmly anchored in the tradition of Western liberalism. That these traditions would serve as reference points for postwar reconstruction and development in Asia, Africa, and Latin America was hardly surprising at a time when the Soviet Union had collapsed and socialism seemed a defunct concept. In ideological terms, political and economic liberalism was the dominant paradigm in the post–Cold War world. Recent Western scholarship, as we have seen, also seemed to affirm that this was a solid foundation for domestic and international peace. World Bank research recommended rapid postwar growth to sustain the peace. The case for political democracy and peace was celebrated in triumphalist terms by an American scholar and co-founder of the new *Journal of Democracy*:

> The experience of this century offers important lessons. Countries that govern themselves in a truly democratic fashion do not go to war with one another . . . [they] do not 'ethnically' cleanse their own populations . . . [they]

do not sponsor terrorism . . . [they] do not build weapons of mass destruction to use on or to threaten one another. . . . [They] form more reliable, open and enduring trading partnerships . . . [they] are more environmentally responsible because they must answer to their own citizens' (Diamond, cited in Paris 2004, 35).

The limitations of the liberal theory of violence as a guide to understanding the relationship between development and conflict have been noted above. In addition, some scholars now asked whether liberal institutions were particularly *ill*-suited as a framework for postwar reconstruction. A trenchant critical analysis in this regard was developed by Roland Paris in the book *At War's End* (Paris 2004). Liberalism, he noted,

invites open competition, be it in the market or in the political arena. Countries emerging from civil war, however, are more in need of integrative mechanisms to overcome the divisive events of the past and reconstitute themselves as functioning societies. This requires above all structures of guidance, stability, and predictability—in short, institutions that can regulate access to economic and political power. Hence, in an echo of the Huntingtonian prescription of the 1960s, Paris recommended the development of institutions before introducing liberal reforms in order to strengthen peace.

The combination of large aid flows and high policy relevance have turned peacebuilding studies into a massive growth industry. Much has been applied research to assess the impact of particular projects, but there is also a growing body

Figure 21.6   Reconstruction in Afghanistan

Source: Chr. Michelsen Institute/Merete Taksdal

of more academic work. Some used comparative analysis to study the causes of peace—what determines the degree and kind of peace being established? The post-conflict package, they found, helped to stabilize peace at least in the sense that it prevented relapse into full-scale war (Doyle and Sambanis 2006).[7] Others worked in the tradition of critical analysis to understand the functions of peacebuilding in relation to the political, strategic, or organizational interests of the 'peacebuilders' (see Box 21.5). The very term, of course, served to legitimize and partly also to mystify a variety of activities. For example, NATO often presented its role in Afghanistan as part of a peacebuilding task even though it involved offensive military operations and rested on a complex strategic rationale related to the global mission of the alliance.

CONCLUSIONS

Prepositions and conjunctions can be tricky. The title of this chapter, 'Conflict *and* development', suggests that violence is a separate thing that can be extracted from a country's historical development. This is certainly the starting point of many studies, particularly contemporary research that relies on statistical analysis. But the chapter could also be titled 'Conflict *in* development' to convey a different perspective—namely, that conflict is embedded in development understood as social change. Such change often becomes violent, especially during major social transformations. To study conflict 'in' development therefore requires placing events in their broader historical and deeper sociological context. The careful student can learn from both approaches.

BOX 21.5   MARK DUFFIELD: THE MERGING OF DEVELOPMENT AND SECURITY

Mark Duffield's 2001 book *Global Governance and the New Wars: The Merging of Development and Security* is a radical analysis of Western development aid that also applies to peacebuilding efforts. A former aid worker, Duffield claims that the increased interaction between development practice and peacebuilding has enabled the West to control the developing world in novel ways. His argument is complex, but in a simplified version it goes as follows: In a increasingly deregulated world economy, the same processes that have increased global trade, communications, and financial transfers have enabled the emergence of networks for arms trade, money laundering, and drug trafficking that generate instability in the developing world—the South. However, the developed countries in the North do not recognize this connection. Rather, instability is interpreted as a symptom of underdevelopment, the causes of which are internal to the developing countries.

Moreover, this underdevelopment and the instability it leads to is perceived as a threat to the North as well in the form of refugee flows, transnational crime, epidemic diseases, and terrorism. Thus, 'the promotion of development has become synonymous with the pursuit of security' (Duffield 2001, 37), what Duffield terms *the merging of development and security*. Yet, he argues, the underlying structures that perpetrate both instability and underdevelopment—that is, the global economic system—have been taken out of the equation. In reality, therefore, development and security interventions—and hence peacebuilding as well—are really about managing exclusion: controlling and containing the global poor.

A related implication is the geographic location of conflict. If we understand conflict as part of development, we can more readily recognize conflict—and its potential for violence—as part of the history of nations that today are 'developed'. The prosperous, industrialized political democracies of the North are in direct and indirect ways founded on conflict, violence, and suffering.

Violent conflict is not something that primarily afflicts the latecomers to development or involves gruesome war tactics (such as amputating limbs, as RUF rebels in Sierra Leone did) that are uniquely barbarian. Exercising 'memory' in relation to our own past, as Christopher Cramer calls it, is a precondition for understanding and addressing the conflict potential in all forms of development.

QUESTIONS FOR DISCUSSION

1. Taking a developed country you are familiar with, what do you think the role of conflict, especially violent conflict, has been in its development?

2. Taking a developing country today that you are familiar with, do you see any parallels with the role of conflict in its development? What accounts for similarities and differences?

3. What are the implications of using the term 'conflict and development' versus 'conflict in development'?

4. Why, and in what ways, does choice of methodology matter in analyzing the relationship between conflict and development?

5. What are the strength and weakness of the prevailing peacebuilding strategies?

6. Take one or several components of the strategy (e.g., UN peacekeepers, refugee return, elections, economic reconstruction), and consider how they can promote peace or have unintended consequences.

FURTHER READING

Ballentine, K., and J. Sherman. 2003. 'Introduction'. In *Beyond Greed and Grievance: The Political Economy of Armed Conflict*. London: Lynne Rienner.

Collier, P., et al. 2003. 'Breaking the conflict trap: Civil war and development policy'. *World Bank Report 2003*.

Cramer, C. 2006. *Civil War Is Not a Stupid Thing Accounting for Violence in Developing Countries*. London: Hurst.

Duffield, M. 2001. *Global Governance and the New Wars*. London: Zed Books.

Huntington, S.P. 1968. *Political Order in Changing Societies*. New Haven, CT: Yale University Press.

Paris, R. 2004. *At War's End*. New York: Cambridge University Press.

Pugh, N., N. Cooper, and J. Goodhand. 2004. *War Economies in a Regional Context: Challenges of Transformation*. Boulder, CO, and London: Lynne Rienner.

Richards, P. 2005. *No War, No Peace: An Anthropology of Contemporary Armed Conflicts*. Oxford: James Currey.

Tilly, C. 1985. 'War making and state making as organised crime'. In Peter B. Evans, Dietrich Rueschemeyer, and Theda Skocpol, eds, *Bringing the State Back In*, 169–91. Cambridge: Cambridge University Press.

Wood, E.J. 2003. *Insurgent Collective Action and Civil War in El Salvador*. New York: Cambridge University Press.

INTERNET RESOURCES

ReliefWeb: http://www.reliefweb.int. United Nations website providing information to relief organizations on humanitarian emergencies and disasters, administered by the UN Office for the Coordination of Humanitarian Affairs (OCHA).

Crisis States Research Centre: http://www.crisisstates.com. Research centre based at the London School of Economics focusing on development, war, and violence in fragile states.

Small Arms Survey: http://www.smallarmssurvey.org. Independent research project on small arms issues, located at the Graduate Institute of International Studies in Geneva.

MICROCON: http://www.microconflict.eu. Research program on micro-level aspects of conflict, co-ordinated by the Institute of Development Studies, University of Sussex.

Governance and Social Development Research Centre: http://www.gsdrc.org. Resource centre on governance, conflict, and development, administered by the UK Department for International Development.

Carnegie Endowment for International Peace: http://www.ceip.org. Policy-oriented research institute with focus on internal and international peace and conflict, including state-building and democratization.

NOTES

1. For instance, Polity on democracy (http://www.cidcm.umd.edu/polity), the World Bank on economic statistics (http://econ.worldbank.org), and UNDP on socio-economic indicators (http://hdr.undp.org).
2. Among the best known are the Correlates of War project (http://www.correlatesofwar.org) and UCDP/PRIO Armed Conflict Dataset (http://new.prio.no/CSCW-Datasets/Data-on-Armed-Conflict/UppsalaPRIO-Armed-Conflicts-Dataset).
3. Robert Kaplan's 'The coming anarchy' was hugely influential in the US.
4. Collier was at the time research director at the World Bank.
5. '[I]in the former case [transition from feudalism to capitalism], we had the expropriation of the mass of the people by a few usurpers: in the latter [transition from capitalism to socialism], we have the expropriation of a few usurpers by the mass of the people' (*Capital*, vol. I, ch. 32).
6. The Development Assistance Committee (DAC), a powerful committee of the 30-member OECD organization, was in 2007 drafting guidelines for evaluating such activities—i.e., a powerful tool for harmonization.
7. Some estimates of the recurrence of war were highly inflated (see Suhrke and Samset 2007).

CHAPTER 22

INTERNATIONAL MIGRATION AND DEVELOPMENT

KHALID KOSER

LEARNING OBJECTIVES

- To understand the main trends, patterns, and processes of contemporary international migration.
- To understand how globalization and global disparities explain migration.
- To understand how migrants and migration influence development in origin countries.

To set the scene, this chapter begins with a brief overview of contemporary **international migration**. It then turns to examining the relationship between international migration and development in two main ways. First, it demonstrates how international migration has become inextricably linked with the process of **globalization** and specifically how **disparities** in development can be an incentive to migrate. It then goes on to consider the relationship in reverse, demonstrating how international migration influences development in origin countries. In the final section, the chapter turns to the interactions between displacement—or involuntary migration—and development.

CONTEMPORARY INTERNATIONAL MIGRATION

The United Nations defines as an **international migrant** a person who stays outside their usual country of residence for at least one year (see Box 22.1). According to that definition, the UN estimated that in 2006 there were about 200 million international migrants worldwide, including about 10 million **refugees**. This is roughly equivalent to the population of the fifth most populous country on earth, Brazil. One in every 35 people in the world today is an international migrant. But

migration also affects far more people than just those who migrate—it has important social, economic, and political impacts at home and abroad.

The number of international migrants has more than doubled in just 25 years, and about 25 million were added in only the first five years of the twenty-first century. Before 1990, most of the world's international migrants lived in the developing world; today, the majority live in the developed world, and their proportion is growing. In 2005, there were about 65 million migrants in Europe, 54 million in Asia, 45 million in North America, 17 million in Africa, 7 million in Latin America, and 5 million in Oceania. Almost 20 per cent of the world's migrants in 2000—about 38 million—lived in the US. The Russian Federation was the second most important host country for migrants, with about 13 million, or nearly 8 per cent of the global total. Germany had 10 million migrants, followed in the rankings by Ukraine, France, and Canada with between six and seven million migrants each. It is much harder to say which countries most migrants come from, but it has been estimated by the Global Commission on International Migration that at least 35 million Chinese, 20 million Indians, and 7 million Filipinos currently live outside their country.

BOX 22.1   WHO IS A MIGRANT?

Ostensibly, the answer to the question 'who is a migrant' is very straightforward: most countries have adopted the UN definition of someone living outside their own country for a year or more. In reality, however, the answer is more complicated. First, the concept 'migrant' covers a wide range of people in a wide variety of situations—for example, voluntary and forced migrants, low-skilled and high-skilled migrants, legal and illegal migrants. Second, it is very hard to actually count migrants and to determine how long they have been abroad. Third, just as important as defining when a person becomes a migrant is to define when they stop being a migrant. One way for this to happen is to return home; another is to become a citizen of a new country, and the procedures governing that transformation vary significantly. Finally, it has been suggested that as a result of globalization, there are now new 'types' of migrants with new characteristics, at times described as members of transnational communities or diasporas.

Besides the dimensions and changing geography of international migration, there are at least three trends that signify an important departure from earlier patterns and processes. First, the proportion of women among migrants has increased rapidly (see Box 22.2). Very nearly half the world's migrants were women in 2005; according to UN statistics, in 2005 there were more female than male migrants in Europe, Latin America and the Caribbean, North America, Oceania, and the former USSR. What is more, whereas women have traditionally migrated to join their partners abroad, an increasing proportion who migrate today do so independently; they are often the primary breadwinners for the families they leave behind.

Second, the traditional distinction between countries of origin, transit, and destination for migrants has become increasingly blurred. Today, almost every country in the world fulfills all three roles—migrants leave, pass through, and head for all of them. Perhaps no part of the world better illustrates the blurring boundaries between origin, transit, and destination countries than the Mediterranean region (see Box 22.3). Finally, while most of the major movements that took place over the past few centuries were permanent, temporary migration has become much more

important today. Furthermore, the traditional pattern of migrating once, then returning home seems to be phasing out. An increasing number of people migrate several times during their lives, often to different countries or parts of the world, returning home in the intervening periods. Even those who are away for long periods of time return home at more and more frequent intervals, since international travel has become so much cheaper and more accessible.

DEVELOPMENT AND MIGRATION

International migration is an important dimension of globalization and has become increasingly embedded in changes in global economic and social structures. Growing developmental, demographic, and democratic disparities provide powerful incentives to move, as does the global jobs crisis affecting large parts of the developing world. The segmentation of labour markets in richer countries is creating increasing demand for migrant workers there. A revolution in communication has facilitated growing awareness of disparities and opportunities for would-be migrants, while transformations in transportation have made mobility cheaper and more readily accessible.

Figure 22.1   A currency exchange house in rural central Mexico, established because of remittances from migrant family members working in the United States

Source: Paul Haslam

BOX 22.2   THE FEMINIZATION OF INTERNATIONAL MIGRATION

There are a number of reasons why women comprise an increasing proportion of the world's migrants. One is that the demand for foreign labour, especially in more developed countries, is becoming increasingly gender-selective in favour of jobs typically fulfilled by women—services, health care, and entertainment. Second, an increasing number of countries have extended the right of family reunion to migrants—in other words, allowing them to be joined by their spouses and children. Most often, these spouses are women. Changing gender relations in some countries of origin also means that women have more independence to migrate than previously. Finally, and especially in Asia, there has been a growth in the migration of women for domestic work (sometimes called the 'maid trade'), organized migration for marriage (sometimes referred to as 'mail order brides'), and the trafficking of women, especially into the sex industry.

BOX 22.3   ORIGIN, TRANSIT, AND DESTINATION COUNTRIES IN THE MEDITERRANEAN REGION

Perhaps no part of the world better illustrates the blurring boundaries between origin, transit, and destination countries than the Mediterranean. About 50 years ago, the situation was fairly straightforward. All the countries of the Mediterranean—in both North Africa and southern Europe—were countries of origin for migrants who mainly went to northern Europe to work. About 20 years ago, southern Europe changed from a region of emigration to a region of immigration as increasing numbers of North Africans arrived to work in their growing economies and at the same time fewer southern Europeans had an incentive to head north for work anymore. Today, North Africa is changing from an origin to a transit and destination region. Increasing numbers of migrants from sub-Saharan Africa are arriving in countries like Libya, Morocco, and Tunisia. Some remain, others cross the Mediterranean into southern Europe, usually illegally, where again some stay and others try to move on into northern Europe.

Migration networks have expanded rapidly and further facilitate migration. New individual rights and entitlements allow certain people to cross borders and stay abroad more easily (although many more face growing restrictions). And the growth of a migration industry adds further momentum to international migration, even where it is not officially permitted. In this section, we examine why there are more reasons and additional means to migrate than ever before.

Growing disparities

Development is a difficult concept to measure. The United Nations Development Programme (UNDP) has produced a widely cited **Human Development Index** (HDI), which ranks countries according to a combination of three dimensions—income, health, and education. According to the 2005 report, while the HDI has risen across the developed world and most of the developing world, there have been unprecedented reversals in some of the very poorest countries. In 2005, 18 countries recorded lower HDIs than they had in 1980; 12 of them were in sub-Saharan Africa. Not only

is human welfare in those countries deteriorating, but at the same time the gaps between them and the rest of the world are increasing.

Some of the statistics provided by UNDP are very depressing indeed. Around 550 million of the people in work around the world earn less than one US dollar per day. More than 850 million people, including one in three preschool children worldwide, suffer from malnutrition. More than 1 billion people lack access to safe water, and 2.6 billion do not have adequate sanitation. Worldwide, about 115 million children are denied even basic primary education—most of them in sub-Saharan Africa and South Asia. On average, girls can expect to receive one year of education less than boys in African and Arab states and two years less in South Asia. In the developing world as a whole, only 58 per cent of women are literate, compared to 68 per cent of men.

A lack of development is compounded by growing population pressure. Almost five billion people, or 80 per cent of the world's population, currently live in poor or at best middle-income countries. While many of the world's more prosperous countries have declining populations, they are burgeoning in many poorer countries: virtually all of the world's population growth currently takes place in developing nations. The average woman in Africa today has 5.2 children, while the average European woman has just 1.4. These trends mean that the share of the world's population residing in developing countries will rise even further. And as a result of such high rates of childbirth in the developing world, there is also a far higher proportion of younger people there than in the developed world, people who need to be absorbed into the labour market or will have to migrate elsewhere to find work.

It is no coincidence that a good number of poor countries are also states where the democratic process is fragile, where the rule of law is weak, and where corruption is rife (although corruption is certainly not limited to poor countries). By migrating, people try to protect themselves and their families from the effects of a weak economy and volatile market and from political crises, armed conflicts, and other risks. In some cases, people are forced to flee as refugees because the state can no longer protect them from the impact of conflict or from persecution. In the very worst cases, it is the states themselves that are responsible for these offences.

But it is important to stress that underdevelopment or overpopulation or poor governance per se are not necessarily the cause of migration but rather differentials between different parts of the world. Per capita Gross Domestic Product

Figure 22.2   The wall separating Israel and Palestine

Source: Alternatives/Michel Lambert

(GDP) is 66 times higher in the developed world than in the developing world. A child born in Burkina Faso today can expect to live 35 years less than a child born in Japan, and somebody born in India can expect to live 14 years less than somebody born in the United States. Limited school enrolment and low literacy levels in poorer countries contrast with almost universal enrolment and full literacy in the richer ones. And with very few exceptions, the most corrupt and undemocratic governments are in the poorest countries.

The global jobs crisis

One of the most powerful incentives to migrate is the need to find work. Although there are important variations, overall unemployment has declined in the developed world in recent years. In contrast, it has increased or remained at a stable but high level in large parts of the developing world. The highest incidence of unemployment in the world's major regions is in the Middle East and North Africa at over 12 per cent, compared with about 6 per cent across the industrialized economies.

Being out of work is not the only dimension of the current global jobs crisis. Many people are underemployed. Usually, these people work in the informal sector where employment is unpredictable, opportunities come and go by the season and in some cases by the week or even day, and working conditions can be appalling. Even for those who are employed, wages are often barely sufficient for survival. UNDP estimates that although poverty is likely to decrease, it will still remain substantial for the foreseeable future and that in 2015, some 380 million people will still be trying to survive on less than one US dollar per day. Another aspect of the global jobs crisis is the 12 million people who the International Labour Organization (ILO) estimates are currently working in situations of forced labour.

Populations under particular stress in the developing world are those who rely on agriculture for their income. They comprise about half of the entire labour force—some 1.3 billion people. Many have small farms that are threatened by commercial expansion and environmental degradation. They are also often taxed disproportionately because of their weak political position. The income gap between farming and non-farming activities in developing countries has increased dramatically in recent years. One result has been increasing rural-urban migration as farmers and their families head for towns and cities to try to find a better source of livelihood. For many of these people, internal migration to the city is the first step towards international migration out of their country.

The segmentation of labour markets

High-income economies are increasingly becoming characterized by the segmentation of labour markets. This occurs when national workers eschew sectors of the labour market because they are low-paying, offer little security, and are low-status and thus have become dominated by migrant workers. These occupations are often described as '3D jobs', entailing work that is dirty, dangerous, or difficult—often a combination of all three. They are concentrated in sectors such as agriculture, forestry, plantations, heavy industry, construction, and domestic services. Often, the migrants who work in these sectors are undocumented or have irregular status, since they are the people most willing to work for very low wages and in insecure conditions.

The communication and transportation revolutions

The communication revolution is a central element of the globalization process. Much of the academic literature on globalization has focused on the recent explosion in hi-tech developments such as email and the Internet, electronic bulletin boards, and satellite television stations, as well as cellphones and cheap international telephone calls. It has been estimated, for example, that between 1990 and 2000, the number of telephone lines worldwide increased from 700 million to

2.5 billion, while the number of Internet users increased from scarcely one million to more than one billion. This revolution has facilitated global linkages and, in effect, reduced the distance between different parts of the world. It is relevant to migration for two reasons. First, it makes people aware of disparities—of what life is like in other parts of the world. Second, it makes people aware of opportunities to move and to work abroad.

At the same time, it is possible to overstate the communication revolution. There is still a significant global 'digital divide', which is the term given to the gap in access to information resources that exists between poor and rich countries (see chapter 24). This was most strikingly illustrated in a speech by UN secretary-general Kofi Annan in 2000, who said that 'Half the world's population has never made or received a phone call', although this statistic has been widely debated ever since. Bridging the digital divide is nevertheless considered important for achieving global equality, increasing social mobility, encouraging democracy, and promoting economic growth.

Another 'revolution' often referred to in the globalization literature is in transportation. This refers on the one hand to the increasing range of options for international travel and on the other to decreasing costs. It has arisen particularly because of the proliferation of competition among airline companies. Once again, it would be a mistake to assume that this revolution has reached every part of the world, but it is nevertheless estimated that today it costs no more than US $2,500 to travel legally between any two places in the world. It can be far more expensive—although still possible—to travel illegally (see Box 22.5). If the communication revolution has made many would-be migrants more aware of reasons to migrate, the transportation revolution has made migration more feasible. At the same time, travelling internationally is still prohibitively expensive for the majority of the world's population, and many face administrative obstacles such as the difficulty of obtaining passports and visas.

Migration networks

Most migrants move to countries where they have friends or family already established, forming what is often referred to as transnational migration networks. It has been argued that these networks, which establish a self-perpetuating cycle, are one of the main reasons why migration is increasing today. The expansion of migration means that more people than ever before have friends or family already living abroad, and the changing geography of migration means that more often than previously, these networks link would-be migrants in poor countries with potential destinations in richer countries.

BOX 22.4   THE CELLPHONE REVOLUTION IN AFRICA

It is estimated that worldwide there are 2.4 billion cellphone users and that 1,000 new customers subscribe every minute. Fifty-nine per cent of cellphone users are based in developing countries, making cellphones the first telecommunication technology in history to have more users there than in the developed world. Cellphone usage in Africa is growing faster than in any other region and jumped from 63 million users two years ago to 152 million today. There are 3.2 million cellphone customers in the Democratic Republic of Congo alone, and 8,000 new cellphone customers sign up each day. This compares with just 20,000 conventional land lines there.

BOX 22.5   THE COSTS OF MIGRANT SMUGGLING

A 2005 review of more than 600 sources in which the costs charged to migrants by smugglers were reported yielded the following mean costs for movement between world regions:

Routes	Mean costs (US$)
Asia–Americas	26,041
Europe–Asia	16,462
Asia–Australasia	14,011
Asia–Asia	12,240
Asia–Europe	9,374
Europe–Australasia	7,400
Africa–Europe	6,533
Europe–Americas	6,389
Americas–Europe	4,528
Americas–Americas	2,984
Europe–Europe	2,708
Africa–Americas	2,200
Africa–Australasia	1,951
Africa–Africa	203

Source: Petros 2005, 4–5.

Migration networks have been shown to encourage migration in three main ways. First, they provide information, often taking advantage of the new communications technologies described above. Second, they finance trips by lending would-be migrants money. Third, they can play a crucial role in helping new migrants to settle by providing an initial place to stay, helping them find a job, and providing other economic and social assistance.

New rights and entitlements

There has been a significant expansion of rights and entitlements that allow certain people to cross borders and stay abroad far more easily than ever before. The dismantling of internal borders in the European Union (EU), for example, allows for the free movement of EU citizens within the region, while the North American Free Trade Agreement (NAFTA) and regional economic agreements in other parts of the world, including Africa and South America, also contain some provisions for the free movement of workers. Furthermore, certain categories of people—such as business-people, academics and students, sports and entertainment performers—often either do not require visas or can apply via fast-track procedures. Almost every country in the developed world allows long-term migrant workers to be joined by members of their immediate family. Furthermore, most countries in the world have also signed the 1951 UN Refugee Convention, which guarantees protection and assistance to refugees outside their country (perhaps the most significant non-signatory is India).

However, the extent of these new rights and entitlements can be exaggerated. The free movement of labour has not yet been realized in most regional economic agreements outside the EU. Applicants for family reunion face increasingly rigorous administrative processes. There are also increasing restrictions on the mobility of many other people—the low-skilled and asylum seekers, for example. In particular, the phenomenon of 'irregular' migration (also referred to as 'undocumented' or 'unauthorized' migration) has risen quickly on political agendas worldwide (see Box 22.6).

The migration industry

Migration is facilitated by a wide range of individuals and agents, including labour recruiters, immigration lawyers, travel agents, brokers, housing providers, **remittances** agencies, and immigration and customs officials, as well as by entire institutions such as the International Organization for Migration (IOM), which is often responsible for transporting migrants and refugees for official resettlement or return programs, and NGOs that provide assistance and shelter to migrants and refugees. These individuals and organizations have been described by some analysts as forming a new migration 'industry' or migration 'business'. There is also an illegitimate part of the migration industry, comprising human traffickers and migrant smugglers (see Box 22.7). The enormous profits that the immigration industry makes from migration, it has been argued, add considerable momentum to the process.

BOX 22.6   IRREGULAR MIGRATION

Irregular migration is itself a complex and diverse concept. First, it is important to recognize that there are lots of ways that a migrant can become irregular. Irregular migration includes people who enter a country without the proper authority—for example, by entering without passing through a border control or entering with fraudulent documents. It also includes people who may have entered a country perfectly legally but then remain there in contravention of the authorities—for example, by staying after the expiry of a visa or work permit, through sham marriages or fake adoptions, or as bogus students or fraudulently self-employed. The term also includes people moved by migrant smugglers or human traffickers and those who deliberately abuse the asylum system.

Second, there are important regional differences in the way that the concept irregular migration is applied. In Europe, for example, where the entry of people from outside the European Union is closely controlled, it is relatively easy to define and identify migrants with irregular status. That is not the case in many parts of Africa, where borders are porous, ethnic and linguistic groups straddle state borders, some people belong to nomadic communities, and many people do not have proof of their place of birth or citizenship.

A final complexity arises because migrants' status can change, often quite literally overnight. For example, migrants might enter a country in an irregular fashion but then regularize their status, perhaps by applying for asylum or entering a regularization program. Conversely, migrants might enter regularly, then become irregular when they work without a work permit or overstay a visa.

BOX 22.7   MIGRANT SMUGGLING AS A BUSINESS

The author spent some time in 2004 interviewing migrant smugglers in Afghanistan and Pakistan. They reported that over time, not only had the amount they charge changed but the way they received payments had as well. About 10 years ago, migrant smugglers apparently insisted that payments be made in full in advance. The danger for migrants was that smugglers might take their money and disappear before moving them. In response to these fears, some smugglers changed their practice, asking only for a deposit in advance of movement, with the balance to be paid after arrival in the destination country. The problem here was that some migrants were exploited by smugglers to whom they were indebted after they had arrived. In the past two or three years, smugglers have responded to their clients' concerns and demands once again. Now payment is made in full in advance but is deposited with a third party rather than being paid to the smuggler directly. The money is released to the smuggler only after the migrant has called to confirm that he or she has arrived safely at the destination. What this amounts to is a money-back guarantee on migrant smuggling.

Figure 22.3   Surveillance on the US side of the wall that separates San Diego, California, from Tijuana, Mexico

Source: Paul Haslam

Explaining migration

This section has briefly explained some of the key structural changes in the global economy that together provide increasing incentives and opportunities for people to migrate. Yet these factors need to be reconciled with the fact that international migrants still make up only about 3 per cent of the world's population. Given growing inequalities, widening awareness of opportunities for a better life elsewhere, and increasing access to transportation, a legitimate question to ask is why so few people migrate.

Some of the answers to this question have already been alluded to. The very poorest people, those most affected by global inequalities, simply cannot afford to move. Many people who do migrate in response to poverty move internally, normally from the countryside to the city, and not internationally. There are far more unemployed or underemployed people in the poor world than jobs for them, even in the segmented labour markets of the rich economies. The communication and transportation revolutions are not as far-reaching as some commentators believe, nor are migration networks. Rights and entitlements to move apply on the whole to the privileged few. And the migration industry depends on profit and therefore has an incentive to keep migration costs up.

At least three other reasons emerge from the literature. The most important is inertia. Most people do not want to move away from family, friends, and a familiar culture, so they tend to stay in the country where they were born. Another reason is that governments can control migration. Communist countries used to stop people leaving, but since the collapse of the Soviet Union and end of the Cold War, this is rarely the case anymore (Cuba and North Korea are notable exceptions). However, certain countries in Africa and the Middle East still require citizens to obtain permission before they can leave. Much more common today is migration control on the part of destination countries, although their efforts are not always effective. An additional reason is that as countries develop, emigration eventually

declines, and despite the depressing statistics cited earlier in this section, most countries in the world are developing, albeit sometimes at a painfully slow rate. The next section turns to the links between migration and development.

MIGRATION AND DEVELOPMENT

Migration can have profound impacts on the development of countries of origin. On the positive side, migrants often send home vast sums of money and make other contributions from abroad too, and when they return they can bring home new skills, experiences, and contacts. On the negative side, migration can deplete countries of skills that are in short supply through the **brain drain**.

Remittances

The term remittance usually refers to money sent home by migrants abroad. The true scale of remittances worldwide is hard to gauge. While some money is sent home through banking systems and can thus be formally tracked, it is likely that more is sent home through informal channels. One reason is the high costs that are often charged by banks and agents. Channels for informal remittances include migrants taking home cash when they return for visits or sending home money with friends or relatives. Sometimes entrepreneurs and traders who travel regularly to and from home carry money back for migrants for a small commission—in Cuba, for example, these entrepreneurs are known as *mulas*. Perhaps the most elaborate mechanism for informal transfers, however, is the Somali *hawilaad* system (see Box 22.8). The point is that the scale of these informal transfers is simply not known. Furthermore, even formal remittances cannot always be accurately quantified, because banks are often unwilling or unable to release specific details about personal transfers.

These data problems notwithstanding, the World Bank produces annual estimates of the scale of remittances worldwide. They estimate that in 2006, some US $276 billion was sent home by migrants. This is a quite staggering sum, which

BOX 22.8   THE *HAWILAAD* SYSTEM

The *hawilaad* (or *xawilaad*) system is based on Somali traders. They collect hard currency from Somali migrants abroad, then use the money to purchase commodities that can be sold in Somalia. They return periodically to Somalia, sell their goods, then pay the equivalent in Somali currency to the migrants' families. Profit made on the sale of the goods effectively becomes the traders' commission. This system of transfer is very common among Somali communities across the world. In the aftermath of 9/11, attempts were made to monitor it or close it down because of some evidence that funding for the attacks was channelled through Somalia. However, the system has proved hard to formalize and still appears to be widespread.

is also striking because it represents a 50 per cent increase in the flow of remittances in just five years—the main reason being the impact of globalization (see Box 22.9). In developing countries, remittances amount to almost three times the value of donations through development assistance and charity.

The top three remittance-receiving countries in 2004 were Mexico (US $16 billion), India (US $9.9 billion), and the Philippines (US $8.5 billion). However, remittances as a proportion of GDP were highest in small countries, amounting to 23 per cent in Jordan, 27 per cent in Lesotho, and 37 per cent in Tonga. Compared with other developing regions, sub-Saharan Africa received the lowest level of remittances, amounting to just 1.5 per cent of the global total. The top countries from which remittances were sent in 2004 were the United States (US $28 billion), Saudi Arabia (US $15 billion), and Belgium, Germany, and Switzerland (US $8 billion each).

There is still significant debate about the impact of remittances at home. It is clear that they benefit those who receive them directly—who are

BOX 22.9   REMITTANCES, GLOBALIZATION, AND THE '3Ts'

The main reason remittances have increased so rapidly in recent years is the globalization process. Specifically, there are '3Ts' that have been generated by globalization and at the same time promote remittances. One is transportation—particularly, cheap air transportation. The second is the growth in tourism—many migrants carry home money when they visit for a holiday. The third is telecommunication—cheap telephone calls and widening Internet access mean that migrants and their families can stay in contact more regularly than previously and friends and families can more easily request assistance.

often among the poorest in society. Remittances can lift people out of poverty: it has been estimated that in Somaliland, for example, the average household income is doubled by remittances, while in Lesotho they represent up to 80 per cent of the income of rural households. Besides increasing incomes, remittances also diversify them, meaning that households are less reliant on a single source of income. In this way, remittances also provide insurance against risk. In addition, they are often spent on the education of children and health care for the elderly.

The extent to which remittances benefit those outside the immediate family, however, largely depends on how the money is spent. If used to establish small businesses, for example, or invested in community-based enterprises such as wells, schools, or health clinics, then remittances can provide employment and services for people other than the direct recipients. On the other hand, if as is often the case they are spent on consumer goods such as cars and television sets or on repaying debt, their wider benefit is limited. Additionally, when some households receive remittances and others do not, disparities among households can be exacerbated and communities undermined. It is also worth remembering that migrants tend to originate in certain parts of origin countries, which means that their remittances can increase regional disparities too. There is also some evidence that receiving remittances can create a 'culture of migration' in origin countries whereby young people see the apparent rewards of migrating and have unrealistic expectations about moving abroad. Alternatively, relying on remittances can be a disincentive for some people at home to work at all.

Diasporas

In places where there are considerable numbers of migrants from one town or city, region or country living together in the same country of destination, they often come together in formal organizations. These organizations take a variety of forms. They include professional associations, bringing together migrant doctors, lawyers, or teachers from the same origin, for example. They also include organizations based on common interests such as sport, religion, gender, charitable work, and development. Another type of organization is the home town association (HTA) that brings together people from the same town or city who direct their activities on development in their home town (see Box 22.10). The catch-all term **diaspora** is often used to describe these various migrant organizations.

These diaspora organizations commonly collect donations from their membership and send them back to the country of origin for specific purposes, including ongoing development and emergency assistance. Diaspora organizations rallied quickly to send home money, medical equipment, tents, and food in response to the 2005 earthquake in northern Pakistan, for example. As well as making economic contributions by sending home money and material goods, diaspora organizations can also participate in the political, social, and cultural affairs of their home country and community. A good example can be seen in Somalia, where Somali diaspora organizations largely paid for the construction of the University of Hargeisa and Amoud University in Borama.

While diasporas can contribute to development, they can also contribute to warfare. Remittances from Ethiopian and Eritrean diaspora organizations certainly helped fund the recent conflict between these two countries. In addition, diaspora organizations are often dominated by a particular religious or ethnic group, and their contributions often target those particular groups, thus exacerbating disparities. An associated point is that diaspora organizations are often comprised of the educated and elite, and their contributions reflect this. Building a university, for example, probably does not directly benefit poor rural peasants.

Return

Besides sending home remittances and making a collective contribution through diaspora organizations, a third way that migrants can potentially

Figure 22.4 Migrants in a poor Bolivian barrio on the outskirts of Buenos Aires, Argentina, celebrate their culture and traditions on their national day

Source: Paul Haslam

contribute to development is by returning. Migrants can bring home savings from abroad to invest at home when they return, often establishing small businesses, for example. They may come home with a good network of contacts abroad that can form the basis for small-scale trade and import–export activities. They may also bring back new ideas that can spur entrepreneurial attitudes and activities among the people with whom they settle on return.

BOX 22.10   HOME TOWN ASSOCIATIONS

Mexican HTAs have a long history—the most prominent were established in the 1950s. There are currently more than 600 Mexican HTAs in 30 cities in the US. They support public works in their localities of origin, including the construction of public infrastructure (for example, new roads and road repairs), donating equipment (for example, ambulances and medical equipment), and promoting education (for example, establishing scholarship programs, constructing schools, and providing school supplies).

Once again, it is important not to overestimate the impact of return. Some people return because they have not succeeded abroad—they may come home with no savings and no new experiences and return to whatever they did before leaving. It is often the case that migrants go home to retire, having spent their working lives abroad. While they may take home money and experience, they are not economically active themselves upon return. Also, the extent to which return has an impact really depends on conditions at home. If there is no access to land, or taxes are too high, or there is an inadequate supply of skilled labour, for example, return migrants with good intentions to set up a new business can easily become frustrated and have their plans thwarted.

The brain drain

When there are high levels of unemployment at home, emigration can be positive in that it reduces competition for limited jobs. This is one reason why the government of the Philippines, for example, positively encourages emigration; another reason, of course, is the money that these migrants send home.

Migration, however, can be selective, and those who leave are at times among the most entrepreneurial, best educated, and brightest in society. If their particular skills are readily available in the society, once again this need not be a problem. India, for example, can afford computer experts and technical workers leaving in substantial numbers, since so many young people in India today have these skills. It is more usually the case, however, that these movements deplete the country of origin of skills that are scarce. This process is usually referred to as the brain drain. Besides removing skills, the brain drain also means that countries do not see any return on their investment in educating and training their own citizens.

Of special concern is the migration of health personnel—nurses and doctors—from countries in sub-Saharan Africa. Some of the figures are startling: since 2000, for example, nearly 16,000 nurses from sub-Saharan Africa have registered to

work in the UK alone. Only 50 out of 600 doctors trained since independence are still practising in Zambia. It has been estimated that there are currently more Malawian doctors practising in Manchester, England, than in the whole of Malawi. Although it has attracted less attention, the brain drain of teachers from Africa is generating growing concern.

Reactions to the brain drain are divided. It can be argued that the brain drain represents people moving in order to improve their lives and realize their potential and that there is nothing wrong with that. In addition, if their own countries cannot provide adequate employment, career opportunities, and incentives to stay, then the problem lies with those countries. On the other hand, there has been criticism of the richer countries to which skilled migrants head, especially when they actively recruit those skills. Furthermore, many migrants fail to find jobs commensurate with their skills, a phenomenon often referred to as the 'brain waste'.

DISPLACEMENT AND DEVELOPMENT

So far, this chapter has focused mainly on voluntary migrants—people who by and large choose to move abroad. This final section briefly considers the interactions between involuntary migration—or displacement—and development. Most people who are forced to leave their own countries are described as refugees, although in fact the legal definition of a refugee is very specific (see Box 22.11). The majority of the world's 10 million or so refugees are currently located in sub-Saharan Africa, the Middle East, and Central Asia.

The literature on links between refugees and development focuses on three specific interactions. The first is the link between development—or lack of development—and displacement. The second is the developmental impacts of refugees in host countries. And the third is the implications of the return of refugees for development in their home countries.

BOX 22.11 WHO IS A REFUGEE?

According to the United Nations Convention relating to the Status of Refugees (1951), a refugee is someone who is '. . . outside his own country, owing to a well-founded fear of persecution, for reasons of race, religion, nationality, membership of a particular social group, or political opinion'. There are regional variations on this basic formula, and it has been criticized as being out-of-date; yet it remains the most commonly accepted definition. There are two defining characteristics of this definition. First, it only covers people who have been displaced outside their own country—many more people have been forcibly displaced within their countries. Second, it focuses on people who are displaced by persecution and conflict—not those who flee natural disasters or extreme poverty.

There is considerable debate about the extent to which a link exists between refugee displacement and poverty or underdevelopment in their home countries. In 1995, the Office of the United Nations High Commissioner for Refugees (UNHCR) conducted a basic analysis comparing refugee numbers and development indicators. It found that countries with the highest ranking on the Human Development Index were the least likely to experience population displacements, whereas those with the lowest ranking had the highest propensity to generate large movements of refugees. The same broad correlation remains true today.

What is difficult, however, is to establish a causal relationship. Many poor countries have not generated refugees—Tanzania is a good example. Conversely, some wealthier countries have, and the best recent example is the former Yugoslavia. Furthermore, many recent refugee movements have been provoked by events such as conflict, which are not necessarily directly linked with economic development—the recent interventions in Afghanistan and Iraq are examples.

The second main focus of literature considering interactions between refugees and development considers the developmental implications of refugees in host countries. It is often assumed that refugees have a negative impact, and there is a par-

ticular focus in the literature on the environmental impacts of refugees. Refugees often need wood for cooking and construction, and significant deforestation can occur around their settlements, resulting in the longer term in deteriorating soil quality. The water table may also be lowered and groundwater polluted. Their potentially negative impact on the environment has been cited recently by several countries (for example Honduras, Pakistan, and Turkey) as one reason to turn refugees away. In this light, it is important to place the environmental impact of refugees in proper context. It varies according to the number of refugees and the length of time they stay. It is likely to be more severe when they settle on marginal land, when they live in camps rather than within local settlements, and when their movement is restricted. And recent evidence suggests that even where environments are damaged, they can rebound quickly once refugees have gone home.

A more limited literature considers various other impacts that refugees can have. Because they receive aid, they can sometimes undercut the wage rates of local people, thus introducing an element of competition that benefits some and disadvantages others within the local community. Social tensions can arise between refugees and the local community. Sometimes refugee camps can also become the focus for political activities.

Perhaps the clearest example of a positive impact of refugee settlement is the 'integrated zonal developments' that emerged in several East African countries during the 1960s and 1970s. Rural refugee settlements were planned and deliberately integrated into the local economy, and in some cases they formed the focus for the growth of new villages and even towns. The reasons these developments succeeded were, first, that there were relatively few refugees involved and second, that host governments had a largely positive attitude towards them.

The final interaction to consider is the implications of the return of refugees for development at home. The first thing to bear in mind, however, is that refugees often return to countries that have been affected by conflict for long periods of time (for example, Afghanistan or Mozambique), and in this context it may be premature to talk of development, at least in the short-term. It also needs to be noted that there is a significant shortage of research on what happens to refugees after they return, at least in part because they no longer fall under the institutional responsibility of any international organization.

The limited literature, nevertheless, indicates that return can pose significant obstacles for refugees. Recurrent physical problems include the presence of land mines and the destruction of housing. Economic activity largely depends on access to key resources such as land, labour, working capital, and skills. And social confrontation can often arise in the context of the reintegration of returnees with the internally displaced, with those who never fled, and also with demobilized soldiers.

One of the most important variables that can influence the reintegration process is conditions in refugee settlements in exile and, specifically, the extent to which refugees have been allowed to gain a degree of self-reliance. Other variables include the type and management of settlements for returnees and the extent and type of assistance made available to them.

A recent extension of the literature considering the links between refugee return and develop-ment at home focuses on situations in which refugees do not return but instead remain in host countries permanently and form a 'refugee diaspora'. It must be acknowledged straightaway that this situation probably only applies to that very small percentage of refugees who move long distances and settle in richer countries. Despite their small numbers, they can nevertheless have a significant impact on development at home. They often send home remittances and invest in land or property. They can participate in elections from abroad. And they can contribute to intellectual debate via the Internet. Clearly, however, the desire and ability of refugees to contribute in these sorts of ways vary over time and cannot always be taken for granted.

CONCLUSIONS

This chapter has focused almost exclusively on international migration—both voluntary and involuntary. This topic has been the subject of far more research and writing than internal migration and has also attracted far more political and media attention and public discourse. Yet the number of internal migrants—both voluntary and involuntary—is far higher than the number of international migrants. In the conclusion, we will look at specific interactions between internal migration and development that are worth considering.

Worldwide, far more people choose to move within their own countries than to cross an international border. It is estimated that in China alone, there are 140 million internal migrants, compared to 200 million international migrants worldwide. What is more, internal migration appears set to grow at an even faster rate than international migration over the next few years. In the next 20 years, a further 300 million Chinese citizens are expected to migrate within their country.

Like international migration, internal migration is both a symptom and a cause of development processes. Most people who move within their country move from the countryside to towns and cities, normally in search of work, better incomes, and greater opportunities. Internal migration can also contribute to development. It has been estimated that internal migration has contributed up to 16 per cent annually to the growth of China's GDP in recent years. The main reason is that internal migration is one way of relieving unemployment in certain areas and filling labour market gaps in other areas. Limited research indicates that internal migrants also send home significant remittances. According to one estimate, the equivalent of over US $30 billion is sent home each year by Chinese internal migrants—mainly to rural areas by workers who have moved to the city. Their remittances have helped to reduce the rural–urban income gap in China, decrease regional disparities in wealth,

reduce rural poverty, pay for education and health care, and promote consumption and investment.

Similarly, far more people have been displaced inside than outside their own countries. Many of these people have been affected by 'development-induced displacement', particularly in the context of dam construction. In such development schemes, planned reservoir areas can necessitate the relocation of entire settlements. The scale of these displacements is hard to assess, but it is estimated by the World Bank that in the past decade, more than 100 million people have been affected. Particular controversy surrounds the ongoing construction of the Three Gorges dam on the Yangtze River in China. It is estimated that this project will lead to the inundation of two cities, 140 towns, and 1,350 villages and necessitate the resettlement of more than one million people.

QUESTIONS FOR DISCUSSION

1. Who is an international migrant?
2. What are the main causes of migration?
3. Why are there not more international migrants?
4. What is the impact of remittances on development in poor countries?
5. What is the 'brain drain'?
6. What are the links between displacement and development?
7. What are the links between internal migration and development?

FURTHER READING

Castles, Stephen, and Mark Miller. 2003. *The Age of Migration: International Population Movements in the Modern World*. 3rd edn. London: Macmillan.

IOM (International Organization for Migration). 2005. *World Migration 2005: Costs and Benefits of International Migration*. Geneva: IOM.

Koser, Khalid. 2007. *International Migration: A Very Short Introduction*. Oxford: Oxford University Press.

Skeldon, Ron. 1997. *Migration and Development: A Global Perspective*. London: Longman.

UNDESA (UN Department of Economic and Social Affairs). 2005. *World Economic and Social Survey 2004*. New York: UNDESA.

UNHCR (UN High Commissioner for Refugees). 2006. *The State of the World's Refugees*. Oxford: Oxford University Press.

INTERNET RESOURCES

Centre on Migration, Policy and Society (COMPAS): http://www.compas.ox.ac.uk.
Global Commission on International Migration (GCIM): http://www.gcim.org.
International Organization for Migration (IOM): http://www.iom.int.
Migration Policy Institute (MPI): http://www.migrationinformation.org.
UN High Commissioner for Refugees (UNHCR): http://www.unhcr.org.

CHAPTER 23

INDIGENOUS PEOPLES: A CATEGORY IN DEVELOPMENT

NATACHA GAGNÉ

LEARNING OBJECTIVES

- To understand the principal factors shaping the definition of indigenous peoples at the United Nations.
- To understand the history and the context of the mobilization of indigenous peoples at the international level.
- To understand the main issues surrounding indigenous rights claims at the international level from the perspective of indigenous peoples as well as the states that they are part of.

Today, we estimate that between 300 and 350 million people in the world can be considered indigenous (IWGIA 2007, 10; WGIP 2001; for regional estimates, see Maybury-Lewis 2006, 22). Indigenous people represent almost 6 per cent of the world population and constitute no less than 5,000 groups in 77 countries. The term 'indigenous', in addition to being an expression of political identity, is today a legal category recognized by international law. For a few decades, indigenous people have demanded in great numbers to be heard and to have their rights to cultural survival and to economic and political development recognized across the institutions of the United Nations (UN) and more broadly.

This chapter consists of three parts, which aim to give a general overview of the struggles and conditions of indigenous peoples in the world. First, we will see how the term 'indigenous', a word with ancient roots, has been mobilized politically in recent years by various populations asserting a distinct community of experience and demanding recognition of their rights. Subsequently, we will review the history of the struggle of indigenous peoples and the emergence of the descriptor 'indigenous' as a legal category in the international arena. Finally, we will examine some developments and current issues in relation to the indigenous question.

WHAT IS INDIGENEITY?

Who are these people who call themselves indigenous and demand rights on that basis? What does it mean to be indigenous today? What are the common experiences that unite indigenous people worldwide? What rights do they claim? What recognition and what rights do they enjoy on the international scene?

There is an important distinction between the two meanings of the term 'indigeneity': one denotes a universal category based on ancient usage; the other is a specific term referring to a political and identity category as well as a legal category defined under international law since the end of the 1970s.

If we examine the general definition of the word 'indigenous', the word signifies originating from a country or region and not arriving by immigration. The synonyms of 'indigenous' are 'native', 'aboriginal', and 'autochtonous'. This last word comes from the Greek expression *autokhthōn*, which breaks down into two words: '*autos*', signifying 'self', and '*khthōn*', signifying 'earth, land'. Consequently, the Greek word means 'that which comes from the earth itself, from this very land'. In common parlance, 'indigenous' is the antonym of 'foreigner'. Therefore, an indigenous custom is a custom relating to the inhabitants of a country, an indigenous species of tree is a species from the region that has not been imported, and being indigenous to a place signifies originating from that place. In common parlance, then, the word has a universal meaning.

Throughout history, the propensity for societies to distinguish between those who come from here and those who come from elsewhere has been universal. For all societies, it means defining one's own borders by identifying the Other or otherness, using specific criteria that vary from one society to another. No matter what language it is expressed in, the term 'indigenous' has been used throughout history to mark the difference between those who originate from here in contrast to those who came from elsewhere, the immigrants. This distinction was made by the ancient Greeks, the Celts, the Romans, the Kanaks of New Caledonia, the Amazon peoples, the Mossi from sub-Saharan Africa, the Egyptians during the time of the pharaohs, just to mention a few classical examples (see, among others, Bensa 2008; Detienne 2003).

In all these societies, the term 'indigenous' is used as a basis for spatial, juridical, and political legitimacy. This legitimacy is based on the privileged relationship of one group with the land they occupy and the fact that they were the original occupants of the territory. In all these cases, indigeneity is a characteristic of the majority, and it can be used either to reject and ward off immigrants or to establish a relationship with them. Among the Kanaks, the Mossi, and the Fijians for example, the difference between two distinct, if not antagonistic, groups is the basis of their legal and political ideology: indigenous people hold sway over land and have legal and religious control over it, while foreigners have political power over society (Bensa 2008).

Since the 1920s, but even more since the end of the 1970s, the term 'indigenous' has been remobilized in the international arena in a precise political-historical context within the larger framework of the decolonization movement and civil rights struggles.

This remobilization had two important dimensions. First, it helped to form a social movement that reclaimed the designation 'indigenous' for precise identity and political purposes. The term 'indigenous' has since been used by marginalized populations to demand justice for human rights violations suffered since **colonization** or for the invasion of their lands, basing these claims on their historical precedence in the occupation of a territory.

Second, it has led to the emergence at the UN—mainly through human rights activities, the Economic and Social Council (ECOSOCO), and the International Labour Organization (ILO)—of a legal category corresponding to a particular set of populations that has been discriminated against by states. Even if a formal definition of this category has not yet been formulated, certain criteria have been established. These criteria are found for the most part in the working definition provided by José Martinez Cobo, the special rapporteur who in 1971 was authorized by the UN Sub-Commission on the Prevention of Discrimination and the Protection of Minorities to study the problem of **discrimination** against indigenous populations. This definition, which has guided the work of the United Nations for several years, reads as follows:

> 379. Indigenous communities, peoples and nations are those which, having a historical continuity with pre-invasion and pre-colonial societies that developed on their territories, consider themselves distinct from other sectors of the societies now prevailing in those territories, or parts of them. They form at present non-dominant sectors of society and are determined to preserve, develop and transmit to future generations their ancestral territories, and their ethnic identity, as the basis of their continued existence as peoples, in accordance with their own cultural patterns, social institutions and legal systems.

> 380. This historical continuity may consist of the continuation, for an extended period

reaching into the present, of one or more of the following factors:

(a) Occupation of ancestral lands, or at least of part of them;

(b) Common ancestry with the original occupants of these lands;

(c) Culture in general, or in specific manifestations (such as religion, living under a tribal system, membership of an indigenous community, dress, means of livelihood, lifestyle, etc.);

(d) Language (whether used as the only language, as mother-tongue, as the habitual means of communication at home or in the family, or as the main, preferred, habitual, general or normal language);

(e) Residence in certain parts of the country, or in certain regions of the world;

(f) Other relevant factors.

381. On an individual basis, an indigenous person is one who belongs to these indigenous populations through self-identification as indigenous (group consciousness) and is recognized and accepted by these populations as one of its members (acceptance by the group).

382. This preserves for these communities the sovereign right and power to decide who belongs to them, without external interference (UN Document E/CN.4/Sub.2/1986/7).

Although not an absolute definition, the category 'indigenous' refers to a specific configuration of power relations, including the fact that indigenous peoples are the last remaining peoples still being colonized and victimized by expansionist activities. In practice, indigenous populations:

1. are under domination;
2. have few or no rights or access to their own natural resources;
3. are a political minority that is often not recognized as such;
4. are exploited economically by neighbouring societies;

5. are culturally dominated (Schulte-Tenckhoff 1997; see also Maaka and Andersen 2006 and Niezen 2003).

The category 'indigenous' assumes a historical continuity with the ancient societies that existed prior to invasion or colonization. It also assumes a distinct cultural background in terms of ontology, cosmology, language, custom, and religion. Cobo's definition stresses the existence of a desire among indigenous peoples to maintain and perpetuate their environments, ancestral systems, and thus their cultural specificity. What is more, despite living under diverse conditions, indigenous peoples differentiate themselves as among the most underprivileged populations in

Figure 23.1   A woman cooking on a wood burning oven near Cheran, Michoacan State, Mexico

Source: Denis Marchand, IDRC

BOX 23.1   INDIGENOUS WOMEN: DOUBLE MARGINALIZATION

Among indigenous people, women have the most difficult living conditions. In fact, indigenous women are known to be one of the most underprivileged categories of people, and they suffer from the greatest socio-economic disadvantages. Statistics reveal that among other difficult conditions, indigenous women, to a greater extent than indigenous men, suffer from extreme poverty, various diseases, illiteracy, and violence, including sexual violence (see, for example, Rights and Democracy 2006). Many of these women, especially those who live in big cities, are involved in the sex trade and international tourism (Smith 1999; Trask 1993). Indigenous women's access to their ancestral lands is also much more restricted than that of indigenous men. Moreover, indigenous women are often left behind by development projects, and their experiences and knowledge are often marginalized, reduced to folklore, or neglected. The living conditions of indigenous women can be explained by the fact that they are victims of a double discrimination: both **sexism** and racism.

In Canada, for example, the body of legislation known as the Indian Act, adopted in 1876 (and revised several times since), systemically discriminated against indigenous women. After many years of mobilization and struggle by indigenous women in Canadian courts and before the Human Rights Committee of the United Nations, this situation was partly corrected in 1985 with the enactment of Bill C-31 (for more information, see Jamieson 1986; Fiske and George 2006). Before 1985, the law governed all aspects of indigenous women's lives and accorded them fewer rights than other Canadian citizens, including indigenous men and other Canadian women. Indigenous women were considered as minors under the law and therefore dependent on their husbands. They were automatically 'disenfranchised'[1] when they married non-Indians or non-status Indians. This meant that they lost their legal Indian status. In this respect, by marrying a non-Indian or a non-status Indian, indigenous women automatically renounced their inheritance rights and their right to vote in band council elections, to participate in band council business, or to manage property belonging to their husbands even after their husbands were deceased. They even had to leave the community and live off-reserve in order to live with their non-Indian husbands, depriving them of participation in the life of their community of origin. This exclusion was intensified by the dominant society's rejection of indigenous women (Jamieson 1986). According to the terms of the Indian Act, the children of these women did not inherit the Indian status of their mothers, even though Indian men who married non-Indian women could pass on their status to their children and also to their non-Indian wives. Since women are often responsible for passing down their culture to children, the Indian Act has been a significant factor in assimilation.

Bill C-31 gave indigenous women married to non-Indians or to non-status Indians the right to keep their legal Indian status. However, sex discrimination persists in the law: although Indian women who marry non-Indians and their children can regain their status, these children cannot pass down their status unless they marry status Indians.

the world. This is why indigenous peoples are often considered as part of the Fourth World, the most underprivileged and oppressed peoples within developed countries and in the Third World. (Box 23.1 describes the added difficulties facing indigenous women.)

Another important factor defining the category 'indigenous' is the self-definition or self-identification factor. This factor is now widely recognized in the official organs of the United Nations. So, for example, ILO Convention no. 169, which is very important in the indigenous struggle, as we will see later on, reads that the 'indigenous and tribal peoples' sense of belonging needs to be considered as a fundamental factor in determining to which groups the provisions of the present convention apply [author's translation]' (Schulte-Tenckhoff 1997, 141). In addition, Article 9 of the United Nations Declaration on the Rights of Indigenous Peoples, adopted by the Human Rights Council in June 2006 and by the General Assembly in September 2007, states that 'Indigenous peoples and individuals have the right to belong to an indigenous community or nation, in accordance with the traditions and customs of the community or nation concerned.'

In many cases, the self-definition criterion is in direct conflict with the categories defined by states. For example, in the case of the Kanaks of New Caledonia and the Amerindians of French Guyana, their affirmation as indigenous people and their demand for recognition of their indigenous rights is not compatible with French law, which does not recognize the presence of indigenous populations on its territory because it does not recognize the possibility of **collective rights**. Since French law is based on the indivisibility of the republic, the equality principle, and its corollary, the principle of non-discrimination, collective rights cannot prevail over individual rights. This was evident in the ambiguous position expressed by the French representative in the debates prior to the vote on the Declaration on the Rights of Indigenous Peoples by the Human Rights Council. The French supported the decla-

ration while knowing that at the national level, 'France would have legal difficulties [author's translation]' in terms of enforcement.[2]

Another fundamental point regarding the category 'indigenous' is precisely that it underpins claims for collective rights. This characteristic distinguishes the category from that of 'minority', which remains associated, at least at the UN, with claims for individual rights, as illustrated by the 1992 Declaration on the Rights of Persons Belonging to National or Ethnic, Religious and Linguistic Minorities. Historically, minorities have struggled for the equality (racial, sexual, religious, or other) of individual persons within a national framework, while indigenous peoples have demanded distinct collective rights, including the recognition of their sovereignty and their right to self-determination, their emancipation through the exercise of power, their territorial rights or the right to be compensated for the loss or the exploitation of their territory, and their right to protect, develop, and transmit their cultural heritage (see, among others, Bellier 2006; Maaka and Fleras 2005; Niezen 2003; Schulte-Tenckhoff 1997).[3]

Thus, it is clear that the category 'indigenous' questions the primacy of individual rights—defended by modern states—over the collective rights claimed by indigenous peoples. The conceptual conflict between two options considered irreconcilable is important (although not much effort has been made to reconcile them). On the one hand is the position that only individuals have rights and on the other, the position recognizing rights of communities (other than states). Claims formulated in terms of collective rights by indigenous peoples are based on a history of dispossession, exclusion, and domination, on their particular lifestyles and their capacities as autonomous societies predating colonization, and on their current status as threatened communities and cultures.

The kinds of domination suffered by populations self-identifying as indigenous and claiming rights in line with the legal category of 'indigenous' seem much clearer in societies resulting from Western colonization, since the distinctions between the aboriginal population and the populations stemming from European settlement and subsequent immigration are obvious (Schulte-Tenckhoff 1997). Initially at the UN, the definition of indigenous peoples only concerned the original inhabitants of European settlement colonies. This reference was implicit in the working definition provided by Cobo. Although a list was never established at the UN, the emblematic representatives of indigeneity are the Amerindians of the Americas, the Inuit of the circumpolar regions, the Maoris of New Zealand, and the Aboriginals of Australia (see, among others, Schulte-Tenckhoff 1997; Sissons 2005). Moreover, the leaders of these peoples, with specific political and legal aims, were responsible for the remobilization of the category 'indigenous' at the international level.

Representatives of other peoples who define themselves as indigenous subsequently joined their ranks, including the Saamis of Scandinavia, the indigenous peoples of Siberia, the Torres Strait Islanders of Australia, and the Ainus of Japan. These peoples are today widely recognized as indigenous peoples. The situation is a lot less clear for the so-called 'tribal' peoples of Asia and Africa to whom the category 'indigenous' is sometimes applied—for example by the ILO (Schulte-Tenckhoff 1997). For several tribal peoples, the situation is very similar to that of indigenous peoples in terms of the threat that industrial society poses for their lands, their traditional economies, their ontology, and their distinct identity.

Another element of Cobo's definition points to the marginalization and subjugation experienced by some groups even though they were not victims of conquest, genocide, or forced assimilation:

Although they have not suffered conquest or colonization, isolated or marginal groups existing in the country should also be regarded as covered by the notion of 'indigenous populations' for the following reasons:
- they are descendants of groups which were in the territory at the time when other groups of different cultures or ethnic origins arrived there;
- precisely because of their isolation from other segments of the country's population they have preserved almost intact the customs and traditions of their ancestors which are similar to those characterized as indigenous, and
- they are, even if only formally, placed under a State structure which incorporates national, social and cultural characteristics alien to theirs (UN Document E/CN.4/Sub.2/L.566).

It was in the spirit of this last element of Cobo's definition that the situation of several peoples in Asia and Africa was treated at the UN as an indigenous question. Nevertheless, as emphasized by Schulte-Tenckhoff, the text seemed to focus on 'populations occupying ecologically fragile habitats like forest and desert regions that had adopted particular lifestyles [author's translation]' (Schulte-Tenckhoff 1997, 136). Thus, cross-border and nomadic peoples as well as peoples from African, Asian (and Oceanian) states who emerged from the decolonization movement and who are victims of diverse forms of neo-colonialism still pose a problem in the definition of 'indigeneity' (for examples, see Schulte-Tenckhoff 1997, 136–7). This situation endures in spite of the fact that in the past few years, these groups have increasingly found themselves on the agenda of UN institutions interested in indigeneity.

A SHORT HISTORY OF INDIGENEITY AT THE INTERNATIONAL LEVEL

How were indigenous actors able to assert themselves internationally? How was recent political mobilization around the category 'indigenous' made possible? How did it emerge historically?

The frustration engendered by the inability of indigenous people to obtain justice from their own national governments, and the refusal of indigenous peoples to define themselves by the political categories established by these states, has led self-defined indigenous peoples to look beyond their national borders and establish international solidarity networks with other indigenous groups and non-indigenous actors who are sensitive to the indigenous cause. These networks have allowed them to use international forums, especially through the UN system, to air their grievances and demands. One of their strategies has been to criticize their states by exposing examples of abuse on the international scene, using what Blaser, Feit, and McRae (2004, following Keck and Sikkink 1998) call the **boomerang strategy**. The boomerang strategy involves using the international arena to put pressure on states in the hope that international opinion will influence decisions at the national level. Indeed, Niezen (2003) and Morin (2005) note that the UN has become the new focus of efforts on the part of the international indigenous movement. At this level, another important objective of the indigenous struggle is to have their situation and specific issues recognized and to ensure that international standards are put in place to guarantee their protection, their development, and their rights.

Minde (1996) identifies two phases in the relatively long history of indigenous struggles. The first phase occurred during the early decades of the twentieth century when the first indigenous movements developed at the national level in Canada, the United States, New Zealand, Australia, and the Scandinavian countries. At that time, indigenous people decided to concentrate on indirect opposition and symbolic actions, because direct opposition was viewed as too risky in the context of the oppression, political assimilation, and imperialism of the era (Minde 1996; C. Allen 2002).

It was during this period that the first regional organizations were established, such as the Alaska Native Brotherhood (1912), the Allied Tribes of British Columbia (1916), and the Native Brotherhood of British Columbia (1931, 1936), as well as the first national organizations, such as the League of Indians of Canada (1918). It was also during that time that the first indigenous delegations at the international level were formed (Minde 1996; Schulte-Tenckhoff 1997). These

initial initiatives delivered few benefits, and many organizations disappeared rapidly.

Nonetheless, new opportunities opened up for indigenous peoples after the First World War with US President Woodrow Wilson's promotion of the right of peoples to **self-determination**, now elevated to the status of a commonly accepted principle in international law. However, indigenous leaders, with a few exceptions, were unable to exploit this new opportunity and faced opposition from state representatives. Indigenous leaders lacked the international experience and the political capacity needed to be effective (Minde 1996). Furthermore, another important condition that could have given more power to indigenous peoples did not exist at the time—namely, any general international standards governing the protection of this distinct genre of minority.

The second phase of the national and international indigenous movement began after the Second World War and was characterized by real presence and expansion, even though the momentum did not pick up until the 1970s. From that moment onward, indigenous and non-indigenous NGOs played a very important role at the UN by denouncing human rights violations experienced by indigenous peoples and thus forming a counterweight to the governments that dominate the UN system even today (see Niezen 2003). The National Indian Brotherhood of Canada, created in 1969, was accredited in 1974 as the first indigenous NGO having consultative status at the UN (Minde 1996). Moreover, this organization was behind the creation of the World Council of Indigenous Peoples in 1975 after a meeting between representatives of the Saamis, the Inuit, the Maoris of New Zealand, the Aboriginal people of Australia, and Amerindians at Port Alberni, British Columbia, with the support of NGOs like the International Work Group for Indigenous Affairs (IWGIA), the Scandinavian governments, and the Council of Churches (Morin 2008). (See Box 23.2 for details on the Maori struggle.) The World Council of Indigenous Peoples obtained its accreditation to the UN in 1981.

BOX 23.2   THE MAORI STRUGGLE

As urbanization increased following the Second World War, the impoverishment, marginalization, and proletarianization of the Maori people became more evident, spurring their mobilization. In the beginning, Maori protests were linked to the broader protest movement for labour rights. This was also the case elsewhere, such as in Hawaii. Subsequently, the association between the Maoris and Pakehas militants (people of predominantly European ancestry) gradually weakened (Poata-Smith 1996; Greenland 1991), a situation that could for the most part be attributed to lack of concern among the Pakehas over racism in New Zealand even though they protested against racism elsewhere in the world. A visit to New Zealand by the South African team during the Springbok Rugby Tour in 1981 was a catalyst for the Maoris, giving them an opportunity to draw attention 'to Paakehaa hypocrisy in fighting for justice overseas but ignoring apartheid-like inequities at home' (Fleras and Spoonley 1999, 45).

In the 1960s and at the beginning of the 1970s, Maori protest movements were very much influenced by the revolutionary wing of the Black Power movement in the United States (Poata-Smith 1996; Greenland 1991). Drawing on this

Figure 23.2   Whina Cooper during the 1975 Maori Land March

Source: Christian F. Heinegg Collection, PA7-15-18, Alexander Turnbull Library, Wellington, New Zealand

movement, they used the rhetoric 'Brown Power' to represent their rejection of the institutions and racist values of New Zealand society. From the mid-1970s, however, they took inspiration from the liberation movements of the Third and Fourth Worlds (Greenland 1991). Emphasis was increasingly placed on concepts like 'indigeneity', their distinct link to the land based on their *tangata whenua* status (literally, people of the land) as the first inhabitants, and the principle of *rangatiratanga* (usually translated in English as chieftainship, indicating the capacity to manage one's own affairs), a principle recognized in the Treaty of Waitangi, signed in 1840 between the Maori chiefs and the British Crown.

Many rallies were held, and in 1975 a large protest march culminated at the Wellington Parliament in opposition to the Maori Affairs Amendment Act (1967), which sought to deprive the Maori of the last lands owned by them. Several land occupations followed the 1975 march, such as the Bastion Point occupation—a real estate development zone in a very desirable section of Auckland—from 1977 to 1978 and the Raglan golf club occupation in 1979. These land occupations ended with police intervention and several arrests.

Figure 23.3   1975 Maori Land March

Source: Dominion Post Collection, EP/1975/4202/8a, Alexander Turnbull Library, Wellington, New Zealand

The international arena has been very important for Maori strategy. The Maoris have always been very active at the UN, standing with representatives of the First Nations of Canada and the United States and the Aboriginals of Australia (Minde 1996; C. Allen 2002; Smith 1999). Many links with other indigenous organizations have been established, thanks to George Manuel, who was the president of the National Indian Brotherhood of Canada from 1970 to 1976 and organized several visits with Amerindian representatives to New Zealand. A large gathering of indigenous peoples was subsequently organized by the American Indian Movement in which Maori representatives participated. They later became involved in the International Indian Treaty Council created in 1974, the World Council of Indigenous Peoples created in 1975, and the indigenous missions at the UN.

In 1977, the first conference dealing directly with indigenous questions took place at the UN's Palais des Nations in Geneva. The International Non-Governmental Organization Conference on Discrimination against Indigenous Populations in the Americas brought together almost 60 indigenous organizations. It was followed in 1981 by another conference on indigenous populations and the land claims question.

These meetings, as well as the Cobo study (then ready to be submitted[4]) greatly contributed to the creation of the UN Working Group on Indigenous Populations (WGIP) in 1982 within the framework of the UN Sub-Commission on

Prevention of Discrimination and Protection of Minorities, a branch of the Commission on Human Rights. The working group is one of the most important steps forward in the indigenous struggle at the UN. One of its principles is to promote the participation of a large number of representatives from other organizations (governmental and non-governmental) and from indigenous communities. Each year, about 700 people participate in WGIP sessions, notably representatives from governments, NGOs, and indigenous peoples, as well as specialists and academics.[5]

Beginning in 1985, the working group focused on drafting a declaration on the rights of indigenous peoples. The public launching of this project took place in 1994 under the title Draft United Nations Declaration on the Rights of Indigenous Peoples. The document was submitted to the Commission on Human Rights for their consideration. The commission in turn created its own working group in 1995, the Working Group on the Draft Declaration on the Rights of Indigenous Peoples, with a mandate to examine the text further with a view to its adoption by the UN General Assembly.

Several other initiatives, such as specialized seminars and expert meetings on indigenous rights, have been pursued by the international community. Reports and conferences on other general themes increasingly refer to indigenous peoples. Other initiatives of a more symbolic nature included the UN's proclamation of 1993 as the International Year of the World's Indigenous People and the decades of 1995–2005 and 2005–15 as the first and second International Decades of the World's Indigenous People. The UN also declared 9 August as the International Day of the World's Indigenous People. At the World Conference on Human Rights, which took place in 1993 in Vienna and in which hundreds of indigenous people participated, it was recommended that the General Assembly examine the possibility of establishing an indigenous forum at the UN. In 2000, the UN Permanent Forum on Indigenous Issues was created (see Box 23.3).

What has led to a widening of the indigenous field of action—or their 'political space' (Bellier and Legros 2001, 31)—over the past few decades from the local to the international and from indirect and symbolic opposition to direct opposition? What were the contexts and conditions that made it possible for indigenous activists to use new springboards beyond the state to advance their claims?

In fact, the international context favoured the creation of a new political space that enabled the indigenous movement to succeed. The period following the Second World War was marked at first by a dominant vision in favour of the protection of minorities. However, instead of supporting the self-determination of ethnic groups such as occurred after the First World War, this vision emphasized the protection of individual human rights, particularly those of people belonging to a minority. Nonetheless, this hostility towards special cultural protection for ethnic groups in general and for indigenous peoples in particular diminished rapidly—for reasons explained by Minde (1996, 231):

1. The anti-Nazi campaign, which by and large became an anti-racist campaign in favour of human rights, made it difficult to close one's eyes to the demands made by ethnic groups previously considered non-civilized or in danger of extinction.

2. The global postwar experience of industrial and technological colonialism in the peripheral regions, such as tropical rain forests and Artic regions, raised awareness of the need to protect the most exposed populations (for example, those in South America).

3. The wave of Third World decolonization generated sympathy for ethnic groups who were victims of internal colonization. This led in 1960 to the adoption of a UN resolution that enunciated the principle that all peoples had the right to self-determination and were free to determine their own social and cultural development.[6]

BOX 23.3   THE UN PERMANENT FORUM
ON INDIGENOUS ISSUES

Founded on 28 July 2000 by Resolution 2000/22 of the UN Economic and Social Council following the recommendation of the Commission on Human Rights, the Permanent Forum on Indigenous Issues is a consultative organ with a mandate to discuss indigenous questions concerning economic and social development, the environment, culture, education, health, and human rights. The permanent forum is at the same level in the UN structure as the Human Rights Council and does not replace the Working Group on Indigenous Populations (for more information on the two organizations, see Martinez 2003).

After many years of struggle, the permanent forum represents a very important gain in the international arena for indigenous peoples. In effect, it is an important step in that it formally and permanently integrates indigenous peoples and their representatives into the official UN structure. It is also the first high-level, official UN organization ever to grant state representatives and non-state representatives alike an equal voice.

Sixteen independent experts are seated at the permanent forum for a mandate of three years, renewable once. Eight of the members are nominated by governments and elected by the Economic and Social Council according to the five regional groupings used at the UN (Africa, Asia, eastern Europe, Latin America and the Caribbean, and western Europe and other States). In addition to the five regional seats, three seats rotate among the regional groupings. The eight other members are designated by the president of the Economic and Social Council following extensive consultations with indigenous groups and respecting the principles of diversity, representation, and geographical distribution among the seven large socio-cultural regions of Africa, Central and South America and the Caribbean, the Artic, eastern Europe, central Asia, the Russian Federation and Transcaucasia, and North America and the Pacific. One of these eight seats rotates among the three biggest regions: Asia, Africa, and Central and South America and the Caribbean. The permanent forum shares its experience, advice, and recommendations on indigenous issues at the UN through the Economic and Social Council. Another of the permanent forum's tasks is to 'raise awareness and promote the integration and coordination of relevant activities within the UN system; and prepare and disseminate information on indigenous issues' (visit the permanent forum site at http://www.un.org/esa/socdev/unpfii/en/structure.html).

The Permanent Forum on Indigenous Issues meets annually over 10 working days, generally during May. The first session was held in May 2001, and so far they have always taken place at UN headquarters in New York, but they can also be held in Geneva. The General Assembly granted the permanent forum a secretariat in 2002 to prepare the sessions and ensure the co-ordination and execution of its recommendations within the UN. The secretariat came into operation in February 2003.

The sessions of the permanent forum are open to observers who want to enter into dialogue with members. Observers can be specialized agents from official UN bodies, governments, intergovernmental organizations, non-governmental organizations, and indigenous peoples. Each year, about 1,200 participants—consisting of some 1,000 indigenous representatives and representatives of 70 member states—take part in the session. The permanent forum submits an annual report on its activities and recommendations to the Economic and Social Council for approval.

According to Minde (1996), other conditions also favoured the indigenous struggle:

1. the establishment of minimum standards for the protection of minorities with the ILO's Convention no. 107 (1957) and two 1966 UN conventions relating to the principle of self-determination (albeit limited) for minorities;
2. the formation of the World Council of Indigenous Peoples in 1975, which facilitated the sharing of information and strategies and the co-ordination of common initiatives linked to the UN;
3. increasing concern with questions of internal human rights in the 1970s and 1980s in the context of the Cold War;
4. support by anthropologists for the indigenous struggle and their call for active political engagement as a result of numerous examples of genocide in Brazil, Paraguay, and Colombia.

Two important organizations were created by anthropologists: the International Work Group for Indigenous Affairs (1968) and the Primitive Peoples' Fund (1969), which became Survival International (1971). In 1971, a symposium of anthropologists also adopted the Declaration of Barbados: For the Liberty of the Indians. As discussed above, such international efforts focused on human rights greatly contributed to improving the access of indigenous peoples to a system from which they had previously been largely excluded (Schulte-Tenckhoff 1997).

Since 1916, the ILO has played an important role in the indigenous struggle by drawing attention to the lot of indigenous labourers. The ILO's Convention no. 107 (1957) was in effect the first international instrument concerned with the rights of indigenous and tribal peoples and state obligations towards these populations. Although it was innovative, the convention had a paternalistic tone. According to Morin (2008) and Schulte-Tenckhoff (1997), the convention described the populations subject to it as 'less advanced', and it privileged an assimilation-ist approach to the 'Protection and Integration of Indigenous and Other Tribal and Semi-Tribal Populations in Independent Countries'.[7] Convention no. 169, which was adopted in 1989, also focused on the rights of indigenous and tribal peoples but without the assimilation-ist aims of the previous convention. Certain collective rights are ensured, since 'Convention no. 169 takes the approach that the cultures and institutions of indigenous and tribal peoples must be respected, and presumes their right to continued existence within their national societies, to establish their own institutions and to determine the path of their own development' (UN 2001). As emphasized by Schulte-Tenckhoff (1997, 128), efforts to recognize collective rights remain weak, since the interests of states are prioritized. Convention no. 169 came into effect in 1991 and had been ratified by 19 states at the time of writing.[8] Several organizations and programs like the United Nations Development Programme (UNDP) and the World Bank refer to Convention no. 169 when developing their policies and programs related to indigenous populations, thus strengthening the convention and developing it as a reference in international law.

Apart from the international context, the indigenous political space also expanded within the larger context of movements promoting the rights of blacks, women, and gays and lesbians, student uprisings, and protests against the war in Vietnam. Moreover, among indigenous people themselves, changing conditions favoured a remodelling of political activism:

(1) young leaders educated in the Western school system leading activism onto the national and international scene; (2) the ambition of indigenous peoples to create 'spaces of meaning' beyond the national borders of the state that engulfed them and not only deprived them of the ability to access institutions of meaning but also did not correspond to their image of their own world;

Figure 23.4   Chief Haudenosaunee Deskaheh travelled to the League of Nations in Geneva in 1923 to defend the autonomy of his people but was denied permission to speak

Source: Bibliothèque de Genève

(3) growing awareness of threats to their societies resulting from new economic networks and new methods of production, particularly environmental ones [author's translation] (Bellier and Legros 2001, 9).

RECENT DEVELOPMENTS AND CURRENT ISSUES

How has the struggle of indigenous peoples to be recognized developed recently? After many decades of struggle and significant gains in recognition at the international level, what issues do indigenous people face today?

On 29 June 2006, after more than 20 years of discussion,[9] the Declaration on the Rights of Indigenous Peoples was adopted during the first session of the new UN Human Rights Council (which replaced the Commission on Human Rights earlier that year). The council also recommended that the declaration be adopted by the UN General Assembly.[10] An important step had been taken in the advancement of the indigenous cause.

However, a broad consensus did not exist in favour of the adoption of the declaration, and a formal vote was demanded: 30 states voted in favour of adoption, 2 states (Canada and the Russian Federation—see Box 23.4 for Canada's position) voted against, and 12 states abstained, six of which were African states (Algeria, Ghana, Morocco, Nigeria, Senegal, and Tunisia). The collective nature of certain rights stipulated in the text was controversial.

The Declaration on the Rights of Indigenous Peoples is perceived by some states and majority populations as a threat. If we take a much closer look, we note that countries such as France and the United Kingdom, although expressing their support in the name of human rights, strongly circumscribe this support by stating that the declaration is not applicable in their territory. They also insist that they will not recognize collective rights that infringe on individual rights. Like Canada, they also emphasize that the declaration is legally non-binding because according to the doctrine of non-intervention codified in the United Nations Charter, international declarations are not legally binding on sovereign states.

In the fall of 2006, many procedural questions slowed down the General Assembly's consideration of the declaration. It was decided that

BOX 23.4   THE CANADIAN POSITION

On the website of the Minister of Indian and Northern Affairs Canada (MINAC), the Canadian Conservative government (elected in January 2006) explained its position on the United Nations Declaration on the Rights of Indigenous Peoples project in advance of the vote in the General Assembly:

> As Canada expressed in its statement to the Human Rights Council, the current provisions on lands, territories and resources are broad, unclear and capable of a wide variety of interpretations. They could be interpreted to support claims to broad ownership rights over traditional territories, even where rights to such territories were lawfully ceded through treaty. These provisions could also hinder our land claims processes in Canada, whereby Aboriginal land and resource rights are premised on balancing the rights of Aboriginal peoples with those of other Canadians, within the Canadian constitutional framework—our framework for working together.
>
> In addition, the concept of free, prior and informed consent is used in many contexts within the Draft Declaration. It could be interpreted as giving a veto to indigenous peoples over many administrative matters, legislation, development proposals and national defence activities which concern the broader population and may affect indigenous peoples.
>
> Also, in relation to self-government provisions, the text does not provide effective guidance about how indigenous governments might work with other levels of government, including laws of overriding national importance and matters of financing (http://www.ainc-inac.gc.ca/nr/spch/unp/06/ddr_e.html, accessed 25 July 2007).

Canada's vote caught several actors by surprise, such as the First Nations of Canada. Its position was viewed as disappointing, especially since Canada had collaborated from the very beginning in the drafting of the declaration. This disappointment deepened in September 2007 when Canada did not vote in favour of the declaration at the UN General Assembly despite extensive pressure to change its view since June 2006.

the Third Committee (responsible for social, humanitarian, and cultural questions) would first consider it. It quickly became apparent that several African countries had significant concerns with the text of the declaration, notably in relation to the definition of 'indigenous peoples', the right to self-determination (which was interpreted as a right to secession), the right to belong to a community or an indigenous nation, the right to land and exploitation of natural resources, and the right to create distinct political and economic institutions. These points were seen as threats to the national and territorial integrity of African states and/or as violating the constitutional provisions of African states.[11]

On 28 November 2006, Namibia, supported by 29 African states, presented to the Third Committee an amendment demanding the deferment of the vote to September 2007. This resolution was approved (82 votes for and 67 against) and subsequently ratified by the General Assembly on 23 December 2006 (86 votes for and 89 abstentions) (IWGIA 2007, 560). It appears that strong pressure was exerted by Canada, the

United States, Australia, and New Zealand. Evidently, the emergence of universal indigenous rights was posing problems.

Not only did states have to confront several issues related to the emergence of these universal rights (because, among other things, the definition of the legal category 'indigenous' and the identification of indigenous peoples remained somewhat ambiguous), but indigenous peoples themselves also had to face a number of issues for the same reason. We will only explore a few here. It must be remembered that neither the UN Declaration on the Rights of Indigenous Peoples nor the ILO, which established minimum standards for the protection of indigenous populations, had identified or precisely defined the meaning of 'indigenous peoples'. Nonetheless, the notion of 'indigenous peoples' is presumably sufficiently clear to prevent an unending series of rights claims based on indigeneity, since 'indigeneity' could not be applied to any and all groups that asserted a certain historical precedence over other groups (see Box 23.5 for the Afrikaner example).

One advantage of a definition without absolute criteria or a list of peoples is that the choice of indigeneity as political strategy remains open for peoples who may have, until now, used other means to make themselves heard. This is the case of the Kanaks of New Caledonia, for example, who have seen movements claiming to act in their interest as 'indigenous people' increase their influence since 2001 (Demmer 2007). These efforts represent a departure from the Kanak strategy of the 1970s, which insisted on full sovereignty modelled on the approach of other Melanesian states.

Another advantage of a definition with no absolute criteria is that it permits the expression and recognition of the diversity of indigenous populations. Several analysts have emphasized the inherent dangers of a single universal or narrow definition of indigenous peoples and indigenous rights. The Maori researcher Linda Tuhiwai Smith suggests that '[the] term "indigenous" is problematic in that it appears to collectivize many distinct populations whose experiences under imperialism have been vastly different' (1999, 6). Indigenous leaders vigorously insist on the pluralized 'indigenous peoples' rather than 'indigenous people'. Indigeneity is heterogeneous: it consists of a multiplicity of identities and of local, territorial, tribal, and community issues.

Poirier (2000) also emphasizes the danger that indigenous rights can represent, not only in

BOX 23.5   THE AFRIKANERS

This case remains controversial. At the 1994 and 1995 meetings of the Working Group on Indigenous Populations, Afrikaner representatives claimed the status of indigenous peoples. Several indigenous people left the room to protest what they considered an inappropriate assertion of identity. Subsequently, a petition was signed by 82 indigenous representatives to show their concern over the presence of the Afrikaner representatives at the working group (Larson 2007; Schulte-Tenckhoff 1997, 133). In practice, the Afrikaners do not unambiguously fit at least one criterion of indigeneity—namely, that of having been dominated. Their prior claim to occupation of the territory is also questionable, since they are the descendants of European settlers who arrived in South Africa during the seventeenth century and displaced other populations.[12]

relation to their multiplicity but also in undermining the dynamic character of indigenous peoples by casting them in terms of a generalized historical experience of dispossession and exclusion. This danger is compounded by the rigid and ahistorical conceptions of indigenous people typically perpetuated by political and legal institutions in Western democracies. The international recognition of indigenous rights could effectively essentialize what is considered indigenous and make it difficult, for example, to advance in ways that depart from lifestyles recognized as 'traditional'. This situation is especially tragic for indigenous people living in urban areas, which is the case for the majority of indigenous people in countries like New Zealand, Canada, and the United States.

Bowen (2000) also warns that references to indigeneity in development policies, besides leading to the neglect of locally specific meanings, can also contribute to framing debates in terms of ethnicity, thus potentially undermining the peaceful and constructive coexistence between indigenous people and other people in the same region or state. On the other hand, one of the drawbacks of the absence of an absolute definition is that indigenous people are often defined unilaterally by national governments and these definitions vary greatly from one state to another.

Several important problems emerge from the absence of a specific definition of 'indigeneity',

particularly because it allows states, in line with their own legal frameworks, to affirm that indigenous issues do not concern them (Schulte-Tenckhoff 1997). For example, the United Kingdom representative made the following declaration before the Human Rights Council on 29 June 2006:

> The United Kingdom observed that it did not accept the concept of collective rights in international law. The United Kingdom clarified that it understood the right of self-determination as set out in the declaration as one which was to be exercised within the territory of a State and which was not designed to impact in any way on the territorial integrity of States. The United Kingdom emphasized that the declaration was not legally binding and that the citizens of the United Kingdom and its territories overseas did not fall within the scope of the declaration.[3]

While making a link to the definition of indigeneity, some authors, such as Sissons (2005), have recently held that the struggles of the indigenous populations of the New World and the settler colonies and those of the so-called tribal and nomadic peoples who have been victims of neo-colonialism in recently independent countries in Africa, Asia, and Oceania should not be considered the same, since they emerged in different socio-historic contexts. As Schulte-Tenckhoff writes:

BOX 23.6   WHO IS HAWAIIAN?

In the United Sates, the legal definition of the category 'native Hawaiians', still valid today, is found in the 1920 Hawaiian Homes Commission Act. This federal law, in addition to defining the category, contributed to its 'racialization' by limiting the definition to individuals able to prove that they have more than 50 per cent Hawaiian blood (50 per cent blood quantum criterion) (Kauanui 2007).

The distinct situation of the countries of the Afro-Asiatic world rests in the paradoxical character of the process of 'indigenization' brought about by decolonization: colonialism was overcome by virtue of the right of peoples to self-determination, yet these new states were unwilling to grant the same right to the peoples incorporated within their often arbitrarily drawn borders [author's translation] (Schulte-Tenckhoff 1997, 140).

As Fritz and Fritz-Legendre point out, 'the claim to rights no longer pits "natives" against the descendents of European settlers but rather against other populations who were also often considered natives during the colonial era [author's translation]' (2005, 41–2).

According to Sissons (2005, 16), the downplaying of these distinctions in international forums over the past few years has led to certain disagreements and to a loss of political direction. In addition, Sissons (2005) notes that ever since representatives of the 'tribal' populations of Asia and Africa joined the UN Working Group on Indigenous Populations, more emphasis has been placed on the relationship between being indigenous and relying on a subsistence economy and living in close proximity with nature. This marked a change from the previous emphasis on the claim to precedence in territorial occupation and a lack of governmental control. Sissons describes this trend as eco-indigenism and suggests that it has two consequences: 'On the one hand, it primitivizes indigenous peoples living in settler states who have adopted urban lifestyles or it calls into question their authenticity; on the other hand, it opens up the possibility for almost any people with a subsistence-based culture to claim membership in international indigenous forums' (Sissons 2005, 16–17; see also Schulte-Tenckhoff 2008 on the larger issue of culturalist biases). These arguments have also been taken up by critics of indigenous rights claims, including researchers as well as states and members of majority populations in countries where indigenous populations assert themselves.

Finally, on 13 September 2007, a few days before the close of the 61st session, the UN General Assembly adopted the Declaration on the Rights of Indigenous Peoples. The result of the vote was 143 votes for, 4 against (Australia, Canada, the United States, and New Zealand[14]), and 11 abstentions (Colombia, Azerbaijan, Bangladesh, Georgia, Burundi, the Russian Federation, Samoa, Nigeria, Ukraine, Bhutan, and Kenya). The adoption was made possible by an intense dialogue among African states, states supporting the declaration, and indigenous representatives between November 2006 and September 2007.[15] At the beginning of September 2007, an understanding was finally reached with the African states on nine amendments, which did not undermine the substance of the declaration text. It was the amended text that was adopted on 13 September.[16] The UN Secretary-General Ban Ki-moon welcomed the historic event, which he described 'as a triumph for indigenous peoples around the world', and challenged governments and civil society to integrate the declaration's rights into international law, development programs, and policies at all levels 'so as to ensure that the vision behind the Declaration becomes a reality'.

Finally, it should be noted that even before it was adopted and despite the fact that the Declaration on the Rights of Indigenous Peoples is not legally binding, it has had and will continue to have an impact on the laws and policies of some countries, the practices of multinational corporations, and international and regional agencies. Even more significantly, for several years the draft declaration has enjoyed great legitimacy in the eyes of the indigenous peoples of the world (Schulte-Tenckhoff 1997) and has allowed for improvements and even successes even as the struggle continues.

QUESTIONS FOR DISCUSSION

1. Why do indigenous claims to collective rights pose problems for modern states?
2. What particular problem regarding indigenous rights claims do the populations of Africa and Asia face?
3. How can the category 'indigenous' be described as both ethnic and political? In what contexts?
4. Why is the Declaration on the Rights of Indigenous Peoples not legally binding for states even though it was adopted by the UN General Assembly?
5. What is the scope of the right to self-determination as defined in the Declaration on the Rights of Indigenous Peoples?

FURTHER READING

Barker, Joane, ed. 2005. *Sovereignty Matters: Locations of Contestation and Possibility in Indigenous Struggles for Self-Determination*. Lincoln: University of Nebraska Press.

Coates, Ken S. 2004. *A Global History of Indigenous Peoples: Struggle and Survival*. New York: Palgrave Macmillan.

Maaka, Roger C.A., and Chris Andersen, eds. 2006. *The Indigenous Experience: Global Perspectives*. Toronto: Canadian Scholars' Press.

Niezen, Ronald. 2003. *The Origins of Indigenism: Human Rights and the Politics of Identity*. Berkeley: University of California Press.

United Nations. 2007. *Declaration on the Rights of Indigenous Peoples*. UN General Assembly, A/RES/61/295. http://daccessdds.un.org/doc/UNDOC/GEN/N06/512/07/PDF/N0651207.pdf.

INTERNET RESOURCES

United Nations Guide for Indigenous Peoples: http://www.unhchr.ch/html/racism/00-indigenousguide.html.
United Nations Permanent Forum on Indigenous Issues: http://www.un.org/esa/socdev/unpfii/.
International Work Group for Indigenous Affairs (IWGIA): http://www.iwgia.org.

NOTES

* I would like to thank my colleague Marie Salaün for our discussions on issues related to indigenous peoples and her comments on this text. The author is also a researcher at the joint research unit IRIS (Institut de recherche interdisciplinaire sur les enjeux sociaux: sciences sociales, politique, santé), which is associated with the École des hautes études en sciences sociales (EHESS), the Centre national de la recherche scientifique (CNRS), the Institut de la santé et de la recherche médicale (INSERM), and the University of Paris 13, Paris, France.

1. Note that the Indian Act, aimed to assimilate indigenous people into the majority population and to appropriate their lands and resources.

2. See UN Human Rights Council press release at http://www.unhchr.ch/huricane/huricane.nsf/view01/BCE215C018CE4384C125719A007055F7?opendocument, accessed 24 July 2007.

3. For a more detailed and nuanced discussion on the distinctions between individual rights, collective rights, and group rights, see Koubi 1998; Koubi and Schulte-Tenckhoff 2000; and Schulte-Tenckhoff 2008.

4. The study carried out by José Martínez Cobo consists of five volumes, which were submitted between 1981 and 1984.

5. For more details on how the group operates, see http://www.unhchr.ch/html/menu6/2/fs9.htm (accessed 24 July 2007).

6. This concerns the Declaration on the Granting of Independence to Colonial Countries and Peoples, adopted in UN General Assembly Resolution 1514 (XV) on 14 December 1960.

7. For the complete text of Convention no. 107, see http://www.ilo.org/ilolex/cgi-lex/convde.pl?C107 (accessed 23 July 2007).

8. For the complete text of Convention no. 169 and an up-to-date list of the states that have ratified it, see http://www.ilo.org/ilolex/cgi-lex/convde.pl?C169 (accessed 23 September 2007).

9. For details on the drafting of the declaration, its adoption by the Working Group on Indigenous Populations, and developments since 2006, see IWGIA 2007.

10. See the complete text of the recommendation and the declaration at http://www.ohchr.org/english/issues/indigenous/docs/declaration.doc (accessed 18 July 2007).

11. For information relating to these concerns, see the African group's *Draft Aide Memoire* at http://www.iwgia.org/graphics/Synkron-Library/Documents/InternationalProcesses/DraftDeclaration/AfricanGroupAideMemoireOnDeclaration.pdf (accessed 19 September 2007). It should be noted that over the past 20 years, the majority of African states have barely participated in the negotiations surrounding the elaboration of the declaration's text, which could explain the numerous misinterpretations.

12. See Niezen 2003 (21–2) for a similar event, which took place in 1999 and involved the Rehoboth Baster Community in Namibia, the descendents of Afrikan settlers and indigenous Khoi. Morin (2008) mentions other contentious cases.

13. See http://www.unog.ch/80256EDDOO6B9C2E/(httpNewsByYear_en)/BE82C77003776B9EC1257 19C005D5994?OpenDocument. Accessed 16 October 2007

14. The arguments evoked were the same as those put forward by Canada in June 2006. This statement echoes that of France, cited earlier.

15. For details on this dialogue, see the IWGIA website at http://www.iwgia.org/sw21505.asp and Morin 2008.

16. See the resolution to adopt the declaration and the text of the declaration that was adopted at http://daccessdds.un.org/doc/UNDOC/GEN/N06/512/07/PDF/N0651207.pdf (accessed 8 January 2008).

CHAPTER 24

TECHNOLOGY, INFORMATION, AND DEVELOPMENT

ERWIN A. ALAMPAY

LEARNING OBJECTIVES

- To understand the role of technologies in development.
- To develop a critical understanding of the effects of technologies, both good and bad, on societies, institutions, work, and individuals.
- To understand the role of technology, in particular information and communication technologies (ICTs), in development.
- To identify the causes of the 'digital divide' that exists between and within nations and its implications on development.

Information is central to the things people do every day. Access to information is crucial in the development of people and their communities. People need information to find ways of meeting their needs, access basic services like water and health care, and look for opportunities. This chapter explains how information and systems for sending and receiving it can be used for development and governance. We begin with a brief discussion of the relationship between technology and development, then focus on information and communication technologies (ICTs).

In discussing the role of ICTs in development, the chapter is not limited to computers and the Internet. It includes other ICTs such as radio, TV, telephone, and indigenous information systems that may be available and more appropriate for some situations in the real world. We also look at how ICTs are affecting economies, how we organize, and work. We discuss important policy issues, such as open access, intellectual property rights, censorship, and freedom of expression.

TECHNOLOGY AND SOCIETY

> Every technology is both a burden and a blessing; not either-or, but this-and-that.
> Neil Postman 1992, 4–5.

Defining technology

Technology is considered 'the science and art of getting things done through the application of skills and knowledge' (Smillie 2000, 69). The nongovernmental organization Practical Action defines it as the capacity to organize and use physical infrastructure, machinery and equipment, knowledge, and skills. In this respect, benefiting from technology is not simply a matter of getting new equipment, tools, and infrastructure but also putting people's knowledge and skills to use and applying it to their problems.

Technology creation and diffusion

Technology can be developed and transferred in a number of ways. Resource abundance and shortages play an important role in the development and diffusion of technologies. A good example of this is the need for grain and the resulting Green Revolution in the 1970s (see chapter 18). The Green Revolution was a by-product of work conducted in the 1960s to develop higher-yielding strains of rice and wheat. A cross-bred variety of rice was developed that doubled traditional yields, and from 1982 to 1992, production of cereals grew in Asia by 25 per cent and in Africa by 41 per cent (Smillie 2000).

Technologies can be independently created, but they can also be bought, copied, and stolen. Commerce and warfare have been among the most important contributors to technological development and diffusion. Early trading between China and other Asian countries, for instance, brought with it the diffusion of technologies on paper, textiles, gunpowder, and porcelain. Aztec, Maya, and Inca technology for intercropping *ipil-ipil* with maize was transferred to Asia by the galleon trade (Smillie 2000). Arabian traders helped to spread Chinese steel technology and Arabian medical knowledge. In more recent times, the Japanese, Koreans, and Taiwanese developed their automobile and electronics industries from products that were originally developed in the West.

The contribution of warfare to technological innovation has included the use of crossbows, guns and gunpowder, and mathematics to optimize distribution systems and decode messages. Space technology, for instance, traces its roots to the development of land-based missiles that can carry bombs across vast distances. Similarly, the Internet had its origins in the need to secure communications in the event of a nuclear attack. Moreover, technological disparities between civilizations have led to the conquest of nations. A good example of this is the way that the greatly outnumbered Spaniards were able to defeat the Incas in the 1500s because of their guns, steel weapons, armour, and horses (Diamond 1999).

Appropriate technology

The transfer of technology, however, is not that easy to accomplish. In developing countries and marginalized communities, it is necessary to consider the socio-economic and environmental context into which a technology will be transplanted. The term **appropriate technology** has its origin in the work of Dr. Fritz Schumacher on the kinds of technology that fit small-scale, grassroots, and community-centred organizations. These are technologies that are appropriate to the environmental, cultural, and economic context to which they are transferred. An appropriate technology does not mean it is a 'lesser' kind of technology. What is important is that it works, is suitable for the context, and is sustainable. Some examples of appropriate technologies include a polio vaccine that only requires a drop on the tongue, heat-stable vaccines that do not require refrigeration, vaccine cocktails in a single shot (UNDP 2001, 28), inexpensive water hand pumps, fuel-efficient stoves, cheap electricity provided by windmills (Smillie 2000), and (strange as it may seem) building simple latrines to help reduce the incidence of blindness (see http://www.carter-center.org). Appropriate technologies typically require fewer resources, cost less, and have a minimal impact on the environment. They also tap the existing knowledge of local people and use local natural resources.

Technological determinism versus social determinism

Social scientists have looked at the interaction between technology and society in two ways: either through technological determinism or through social determinism.

Technological determinism suggests that it is technology that drives the evolution of society. The idea is that technology begets technology and that society is continually reformed in the wake of this process (Ling 2007). An example of this is the way the printing press contributed to the Protestant Reformation by giving more people access to the Bible and permitting individual interpretations of God's word.

Social determinism, on the other hand, considers social interaction as having primacy in terms of the development and use of tools. Thus, tools, while originally intended to function in one particular way, can be reinterpreted and used in another way. Viewed this way, technology is not inherently good or bad, since the outcome depends largely on how it is used. For example, nuclear technology has been used constructively to support industries and communities but has also been used destructively for war. A hand tractor originally intended for ploughing and farm use has been reinvented as a means of public transportation in some rural villages in the Philippines. In the context of development, this interpretation highlights the importance of focusing on people, on what they can do with technology, and on building their capacities.

Some technologies, however, are particularly closed. They are difficult to reinterpret and use in ways other than originally intended, while others are particularly open. Information and communication technologies, for instance, are particularly open. Hence, while the telephone was originally intended for use by business, people soon found other more social and personal applications for it. The same goes for the Internet, which is used not only by scientists, researchers, and the military (as originally intended) but also by ordinary people looking for recipes, life-partners, or entertainment. In India, for instance, engineers conducted an experiment to test whether people in slum areas can independently learn to use an Internet-connected computer without instruction. Among the findings was how quickly children embraced the technology and were able to develop their own vocabulary for teaching each other about it.[1]

In the context of development studies, however, the issue of whether technology shapes organizations or whether society defines how technologies are used may not be as important as the effects that result from the interaction between society and technology.

Technology and development

According to the United Nations Development Programme (UNDP 2001, 27), many technologies can be used for human development to increase people's incomes, improve their health, allow them to live longer and enjoy better lives, and permit them to participate more fully in their communities. However, as Postman

Figure 24.1   The Asháninka, an indigenous tribe in the village of Marankiari Bajo, Perv, view the Internet as a means to share their traditions, while strengthening their culture and language.

Source: Luis Barnola/IRDC

(1992) suggests, technology is both a burden and a blessing.

Fire, gunpowder, steam engines, electricity and nuclear energy, trains, airplanes, the telegraph, and telephones . . . history is full of examples of technologies that have changed the course of human development—and not all of them necessarily for the better. Thus, while technologies are often seen as indicators of modernization and material progress, they have also created new social conflicts. During the **Industrial Revolution**, for instance, technology created tensions not only between man and nature but also among men with different relationships to technology. Owners of capital were pitted against owners of land, progress against tradition, and capital against labour (Briggs 1963). As Jared Diamond aptly puts it, 'technology, in the form of weapons and transport, has provided the direct means by which some peoples have expanded their realms and conquered other people' (1997, 2,441).

Technologies are also identifiable with historical eras. For instance, some would consider what mechanization did for the Industrial Revolution, computer technology is doing for the Information Age (Naisbitt 1984, cited in Webster 2000, 8). The discovery of the steam engine and later electrical production spurred the Industrial Revolution and resulted in the transformation of major social institutions such as the family, the church, cities, and working life. The family moved from being multi-generational to today's nuclear mom, dad, and kids. The church lost much of its power, cities grew larger, and organizations became bureaucratized (Ling 2007). Similarly, an important question today is how information and communication technologies are also changing society and these same institutions (see Table 24.1).

THE INFORMATION SOCIETY

Information and communication technologies (ICTs) are arguably the defining technologies of contemporary life. ICTs encompass both the equipment and the services that facilitate the electronic capture, processing, and display of information (Torrero and Braun 2006, 3). They include computer technologies (computers, the Internet), telecommunications (cellular and land-line phones), audio-visual technologies (DVDs, cameras, MP3s), and broadcasting (radio, television).

Convergence and interactivity

New ICTs are the product of technological convergence between old and new networks of technologies. Older technologies, such as radio and television, were characterized by one-way provision of communication. People were passive recipients of information. Newer ICTs are characterized by 'interactivity' whereby communication is two-way and people have a choice in selecting the information they want.

Table 24.1 Comparison between the Industrial Age and the Information Age

	Industrial Age	Information Age
Productive input	Energy (steam; electricity); machines	Information; ICTs
Output	Products	Services
Organizations	Large factories	Networked organizations
Workers	Organized labour	Individualization

Source: Adapted from Castells 2000; Rubery and Grimshaw 2001; Ling 2007; Winter and Taylor 2001.

Figure 24.2 The satellite dish used by the Tombouctou Multipurpose Community Telecentre, Mali, Africa

Source: H. Hudson/IDRC

Developed countries tend to be more interested in the newer technologies, largely because they have achieved widespread penetration, superseding the older ones (Sciadas 2003). However, in developing countries, where access to older ICTs has remained problematic, it is necessary to consider alternative ways of gaining access to needed information, including the use of appropriate ICTs, whether old, new, or a combination of these technologies. In the near future, this issue may no longer be salient, since *convergence* has resulted in the 'old' media of TV, radio, and telephones becoming digital.

Theories of the information society

There are five arguments for considering the world today as an 'information society': technological, economic, occupational, spatial, and cultural (Webster 2000).

The *technological* argument emphasizes the impressive technological innovations in information processing, storage, and transmission. It touches on the issue of 'convergence' of telecommunications, broadcasting, and computing and the creation of networks of terminals among organizations, offices, schools, homes, and so on. These technologies, in turn, have provided people with new ways of working—flexible specialization and greater customization of products and services.

The *economic* perspective on the information society derives from the work of Fritz Machlup (Machlup 1984, cited in Webster 2000), who developed a framework for measuring the information society in economic terms by classifying technologies according to five broad primary industry groups: education (e.g., schools, libraries, universities), media (radio, television, advertising), information machines (computer equipment, musical instruments), information services (law, insurance, medicine), other information activities (research and development, non-profit work). He also identified secondary-level organizations, such as research and development (R&D) within companies, information produced by institutions, and the library resources of organizations. By quantifying the economic contributions of these industries, one can calculate the growing economic significance of information and knowledge in today's society.

The *occupational* argument focuses on occupational change and the apparent predominance of occupations based on informational work (more teachers, lawyers, and entertainers than builders and coal miners, for example). This perspective is often combined with the economic approach. In this view, there is a progressive shift in the distribution of occupations towards a 'white collar society' and a decline in industrial labour. A simplification of this dichotomy argues that in the industrial sector, workers create, process, and handle physical goods, while in the information sector, workers create, process, and handle information.

The *spatial* perspective is based on the informational networks that now connect locations and affect how society organizes around time and space, thereby leading to a 'flat world' (Friedman 2005). An example of this phenomenon is that multinational organizations can operate 24 hours a day, with offices, factories, suppliers, and employees located all over the world, as a result of the ICT infrastructure that links them together. This perspective sees ICTs as crucial drivers of globalization today.

The *cultural* argument recognizes the extraordinary increase in information in social circulation because of television, the Internet, cellphones, and other devices. As a result, the behaviour and values of people in cities as diverse as Tokyo, London, New York, Manila, and Kuala Lumpur may be more similar than they are to those of people within the same country who are less connected to the network of information technologies. Furthermore, given the role that technology plays in people's lives, it affects the way that homes, workplaces, and even clothes are designed. Homes and offices are equipped with ports for plugging into the Internet; clothing comes with special pockets for iPods™; and cars contain cordless phone jacks.

These five typologies, however, remain problematic. Identifying the types of economic activity that constitute the information society is somewhat subjective. It can be argued that just about every profession deals with information and that many of these professions have existed for a long time. Furthermore, at what point (in terms of percentage of GNP or types of employment) can we say that a nation already constitutes an information society?

India, for example, is often cited as one of the beneficiaries of the information revolution, yet its society is also mired in a wide divide among the haves and have-nots, and its employment profile has barely changed over the 1990 to 2004 period (see Table 24.2). Over the same time span, Kazakhstan's economy actually became more agricultural. According to the same table, which countries could be described as information societies? The stark differences among these countries suggest that there are clearly more informatized and less informatized societies and that the world cannot collectively be described as an information society (see Box 24.1).

Finally, networks among people in the same occupation or profession have been around since long before the creation of the Internet. Examples include machine technicians, salespersons, lawyers, academics, and doctors who meet regularly to discuss their respective professions. Taking such phenomena into account, how does one identify the point at which the information society came to be? From a pragmatic viewpoint, however, it does not really matter whether we are an information society or not. Even though the concept of an information society may be debatable, what matters (and is not debatable) is that ICTs are here to stay and that they are affecting society economically, socially, and culturally. Societies are confronted with the growing importance of information products, an increase in information itself, the essential role of ICTs in many services and activities, and the need for information processing in trading and finance. It is important to understand what is happening in the interaction between society and ICT. These interactions have technological, cultural, socio-political, and economic dimensions. For that reason, just about every field in the social sciences has begun investigating the implications of ICTs.

Development theories and the information society

The idea of the 'information society' can be linked to the ideas of *modernization* and *globalization*.

Table 24.2 Labour and employment by economic activity

		% employment					
		1990			**2007**		
Year	**Country**	**Agriculture**	**Industry**	**Services**	**Agriculture**	**Industry**	**Services**
2004	Afghanistan	70	15	15	70	5	26
2003	Bangladesh	64	15	21	52	10	38
2004	Cambodia	81	2	17	60	10	30
2004	Hong Kong	1	28	72	0	7	93
2004	India	5	28	67	5	27	69
2005	Korea	18	28	55	8	19	73
1997	Myanmar	66	8	27	63	10	28
2005	Philippines	45	10	44	37	10	53
2005	Thailand	64	10	26	43	15	43
2005	Kazakhstan	19	21	60	32	12	56

Source: Asian Development Bank statistical database, http://sdbs.adb.org:8030/sdbs/index.jsp.

Modernization theory explains how societal development must go through a series of stages, with each phase having a different technological base of production (see chapter 3). In an information society, that base would be information technology. Furthermore, economies of the world have become more integrated, aided by information technology, as a result of globalization (see chapter 6). It is only over the past few decades that a technological infrastructure has developed to permit the global economy to function as a unit on a planetary scale. This technological infrastructure includes telecommunications, information systems, micro-electronic processing, air transportation, cargo systems, and international business services all over the world (Castells 1999).

In both the modernization and the globalization perspectives, information technologies play a part in development. According to modernization theory, they can be seen as a potential means of closing the gap between nations. In fact, ICTs even allow countries to leapfrog stages of economic growth by modernizing a country's production system and increasing competitive-ness at a faster rate than in the past (Castells 1999). ICTs are viewed as an important aspect of nations' ability to participate in the economic process of globalization.

However, these development perspectives have also been questioned. The *dependency* paradigm, in particular, holds the view that development in one country implies underdevelopment in another and that this is implicit in the nature of capitalism (see chapter 3). This view is consistent with the world systems view of development that sees a dynamic link between core regions of development and peripheral areas. Core regions are characterized by high income, advanced technologies, and diversified products, while peripheral areas have lower wages, rudimentary technology, and simple production mixes (Taylor 1989, cited in Malecki 1997). For instance, call centre work, which has been a growth industry in English-speaking developing countries such as India and the Philippines, is also seen by some as just another modern-day sweatshop. For example, once a call centre operator ends a conversation and drops the call, the system immediately and automatically

BOX 24.1   THREE WORLDS OF THE INFORMATION SOCIETY

As Table 24.2 shows, no country is purely service-based (or information-based). Verzola (1998), however, argues that one of three sectors will dominate: agricultural, industrial, or informational. This creates three disparate worlds and could lead to a widening gap between the rich and poor societies.

The agricultural sector produces and consumes living matter. The industrial sector extracts raw materials from nature to produce non-living finished goods, while the information sector produces non-material goods that are based on high information content. In trade terms, this equates producing 160 pounds of coffee (if coffee costs $1 per pound) with producing one television set at $160 or selling one copy of the latest Microsoft Office Professional™ for the same price.

The unique characteristic of information—never wearing out, never being used up, and easily copied with minimal input of labour and materials gives a significant advantage to societies with economies that are more information-based over agriculture- and industry-based economies.

diverts the next call in order to minimize idle time among workers. According to Hechanova (2007), the negative effects of call centre work include lack of sleep, lack of exercise, increase in drinking and smoking, and less time for the family. Odd work schedules, coupled with the mentally and physically stressful nature of the work, are leading to high turnover rates in these kinds of jobs.

Hence, the core-periphery dichotomy that was evident during colonial times and the industrial era continues in the information age, with the idea of *divides* continuing to persist. As Castells explains, a network society has the 'simultaneous capacity to include and exclude people, territories and activities that characterizes the new global economy as constituted in the information age' (1999, 5).

Just as nations have to clarify their position with respect to these development perspectives, they also have to clarify the role of ICTs in their development policies, since ICT use is also value-laden, cultural, and contextual. For instance, as a tool for governance, ICTs can be used to increase control just as they can be used to empower. They can be used to develop national identity, just as

they can be used to better understand other cultures. In the end, ICT is a tool, and it is up to the owners or users of the technology to decide how it will be used for development—whether in commerce, education, health, or governance.

THE IMPACT OF ICTs ON SOCIETY

ICTs and development: Why are ICTs crucial in today's society?

ICTs and society

There are a number of ways by which access to ICTs can help communities. Most important are the efficiency gains they provide. Access to telephones, for example, helps to reduce travel time and transportation costs because people do not have to physically commute to communicate with each other. It also provides more security, especially for those who are isolated, in remote areas, or in dangerous locations, since access to ICTs enables them to communicate more quickly with police, hospitals, and emergency response services. Furthermore, with an increasingly mobile population, ICTs are useful in maintaining family ties and in some cases have stemmed migration because businesses have outsourced various processes to developing countries. However, the primary function of ICTs has in fact been social in nature, allowing people to keep in touch, rather than in the economic sphere for which they may have originally been intended (Alampay 2006).

In that context, there are various views on how ICTs affect society and development. Some are optimistic, focusing on the potential benefits that ICTs can bring, including access to economic opportunities, more efficient work, and instantaneous access to better and more relevant information. In a 'networked economy', those included in the network have the opportunity to share and increase their life chances, while those who are excluded have fewer opportunities and roles (Castells 1999). Hence, to keep pace with other countries, every nation must be able to participate in the information economy. This fact creates scepticism among some observers, who caution that ICTs simply support existing social divides. For them, the information society widens the gap between the rich and the poor because of differences in their access to ICTs, their capabilities for using them, and the ways that they can apply them. Some also view ICTs as irrelevant to the majority of the poor and a possible negative influence on people's culture and lives (see Box 24.2).

More pragmatic observers, however, see ICTs as having varied effects on different groups and regions across the world. Consequently, they see the challenge as how ICTs can be made relevant for different groups.

Optimistic view

The optimists see the use of ICTs as a necessity that helps to encourage the sustainable development of individuals, communities, and nations. At the World Summit on the Information Society (WSIS) in 2003, ICTs were considered crucial to development because they can be used in public administration,

business, education, health, and environmental protection. They are seen as useful in alleviating poverty by expanding people's opportunities for economic development. They are also seen as tools that provide people with access to information that can be used to undertake production, participate in the labour market, and conduct reciprocal exchanges with other people.

The growing share of ICTs in world economic output is cited as evidence of their importance. The most optimistic see ICTs as providing developing countries with an opportunity to 'leapfrog' stages of development and achieve the level of development of the West (see Box 24.3). In fact, a recent study has found a beneficial relationship between access to mobile phones and economic growth, with the impact more significant in developing than in developed countries (Waverman, Mesch, and Foss, cited in *The Economist* 2005b).

Pessimistic view

An opposing view about ICTs is that they will only increase existing inequalities and social divides. Evidence for this perspective is taken from cases demonstrating that areas that have long benefited from excellent physical access and have been dominant politically and economically are the ones benefiting from greater access to information technologies (Niles and Hanson 2003). Historically, telecommunications roll-out has generally increased inequality, benefited mostly the wealthy, and had little impact on quality of life for the poor (Forestier, Grace, and Kenny 2003). The idea that development results from linking poor nations to ICTs—the Internet in particular—is also considered a myth (*The Economist* 2005a). Indeed, there are legitimate questions regarding the real effects of ICTs on national development, considering the limited evidence regarding any correlation (Heeks 1999). For instance, while ICTs have been instrumental in the development of India's information technology industry, this has not helped to reduce inequality between the rich and poor in Indian society (UNDP 2001; Warschauer 2004). To under-

BOX 24.2   GLOBAL CARE CHAINS

An interesting example of the balance between positive and negative views of ICTs is the concept of 'global care chains', which are a 'series of personal links between people across the globe based on paid or unpaid work of caring' (Hochschild 2001, 131, cited in Munk 2005). These chains emerged as a result of greater numbers of women obtaining employment in 'post-industrial' occupations created by the informatization of the economy. The growing need for non-manual skills has particularly benefited women. However, the increase in the proportion of women in the labour force has had an impact on the nuclear family in developed countries. It has fuelled a need for migrant domestic workers from the South to serve the needs of families in the North. Similarly, those who stay in their countries of origin but serve the needs of the North through outsourced services do so at odd hours. Thus, traditional family arrangements in developing countries are also affected.

stand why the gap continues to increase, one simply needs to visualize the price and cost differential between commodities. Original software on a disk may cost $100 and can be duplicated at almost zero cost with minimal expenditure of time. Contrast that to the situation of a farmer who would need vast inputs in resources and time to produce the same value in agricultural produce. Finally, for some countries, the utopian ideal of an information society requiring investment in ICTs is overshadowed by more pressing basic needs, like shelter, food, and health care.

Pragmatic view

The pragmatic point of view sees ICTs as playing a role in a country's development if applied appropriately. There is anecdotal evidence showing that access to a telephone, for instance, can have a dramatic effect on the quality of life of the rural poor. For example, the Grameen Village phone ladies in Bangladesh have been celebrated as a good model for areas where there is no widespread access to telephones. At one point, village phone ladies were earning three times the national average income. However, as access to mobile phones

in Bangladesh increased, the income from this 'shared-access model' has declined. Nonetheless, the model would still seem viable in places like Uganda, Rwanda, and Indonesia, where telephone access remains limited.[2]

Hence, whether ICTs are useful for development or not still depends on overcoming the same socio-economic barriers that contribute to underdevelopment in the first place. Strategies for using ICTs should consider their fit in the local context. Innovative public policies are also required to make sure that technologies are not only tools for progress but also socially inclusive.

THE DIGITAL DIVIDE

At the World Summit on the Information Society, representatives of governments and civil society organizations from 175 countries declared their common desire and commitment to building

'. . . a people-centred, inclusive and development-oriented Information Society, where everyone can create, access, utilize, and share information and knowledge, enabling individuals, communities and peoples to achieve their full potential in promoting their sustainable development and improving their quality of life' (WSIS 2003, 1).

The challenge of making a more inclusive information society means overcoming the so-called **digital divide**. The digital divide is generally defined as the difference between groups in their access to and use of ICTs. Manifestations of this divide are commonly seen between the North and the South, rich and poor, genders, urban and rural areas, young and old, and the educated and uneducated. The divide is usually measured in terms of number of phone lines per inhabitant and the number of Internet users or mobile phones in a population (see Figure 24.3).

The digital divide, however, is a relative concept. Optimists would argue that access is always on the upswing, given that the technology is rapidly developing (see Box 24.3) and its capacity exponentially increasing at the same time that the cost is decreasing. Pragmatists, however, would argue that any progress towards access among the

marginalized should be examined against the progress made by developed countries. For others, the idea of a digital divide may be passé or irrelevant, because those who need ICTs in the more developed countries already have them and those who do not have access do not really need them. There is anecdotal evidence, however, that access to ICTs can make a difference to people who have been deprived of it, even as there is clear evidence that such a divide exists between and within countries (see the case study of Nepal Wireless below).

In the end, the issue of whether the divide is increasing or not is less important than the question of how to bridge it. Bridging the digital divide is important for a number of reasons. The primary reasons are to provide access to basic services and to promote social equality.

Access to basic services

Access to ICTs is a basic component of civic life that some developed countries aim to guarantee for their citizens. The primary argument for universal access to ICTs, in fact, is security-related, not economic.

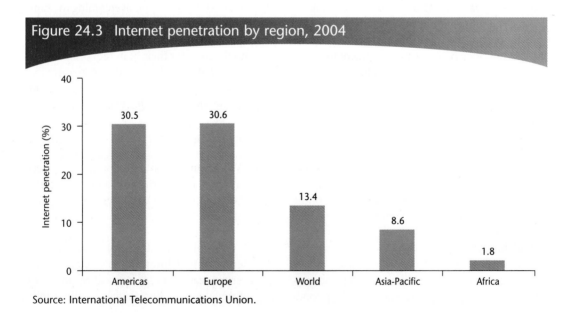

Figure 24.3   Internet penetration by region, 2004

Source: International Telecommunications Union.

BOX 24.3   LEAPFROGGING STAGES OF ICT DEVELOPMENT

Given how rapidly ICTs are developing today, many are optimistic that developing societies and communities are likely to catch up quickly. Part of this optimism has to do with the fact that ICTs are not only becoming more powerful, they are also becoming more affordable. This is attributable to Moore's Law, which states that the number of transistors on a chip doubles about every two years. This leads to a rapid and continuing advance in computing power per unit cost because the increase in transistor count is also a rough measure of computer processing power. On this basis, the power of computers per unit cost doubles every 24 months. A similar law has held for hard disk storage cost per unit of information, as well as for RAM (random access memory). Hence, not only is the technology getting better, it is also becoming more affordable and therefore more accessible to poorer segments of the population. In turn, this fuels the worldwide ICT revolution.

Thus, advancements in the development of ICTs contributes to the concept of *leapfrogging*, which is a theory of development in which developing countries skip inferior, less efficient, more expensive, or more polluting technologies and industries and move directly to more advanced ones. A frequent example is countries that move directly from having no telephones to having cellular phones, skipping the stage of land-line telephones altogether. Similarly, first-time computer users do not have to start with old 286 models but instead use the much faster and more powerful computer systems available in the market. The benefit of leapfrogging in information technologies is that it promotes greater access to information and ICTs that are at par with the developed world.

Telephone service is often considered important for the security and reduced isolation of remote areas. Health, crime, disaster, and other types of emergencies can be handled better if the person in trouble has access to telecommunication systems. Also important is the fact that much vital information for educational, career, civic life, and safety purposes is increasingly available on the Internet, especially on websites. Even social welfare services can be administered and offered electronically.

Social equality

For people in developing countries without access, bridging the digital divide is a means of sharing the wide range of opportunities already available to those who are connected (i.e., the rich, people in urban areas, the educated). It gives them a means not only of making better decisions but also of participating in decisions (see Sen 1999, chapters 1 and 13). This is especially important in the exercise of **good governance**. It varies from the simple ability to search and access government information to more ambitious visions of increased public participation in elections and decision-making processes. Direct participation through ICTs would only be possible if access to these technologies were available to all strata of the population.

From an economic standpoint, the development and use of ICTs is widely believed to be a source of competitive advantage. Hence, the

Case Study
Bridging the Digital Divide: The Case of Nepal Wireless

This is Mahibur Pun's story on how he brought the Internet to his village.

In 1997, I wished to get Internet in my village for the first time after Himanchal High School got four used computers as presents from the students of a school in Australia. Internet and e-mail were quite new terms then. Students from Billanook College in Melbourne collected the computers and raised money to ship them to Nepal. Our dream then was to have the students of the two schools communicate with each other through e-mail. That dream did not come true instantly because there was no phone line in the village to connect to the Internet.

I tried everything to get a telephone line. Initially we got a radio phone for the village, but it did not work well. I tried to find ways to get a satellite phone; however, the cost was beyond our means. I asked political leaders and officers of Nepal telephone company for help, but nothing happened. I kept asking people for ideas. I wrote a short e-mail to the BBC in 2001, asking if they knew anyone who could suggest ideas for getting cheaper Internet connection to my village. They wrote articles about my school and the computers we had built in wooden boxes. That article changed everything: I got responses with ideas from people all over the world.

As a result of the BBC article, we received two volunteers in early 2002 who knew about wireless networking. We experimented with wireless cards to test the connection between two villages which were 1.5 kilometres apart across a river valley. We used ordinary TV dish antennas and home-built antennas for the testing. The test was successful. Later on, many people from around the world helped provide more ideas about the wireless technology. Others donated equipment for access points for the project. Additional tests were done to connect my village to Pokhara (the nearest city with an Internet Service Provider [ISP]) using an ordinary TV satellite antenna. We pointed the antenna towards the mountain range that was stretching between Pokhara and my village. These mountains were the main obstacle for us. To overcome it, we used a tall tree on the top of the mountain as a relay station.

We had partial success. We found that we could connect to Pokhara because we could connect to Pokhara from a relay station hill. However, we could not connect to Pokhara directly from the village that time even though we tried everything we could. I played with the access points for a few more weeks. I figured out that I could connect to Pokhara if I set the transfer rate of the radio at 2 Mbps, put the access points further apart, and put a screen made of aluminum foil in between them. It worked well but there was shortage of power to run the radios all day. We had connection only for a couple of hours every day.

It took seven years for my wish to be fulfilled. Eventually, we got a grant from a foundation, which was used to buy additional equipment. We have come a long way in the past three years, but we still have to go further to bring the full benefit of the Wi-fi technology to the villagers.

Source: Abridged from http://nepalwireless.net/story01.php.

ability to harness its potential is important so that no one is left behind.

If ICTs play an increasingly important role in continued learning and career advancement, then meaningful education in ICT use is necessary to prepare everyone. Unless such education is widely available, the existing digital divide discriminates against children of lower socio-economic status. However, offering long-distance education through ICTs can potentially reduce the cost of education,

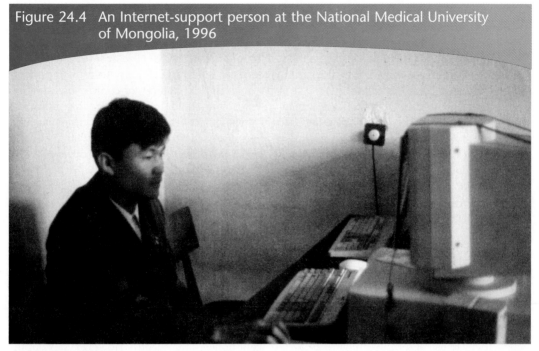

Figure 24.4   An Internet-support person at the National Medical University of Mongolia, 1996

Source: G. Long/IDRC

especially at the post-secondary level, since the cost of relocation and travel can be a disincentive to continuing in school. In fact, this was the prime motivation behind Mahabir Pun's quest to provide Internet service to his high school (see the case study on Nepal Wireless). Students in the villages can now not only access more information but also listen to guest teachers from distant places through the Internet.

Factors contributing to the digital divide

1. **Unequal diffusion/distribution of technologies**: The disparity between nations often begins with a lack of access to technological infrastructure. Access is often prioritized for urban centres and business areas. This explains the divide between urban and rural communities.

    The availability of technologies in a community, however, does not guarantee usage. Social barriers also need to be overcome in order for technologies to become useful. Foremost among these barriers are high costs, lack of education, and insufficient motivation.

2. **Affordability**: Even within urban enclaves where ICTs are commonplace, one barrier to usage is the cost of obtaining and using them. This contributes to disparities in the use of ICTs between the rich and the poor. The popularity of cellphones over land-line telephones in developing countries, for instance, was driven by the lower cost of short messaging systems (SMS) and the availability of pre-paid cards that allowed customers to overcome barriers to ownership when credit histories were often a prerequisite.

3. **Skills**: In many countries, differences in the use of ICTs are related to educational attainment. The more educated tend to use ICTs more. A gender dimension is also apparent, especially in places where women have less

access to education and are therefore less likely to have access to or use for ICTs.

4. **Motivation**: Another reason for the marked differences in usage within societies is motivation. This is especially true with regard to the young and the old. Older people tend to have a harder time adapting to new technologies, partly because they are quite used to life without them. Motivation is also related to the relevance of the technologies to a person's occupation. People working in white-collar professions, for instance, may find more uses for ICTs than farmers and fishermen.

USING ICTs FOR DEVELOPMENT

Using ICTs for development requires an integrated approach that takes into consideration access to the ICT itself, the content and applications that can be used, and building the necessary skills among people to make use of them (see Figure 24.5).

Access and equity: Providing people with universal access to ICTs

Universal service/universal access policies deal with bridging the ICT divide.

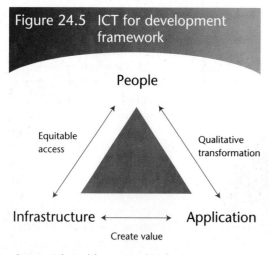

Figure 24.5   ICT for development framework

People

Equitable access

Qualitative transformation

Infrastructure ⟷ Application

Create value

Source: Adapted from NITA of Malaysia

Universal service in telecommunications is defined as 'making affordable a defined minimum service of specified quality to all users at an affordable price' (Prosser 1997, 80). The focus of universal service policies is to promote '"universal" availability of connections by individual households to public telecommunications networks' (Intven 2000, 1). This means that universal service is based on the availability of ICTs in homes (i.e., the percentage of households with a telephone).

Universal access, on the other hand, refers to 'a situation where every person has a reasonable means of access to a publicly available telephone . . . [which] may be provided through pay telephones, community telephone centers, teleboutiques, community Internet access terminals and similar means' (Intven 2000, 1). It is often measured in terms of the proportion of people in the population with access (i.e., telephone lines per 100 inhabitants, percentage of people with cellphones, and so on). However, developing countries have varied definitions of access. Some define it in terms of distance, while others define it with respect to time. For instance, in Burkina Faso, access is defined as a pay phone within 20 kilometres of most people. In Bangladesh, it is every villager having access to a telephone within a 10-minute walk (PANOS 2004).

Both universal service and universal access are based on the *affordability, accessibility,* and *quality* of basic telecommunication services. The primary difference is that universal service is focused on the availability of services in all homes, whereas universal access aims to have basic telecommunication services available in all communities. Developed countries tend to aspire for universal service, whereas developing countries aim for the more modest goal of universal access, considering the limitations of their markets and resources. Policies are crucial in making this possible (see Box 24.4).

Historically, universal access and universal service have referred to land-line telephones. However, with the convergence of technologies and the development of wireless devices such as the cellphone and Wi-fi, universal access and universal service have evolved to refer to access to the types of services or functions a technology can deliver. Developing countries are now moving towards access to the Internet as their primary universal access objective.

Creating value: Developing relevant content

Using ICTs for development requires understanding, first and foremost, the information needs and rights of people (see Box 24.5). This understanding should come from the intended users in the community themselves.

There are various ways in which the community's information needs can be assessed, including observation, surveys, focus group discussions, and community consultations. Some of the basic information that can be collected may include:

1. the different groups in the community;
2. the tasks these groups perform and the information they require to perform them;
3. the different media and ICTs that are used and can be used to access information;
4. the places where information can be obtained and how often it is needed.

Providing qualitative transformation: Making ICT use relevant to people

It is not enough to assume that ICTs alone can make a significant impact on an individual, an organization, or a government. Effects depend on the capacities and values of the people using the technology. Thus, investing in ICTs requires shaping people and developing the necessary skills to permit them to succeed.

In fact, even though newer ICTs are more 'user-friendly' than those of the past, they still require

BOX 24.4   IMPLEMENTING UNIVERSALITY: REGULATORY MEASURES TO FUND IT

1. Market-based reforms: In most countries, telecommunication services have historically been provided by a monopoly supplier, whether publicly or privately owned. In cases where the government had owned the telecommunication operations, evidence has shown that a marked improvement in access to services occurred following privatization. Other reform measures include opening the market to more competition and cost-based pricing.
2. Mandatory service obligations: Service obligations are imposed through licence conditions or other regulatory measures. This is often described in some countries as a provider's duty to serve all customers who are willing to pay the prescribed rates. The government may also prescribe geographic limits to areas where service is mandatory.
3. Cross-subsidies: This involves using surplus revenue earned from profitable services to cover losses from unprofitable areas or services (e.g., long-distance rates subsidizing local rates, business rates subsidizing residential rates).
4. Universality funds: This refers to independently administered funds that collect revenue from various sources and provide targeted subsidies to implement universality programs. These sources may include government appropriated budgets, charges for interconnection services, levies on subscribers, or levies on service operators. Countries that have used this system include Chile and Peru (Intven 2000).

BOX 24.5   COMMUNICATION RIGHTS ISSUES PERTAINING TO CONTENT

There are a number of pressing issues with respect to developing content for the information society. Among these issues are free access to useful and relevant information, freedom of expression, and the preservation of local cultures.

Open access versus intellectual property rights: Open access is important, especially when considering the importance of sharing the benefits of technological developments. It becomes a controversial issue, however, when pitted against commercial interests in terms of ownership and intellectual property rights. A good example of this is the battle between propriety software like Microsoft Explorer™ and open source software that does the same thing like Firefox™. This development is similar to the growth of non-profit organizations in the West as an offshoot of the backlash against corporate greed. Interestingly, in the World Wide Web, voluntarism and sense of community remain very much alive. This is evident in the numerous journals and websites that provide open access—i.e., free, immediate, permanent, full-text, on-line access—for any user, Web-wide, to digital scientific and scholarly materials and the growth of open source software available online.

Censorship versus freedom of expression: On the negative side, people are concerned about the dangerous content carried in ICTs, especially pornography and gambling sites on the Internet. Hence, states are concerned about regulating its use. However, some people worry that increased regulation, especially in the form of censorship, can be abused and curtail people's freedom to express themselves, communicate, and access useful information. A good example of this occurred in 2007 in Burma when thousands of Buddhist monks marched for freedom in the streets of Yangon. The state tried to curtail access to the Internet to prevent the story from coming out. Nonetheless, activists and journalists were still able to smuggle images and video captured on mobiles phones and broadcast them on the Internet via YouTube™. Their action generated worldwide condemnation of and concern over the events occurring in Burma.

Diversity of content: One important issue with ICTs is the dominance of content created in the West. For example, the predominant language on the Internet is English, which may not be the first language of choice in many countries of the world. That is why some countries fear that ICTs can endanger local cultures and heritage. Furthermore, news conglomerates, often owned by a few powerful people, may present biased perspectives on world events. Thus, an important challenge is to diversify the content, provide information that celebrates different cultures, acknowledge differences in viewpoints, and provide more information in local languages.

some degree of skill to operate. Being able to navigate the Internet to find useful information still requires the ability to discriminate between what is useful and relevant and what is not. This is why the more educated have been better able to take advantage of the benefits offered by the Internet such as surfing the World Wide Web and emailing.

ICTs and organizations

Since ICTs are tools, their impact on organizations depends on the people who design what the system is supposed to do and on how people, in the end, use it. Thus, its impact also depends on what the user wants it to be rather than just on the technology itself. While the available technology defines the limits of what can and cannot be done in an organization to some extent, in the final analysis, how ICTs are used tends to be socially determined by its managers.

Internal versus external focus

ICTs can be used to make internal processes more efficient (e.g., automation). They can also be used to network different systems within the organization. In this sense, the focus of ICTs is internal to the organization. However, systems can also be designed to increase interaction between the organization and its clients. This can be done by offering feedback mechanisms through telephone hotlines, websites, or email. Automated systems and business process outsourcing to other parts of the world can also enable an organization to offer services around the clock, seven days a week.

Flexibility versus control

ICTs can be used to help make work easier and empowering. This can be done by giving people greater access to different kinds of information within (e.g., through local networks with access to internal databases) and outside the organization (e.g., providing Internet access during working hours). However, ICTs can also expand control over what employees are doing because they increase managers' span of control (e.g., thanks to cellphones, employees can be reached any time and anywhere).

ICTs and work

The impact of ICTs on employment is mixed, just as it is in other facets of development. On the plus side, new kinds of jobs have been created. Some examples are call centre operators, computer programmers, knowledge managers, systems administrators, web designers, online tutors, and medical transcribers. ICTs can also provide flexibility in careers and work opportunities, since people are no longer limited by their location and the opportunities available there. They expand work opportunities available to people, giving them easier access to information about work in different parts of the world. Such information could enable people in developing countries to earn higher pay than what the local market would normally provide. It could also help workers balance their work and family life.

On the negative side, however, jobs can be destroyed. Automated teller machines, for instance, take the place of bank tellers. Lawyers no longer rely heavily on secretaries to type their briefs. With email, the need for messengers and telegraph operators declines. Services outsourced to developing countries take jobs away from other parts of the world. Hence, even though people may have more employment opportunities, they face more competition for those jobs.

There are other drawbacks to always being 'connected'. For some people, being accessible at all times opens the way to intrusion in their private space rather than helping them to balance work and family life. Moreover, ICTs can create an irresistible distraction that could lead to lower productivity—even abuse and addiction. Because the Internet is so content-rich, people sometimes venture to websites and activities that are not work-related while on the job. These activities include answering personal email, instant messaging, reading news, games, music and movies, pornography, and gambling.

Thus, balancing the benefits and hazards of providing Internet access in the workplace has become a policy decision in organizations. Determining who should have access and restrictions in terms of time and content are pertinent issues in the workplace today.

In the end, ICTs are not a panacea for making corrupt governments less corrupt, bad organizations good, or incompetent individuals competent. However, as with other technologies, ICTs in the hands of good people can make the people themselves and their society better. That is what ICT for development strives for.

QUESTIONS FOR DISCUSSION

1. What were the initial factors that contributed to the digital divide in the Nepalese case discussed above? How did the community overcome these problems? Do you think that their solution to the digital divide could be replicated in other developing communities? Can such technology transfer be sustained?

2. Think of a technology today, and list the benefits and problems it brings to society. (For example, cars have helped communities become more mobile. However, they have also contributed heavily to pollution and have been among the leading causes of deaths due to accidents.)

3. Which of the countries in Table 24.2 would you consider information societies? Explain your answer. Would you say that the concept of an information society is an inclusive one? When is a person part of the information society?

4. What are some of the policies and strategies that organizations can implement to balance the advantages and disadvantages of Internet access? What do you think are the pros and cons of applying these policies to an organization?

FURTHER READING

Smillie, I. 2000. *Mastering the Machine Revisited: Poverty, Aid and Technology*. Bourton on Dunsmore, Rugby, UK: ITDG.

UNDP (UN Development Programme). 2001. *Human Development Report 2001: Making New Technologies Work for Human Development*. New York: United Nations. http://hdr.undp.org/reports/global/2001/en.

Webster, F. 2000. *Theories of the Information Society*. London and New York: Routledge.

INTERNET RESOURCES

Technology and development:
Practical Action: http://practicalaction.org/?id=home.
The Carter Center: http://www.cartercenter.org/health/index.html.

ICTs and development:
Information for Development Program (InfoDev): http://www.infodev.org/en/index.html.
ICTs and development online resources: http://www.sed.man.ac.uk/idpm/research/is/ictdev.htm.
Women and ICT-based enterprises: http://www.womenictenterprise.org/home.htm.

ICT for development cases:
The Hole in the Wall Project: http://www.ncl.ac.uk/egwest/holeinthewall.html.
Grameen Village phones: http://mobileactive.org/grameen-village-phone-ladies.

Communication rights:
Handbook on Communication Rights: http://www.crisinfo.org.
The Open Net Initiative: http://opennet.net.

NOTES

1. See the Hole in the Wall Project, http://www.ncl.ac.uk/egwest/holeinthewall.html.
2. See http://mobileactive.org/grameen-village-phone-ladies.

CHAPTER 25

CULTURE AND DEVELOPMENT

NISSIM MANNATHUKKAREN

LEARNING OBJECTIVES

- To understand the concept of culture and to dispel the many myths surrounding it.
- To understand the relationship between culture and development.

INTRODUCTION

Culture is one of the most misunderstood concepts in the lexicon. It is often used rather loosely, denoting entirely contradictory meanings. Misunderstandings about culture have very serious implications. In fact, in recent history, there are hardly any conflicts, major or minor, that have not entailed invoking the concept of culture in some way. It seems that in an age when humankind has achieved the highest level of economic prosperity and scientific and technological advancement, culture and its varied manifestations have acquired an all-pervasive influence as a concept that can explain almost anything. In academia, one of the most important examples of this is the theorist Samuel Huntington's revival of his 'clash of civilizations' argument to explain the post-9/11 world reality. Such arguments, as we will discuss in this chapter, have only solidified misunderstandings about the concept of culture in popular discourse, thus further exacerbating the conflicts ostensibly rooted in culture. This possibility for aggravating or even causing conflict places a greater responsibility on academics to develop a better understanding of the term.

In the sphere of development, culture has also assumed an unprecedented significance in explaining phenomena such as poverty, economic growth, violence, and so on. From the policy formulations of international financial institutions such as the World Bank and the International Monetary Fund (IMF) to the theoretical and practical programs of non-governmental organizations (NGOs), culture has become the centre of attention. Hence, we see the ubiquity of words such as 'community', 'ethnicity', and 'gender' in the development discourse and the differences associated with these concepts. This is in marked contrast to the dominant tendency of twentieth-century development theory and practice, which excluded questions of culture.

Since the Enlightenment (in eighteenth-century Europe), Western thought has been dominated by an outlook that placed its faith in human reason instead of in an extraneous supernatural authority such as the God of Judeo-Christian religions. Reason was a universal human trait and hence was not the property of any one cultural group or formation. Reason was supposed to liberate human beings from superstitions, serfdom, and poverty and take them on the path of progress. Development, until quite recently, was based on this philosophical assumption. The means of realizing this assumption was through a project of modernization, which would destroy archaic institutions and relations. Industrialization and urbanization were the ideal and the necessary outcomes of this process of modernization (Escobar 1997, 86). All this was made possible by 'rationality, the highest expression of which was science' (Shanin 1997, 65).

Irrespective of cultural differences, all societies could follow this path of modernization. But this universal project of development based on reason, and above culture, did not materialize. Moreover, the glorious tenets of the Enlightenment—liberty, equality, and fraternity—have still not been accepted by all societies. Even in societies that have accepted these values as core constitutional principles, it is liberty (mainly economic liberty) that has gained precedence. Since the emergence of capitalism, and more specifically, the **Industrial Revolution**, 'the ceaseless production of endlessly proliferating material goods' (Shanin 1997, 66) has increasingly connoted progress. Therefore, it was not surprising that the entire development enterprise, as implemented in the Third World, mainly meant revolutionizing the economic forces of production, a cause towards which all other questions, including cultural, were sacrificed (see Box 25.1).

Recent criticisms that have emerged from a *post-modern* and *post-colonial* perspective have looked at the Enlightenment values, including the crowning of reason and science, as European constructions that have been imposed on the rest of the world. Thus, the experience of **colonialism**, **imperialism**, and development, and the monstrosities that were caused by them, put a serious question mark on the efficacy of reason itself. We stand at a juncture, therefore, in which the ideas and values that ruled our consciousness for two to three centuries have been deeply questioned—chief among them being the conception that all societies have a similar path to pursue and a similar goal to achieve. Instead, we see the emphasis on diversity and 'difference' and the multiple paths and endeavours characterizing different cultural formations. Therefore, the current explosion of the use of the concept of culture can be seen as a justifiable backlash against ignoring culture for so long.

In the course of this chapter, we will look at culture in its varied manifestations and its relationship to development. One of the main goals will be to dispel the many myths that surround the concept of culture. After setting out a plausible definition of culture, we will deal with one of the important debates that characterizes the field:

BOX 25.1   DEVELOPMENT *SANS* CULTURE

The adoption of modernization and scientific rationality has led to an inevitable conflict between the world views of the modernizing elites and the masses who still continue traditional ways of living. Therefore, development in many Southern societies has seen rural peasants being subjected to policies constructed by the educated bureaucrats from the cities. One example is the relief package announced by the government of India in 2006 for the debt-ridden farmers of western India, which included the distribution of cattle to people who had never used them before and in a region that is deficient in water and fodder. Ultimately, the result of the government promoting dairying in a region not suited for it was that the farmers spent a lot of labour time in tending to the cattle, as well as the equivalent of three people's daily wages on the sustenance of one cow, with hardly any return from it (Sainath 2006)! Such examples abound in the history of the development era, not only in the South but also in the North–South relationship seen especially in the devastating policies designed by institutions like the World Bank without due consideration to the local, material, and cultural contexts of a region.

the cultural versus the material. Understanding the relationship between these two spheres is crucial to clearing up some of the misconceptions about the concept of culture. In the following sections, we elaborate on two commonly used, and often confused, terms—**mass culture** and **popular culture**. In the final section, we focus on the turn towards culture as an explanation and the reasons and implications of such a turn.

WHAT IS CULTURE?

If we are to clear up misunderstandings about the term culture, the first step is to develop a precise definition of the concept. The word culture derives from the Latin word *cultura* and in its initial usage referred to the cultivation or the nurturing of animals or crops. From the sixteenth century onward, this original usage was extended to include human beings and the cultivation of the mind. Gradually, it took on the connotation of a 'progressive process of human development, a movement towards refinement and order and away from barbarism and savagery' (Thompson 1990, 124, 126). Affinities with the Enlightenment idea of progress are visible here. Similarly, culture can be seen as 'a state or process of human perfection, in terms of certain absolute or universal values' (Williams 1961, 41). One of the problems in defining culture in this fashion is that it can acquire an elitist and evolutionary connotation, suggesting that culture is the property of a few people while the majority lack culture and that culture can be attained only at a certain stage of development. This elitist belief is common in many societies, but it took its most pronounced form in the European encounter with non-Europeans, especially colonized people. This is the reason why the colonizing enterprise was also a civilizing mission—to bring culture to the 'primitives'.

This notion of the inferiority of non-European cultures began to be corrected only with the emergence of the discipline of anthropology towards the end of the nineteenth century. Rather than seeing culture as an evolutionary movement to a predestined state of perfection defined by Europeans, anthropology began to look at cultures, especially non-Western ones, without any preconceived notions of inferiority (Benhabib 2001, 3). E.B. Tylor, one of the famous first-generation anthropologists, described culture as 'that complex whole which includes knowledge, belief, art, morals, law, custom, and any other capabilities and habits acquired by man as a member of society' (quoted in Thompson 1990, 128). Similarly, culture can be seen as 'a description of a particular way of life, which expresses certain meanings and values not only in art and learning but also in institutions and ordinary behaviour'. This definition will 'include analysis of elements in the way of life that to followers of the other definitions are not "culture" at all: the organization of production, the structure of the family, the structure of institutions which express or govern social relationships, the characteristic forms through which members of the society communicate' (Williams 1961, 41, 42). These definitions are devoid of the ethnocentric (Europe-centred) assumptions of the evolutionary and elitist concept of culture that we saw above. They do not seek to pass an evaluative judgment about what is good or bad. However, these definitions can become very broad, encompassing almost everything that human beings do. This renders them somewhat vague and imprecise (Thompson 1990, 130). It is therefore imperative that we move beyond both the elitist and the anthropological understandings of culture, while retaining what is useful in them.

It has been argued that the distinctive feature of human life is the fact that it has a fully developed language (Thompson 1990, 130). Therefore, a good starting point is to focus the study of culture on the symbolic. According to the distinguished anthropologist Clifford Geertz, 'man is an animal suspended in webs of significance he himself has spun' (Geertz 1973, 5). Culture becomes important because human beings do not just inhabit a world that is objective and natural. It is also simultaneously a world that is constructed and subjective. This means that human beings develop and attribute their own meanings to the objective world they inhabit. And these meanings may vary from one society to another. Here, it would be productive to follow Thompson: 'culture is the pattern of meanings embodied in symbolic forms, including actions, utterances and meaningful objects of various kinds, by virtue of which individuals communicate with one another and share their experiences, conceptions and beliefs' (Thompson 1990, 132). But this is only the first step towards a proper understanding, especially when we are seeking to understand culture's relationship with development.

The variety of understandings about culture is mainly a result of the genuine complexity of cultural formations that exist in the world. At the same time, it would be fruitful to develop a definition that eliminates some of the myths that surround culture. Thus, the evolutionary definition, which holds that culture is a constant movement towards perfection, would not make sense unless we understood the elements that constitute this idea of perfection and the actual social and historical contexts that produce different ideas of perfection. At the same time, we have to account for values that do not meet the criteria of perfection. There is also the need to avoid definitions that narrowly treat culture as a mere by-product of other, 'real' interests in society (Williams 1961, 43–4, 46). That does not help us to understand what is intrinsic to the sphere of culture. However, the study of culture cannot remain at the level of culture alone either; it should move on from a mere study of symbolic forms to a study of them in 'relation to the historically specific and socially structured contexts and processes within which, and by means of which, these symbolic forms are produced, transmitted and received' (Thompson 1990, 136). For example, while we can easily identify with many of the themes in William Shakespeare's plays, it would be wrong to assume that we can learn all about the culture of the period from the plays alone; instead, they have to be placed and understood in relation to the context of sixteenth-century England.

THE CULTURAL VERSUS THE MATERIAL

It would be a fascinating enterprise to study transformations throughout history in the cultural sphere along with transformations in the material sphere. Of course, we must acknowledge that in reality, these spheres are inextricably intertwined and that it is only for heuristic purposes that we try to make such distinctions. It would be going along with a wrong, though commonsensical, understanding that the symbolic is somehow beyond all determinations and influences. The economic aspect, for example, is a very important facet of the interrelationship between culture and other elements in society. In fact, many misunderstandings about culture stem from the belief that culture can be analyzed without understanding its interlinkages with the economic dimension, which would include the forces of production (land, labour, machinery) and the relations of production (the relationship between classes in the process of economic production). How can we understand the cultural forms of the present without an in-depth look into how capitalism—the dominant mode of production of our time—functions? It has to be kept in mind that the practice and interpretation of cultural forms cannot be entirely random. The capitalist mode of production (as any other mode of production) structures in various ways the cultural forms that are produced. How is it possible to study multiculturalism without studying the movement of labour and people that created it in the first place? How is it possible to study mass-mediated cultural forms without understanding the broadcasting institutions that produced them? Similarly, how can we understand shopping and advertising without understanding the processes of manufacturing and retailing? (Garnham 1998, 611). These questions are especially relevant considering the fact that modern culture is inextricably linked with mass media. It has been 'caught up in processes of commodification and transmission that are now global in character' (Thompson 1990, 124).

Technology plays a crucial role in present-day culture. The ways in which modern means of communication and commodification have shaped culture show that culture does not exist in a vacuum but is constantly shaped by material forces. For example, the development of communication technologies like the Internet and mobile phones has had a significant impact on the cultural meanings of human relationships and interaction, especially in the South where the paradoxes produced by the coexistence of modern and traditional ways of life are very pronounced. The availability of technologies such as photography and printing has also completely altered our relationship to the past. This new way of recording culture has a significant impact (both negative and positive), especially on indigenous cultures that have oral traditions, societies that transmit their culture across generations without a writing system. Similarly, science exerts an influence on cultural forms. The detective story genre, for example, would not have been possible in any age other than the scientific age. Detective stories 'could only appeal to—in fact, only be *comprehensible* to an audience accustomed to think in scientific terms: to survey the data, set up a hypothesis, test it by seeing whether it caught the murderer' (Macdonald 1964, 37; emphasis in the original).

Even as the mode of production, along with the level of science and technology, sets a limit to the kind of cultural forms that are produced, we have to avoid conceiving of this relationship as mechanical. The most difficult task is to understand this relationship in a non-reductive manner—that is, to study culture without reducing it to changes in the economic sphere (or vice versa) (see Box 25.2). Development, for a long time, was undertaken with the belief that culture did not matter and that culture would mechanically adjust itself to changes in the economic sphere, the consequences of which could be deleterious (one example is the introduction of smallpox vaccination by the British in colonies while outlawing existing indigenous techniques that were intrinsically linked with religious practice and worship [see Marglin 1990, 8]). Cultural forms produced under capitalism are not necessarily homogeneous, since 'the capitalist mode of production does not demand, require, or determine, any one form of politics' (Garnham 1998, 605). While the United States, Japan, and the United Kingdom are all capitalist societies, their cultures are not identical. These cultural variations show that culture cannot be explained merely by the distinction between the owners of the means of production and wage labour, as is the case in capitalism (Grossberg 1998, 614).

BOX 25.2   ARE HUNTER-GATHERERS POOR?

The ideology of modernization and development characterized pre-modern subsistence economies as societies existing in precarious and extremely difficult conditions. The anthropologist Marshall Sahlins, in a famous study on the hunting and gathering tribes, has questioned characterizing a lack of material possessions as poverty. Sahlins instead argues that the lack of material possessions does not make these tribes poor but free. In their own evaluation, this lack is a positive cultural fact, for they privilege the freedom of movement over material accumulation (see Sahlins 1997). It is important to ask here why our modern criteria would label people with such few wants as poor rather than as affluent, as Sahlins does.

While economic practices 'determine the distribution of practices and commodities', they do not totally determine the meanings that are circulated by these practices (Grossberg 1998, 618).

One of the most important debates that have characterized the social science tradition since its origin has been the materialism versus idealism debate. The former asserts the primacy of material factors in social change, while the latter focuses on cultural factors, mental phenomena, and ideas. As we said before, this kind of binary distinction is problematic because of the interlinked nature of social phenomena. Privileging one over the other does not aid us in arriving at a proper understanding of culture or development. For instance, it has been a common practice among modernization theorists and also within popular discourse to blame the slowness of economic growth on the 'backward' mentality and superstitious beliefs of 'traditional' societies. These views, in the absence of an understanding of material factors, come to portray development

as primarily governed by thought processes. Here, social phenomena such as poverty can be blamed on the poor themselves for their lack of 'correct' thinking (T. Allen 2002, 454). On the other hand, material factors such as forces of production do not develop on their own. Labour is not a physical activity alone but also involves a mental component. Modern science and technology could not have originated unless the previous belief in the sacredness of nature had been substantially altered. Similarly, capitalism could not have originated or flourished without continuous savings and investments, which required a radical change in the meanings attributed to money and its use.

Nonetheless, it should be understood that conscious acts and agency themselves can turn into a structure: 'structures created and perpetuated by a multitude of conscious, individual acts [can] develop some sort of internal logic, or institutional imperative, over and above these acts' (Femia 1981, 119). Very often, the economic realm, because of its centrality to the sustenance

Figure 25.1   Argentines celebrate a goal by their national soccer team during the 1998 World Cup

Source: Paul Haslam

and reproduction of human life, develops such structures with their own logic and dynamism that are not easily circumvented except by the combined agency of a very large number of people. It is in this sense that the economic sphere, along with other material factors such as natural and physical resources, is seen to limit the 'the range of possible outcomes' of cultural imagination without mechanically determining them. Ultimately, what outcome becomes a reality is still decided by 'free political and ideological activity' (Femia 1981, 119). Here, it is also important to recognize what is intrinsic and unique to each sphere beyond its interlinkages with and determinations by other spheres.

Culture and development thus are intrinsically interlinked. With recent revisions to our understanding of development, following theorists such as the Nobel laureate Amartya Sen, from mere economic development to the enhancement of human freedom in the broadest sense, development has begun to include the enhancement of cultural freedom as well. Economic development can also lead to enhanced resources that can enable the exploration of a society's cultural history through historical excavations and research. Sen argues that culture can thus become one of the basic ends of development. Culture plays another role for Sen: as a means of development. As we observed above, symbolic understandings can govern behaviour, including peoples' economic behaviour (see Box 25.3). Thus, cultural traditions and norms can play an important role in influencing economic success and achievement. They can also constitute an important source of economic investment and returns through activities such as tourism promotion, which has other positive benefits, including cultural contact and interaction (Sen 2001, 1–4).

CULTURE AS DOMINATION AND CULTURE AS RESISTANCE

One of the biggest myths about culture is that it is an ahistorical entity—something that persists without change. Thus, for example, whenever there is a discussion about religion or religious texts, especially from the point of view of the

BOX 25.3 THE PROTESTANT ETHIC

The most famous theory regarding cultural influence on economic behaviour is Max Weber's theory of the **Protestant ethic** in which certain characteristics of Protestantism (especially Calvinism), such as valuing austerity, discipline, and hard work to attain material wealth and success as a route to personal salvation, were considered as having played a major role in the origin of capitalism. The theory has been criticized heavily for its inability to explain the economic success of Catholic countries such as France and Italy and non-Christian Asian countries in the twentieth century. However the Japanese economic miracle has been attributed to a different set of cultural values, 'which emphasized group responsibility, company loyalty, interpersonal trust and implicit contracts that bind individual conduct'. These values originate from a variety of cultural traditions including Japan's history of feudalism, Confucian ethics, and the 'Samurai code of honour' (Sen 2001, 6–7, 11). In 'transitional' and 'developing' countries, it is claimed that one of the important cultural barriers to efficient economic growth is the problem of corruption. Former socialist economies such as those of Russia and eastern European countries are examples of this phenomenon (Sen 2001, 14).

faithful, the general tendency has been to see them in abstract, universal, and essentialist terms. The fact that they originated in a particular period, respond to particular needs, are subject to many kinds of contestation, and change accordingly throughout history is rarely recognized. Culture is as much determined by relations of power as any other sphere is. There is no work of art or ritual that is above a particular point of view or interest. Cultural forms 'are always produced or enacted in particular social historical circumstances, by specific individuals drawing on certain resources and endowed with varying degrees of power and authority' (Thompson 1998, 135). Cultural phenomena are distributed, received, and interpreted by individuals and groups placed in different power locations and with different material interests. The interpretation of cultural phenomena varies according to these differences. In short, cultural phenomena are not benign; they, like any other social phenomenon, are immersed in relations of power. And these relations of power cannot be reduced to economic relations or class power. They exist in other spheres, such as gender relations, relations between ethnic and religious communities, and nation-states.

Thus, the practice of cultural forms and the enjoyment of symbolic objects are not activities devoid of ideological aspects. Very often, they serve to provide the cultural underpinnings of a dominant mode of development. Not all classes and groups in society influence the formation of culture equally. In this sense, the ideological and material interests of the ruling class and the dominant groups tend to dominate the art and culture of any period. The social scientific tradition inaugurated by Karl Marx and Friedrich Engels was the first to theorize about this phenomenon.

Once we understand that culture is characterized by power relations and the obvious resistances they produce, it becomes easier to dispel the myth that cultures are homogeneous wholes. This myth essentializes 'the idea of culture as the property of an ethnic group or race'; it reifies 'cultures as separate entities by overemphasizing their boundedness and distinctness' (Terence Turner,

quoted in Benhabib 2001, 4). Such claims of cultural homogeneity and distinctness, for instance, are routinely made in relation to nationalism, one of the most potent cultural forces in the present world. The culture-development linkage is very clearly demonstrated in the nation-state: the nation provides the cultural underpinning for the state's pursuit of development. But what is crucial from our perspective is the two-faced nature of nationalism: even when the nation seeks to be a community of people, it is in reality characterized by hierarchy and domination and the perpetration of exploitation and exclusions. Nationalism, in the present, becomes a cultural ideology that seeks to paper over the inequities generated by the development process (see Box 25.4).

Thus, culture is not a static entity. Since all the elements of the bygone cultural past cannot be known or practised as a part of a tradition, the question of selection invariably crops up. Here, the selection of particular aspects of a period's culture will be governed by many kinds of dominant interests, including class interests. The student of development should relate the particular selection and interpretations of tradition and culture to each period's development context to see how the interplay between material and cultural factors is influenced by various classes and groups in society. Development studies should endeavour to examine how certain symbolic forms and ideas gain dominance rather than seeing them as natural phenomena. It may then be obvious that many of the ideas and symbolic forms that appear as universal and abstract actually originate in particular dominant groups—either class-based or otherwise (see Box 25.5).

Mass Culture

We have seen above that the distinguishing feature of modern culture is the fact that it is inextricably linked with modern means of technology and transmission and that it is primarily driven by commercialization. In that sense, much of present-day culture can be called as **mass culture**. 'Mass culture's distinctive mark is that it is

BOX 25.4   THE MYTH OF NATIONALISM

Many homogeneous nationalisms that exist or are pursued today actually mirror the dominant ethnic group's culture at the cost of the minority nationalities and ethnic groups. A good example would be the recent efforts by Hindu fundamentalists to define Indian nationalism as Hindu, an approach that seeks to erase the diversity of one of the most multicultural societies in history. Indian society is home to all the major religions of the world. Despite Hindus being the majority, it has the third largest Muslim population in the world and a substantial number of Christians. The Hindu nationalists' attempt to build a majoritarian nationalism, often through violent means, has led to the loss of many lives. Nationalists have also used religion in an instrumental fashion to garner the support of the majority Hindus. In placing religious and cultural issues such as the building of temples and protection of Hinduism at the top of the agenda and in positing religious minorities such as Muslims (or other nations such as Pakistan) as the main enemy, Hindu nationalists glossed over the fundamental divisions in society between the owners of capital and land and the labouring masses, high and low castes, and men and women that mark all religious communities, including the Hindu majority. As a result, during their tenure in government, no attempt was made to level these hierarchies. For example, despite the fact that the Indian economy was growing at one of the fastest rates in the world, the country actually went down the Human Development Index (HDI) from 124 to 127, showing that the boom in the economy benefited only the rich and the middle classes. Here, nationalism becomes a rhetoric and is hollow, not capable of meeting the material needs of even the majority community it claims to speak for. It merely becomes a symbolic tool in the hands of the powerful to mobilize the support of the powerless while also constituting a source of cultural pride for the classes that are included in the economic growth.

BOX 25.5   THE 'AMERICAN DREAM'

An example of how certain ideas gain universal acceptance and acquire an ideological form is the idea of the 'American Dream' according to which if a person has talent and works hard, she can lead a very successful life. This dream drives millions of people, from all over the world to move to the US. While the concept contains an element of truth, it hides the fact that the United States, despite its wealth, is the most non-egalitarian society among the Northern countries, and structural inequalities based on class and race (among other factors) would prevent a majority of immigrants from attaining their dream.

solely and directly an article for mass consumption, like chewing gum' (Macdonald 1964, 59). Unlike folk art, which grew from below and belonged to the common people, mass culture is something that is imposed from above. This means that the people who consume it have very little say in its production. They contribute to it only in the sense of buying it or not buying it. Thus, a few people produce cultural forms that are consumed by the vast majority. And the people who produce culture belong overwhelmingly to the capitalist cultural industry. This has serious implications for development in the Third World. Leslie Sklair has argued that the value system that is key to capitalist modernization is the 'culture-ideology of consumerism' (Sklair 1991). Capitalism is a system built on the relentless pursuit of profits, which can happen only with production of more and more goods, the commodification of new objects, and the creation of new wants. The mass media and the entertainment industry have been the main vehicles for promoting new practices of the culture-ideology of consumerism in the Third World. '[T]he promise of the 1970s that satellite television would revolutionize education, public health and nutrition, and eliminate illiteracy throughout the urban and rural Third World, has been largely unrealized' (Sklair 1991, 165).

The emergence of mass culture is linked with the emergence of a new mode of production—industrial capitalism—and the associated development of science and technology. Capitalist industrialization broke down agrarian-based feudal modes of production. Under feudalism, labour was closely tied to the land and the landlord and did not have mobility. People lived in close-knit communities, and culture, especially that of the labouring classes, was collectively produced. Industrial capitalism broke down these relationships. Labour was detached from land and other means of production to constitute the wage labour for urban-based factories. With increasing division of labour, jobs began to take on a mechanical and fragmented shape, requiring no special skills. The increasing number of people with monotonous jobs and with highly individu-

alized (and atomized) lifestyles began to constitute the biggest base for mass culture. Mass culture is deemed by many as a debased phenomenon that does not lead to the ennoblement of the intellectual and aesthetic faculties with which human beings are endowed because it seeks to satisfy the lowest common denominator and panders to the tastes of the 'most ignorant' (Macdonald 1964, 70). Mass culture is criticized as mere entertainment, and 'entertainment is betrayal', in the famous words of the philosopher Theodor Adorno, for it promises happiness to the masses that is subsequently denied by capitalism (Benhabib 2001, 3). This can especially be deemed true for the Third World, where consumption practices modelled on Western lifestyles engineered by the mass media have brought about serious contradictions and a skewed relationship between production and consumption. The masses have been exposed to the glitzy and glamorous world of new global market culture without the material means to afford this culture (see Figure 25.2). And culture-based economic activities such as tourism can have harmful consequences because of excessive commercialization—selling exoticized versions of 'traditional' cultures primarily to rich Western tourists (see Box 25.6).

Popular Culture

Very often, the term **popular culture** is used to connote mass culture. Following Stuart Hall, it would be better to make a distinction between the two. Popular culture does not mean whatever is followed or appreciated by the most number of people, as the market definition would put it. For Hall, popular culture refers to those elements of culture that are in continuous tension with the dominant culture. These elements invariably belong to the culture of the marginalized and oppressed classes, working people, and the poor (Hall 1998, 449). There is a double movement in the domain of culture. While the dominant elements seek to control and rein in the popular elements, the latter are not passive actors; they are constantly seeking to resist these attempts despite the fact that the contest is unequal because of the

Figure 25.2 'Prototype for New Understanding #8', 1999

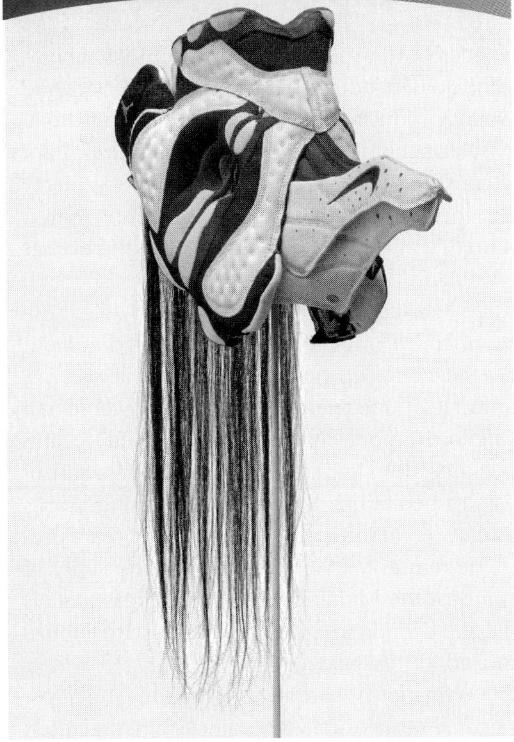

Brian Jungen, a Canadian artist, uses modern consumerist artifacts (such as the Nike footwear here) to rework them to resemble specified references to First Nations cultures, thus creating new meanings to represent the complex relationship of the indigenous people to the modern capitalist world.
Source: Brain Jungen *Prototype for New Understanding #8*, 1999 Nike Air Jordans 58.5 x 19 x 38.1 cm. Collection of Collin Griffiths, Vancouver. Courtesy of Catriona Jeffries Gallery.

power possessed by the dominant elements (Hall 1998, 443, 447). This follows the Marxist theoretician Antonio Gramsci, who famously argued that it is not a one-sided process in which the ruling or dominant culture simply overruns or decimates the subordinate culture—as is a common misconception—but is a complex process of struggle in which the former can become dominant only by accommodating the latter in some measure (Bennett 1986, xv). Therefore, against the common belief that cultural practices and objects come with inherent meanings, it has to be emphasized that meanings are created in the process of struggle and contestation. What belongs to dominant elite culture or popular culture shifts over time, depending on these contestations. Thus, all cultures are contradictory, containing different elements that intersect and overlap in the course of struggle (Hall 1998, 452). Culture, therefore, is a process rather than a finished form (see Box 25.7).

As a result of these contestations and struggles, mass culture (which is mainly a part of dominant culture) is not merely manipulative but serves other functions as well. In fact, an entire stream of literature (called cultural populism) has emerged focused on the practices of consumption of mass cultural products and the agency and pleasures involved in them (see Storey 1998; During 1993; Grossberg 1998). Moreover, the unintended consequences of mass culture have to be recognized. It contributes to a kind of levelling process: a proliferation of information, a scaling down of hierarchy (Anderson 1998, 111), and making (at least some of the) cultural products accessible to the masses. This is significantly different from the pre-capitalist situation when there was a stark distinction between high and low culture, with the latter completely excluded from the former. But ultimately, one of the main reasons for the appropriation of popular culture by the dominant culture is the fact that the power and the means of cultural production are concentrated in the hands of cultural industries. For example, in the early 1990s, the international music recording industry was an oligopoly consisting of six companies (During 1993, 16). This is an instance of the economic mode of production, in a particular period, acting as the limiting force, and it shows the inevitable intertwining of cultural and material domination (see Box 25.8).

Mass culture and popular culture thus show the two sides of culture: as domination and as resistance.

BOX 25.6   BOLLYWOOD AND RAI

Mass culture is an important facet even in the societies of the South today. In countries such as India, its reach and popularity are phenomenal. The Indian film industry, which includes Bollywood (films in the Hindi language) is the largest in the world, producing more than 800 films and selling almost four billion tickets every year. Being a visual medium, it has played a very important role, as in many other post-colonial societies, in the construction of a national identity in a society that has a substantial number of poor and illiterate people who are also divided by ethnic differences and geographical distance. It became a great unifier in a country emerging from the bruises of a 200-year period of colonial rule. It also became a tool for spreading political messages, so much so that in some Indian states, many of the important political figures are also film stars. While these commercial films are mainly for entertainment and uncritically reinforce many of the dominant values, such as patriarchy and the naturalness and necessity of economic and social hierarchies, there are contrary tendencies too. They portray a universe of unequal power relations, even if in a simplistic fashion, in which the exploiters are the landlords, moneylenders, and industrialists and the exploited are the poor, the landless, and the illiterate. More important, they provide a sort of anchor in a rapidly modernizing society that appears to be continuously eroding existing norms and ways of life. These films try to provide some kind of resolution to the anxieties and fears produced in such conditions (see Nandy 1995, 205). One reason for the phenomenal popularity of Bollywood films in Afghanistan and in countries in Africa, the Middle East, and Southeast Asia is the fact that these societies, undergoing similar social and economic changes, find (despite linguistic barriers) an affinity with the moral universe portrayed in these films.

Mass culture has also occasionally sought to question the norms of dominant culture. The genre of Rai music in Algeria is a good example: it has become a major rallying point against religious fundamentalism. Despite the fact that it is disseminated by the capitalist market using widely available cheap consumer electronics, the music has often raised issues such as sexuality, women's rights, political freedom, and drug and alcohol use—all considered taboo by the orthodox Islamic leaders. Rather than just imitate Western pop culture, as the Islamic forces allege, Rai musicians actually revived the centuries-old tradition of libertinism and religious scepticism present in Arab culture and mixed it with Western genres of music (Freund 2002).

THE CULTURAL TURN

We have seen briefly how the values of the Enlightenment have been subject to scrutiny in the recent past. In fact, the biggest theme animating the field of development is the cultural question: 'culture is . . . foundational. [It] is neither reflective nor instrumental. Culture is not a superstructure that emerges from and reflects a given material base. Nor is culture to be understood as the instrument which may facilitate or obstruct improvement in the material standard of living' (Marglin 1990, 23). The supposed failure of grand projects based on capitalism and socialism has set the stage for a new path. Recourse to explanations based on culture has also been the result of a general consensus about the fact that there is an impasse in development studies: the inability or the failure of much of development theory to explain reality, especially in the South (Booth

BOX 25.7   SYMBOLIC STRUGGLES

Even as the culture of dominant groups and ruling classes tries to control the culture of subordinate people, the latter mounts resistance. This has been a constant feature in all societies across the ages. Thus, no dominant ideology can ever be completely dominant. Unless we factor in resistance waged at the symbolic and material levels, we will not be able to explain social change. Such resistance has been brilliantly theorized by James Scott, especially through his study of the peasantry in Malaysia. According to Scott, despite the lack of material means and avenues to challenge the dominance of powerful groups, the powerless resort to symbolic struggles in innovative and anonymous ways. Beyond the surface appearance of a placid acceptance of dominant culture, the cultural sphere is actually simmering with 'gossip, folktales, songs, gestures, jokes, and theater of the powerless' through which they mount a critique of power (Scott 1990, xii). We would not generally associate these things (along with others, such as rumour, linguistic tricks, metaphors, and euphemisms) as anything to do with politics or the struggle for power, but they do constitute an important part of the symbolic armoury of the powerless. Gossip, for instance, especially gossip that seeks to destroy the reputation of superiors, is a tool used by the dominated to ensure that the former do not exceed acceptable levels of oppression (Scott 1990, 137, 142–3). Similarly, symbolic resistance to new economic modes of production, such as capitalism, that cause a tremendous disruption to traditional ways of agrarian life (which despite the lack of many modern freedoms were secure in many other aspects) can be seen in many parts of the South. One example is the belief by displaced peasantry in Colombia and Bolivia that capitalist proletarianization and commoditization are intimately associated with the sprit of evil and thus unnatural (see Taussig 1980).

1994). From the 1980s, the endeavour has been to envision an alternative path to development—of which the building block is culture. It can be summarized as 'the challenge . . . to find ways of increasing well-being without indiscriminately destroying valued ways of living and "knowing" and without placing unbearable strains on the environment' (Jayawardena 1990, vi). This search for an alternative was premised on the supposed failure of the Western model of development, which had been dominant especially over the past 60-odd years. The blind imitation of this model by the non-West, especially poor countries, has led to their ruin, according to critics:

It is taken as axiomatic that intellectual frameworks borrowed from other historical, cultural and political environments can no longer be effective in understanding the complex realities of the other, fundamentally different cultures and contexts, or in giving direction to social changes underway in them. The additional question is how to use the total knowledge systems that are available in the South to facilitate this understanding (Wignaraja 1993, 6).

It was as much a case of the West dominating the non-West as the latter actively looking towards the former in awe. After all, throughout the years of colonialism, the colonized were inculcated in systems of education that glorified Western ways of living. Colonialism drew its justification by portraying the colonized as 'children' who needed to be looked after (Nandy 1983). What this did was largely erase indigenous ways

Figure 25.3   A billboard promoting Guyanese export, 1980

THE WORLD IS NOW PAYING MORE FOR RICE, SUGAR, BAUXITE AND GOLD

SO WE GUYANESE MUST SEIZE THE TIME !

Source: Neill McKee/IRDC

of life and knowledge. This erasure altered the course of the histories of colonized societies and has had real effects in the post-colonial period. Almost all of these societies are victims not only of economic underdevelopment but also of cultural underdevelopment. Hence, we see the adoption of the languages of the erstwhile European rulers as official languages in these societies. For example, 38 African countries have adopted a European language as their official language (Dhaouadi 1988, 220). This has very serious implications, for it systematically undermines native languages and also creates a divide between elites, who have fluency in European languages, and subordinate groups, who do not. Equally significant are the substantial changes brought about

in the sphere of family and personal law. The diversity in the type of families that characterized 'traditional' societies was replaced by the ideal of the European nuclear family. The collapse of joint and extended families, for example, has had deep psycho-social consequences that have not been overcome in the rapidly modernizing societies of the South (see Box 25.6).

According to those who have questioned this domination, '[w]hat passes today for the truth of the history of humankind (that is, progressive access of every nation to the benefits of development) is actually based upon the way in which Western society— to the exclusion of all others—has conceptualized its relationship to the past and the future' (Rist 1997, 44). Or, as more emphatically put by

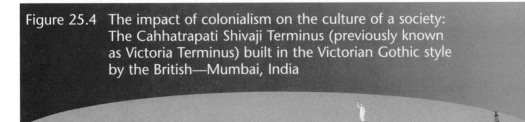

Figure 25.4 The impact of colonialism on the culture of a society: The Cahhatrapati Shivaji Terminus (previously known as Victoria Terminus) built in the Victorian Gothic style by the British—Mumbai, India

Source: Christophe Boisvieux/Corbis

BOX 25.8 CHE AS A CAPITALIST ICON

One of the best examples of the appropriation of popular culture by dominant culture is the symbolic figure of Che Guevara, one of the leading Marxist revolutionaries of the twentieth century. If he was the inspiration of many a communist insurrection in the 1960s and 1970s, he now mainly adorns billboards and designer wear created by the capitalist market. Here, the symbol of Che acquires a totally different meaning from the one he intended as a result of its appropriation by forces of capital (see Figure 25.5).

Figure 25.5   Che Guevara—The appropriation of a radical symbol by the capitalist mass culture

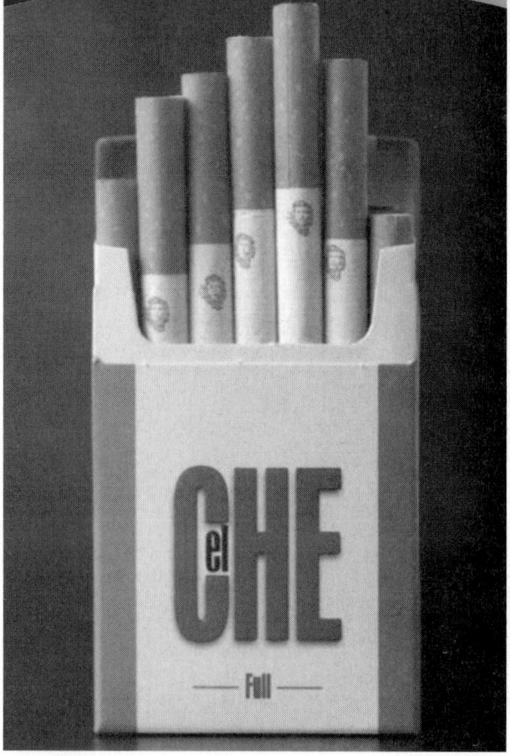

Source: AFP/Getty Images

Jonathan Crush: 'development discourse is rooted in the rise of the West, in the history of capitalism, in modernity and globalization of Western state institutions, disciplines, cultures and mechanisms of exploitation' (Crush 1995, 11).

Academic theories were also implicated in ethnocentrism. This was very obvious with theories such as modernization that posited one end-goal for the so-called Third World countries—that is, to become like the West (see chapter 3). Modernization theory operated with dichotomies such as tradition/modernity, backward/advanced, with a clear privileging of the second category. It was as if the entire history of Third World coun-tries did not matter and what mattered was the future alone, in which they would become like the West. Even dependency and other Marxist-inspired theories that arose as a critique of mod-ernization were deemed ethnocentric because they operated 'within the same discursive space of development' (Arturo Escobar, cited in Crush 1995, 20) by not questioning the basic assump-tions of development such as industrialization and growth. Moreover, they unwittingly repli-cated the structure of modernization through cat-egories such as developed/underdeveloped and centre/periphery. Again, what happened inside the periphery (the 'Third World' countries) was less important than what the core (the 'First World' countries) did to it. It was disenchantment with these theories that led to the emergence of the 'post' discourse (e.g., post-modern, post-colo-nial, post-development; see, for a representative sample, Rahnema and Bawtree 1997), which seeks to go beyond the assumptions of many of the interrelated projects that governed humankind in the recent past: modernity, colo-nialism, development, and so on. This discourse has sought to lay the blame for the current state of the world on modernity, or the period since the Enlightenment that has elevated reason to a priv-ileged position (see chapter 4).

In their search for an alternative, the critics of modernity looked towards traditional and indigenous cultural systems and a recovery of the practices associated with them, which had been dismissed as 'backward, irrational, superstitious, obscurantist' by the Western paradigm of devel-opment. If the West is characterized by *episteme*—the impersonal, a negative moral connotation attached to labour, control over nature, and a neg-ative view of illness—non-Western traditional societies are characterized by *techne*—the per-sonal, a divine conception of manual labour, con-trol over the self, and illness as a necessary imbalance (Marglin 1990, 8–25). Moreover, non-Western societies embraced the 'participation of the people in decisions that affected their lives; sharing and caring for the community beyond individual self-interest; trust, innocence, simplic-

Figure 25.6   A young sidewalk vendor in Bamako, Africa

Source: Stephanie Colvey/IDRC

ity, thrift; a work ethic with a fine-tuned balance between work and leisure; harmony with nature and a rational use of resources; communal ownership of the commons; and complementarity between men and women' (Wignaraja 1993, 20). These values would constitute the fulcrum of an alternative path.

The theories that have arisen under the 'post' rubric have taught us to look at non-Western societies without the coloured lens constructed elsewhere. Classic texts such as Edward Said's *Orientalism* deconstructed many commonplace assumptions about the Orient. Said's work showed that the Orient the Occident knew was more a construction than reality. It exposed the deep linkages between knowledge and power (in this case, colonial power). According to Said, 'the essence of Orientalism is the ineradicable distinc-

tion between Western superiority and Oriental inferiority' (Said 1978, 42). What the critique of modernity, colonialism, and development did was reclaim the history, the culture, and the agency of the colonized, thus giving them a sense of identity. More important, it put a question mark over the assumption that the Western way constituted the only path to civilization and development. The concept of development, which until recently connoted mere economic development, was redefined and expanded as a result.

Despite these achievements, the theories inspired by post-modernism are ridden with problems. Most have adopted an extreme stance vis-à-vis modernity and development, ultimately proving counterproductive for the marginalized and oppressed for whom the theories claim to speak. The fundamental problem is that culture becomes an all-encompassing explanatory variable. At the same time, culture appears to be detached from all other elements in society. Culture is seen as a homogeneous and essentialist whole, without fissures and conflicts. Hence, the large generalized categories such as the West/East, colonizer/colonized, tradition/modernity replicate the dichotomies that were created by mainstream theories such as modernization. Fear of the universalizing tendencies of modernity and the Western development model makes the post-modern-inspired theories essentialize tradition and adopt an uncritical attitude towards it. Consider, for example, Marglin's comment, 'it may be readily agreed that the sacrifice of a young woman on an altar in traditional society is barbarous, but in and of itself it is no more barbaric than the sacrifice of a young man on a battle field in modern society' (Marglin 1990, 12). This statement ignores (despite the presence of ideological inculcation in both) the fact that in the second case, physical coercion is absent (except in conscription).

Similar exercises of seeing culture in benign terms can lead to defending practices such as female circumcision rather than analyzing them in terms of power relations—in this case, patriarchy. Therefore, these theories ultimately end up as a nativist and 'Third Worldist' discourse, uncritically upholding tradition, religion, community, and so on while ignoring issues such as internal hierarchies and oppression within these categories. A critique of practices such as the sacrifice of women on their husbands' funeral pyre and female circumcision do not have to come from a perspective that glorifies Western standards of justice. Criticism and opposition are already present in these 'traditional' societies, as demonstrated by the fact that coercion, especially physical coercion, is often required to enforce norms.

Societies in the non-Western world are supposed to have a divine conception of manual labour. But then how did a caste system based on an occupational division of labour with a clear privileging of mental over manual labour emerge in India, for example? Why were the 'lower' castes performing the menial tasks subjected to deep

oppression for centuries? Similarly, the non-Western world is supposed to be characterized by a harmonious relationship with nature. But, as David Harvey points out regarding 'pre-modern' China, '[t]he Chinese may have ecologically sensitive traditions of Tao, Buddhism and Confucianism . . . but the historical geography of de-forestation, land degradation, river erosion and flooding . . . contains not a few environmental events which would be regarded as catastrophes by modern-day standards' (Harvey 1993, 29). These contradictions cannot be explained by the simple categorization of East/West and tradition/modernity. Ultimately, although post-modern theories start out 'with the intention of preaching tolerance and the recognition of difference, . . . [they come] dangerously close to a celebration of repression' (Kiely 1995, 159).

These theories cannot avoid the slide into **cultural relativism**, because they refuse to acknowledge any kind of universalism. Once they argue that cultural practices are not necessarily right or wrong because 'there is no way of assessing their truth or falsity apart from people's beliefs' (Marglin 1990, 13), their justification of repressive practices becomes inevitable. Despite the fact that colonialism and the Western development model have used universalism instrumentally to their own benefit and subverted some of its core principles, there are problems in abandoning the concept itself. Post-modern accounts have one-sidedly reduced modernity and the Enlightenment to being indissolubly associated with domination, alienation, deprivation, and so on. This ignores the fact that the Enlightenment was also founded on values such as liberty, equality, and fraternity, which have inspired countless struggles against oppression all over the world, not just in Europe. More important, these values are attractive because of their deep affinity to at least some of the values in non-Western societies (see Box 25.9). As we saw above, criticism of oppression or the struggle for equality cannot be said to be merely European or modern; intimations of Enlightenment can be found in different parts of the world and in previous periods of history. They are embedded in various ritual prac-

BOX 25.9   UNIVERSAL VALUES

The traditional and modern ways of living do not have to be absolutely disparate as post-modern criticisms imply. For example, among the Boran tribes people, traditionally pastoral nomads living mainly in Ethiopia, the concept that comes closest to development is *fidnaa*. It basically denotes a variety of things ranging from growth and reproduction of vital resources, 'lack of fear and hunger, freedom from worries about one's nearest and dearest . . . [an] egalitarian and expanding social order that extends to neighbouring peoples' (Dahl and Megerssa 1997, 55). The commonalities between this concept and the modern development enterprise are striking.

tices, such as the 'carnival in Catholic countries, the Feast of Krishna in India, the Saturnalia in classical Rome, the war festival in Buddhist Southeast Asia . . . [and] have provided the ideological basis of many revolts' (Scott 1990, 80).

The abuse of Enlightenment values does not mean that we should therefore dismantle the entire European critical tradition. An abandonment of universalism would make any talk of social justice impossible, and any oppression, including slavery, could be justified on cultural grounds. As Martha Nussbaum argues, 'to give up on all evaluation and, in particular, on a normative account of the human being and human functioning [is] to turn things over to the free play of forces in a world situation in which the social forces affecting the lives of women, minorities, and the poor are rarely benign' (Nussbaum 1992, 212). To overcome cultural relativism, Charles Taylor proposes that we talk in a 'language of perspicuous contrast' that would allow us to 'formulate both their way of life and ours as alternative possibilities in relation to some human constants at work in both' (Taylor 1985, 125). Such constants obviously rise above the particularities of different cultures and constitute the basis of a universalist understanding. This is a dialogic process in which the West has as much to learn from the non-West as the latter from the former (see Box 25.10). Only such an understanding will act as a

check on the use of culture by the ruling classes to justify authoritarianism (see Box 25.11).

Thus, we come back to the problem that we started out with: culture is as marked by relations of power as any other sphere in society and is continuously changing according to the nature of contestation and struggle. The other major flaw in the post-modern theoretical framework is the near total absence in it of an analysis of material relationships. This is very obvious in the post-colonial analysis of colonialism in which colonial exploitation without material relations becomes mere Western cultural domination. Economic exploitation itself takes a back seat. Therefore, European domination appears unrelated to capitalism. As Dirlik argues, 'Without capitalism as the foundation for European power and the motive force of its globalization, Eurocentrism would have been just another ethnocentrism . . . [post-colonialism] fails to explain why this particular ethnocentrism was able to define modern global history, and itself as the universal aspiration and the end of that history, in contrast to the regionalism or localism of other ethnocentrisms' (Dirlik 1997, 68).

In post-colonial theory, there is an obsessive focus on the colonial past and **Eurocentrism** that takes away an engagement with the present. Thus, the current internationalization and globalization, of a scale unimaginable before, initiated by late capitalism, and the exploitation inherent in these

BOX 25.10   CULTURE SHOCK

Culture shock is a common phenomenon experienced by students of international development and others when they travel to a foreign culture, especially for long periods of time. It is, according to the anthropologist Kalervo Oberg, who coined the term, 'precipitated by the anxiety that results from losing all our familiar signs and symbols of social intercourse' (quoted in Irwin 2007). When human beings are not able to communicate and understand, the bases of existence and identity are threatened. Some of the common themes that run through the experiences of culture shock faced by people from the West travelling to 'developing countries' include: excruciating poverty and the resulting low quality of life, poor levels of cleanliness, paternalistic attitudes towards women, high levels of violence, and anxiety over health. At the same time, pleasant experiences are also common, such as what many describe as the extraordinary hospitality shown by people despite extremely trying conditions. The only way to cope with culture shock, especially for students of development, is to overcome their lack of familiarity by developing a genuine understanding (through a certain amount of socio-historical study) of the foreign culture rather than relying on stereotypical notions. Much of the misconception about issues like poverty, hygiene, and even violence stems from seeing them as merely cultural issues and not understanding their material dimensions. Another way of eliminating some of the strangeness of the unfamiliar is to turn a critical lens on the 'developed societies' and to realize that many of these 'shocking' practices were not completely alien during the history of these societies themselves. This perspective can help to solve some of the problems that some face in adjusting to the comfort of their own societies when they return. Ultimately, culture shock can become a positive and intensive learning experience, because it highlights contrasts that force one to take a critical perspective on both one's own and the alien culture. Sometimes, just a small dose of the unfamiliar can shake the complacency and arrogance of the familiar and lead to social transformation.

processes cannot be countered by culturalism, especially when capitalism is increasingly becoming Asian-dominated. When almost the entire globe has come under the sway of capital and commodification, it is not feasible to simply *reject* modernity or development. This is all the more true when the poor and marginalized, who constitute the vast majority of the world's population, also embrace values such as equality and democracy and seek goods such as health, education, shelter, and security that modernity has to offer yet so far have been available to only a minority. Without an internally differentiated view that takes into account the different classes, castes, and groups within broad categories such as the East, the South, or traditional societies and their different (as well as common) experiences under modernity and capitalism, any alternative proposal based on culture alone that aims to go beyond development can only be incoherent. More important, it can only help the ruling classes and elites in these deeply non-egalitarian societies to maintain their power, using the legitimacy of cultural difference. Rather than indulge in a romantic celebration of Eastern cultures, an alternative development project should not only include cultural decolonization but also a material transformation that would eliminate all kinds of

BOX 25.11 'ASIAN VALUES'

The resort to culture for legitimacy (of rule) by the elites is seen in the propagation of the 'Asian values' thesis by the first prime minister of Singapore, Lee Kuan Yew, who argued that Asian culture is more conducive to discipline and order rather than to freedom and liberty (which suited the West). Such vast generalizations justifying authoritarianism are grievously erroneous, for they completely ignore the enormous diversity that exists within these large blocks called Asia and the West. Once we examine this diversity, we might find a different reality from the one outlined by Lee Kuan Yew. It would be even more obvious if we looked into the accounts of the marginalized and the oppressed, who would have a totally different understanding of discipline and order from that of the ruling classes.

The 'Asian values' thesis has also been used as a cultural explanation for the economic success of Japan, China, and Southeast Asian countries. But again, the problem is that the thesis is too broad, ultimately inadequate for explaining the specificities of the different countries. For example, how do the different traditions of Confucianism, Buddhism, and Shintoism prevalent in the region explain the same phenomenon of capitalist success? Moreover, the application of the thesis is further complicated by the success of Islamic Indonesia and Malaysia and the emerging economic power of Hindu-dominated India. Thus, the thesis boils down to a cultural 'grand theory' that seeks to explain major economic, political, and social outcomes across the world in terms of cultural differences—the kind of theory that, as in this case, does so rather unsuccessfully (Sen 2001, 11–13).

exploitation, including economic exploitation, perpetrated not only by the West but also by indigenous classes and groups within the 'Third World'. To this end, the critical resources of the West and the East, as well as modernity and tradition, would have to be mobilized (see Box 25.12).

BOX 25.12 BEYOND THE TRADITION–MODERNITY DIVIDE

A few cases have given great hope to development practitioners seeking to bridge the divide between the modern and the traditional and to end development as oppression. One such case is that of the Irulas, an indigenous people in India who mainly live by catching rats. Over the past few years, they have only just managed to survive, and some have starved to death. A development organization developed a new rat trap technology that has improved rat-catching success rates from 40 per cent to 95 per cent. The Irulas have doubled or tripled their incomes, which has led to better health care and education for them (*The Hindu* 2007). This is a classic demonstration of how modern technology can help development of an indigenous people without necessarily robbing them of their cultural practices.

CONCLUSION

We have tried to make sense of a very difficult concept as well as its relationship with development. As we have seen, culture has acquired a lot of importance in recent years—and justifiably so. What has to be guarded against is reducing societal processes to one single explanatory variable. In reality, they cannot as easily be broken down into various elements, such as culture, politics, and economics, as they are in an academic analysis. All elements are interlinked and cannot be abstracted and studied in isolation. Therefore, development does not make sense at all without an understanding of the meanings and the cultural value attributed to it by the people who are subjected to it. At the same time, these meanings cannot be entirely disparate because of certain universal features of the human condition—and also because the same material processes of commodification and marketization are taking place across the world. The task for the development studies student is to negotiate the lines between acknowledging the importance of agency, the process of creating meanings, and understanding the structural limitations imposed by material factors on the imagination of the symbolic.

QUESTIONS FOR DISCUSSION

1. How can culture be defined?
2. Why has culture acquired prominence in recent years?
3. What is the relationship between the cultural and the material?
4. Can any distinction be drawn between mass culture and popular culture?
5. What are the pitfalls of cultural relativism?

FURTHER READING

Dahl, G., and A. Rabo, eds. 1992. *Kap-Am or Take-Off: Local Notions of Development*. Stockholm: Stockholm Studies in Social Anthropology.

Fabian, J. 1983. *Time and the Other: How Anthropology Makes Its Object*. New York: Columbia University Press.

Ferguson, J. 1990. *The Anti-politics Machine: 'Development', Depoliticization and Bureaucratic Power in Lesotho*. Cambridge: Cambridge University Press.

Ong, A. 1987. *Spirits of Resistance and Capitalist Discipline: Factory Women in Malaysia*. Albany: SUNY Press.

Pigg, S.L. 1992. 'Constructing social categories through place: Social representations and development in Nepal'. *Comparative Studies in Society and History* 34 (3): 491–513.

INTERNET RESOURCES

American Anthropological Association: http://www.aaanet.org/index.htm.
Centre for Study of Culture and Society: http://cscsban.org/index.html.
Testimonio: http://digitalunion.osu.edu/r2/summer06/herbert/index.html.
UNESCO: http://portal.unesco.org/.

CHINA, GLOBALIZATION, AND DEVELOPMENT

SAMIR AMIN

LEARNING OBJECTIVES

- To understand the importance of the Chinese Revolution for its subsequent economic development.
- To understand the importance of the agrarian question in the current and future development of China.
- To consider whether China is following a 'market socialist' or capitalist development trajectory.

INTRODUCTION

According to the dominant discourse of our times, Asia is in the process of overcoming the legacy of underdevelopment. In this view, the region is 'catching up' within the capitalist system rather than breaking away from it. This suggests that capitalism might be shedding its imperialist nature, at least as far as East and South Asia are concerned. Countries such as China and India are seen to be in the process of becoming great powers, including in the nuclear arena.

The eventual result of this process of evolution would be a multi-polar world, organized around at least four poles: the United States, Europe, Japan, and China (and perhaps even six poles, if we include Russia and India). Together, these poles and the countries and regions directly associated with them (Canada and Mexico, eastern Europe, Southeast Asia, and Korea) contain the vast majority of the Earth's population. This multi-polar system would thus be different from the successive versions of imperialism, from multi-polar (up to 1945) to unipolar (with the emergence of the collective imperialism of the **triad** among the United States, the European Union, and Japan), which included only a minority of the world's people.

But the analysis on which this reasoning rests appears shallow to me. First of all, this vision does not take into account the policies that Washington deploys to undermine the diverse projects that might eventually threaten its hegemony, such as the ambitions of the principal actors concerned, including China. In the meantime, the triad remains dominant. Despite some differences with Washington, Europe has not yet begun to contemplate the possibility of breaking the Atlantic ties that leave it in the shadow of the United States. For both similar and distinct reasons, Japan remains deferential with regard to its trans-Pacific protector. As a result, the days of the triad's collective imperialism are still far from over.

Second, it is problematic to predict the emergence of new economic powers simply on the basis of economic growth rates. It would present a deceptive picture, and in addition, the validity of such projections beyond a few years into the future is doubtful. In reality, the pursuit of growth in Asia depends on numerous internal and external factors that are articulated in various ways according to, on the one hand, the strategic models of social modernization chosen by the dominant local classes and, on the other hand, reactions from outside (that is, by the imperialist powers who constitute the triad). In addition to its possible consequences for the planet's ecological equilibrium, this pursuit of growth also has the clear potential to trigger conflict with the countries of the triad, who have until now been the exclusive beneficiaries of the world's resources.

CONTRASTING LEGACIES OF THE CHINESE REVOLUTION

The dominant discourse attributes China's post-Maoist success entirely to the virtues of the market and its opening to the outside world. This discourse is an extremely simplistic analysis of the realities of Maoist China, and it also ignores the problems surrounding the capitalist option.

Exceptional trajectory

During the three decades of **Maoism** (1950 to 1980), China registered an exceptional level of growth, double the rate of India's and that of all the other large regions of the Third World. Nonetheless, its performance during the final two decades of the century was even more extraordinary. What has to be remembered, however, is that these unparalleled recent results would not have been possible without the economic, political, and social foundations that were laid during the preceding period—although this should not be taken to imply that there were not also changes. Thus, during the Maoist period, priority was given to laying down a solid basis for the long term. Today, the new economic policy places the emphasis on immediate improvements in consumption, which were made possible by the earlier efforts. It is not absurd to argue that the Maoist decades were characterized by a tendency to favour the building of long-term foundations. But inversely, the emphasis placed on light industry and services from 1980 onward cannot last forever, since China is still in a phase that requires the expansion of its basic industries.

'Workshop of the world' or 'market socialism'

While economic power formerly rested on the monopoly of industrial strength by the world's great powers, today the imperialism of the triad is based on new monopolies, notably the control of technology, the flows of finance, access to the planet's natural resources, information and communication, and weapons of mass destruction (on the five monopolies of new imperialism and the polarization of its construction, see Amin 1997, 3–5). However, these new privileges of the imperialist centres act to deepen global polarization rather than to counteract or attenuate it. In this sense, the term 'emerging country', which appears to suggest that the triad is 'threatened' by countries such as China, India, Brazil, and the others, is deceptive. These are in fact countries that, far from 'catching up', are building tomorrow's **peripheral capitalism**. China is no exception. China is already the workshop of the world, a subcontracting workshop for the benefit of capital and consumers in the countries of the triad. In contrast with this model, the path toward a socialist alternative will be longer and very different from the paths imagined by the Second and Third Socialist International. Following this perspective, **market socialism** could constitute a first phase. But in order for that to happen, several conditions must be met.

China and Russia: Two different itineraries

The Marxism of the socialist movements of the early twentieth century was essentially worker-oriented and Eurocentric. This Marxism shared the dominant ideology's linear vision of history, according to which all societies had to pass first through a phase of capitalist development (for which colonization—in this respect 'historically positive'—laid the ground) before being capable of aspiring to 'socialism'. The idea that the 'development' of some (the dominant centres) and the underdevelopment of others (the dominated peripheries) were indissolubly linked, both imminent products of the global expansion of capitalism, was entirely foreign to this vision.

Initially, some socialists, including Lenin, kept their distance from this dominant theory. Lenin notably led a successful revolution in the

Figure Ep.1   Making rattan furniture in Haimen, China, 1986

Source: Denis Sing, IDRC

'weak link' country (Russia) but always with the conviction that this would be followed by a wave of socialist revolutions in Europe. As we know, this dream was never fulfilled. Lenin thus propounded a vision that placed more emphasis on the transformation of the eastern rebellions into revolutions. But it was left to the Communist Party of China and to Mao to turn this new vision into concrete reality.

The Russian Revolution was led by a party that was deeply rooted within the working class and the radical intelligentsia. Its alliance with the peasantry followed naturally. The resulting radical agrarian reform finally fulfilled the long-standing dream of Russian peasants: to become landowners. But this historical compromise contained the seeds of its own limitations: the 'market' itself inevitably increased economic and social differentiation within the peasantry (the well-known phenomenon of 'kulackization').[1]

The Chinese Revolution that followed later, however, was rooted in different social bases right from the start, which guaranteed a strong alliance between the poor and middle peasantry. In addition, the war of resistance against Japanese aggression allowed the formation of a united front led by the communists, recruited largely from the dominant classes who were disappointed by the betrayals of the Kuo Min Tang (KMT).[2] The Chinese Revolution thus produced a novel outcome, different from that of post-revolutionary Russia. A radical peasant revolution rejected the very idea of private property in land and replaced it with the guarantee of equal access to land for all peasants. To the present day, this decisive advantage, which is shared by only one other country (Vietnam), constitutes the major obstacle to a devastating expansion of agrarian capitalism. It should be noted that current debates in China are largely over this question.

The success of Maoism

Moreover, Maoist China achieved these results by avoiding the worst excesses of the Soviet Union. **Collectivization** was not imposed through murderous violence, as occurred under Stalinism. Conflicts within the party did not lead to a reign of terror (Deng Xiaoping was pushed aside but then later returned). The goal of an unprecedented relative equality, in the distribution of incomes between peasants and workers as well as within these classes and between them and the leadership, was pursued—with highs and lows, of course—with tenacity and formalized by strategic development choices that contrasted with those taken by the Soviet Union (these options were formulated in China in the '10 great reports' at the beginning of the 1960s). These achievements laid the ground for the subsequent development successes of post-Maoist China from 1980. This explains why post-Maoist China, while inscribing its development within the framework of the new capitalist globalization, did not experience the same destructive shocks that followed the breakup of the Soviet Union.

Mao's failure

The successes of Maoism nonetheless did not irreversibly resolve the question of the long-term success of socialism. First, the development strategy of the 1950–80 period, based on heavy industry and the construction of a vast infrastructure, exhausted its potential, in part because it came to fruition and in part because it could not maintain growth without expanding the internal market at the same time as opening, even in a limited way, to external markets. It then became clear that some kind of opening (albeit controlled) was necessary. The Chinese Maoist system simultaneously combined the contradictory tendencies of a reinforcement of socialist options and their weakening. Mao, conscious of this contradiction, tried to shift the tide in favour of socialism through the **Cultural Revolution** (from 1966 to 1974). This

was the reasoning behind his call to set 'fire to the headquarters' (the central committee of the Chinese Communist Party), which to his eyes was the source of the bourgeois aspirations of the ruling political classes. Mao thought that he could rely on the 'youth' to lead this correction in the course of the revolution. The unfolding of events, however, showed that this judgment was mistaken. Once the page was turned on the Cultural Revolution, supporters of the capitalist route were emboldened to go on the offensive.

What legacy?

Maoism contributed decisively to setting the precise parameters of the pitfalls and challenges posed by the expansion of globalized imperialism/capitalism. Maoism made it possible to put the centre/periphery contrast inherent in the expansion of 'truly existing',[3] imperialist, and polarizing contemporary capitalism at the centre of its analysis of this challenge and to draw out all of the lessons it offered for the socialist struggle in both the dominant centres and the dominated peripheries. These conclusions were summarized in a tidy formula 'Chinese style': 'States want independence, nations want liberation, people want revolution.' States (that is, the ruling classes) attempt to increase their room for manoeuvre within the global system and to go beyond the status of 'passive' actors (condemned to suffer a unilateral adaptation to the demands of the dominant imperialist power) to become 'active' actors (who participate in shaping the global order). Nations (historic blocs of classes) want liberation—that is, 'development' and 'modernization'. People (the dominated and exploited masses) aspire to socialism. The formula allows us to understand the real world in all its complexity and hence to formulate effective strategies. Given this formulation, the transition from capitalism to global socialism will be a very long-term process, and thus we break with the idea of a 'short transition' that dominated socialism for most of the twentieth century.

Figure Ep.2   Men and women participating in an exercise drill

Source: IDRC/CRDI

THE CHALLENGES OF CONTEMPORARY CHINA

The Chinese ruling class has chosen the capitalist route, if not since the beginning of Deng Xiaoping's rule, then at least after it. But it will not explicitly recognize this fact because its legitimacy rests entirely on the revolution, which it cannot repudiate without committing political suicide. We must nonetheless judge political forces by what they do and not by what they say.

The capitalist project

The true project of the Chinese ruling class is of a capitalist nature, and 'market socialism' is a shortcut that allows them to gradually put in place the fundamental structures and institutions of capitalism, while keeping the frictions and pains of the transition to a minimum. This method is

diametrically opposed to the one that has been adopted by the new ruling class in Russia, who accepted the simultaneous negation of the revolution and the evolution that followed it, which allowed it to reconstruct itself as the new bourgeois class. In contrast, the Chinese ruling class knows that the path it is following leads to capitalism, and it is content with this, even if a fraction (no doubt a minority) remain imprisoned in the rhetoric of 'Chinese socialism'. The ruling class also knows that the people are attached to 'socialist values' (equality above all) and to the real progress associated with these values (the right to equal access to land for all peasants above all). It knows that it must move towards capitalism slowly, with great caution and deliberateness.

The structure of the worldwide capitalist project and the degree of stability it enjoys are the products of 'historical compromises', social alliances defining the hegemonic blocs that succeed each other during the process of establishing the system. The specificity of each of the different historical paths (the English, the French, the German, the American) defined by these successions has produced, in turn, the specific characteristics of the contemporary form of capitalism in each of these societies. It is because each of these distinct approaches was carried out successfully in the countries at the centre of the world system that capitalism became 'stabilized' (which is not synonymous with 'eternal'!).

New alliances

What are the possibilities open to the capitalist option in China today? Alliances are already in place among state powers, the new class of large 'private capitalists', peasants in the areas that have profited from the openings offered by urban markets, and the rapidly expanding middle classes. Nonetheless, this hegemonic bloc excludes the great majority of workers and peasants. Thus, the Chinese structure is not perfectly analogous to the historical alliances built by certain European bourgeoisies with the peasantry (against the working class) and the subsequent social democratic approach, the historic compromise between capital and labour. The model of capitalist development underway in China is based on prioritizing exports to satisfy the growing consumption demands of the middle classes. This is the model that I characterized as being the perfect example of peripheral accumulation. The pursuit of this model implies what we have already seen: a barbaric exploitation of workers that is reminiscent of the nineteenth century (not to mention the associated ecological disaster). In contrast, a more balanced model of development must be based on prioritizing the growth of internal markets to benefit the majority of the population, reinforced by the development of capital goods production. Current political and social conflicts in China, which are taking place within the party as well as between the party and the various lower-class social groups, are in large part a reflection of these two fundamental positions. On one side, the par-

tisans of peripheral capitalism need to exploit the masses as much as possible, because the model of accumulation they propose is outward-oriented. And on the other side, the proponents of the model based on the growth of an internal market have to establish a relationship with the popular classes so that they can gain access to capitalist production, as occurred with the 'great Keynesian compromise' that took place in Western countries after 1945.

This weakness within the hegemonic pro-capitalist bloc in China is the origin of the difficult problem of the political management of the system. I leave the task of arguing that markets equal democracy to the propagandists. Capitalism functions, under certain conditions, in parallel with the political practice of limited democracy in that the former manages to control democratic usage and thus prevent the anti-capitalist 'drift' that authentic democracy inevitably entails. When this is not possible, capitalism simply avoids democracy and does not fare any less well.

The democracy question

The issue of democracy in China is more complex as a result of the legacy of the Third International and its particular beliefs concerning the 'dictatorship of the proletariat'. The party line put in place during the Maoist period, breaking with the Soviet tradition, was a genuine step towards participatory democracy, though insufficient. Today, this approach has been abandoned, and it is clear that maintenance of the current political structures is not compatible with the capitalist route that is becoming harder to deny. How will the party-state retain its name (the Communist Party!) and its reference, though purely rhetorical, to Marx and Mao? If they were abandoned in favour of the model of 'Western democracy' (essentially the multi-party electoral system), could that model function within the country's specific circumstances? I doubt it, not for supposedly historical cultural reasons (along the lines that 'democracy is a foreign concept to Chinese culture') but because the social struggles in which the majority of the lower classes are likely to become engaged would render it impracticable. China has to invent another form of democracy, associated with market socialism, understood as a phase in a long socialist transition. Otherwise, I can only foresee a succession of autocrats lacking legitimacy, with intervals of unstable, 'superficial democracy', which is the current fate of the capitalist Third World.

What is socialism?

Socialism is defined as the emancipation of humanity. 'True' socialism, if we can speak of any social system in such qualified terms, cannot be described a priori in terms of precise organizational structures or institutions but according to democratic principles that shape the creative imagination and the full exercise of the powers of the people, as yet unrealized. Here, the creative utopia inspired by Marx provides much more substance for reflection than a mediocre, so-called realist sociology. The path towards socialism will be long, much longer than (and taking a different form from) that imagined by earlier movements. And from this perspective, 'market socialism' could constitute a first phase. But for this to work, some conditions must be fulfilled, to which I now turn.

Forms of collective property must be created, maintained, and reinforced throughout the process of social advancement. These forms can, and in fact must, be multiple: through the state, regional groups, workers' and citizens' collectives. But for them to successfully meet the needs of market exchange, they will have to be designed and understood as authentic forms of ownership (though not private) and not as an expression of ill-defined powers. I do not accept in this regard the fashionable simplification—invented by von Mises and von Hayek—that confuses property with private property. This reductionism/simplification arises from the false elision of Soviet-style centralized planning with socialism. At the same time, the dominance of collective property does not preclude the recognition of a role for private property. I refer not only to local, 'small' property

(artisans, small and medium-sized businesses, small trades and services) but even to 'big business' or arrangements with transnational capital, as long as the framework within which they are allowed to relocate and shift is clearly defined. Owners' (state, collective, and private) use of their rights must be regulated. Such regulation will have to balance the tension between the requirements of capitalist accumulation (despite the collective nature of property) and those of the progressive imposition of the values of socialism (equality first, inclusion of all social groups in the process of change, public service in the most noble sense of the term). Democracy is thus not a single formula that is set once and for all and that need only be 'applied' but a process that is never complete, leading me to prefer the term 'democratization'. Democratization must therefore combine, in its increasingly rich and complex formulations, precise 'procedural' definitions (the rule of law, in common parlance) as well as 'substantive' elements that reinforce the values of socialism within decision-making processes at all levels and in all areas.

The centrality of the agrarian question

Present-day China is already outside of the 'market socialist' model proposed in this chapter. The country advanced along a capitalist path when it accepted, effectively, the dominance of a private property system over public and collective ownership. Many critiques of the current system based on solid factual evidence, Chinese in particular, affirm that it is 'already too late'. This is not exactly my point of view. As long as the principle of equal access to land remains recognized and effectively implemented, I believe it is possible to conclude that it is not yet too late for social action to modify the evolution of the Chinese model.

The population of China grew in the year 2000 to 1.2 billion inhabitants, of which two-thirds live in rural areas (800 million). A simple projection 20 years into the future demonstrates that it would be illusory, if not dangerous, to believe that urbanization could significantly reduce the number of rural inhabitants, even if the proportion could be reduced. Annual demographic growth of 1.2 per cent would increase the population of China to 1.52 billion by 2020. We can assume that China could achieve an annual growth rate of 5 per cent in industry and modern services located in urban zones. Realizing this growth rate in a context of modernization and competition would require the intensification of accumulation based on an increase in the productivity of labour (of around 2 per cent annually), rather than an expansion of existing industries and services. The growth in urban employment would therefore be in the order of 3 per cent per year, making it possible to absorb a total of 720 million people in urban areas. This figure assumes no change in the number of people who are currently unemployed or working in precarious or informal employment (and this number is not negligible). Nonetheless, the proportion of people in this situation would be significantly reduced (and this would certainly be a good outcome). Basic mathematics reveals that some 800 million Chinese—the same number as today, but reduced from 67 per cent to 53 per cent as a proportion of total population—would have to remain rural. If they were condemned to migrate to the cities because of a lack of access to land, they would swell the marginalized population of urban slums, as has frequently been the case elsewhere in the capitalist Third World. A projection 40 years into the future simply reinforces this conclusion (see, for example, Tiejun 2001, 287–95). This problem is far from being confined to China. It concerns the whole of the Third World—that is, 75 per cent of the world's population.

The argument of those who would defend capitalism is that the agrarian question in Europe was solved by a rural exodus. Why would the countries of the South not reproduce, one or two centuries later, a similar model of transformation? It is easy to forget that the urban industries and services of the nineteenth century required abundant manual labour and that surplus population could emigrate en masse to the Americas. The

contemporary Third World does not have this option, and if it wants to be competitive, as we ordered it to be, it must immediately adopt modern technologies that require little labour. The polarization produced by the global expansion of capital prevents the South from reproducing, in a delayed fashion, the model of the North.

Is peasant agriculture an option?

What is to be done? We must accept the preservation of peasant agriculture for all the foreseeable future of the twenty-first century—not for reasons of romantic nostalgia for the past but simply because the solution to the agrarian problem can only come from going beyond the logic of capitalism and positioning it within the long secular tradition of global socialism. The agrarian question, far from having been solved, is more than ever at the centre of the major challenges of the future to be faced by humanity.

And yet in this area, China has a major asset at its disposal—the legacy of its revolution—which could allow it to construct one of the possible 'models' of what to do. Access to land is, in effect, a fundamental right for half of humanity, the recognition of which is necessary for survival. This right, ignored by capitalism and not even mentioned in the United Nations Declaration of Universal Human Rights, is recognized to this day in China (and in Vietnam). It would be a supreme illusion to think that by renouncing these rights (that is, by giving land the status of a saleable good, as has been suggested by capitalism's apologists in China and elsewhere), it would be possible to 'accelerate modernization'.

The modernization of agriculture was indeed one of the four modernizations decreed by the Communist Party during the turning point of the 1970s. This most definitely does not mean that encouraging the needed growth of agricultural production requires the abandonment of the right to land for all in favour of profit for the few. Taking this path would certainly yield decent growth in production for a few but at the cost of stagnation for many. Growth would likely be meagre over the

Figure Ep.3   Workers collecting rice for transportation

Source: Denis Sing, IDRC

long haul, both for the majority of the peasants remaining on the land and for those who migrated to the urban slums. This reality is of little concern to the unconditional champions of capitalism. The accumulation and enrichment of the few is the only law they know. The exclusion of the 'inefficient', be it billions of human beings, is not their problem.

The history of China over the course of the past half century has revealed another path that has sought to engage the whole of the peasantry in the process of modernization (respecting the right to land for all) and that has yielded results that compare favourably with the capitalist path to development. The error of both the Soviet and the Chinese 'commune' model (like the central

planning model) was precisely its claim to have established such formulas as definitive solutions. I share the ideas, for example, of numerous peasant organizations in China who promote and support a diverse movement of cooperatives managed by local communities themselves and not controlled from above by the state.

The national question

The national question also plays a central role in debates and political struggles in China between partisans of different political stripes. China was the victim of uninterrupted imperialist aggression by Western powers and Japan between 1840 and 1949. The invaders operated by means of alliances with the dominant and reactionary local classes, often described as 'feudal' or 'compradore' (a term coined by the Chinese communists). Subsequently, a war of national liberation led by the Communist Party restored China's dignity and reconstructed its territorial unity (with the exception of Taiwan, the status of which remains unresolved). All of China is aware of this history. Despite the regionalisms that the size of the country inevitably generates, the Chinese (Han) nation is a reality. Certain elements of the national question are managed in a questionable manner, notably the situations in Tibet and East Turkistan. Multiple conflicts have developed around these situations. Furthermore, the conflicts have been exacerbated by various attempts by the dominant countries to 'pour oil on the fire' in the hope of exploiting these weaknesses of the Chinese regime.

The Chinese are well aware of the place that their nation holds in history. This is why the Chinese intelligentsia has always looked towards those outside 'models' that, in their opinion, showed what had to be done for China to take its place in the modern world. The first models appeared at the time of the great social movements of May 1919, first in Japan (inspiration for the Kuo Min Tang), then in revolutionary Russia (which finally triumphed because it brought together the struggle against imperialism and a revolutionary social transformation that inspired the people).

Today, with Japan in crisis, Russia dissolved, and Europe itself seeking to imitate the United States, China runs the risk of interpreting its quest for modernity and progress as a failure if it does not adopt the 'American model'—the model of its adversary—just as it had followed the example set by Japan in the past. China, that great nation, always compares itself with the most powerful.

What 'miracle'?

The legacy of the Chinese Revolution is weighty and continues to weigh in the future of China and the world itself. The successes achieved over the past 20 years would not have been possible without the revolution. Only propagandists for American imperialism and their emulators elsewhere in the world, including China, seem not to know this fact.

An oft-repeated saying is that 'China is a poor country where one sees little poverty.' China feeds 22 per cent of the world's population even though it only has 6 per cent of the planet's arable land. That is the real miracle. It is not correct to suggest that the source of this miracle can be found in the antiquity of Chinese civilization. Although it is true that on the eve of the Industrial Revolution, China was more technologically advanced than all the other large regions of the world, its situation had deteriorated over the preceding century and a half, resulting in large-scale misery comparable to that found in countries ravaged by imperialism, such as India. China owes its remarkable turnaround to its revolution. At the other extreme of the range of conditions created by the expansion of global capitalism, I would place Brazil, often described as 'a rich country where one only sees poverty'.

The China of 'modernity'

The Chinese Revolution brought Chinese society into modernity. Modernity expresses itself in all aspects of the behaviour of its citizens, who consider themselves responsible for their own history. This modernity is an explanation for why China does not exhibit the para-cultural neuroses that hold sway in other environments, including the Muslim countries, India, and sub-Saharan Africa. China lives its moment in history. It does not feed on the nostalgia for a reconstructed mythological past that seems to define the spirit of our times. China does not have an 'identity' problem. If modernity does not produce ipso facto democracy, it at least creates the necessary conditions that would otherwise be unthinkable. Relatively few societies in the periphery of the capitalist system have made this jump into modernity (Korea and Taiwan are also exceptions). On the contrary, the current historical moment is, as a whole, characterized by appalling back-pedalling in this regard—another expression of the bankruptcy of capitalism. Indeed, Gramsci wrote, 'the old is dying and the new cannot be born; in this interregnum a great variety of morbid symptoms appears' (Gramsci 1971, 275–6).

In this respect, the dominant discourse regarding the cultural traits that are supposedly favourable or unfavourable to democracy only feeds the confusion. This discourse attributes an invariable and trans-historical character to those 'cultures' and does not recognize that modernity is a rupture with all other pasts. The modernity that has engulfed China is a major advantage for its future development. The revolution and its dive into modernity have transformed the Chinese people more than any other in the contemporary Third World. China's popular classes are self-confident. They know how to struggle, and they know that doing so pays off. Submissive attitudes have largely been banished, and the idea that citizens have equal rights and are not subject to the arbitrary rule of the dominant is well anchored in society. The people show a remarkable fighting spirit in social struggles, which number in the thousands, occasionally take the form of violence, and do not always end in failure. Those in power know it, sometimes applying repression in order to avoid the crystallization of battlefronts beyond local horizons (by forbidding the independent organization of the popular classes) and further limiting the danger by the art of 'dialogue' and manipulation. These struggles rarely catch the attention of Western defenders of 'human rights'. Democracy in the service of class struggle does not interest them; indeed, many find it worrying. On the contrary, their desire for democracy, systematically defended and harped upon by all, comes from the 'liberals' who once in power will weaken in comparison to their defence of the virtues of capitalism!

Shifting futures

The future of China remains unclear (see Amin 1983). The struggle for socialism has not been won. But it has not (yet) been lost either. And in my opinion, it will not be lost until the day when the Chinese system renounces the right to land for all its peasants. Until that point, political and social struggle can change the country's evolution. The leadership class has tried to control these popular struggles by means of its bureaucratic dictatorship. Some fragments of this same class think that the same methods will prevent the emergence of a bourgeoisie. The bourgeoisie and the middle classes as a whole have not decided to fight for democracy and have accepted without difficulty the 'Asian style' autocratic model as long as they are able to satisfy their consumer appetites. At the same time, the popular classes struggle to defend their economic and social rights. Will they be able to unify their struggle, invent new forms of organization, formulate an alternative and positive program, and define the content and practices of a democracy that would benefit them?

In this contradictory context, three futures under construction can be envisaged. These three scenarios correspond to:

- the imperialist project of breaking up the country and the compradorization of its coastal regions;
- a 'national' project of capitalist development;
- a national and popular development project that brings together, in a complementary and conflictual way, the logic of market capitalism and the logic of a long-term commitment to socialism.

The option of market deregulation and maximum economic opening is preferred by both Chinese and foreign liberals and plays into the imperialist strategy. Their argument stresses depoliticization and knee-jerk opposition to the popular classes at the same time that it would deepen the external vulnerability of the Chinese nation and state. This is not a path to democracy. Furthermore, this option would not lift China out of its dominated and peripheral status and would leave it subordinated to the logic of the expanding imperialism of the triad (see Amin 1974, 9–26).

The difference between the second and third models is difficult to identify at first glance, but it can be summarized in the fact that the third implies an assertive foreign policy and the maintenance of modes of redistribution that ensure an acceptable level of social and regional solidarity. But in fact, the difference is one of the nature and not the degree of state intervention. The real core of the debate is found here. The progressive (third) option can only be based on prioritizing the expansion of the internal market and on regulating social relations in such a way as to reduce social and regional inequality as much as possible. Consequently, foreign relations must be subordinate to the needs of this driving logic.

This approach can be contrasted with the option that involves ever-deepening insertion into the world capitalist system as the principal motor of economic development. This option is inevitably associated with a worsening of regional and, above all, social inequalities. With that as a necessary outcome, there is limited space to pursue the alternative option of a 'national capitalism' that would allow China to catch up over time with the developed capitalist world and make it a new great power—indeed a superpower that would force the current powers to renounce their hegemony. It is hard to imagine that any political authority could hold this course within the permissible margins or that a strategy inspired by this goal could avoid turning to the right (and ending up subordinated to the imperialist plan) or to the left (and evolving towards the third model) (Chun 2006).

CONCLUDING THOUGHTS: CHINA IN THE DEBATE ON DEVELOPMENT

The Maoist and post-Maoist periods of the Chinese experiment do not support the dominant discourse of 'development in global capitalism' at all. On the contrary, despite first impressions, they invalidate these claims and support the analysis that I present of the polarization inherent in the global expansion of actually existing capitalism. China is not an emerging superpower, but if the country continues along the path on which it is currently travelling, it will become the model, par excellence, of the periphery of tomorrow.

Another path is possible, initiated by Maoism. That path found the necessary solution to the agrarian problem and in that respect constitutes an important model for the peoples of the periphery (75 per cent of humanity). Maoism initiated the building of 'another world', one that was not 'invented' by the (justifiably) angry young Westerners at Seattle. In other respects, those Westerners would do well to round out their knowledge of the realities of our world and develop a deeper consciousness of the real challenges confronting humanity. Certainly, Maoism had its limits. In any case, it was not a replica of Sovietism, as some say unreflectively, and it was able to open up new avenues for advancement.

As for the achievements of post-Maoism, they are certainly impressive: 200 million more urban dwellers, better lodged and nourished than anywhere else in the Third World; industry capable of exporting and absorbing technological progress; reduction of pockets of rural poverty. But these achievements remain vulnerable. Forty per cent of China's exports are manufactured by the branch plants of multinationals and their subcontractors (Plantade and Plantade 2006). This is, above all, associated with an increasing inequality in the social and regional distribution of income. But it also gives hope that with a possible shift to the left, China could contribute to the construction of 'another world', a better world.

QUESTIONS FOR DISCUSSION

1. How does this chapter engage the states versus markets debate?
2. Does the 'emergence' of China as a global player represent a challenge to existing theories and practices of development? Discuss with reference to the theories and concepts learned in this course.
3. What is market socialism and is it being pursued in China?
4. Why is the agrarian question central to China's development?

FURTHER READING

Amin, Samir. 1997. *Capitalism in the Age of Globalization: The Management of Contemporary Society*. London: Zed Books.
Chun, Lin. 2006. *The Transformation of Chinese Socialism*. Durham, NC: Duke University Press.

INTERNET RESOURCES

World Social Forum: http://www.forumsocialmundial.org.br.
World Forum for Alternatives: http://www.forumdesalternatives.org/EN/inicio.php.
Focus on the Global South: http://www.focusweb.org.
Asia Monitor Research Center: http://www.amrc.org.hk.
Globalization Monitor: http://www.globalmon.org.hk/en/index.html.

NOTES

1. From 'kulacks', a new class of rich peasants who took the place of the feudal structures and developed capitalist agriculture. This social group was physically liquidated by Stalin in the 1930s.
2. Nationalist political party created at the beginning of the century by Sun Yatsen. Until 1927, the KMT and the Communist Party were allies. Subsequently, the civil war broke out and ended in 1949 with the victory of the Communists.
3. 'Truly existing' and therefore very different from the idealized vision generally portrayed by those who are in favour of the expansion of capitalism.
4. Although I do not at all share the point of view of those supposed 'defenders of democracy' whose opinions converge with the lamas and mullahs.

GLOSSARY

Agricultural extensification: A means of increasing food production only through an expansion of the total area cultivated and not by increasing the rate of labour or capital inputs.

Agricultural intensification: A means of increasing the amount of food produced by a given area of land through the use of additional labour or capital, such as the increased use of manure or fertilizer, planting more crops per year or using higher-yielding crop varieties, irrigating, or using more labour or chemicals for weed and pest control.

Ahistorical: Neglect of the historical experiences of countries in the differentiated **Global South** in theoretical frameworks. For example, the legacies and influence of colonial political and economic structures are ignored in studies of social change situated within leading development theories such as modernization and **neo-liberalism**.

Appropriate technology: Technologies that are appropriate to the environmental, cultural, and economic context to which they are transferred.

Authoritarian regimes: Regimes in which state officials prevent society from participating in the decision-making process; frequently resort to arbitrary violence against society; extract, use, and distribute economic resources in an arbitrary and often violent fashion; and are rarely held accountable (Médard 1991).

Basic human needs: Minimum acceptable levels for food, nutrition, drinking water, health, education, and shelter.

Bilateral: Agreements or relations implicating only two governments. Often distinguished from broader **multilateral** agreements, institutions, or relationships.

Bilateral aid or **bilateral assistance**: Foreign aid provided by the government of an industrialized country directly to the government of a developing country.

Bilateral investment treaties: Agreements that enunciate the principles of treatment that foreign investors are entitled to receive from host governments and that permit **multinational corporations** to sue host governments in international arbitral tribunals for breach of obligations.

Boomerang pattern, **effect**, or **strategy**: A concept developed by Margaret Keck and Kathryn Sikkink to explain how local **non-governmental organizations** can influence their own governments by pressuring actors external to the country, such as international organizations or the home government of a **multinational corporation**, which in turn directly pressure the host government in question.

Brain drain: The emigration of a significant proportion of one country's trained and talented people to another country.

Bretton Woods Institutions: The World Bank and the International Monetary Fund, so called because they were founded in Bretton Woods, New Hampshire, in 1944.

Bretton Woods System: A system of fixed exchange rates between countries implemented following the Second World War in order to promote financial stability and international trade. This system laid the basis for the original roles of the International Monetary Fund and the World Bank.

Capabilities approach: A method of understanding poverty and development developed by Nobel Prize–winning economist Amartya Sen. Sen argues that development should not be seen simply as rising income levels but rather as an increase in individuals' substantive freedoms and ability to make choices they value.

Capitalism: The economic organization of society in which there is private ownership and control of the means of production and people are free to sell their labour in the marketplace. Owners of the means of production are able to make profit, and accumulate more capital, by paying wage workers less than what the owners earn through the sale of the products.

Carrying capacity: The hypothetical maximum number of all species, including people, that can be supported with available resources and with a given level of human technology.

Chartered company: A company that received monopoly commercial rights from a state ruler for the purpose of promoting trade and exploration in a specific geographic area. Chartered companies served as vehicles for European overseas expansion, becoming vitally important in the seventeenth century.

Citizenship: A status conferred on the inhabitants of a state, which provides them with a wide range of social and political rights, including the right to vote, to access state services (such as education and legal counselling), and to have a fair trial. For a regime to be truly democratic, these rights must be applied *equally*, *fairly*, and *systematically* (everywhere and at any time) (O'Donnell 2004).

Civil society: The collectivity of social organizations that are not controlled by the state—church groups, environmental lobbies, and so on. The presence and active participation of civil society organizations is thought to be a necessary if not sufficient guarantee of democracy, **good governance**, and participatory development.

Collective rights: Rights that are held and exercised by a group of people. They stand in contrast to individual rights, which are held only by individuals. Collective rights thus protect groups of people, taking into account collective dimensions of some violations of human rights and aiming at the improvement of a collective situation.

Collectivization: The reorganization of peasants into rural collectives in which property was held collectively. This process occurred in the aftermath of communist revolutions in Russia and China.

Colonialism: The territorial conquest, occupation, and direct control of one country by another. In some instances, it also involved large-scale settlement and nearly always brought systems of great political inequality and economic exploitation.

Colonization: The processes of occupation and administration of a territory, country, or region by another and the consequences of these processes.

Commodity control schemes: Internationally managed commodity agreements that entailed participating nation-states agreeing to adhere to country-specific quotas for the amount of their product they could sell on the market in order to force prices up and keep them relatively stable. Agreements were signed for most major tropical commodities in the 1950s; by the end of the 1980s, most of them had become defunct.

Communitarianism: The ethical standpoint that individuals belong to a political and social community, that this is a factor of key moral relevance, and that a social order that fosters communal bonds is morally preferable to an individualistic social order. Often contrasted with liberalism.

Comparative advantage: A theory of international trade formulated by David Ricardo in the nineteenth century according to which each nation has an economic advantage relative to other nations for the production of some goods. Consequently, the theory assumes that it would be to the relative benefit of all nations to focus on producing those goods for which they have the strongest comparative advantage and then trade with each other for the goods for which they do not.

Conflict trap: Grounded in the **liberal theory of violence**, an argument claiming that countries that have experienced civil war are likely to plunge into renewed violence unless the conditions that gave rise to war in the first place—underdevelopment—are addressed. The concept was promoted in a 2003 World Bank report, *Breaking the Conflict Trap*.

Consequentialist ethics: An ethical standpoint that judges whether an action is morally right or wrong by the consequences of the action.

Contractarian ethics: An ethical standpoint that holds that moral norms are justified according to the idea of a contract or mutual agreement (as in the political philosophy of Thomas Hobbes, John Locke, and most recently John Rawls).

Corporate social responsibility: The idea that corporations have a moral responsibility beyond their shareholders to a broader set of groups known as stakeholders affected by the activities of the firm, including employees and local communities. Corporate social responsibility is a voluntary commitment of firms to improve the quality of their relationship with stakeholders.

Cosmopolitanism: An ethical position that holds national boundaries to be irrelevant to questions of justice and argues that our common humanity entails a set of shared values and responsibilities to people around the world regardless of where we were born or currently live.

Cultural relativism: The theoretical position that holds that the values and beliefs of a cultural formation have to be evaluated on the basis of standards internal to that culture. While cultural relativism is helpful in countering notions of ethnocentrism—the belief in the superiority of one's own culture—if taken to the extreme, it can ignore the many universal features of human physical and social life across different cultures.

Cultural Revolution: The 1966–74 period in China when Mao Zedong turned to students and the Red Guard to support him in a struggle against 'bourgeois' elements that he claimed threatened the socialist revolution.

Cultural turn: The theoretical trajectory that many disciplines in the social sciences have taken in the past couple of decades. It basically uses **culture** as an explanatory variable to understand society and social transformation.

Culture: A complex concept referring to the web of meanings and understandings generated by human beings about themselves and the natural world and the ability to convey these meanings and understandings through symbols, actions, and utterances.

Democratic consolidation: A phase of democratization characterized by a solidification of the democratic foundations in which there is no uncertainty as to *whether* political actors want to conserve the **authoritarian regime** or adopt a democracy but rather about how they should go about reinforcing the democratic system (Schedler 2001).

Democratic transition: The period when authoritarian institutions and practices are in the process of being reformed and replaced by institutions and practices that are more democratic (or that are less authoritarian). It is an uncertain phase in which actors or forces pushing for democracy are struggling with those attempting to maintain the authoritarian status quo.

Depoliticization: Conceptual practices that present political-economic issues as technical matters requiring technical solutions.

Desertification: The process of overexploitation, such as overgrazing and/or deforestation, through which an ecosystem loses its ability to retain moisture, thus becoming increasingly dry and unable to adequately support human populations.

Development tourist: A derogatory term to describe well-paid development consultants who jet in and out of countries, stay in five-star hotels, and dispense advice with little knowledge of local conditions.

Diaspora: A term traditionally used to refer to any people or ethnic population forced to leave their traditional homelands, their dispersal, and the ensuing developments in their culture. More recently, the term has been used more broadly to describe migrant populations that maintain an attachment to and link with their home country.

Digital divide: The difference between groups in their access to and use of **information and communication technologies**.

Discrimination: The unfair treatment of a person or group as a result of prejudice. It includes **sexism** and sexual discrimination.

Disparities: Differences between countries and regions of the world. Disparities in development, demography, and the democratic process are particularly significant causes of **international migration**.

Distribution of income (inequality in the): How the average wealth of a country is divided among the population. Distribution of income may be measured by comparing the average wealth of different deciles (tenths) or quintiles (fifths) of the population or by a measure such as the Gini coefficient.

Donor: A government of an industrialized country or an international agency that provides foreign aid.

Double burden of disease: A pattern in which continued substantial prevalence of communicable diseases, which have historically been regarded as 'diseases of poverty', coexists with rising incidence of non-communicable 'diseases of affluence' like cardiovascular disease, diabetes, and cancer.

Elite: Groups within societies who have access to and who seem to enjoy the concentration of wealth and power and consequently are able to disproportionately sway decision-making.

Emancipatory (as in **emancipatory social movements, emancipatory ideas, emancipatory outcomes**): An adjective used to describe civil, social, and political freedoms-enhancing activities and practices.

Embedded liberalism: A concept referring to the international trade and development regime that emerged out of the Bretton Woods negotiations in 1944 and lasted until the 1970s. It entailed a mixture of international state intervention to control capital and investment flows with liberal trade objectives.

Empowerment: The capacity of individuals for self-development—to act and participate in decisions that affect their livelihoods and living standards. In practice, it refers to an enhanced sense of participation, to change oneself rather than the operating structures of the 'system'. In reference to gender, it indicates change in gender relations that challenges assumptions about power, helping, achieving, and succeeding.

Environmental justice: Notion calling for efforts to rectify the fact that the burdens of environmental degradation are disproportionately borne by less powerful groups, such as populations in the developing world, racial minorities, and many women.

Ethnic conflict: A form of conflict that some analysts see as generated by ethnic difference and animosities per se, requiring little additional explanation. Others regard ethnicity as one among several factors, and some reject the term's analytical value altogether.

Eurocentric, Eurocentrism: A bias towards glorifying the values, practices, and historical developmental experience of Europe and the United States. It is important to remember that the rise of Europe and the US had multiple causes, which may or may not support the idea that development elsewhere should follow the same steps.

Export processing zones: Industrial parks, usually in developing countries, that are specially designated as manufacturing-for-export areas. These zones aim to attract efficiency-seeking **foreign direct investment** by reducing regulations that increase costs for **multinational corporations**, such as import-export duties, corporate taxation rates, labour and minimum wage legislation, and health and safety standards.

Fair trade: A political-economic concept that has gained popularity since the Second World War premised on a belief in the need for international market regulation in the interests of poorer Southern nations to combat the historical legacy of **colonialism**, dependency, and underdevelopment. Proponents of fair trade tend to focus on two key demands: the development and expansion of interventionist mechanisms to ensure fair prices and living standards for Southern farmers and workers and the elimination of 'unfair' protectionist policies in the North.

Fair trade network: A network that connects small farmers, workers, and craftspeople in the South with organizations and consumers in the North through a system of 'fair trade' rules and principles, including democratic organization (of cooperatives or unions), no exploitation of child labour, environmental sustainability, a minimum guaranteed price, and social premiums paid to producer communities to build community infrastructure.

Food security: The ability (derived from land, labour, capital, and/or political power) to meet food consumption needs either directly from farming, livestock keeping, fishing, or hunting or indirectly through purchase or trade.

Foreign direct investment: A catch-all phrase that refers to investment made across borders. The word 'direct' in foreign direct investment indicates that the investment has a physical presence or corporate form (such as a branch plant) and differentiates this mode of investment from indirect investment, also known as portfolio capital.

Foreign portfolio investment: Investments that are not made in an enterprise form and include the purchase of foreign debt, loans, and stock market investments. Portfolio capital may flow into or out of a developing country more rapidly than **foreign direct investment**, leading to financial instability and balance of payments crises.

Fourth World: The most underprivileged and oppressed peoples within the so-called developed countries and Third World countries. It is used to speak about a population that suffers from social, economic, and social exclusion and, more generally, to stateless nations. The term is often used more specifically to designate indigenous peoples.

Free trade: A political-economic concept popularized in the nineteenth century, premised on the belief that the removal of barriers to trade and the limitation of state intervention in economic and social interactions within and between nation-states would provide the greatest social gains for all countries involved. Significantly revived since the 1970s, free trade is supported on the grounds that state regulation of the market is inherently inefficient and wasteful while an unregulated market operates as an efficient 'hidden hand' that responds accurately to undistorted market signals of supply and demand.

GDP per capita: The most widely used indicator of economic development that measures the total market value of the goods and services produced in an economy divided by the number of people in that economy. GDP per capita is a measure of the average wealth in a country and does not take account of how that wealth is distributed.

Gender equality: Involves both women and men as partners in the quest for fairness and in the benefits of equality.

Global civil society: Non-state actors acting at the global level and engaging with global institutions and processes.

Global ethics: The field of study examining questions of morality at the level of the world, such as international justice, distribution of wealth between nations or between peoples of different nations, global trade, and humanitarian activity.

Globalization: The economic, sociological, and cultural process by which nation-states, organizations, and individuals become increasingly interlinked and interdependent.

Global South: A concept created by Filipino political economist Walden Bello to underline the unequal global distribution of resources between the developed countries and the less developed countries mostly (though not exclusively) located in the South.

Good governance: The idea that in order for market-orientated development strategies to be effective, the political systems that surround them must be accountable, transparent, responsive, efficient, and inclusive.

Governance: A neologism of the 1980s, extensively used by political scientists working in the area of development. It refers to rules of procedure and regulation designed to maintain order—or political order—without or with as little government as possible by engaging non-state institutions or civil society in the process of maintaining order.

Health (in)equity: An emerging concept in health policy that defines as inequitable those disparities in health status within or between populations that are avoidable, unfair, and systematically associated with social (dis)advantage.

Heavily Indebted Poor Countries Initiative: A 1996 arrangement between the **Bretton Woods Institutions** and some large government **donors** to cancel some of the debts of the poorest countries if they implemented **structural adjustment** programs.

Hegemonic power: A great power or group of powers that can bring great pressures or inducements to bear on other states such that they lose some or most of their freedom of action in practical terms (though not their formal sovereignty). A hegemonic power can affect other states' behaviour by way of economic, military, and other material incentives but also by way of ideology, policy formulas, and other non-material influences.

Hegemony: A term used in critical development studies to refer to a theory that at a given historical conjuncture sets the parameters of, for instance, how we think about the role of the state in political and economic spheres.

Homogenization: The tendency in dominant theories of development to portray the diverse societies comprising the **Global South** as sharing the same history, cultural practices, and political and economic realities.

Homophobia: The irrational fear of, aversion to, or discrimination against homosexuals (from the Greek *homós*: one and the same; and *phóbos*: fear, phobia).

Human Development Index: A composite measure of three equally weighted factors: a long and healthy life, knowledge, and standard of living. A long and healthy life is measured by life expectancy at birth; knowledge is a composite of the adult literacy rate and the combined gross enrolment ratio for primary, secondary, and post-secondary schools; and standard of living is measured by **GDP per capita**. In this respect, the index recognizes that income levels are important but that other factors are also important in human development.

Illegitimate debt: A loan that should not have been made and thus reflects misconduct by the lender. Such a debt is the responsibility of the lender, not the borrower.

Imperialism: A political and economic system by which wealthy and powerful states control the political and economic life of other societies. Most forms of imperialism involve long-distance commercial ties, with or without direct political ties.

Income inequality: See **distribution of income**.

Indirect rule: A system of governance by which colonial powers recognized and supported the legitimacy of indigenous authorities and legal systems insofar as they were subordinate and useful to the colonial state and used those authorities as intermediaries to govern the local population.

Industrial capitalism: Form of **capitalism** in which production shifts from small-scale individual production to large-scale centralized production in factories, with an increasingly complex division of labour. Work tasks are normally split into small, routinized activities, as on an assembly line.

Industrial Revolution: The transition from rural, agrarian economies to urban-based factory production, associated with the harnessing of steam power as an energy source. First identified in eighteenth-century England, the Industrial Revolution eventually brought enormous political, social, and cultural change throughout nineteenth-century Europe.

Informational capitalism: A concept introduced by Manuel Castells, who argues that modern 'globalized' **capitalism** is largely about controlling the flows of strategic information, processes, and patents.

Information and communication technologies: The equipment and services that facilitate the electronic capture, processing, and display of information. These include computer technologies (computers, the Internet), telecommunications (cellular and land-line phones), audio-visual technologies (DVDs, cameras, MP3), and broadcasting (radio, television).

Integrated approach: An interdisciplinary ideal that acknowledges the complexity and interconnected, interdisciplinary nature of rural development problems. Such approaches and projects attempt to co-ordinate teams of disciplinary specialists, including agricultural, environmental, nutritional health, social, economic, and political expertise.

Interest: The amount that must be paid by the borrower in addition to the **principal** and that provides the lender's profit and security against risk.

Intergovernmental: Relations or agreements between governments.

International aid regime: The principles, norms, rules, and procedures and institutions concerning **official development assistance** associated with multilateral and bilateral aid **donors** and regulators.

International division of labour: A concept explaining the location of the activities of **multinational corporations** and their benefits and arguing that high-value manufacturing remains in the core countries and commodity and resource extraction is conducted in developing countries, thus maintaining and deepening the underdevelopment of the periphery.

International migrant: As defined by the United Nations, a person who stays outside their home country for at least one year.

International migration: The movement of people away from their home countries.

Keynesian policies: Policies to stimulate economic growth through state intervention in market processes, based on the idea that capitalist markets require state regulation in order to correct problems that emerge from the operation of free markets.

Knowledge-based (as in **knowledge-based institutes**, **knowledge-based activities**): Institutions and activities that owe their influence to the scientific generation of new ideas, techniques, and processes. Many organizations of the United Nations system exhibit influence based on knowledge.

Laissez-faire: Literally, 'leave to do', the idea being to allow individuals to pursue their own interests through market transactions. 'Perfect competition' is believed to result in optimal and more rational outcomes than state regulation.

Legitimacy: The idea that governments require the consent of their populations to rule. A government that lacks general support from its population is said to be illegitimate.

Liberal theory of violence: A view that progress or development reduces the likelihood of violent conflict. In this view, conflict is regarded as a setback for development.

Libertarianism: The ethical standpoint that holds individual freedom to be the highest moral principle and that it should not be infringed upon by the collectivity, society, or the state. Key individual rights, according to libertarianism, include the rights to acquire and retain property.

Individual rights should never be breached in favour of the collective good.

Listian industrialization: Also known as infant industry protection, the idea that national industries may need to be protected from external competition, at least in the early phase of development, by tariffs that raise the cost of products exported by other countries' industries.

Livelihood: The capabilities, assets (material and social), and activities required for a means of living (Scoones 1998, 5).

Loan pushing: Banks or lending agencies encouraging borrowers to take loans they do not need or cannot afford to repay.

Maoism: The philosophy associated with Mao Zedong's rule and interpretation of communism in China from 1949 until his death in 1976. An important characteristic of this philosophy was his focus on the peasantry as a revolutionary class.

Market socialism: The attempt to reconcile features of the socialist political structures, such as a one-party state and a concern for social justice, with a capitalist economy.

Mass culture: Cultural forms produced in the modern industrial age on a mass scale and intended for mass consumption.

Multilateral, multilateralism: Arrangements among three or more states, commonly for peaceful purposes over extended periods. Such arrangements can help governments improve their standing, influence, security, or economic advantage.

Multinational corporation: A corporation that invests across national borders and/or establishes branch plants, subsidiaries, or other operations in more than one country. Usually used as a synonym of '**transnational corporation**' and '**multinational enterprise**' but favoured by social scientists and the media.

Multinational enterprise: A corporation that invests across national borders and/or establishes branch plants, subsidiaries, or other operations in more than one country. Usually used as a synonym of '**transnational corporation**' and '**multinational corporation**' but favoured by international business studies.

Nation: Refers both to a well-defined territorial and political entity and to a population that identifies itself as a common group in juxtaposition to others. The distinction is important; for example, we frequently discuss Basque nationalism even though a Basque government does not exist.

Neo-liberal globalization: An economic doctrine that repudiates the role of the state in the economy, preferring to leave the economy in the hands of the market, and promotes the integration of economies and societies across the world into the 'new world order'—a global economy based on the principles of liberalism and **capitalism**.

Neo-liberalism (also **neoliberalism**): Mainstream international economic theory positing that markets are almost always the best decision-makers in terms of efficient resource allocation and that trade and investment flows across borders are optimized when there are as few restrictions as possible. The term 'neo' distinguishes the creed from classical liberalism and indicates that some mainstream economists do recognize that there are certain market failures that must be addressed.

Neo-liberal orthodoxy: A synonym of the **Washington Consensus**, which advocates a development strategy based on **structural adjustment** to correct external and fiscal imbalances by means of downsizing the state, privatizing public enterprises, and promoting the market as *the* engine of development.

New international division of labour: The result of **multinational corporations** seeking out Third World locations for their low-cost labour while maintaining high-skill and value-added manufacturing in the developed countries.

Non-governmental organizations: First established in the 1960s in the form of 'private voluntary organizations'. They serve a range of contradictory purposes, some charitable, some political. Such organizations are often supported by governments and therefore serve not to promote change but to sustain the existing order. The World Bank favours them as a strategic partner in the war on poverty and as instruments of **good governance**.

Obsolescing bargaining model: A model of state–firm relations developed by Raymond Vernon that argues that each actor—state and firm—wants to capture a greater share of the benefits of foreign investment and that over time the relative strength of each actor changes. At the time of the investment, the **multinational corporation** is in the stronger position, but over time, the initial contract over the terms of investment erodes as the state becomes more powerful.

Odious debt: A loan to a dictatorship or despotic regime that does not benefit the people and may be used to repress the population that fights against the regime. Such a debt is not an obligation for the nation; it is a personal debt of the regime and need not be repaid by the successor regime.

Official development assistance: As defined by Western **donors** in 1969, flows to developing countries and multilateral institutions provided by official agencies that meet the tests of (a) promoting the economic development and welfare of developing countries as the main objective and (b) containing a grant element of at least 25 per cent. Often referred to as *foreign aid*.

OLI Paradigm: Developed by John H. Dunning and also known as the 'eclectic' approach, a theory arguing that the internationalization of **multinational corporations** can be explained through the interaction of three factors related to its ownership (O), location-specific (L), and internalization (I) advantages, relative to non-internationalized firms.

Oppression: The unjust or cruel exercise of authority or power, such as the systematic, institutionalized, and elite-sanctioned mistreatment of and/or discrimination against a group in society by another group or by people acting as agents of the society as a whole.

Paris Club: An informal association of government (bilateral) lenders that meets in Paris.

Participatory approach: An ideological and philosophical commitment to an ideal that rural development is controlled by the full range of rural actors with a stake in it.

Patriarchal system: A political structure that controls and subjugates women so that their rights as citizens are denied and their range of choices is largely confined within their role as mothers.

Patron–client networks: An informal political structure typical of developing countries in which someone who holds power at the national, state, municipal, or local level (a patron) channels resources to the poor (the clients) in exchange for their political support or

votes. Patron–client relationships normally limit the ability of the poor to politically express themselves in an autonomous fashion and tend to maintain existing **elites** in power.

Peacebuilding: In a most general sense, peacebuilding means activities directed towards the establishment or consolidation of peace. A more narrow meaning refers to activities by international actors in countries emerging from civil wars designed to prevent the recurrence of conflict.

Peripheral capitalism: A concept developed by dependency theorists, who argued that the capitalist world economy could be divided into core and peripheral (and in some cases semi-peripheral) regions. In the periphery, **capitalism** develops differently from the way it developed in core countries and is characterized as externally directed, less dynamic, and more exclusionary and unjust than in currently developed countries.

Political economy: Interdisciplinary study of interactions or relationships between production and trade and power and politics.

Political economy of war: A term normally referring to relations between economic activities, power structures, and violence during wartime.

Political regime: The set of principles and rules that govern power relations between society and the state (Przeworski et al. 2000, 18–19).

Popular culture: The cultural forms that are appreciated by the greatest number of people. A more critical perspective would see it as those elements of culture that are mainly associated with the marginalized and oppressed groups and that are in a constant tension with the dominant culture.

Positionality: An awareness by researchers or development practitioners of the social situation and power relationships in which they are embedded. This awareness, particularly their position relative to the local people with whom they interact, helps development researchers and practitioners make better decisions and reduce their negative impact.

Poverty (absolute): The minimum level of income required for physical survival. The World Bank defines this level as US $1 per day measured at international **purchasing power parity**.

Poverty (moderate): An income level that indicates income deprivation and insecurity but at which actual physical survival is not threatened. Moderate poverty is typically considered to be an income of US $2 per day at international **purchasing power parity**.

Poverty (relative): Poverty that does not threaten a person's daily survival but in which that person may not have the income necessary to fully participate in his or her society. Relative poverty is often the principal kind of poverty in developed countries.

Poverty Reduction Strategy Papers (PRSPs): A refashioning of the IMF and World Bank's **structural adjustment** programs in the later 1990s. PRSPs are intended to cover a wide range of social, economic, and political reforms, including a firm commitment to **good governance**.

Power/knowledge regime: A conception of political power that explores not just an international regime's direct political-economic power but also its knowledge-producing power. With this concept, sociologist Michael Goldman argues that an international organization like the World Bank does not produce value-neutral knowledge but rather constructs a 'power/knowledge' regime designed to naturalize and legitimize a world order skewed in the interest of rich Northern countries.

Principal: The amount of money initially borrowed.

Privatization: The policy and practice, universally supported by neo-liberal regimes, of selling off publicly owned assets and publicly controlled services (railways, airlines, prisons, hospitals, water supplies, road maintenance, garbage collection) to private investors. A reversal of the nationalization policy of regimes in the 1950s and 1960s under the state-led strategy of national development.

Protestant ethic: The most famous theory regarding cultural influence on economic behaviour, posited by Max Weber. It holds that certain characteristics of Protestantism (especially Calvinism), such as valuing austerity, discipline, and hard work to attain material wealth and success as a route to personal salvation, played a major role in the origin of **capitalism**.

Purchasing power parity: A comparative indicator based on an exchange rate that equates the price of a basket of identical traded goods and services in two countries.

Real interest rate: The rate of **interest** charged less the rate of inflation.

Recipient (government): A government that receives foreign aid.

Refugee: As defined in the United Nations Convention Relating to the Status of Refugees (1951), someone who is 'outside his own country, owing to a well-founded fear of persecution, for reasons of race, religion, nationality, membership of a particular social group, or political opinion'.

Regulatory chill: The possibility that good public policy could be withdrawn or never proposed because of the government's fear of being sued by affected foreign investors.

Remittances: Transfers of money by migrants to their home countries.

Rights-based philosophy: Justifies moral claims on the basis of fundamental entitlements to act or be treated in specific ways. Justifications for rights-based morality are complex, but they include the idea that we have rights because we have interests or because of our status.

Rule of capture: Policy whereby property rights are granted to individuals who can demonstrate presence or 'productive' use of a resource, such as the cutting of trees to plant crops or raise cattle.

Self-determination: A principle in customary international law and diplomacy according to which all peoples have the right to 'freely determine their political status and freely pursue their economic, social and cultural development' (International Covenants on Civil and Political Rights and on Economic, Social and Cultural Rights). The right of all peoples to self-determination is embodied in several treaties and can be implemented in diverse ways.

Semi-authoritarian regimes (or hybrid regimes): Regimes that have democratized their formal institutions (removed a one-party system and/or the military from political office) but in which **elites** of the old **authoritarian regime** still perpetuate (sometimes informally, sometimes in a more formal fashion) a plethora of heavily authoritative political practices (Brownlee 2002; Levitsky and Way 2002; Ottaway 2003; Schedler 2006).

Sexism: Discriminatory or abusive behaviour towards girls and women.

Social cohesion: A concept introduced by Émile Durkheim at the end of the nineteenth century. Today, it is generally defined as the ongoing process of developing a community of shared values, shared challenges, and equal opportunity in a pluralistic society.

Social determinants of health: Social, economic, and environmental conditions under which people live and work that affect their opportunity to lead healthy lives. Access to health care is only one of many social determinants of health, which lie largely outside the domain of the health care professions and the remit of government ministries or other agencies concerned with health.

Social determinism (of technology): Considers social interaction as having primacy in terms of the development and use of tools and technologies

Social or socio-economic gradient: A pattern, found in rich and poor societies alike, in which health status varies with income, wealth, education, or some other indicator of socio-economic status. In other words, health improves with wealth, income, education, and other assets.

Sphere of influence: Geographical and political areas over which major powers can expect their wishes to be respected because of their ability to threaten, intimidate, or persuade governments and non-state actors. Frequently used in reference to the Cold War partition of much of the world between American and Soviet spheres of influence.

State: A government that makes decisions on behalf of a political and territorially defined entity. It is important to point out that the state itself can be rife with internal conflicts, reflecting wider divisions within society.

Structural adjustment: A controversial series of economic and social reforms promoted by the IMF and World Bank following the 1982 debt crisis that aimed to promote economic development through minimizing the role of the state and liberalizing markets.

Sustainable development: Defined by the World Commission on Environment and Development as development that meets the needs of the present without compromising the ability of future generations to meet their own needs.

Sustainable livelihoods: 'A livelihood is sustainable when it can cope with and recover from stresses and shocks and maintain or enhance its capabilities and assets both now and in the future, while not undermining the natural resources base' (Chambers and Conway 1992, cited in Shaffer 2002, 30).

Technological determinism: The notion that technology drives the evolution of society.

Technology: The science and art of getting things done through the application of skills and knowledge, or the capacity to organize and use physical infrastructure, machinery and equipment, knowledge, and skills.

10/90 gap: The fact that worldwide, less than 10 per cent of health research spending addresses conditions that account for 90 per cent of the global burden of illness and death, almost entirely in low- and middle-income countries.

Tied aid: Foreign aid that must be used to purchase goods and services from the **donor** country.

Time and space (contraction of): An effect of modern communication and transportation techniques that have changed the way in which economic and social relations are constructed and perceived, giving the appearance that time runs more quickly and the distance between places has been reduced.

Traditional ecological knowledge: Non-scientifically based understanding of ecological systems, accumulated and held by local peoples and based on an intimate understanding of the resources upon which they have relied for their livings and that they have managed over long periods of time.

Tragedy of the commons: A misnomer, popularized by Hardin, referring to the overexploitation and resulting degradation of environmental resources as a result of individuals rationally pursing personal gain with resources that are held in common by a group of people.

Tragic view of history: The idea that suffering is or has been necessary for progress. A modified version was put forward by Christopher Cramer (2006), who suggested a melancholy perspective, one that accepts that violence has played a part in progress and is also likely to do so in the future but nonetheless recognizes that progress will not solve all conflict and that not all violence has progressive consequences.

Transnational corporation: A corporation that invests across national borders and/or establishes branch plants, subsidiaries, or other operations in more than one country. Usually used as a synonym of **'multinational corporation'** and **'multinational enterprise'** but favoured by the United Nations system in its reports and publications.

Triad: The most powerful capitalist areas, which dominate the world economy: North America, western Europe, and Japan.

Unequal exchange: A theory of international trade popularized by underdevelopment and dependency theorists in the 1960s and 1970s. It states that Third World countries, rather than being in a position to enhance their **comparative advantage** through international trade, have their national development restricted and distorted by the 'unequal exchange' of lower-priced primary commodities (such as coffee, tea, cocoa, and bananas) for higher-priced industrial goods, technology, and services from the First World.

United Nations (UN): Founded in 1945 to replace the League of Nations and aimed at facilitating cooperation in international law, international peace and security, and economic and social development, as well as in human rights issues and humanitarian affairs. The UN is currently composed of 192 recognized independent states, and its headquarters is located in New York City on international territory.

Universal access (to ICTs): A situation in which every person has a reasonable means of access to a publicly available telecommunication service, which may be provided through pay telephones, community telephone centres, teleboutiques, community Internet access terminals, or similar means.

Universalizing logic: The representation of the European and American political, cultural, and economic historical developments as the reference point for all societies in the world.

Universal service (to ICTs): Making available a defined minimum telecommunication service of specified quality to all users at an affordable price.

Usury: Excessive **interest** rates.

Washington Consensus: A tacit agreement between the International Monetary Fund, the World Bank, and the US executive branch over the development policies that developing countries should follow. The consensus formed around the key issues of macroeconomic prudence, export-oriented growth, and economic liberalization. See **neo-liberal orthodoxy**.

White man's burden: The idea that (white) Europeans and Americans have a duty to colonize and rule over peoples in other parts of the world because of the alleged superiority of European culture. Both the subject peoples and the act of **colonization** are seen as the 'burden'. This idea was used as a justification for colonization in the nineteenth century.

LIST OF REFERENCES

AbouZahra, C., and Wardlaw, T. 2000. *Maternal Mortality in 2000: Estimates Developed by WHO, UNICEF and UNFPA*. Geneva: World Health Organization.

Adams, P. 1991. *Odious Debts*. London: Earthscan.

Adams, W.M. 1995. 'Green development theory? Environmentalism and sustainable development'. In J. Crush, ed., *Power of Development*, 87–99. London and New York: Routledge.

Adams, W.M., and C.C. Megaw. 1997. 'Researchers and the rural poor: Asking questions in the Third World'. *Journal of Geography in Higher Education* 21 (2): 215–29.

Afoaku, Osita G. 2000. 'US foreign policy and authoritarian regimes: Change and continuity in international clientelism'. *Journal of Third World Studies* 17(2): 13–40.

African Development Bank. 2004. *Africa in the World*. African Development Report 2004. Oxford: Oxford University Press.

Afrobarometer. 2006. *The Status of Democracy, 2005–2006: Findings from Afrobarometer Round 3 for 18 Countries*. Afrobarometer Briefing Paper no. 40.

Agarwal, Bina. 1997. 'Gender, environment, and poverty interlinks: Regional variations and temporal shifts in rural India, 1971–91'. *World Development* 25 (1): 23–52.

Agence de la santé et des services sociaux de Montréal. 2007. *Atlas santé Montréal*. http://www.cmis.mtl.rtss.qc.ca/fr/atlas.

Agence française de développement. 2007. 'About us'. www.afd.fr/jahia/Jahia/home/Qui-Sommes-Nous (accessed 18 September 2007).

Agrawal, Arun. 2001. 'Common property institutions and sustainable governance of resources'. *World Development* 29 (10): 1649–72.

Ahmad, A. 1992. 'Three worlds theory'. In *In Theory: Nations Classes Literatures*. London: Verso.

Akin, J., N. Birdsall, and D. de Ferranti. 1987. *Financing Health Services in Developing Countries: An Agenda for Reform*. Washington: World Bank.

Alampay, E.A. 2006. 'Analysing socio-demographic differences in the access and use of ICTs in the Philippines using the capability approach'. *The Electronic Journal of Information Systems in Developing Countries*, 27. http://www.ejisdc.org/ojs2/index.php/ejisdc.

Allen, Chadwick. 2002. *Blood Narrative: Indigenous Identity in American Indian and Maori Literary and Activist Texts*. Durham, NC: Duke University Press.

Allen, Tim. 2002. 'Taking culture seriously'. In Tim Allen and Alan Thomas, eds, *Poverty and Development into the 21st Century*, revised edn, 443–66. Oxford and New York: Open University in association with Oxford University Press.

Ambrose, S. 2006. 'Preserving disorder: IMF policies and Kenya's health care crisis'. *Pambazuka News*. http://www.pambazuka.org/en/category/features/34800.

Amin, Samir. 1974. 'Accumulation and development: A theoretical model'. *Review of African Political Economy* 1 (1): 9–26.

———. 1983. *The Future of Maoism*. New York: Monthly Review Press.

———. 1990. *Delinking: Towards a Polycentric World*. London: Zed Books.

———. 1997. *Capitalism in the Age of Globalization: The Management of Contemporary Society*. Michael Wolfers, trans. London: Zed Books.

———. 2004. *Obsolescent Capitalism: Contemporary Politics and Global Disorder*. London: Zed Books.

Amsden, Alice H. 1989. *Asia's Next Giant: South Korea and Late Industrialization*. New York: Oxford University Press.

Anderson, P. 1998. *The Origins of Modernity*. London: Verso.

Apentiik, C.R.A., and J.L. Parpart. 2006. 'Working in different cultures: Issues of race, ethnicity and identity'. In V. Desai and R.B. Potter, eds, *Doing Development Research*, 34–43. London: Sage.

Arreaza, T. 2004. 'ALBA: Bolivarian Alternative for Latin America and the Caribbean'. In Venezuelanalysis.com. http://www.venezuelanalysis.com/docs.php?dno=1010.

Arrighi, G. 2003. 'The social and political economy of global turbulence'. *New Left Review* II/20.

———. 2005. 'Hegemony unravelling I and II'. *New Left Review* II/32, II/33.

Ashley, C., and S. Maxwell. 2001. 'Rethinking rural

development'. *Development Policy Review* 19 (4): 395–425.

Attaran, A. 2004. 'How do patents and economic policies affect access to essential medicines in developing countries?'. *Health Affairs* 23 (3): 155–66.

———. 2007. 'A tragically naive Canadian law for tragically neglected global health'. *Canadian Medical Association Journal* 176: 1726–7.

Ayres, R.L. 1983. *Banking on the Poor: The World Bank and World Poverty.* Cambridge, MA: MIT Press.

Baby Milk Action. 2007. http://www.babymilkaction.org/press/press11may07.html.

Baer, W. 1972. 'Import substitution and industrialization in Latin America: Experiences and interpretations'. *Latin American Research Review* 7 (1): 95–122.

Baeza-Rodriguez, Cecilia, and Marielle Debos. 2004. 'Féminisme et altermondialisme: Des affinités electives'. In Lilian Halls-French and Josette Rome Chastanet, eds, *Féministes et Féminismes*, 101–4. Paris: Éditions Syllepse, Collection Espaces Marx.

Ballentine, K., and J. Sherman. 2003. 'Introduction'. In *Beyond Greed and Grievance: The Political Economy of Armed Conflict.* London: Lynne Rienner.

Banaji, J. 1977. 'Modes of production in a materialist conception of history'. *Capital and Class* 3: 1–44.

Barder, Owen. 2007. 'Reforming development assistance: Lessons from the UK experience'. In Lael Brainard, ed., *Security by Other Means: Foreign Assistance, Global Poverty, and American Leadership*, 277–320. Washington: Brookings Institution Press.

Barratt Brown, M. 1993. *Fair Trade: Reform and Realities in the International Trading System.* London: Zed Books.

Barrett, C.B., T. Reardon, and P. Webb. 2001. 'Nonfarm income diversification and household livelihood strategies in rural Africa: Concepts, dynamics, and policy implications'. *Food Policy* 26: 315–31.

Baviskar, Amita. 1995. *In the Belly of the River: Tribal Conflicts over Development in the Narmada Valley.* New Delhi: Oxford University Press.

Bayart, Jean-François, Peter Geschiere, and Francis Nyamnjoh. 2001. 'Autochtonie, démocratie et citoyenneté en Afrique'. *Critique Internationale* 10: 177–94.

Beckerman, Wilfred. 1974. *In Defence of Economic Growth.* London: Cape.

Beissinger, Mark, and Crawford Young. 2002. *Beyond State Crisis: Postcolonial African and Post-Soviet Eurasia in Comparative Perspective.* Washington: Woodrow Wilson Center Press; Baltimore, MD: Johns Hopkins University Press.

Bell, M.M. 2007. 'The two-ness of rural life and the ends of rural scholarship'. *Journal of Rural Studies* 23 (4): 402–15.

Bellier, Irène. 2006. 'Les peuples autochtones à la recherche de droits collectifs'. *Sciences Humaines* 169: 30–1.

———, and Dominque Legros. 2001. 'Mondialisation et redéploiement des pratiques politiques Amérindiennes: Esquisses théoriques'. *Recherches Amérindiennes au Québec* 31 (3): 3–11.

Bello, Walden. 2002. 'What's wrong with the Oxfam trade campaign?'. *Focus on Trade* 77.

———. 2004. *Deglobalization: Ideas for a New World Economy.* London: Zed Books.

———. 2006. *Dilemmas of Domination: The Unmaking of the American Empire.* New York: Metropolitan Books.

Benaría, Lourdes. 2003. *Gender, Development and Globalization.* New York and London: Routledge.

Benhabib, S. 2001. *The Claims of Culture: Equality and Diversity in the Global Era.* Princeton, NJ: Princeton University Press.

Bennett, T. 1986. 'Introduction: Popular culture and the "turn to Gramsci"'. In T. Bennett, C. Mercer, and J. Woollacott, eds, *Popular Culture and Social Relations*, xi–xix. Milton Keys, UK, and Philadelphia: Open University Press.

Bensa, Alban. 2008. 'Usages savants et politiques de la notion d'autochtonie'. In Natacha Gagné, Thibault Martin, and Marie Salaün, eds, *L'Autochtonie en question: Vues de France et du Québec.* Québec: Presses de l'Université Laval, collection Les mondes autochtones contemporains.

Berkes, Fikret. 1989. 'Common property resources: Ecology and community-based sustainable development'. *World Development* 20 (4): 557–70.

———, and Iain Davidson-Hunt. 2006. 'Biodiversity, traditional management systems, and cultural landscapes: Examples from the boreal forest of Canada'. *International Social Science Journal* 58 (187): 35–47.

Berry, Sara. 1992. 'Hegemony on a shoestring: Indirect rule and access to agricultural land'. *Africa* 62 (3): 327–55.

Bertrand, Romain. 2002. *Indonésie: La démocratie invisible*. Paris: Karthala.

Bhagwati, J. 2002. *Free Trade Today*. Princeton, NJ: Princeton University Press.

Binns, T. 2006. 'Doing fieldwork in developing countries: Planning and logistics'. In V. Desai and R.B. Potter, Eds, *Doing Development Research*, 13–24. London: Sage.

Birn, A.-E. 2005. 'Gates's grandest challenge: Transcending technology as public health ideology. *Lancet* 366: 514–19.

Bisilliat, Jeanne, Ed. 2003. *Regards de femmes sur la globalisation. Approches critiques*. Paris: Karthala.

Blaser, Marie, Harvey A. Feit, and Glenn McRae, Eds. 2004. *In The Way of Development: Indigenous Peoples, Life Projects and Globalization*. London: Zed Books; Ottawa: International Development Research Centre.

Blouin, C., N. Drager, and R. Smith, Eds. 2006. *International Trade in Health Services and the GATS: Current Issues and Debates*. Washington: World Bank.

Boix, Carles. 2003. *Democracy and Distribution*. Cambridge: Cambridge University Press.

Bond, Patrick. 2001. *Against Global Apartheid: South Africa Meets the World Bank, IMF and International Finance*. Cape Town: University of Cape Town Press.

———. 2005. 'Imperialism's African Helpers'. *Socialist Review* June.

Booth, D. 1985. 'Marxism and development sociology: Interpreting the impasse'. *World Development* 13 (17).

———. 1994. 'Rethinking social development: An overview'. In D. Booth, Ed., *Rethinking Social Development: Theory, Practice and Research*, 277–97. London: Longman.

Bose, Sugata, and Ayesha Jalal. 2004. *Modern South Asia: History, Culture, Political Economy*. 2nd edn. New York: Routledge.

Boserup, Ester. 1965. *The Conditions of Agricultural Growth*. New York: Aldine.

———. 1970. *Women's Role in Economic Development*. New York: St Martin's Press.

———. 1981. *Population and Technological Change: A Study of Long Term Trends*. Chicago: University of Chicago Press.

Bowen, John R. 2000. 'Should we have a universal concept of "indigenous peoples" rights? Ethnicity and essentialism in the twenty-first century'. *Anthropology Today* 16 (4): 12–16.

Braveman, P. 2006. 'Health disparities and health equity: Concepts and measurement'. *Annual Review of Public Health* 27: 167–94.

———, and S. Gruskin. 2003a. 'Defining equity in health'. *Journal of Epidemiology and Community Health* 57: 254–8.

———, and ———. 2003b. 'Poverty, equity, human rights and health'. *Bulletin of the World Health Organization* 81: 539–45.

Bray, D., L. Merino-Pérez, P. Negreros-Castillo, et al. 'Mexico's community-managed forests as a global model for sustainable landscapes'. *Conservation Biology* 17 (3): 672–7.

Brenner, R. 1978. 'The origins of capitalist development: A critique of neo-Smithian Marxism'. *New Left Review* I/104 (March/April).

Briggs, A. 1963. 'Technology and economic development'. In *Technology and Development*, 3–18. *Scientific American*. New York: Alfred A. Knopf.

Bringa, T. 2003. *Returning Home: Revival of a Bosnian Village*. Documentary film.

Brown, T.M., M. Cueto, and E. Fee. 2006. 'The World Health Organization and the transition from "international" to "global" public health'. *American Journal of Public Health* 96 (1): 62–72.

Browne, S. 2006. *Aid and Influence: Do Donors Help or Hinder?* London: Earthscan.

Brownlee, Jason. 2002. 'And yet they persist: Explaining survival and transition in neopatrimonial regimes'. *Studies in Comparative International Development* 37 (3): 35–63.

Brown-Syed, C. 1993. 'The new world order and the geopolitics of information'. *LIBRES: Library and Information Science Research*. 1999 edition available at http://valinor.ca/csyed_libres3.html# Unesco.

Bryce, J., R.E. Black, N. Walker, et al. 2005. 'Can the world afford to save the lives of 6 million children each year?' *Lancet* 365 (9,478): 2, 193–200.

Brydon, L. 2006. 'Ethical practices in doing development research'. In V. Desai and R.B. Potter, eds, *Doing Development Research*, 25–33. London: Sage.

Buchert, L. 2002. 'Towards new partnerships in sector-wide approaches: Comparative experiences from Burkina Faso, Ghana and Mozambique'.

International Journal of Educational Development 22 (1): 69–84.

Bunting, M. 2005. 'The world pays a heavy price for our cheap Christmas miracles'. *The Guardian Unlimited*, 19 December. http://www.guardian.co.uk/comment/story/0,,1670279,00.html.

Burnell, P. 1997. *Foreign Aid in a Changing World*. Buckingham, UK: Open University Press.

Caldeira, Teresa P.R., and James Holston. 1999. 'Democracy and violence in Brazil'. *Comparative Studies in Society and History* 41 (4): 691–729.

Callan, Eamonn. 1997. *Creating Citizens: Political Education and Liberal Democracy*. Oxford: Clarendon.

Cammack, P. 2004. 'What the World Bank means by poverty reduction and why it matters'. *New Political Economy* 9 (2): 189–211.

Cardoso, F.H. 2007. *The Accidental President of Brazil: A Memoir*. Washington: Perseus.

Carruthers, David. 2001. 'From opposition to orthodoxy: The remaking of sustainable development'. *Journal of Third World Studies* 18 (2): 93–112.

Case, A., C. Paxson, and J. Ableidinger. 2004. 'Orphans in Africa: Parental death, poverty, and school enrolment'. *Demography* 41: 483–508.

Cassen, R. 1994. *Does Aid Work?* Oxford: Clarendon.

Castells, Manuel. 1996. *The Information Age: Economy, Society and Culture*, vol. 1: *The Rise of the Network Society*. Cambridge, MA: Blackwell.

———. 1999. 'Information technology, globalization and social development'. UNRISD Discussion Paper no. 114, September.

———. 2000. *The Information Age: Economy, Society and Culture*, vol. 1: *The Rise of the Network Society*. 2nd edn. Cambridge, MA: Blackwell.

Caufield, Catherine. 1996. *Masters of Illusion: The World Bank and the Poverty of Nations*. New York: Henry Holt.

Cayford, Steven. 1996. 'The Ogoni uprising: Oil, human rights and a democratic alternative in Nigeria'. *Africa Today* 43(2): 183–98.

CCIC (Canadian Council for International Co-operation). 2004. *Code of Ethics*. http://www.ccic.ca/e/docs/002_ethics_code.pdf. Ottawa: CCIC.

———. 2005. *A Summary Report of a CCIC-NSI Conference on 'The Politics of the Millennium Development Goals'*. www.ccic.ca. Ottawa: CCIC.

Center for Global Development. 2007. *Commitment to Development Index 2007*. Washington: Center for Global Development.

Cerny, P.G., G. Menz, and S. Soederberg. 2005. 'Different roads to globalization: Neoliberalism, the competition state, and politics in a more open world'. In S. Soederberg, G. Menz, and P.G. Cerny, eds, *Internalizing Globalization: The Rise of Neoliberalism and the Decline of National Varieties of Capitalism*, 1–30. Houndmills, UK: Palgrave Macmillan.

Chambers, R. 1983. *Rural Development: Putting the Last First*. London: Longman.

———. 1997a. 'Responsible well-being: A personal agenda for development'. *World Development* 25 (11): 1,743–54.

———. 1997b. *Whose Reality Counts? Putting the Last First*. London: Intermediate Technology Publications.

Chang, Ha-Joon. 2002. *Kicking Away the Ladder: Development Strategy in Historical Perspective*. London: Anthem Press.

———. 2003. *Rethinking Development Economics*. London: Anthem Press.

———, and Ilene Grabel. 2004. *Reclaiming Development: An Alternative Economic Policy Manual*. London: Zed Books.

Chen, L., T. Evans, S. Anand, et al. 2004. 'Human resources for health: Overcoming the crisis'. *Lancet* 364: 1,984–90.

Chen, L., and V. Narasimhan. 2003. 'A human security agenda for global health'. In L. Chen, J. Leaning, and V. Narasimhan, eds, *Global Health Challenges for Human Security*, 3–12. Cambridge, MA: Global Equity Initiative, Asia Center, Harvard University.

Chen, S., and M. Ravallion. 2004. 'How have the world's poorest fared since the early 1980s?'. *World Bank Research Observer* 19 (2): 141–69.

———, and ———. 2007. *Absolute Poverty Measures for the Developing World, 1981–2004*. Washington: Development Research Group, World Bank. http://siteresources.worldbank.org/INTDECINEQ/Resources/AbsolutePovertyMeasures.pdf.

Chenery, H., M.S. Ahluwalia, C.L.G. Bell, et al. 1974. *Redistribution with Growth*. London: Oxford University Press.

Cheru, F. 2001. *Economic, Social and Cultural Rights: The Highly Indebted Poor Countries (HIPC) Initiative:*

A Human Rights Assessment of the Poverty Reduction Strategy Papers (PRSP). E/CN.4/2001/56. Geneva: UN Economic and Social Council.

Chirac, P., and E. Torreele. 2006. 'Global framework on essential health R&D'. *Lancet* 367: 1,560–1.

Chopra, M., and I. Darnton-Hill. 2004. 'Tobacco and obesity epidemics: Not so different after all?' *British Medical Journal* 328: 1,558–60.

Chun, Lin. 2006. *The Transformation of Chinese Socialism*. Durham, NC: Duke University Press.

Clapham, Christopher. 1996. *Africa in the International System: The Politics of State Survival*. Cambridge: Cambridge University Press.

Clapp, Jennifer, and Peter Dauvergne. 2005. *Paths to a Green World: The Political Economy of the Global Environment*. Cambridge, MA: MIT Press.

Clayton, T., ed. 2006. *Re-thinking Hegemony*. Melbourne: James Nicholas.

Cobridge, S. 1993. 'Ethics in development studies: The example of debt'. In F. Schuurman, ed., *Beyond the Impasse: New Directions in Development Theory*, 123–39. London: Zed Books.

Coes, Donald V. 2005. 'Income distribution trends in Brazil and China'. Unpublished paper. Presented at the University of Illinois/University of Manchester/Universidade de São Paulo Conference on Regulation, Competition, and Income Distribution, Paraty, Brazil, 18–21 November. http://www.competition-regulation.org.uk/conferences/Brazil/Papers/Coes.

Cohen, S.F. 2000. *Failed Crusade: America and the Tragedy of Post-communist Russia*. New York: W.W. Norton.

Collier, D., and S. Levitsky. 1997. 'Democracy with adjectives: Conceptual innovation in comparative research'. *World Politics* 49 (3): 430–51.

Collier, P. 2007. *The Bottom Billion*. Oxford: Oxford University Press.

———, V.L. Elliott, H. Hegre, et al. 2003. *Breaking the Conflict Trap: Civil War and Development Policy*. Washington: World Bank.

Collins, Jane L. 1995. 'Smallholder settlement of tropical South America: The social causes of ecological destruction'. In V.K. Pillai and L.W. Shannon, eds, *Developing Areas: A Book of Readings*, 453–67. Oxford: Berg.

Commission for Africa. 2005. *Our Common Interest: Report of the Commission for Africa*. London: Commission for Africa. http://www.commissionforafrica.org/english/report/thereport/english/11-03-05_cr_report.pdf.

Commission on Macroeconomics and Health. 2001. *Macroeconomics and Health: Investing in Health for Economic Development*. Geneva: World Health Organization.

Cook, D. 2006. 'Ways to fight the AIDS pandemic' (interview with Stephen Lewis, UN special envoy for AIDS). *Africa Report* October: 109–11.

Cook, Joanne, and Jennifer Roberts. 2000. 'Towards a gendered political economy'. In Joanne Cook, Jennifer Roberts, and Georgina Waylen, eds, *Towards a Gendered Political Economy*. London: Macmillan.

———, ———, and Georgina Waylen, eds. 2000. *Towards a Gendered Political Economy*. London: Macmillan.

Cooke, B., and U. Kothari. 2001. *Participation: The New Tyranny?* London: Zed Books.

Coombs, P.H. 1985. *The World Crisis in Education: The View from the Eighties*. New York: Oxford University Press.

Cooper, Frederick. 1997. 'Modernizing bureaucrats, backward Africans, and the development concept'. In F. Cooper and R. Packard, eds, *International Development and the Social Sciences: Essays on the History and Politics of Knowledge*, 64–92. Berkeley: University of California Press.

———. 2006. 'A parting of the ways: Colonial Africa and South Africa, 1946–48'. *African Studies* 65 (1): 27–44.

———, Thomas C. Holt, and Rebecca J. Scott. 2000. *Beyond Slavery: Explorations in Race, Labor, and Citizenship in Postemancipation Societies*. Chapel Hill: University of North Carolina Press.

Cornia, G.A., R. Jolly, and F. Stewart, eds. 1987. *Adjustment with a Human Face*, vol. 1: *Protecting the Vulnerable and Promoting Growth*. Oxford: Clarendon.

Cowen, M., and R.W. Shenton. 1996. *Doctrines of Development*. London and New York: Routledge.

Cox, R.W. 1999. 'Civil society at the turn of the millennium: Prospects for an alternative world order'. *Review of International Studies* 25: 3–28.

Cramer, C. 2002. 'Homo economicus goes to war: Methodological individualism, rational choice and the political economy of war'. *World Development* 30 (11): 1,845–64.

————. 2006. *Civil War Is Not a Stupid Thing Accounting for Violence in Developing Countries.* London: Hurst.

CRS (Congressional Research Service). 2006. *United Nations System Funding: Congressional Issues.* Washington: CRS.

Crush, J. 1995. 'Introduction: Imagining development'. In J. Crush, ed., *Power of Development,* 1–23. London and New York: Routledge.

Cumings, B. 1999. 'Webs with no spiders and spiders with no webs: The genealogy of the developmental state'. In Meredith Woo-Cumings, ed., *The Developmental State.* Ithaca, NY: Cornell University Press.

Dahl, G., and G. Megerssa. 1997. 'The spiral of the Ram's horn: Boran concepts of development'. In M. Rahnema and V. Bawtree, eds, *The Post-development Reader,* 51–64. Atlantic Highland, NJ: Zed Books.

Dakar Framework for Action. http://unesdoc.unesco.org/images/0012/001211/121147e.pdf.

Darbon, Dominique. 1995. 'Une transaction démocratique: Le "miracle" de la refondation'. *Temps modernes* 585: 294–313.

Darity, W., and B. Horn. 1988. *The Loan Pushers: The Role of Commercial Banks in the International Debt Crisis.* Cambridge, MA: Ballinger–Harper and Row.

Davies, L. 1993. 'Teachers as implementers or subversives'. *International Journal of Educational Development* 13 (1): 161–70.

Davis, M. 2006. *Planet of Slums.* London: Verso.

Deaton, A. 2006. 'Global patterns of income and health'. *WIDER Angle* 2006 (2): 1–3.

Delang, Claudio. 2005. 'The political ecology of deforestation in Thailand'. *Geography* 90 (3): 225–37.

Demmer, Christine. 2007. 'Autochtonie, nickel et environnement: Une nouvelle stratégie Kanake. *Vacarme* 39 (printemps): 43–8.

Department of Vaccines and Biologicals, World Health Organization. 2002. *State of the World's Vaccines and Immunization.* Geneva and New York: WHO, UNICEF.

De Savigny, D., H. Kasale, C. Mbuya, et al. 2004. *Fixing Health Systems.* Ottawa: International Development Research Centre.

Desmarais, Annette Aurélie. 2007. *La Vía Campesina: Globalization and the Power of Peasants.* Halifax: Fernwood; London: Pluto Press.

De Soto, Hernandez. 2000. *The Mystery of Capital: Why Capitalism Triumphs in the West and Fails Everywhere Else.* New York: Basic Books.

DeStefano, J., A.M. Schuh Moore, and A. Hartwell. 2006. 'Meeting EFA: Reaching the underserved through complementary models of effective schooling'. EQUIP 2 Working Paper. Washington: USAID. http://www.equip123.net/docs/e2-MeetingEFASynth_WP.pdf.

Detienne, Marcel. 2003. *Comment être autochtone: Du pur athénien au français raciné.* Paris: Seuil.

De Vogli, R., and G.L. Birbeck. 2005. 'Potential impact of adjustment policies on vulnerability of women and children to HIV/AIDS in sub-Saharan Africa'. *Journal of Health Nutrition and Population* 23: 105–20.

Deyo, Frederic C., ed. 1987. *The Political Economy of the New Asian Industrialism.* Ithaca, NY: Cornell University Press.

Dhaouadi, M. 1988. 'An operational analysis of the phenomenon of the other underdevelopment in the Arab world and in the Third World'. *International Sociology* 3 (3): 219–34.

Diamond, Jared M. 1997. *Guns, Germs, and Steel: The Fates of Human Societies.* New York: W.W. Norton.

Diamond, Larry. 2002. 'Thinking about hybrid regimes'. *Journal of Democracy* 13 (2): 21–35.

Diderichsen, F., T. Evans, and M. Whitehead. 2001. 'The social basis of disparities in health'. In M. Whitehead, et al., eds, *Challenging Inequities in Health: From Ethics to Action,* 13–23. New York: Oxford University Press.

Diffie, Bailey W., and George D. Winius. 1977. *Foundations of the Portuguese Empire, 1415–1580.* Minneapolis: University of Minnesota Press.

Dirlik, A. 1997. *The Postcolonial Aura: Third World Criticism in the Age of Global Capitalism.* Boulder, CO: Westview.

Djurfeldt, G., H. Holmér, M. Jirstrom, et al., eds. 2005. *The African Food Crisis: Lessons from the Asian Green Revolution.* London: CABI.

Dollar, David. 2002. 'Spreading the wealth'. *Foreign Affairs* 81 (1): 120–33.

Dower, Nigel. 1998. *World Ethics: The New Agenda.* Edinburgh: Edinburgh University Press.

Doyle, Michael W. 1983. 'Kant, liberal legacies, and foreign affairs', parts 1 and 2. *Philosophy and Public Affairs* 12: 205–35, 324–53.

————. 2006. 'One world, many peoples: International justice in John Rawls's *The Law of Peoples*'. *Perspectives on Politics* 4 (1): 109–20.

————, and Nicholas Sambanis. 2006. *Making War and Building Peace: United Nations Peace Operations*. Princeton, NJ: Princeton University Press.

Drake, Paul. 1989. 'Debt and democracy in Latin America, 1920–1980s'. In Barbara Stallings and Robert Kaufman, *Debt and Democracy in Latin America*, 43. Boulder, CO: Westview.

Dreier, P., J. Mollenkopf, and T. Swanstrom. 2001. *Place Matters: Metropolitics for the Twenty-first Century*. Lawrence: University of Kansas Press.

Dryzek, John S. 2005. *The Politics of the Earth: Environmental Discourses*. 2nd edn. New York: Oxford University Press.

Duffield, M. 2001. *Global Governance and the New Wars*. London: Zed Books.

Dunning, John. H. 1993. *Multinational Enterprises and the Global Economy*. Reading, MA: Addison-Wesley.

During, S. 1993. 'Introduction'. In S. During, ed., *The Cultural Studies Reader*, 1–25. London and New York: Routledge.

Durston, J. 1999. 'Building community social capital'. *CEPAL Review* 69: 103–18.

Dwivedi, Ranjit. 2001. 'Environmental movements in the Global South: Issues of livelihood and beyond'. *International Sociology* 16 (1): 11–31.

Easterly, William. 2001. *The Effect of International Monetary Fund and World Bank Programs on Poverty*. Washington: World Bank.

————. 2006. *The White Man's Burden: Why the West's Efforts to Aid the Rest Have Done So Much Ill and So Little Good*. New York: Penguin.

————, ed. 2008. *Reinventing Foreign Aid*. Cambridge, MA: MIT Press.

ECLAC (Economic Commission for Latin America and the Caribbean). 2000. *Social Panorama of Latin America 1999–2000*. Santiago: ECLAC.

Economist, The. 2005a. 'The real digital divide'. 12 March: 9.

————. 2005b. 'Economics focus: Calling across the divide'. 12 March: 9.

Eden, Lorraine. 1991. 'Bringing the firm back in: Multinationals in international political economy'. *Millennium: Journal of International Studies* 20 (2): 197–224.

Eichengreen, Barry, and Peter Lindert. 1989. *The International Debt Crisis in Historical Perspective*. Cambridge, MA: MIT Press.

Ellis, F. 2000. *Rural Livelihoods and Diversity in Developing Countries*. Oxford: Oxford University Press.

————, and S. Biggs. 2001. 'Evolving themes in rural development: 1950s–2000s'. *Development Policy Review* 19 (4): 437–48.

Emmanuel, A. 1969. *Unequal Trade: A Study in the Imperialism of Trade*. London: New Left Books.

Escobar, A. 1995a. *Encountering Development: The Making and Unmaking of the Third World*. Princeton, NJ: Princeton University Press.

————. 1995b. 'Imagining a post-development era'. In J. Crush, *Power of Development*, 211–27. London: Routledge.

————. 1997. 'The making and the unmaking of the Third World through development'. In M. Rahnema, and V. Bawtree, eds, *The Post-development Reader*, 85–93. Atlantic Highland, NJ: Zed Books.

————, and Sonia Alvarez, eds. 1992. *The Making of Social Movements in Latin America: Identity, Strategy and Democracy*. Boulder, CO: Westview.

Esping-Andersen, Gøsta. 1990. *The Three Worlds of Welfare Capitalism*. Princeton, NJ: Princeton University Press.

Esteva, Gustavo, and Madhu Suri Prakash. 1997. 'From global thinking to local thinking'. In Majid Rahnema and Victoria Bawtree, eds, *The Post-Development Reader*, 277–89. Atlantic Highland, NJ: Zed Books.

————, and ————. 2006. 'From global thinking to local thinking'. In M. Rahnema and V. Bawtree, eds, *The Post-Development Reader*. Atlantic Highland, NJ: Zed Books.

EU Commission. 2007. http://ec.europa.eu/development/ICenter/Pdf/COMM_PDF_COM_2007_0100_F_EN_ACTE.pdf.

Evans Peter. 1979. *Dependent Development: The Alliance of Multinational, State and Local Capital in Brazil*. Princeton, NJ: Princeton University Press.

————. 1995. *Embedded Autonomy: States and Industrial Transformation*. Princeton, NJ: Princeton University Press.

Ezzati, M., S. Vander Hoorn, C.M.M. Lawes, et al. 'Rethinking the "diseases of affluence" paradigm: Global patterns of nutritional risks in relation to economic development'. *PLoS Medicine* 2 (5).

Falquet, Jules. 2003. 'L'ONU, alliée des femmes? Une analyse féministe critique du système des organisations internationales'. http://multitudes.samizdat.net/article112.html.

FAO (Food and Agriculture Organization). 2004. *Globalization of Food Systems in Developing Countries: Impact on Food Security and Nutrition*. Rome: FAO.

——. 2006. *The State of Food Insecurity in the World 2006*. Rome: FAO.

——. 2007. *Information Sheet: Division of Labour. Gender and Food Security*. http://www.fao.org/Gender/en/lab-e.htm.

Farmer, P. 2003. *Pathologies of Power: Health, Human Rights and the New War on the Poor*. Berkeley: University of California Press.

Farrell, J.P. 1999. 'Changing conceptions of equality of education: Forty years of comparative evidence'. In R.F. Arnove and C.A. Torres, eds, *Comparative Education: The Dialectic of the Global and the Local*. Lanham, MD: Rowman and Littlefield.

Feachem, R.G.A. 2001. 'Globalisation is good for your health, mostly'. *British Medical Journal* 323: 504–6.

Fearon, J.D., and D.D. Laitin. 2003. 'Ethnicity, insurgency, and civil war'. *American Political Science Review* 97 (1): 75–90.

Femia, J.V. 1981. *Gramsci's Political Thought: Hegemony, Consciousness, and the Revolutionary Process*. Oxford: Clarendon.

Ferguson, J. 1992. 'De-moralizing economies, African socialism, scientific capitalism and the moral politics of structural adjustment'. Paper presented to the Conference of the Canadian Association for the Study of International Development, Charlottetown.

——. 1994. *The Anti-Politics Machine: 'Development,' Depoliticization, and Bureaucratic Power in Lesotho*. Cambridge: Cambridge University Press.

Field, M.G. 2000. 'The health and demographic crisis in post-Soviet Russia: A two-phase development'. In M.G. Field and J.L. Twigg, *Russia's Torn Safety Nets: Health and Social Welfare during the Transition*, 11–42. New York: St Martin's Press.

——, D.M. Kotz, and G. Bukhman. 2000. 'Neoliberal economic policy, "state desertion," and the Russian health crisis'. In J.Y. Kim, et al., *Dying for Growth: Global Inequality and the Health of the Poor*, 155–73. Monroe, ME: Common Courage Press.

Fink, C. 2006. 'Intellectual property and public health: The WTO's August 2003 decision in perspective'. In R. Newfarmer, ed., *Trade, Doha, and Development: A Window Into the Issues*, 187–95. Washington: World Bank.

Fiske, Jo-Anne, and Evelyn George. 2006. *Seeking Alternatives to Bill C-31: From Cultural Trauma to Cultural Revitalization through Customary Law*. Ottawa: Status of Women Canada. http://www.swc-cfc.gc.ca/pubs/pubspr/066243773X/200609_066243773X_1_e.pdf (accessed 23 September 2007).

Fleras, Augie, and Paul Spoonley. 1999. *Recalling Aotearoa: Indigenous Politics and Ethnic Relations in New Zealand*. Auckland: Oxford University Press.

Floro, M., and G. Dymski. 2000. 'Financial crisis, gender, and power: An analytical framework'. *World Development* 28: 1,269–83.

Forbes. 2007. 'Special report: The world's billionaires'. 8 March. http://www.forbes.com/lists/2007/10/07billionaires_The-Worlds-Billionaires_Rank.html.

Forero, J., and P.S. Goodman. 2007. 'Continental drift towards Venezuela'. *The Guardian Weekly* 30 March. http://www.guardian.co.uk/guardianweekly/outlook/story/0,,2044793,00.html.

Forestier, E., J. Grace, and C. Kenny. 2003. 'Can information and communication technologies be pro-poor?' *Telecommunications Policy* 26: 623–46.

Forsyth, Tim. 2002. 'The brown environmental agenda'. In V. Desai and R. Potter, eds, *The Companion to Development Studies*, 294–7. New York: Arnold Press.

Fourie, P. 2007. 'The relationship between the AIDS pandemic and state fragility'. *Global Change, Peace and Security* 19: 281–300.

Frank, Andre Gunder. 1969. *Capitalism and Underdevelopment in Latin America*. New York: Monthly Review Press.

——. 1972. *Lumpenbourgeoisie: Lumpendevelopment*. New York: Monthly Review Press.

——. 1991. 'The underdevelopment of development'. *Scandinavian Journal of Development Alternatives* 10 (3: special issue): 5–72.

Fraser, Arvonne S., and Irene Tinker. 2004. *Developing Power: How Women Transformed International Development*. New York: Feminist Press.

Freeman, A. 2004. 'The inequality of nations'. In Alan Freeman and Boris Kagarlitzky, eds, *The Politics of Empire*. London: Pluto.

Freeman, T., and S.D. Faure. 2003. *Local Solutions to Global Challenges: Towards Effective Partnership in Basic Education*. The Hague: Netherlands Ministry of Foreign Affairs.

Freund, Charles Paul. 2002. 'In praise of vulgarity: How commercial culture liberates Islam—and the West'. March. http://www.reason.com/news/show/28344.html (accessed 21 September 2007).

Fridell, G. 2007. *Fair Trade Coffee: The Prospects and Pitfalls of Market-Driven Social Justice*. Toronto: University of Toronto Press.

Fridell, M., I. Hudson, and M. Hudson. 2008. 'With friends like these: The corporate response to fair trade coffee'. *Review of Radical Political Economics* 40 (1).

Friedman, M. 1962. *Capitalism and Freedom*. Chicago: University of Chicago Press.

Friedman, T.L. 2005. *The World Is Flat: A Brief History of the Twenty-First Century*. New York: Farrar, Strauss and Giroux.

Fritz, Jean-Claude, and Myriam Fritz-Legendre. 2005. 'Les mutations de la question indigène: De "l'indigène" à "l'autochtone": Mise en perspective historique'. In Jean-Claude Fritz et al., *La nouvelle question indigène: Peuples autochtones et ordre mondial*, 23–46. Paris: L'Harmattan.

Fröbel, F., J. Heinrichs, and O. Kreye. 1980. *The New International Division of Labour*. Cambridge: Cambridge University Press.

Frohlich, K.L., N. Ross, and C. Richmond. 2006. 'Health disparities in Canada today: Some evidence and a theoretical framework'. *Health Policy* 79: 132–43.

Fry, G., and G.R. Martin, eds. 1991. *The International Development Dictionary*. Santa Barbara, CA: ABC-CLIO.

Fukuyama, F. 1992. *The End of History and the Last Man*. London: Hamish Hamilton.

———. 1995. *Trust: The Social Virtues and the Creation of Prosperity*. New York: Free Press.

Fuller, B. 1991. *Growing up Modern: The Western State Builds Third World Schools*. New York and London: Routledge.

———, and R. Rubinson. 1992. 'Does the state expand schooling? A review of the evidence'. In B. Fuller and R. Rubinson, eds, *The Political Construction of Education*. New York: Praeger.

Fung, A., and E.O. Wright. 2003. *Deepening Democracy: Institutional Innovations in Empowered Participatory Governance*. London: Verso.

Furtado, C. 1976. *Economic Development of Latin America*. Cambridge: Cambridge University Press.

G-8. 2000. 'Global Poverty Report'. Okinawa Summit, July. http://www.worldbank.org/html/extdr/extme/G8_poverty2000.pdf.

Garnham, N. 1998. 'Political economy and cultural studies: Reconciliation or divorce?' In J. Storey, ed., *Cultural Theory and Popular Culture: A Reader*, 2nd edn, 604–12. Hemel Hempstead, UK: Prentice Hall.

Gasper, Des. 1986. 'Distribution and development ethics: A tour'. In R. Apthorpe and A. Krahl, eds, *Development Studies: Critique and Renewal*, 136–203. Leiden, Netherlands: E.J. Brill.

———. 1999. 'Ethics and the conduct of international development aid: Charity and obligation'. Institute of Social Studies Working Paper Series no. 297. The Hague: Institute of Social Studies.

———. 2005. 'Beyond the international relations framework: An essay in descriptive global ethics'. *Journal of Global Ethics* 1 (1): 5–23.

Gasser, R. 2007. *UN and Business: Where Do We Stand?* Geneva: Centre for Applied Studies in International Negotiations, Programme on Global Issues and Civil Society.

Geertz, C. 1973. *The Interpretation of Cultures*. New York: Basic Books.

Gellner, E. 1983. *Nations and Nationalism*. Ithaca, NY: Cornell University Press.

George, S. 1988. *A Fate Worse Than Debt*. New York: Grove Press.

———, and F. Sabelli. 1994. *Faith and Credit: The World Bank's Secular Empire*. Boulder, CO: Westview.

Gereffi, Gary, and Miguel Korzeniewicz, eds. 1994. *Commodity Chains and Global Capitalism*. Westport, CT: Greenwood.

———, and Donald L. Wyman. 1990. *Manufacturing Miracles: Paths of Industrialization in Latin*

America and East Asia. Princeton, NJ: Princeton University Press.

Gerschenkron, Alexander. 1962. *Economic Backwardness in Historical Perspective*. Cambridge, MA: Belknap Press.

Gibbs, T. 2006. 'Business as unusual: What the Chávez era tells us about democracy under globalisation'. *Third World Quarterly* 27 (2): 265–79.

Gibson, Clark, Margaret A. McKean, and Elinor Ostrom. 2000. *People and Forests: Communities, Institutions, and Governance*. Cambridge, MA: MIT Press.

Gibson-Graham, J.K. 2005. 'Building community economies: Women and the politics of place'. In Wendy Harcourt and Arturo Escobar, eds, *Women and the Politics of Place*. Bloomfield, CT: Kumarian Press.

Gilgan, M. 2001. 'The rationality of resistance: Alternative for engagement in complex emergencies'. *Disasters* 25 (1): 1–18.

Gill, S. 2003. 'National in/security on a universal scale'. In I. Bakker and S. Gills, eds, *Power, Production and Social Reproduction*, 208–23. New York: Palgrave Macmillan.

Gilman, N. 2003. *Mandarins of the Future: Modernization Theory in Cold War America*. Baltimore, MD: Johns Hopkins University Press.

Gilpin, Robert. 1975. *U.S. Power and the Multinational Corporation: The Political Economy of Foreign Direct Investment*. New York: Basic Books.

Glassman, A., M. Reich, K. Laserson, et al. 1999. 'Political analysis of health reform in the Dominican Republic'. *Health Policy Plan* 14: 115–26.

Global Forum for Health Research. 2004. *The 10/90 Report on Health Research, 2003–2004*. Geneva: Global Forum for Health Research.

Göçmen, Dogan. 2007. *The Adam Smith Problem: Reconciling Human Nature and Society in* The Theory of Moral Sentiments *and* The Wealth of Nations. London: Tauris Academic Studies.

Goldman, M. 2005. *Imperial Nature: The World Bank and Struggles for Social Justice in the Age of Globalization*. New Haven, CT: Yale University Press.

Goodhand, Jonathan. 2006. *Aiding Peace? The Role of NGOs in Armed Conflict*. Bourton on Dunsmore, Rugby, UK: ITDG.

Gordon, Raymond G., Jr, ed. 2005. *Ethnologue: Languages of the World*. 15th edn. Dallas, TX: SIL International.

Gore, C. 2004. 'MDGs and PRSPs: Are poor countries enmeshed in a global-local double bind?' *Global Social Policy* 4: 277–83.

Gosovic, B. 2000. 'Global intellectual hegemony and the international development agenda'. *International Social Science Journal* 166: 447–57.

Goulet, Denis. 1971. *The Cruel Choice: A New Concept in the Theory of Development*. New York: Atheneum.

Government of Norway. 2006. *The Soria Moria Declaration on International Policy*, chapter 2: 'International policy'. Oslo. http://odin.dep.no/smk/english/government/government/001001-990363/dok-bn.html.

Gowan, P. 1999. *The Global Gamble: Washington's Faustian Bid for World Dominance*. London: Verso.

Gramsci, Antonio. 1971. *Selections from the Prison Notebooks*. Quintin Hoare and Geoffrey Nowell Smith, trans. New York, International Publishers.

Grant, H. 2006. 'From the Transvaal to the Prairies: The migration of South African physicians to Canada'. *Journal of Ethnic and Migration Studies* 32: 681–95.

Gray, Andrew, Alejandro Prellada, and Hellen Newing. 1998. *From Principles to Practice: Indigenous Peoples and Biodiversity Conservation in Latin America*. Copenhagen: IWGIA.

Greenland, Hauraki. 1991. 'Maori ethnicity as ideology'. In Paul Spoonley, David Pearson, and Cluny MacPherson, eds, *Nga Take: Ethnic Relations and Racism in Aotearoa/New Zealand*, 90–107. Palmerston North, NZ: Dunmore Press.

Griffith-Jones, S., and B. Stallings. 1995. 'New global financial trends: Implications for development'. In B. Stallings, ed., *Global Change, Regional Response: The New International Context of Development*, 143–73. Cambridge: Cambridge University Press.

Grindle, M.S. 1996. *Challenging the State: Crisis and Innovation in Latin America and Africa*. Cambridge: Cambridge University Press.

Grinter, L. 1975. 'How they lost: Doctrines, strategies and outcomes of the Vietnam War'. *Asian Survey* 15: 12.

Grossberg, L. 1998. 'Cultural studies vs. political economy: Is anybody else bored with this debate?' In J. Storey, ed., *Cultural Theory and Popular Culture: A Reader*, 2nd edn, 613–24. Hemel Hempstead, UK: Prentice Hall.

Grossman, G., and A. Krueger. 1995. 'Economic growth and the environment'. *Quarterly Journal of Economics* 110 (2): 353–377.

Guha, Ramachandra. 1989. *The Unquiet Woods: Ecological Change and Peasant Resistance in the Himalaya*. London: Oxford University Press.

Guilmoto, Christophe Z., and P.M. Kulkarni. 2004. 'Les femmes, la caste et l'état: Cinquante ans de planification familiale en Inde'. In A. Gautier, ed., *Les politiques de planification familiale: Cinq expériences nationales*, 25–74. Paris: DEPED.

Gurr, T. 1970. *Why Men Rebel*. Princeton, NJ: Princeton University Press.

Gwatkin, D., K. Johnson, A. Wagstaff, et al. 2000. 'Socio-economic differences in health, nutrition and population: 45 countries'. http://poverty2. forumone.com/library/view/15080.

Haakonsson, S.J., and L.A. Richey. 2007. 'TRIPs and public health: The Doha Declaration in Africa'. *Development Policy Review* 25 (1): 71–90.

Haggard, Stephan. 1990. *Pathways from the Periphery: The Politics of Growth in the Newly Industrializing Countries*. Ithaca, NY: Cornell University Press.

Hall, J.J., and R. Taylor. 2003. 'Health for all beyond 2000: The demise of the Alma-Ata Declaration and primary health care in developing countries'. *Medical Journal of Australia* 178 (1): 17–20.

Hall, Peter. 1989. *The Political Power of Economic Ideas: Keynesianism across Nations*. Princeton, NJ: Princeton University Press.

Hall, S., ed. 1997. *Representation: Cultural Representations and Signifying Practices*. London: The Open University.

———. 1998. 'Notes on deconstructing "the popular"'. In J. Storey, ed., *Cultural Theory and Popular Culture: A Reader*, 2nd edn, 442–53. Hemel Hempstead, UK: Prentice Hall.

Hanlon, J. 2006. '"Illegitimate" loans: Lenders, not borrowers, are responsible'. *Third World Quarterly* 27 (2): 211–26.

Hansen, S.J. 2003. 'Warlords and peace strategies: The case of Somalia'. *Journal of Conflict Studies* 22 (2).

Harcourt, Wendy, and Arturo Escobar. 2005. *Women and the Politics of Place*. Bloomfield, CT: Kumarian Press.

Hardin, Garrett. 1968. 'The tragedy of the commons'. *Science* 162: 1,243–8.

Hardt, Michael, and Antonio Negri. 2000. *Empire*. Cambridge, MA: Harvard University Press.

Harriss, John. 2001. *Depoliticising Development: The World Bank and Social Capital*. New Delhi: Left Word Books.

———, Janet Hunter, and Colin M. Lewis, eds. 1995. *The New Institutional Economics and Third World Development*. London: Routledge.

Hart-Landsberg, M., and P. Burkett. 2005. *China and Socialism: Market Reforms and Class Struggle*. New York: Monthly Review Press.

Harvey, David. 1990. *The Condition of Postmodernity: An Enquiry into the Origins of Cultural Change*. Oxford: Blackwell.

———. 1993. 'The nature of environment: Dialectics of social and environmental change'. *Socialist Register* 1–51.

———. 2005. *A Brief History of Neoliberalism*. Oxford: Oxford University Press.

Haslam, Paul Alexander. 2007. 'The firm rules: Multinationals, policy space and neoliberalism'. *Third World Quarterly* 28 (6): 1,167–83.

———. 2008. 'Is there a post-neoliberal policy towards foreign direct investors in Argentina and Chile?'. In L. Macdonald and A. Ruckert, eds, *Post-neoliberalism in the Americas*. New York: Palgrave Macmillan.

Hassan, Rashid, Robert Scholes, and Nevelle Ash, eds. 2005. *Ecosystems and Human Well-Being: Current State and Trends*, vol. 1: *Findings of the Condition and Trends Working Group of the Millennium Ecosytem Assessment*. Washington and London: Island Press.

Hawkes, C. 2005. 'The role of foreign direct investment in the nutrition transition'. *Public Health Nutrition* 8: 357–65.

———. 2006. 'Uneven dietary development: Linking the policies and processes of globalization with the nutrition transition, obesity and diet-related chronic diseases'. *Globalization and Health* 2 (4).

Hayami, Y., and V.W. Ruttan. 1985. *Agricultural Development: An International Perspective*. 2nd edn. Baltimore, MD: Johns Hopkins University Press.

Hayden, Robert. 2002. 'Dictatorships of virtue'. *Harvard International Review* (summer).

Hayter, T., and C. Watson. 1985. *Aid: Rhetoric and Reality*. Hammondsworth, UK: Penguin.

Hechanova, R. 2007. 'The view from the other side: The impact of business process outsourcing on the wellbeing and identity of Filipino call center workers'. Paper presented at the Living the Information Society Conference, 23–24 April 2007, Makati City, Philippines.

Heeks, R. 1999. 'Information and communication technologies, poverty and development'. *Development Informatics* Working Paper no. 5, June.

Hegre, H., T. Ellingsen, S. Gates, et al. 2001. 'Toward a democratic civil peace? Democracy, political change and civil war 1816–1992'. *American Political Science Review* 95 (1): 33–48.

Held, David, and Anthony McGrew. 2003. *The Global Transformations Reader*. 2nd edn. Cambridge: Polity Press.

Helleiner, E. 1994. *States and the Reemergence of Global Finance: From Bretton Woods to the 1990s*. Ithaca, NY: Cornell University Press.

Helsinki Process on Globalization and Democracy. 2007. http://www.helsinkiprocess.fi/.

Hettne, B. 1990. *Development Theory and the Three Worlds*. Harlow, UK: Longman.

Hewett, P.C., and C.B. Lloyd. 'Progress toward education for all: Trends and current challenges for sub-Saharan Africa'. In C. Lloyd et al., *The Changing Transitions to Adulthood in Developing Countries: Selected Studies*, 84–117. Washington: National Academies Press.

Hill, Kevin A. 1996. 'Zimbabwe's wildlife utilization program: Grassroots democracy or an extension of state power?'. *African Studies Review* 39 (1): 103–21.

Hindu, The. 2007. 'New improved rat traps at work'. 30 November.

Hira, Anil. 1998. *Ideas and Economic Policy in Latin America: Regional, National and Organizational Case Studies*. Westport, CT: Greenwood.

———. 2007. *An East Asia Model for Latin America: The New Path*. Burlington, VT: Ashgate.

Hira, Ron, and Anil Hira. 2005. *Outsourcing America*. New York: Amacom.

Hirschman, Albert O. 1971. *A Bias for Hope: Essays on Development and Latin America*. New Haven, CT: Yale University Press.

Hirst, Paul, and Grahame Thompson. 1996. *Globalization in Question: The International Economy and the Possibilities of Governance*. Cambridge: Polity Press.

Hobsbawm, E. 1994. *Age of Extremes: The Short Twentieth Century: 1914–1991*. London: Viking.

Hobson, John A. 1902. *Imperialism: A Study*. London: J. Nisbet.

Holdcroft, L.E. 1976. 'The rise and fall of community development in developing countries, 1950–65: A critical analysis and an annotated bibliography'. MSU Rural Development Papers no. 2. East Lansing: Department of Agricultural Economics, Michigan State University.

Hoogvelt, Antony. 2001. *Globalization and the Postcolonial World: The New Political Economy of Development*. Baltimore, MD: John Hopkins University Press.

Hopkins, S. 2006. 'Economic stability and health status: Evidence from East Asia before and after the 1990s economic crisis'. *Health Policy* 75: 347–57.

Horowitz, D.L. 1985. *Ethnic Groups in Conflict*. Berkeley: University of California Press.

Huber, Evelyne, et al. 2006. 'Politics and inequality in Latin America and the Caribbean'. *American Sociological Review* 71 (6): 943–63.

Huntington, Samuel. 1968. *Political Order in Changing Societies*. New Haven, CT: Yale University Press.

———. 1969. *Political Order in Changing Societies*. New Haven, CT: Yale University Press.

———. 1993a. 'The Clash of Civilizations'. *Foreign Affairs* (summer): 72–3.

———. 1993b. *The Third Wave: Democratization in the Late Twentieth Century*. Norma: University of Oklahoma Press.

Hymer, S. 1972. 'The multinational corporation and the law of uneven development'. In J. Bhagwati, ed., *Economics and the World Order from the 1970s to the 1990s*. New York: Collier-Macmillan.

IFAD (International Fund for Agricultural Development). 2001. *Rural Poverty Report 2001: The Challenge of Ending Rural Poverty*. Oxford, UK: Oxford University Press.

IFBAN (International Baby Food Action Network). http://www.ibfan.org/french/ibfan00-fr.html.

Igoe, Jim. 2004. *Conservation and Globalization: A Study of National Parks and Indigenous Communities from East Africa to South Dakota*. Toronto: Wadsworth/Thomson.

Illich, I. 1997. 'Development as planned poverty'. In R. Majid and V. Bawtree, *The Post-development Reader*. London: Zed Books; Dhaka: University Press; Halifax: Fernwood; Cape Town: David Philip.

IMF (International Monetary Fund). 2001. *External Comments and Contributions and IMF Conditionality*. Washington: IMF.

Imhof, Aviva, Susanne Wong, and Peter Bosshard. 2002. *The Citizen's Guide to the World Commission on Dams*. Berkeley, CA: International Rivers Network.

Inaugural Addresses of the Presidents of the United States. 1989. Washington: US GPO; Bartleby.com, 2001, www.bartleby.com/124 (accessed 11 June 2007).

Independent Evaluation Office, IMF. 2007. *The IMF and Aid to Sub-Saharan Africa*. Washington: International Monetary Fund.

Inkeles, A., and D.H. Smith. 1974. *Becoming Modern: Individual Change in Six Developing Countries*. Cambridge, MA : Harvard University Press.

International Forum on Globalization. 2002. 'Alternatives to economic globalization'. http://www.ifg.org/alt_eng.pdf.

Intven, H., ed. 2000. *Telecommunications Regulations Handbook, Module 6: Universal Service*. Washington: InfoDev, World Bank.

Irwin, R. 2007. 'Culture shock: Negotiating feelings in the field'. *Anthropology Matters* 9 (1). http://anthropologymatters.com/journal/2007-1/irwin_2007_culture.htm (accessed 4 January 2008).

IUCN (International Union for Conservation of Nature and Natural Resources) with UN Environment Programme and World Wide Fund for Nature. *World Conservation Strategy: Living Resource Conservation for Sustainable Development*. IUCN.

IWGIA (International Work Group for Indigenous Affairs). 2007. *The Indigenous World 2007*. Copenhagen: IWGIA.

Jacobsen, K., and L.B. Landau. 2003. 'The dual imperative in refugee research: Some methodological and ethical considerations in social science research on forced migration'. *Disasters* 27 (3): 195–206.

Jaffee, D. 2007. *Brewing Justice: Fair Trade Coffee, Sustainability, and Survival*. Berkeley: University of California Press.

Jamieson, Kathleen. 1986. 'Sex discrimination and the Indian Act'. In Rick Ponting, ed., *Arduous Journey: Canadian Indians and Colonization*, 112–36. Toronto: McClelland and Stewart.

Jansen, J.D. 2005. 'Targeting education: The politics of performance and the prospects of "Education for All"'. *International Journal of Educational Development* 25 (4): 368–80.

Jansen, K., and E. Roquas. 1998. 'Modernizing insecurity: The land titling project in Honduras. *Development and Change* 29: 81–106.

Jayawardena, L. 1990. 'Foreword'. In F. Apffel Marglin and S. Marglin, eds, *Dominating Knowledge: Development, Culture and Resistance*. London: Clarendon.

Jenkins, R. 2004. 'Globalization, production, employment and poverty: Debates and evidence'. *Journal of International Development* 16: 1–12.

Jepma, Catrinus J. 1991. *The Tying of Aid*. Paris: Organisation for Economic Co-operation and Development.

Jha, P., A. Mills, K. Hanson, et al. 2002. 'Improving the health of the global poor'. *Science* 295: 2,036–9.

Johnson, Chalmers. 1982. *MITI and the Japanese Miracle: The Growth of Industrial Policy, 1925–75*. Stanford, CA: Stanford University Press.

Johnson, H., and G. Wilson. 2000. 'Biting the bullet: Civil society, social learning and the transformation of local governance'. *World Development* 28 (11): 7–29.

Jomo, K.S., and Erik Reinert, eds. 2005. *The Origins of Development Economics*. London: Zed Books.

Jones, Charles. 1999. *Global Justice: Defending Cosmopolitanism*. Oxford: Oxford University Press.

Jones, P. 2007. 'Education and world order'. *Comparative Education* 43 (3), 325–37.

Jones, S. 2000. *Of Centaurs and Doves: Guatemala's Peace Process*. Boulder, CO: Westview.

Kabeer, Naila. 2004. 'Globalisation, labour standards and women's rights: Dilemmas of collective (in)action in an interdependent world'. *Feminist Economics* 10 (1): 3–35.

———. 2005. *Objectifs du millénaire pour le développement. Manuel à l'intention des instances de décision et d'intervention*. Québec: Les Presses de l'Université Laval.

———, and S. Mahmud. 2004. 'Globalization, gender and poverty: Bangladeshi women workers in export and local markets'. *Journal of International Development* 16 (1): 93–109.

Kaiser, Jocelyn. 2001. 'Bold corridor project confronts political reality'. *Science* 293 (5,538): 2,196–9.

Kamat, S. 2003. 'NGOs and the new democracy: The false saviours of international development'. *Harvard International Review* (spring).

Kanbur, R., and L. Squire. 1999. 'The evolution of thinking about poverty: Exploring the interactions'. www.people.cornell.edu/pages/sk145/papers. Revised 2001 in G. Meier and J. Stiglitz, eds, *Frontiers of Development Economics*. Oxford: Oxford University Press.

Kaplan, R.D. 1994. 'The coming anarchy'. *The Atlantic Monthly* (February).

Karega, Regina G.M. 2002. *Violence against women in the workforce in Kenya: Assessment of workplace sexual harassment in the commercial agriculture and textile manufacturing in Kenya*. International Labour Rights Fund.

Kauanui, J. Kēhaulani. 2007. 'Diasporic deracination and "off-island" Hawaiians'. *The Contemporary Pacific* 19 (1): 137–60.

Kawachi, I., and S. Wamala. 2007. 'Poverty and inequality in a globalizing world'. In I. Kawachi and S. Wamala, eds, *Globalisation and Health*, 122–37. Oxford: Oxford University Press.

Kay, G. 1975. *Development and Underdevelopment: A Marxist Analysis*. New York: St Martin's Press.

Keck, Margaret E. 1998. *Activists beyond Borders: Advocacy Networks in International Politics*. Ithaca, NY: Cornell University Press.

———, and Kathryn Sikkink. 1999. 'Transnational advocacy networks in international and regional politics'. *International Social Science Journal* 159: 89–101.

Keen, D. 2001. 'The political economy of war'. In Frances Stewart, Valpy Fitzgerald and Associates, eds, *War and Underdevelopment*, vol. 1: *The Economic and Social Consequences of Conflict*. Oxford: Oxford University Press.

Keer, Dhananjay. 2005. *Dr. Ambedkar: Life and Mission*. Mumbai: Popular Prakashan.

Keilly, R. 1995. *Sociology and Development: The Impasse and Beyond*. London: UCL Press.

Kennedy, Paul M. 1977. 'The theory and practice of imperialism'. *The Historical Journal* 20 (3): 761–9.

Kepe, Thembela, Ben Cousins, and Stephen Turner. 2001. 'Resource tenure and power relations in community wildlife: The case of Mkambati area, South Africa'. *Society* 14: 911–25.

Kerala. 2003. 'India marches ahead. . . Kerala calling'. (August): 12. http://www.kerala.gov.in/kerala_callingaug/p12-13.pdf.

Kerry, V.B., and K. Lee. 2007. 'TRIPs, the Doha Declaration and paragraph 6 decision: What are the remaining steps for protecting access to medicines?'. *Globalization and Health* 3 (3).

Keynes, J.M. 1936. *The General Theory of Employment, Interest, and Money*. New York: Harcourt Brace.

Khan, Sona. 2006. 'Imrana ou la sécurité des femmes musulmanes en Inde'. In Christine Ockrent, ed., *Le livre noir de la condition des femmes*, 123–34. Paris: Éditions XO.

Kian-Thiébaut, Azadeh. 2006. 'Les lapidations en Iran'. In Christine Ockrent, ed., *Le livre noir de la condition des femmes*, 109–22. Paris: Éditions XO.

Kickbusch, I., and L. Payne. 2004. 'Constructing global public health in the 21st century'. Paper presented at meeting on Global Health Governance and Accountability, Geneva. http://www.ilonakickbusch.com/en/global-health-governance/GlobalHealth.pdf.

Kim, H., W.J. Chung, Y.J. Song, et al. 2003. 'Changes in morbidity and medical care utilization after the recent economic crisis in the Republic of Korea'. *Bulletin of the World Health Organization* 81: 567–72.

Kindleberger, C. 1978. *Manias, Panics and Crashes*. 1st edn, London: Basic Books–Macmillan; 1996, 3rd edn, New York: John Wiley.

Kitching, G. 1982. *Development and Underdevelopment in Historical Perspective: Populism, Nationalism and Industrialization*. London: Methuen.

Kiwanuka, M. Semakula. 1970. 'Colonial policies and administrations in Africa: The myth of the contrasts'. *African Historical Studies* 3(2): 295–315.

Klein, Naomi. 2000. *No Logo: Taking Aim at Brand Bullies*. Toronto: Knopf Canada.

Kline, R. 2002. 'A model for improving rural schools: Escuela nueva in Colombia and Guatemala'. *Current Issues in Comparative Education* 2 (2): 170–80.

Klitgaard, R. 1991. *Tropical Gangsters*. London: I.B. Taurus.

Kobrin, Stephen J. 1987. 'Testing the bargaining hypothesis in the manufacturing sector in developing countries'. *International Organization* 41 (4): 609–38.

Kohl, B., and Linda Farthing. 2006 *Impasse in Bolivia: Neoliberal Hegemony and Popular Resistance*. London: Zed Books.

Körner, Peter. 1986. *The IMF and the Debt Crisis: A Guide to the Third World's Dilemma*. London: Zed Books.

Koubi, Geneviève. 1998. 'Réflexions sur les distinctions entre droits individuels, droits collectifs et "droits de groupe"'. In *Mélanges Raymond Goy, ed., Du droit interne au droit international*, 105–17. Rouen: Publications de l'Université de Rouen.

———, and Isabelle Schulte-Tenckhoff. 2000. '"Peuple autochtone" et "minorité" dans les discours juridiques: Imbrications et dissociations'. *Revue interdisciplinaire d'études juridiques* 45: 1–26.

Krueger, Anne O. 1974. 'The political economy of the rent-seeking society'. *American Economic Review* 64: 291–303.

———, ed. 2000. *Economic Policy Reform: The Second Stage*. Chicago: University of Chicago Press.

Krugman, P., and A.J. Venables. 1995. 'Globalization and the inequality of nations'. *The Quarterly Journal of Economics* 110 (4): 857–80.

Kurtz, Marcus. 2004. 'The dilemmas of democracy in the open economy: Lessons from Latin America'. *World Politics* 56: 262–302.

Kuziemko, I., and E. Werker. 2006. *How Much Is a Seat on the Security Council Worth? Foreign Aid and Bribery at the United Nations*. Cambridge, MA: Harvard University Press. http://www.hbs.edu/research/pdf/06-029.pdf.

Labonte, R., and T. Schrecker. 2007a. 'Globalization and social determinants of health: Introduction and methodological background', part 1. *Globalization and Health* 3 (5).

———. 2007b. 'Globalization and social determinants of health: Promoting health equity in global governance', part 2. *Globalization and Health* 3 (6).

———. 2007c. 'Globalization and social determinants of health: The role of the global marketplace', part 3. *Globalization and Health* 3 (7).

Laclau, E. 1977. 'Feudalism and capitalism in Latin America'. In *Politics and Ideology in Marxist Theory*. London: NLB.

Laderchi, C.R., R. Saith, and F. Stewart. 2003. 'Does it matter that we do not agree on the definition of poverty? A comparison of four approaches'. *Oxford Development Studies* 31 (3): 243–73.

Landell-Mills, N., and I. Porras. 2002. *Silver Bullet or Fool's Gold? A Global Review of Markets for Forest Environmental Services and Their Impact on the Poor*. London: International Institute for Environment and Development.

Larson, E. 2007. 'Regulatory rights: Emergent indigenous peoples' rights as a locus of global regulation'. In Bronwen Morgan, ed., *The Intersection of Rights and Regulation: New Directions in Sociolegal Scholarship*. Aldershot, UK: Ashgate.

Latinobarometro. 2006. *Latinobarometro Report 2006*. Santiago.

LeClair, M.S. 2002. 'Fighting the tide: Alternative trade organizations in the era of global free trade'. *World Development* 30 (6): 949–58.

Lenin, V.I. 1920 [1916]. *Imperialism: The Highest Stage of Capitalism: A Popular Outline*. Moscow: Foreign Languages Publishing House.

Levitsky, S., and L. Way. 2005. 'International linkage and democratization'. *Journal of Democracy* 16 (3): 20–34.

Lewin, K.M. 1998. 'Education in emerging Asia: Patterns, policies, and futures in the 21st century'. *International Journal of Educational Development* 18 (2), 81–118.

Lewis, Sir W.A. 1955. 'Economic development with unlimited supplies of labour'. *The Manchester School* 22 (May): 139–92.

Leys, C. 1996. *The Rise and Fall of Development Theory*. Oxford: James Currey.

Ling, R. 2007. 'What would Durkheim have thought?' Plenary Paper presented at the Living the Information Society Conference, Makati City, Philippines, 23 April.

Lipietz, A. 1982. 'Marx or Rostow?' *New Left Review* I/132.

Lipset, S.M. 1959. 'Some social requisites of democracy'. *American Political Science Review* 53: 69–105.

Lister, J. 2005. *Driving the Wrong Way? A Critical Guide to the Global 'Health Reform' Industry*. London: Middlesex University Press.

Lockheed, M.E. 1988. *Improving Educational Efficiency in Developing Countries: What Do We Know? Compare* 18 (1) 21–38.

————, and E. Hanushek. 1994. *Concepts of Educational Efficiency and Effectiveness: Human Capital Working Paper*. Human Resources Development and Operations Policy Working Papers no. HRO 24. Washington: World Bank.

Maaka, R.C.A., and C. Anderson, eds. 2006. *The Indigenous Experience: Global Perspectives*. Toronto: Canadian Scholars' Press.

———— and A. Fleras. 2005. *The Politics of Indigeneity: Challenging the State in Canada and Aotearoa New Zealand*. Dunedin, NZ: Otago University Press.

McCully, P. 2001. *Silenced Rivers: The Ecology and Politics of Large Dams*. London and New York: Zed Books.

————. 2006. *Fizzy Science: Loosening the Hydro Industry's Grip on Reservoir Greenhouse Gas Emissions Research*. Berkeley, CA: International Rivers Network.

Macdonald, D. 1964. 'A theory of mass culture'. In B. Rosenberg and D.W. White, eds, *Mass Culture: The Popular Arts in America*, 59–73. Glencoe, IL: Free Press.

McDowell, C., and A. de Haan. 1997. 'Migration and sustainable livelihoods'. IDS Working Paper 65. Brighton, UK: University of Sussex.

Maclure, R. 2006. 'NGOs and education in sub-Saharan Africa: Instruments of hegemony or surreptitious resistance?'. In T. Clayton, ed., *Re-thinking Hegemony*. Melbourne: James Nicholas.

McNally, D. 2002. *Another World Is Possible: Globalization and Anti-Capitalism*. Winnipeg: Arbeiter Ring Publishing.

Maddison, A. 2006. *The World Economy*. Paris: OECD.

Malecki, E. 1997. *Technology and Economic Development: The Dynamics of Local, Regional and National Competitiveness*. 2nd edn. Harlow, UK: Longman.

Malone, D. 2003. 'Developing curriculum materials for endangered language education: Lessons learned from the field'. *International Journal of Bilingual Education and Bilingualism* 6 (5): 332–48.

Malpani, R., and M. Kamal-Yanni. 2006. *Patents Versus Patients: Five Years after the Doha Declaration*. Oxfam Briefing Paper 95. Washington: Oxfam International.

Mamdani, M. 1996. *Contemporary Africa and the Legacy of Late Colonialism*. Princeton, NJ: Princeton University Press.

Marchall, P.A. 1992. 'Research ethics in applied anthropology'. *IRB: A Review of Human Subjects Research* 14 (6): 1–5.

Marglin, S. 1991. 'Towards the decolonization of the mind'. In F. Apffel Marglin and S. Marglin, eds, *Dominating Knowledge: Development, Culture and Resistance*, 1–27. London: Clarendon.

Marmot, M. 2006. 'Health in an unequal world'. *Lancet* 368 (9,552): 2,081–94.

Martinez, M.A. 2003. 'Other matters: Cooperation with other United Nations bodies in the sphere of indigenous issues'. Working paper on ways and means of developing cooperation between the Working Group and the Permanent Forum on Indigenous Issues. Economic and Social Council, E/CN.4/Sub.2/AC.4/2003/8, United Nations. http://www.unhchr.ch/Huridocda/Huridoca.nsf/0/1582f1cae16ae912c1256d6a00480824/$FILE/G0314654.pdf (accessed 24 July 2007).

Marx, K., and F. Engels. 1967 [1848]. *The Communist Manifesto*. London: Penguin.

Maxwell, S., and P. Engel. 2003. *European Development Cooperation to 2010*. Overseas Development Institute (ODI) working paper no. 219. London: ODI.

Maybury-Lewis, D. 2006. 'Indigenous peoples'. In Roger C.A. Maaka and Chris Andersen, eds, *The Indigenous Experience: Global Perspectives*, 17–29. Toronto: Canadian Scholars' Press.

Mayo, P. 2006. '"In and against the state": Gramsci, war of position, and adult education'. In T. Clayton, ed., *Re-thinking Hegemony*. Melbourne: James Nicolas.

Mayoux, L. 2001. 'Vers un nouveau paradigme dans les programmes de micro-crédit'. In Jeanne Bisilliat and C. Verschuur, eds, *Genre et économie: Un premier éclairage*, Cahiers genre et développement no. 2, 325–31. Paris/Genève: Harmattan.

Meadows, D., J. Randers, and W. Behrens. 1972. *The Limits to Growth*. New York: Universe Books.

Médard, J.F. 1991. 'Autoritarismes et démocraties en Afrique noire'. *Politique africaine* 43: 92–104.

Mehrotra, S., and E. Delamonica. 1998. 'Household costs and public expenditure on primary education in five low income countries: A comparative analysis'. *International Journal of Educational Development* 18 (1): 41–61.

————. 2007. *Eliminating Human Poverty:*

Macroeconomic and Social Policies for Equitable Growth. London: Zed Books.

Mendoza, R., and C. Bahadur. 2002. 'Toward free and fair trade: A global public good perspective'. *Challenge* 45 (4): 21–62.

Metcalf, B.D., and T.R. Metcalf. 2006. *A Concise History of Modern India*. 2nd edn. Cambridge: Cambridge University Press.

Meyer, J.W. 1992. 'The social construction of motives for educational expansion'. In B. Fuller and R. Rubinson, eds, *The Political Construction of Education*. New York: Praeger.

Mies, Maria, and Vandana Shiva. 1993. *Ecofeminism*. London: Zed Books.

Milanovic, B. 2005. *Worlds Apart: Measuring International and Global Inequality*. Princeton, NJ: Princeton University Press.

Millennium Ecosystem Assessment. 2005. *Ecosystems and Human Well-being: Synthesis*. Washington: Island Press.

Miller, Richard. 1998. 'Cosmopolitan respect and patriotic concern'. *Philosophy and Public Affairs* 27 (3): 202–24.

Minde, H. 1996. 'The making of an international movement of indigenous peoples'. *Scandinavian Journal of History* 21 (3): 221–46.

Mitchell, T. 2002. *Rule of Experts: Egypt, Techno-Politics, Modernity*. Berkeley: University of California Press.

Mitlin, D. 1998. 'The NGO sector and its role in strengthening civil society and securing good governance'. In Armanda Bernard, Henry Helmich, and Percy Lehning, eds, *Civil Society and International Development*. Paris: OECD Development Centre.

Mohanty, Chandra Talpade. 2004. *Feminism without Borders: Decolonizing Theory, Practicing Solidarity*. Durham, NC, and London: Duke University Press.

Moore, B. 1966. *Social Origins of Dictatorship and Democracy: Lord and Peasant in the Making of the Modern World*. Boston: Beacon Press.

Moran, T.H. 1974. *Multinational Corporations and the Politics of Dependence: Copper in Chile*. Princeton, NJ: Princeton University Press.

———. 1998. 'The changing nature of political risk'. In Theodore H. Moran, ed., *Managing International Political Risk*, 7–14. Malden, MA:

Basil Blackwell.

———. 2005. 'How does FDI affect host country development? Using industry case studies to make reliable generalizations'. In Theodore H. Moran, Edward M. Graham, and Magnus Bloomström, eds, *Does Foreign Direct Investment Promote Development?* 281–313. Washington: Institute for International Economics and Center for Global Development.

Morin, F. 2005. 'L'ONU comme creuset de l'autochtonie'. *Parcours anthropologique* (5): 35–42.

———. 2008. 'L'autochtonie comme processus d'ethnogenèse'. In Natacha Gagné, Thibault Martin, and Marie Salaün, eds, *L'autochtonies: Vues de France et du Québec*. Québec: Presses de l'Université Laval, collection Les mondes autochtones contemporains.

Morrison, D.R. 1998. *Aid and Ebb Tide: A History of CIDA and Canadian Development Assistance*. Waterloo: Wilfrid Laurier University Press.

Mundy, K., and L. Murphy. 2001. 'Transnational advocacy, global civil society? Emerging evidence from the field of education'. *Comparative Education Review* 45 (1): 85–126.

Munk, R. 2005. *Globalization and Social Exclusion: A Transformationalist Perspective*. Bloomfield, CT: Kumarian Press.

Nairn, T. 1981. 'The modern Janus'. In *The Break-up of Britain*. London: Verso.

Nandy, A. 1983. *The Intimate Enemy*. New Delhi: Oxford University Press.

———. 1995. *The Savage Freud and Other Essays on Possible and Retrievable Selves*. Princeton, NJ: Princeton University Press.

Nath, S.R., K. Sylva, and J. Grimes. 1999. 'Raising basic education levels in rural Bangladesh: The impact of a non-formal education programme'. *International Review of Education* 45 (1): 5–26.

Nattrass, N. 2004. 'Unemployment and AIDS: The social-democratic challenge for South Africa'. *Development Southern Africa* 21 (1): 87–108.

Nayyar, D. 2006. 'Economic growth in independent India: Lumbering elephant or running tiger?' *Economic and Political Weekly* 15 April: 1,452–3.

Netherlands Ministry of Foreign Affairs. 1991. *A World of Difference: A New Framework for Development Cooperation in the 1990s*. The Hague.

Netting, R. 1993. *Smallholders, Householders: Farm Families and the Ecology of Intensive,*

Sustainable Agriculture. Stanford, CA: Stanford University Press.

Newitt, M. 2005. *A History of Portuguese Overseas Expansion, 1400–1668*. New York: Routledge.

Niezen, Ronald. 2003. *The Origins of Indigenism: Human Rights and the Politics of Identity*. Berkeley: University of California Press.

Niles, S., and S. Hanson. 2003. 'A new era of accessibility'. *URISA Journal* 15, APA I.

Nolen, S. 2007. *28 Stories about* AIDS *in Africa*. Toronto: Knopf Canada.

North, L. 2003. 'Endogenous rural diversification: Family textile enterprises in Pelileo, Tungurahua'. In L. North and J.D. Cameron, *Rural Progress, Rural Decay: Neoliberal Adjustment Policies and Local Initiatives*, 207–25. Bloomfield, CT: Kumarian Press.

———— and J.D. Cameron. 2003. *Rural Progress, Rural Decay: Neoliberal Adjustment Policies and Local Initiatives*. Bloomfield, CT: Kumarian Press.

Nozick, Robert. 1974. *Anarchy, State and Utopia*. Oxford: Blackwell.

Nussbaum, M. 1992. 'Human functioning and social justice'. *Political Theory* 20 (2): 202–46.

Oakley, A. 1972. *Sex, Gender and Society*. London: Temple Smith.

O'Brien, C. 1971. 'Modernization, order and the erosion of a democratic ideal'. *Journal of Development Studies* 7: 141–60.

Ocampo, J.A., K.S. Jomo, and Sarbuland Khan, eds. 2007. *Policy Matters: Economic and Social Policies to Sustain Equitable Development*. London: Orient Longman; New York: Zed Books; Penang, Malaysia: Third World Network.

O'Connor, A. 2002. 'Poverty in global terms'. In V. Desai and R.B. Potter, eds, *The Companion to Development Studies*, 37–41. London: Arnold.

O'Donnell, G. 2004. *The Quality of Democracy: Theory and Applications*. Notre Dame, IN: University of Notre Dame Press.

OECD (Organisation for Economic Co-operation and Development). 1977, 1991, 1996, 2006. *Development Co-operation: Efforts and Policies of the Members of the Development Assistance Committee*. Paris: OECD.

————. 2001. 'Aid to agriculture'. OECD briefing. December. http://www.oecd.org/dataoecd/40/43/2094403.pdf (accessed 19 October 2007).

————. 2002. *Foreign Direct Investment for Development: Maximising Benefits, Minimising Costs: Overview*. Paris: OECD. http://www.oecd.org/dataoecd/47/51/1959815.pdf.

————. 2003. 'Official development assistance (ODA)'. In *Glossary of Statistical Terms*. http://stats.oecd.org/glossary/index.htm (accessed 23 September 2007).

————. 2007a. 'Donor aid charts'. www.oecd.org/countrylist/0,3349,en_2649_34447_1783495_1_1_1_1,00.html (accessed 18 September 2007).

————. 2007b. 'Final ODA data for 2005'. 3 April. www.oecd.org/document/17/0,3343,en_2649_34447_38341265_1_1_1_1,00.html (accessed 18 September 2007).

————. 2007c. 'Recipient aid charts'. www.oecd.org/countrylist/0,3349,en_2649_33721_25602317_1_1_1_1,00.html (accessed 18 September 2007).

————. 2007d. 'Reference DAC statistical tables'. April. www.oecd.org/dac/stats/dac/reftables (accessed 18 September 2007).

————. 2007e. 'Statistical annex of the 2006 Development Co-operation Report'. 19 January. www.oecd.org/dac/stats/dac/dcrannex (accessed 18 September 2007).

————. 2007f. 'Development aid from OECD countries fell 5.1% in 2006'. Press release, 3 April. http://www.oecd.org/document/17/0,3343,en_2649_34447_38341265_1_1_1_1,00.html (accessed 13 February 2008).

————. N.d. 'International development statistics (IDS) online'. www.oecd.org/dac/stats/idsonline (accessed 20 October 2007).

Ohmae, Kenichi. 1995. *The End of the Nation State: The Rise of Regional Economies*. New York: Free Press.

O'Manique, C. 2005. 'The "securitisation" of HIV/AIDS in sub-Saharan Africa: A critical feminist lens'. *Policy and Society* 24 (1): 24–47.

O'Neill, Onora. 2000. 'Bounded and cosmopolitan justice'. *Review of International Studies* 26 (5): 45–60.

Ooms, G., and T. Schrecker. 2005. 'Viewpoint: Expenditure ceilings, multilateral financial institutions, and the health of poor populations'. *Lancet* 365: 1,821–3.

Ostrom, Elinor. 1990. *Governing the Commons: The Evolution of Institutions for Collective Action*.

Cambridge, New York, and Melbourne: Cambridge University Press.

Ottaway, M. 2003. *Democracy Challenged: The Rise of Semi-Authoritarianism*. Washington: Carnegie Endowment for International Peace.

Oxfam International. 2000. *Growth with Equity Is Good for the Poor*. Oxfam Policy Papers, 6-2000. http://team.univparis1.fr/teamperso/DEA/Cursus/L3/Memoire/Growth_Inequality%20OXFAM.pdf.

———. 2002. *Rigged Rules and Double Standards: Trade, Globalization, and the Fight against Poverty*. Oxfam trade report. Oxford: Oxfam International. http://www.oxfam.org.uk/resources/papers/downloads/trade_report.pdf.

Oxhorn, P. 2001. 'Review: From human rights to citizenship rights: Recent trends in the study of Latin American social movements'. *Latin American Research Review* 36 (3): 163–82.

Pagiola, S., A. Arcenas, and P. Gunars. 2005. 'Can payments for environmental services help reduce poverty? An exploration of the issues and evidence to date from Latin America'. *World Development* 33 (2): 237–53.

Palma, G. 1981. 'Dependency and development: A critical overview'. In D. Seers, ed., *Dependency Theory: A Critical Reassessment*. London: Frances Pinter.

PANOS Institute. 2004. *Completing the Revolution: The Challenge of Rural Telephony in Africa*. The Panos Institute.

Parini, Lorena. 2006. *Le système de genre: Introduction aux concepts et théories*. Zurich: Éditions Seismo, collection Questions de genre.

Paris, R. 2004. *At War's End*. New York: Cambridge University Press.

Paris Declaration on Aid Effectiveness. 2005. Full text and list of participating countries and organizations available at www.oecd.org/dataoecd/11/41/34428351.pdf (accessed 23 September 2007).

Parrado, E.A., and R.M. Zenteno. 2001. 'Economic restructuring, financial crises, and women's work in Mexico'. *Social Problems* 48: 456–77.

Parsons, Talcott. 1937. *The Structure of Social Action*. New York: McGraw-Hill.

Patnaik, P. 2001 'Imperialism and the diffusion of development: Text of the Ansari Memorial Lecture'. 15 March. http://www.macroscan.org/anl/mar01/anl150301Imperialism_Diffusion_Development_1.htm.

Patnaik, U. 2006. 'The free lunch: Transfers from the tropical colonies and their role in capital formation in Britain during the Industrial Revolution'. In K.S. Jomo, ed., *Globalization under Hegemony: The Changing World Economy*. New Delhi: Oxford University Press.

Payer, C. 1991. *Lent and Lost: Foreign Credit and Third World Development*. London: Zed Books.

Peet, Richard. 2003. *Unholy Trinity: The IMF, World Bank, and WTO*. London: Zed Books.

———, and Michael Watts, eds. 1996. *Liberation Ecologies: Environments, Development, and Social Movements*. London and New York: Routledge.

Perkins, J. 2004. *Confessions of an Economic Hit Man*. San Francisco: Berrett-Koehler.

Peters, P. 1994. *Dividing the Commons: Politics, Policy, and Culture in Botswana*. Charlottesville: University of Virginia Press.

Petras, James. 2007. 'The resurgence of the Left'. *New Left Review* 223: 17–47.

Petros, M. 2005. 'The costs of human smuggling and trafficking'. *Global Migration Perspectives* 31, Geneva: Global Commission on International Migration.

Pilger, J. 2003. *The New Rulers of the World*. London: Verso.

Pincus, J., and Winters, J. 2002. 'Reinventing the World Bank'. In J. Pincus and J. Winters, eds, *Reinventing the World Bank*, 1–25. Ithaca, NY: Cornell University Press.

Pineda-Ofreneo, Rosalinda. 1991. *The Philippines Debt and Poverty*. Oxford: Oxfam.

Pink, S. 1998. 'The white "helpers": Anthropologists, development workers and local imaginations'. *Anthropology Today* 14 (6): 9–16.

Plantade, J.M., and Y. Plantade. 2006. *La face cachée de la Chine: Toute la vérité sur la plus grande jungle économique du monde*. Paris: Bourin Editeur.

Poata-Smith, Evan S. Te Ahu. 1996. 'He Pekeke Uenuku i Tu Ai: The evolution of contemporary Maori protest'. In Paul Spoonley, David Pearson, and Cluny Macpherson, eds, *Nga Patai: Racism and Ethnic Relations in Aotearoa/New Zealand*, 97–116. Palmerston North, NZ: Dunmore Press.

Pogge, Thomas. 2002. *World Poverty and Human Rights: Cosmopolitan Responsibilities and Reforms.* Cambridge: Polity Press.

———. 2005. 'World poverty and human rights'. *Ethics and International Affairs* 19 (1): 1–7.

Poggi, G. 1978. *The Development of the Modern State: A Sociological Introduction.* Stanford, CA: Stanford University Press.

Poirier, S. 2000. 'Contemporanéités autochtones, territoires et (post) colonialisme: Réflexions sur des exemples canadiens et australiens'. *Anthropologie et sociétés* 24 (1): 137–53.

Polanyi, K. 1944. *The Great Transformation: The Political and Economic Origins of Our Time.* Boston: Beacon Press by arrangement with Rinehart and Co.

Pollock, A.M, and D. Price. 2003. 'The public health implications of world trade negotiations on the General Agreement on Trade in Services and Public Services'. *Lancet* 362: 1,072–5.

Popkin, B.M. 2006. 'Global nutrition dynamics: The world is shifting rapidly toward a diet linked with noncommunicable diseases'. *American Journal of Clinical Nutrition* 84 (2): 289–98.

Portes, A. 1998. 'Social capital: Its origins and applications in modern sociology'. *Annual Review of Sociology* 24: 1–24.

Postel, S. 1999. *Pillar of Sand: Can the Irrigation Miracle Last?* New York and London: W.W. Norton.

Postman, N. 1992. 'Technopoly'. In *The Surrender of Culture to Technology.* New York: Vintage Books.

Pouligny, B. 2001 'L'humanitaire non gouvernemental face a la guerre: Évolutions et enjeux'. Centre d'études et de recherches internationales (CERI) Working Paper, 25 février, Université de SciencesPo, Paris. http://www.ceri-sciences-po.org/cherlist/pouligny/huma.pdf.

Prebisch, R. 1950. *The Economic Development of Latin America and Its Principal Problems.* New York: United Nations.

Preker, A.S., R.G.A. Feachem, and D. de Ferranti. 2000. *Health, Nutrition, and Population Sector Strategy Paper.* Washington: World Bank.

Prempeh, O-K. E. 2006. *Against Global Capitalism: African Social Movements.* Aldershot, UK: Ashgate.

Prosser, T. 1997. *The Law and Regulators.* Oxford: Clarendon.

Przeworski, A., M.E. Alvarez, J.A. Cheibub, et al. 2000. *Democracy and Development: Political Institutions and Well-being in the World, 1950–1990.* New York: Cambridge University Press.

———, and L. Fernando. 1997. 'Modernization: Theories and facts'. *World Politics* 49: 155–83.

Pschararopoulous, G. 1973. *Returns to Education: An International Comparison.* Amsterdam: Elsevier Scientific Publishing.

Pugh, N., N. Cooper, and J. Goodhand. 2004. *War Economies in a Regional Context: Challenges of Transformation.* Boulder, CO, and London: Lynne Rienner.

Putnam, R.D. 1993. *Making Democracy Work.* Princeton, NJ: Princeton University Press.

Quinlan, M., C. Mayhew, and P. Bohle. 2001a. 'The global expansion of precarious employment, work disorganization, and consequences for occupational health: A review of recent research'. *International Journal of Health Services* 31: 335–414.

———. 2001b. 'The global expansion of precarious employment, work disorganization, and consequences for occupational health: Placing the debate in a comparative historical context'. *International Journal of Health Services* 31: 507–36.

Rahnema, M. 1992. 'Poverty'. In Wolfgang Sachs, ed., *The Development Dictionary,* 158–76. London: Zed Books.

———, and V. Bawtree, eds. 1997. *The Post-Development Reader.* Atlantic Highland, NJ: Zed Books.

Ramirez, F.O., and J. Boli. 1987. 'The political construction of mass schooling: European origins and worldwide institutionalization'. *Sociology of Education* 60: 2–17.

Rathgeber, E. 1994. 'WID, WAD, GAD: Tendances de la recherche et de la pratique dans le champ du développement'. In H. Dagenais and D. Piché, eds, *Femmes, féminisme et développement,* 77–95. Montreal: McGill-Queen's University Press.

———. 2003. 'Gender and development as a fugitive concept'. *Canadian Journal of Development Studies* 26 (special issue).

Rayner, G., C. Hawkes, T. Lang, et al. 2007. 'Trade liberalization and the diet transition: A public health response'. *Health Promotion International* 21 (S1): 67–74.

Redclift, M. 1992. 'Sustainable development and popular participation: A framework for analysis'. In D. Ghai and J.M. Vivian, eds, *Grassroots Environmental Action: People's Participation in Sustainable Development*, 23–49. London: Routledge.

Redford, Kent H. 1996. 'Preface'. In Kent H. Redford and Jane A. Mansour, eds, *Traditional Peoples and Biodiversity Conservation in Large Tropical Landscapes*, ix–x. Arlington, VA: The Nature Conservancy.

Rees, W.E., and L. Westra. 2003. 'When consumption does violence: Can there be sustainability and environmental justice in a resource-limited world?'. In J. Agyeman, R. Bullard, and B. Evans, eds, *Just Sustainabilities: Development in an Unequal World*, 99–125. London: Earthscan.

Richards, P. 1985. *Indigenous Agricultural Revolution: Ecology and Food Production in West Africa*. London: Hutchinson.

———. 2005. *No Peace No War: An Anthropology of Contemporary Armed Conflicts*. Oxford: James Currey.

Richter, Judith. 2001. *Holding Corporations Accountable: Corporate Conduct, International Codes and Citizen Action*. London: Zed Books and UNICEF.

Riddell, R. 1987. *Foreign Aid Reconsidered*. London: James Currey.

———. 2007. *Does Foreign Aid Really Work?* Oxford: Oxford University Press.

Rigg, J. 2006. 'Land, farming, livelihoods, and poverty: Rethinking the links in the rural South'. *World Development* 34 (1): 180–202.

Rights and Democracy. 2006. *Indigenous Women of the Americas*. Montreal: Rights and Democracy. http://www.dd-rd.ca/site/publications/index.php?lang=en&subsection=catalogue&id=1374 (accessed 23 September 2007).

Rist, G. 1997. *The History of Development: From Western Origins to Global Faith*. London: Zed Books.

———. 2002. *The History of Development: From Western Origins to Global Faith*. Revised edn. London and New York: Zed Books.

Rocheleau, D.E., P.E. Steinberg, and P.A. Benjamin. 1995. 'Environment, development, crisis, and crusade: Ukambani, Kenya, 1890–1990'. *World Development* 23 (6): 1,037–51.

Rodney, Walter. 1972. *How Europe Underdeveloped Africa*. London: Bogle-L'Ouverture Publications.

———. 1981. *How Europe Underdeveloped Africa*. Revised edn. Washington: Howard University Press.

Rodriquez-Prieto, I., and E. Fernandez-Juricic. 2005. 'Effects of direct human disturbances on the endemic Iberian frog *rana iberica* at the individual and population levels'. *Biological Conservation* 123 (1): 1–9.

Rondinelli, D.A. 1987. *Development Administration and U.S. Foreign Aid Policy*. Boulder, CO: Lynne Rienner.

———, J. McCullough, and W. Johnson. 1989. 'Analyzing decentralisation policies in developing countries: A political economy framework'. *Development and Change* 20 (1): 57–87.

Ros, Jamie. 2005. 'The pioneers of development economics and modern growth theory'. In K.S. Jomo and Erik Reinert, eds, *Development Economics: How Schools of Economic Thought Have Addressed Development*. London: Zed Books.

Rosa, Kumudhini. 1994. 'The conditions of organisational activities of women in free trade zones: Malaysia, Philippines and Sri Lanka, 1970–1990'. In Sheila Rowbotham and Swasti Mitter, eds, *Dignity and Daily Bread: New Forms of Economic Organizing among Poor Women in the Third World and the First*. New York: Routledge.

Rose, P. 2005. 'Is there a "fast-track" to education for all?' *International Journal of Educational Development* 25 (4): 381–94.

Rosenstein-Rodan, P.N. 1961. *Notes on the Theory of the Big Push in H.S. Ellis and Henry C. Wallach, Economic Development for Latin America*. New York: St Martin's Press.

Rosset, P. 2006. *Food Is Different: Why We Must Get the WTO out of Agriculture*. London: Zed Books.

Rostow, W.W. 1960. *Stages of Economic Growth: A Non-communist Manifesto*. Cambridge: Cambridge University Press.

Rousseau, S., and F. Meloche. 2002. 'Gold and land: Democratic development at stake'. Report of the Observation Mission of the Tambogrande Municipal Consultation Process in Peru. Montreal: Rights and Democracy. http://www.dd-rd.ca/site/publications/index.php?id=1345&subsection=catalogue.

Rowntree, B.S. 1910. *Poverty: A Study of Town Life*. London: Macmillan.

Rubery, J., and D. Grimshaw. 2001. 'ICTs and employment: The problem of job quality'. *International Labour Review* 140 (2).

Rueschemeyer, D., E. Huber Stephens, and J.D. Stephens. 1992. *Capitalist Development and Democracy.* Chicago: Chicago University Press.

Rummel, R.J. 1975–81. *Understanding Conflict and War.* 5 vols. New York: Sage.

———. 1997. *Power Kills: Democracy As a Method of Nonviolence.* Piscataway, NJ: Transaction Publishers.

Sachs, J. 1998. 'The IMF and the Asian flu'. *American Prospect* 37 (March-April).

———. 2005. *The End of Poverty: Economic Possibilities for Our Time.* New York: Penguin.

———. 2007. 'Beware false tradeoffs'. *Foreign Affairs* 23 January. http://www.foreignaffairs.org/special/global_health/sachs.

Sachs, J., and P. Malaney. 2002. 'The economic and social burden of malaria'. *Nature* 417 (6,890): 680–5.

Sachs, S.E., and J. Sachs. 2004. 'Africa's children orphaned by AIDS'. *Lancet* 364: 1,404.

Sachs, Wolfgang. 1993. *The Development Dictionary.* London: Zed Books.

———. 1999. *Planet Dialectics: Explorations in Environment and Development.* London: Zed Books.

Sahle, N.E. 2006. 'Gender states and markets in Africa'. *Studies in Political Economy* 77 (spring). Ottawa: Carleton University Press.

Sahlins, M. 1997. 'The original affluent society'. In M. Rahnema and V. Bawtree, eds, *The Post-development Reader*, 3–21. Atlantic Highland, NJ: Zed Books.

Said, E.W. 1979. *Orientalism.* New York: Vintage Books.

Sainath, P. 2006. 'Till the cows come home'. *The Hindu* 23 November.

Samoff, J., with B. Carrol. 2007. 'Education for All in Africa: Still a distant dream'. In R.F. Arnove and C.A. Torres, eds, *Comparative Education: The Dialectic of the Global and the Local.* Lanham, MD: Rowman and Littlefield.

Sampson, Anthony. 1981. *The Money Lenders.* London: Hodder and Stoughton.

Sanderson, G.N. 1974. 'The European partition of Africa: Coincidence or conjecture?'. *Journal of Imperial and Commonwealth History* 3 (1): 1–54.

Sapir, J. 2000. 'The Washington Consensus and transition in Russia: History of a failure'. *International Social Science Journal* 52 (166): 479–91.

SAPRIN (Structural Adjustment Participatory Review International Network). 2004. *Structural Adjustment: The SAPRI Report: The Policy Roots of Economic Crisis, Poverty, and Inequality.* London: Zed Books.

Schaffer, F. 1998. *Democracy in Translation: Understanding Politics in an Unfamiliar Culture.* Ithaca, NY: Cornell University Press.

Schedler, A. 2001. 'Comment observer la consolidation démocratique?'. *Revue internationale de politique comparée* 8 (2): 225–44.

———. 2006. *Electoral Authoritarianism: The Dynamics of Unfree Competition.* Boulder, CO: Lynne Rienner.

Schieber, G., L. Fleisher, and P. Gottret. 2006. 'Getting real on health financing'. *Finance and Development* 43 (4).

Schoepf, B.G. 1998. 'Inscribing the body politic: AIDS in Africa'. In M. Lock and P. Kaufert, eds, *Pragmatic Women and Body Politics*, 98–126. Cambridge: Cambridge University Press.

Schrecker, T., and R. Labonte. 2004. 'Taming the "brain drain": A challenge for public health systems in southern Africa'. *International Journal of Occupational and Environmental Health* 10: 409–15.

———, ———, and D. Sanders. 2007. 'Breaking faith with Africa: The G8 and population health post-Gleneagles'. In A.F. Cooper, J.J. Kirton, and T. Schrecker, eds, *Governing Global Health: Challenge, Response, Innovation*, 181–205. Aldershot, UK: Ashgate.

Schulte-Tenckhoff, I. 1997. *La question des peuples autochtones.* Bruxelles: Bruylant.

———. 2008. 'Peuples autochtones: Penser le dilemme fondateur de l'état néo-européen'. In Natacha Gagné, Thibault Martin, and Marie Salaün, eds, *L'autochtonies: Vues de France et du Québec.* Québec: Presses de l'Université Laval, collection Les mondes autochtones contemporains.

Schultz, T.W. 1964. *Transforming Traditional Agriculture.* New Haven, CT: Yale University Press.

———. 1971. *Investment in Human Capital: The Role of Education and of Research.* New York: Free Press.

Schuurman, F.J., ed. 1993. *Beyond the Impasse: New Directions in Development Theory.* London and Atlantic Highland, NJ: Zed Books.

Sciadas, G., ed. 2003. 'Monitoring the digital divide . . . and beyond'. Montreal: Orbicom.

Scoones, I. 1998. 'Sustainable rural livelihoods: A framework for analysis'. IDS Working Paper 72. Brighton, UK: University of Sussex.

Scott, J.C. 1976. *The Moral Economy of the Peasant: Rebellion and Subsistence in Southeast Asia*. New Haven, CT: Yale University Press.

———. 1990. *Dominations and the Arts of Resistance*. New Haven, CT: Yale University Press.

Scott, V.C. 1995. *Gender and Development: Rethinking Modernization and Dependency Theory*. Boulder, CO: Lynne Rienner.

Seers, D. 1972. 'What are we trying to measure?' *Journal of Development Studies* 8 (3) 21–36.

———. 1979. 'The meaning of development, with a postscript'. In David Lehmann, ed., *Development Theory: Four Critical Studies*, 9–30. London: Frank Cass.

Sell, S.K. 2003. *Private Power, Public Law: The Globalization of Intellectual Property Rights*. Cambridge: Cambridge University Press.

Sen, Amartya. 1981. *Poverty and Famines: An Essay on Entitlements and Deprivation*. Baltimore, MD: Johns Hopkins University Press.

———. 1999. *Development As Freedom*. New York: Anchor Books.

———. 2001. 'Culture and development'. Paper presented at the World Bank meeting, 13 December 2001, Tokyo. http://www1.worldbank.org/prem/poverty/culture/book/sen.htm (accessed 26 September 2007).

———. 2002. *Rationality and Freedom*. Cambridge, MA: Harvard University Press.

Sender, J. 2003. 'Rural poverty and gender: Analytical frameworks and policy proposals'. In H. Chang, ed., *Rethinking Development Economics*, 407–23. London: Anthem Press.

Shaffer, P. 2002. 'New thinking on poverty: Implications for globalisation and poverty reduction strategies'. Paper for UNDESA Expert Group Meeting on Globalisation and Rural Poverty. www.un.org/esa/socdev/poverty/papers/paper_shaffer.

Shanin, T. 1997. 'The idea of progress'. In M. Rahnema and V. Bawtree, eds., *The Post-development Reader*, 65–72. Atlantic Highland, NJ: Zed Books.

Shiva, V. 1991. *The Violence of the Green Revolution: Third World Agriculture, Ecology and Politics*. London: Zed Books.

———. 2000. 'War against nature and the people of the South'. In Sarah Anderson, ed., *Views from the South: The Effects of Globalization and the WTO on Third World Countries*, 91–125. Oakland, CA: Food First Books.

———. 2001. *Protect or Plunder? Understanding Intellectual Property Rights*. London: Zed Books.

Shkolnikov, V.M., E.M. Andreev, D.A. Leon, et al. 2004. 'Mortality reversal in Russia: The story so far'. *Hygiea Internationalis* 4 (1): 29–80.

Simon, Julian L. 1981. *The Ultimate Resource*. Princeton: Princeton University Press.

Singer, Peter. 2002. *One World: The Ethics of Globalization*. New Haven, CT: Yale University Press.

Sissons, J. 2005. *First Peoples: Indigenous Cultures and Their Futures*. London: Reaktion Books.

Sklair. 1991. *Sociology of the Global System*. Baltimore, MD: Johns Hopkins University Press.

———. 2002. 'Transnational practices, corporations, class and consumerism'. In L. Sklair, *Globalization, Capitalism and its Alternatives*, 3rd edn, 84–117. Oxford: Oxford University Press.

Skocpol, T. 1979. *States and Social Revolutions*. New York: Cambridge University Press.

Smillie, I. 2000. *Mastering the Machine Revisited: Poverty, Aid and Technology*. Bourton on Dunsmore, Rugby, UK: ITDG.

———. 2004. *ODA: Options and Challenges for Canada*. Canadian Council for International Cooperation. www.ccic.ca.

Smith, Adam. 1937 [1776]. *Wealth of Nations*. New York: Modern Library.

Smith, L.T. 1999. *Decolonizing Methodologies: Research and Indigenous Peoples*. London and New York: Zed Books.

Snyder, J. 2000. *From Voting to Violence*. New York: W.W. Norton.

Soederberg, S. 2004. *The Politics of the New International Financial Architecture: Reimposing Neoliberal Domination in the Global South*. London: Zed Books.

Solar, O., and A. Irwin. 2007. *A Conceptual Framework for Action on the Social Determinants of Health*. Geneva: Commission on Social Determinants of Health, World Health Organization. http://www.

who.int/entity/social_determinants/resources/csdh_framework_action_05_07.pdf.

Solow, R. 2000. 'Notes on social capital and economic performance'. In Partha Dasgupta and Ismail Serageldin, eds, *Social Capital: A Multi-Faceted Perspective*. Washington: World Bank.

Stallings, Barbara, and Wilson Peres. 2000. *Growth, Employment, and Equity: The Impact of the Economic Reforms in Latin America and the Caribbean*. Washington: Brookings Institution Press and ECLAC.

Start, D. 2001. 'The rise and fall of the rural non-farm economy: Poverty impacts and policy options'. *Development Policy Review* 19 (4): 491–505.

Stephens, D. 1991. 'The quality of primary education in developing countries: Who defines and who decides?'. *Comparative Education* 27 (1): 223–33.

Stewart, Frances. 2002. 'Horizontal inequalities as a source of conflict'. In Fen Osler Hampson and David M. Malone, eds, *Reaction to Conflict Prevention: Opportunities for the UN System*. Boulder, CO: Lynne Rienner.

———, Ruth Saith, and Barbara Harriss-White. 2007. *Defining Poverty in the Developing World*. London: Palgrave Macmillan.

Stiglitz, J. 2002. *Globalization and Its Discontents*. New York: W.W. Norton.

———. 2003. 'Whither reform? Towards a new agenda for Latin America'. *CEPAL Review* 80 (August): 7–37.

Stopford, J.H., and S. Strange. 1991. *Rival States, Rival Firms: Competition for World Market Shares*. Cambridge: Cambridge University Press.

Storey, J., ed. 1998. *Cultural Theory and Popular Culture: A Reader*. 2nd edn. Hemel Hempstead, UK: Prentice Hall.

Strange, S. 1996. *The Retreat of the State: The Diffusion of Power in the World Economy*. Cambridge: Cambridge University Press.

Streeten, P. 1998. 'Beyond the six veils: Conceptualizing and measuring poverty'. *Journal of International Affairs* 52 (1): 1–31.

Suhrke, Astri, and Ingrid Samset. 2007. 'What's in a figure? Estimating recurrence of civil war'. *International Peacekeeping* 14 (2): 195–203.

Sumner, A. 2005. 'Is foreign direct investment good for the poor? A review and stocktake'. *Development in Practice* 15 (3/4): 269–85.

Sung, Yun-Wing . 2005. *The Emergence of Greater China: The Economic Integration of Mainland China, Taiwan and Hong Kong*. New York: Palgrave Macmillan.

Sylvester, C. 1999. 'Development studies and postcolonial studies: Disparate tales of the "Third World"'. *Third World Quarterly* 20 (4).

Szreter, S. 1999. 'Rapid economic growth and "the four Ds" of disruption, deprivation, disease and death: Public health lessons from nineteenth-century Britain for twenty-first-century China'. *Tropical Medicine and International Health* 4 (2): 146–52.

Talbot, J.M. 2004. *Grounds for Agreement: The Political Economy of the Coffee Commodity Chain*. Oxford: Rowman and Littlefield.

Taussig, M. 1980. *The Devil and Commodity Fetishism in South America*. Chapel Hill: University of North Carolina Press.

Taylor, C. 1985. *Philosophy and the Human Sciences: Philosophical Papers*, vol. 2. Cambridge: Cambridge University Press.

Teschke, B. 2003. *The Myth of 1648*. London: Verso.

't Hoen, E. 2002. 'Trips, pharmaceutical patents and access to essential medicines: A long way from Seattle to Doha'. *Chicago Journal of International Law* 3: 27–46.

Thomas, A. 2000. 'Poverty and the "end of development"'. In Tim Allen and Alan Thomas, eds, *Poverty and Development into the 21st Century*, 3–22. Oxford: Oxford University Press and The Open University.

Thompson, J.B. 1990. *Ideology and Modern Culture: Critical Social Theory in the Era of Mass Communication*. Cambridge: Polity Press.

Tiejun, W. 2001. 'Centenary reflections on the three dimension problem of rural China'. *Inter-Asia Cultural Studies* 2 (2): 287–95.

Tiffen, M., M. Mortimore, and F. Gichuki. 1994. *More People, Less Erosion: Environmental Recovery in Kenya*. Chichester, UK: John Wiley.

Tilly, C. 1985. 'War making and state making as organised crime'. In Peter B. Evans, Dietrich Rueschemeyer, and Theda Skocpol, eds, *Bringing the State Back In*, 169–91. Cambridge: Cambridge University Press.

Tinker, I., and B. Bramsen, eds. 1980. *Women and World Development*. New York: Praeger.

Titmuss, Richard. 1963. *Essays on the Welfare State*. 2nd edn. London: Allen and Unwin.

———. 1968. *Commitment to Welfare*. London: Allen and Unwin.

Todaro, M.P. 1989. *Economic Development in the Third World*. 4th edn. New York: Longman.

Tomich, T., P. Kilby, and B.F. Johnston. 1995. *Transforming Agrarian Economies: Opportunities Seized, Opportunities Missed*. Ithaca, NY: Cornell University Press.

Tomlinson, B. 2005. *The Politics of the Millennium Development Goals: Contributing to Strategies for Ending Poverty?* Ottawa: Canadian Council for International Cooperation. www.ccic.ca.

Toroitich, Isaiah Kipyegon, and African Women and Child Network. 2004. *Women Rights As Human Rights in Kenya: A Contradiction between Policy and Practice*. Norwegian Church Aid, Occasional Paper Series 1, p. 32.

Trask, Haunani-Kay. 1993. *From a Native Daughter*. Monroe, ME: Common Courage Press.

Turner, B.L., G. Hyden, and R.W. Kates. 1993. *Population Growth and Agricultural Change in Africa*. Gainesville: University of Florida Press.

UK Ministry of Defence. Development Concepts and Doctrine Centre. *Global Strategic Trends 2007–2036*. http://www.dcdc-strategictrends.org.uk.

UN (United Nations). 2000. *We the Peoples: The Role of the United Nations in the 21st Century*. New York: United Nations. http://www.un.org/millennium/sg/report/full.htm (accessed 13 February 2008).

———. 2001. *United Nations Guide for Indigenous Peoples*. Geneva: United Nations. http://www.unhchr.ch/html/racism/00-indigenousguide.html (accessed 24 July 2007).

UN General Assembly. 1994. *Declaration on the Elimination of Violence Against Women*. A/RES/48/104. http://www.unhchr.ch/huridocda/huridoca.nsf/(Symbol)/A.RES.48.104.En.

———. 2005. Resolution adopted at the outcome of the World Summit. http://daccessdds.un.org/doc/UNDOC/GEN/N05/487/60/PDF/N0548760.pdf?OpenElement.

UN Millennium Project. 2005. *Investing in Development: A Practical Plan to Achieve the Millennium Development Goals*. London: Earthscan. http://www.unmillenniumproject.org/documents/MainReportComplete-lowres.pdf.

UN Millennium Project. Task Force on Improving the Lives of Slum Dwellers. 2005. *A Home in the City*. London: Earthscan.

UNCTAD (United National Conference on Trade and Development). 1999. *World Investment Report 1999: Foreign Direct Investment and the Challenge of Development*. Geneva: United Nations.

———. 2004a. *Development and Globalization in 2004: Facts and Figures*. New York: United Nations. http://globstat.unctad.org/html/index.html.

———. 2004b. *International Investment Agreements: Key Issues*, vol. 1. Geneva: United Nations.

———. 2006a. *World Investment Report 2006: FDI from Developing and Transition Economies: Implications for Development*. Geneva: United Nations.

———. 2006b. 'Latest developments in investor-state dispute settlement'. IIA Monitor no. 4. Geneva: United Nations.

UNCTAD and IISD (International Institute for Sustainable Development). 2003. 'Sustainability in the coffee sector: Exploring opportunities for international cooperation'. Background document for workshop. Winnipeg: IISD. http://www.iisd.org/pdf/2003/sci_coffee_background.pdf.

UNDP (United Nations Development Programme). 1990. *Human Development Report 1990: Concept and Measurement of Human Development*. Geneva: United Nations. http://hdr.undp.org/reports/global/1990/en.

———. 1994. *Human Development Report 1994: New Dimensions of Human Security*. New York: Oxford University Press. http://hdr.undp.org/en/media/hdr_1994_en.pdf.

———. 1996. 'Good governance and sustainable human development'. Governance Policy Paper. http://magnet.undp.org/policy.

———. 1997. 'The shrinking state: Governance and sustainable human development'. Policy Document. New York: UNDP.

———. 1998. *Human Development Report 1998*. New York: Oxford University Press.

———. 2001. *Human Development Report 2001: Making New Technologies Work for Human Development*. New York: UNDP.

————. 2005. *Human Development Report 2005: International Cooperation at a Crossroads: Aid, Trade and Security in an Unequal World*. New York: Oxford University Press for UNDP.

————. 2006. *Human Development Report 2006: Beyond Scarcity: Power, Poverty and the Global Water Crisis*. Geneva: United Nations. http://hdr.undp.org/hdr2006/statistics.

UNDP, UNEP, World Bank, and World Resources Institute. 2005. *World Resources Report: The Wealth of the Poor: Managing Ecosystems to Fight Poverty*. Washington: World Resources Institute. http://pdf.wri.org/wrr05_full_hires.pdf.

UNEP (United Nations Environment Programme). 2007. *Global Environment Outlook 4: Environment for Development*. UNEP. www.unep.org/geo.

UNESCO (United Nations Educational, Scientific and Cultural Organization). 2003. *Les filles se heurtent encore à de fortes discriminations dans l'accès à l'école*. http://portal.unesco.org/fr/ev.php-URL_ID=17039&URL_DO=DO_TOPIC&URL_SECTION=201.html UNICEF http://www.unicef.org/french.

————. 2007. *EFA Global Monitoring Report: Education for All by 2015: Will We Make It?* Oxford: UNESCO and Oxford University Press. http://unesdoc.unesco.org/images/0015/001547/154743e.pdf.

UNICEF (United Nations Children's Fund). 2006. *Africa's Orphaned and Vulnerable Generations: Children Affected by AIDS*. New York: UNICEF. http://www.unicef.org/publications/index_35645.html.

United Nations Country Team Viet Nam. 2003. *Health Care Financing for Viet Nam*. Ha Noi: United Nations Viet Nam.

USAID (United States Agency for International Development). 2007. *About USAID*. www.usaid.gov/about_usaid (accessed 11 September 2007).

Utting, P., and A. Zammit. 2006. *Beyond Pragmatism: Appraising UN-Business Partnerships*. Geneva: UNRISID Markets, Business and Regulation Programme Paper no. 1.

Valenzuela, J.S. 2000. 'Aux origines de la démocratie chilienne: La création d'institutions électorales au XIXe siècle'. In Christophe Jaffrelot, ed., *Démocraties d'ailleurs*, 161–206. Paris: Karthala.

Van Beusekom, M.M. 2002. *Negotiating Development: African Farmers and Colonial Experts at the Office du Niger, 1920–1960*. Portsmouth, NH: Heinemann.

————, and D.L. Hodgson. 2000. 'Lessons learned: Development experiences in the late colonial period'. *Journal of African History* 41 (1): 29–33.

Van der Hoeven, R., and M. Lübker. 2005. *Financial Openness and Employment: A Challenge for International and National Institutions*. Geneva: International Policy Group, International Labour Office. http://ctool.gdnet.org/conf_docs/Hoeven_Paper_Lunch%20Time%20Session_ILO.pdf.

————, and A. Shorrocks, eds. 2003. *Growth, Inequality and Poverty*. Oxford: Oxford University Press.

Van Doorslaer, E., E.O'Donnell, R.P. Rannan-Eliya, et al. 2006. 'Effect of payments for health care on poverty estimates in 11 countries in Asia: An analysis of household survey data'. *Lancet* 368 (9,544): 1,357–64.

Veeken, H., and B. Pécoul. 2000. 'Drugs for "neglected diseases": A bitter pill'. *Tropical Medicine and International Health* 5: 309–11.

Veltmeyer, H., and J. Petras. 1997. *Economic Liberalism and Class Conflict in Latin America*. London: Macmillan.

————, and ————. 2000. *The Dynamics of Social Change in Latin America*. London: Macmillan.

Vernon, R. 1971. *Sovereignty at Bay: The Multinational Spread of US Enterprises*. New York: Basic Books.

Verzola, R. 1998. 'Towards a political economy of information'. In F. Rosario-Braid and R. Tuazon. *A Reader on Information and Communication Technology Planning for Development*, 94–104. UNESCO National Commission of the Philippines.

Victora, C.G., A. Wagstaff, J.A. Schellenberg, et al. 2003. 'Applying an equity lens to child health and mortality: More of the same is not enough'. *Lancet* 362: 233–41.

Villegas-Reimers, E., and F. Reimers. 1996. 'Where are 60 million teachers? The missing voice in educational reforms'. *Prospects* 23 (3): 469–92.

Von Hayek, F. 1944. *The Road to Serfdom*. London: Routledge.

Wade, R. 1990. *Governing the Market: Economic Theory and the Role of Government in East Asian Industrialization*. Princeton, NJ: Princeton University Press.

————. 2001. 'Showdown at the World Bank'. *New Left Review* 7: 124–37.

Wallace, T. 2003. 'NGO dilemmas: Trojan horses for global neoliberalism?' *Socialist Register 2004.* London: Merlin Press.

Wallerstein, I. 1974a. *The Modern World System.* New York: Academic Press.

———. 1974b. 'The rise and future demise of the world capitalist system: Concepts for comparative analysis'. *Comparative Studies and History* 15: 387–415.

Walley, C.J. 2004. *Rough Waters: Nature and Development in an East African Marine Park.* Princeton, NJ, and Oxford: Princeton University Press.

Warren, B. 1973. 'Imperialism and capitalist industrialization'. *New Left Review* I/81: 3–44.

———. 1980. *Imperialism: Pioneer of Capitalism.* London: New Left Books.

Warschauer, M. 2004. *Technology and Social Inclusion: Rethinking the Digital Divide.* Cambridge, MA: MIT Press.

wa Thiong'o, N. 1977. *Petals of Blood.* London: Heinemann.

———, and E. Sahle. 2004. *Diogenes* May-June.

Watts, M. 1993. 'Development I: Power, knowledge, discursive practices'. *Progress in Human Geography* 17.

———. 1995. 'A new deal in emotions: Theory and practice and the crisis of development'. In J. Crush, *Power of Development.* London: Routledge.

Watts, S. 1999. *Epidemics and History: Disease, Power, and Imperialism.* New Haven, CT: Yale University Press.

WCD (World Commission on Dams). 2000. *Dams and Development: A New Framework for Decision-Making.* London and Stefling, VA: Earthscan.

WCED (World Commission on Environment and Development). 1987. *Our Common Future.* Oxford and New York: Oxford University Press.

Webster, F. 2000. *Theories of the Information Society.* London and New York: Routledge.

Wedel, J.R. 1998. *Collision and Collusion: The Strange Case of Western Aid to Eastern Europe 1989–1998.* New York: St Martin's Press.

Weiler, H.N. 1978. 'Education and development: From the age of innocence to the age of skepticism'. *Comparative Education Review* 14 (3): 179–98.

———. 1984. 'The political economy of education and development'. *Prospects* 14: 667–77.

Weisbrot, M., D. Baker, E. Kraev, et al. 2001. *The Scorecard on Globalization 1980–2000: Twenty Years of Diminished Progress.* Washington: Center for Economic and Policy Research.

Weiss, L. 1998. *The Myth of the Powerless State: Governing the Economy in the Global Era.* Cambridge: Polity Press.

Wells, M., and K. Brandon. 1992. *People and Parks.* Washington: World Bank, World Wildlife Fund, and USAID.

Wen, D., and M. Li. 2006. 'China: Hyperdevelopment and environmental crisis, in coming to terms with nature'. *Socialist Register 2007.* London: Merlin Press.

WGIP (Working Group on Indigenous Populations). 2001. 'Indigenous peoples and the United Nations system'. Leaflet no 1. UN Office of the High Commissioner for Human Rights.

White, H. 2002. 'The measurement of poverty'. In V. Desai and R.B. Potter, eds, *The Companion to Development Studies,* 32–7. London: Arnold.

Whitehead, M., G. Dahlgren, and T. Evans. 2001. 'Equity and health sector reforms: Can low-income countries escape the medical poverty trap?' *Lancet* 358: 833–6.

Whitesell, E.A. 1996. 'Local struggles over rain-forest conservation in Alaska and Amazonia'. *The Geographical Review* 86 (3): 414–36.

WHO (World Health Organization). 2004. News release. http://www.who.int/mediacentre/news/releases/2004/pr_unaids/fr/ONUSIDA/OMS.

Wignaraja, P. 1993. 'Rethinking democracy and development'. In P. Wignaraja, ed., *New Social Movements in the South: Empowering the People,* 4–35. New Delhi: Vistaar.

Williams, G. 1981. 'The World Bank and the peasant problem'. In J. Heyer et al, eds, *Rural Development in Tropical Africa.* London, Macmillan.

Williams, R. 1961. *The Long Revolution.* New York: Columbia University Press.

———. 1983. *Keywords: A Vocabulary of Culture and Society.* Revised edn. New York: Oxford University Press.

Winters, S.J., and S.L. Taylor. 2001. 'The role of information technology in the transformation of work: A comparison of post-industrial, industrial, and proto-industrial organization'. In J. Yates and J.

Van Maanen, eds, *Information Technology and Organizational Transformation: History, Rhetoric, and Practice*. Thousand Oaks, CA: Sage.

Wolfensohn, J. 1999. *A Proposal for a Comprehensive Development Framework*. Washington: World Bank.

Wood, A. 2002. *Could Africa Be More Like America?* http://ssrn.com/abstract=315240 (accessed 19 October 2007).

Wood, E.J. 2003. *Insurgent Collective Action and Civil War in El Salvador*. New York: Cambridge University Press.

Wood, G.D. 1985. 'The politics of development policy labelling'. In G.D. Wood, ed., *Labelling in Development Policy: Essays in Honour of Bernard Schaffer*, 5–31. London: Sage; The Hague: Institute of Social Studies.

Wood, R.E. 1986. *From Marshall Plan to Debt Crisis: Foreign Aid and Development Choices in the World Economy*. Berkeley: University of California Press.

Woodward, S.L. 1999. 'Bosnia and Herzegovina: How not to end civil war'. In Barbara F. Walter and Jack Snyder, eds, *Civil Wars, Insecurity, and Intervention*. New York: Columbia University Press.

Working Group on IMF Programs and Health Spending. 2007. *Does the IMF Constrain Health Spending in Poor Countries? Evidence and an Agenda for Action*. Washington: Center for Global Development.

World Bank. 1989. *Sub-Saharan Africa: From Crisis to Sustainable Growth*. Washington: World Bank.

———. 1992. *World Development Report 1992: Development and the Environment*. New York: Oxford University Press.

———. 1993a. *The East Asian Miracle: Economic Growth and Public Policy*. New York: Cambridge University Press.

———. 1993b. *World Development Report 1993: Investing in Health*. New York: Oxford University Press.

———. 1994. *Governance: The World Bank Experience*. Washington: World Bank.

———. 2000. *World Development Report 2000/2001: Attacking Poverty*. Oxford: Oxford University Press.

———. 2003. *Genre et développement économique*. Montréal: Éditions Saint-Martin.

———. 2004a. *Global Development Prospects: Realizing the Development Promise of the Doha Agenda*. Washington: World Bank.

———. 2004b. *Partnerships in Development: Progress in the Fight against Poverty*. Washington: World Bank.

———. 2007a. Country Papers and JSANs/JSAs. http://go.worldbank.org/SIKR9UVMYO.

———. 2007b. *Global Economic Prospects 2007: Managing the Next Wave of Globalization*. Washington: World Bank.

———. 2007c. 'HNPStats'. Health, Nutrition and Population Program. http://devdata.worldbank.org/hnpstats.

———. 2007d. *World Development Report 2008: Agriculture for Development*. Washington: World Bank. http://go.worldbank.org/ZJIAOSUFUO.

World Commission on the Social Dimensions of Globalization. 2004. *A Fair Globalization Creating Opportunities for All*. Geneva: International Labour Organization. http://www.ilo.org/public/english/wcsdg/docs/report.pdf.

World Declaration on Education for All: Meeting Basic Learning Needs. 1990. http://www.unesco.org/education/wef/en-conf/Jomtien%20Declaration%20eng.shtm.

World Wide Fund for Nature. 2007. *WWF Guiding Principles*. www.panda.org/about_wwf/who_we_are/index.cfm (accessed 8 August 2007).

WSIS (World Summit on the Information Society). 2003. *Declaration of Principles*. Document WSIS-03/GENEVA/DOC/4-E. 12 December.

Zimmerman, F.J. 2000. 'Barriers to participation of the poor in South Africa's land redistribution'. *World Development* 28 (8): 1,439–60.

INDEX